T0344207

Ethical Impact of Technological Advancements and Applications in Society

Rocci Luppicini
University of Ottawa, Canada

Information Science
REFERENCE

Managing Director:	Lindsay Johnston
Senior Editorial Director:	Heather A. Probst
Book Production Manager:	Sean Woznicki
Development Manager:	Joel Gamon
Acquisitions Editor:	Erika Gallagher
Typesetter:	Deanna Jo Zombro
Cover Design:	Nick Newcomer, Lisandro Gonzalez

Published in the United States of America by
Information Science Reference (an imprint of IGI Global)
701 E. Chocolate Avenue
Hershey PA 17033
Tel: 717-533-8845
Fax: 717-533-8661
E-mail: cust@igi-global.com
Web site: http://www.igi-global.com

Library of Congress Cataloging-in-Publication Data

Ethical impact of techological advancemennts and applications in society /
Rocci Luppicini, editor.
     p. cm.
  Includes bibliographical references and index.
  Summary: "This book explores the ethical challenges of technology
innovations, providing cutting-edge analysis of designs, developments,
impacts, policies, theories, and methodologies related to ethical aspects of
technology in society"--Provided by publisher.
  ISBN 978-1-4666-1773-5 (hbk.) -- ISBN 978-1-4666-1774-2 (ebook) -- ISBN 978-
1-4666-1775-9 (print & perpetual access) 1. Technology--Moral and ethical
aspects. 2. Technology--Social aspects. I. Luppicini, Rocci.
  BJ59.E84 2012
  170--dc23
                              2012002097

British Cataloguing in Publication Data
A Cataloguing in Publication record for this book is available from the British Library.

The views expressed in this book are those of the authors, but not necessarily of the publisher.

Table of Contents

Section 2
Technoethics and the Digital Society

Section 3
The Ethical Side of Technological Applications

Section 4
New Trends in Technoethics

Detailed Table of Contents

Section 1
Theoretical Perspectives

We already are hybrid humans, fruit of a kind of co-evolution of both our brains and the common, scientific, social, and moral knowledge we have produced by ourselves starting from the birth of material culture with our ancestors until the recent effects generated by the whole field of technological artifacts and of information and communication technologies (ICTs). We all are "constitutively" natural-born cyborgs, that is biotechnological hybrid minds. Our minds should not be considered to be located only in the head: human beings have solved their problems of survival and reproduction, "distributing" cognitive and ethical functions to external non-biological sources, props, and aids, which originate cultures. The paper also illustrates the interplay between cultures and distributed cognition and stresses the role of some technological artifacts as moral mediators. The second part of the paper is related to the analysis of the interplay between cultures, morality, and cognition and of some consequences concerning the problem of intercultural communication in the light of the role of moral mediators, docility, and cyber-privacy. Finally, I discuss some suggestions concerning the problem of what I call the moral principle of isolation of cultures, with respect to the effects of ICTs.

In this paper, the author examines the idea of respect and makes this the cornerstone of a new approach to ethics that is particularly well suited to addressing the challenges society faces in an age shaped so profoundly by technology. The author uncovers a wealth of meaning in the notion of 'respect' and shows how this relates to the gaze. The attentive gaze is seen as the essence of respect. This thought-provoking analysis is presented in a straightforward way and is certainly open to further development and refinement in fields such as ecology, medicine, education and the promotion of civic-mindedness.

Evandro Agazzi, Università Di Genova, Italy

Two opposite positions are currently dividing the field of discussion regarding the ethical evaluation of science and technology. On the one hand, many people maintain that such a judgment must not be introduced or, less radically, that it needs not be looked for; on the other hand, several scholars maintain that such a judgment is legitimate or, more radically, mandatory. Therefore, it is advisable to examine the arguments of both parties in order to see not so much which viewpoint is right but, perhaps, to what extent both might be right.

Peter B. Crabb, The Pennsylvania State University at Hazleton, USA
Steven E. Stern, University of Pittsburgh at Johnstown, USA

Technologies can have harmful effects on users' psychological health, on society, and on the environment. "Technology traps" arise when users and societies become stuck with technologies and the harmful consequences produced by these technologies. In this paper, the authors describe five technology traps: incompetence, self-miscontrol, misbehavior, techno-centrism, and environmental degradation. The authors then examine the share of ethical responsibility for these traps among end-users, businesses, and government.

J. A. Quilici-Gonzalez, Federal University of ABC, Brazil
G. Kobayashi, Federal University of ABC, Brazil
M. C. Broens, University of São Paulo State, Brazil
M. E. Q. Gonzalez, University of São Paulo State, Brazil

In this article, the authors investigate, from an interdisciplinary perspective, possible ethical implications of the presence of ubiquitous computing systems in human perception/action. The term *ubiquitous computing* is used to characterize information-processing capacity from computers that are available everywhere and all the time, integrated into everyday objects and activities. The contrast in approach to aspects of ubiquitous computing between traditional considerations of ethical issues and the Ecological Philosophy view concerning its possible consequences in the context of perception/action are the underlying themes of this paper. The focus is on an analysis of how the generalized dissemination of microprocessors in embedded systems, commanded by a ubiquitous computing system, can affect the behaviour of people considered as embodied embedded agents.

Section 2
Technoethics and the Digital Society

Chapter 6

Bernd Carsten Stahl, De Montfort University, UK
Richard Heersmink, Delft University of Technology, The Netherlands
Philippe Goujon, Facultés Universitaires Notre-Dame de la Paix, Belgium
Catherine Flick, Facultés Universitaires Notre-Dame de la Paix, Belgium
Jeroen van den Hoven, Delft University of Technology, The Netherlands
Kutoma J. Wakunuma, De Montfort University, UK
Veikko Ikonen, VTT (Technical Research Centre of Finland), Finland
Michael Rader, Karlsruhe Institute of Technology, Germany

Ethical issues of information and communication technologies (ICTs) are important because they can have significant effects on human liberty, happiness, and people's ability to lead a good life. They are also of functional interest because they can determine whether technologies are used and whether their positive potential can unfold. For these reasons, policy makers are interested in finding out what these issues are and how they can be addressed. The best way of creating ICT policy that is sensitive to ethical issues pertain to being proactive in addressing such issues at an early stage of the technology life cycle. The present paper uses this position as a starting point and discusses how knowledge of ethical aspects of emerging ICTs can be gained. It develops a methodology that goes beyond established futures methodologies to cater for the difficult nature of ethical issues. The authors outline how the description of emerging ICTs can be used for an ethical analysis.

Chapter 7

Yasmin Ibrahim, University of London, UK

The increasing use of the body for embedding technology as well as the convergence of multiple features in mobile telephony have made image capture an important phenomenon that presents new ways to capture events and their constructs, which cast new forms of gaze into everyday life. The ways in which one captures and gazes has increasing ethical, legal and social implications for societies. The civilian gaze through mobile recording devices can be empowering in terms of holding authorities accountable, but it can equally debilitate societies by transgressing privacy and enabling new forms of voyeurism and deviance. In recognition of this, many governments and authorities are restricting the ways in which we capture and upload images. This paper looks at how this image economy is creating new ways of looking and how the new rules are, for different reasons, seeking to curb this architecture of capture.

Chapter 8

Peter J. Allen, Curtin University, Australia

Katherine L. Shepherd, Curtin University, Australia

Lynne D. Roberts, Curtin University, Australia

Despite persistent government and industry efforts to stop the sharing and downloading of media such as files over peer-to-peer (P2P) networks, this activity shows no sign of abating. This research investigated whether psychological reactance could account for variance in the intent to engage in, and the extent of such behaviour beyond that accounted for by the standard Theory of Planned Behaviour (TPB) variables. No support for psychological reactance as a predictor of P2P file downloading intent or behaviour was found in this paper. However, the results did indicate that attitude, subjective norms, and perceived behavioural control each accounted for significant variance in P2P file downloading behaviour, and that these relationships were fully mediated by behavioural intent. These findings are consistent with, and provide strong support for, the use of the TPB within this domain.

Chapter 9

Ellen M. Kraft, Richard Stockton College of New Jersey, USA

Jinchang Wang, Richard Stockton College of New Jersey, USA

This article shows the results of a study of the cyberbullying and cyberstalking experiences of students at a public liberal arts college. A survey was administered online to sophomores, juniors, seniors, and graduate students at the college. The prevalence rates were 10% for cyberbullying and 9% for cyberstalking, shown in the sample of 471 respondents. Traditional college students under 25 years of age were experiencing and participating in cyberbullying at higher rates than older college students. Prior experience as a victim of cyberbullying in high school was a significant risk factor for cyberbullying and cyberstalking in college, which implies that students' roles in cyberbullying are maintained from high school to college. The majority of college students are handling cyberbullying incidents themselves rather than utilizing campus resources, but two-thirds of respondents would be more likely to consider reporting an incident if there was a central e-mail address available for reporting incidents.

Chapter 10

José Pinheiro Neves, University of Minho, Portugal

Luzia de Oliveira Pinheiro, University of Minho, Portugal

Cyberbullying has become a major social concern because it raises questions about technoethics. It has been the subject of research, information and prevention activities for different groups to protect against the misuse of technology, and because of that, this paper is based on an exploratory study about the sociological phenomenon of cyberbullying among Portuguese university students. The paper stresses the connection between the concepts of bullying and cyberbullying while promoting a flexible epistemological model that highlights the emerging nature of these phenomena based on the theoretical contribution of Gregory Bateson. In the end, the authors present the main conclusions of the empirical study.

Section 3
The Ethical Side of Technological Applications

Chapter 11

This essay examines Latin American technological development and its connections with regional economic development, ecological deterioration, political freedoms' fluctuations, and globalization processes—understood as the spreading interconnectedness of business, science, technology, politics, and culture through large regions or the entirety of the world. The essay investigates how policy and decision issues resulting from Latin American technological development and its correlates can be plausibly addressed and argues for several theses, most notably, that in dealing with the issues, national legislation and international treaties have attained and are likely to attain their purposes only to a limited extent and in a mixed manner; that less legislation-dependent procedures evidence greater effectiveness and political feasibility; and that some globalization processes help fuel the environmental issues, while others help facilitate their resolution. The essay provides some concrete examples of how the issues can be soundly addressed.

Chapter 12

The increasing level of Internet penetration over the last decade has made web surveying a viable option for data collection in academic research. Software tools and services have been developed to facilitate the development and deployment of web surveys. Many academics and research students are outsourcing the design and/or hosting of their web surveys to external service providers, yet ethical issues associated with this use have received limited attention in academic literature. In this article, the authors focus on specific ethical concerns associated with the outsourcing of web surveys with particular reference to external commercial web survey service providers. These include threats to confidentiality and anonymity, the potential for loss of control over decisions about research data, and the reduced credibility of research. Suggested guidelines for academic institutions and researchers in relation to outsourcing aspects of web-based survey research are provided.

Chapter 13

As long as there has been distance education there has been the question how do you know the student turning in the work is the student registered for the course? As technology has been improving distance education course delivery, online education has been growing in leaps and bounds. The most recent Sloan-C report stated that in the U. S. alone there were almost 3.9 million students taking at least one online course during the fall of 2007 term (Allen and Seaman, 2008). Legislators took a hard look at the issue of student authentication in distance education with the passage of the Higher Education Opportunity Act of 2008. This paper reviews the issues related to student authentication and reviews the current forms of student authentication, reviewing one institution's answer to student authentication in its online programs.

Chapter 14

Scientific and technological expertise is currently experiencing a crisis. The public shows a growing distrust in many aspects related to the techno-scientific development. The birth of that suspicion begins after World War II but has transformed in the past few decades. In this paper, the authors examine how that doubt has specific features in the present moment. Also, there is a reaction to propose another way to make scientific and technological research where there is a more participative spirit. These changes reshape traditional ideas on science, technology and progress. Amateur efforts in science and technology maybe are opening the possibility of a change for these activities and information technology seems to support these efforts. If these can be considered, a consistent trend is difficult to predict.

Chapter 15

The author discusses the ethical issues of using cyberweapons, software that attacks data and other software during warfare. Many people assume these are relatively benign weapons, but we argue that they can create serious harms like any weapon. He defines cyberweapons and describes them in general terms, and survey their status as per the laws of war. He then discusses the unreliability of cyberweapons, the problem of collateral damage, and the associated problems of damage assessment, maintenance of secrecy, and mounting cyber-counterattacks. He examines some possibilities for creating more ethical cyberweapons and discusses the alternative of cyber-blockades. He concludes that cyberattacks should generally be outlawed by international agreement.

Chapter 16

The practice of developing and creating Free Software has been the centre of attention for studies related to economics, knowledge production, laws and the intellectual property framework. However, the practice that constitutes the initiative of Free Software also means a call to rethink current forms of political action and the in-depth meaning of what is understood as "political". This constitutes the field which has been called techno-activism. Along these lines, the authors propose a particular reading of the political challenge that is Free Software from the standpoint of Hardt and Negri's (2000) theoretical work. The authors put forward various contributions -regarding the organization, the agents and the form of political action- that they consider to pose a crisis for traditional proposals and urge society to renew its way of relating to information, the raw material upon which the current exercise of government and practices of techno-activist resistance rest.

Section 4
New Trends in Technoethics

Chapter 17

Alison Anderson, University of Plymouth, UK
Alan Petersen, Monash University, Australia

Nanotechnologies present significant new challenges for the study of technoethics. While they are surrounded by high expectations there is considerable uncertainty about their impact. Discussions about their likely ethical implications have often assumed that ethical issues and standpoints are relatively clear. The commonly held narrow utilitarian conception of benefits versus risks tends to overlook broader issues concerning the operation of power in problem definition, unimagined or unknown effects, and accountability. Drawing upon data from a recent UK-based study, this article examines how scientists' and policymakers' representations of nanotechnologies contribute to shaping thinking about the 'ethics' of this field. It suggests that their particular framing of the field is likely to constrain debate on a range of important matters in need of urgent deliberation, including the direction of current research efforts and whether the investments in particular lines of research are likely to bring about the promised economic and social benefits or have deleterious impacts. Overall, the study found that most of the respondents were optimistic about the perceived benefits of nanotechnologies and sought to distance their work from wider non-technical questions. Scientists and policymakers, it is argued, need to reflect much more upon their own assumptions and consider how these may influence the trajectory of technology development and public responses.

Chapter 18

Keith A. Bauer, Jefferson College of Health Sciences, USA

Transhumanism is a social, technological, political, and philosophical movement that advocates the transformation of human nature by means of pharmacology, genetic manipulation, cybernetic modification, nanotechnology, and a host of other technologies. The aim of this movement is to increase physical and sensory abilities, augment intelligence and memory, and extend lifespan. After providing some background on transhumanism, its philosophical heritage, and its goals, the author looks at three arguments against transhumanism, arguing that they are unpersuasive and should be rejected. This paper presents two arguments against transhumanism that have merit. The first argument is an argument from justice that addresses the distribution of benefits and burdens for funding, developing, and employing enhancement technology. The second argument examines a significant assumption held by many transhumanists, namely, that there is an essential "human nature" that can be transcended.

Chapter 19

Laura Cabrera, Charles Sturt University, Australia

Human implants are among the technology applications that deserve to be carefully assessed as they have the potential to help us treating many devastating human conditions, but also to assist us reaching a stage beyond current human capacities and abilities. Such a development would introduce many challenges for society, governments, and the individual. Human implants can blur the line that lies between what is acknowledged as therapy and enhancement. The lack of a clear distinction between therapy and enhancement will confront governments with new regulatory challenges in public health and funding technology research. This brings to the fore issues of justice, such as how to close instead of widen the 'technology-divide' and how to define priorities for funding, distributing, and using human implants. Given the potential impact that new and improved human implants can have for the individual and for society, a better understanding on the direction and reasons for developing such applications is needed to handle them in a wiser way. One way of assisting such a development is by rethinking our priorities when using technology for human enhancement applications.

Chapter 20

Linda Johansson, Royal Institute of Technology, Sweden

It is often argued that a robot cannot be held morally responsible for its actions. The author suggests that one should use the same criteria for robots as for humans, regarding the ascription of moral responsibility. When deciding whether humans are moral agents one should look at their behaviour and listen to the reasons they give for their judgments in order to determine that they understood the situation properly. The author suggests that this should be done for robots as well. In this regard, if a robot passes a moral version of the Turing Test—a Moral Turing Test (MTT) we should hold the robot morally responsible for its actions. This is supported by the impossibility of deciding who actually has (semantic or only syntactic) understanding of a moral situation, and by two examples: the transferring of a human mind into a computer, and aliens who actually are robots.

Chapter 21

Mahmoud Eid, University of Ottawa, Canada

Terrorism has been a constant threat in traditional and contemporary societies. Recently, it has been converged with new media technology and cyberspace, resulting in the modern tactic, cyber-terrorism, which has become most effective in achieving terrorist goals. Among the countless cyber-terrorist cases and scenarios of only this last decade, the paper discusses four cyber-terrorism cases that represent the most recent severe cyber-terrorist attacks on infrastructure and network systems—*Internet Black Tigers*, *MafiaBoy*, *Solo*, and *Irhabi 007*. Regardless of the nature of actors and their motivations, cyber-terrorists hit very aggressively causing serious damages. Cyber-terrorists are rational actors who use the most advanced technology; hence, the critical need for the use of counter-threat swords by actors on the other side. Given that terrorist goals are mostly dependent on the media's reactions, journalistic practices are significant and need to be most effective. A major tool that can help journalists in their anti- and counter-terrorist strategies with cyber-terrorists is rationalism, merged with the expected socially responsible conduct. Rational behaviour, founded in game theory, along with major journalistic ethical principles are fundamental components of effective media decision-making during times of terrorism.

Preface

TECHNOETHICS AND THE ETHICAL IMPACT OF TECHNOLOGICAL ADVANCEMENTS AND APPLICATIONS IN SOCIETY

The Challenge of Technological Systems and Society

Following the 2011 Fukushima-Daiichi nuclear plant disaster, I was invited to deliver the keynote address for the Value and Ethics Conference hosted by the Canadian Nuclear Safety Commission in Ottawa, Canada. The conference brought together top-level government decision-makers, nuclear energy leaders (public and private), and other stakeholders from the nuclear energy sector. If that had been a decade ago, I would have felt out of place: Why would a government body want to have an outsider lead off a government sponsored event? I was not and had never been a civil servant in the government. And why would a national nuclear energy governing body (public or corporate) wish the expertise of someone who was not an engineer, nuclear physicist, or other nuclear energy expert traditionally sought out to speak on safety standards and regulations within the nuclear energy sector?

However, this type of work was not out of the ordinary in 2011. It made me reflect on the gradual shift in approach to technological advancements and applications I had been witnessing for a number of years within various organizations and areas of public life. I was witnessing a paradigm shift in how society viewed and approached technology. The keynote presentation entitled, "Technoethics and the Future of Nuclear Energy in Canada," explored the ethical implications for human life, public values, and ecological impacts created by society's complex relationship with the development and regulation of nuclear energy technology. Nuclear technology was not a simply hammer that could be disposed of once interest waned in its usefulness. Nuclear waste lasts many lifetimes, cannot be easily disposed of, and poses serious environmental risks for society and the future of society. Like many large-scale technological advancements in the 20th and 21st century, nuclear energy development exemplified a potent technology, which required greater care and caution than previously developed technologies. This required a shift in how society approached it.

Technology, once approached as an empirical object (or collection of objects) that could be built up, isolated, and measured in the external world separate from human beings, was now being treated more and more as a complex social system defined by a complex set of human-technological relations embedded in life and society. In other words, the real world of technology had a human face and the new paradigm that was emerging was one founded on the appreciation of technology as a complex social system within which humans were entrenched. This technological systems paradigm highlighted the need for new types of expertise about social and ethical values in connection with technological systems.

In response, an amassing body of interdisciplinary research dedicated to social and ethical aspects of technology has emerged under the umbrella of Technoethics.

The Changing Face of Academia

Much of the recent popularity of Technoethics stems from a rising pragmatic and interdisciplinary orientation attractive to 21st century academics interested in access to an open (silo-free) forum for academic exchange on real life problems and opportunities of technology in society. In recent years, we have witnessed the landscape of academic move towards inter- and multidisciplinary collaborations to advance a multi-faceted knowledge base of expertise required to solve increasing complex problems faced by our changing society. Discipline specific work has always been recognized for its foundational appeal of possessing unitary knowledge bases and its strong reputation established over time and built up within separate academic departments. As noted by Pierce (1991):

Although most studies fail to define the term explicitly, they typically assume that boundaries of disciplines closely follows those of academic departments. The use of such boundaries may seem to fix overly concrete limits on a highly abstract phenomenon, excluding too large a number of people with interest in the subject. But its importance in creating and maintaining disciplinary communities makes the academic department the building block from which disciplines are created (23).

The discipline dominant approach within traditional academia provided effective coverage of specific domains with established norms and well-defined boundaries to decide what is included and excluded within each discipline. As Foucault (1975, 1979) indicated, "The disciplines characterize, classify, specialize; they distribute along a scale, around a norm, hierarchize individuals in relation to one another and, if necessary, disqualify and invalidate" (p 223), but what happens when what is being studied cannot be easily classified, measured, or placed on a scale? What happens when the nature of what is being studied demands a pragmatic orientation where the creation of new knowledge needs to be context-specific, problem-focused, and multi-faceted in nature? The growth of inter- and multi-disciplinarity, what some scholars are referred to as post academic science (Zimon, 2000), is beginning to take its place alongside disciplinary work, particularity with respect to the study of technology.

Within this new academic landscape, the social and ethical problems surrounding the development and application of new technologies in society stands out as one of the most, if not the most pressing problems of our age. In response, a growing body of work forms the basis of the emerging field known as Technoethics.

The Rise of Technoethics as a Field of Academic Research

The recent emergence of Technoethics as a field of academic research is largely attributable to the coming together of a critical mass of dedicated technology experts (researchers, scholars, administrators, and practitioners) grappling the tough questions arising from the public controversies and ethical dilemmas created by technological development and application in society. The field allowed its contributors to go beyond traditional approaches to the study ethics of technology guided by established philosophical principles, intellectual analysis, and logical reasoning. It pulls together experts from established fields (e.g., bioethics, engineering ethics, computer ethics, etc.) with technology experts working in new areas of technology research where social and ethical issues emerge (i.e., genetic research, nanotechnology, human enhancement, neurotechnology, robotics, reproductive technologies, etc.).

As pioneering breakthroughs are made in technological advancements and applications, novel questions arise regarding human values and ethical implications for society, many of which give rise to ethical dilemmas where conflicting viewpoints cannot be solved by relying on any one ethical theory or set of moral principles. Accordingly, the field of Technoethics takes a practical focus on the actual impacts (and potential impacts) of technology on human beings struggling to navigate the "real world" of technology. In many cases, this leads to the creation of more questions than answers in an effort to discern the underlying ethical complexities connected to the application of technology within real-life situations.

A number of recent publications under the umbrella of Technoethics are responsible for formalizing the field and providing a foundation of research and expertise upon which to build. The two volume Handbook of Research on Technoethics (Luppicini & Adel, 2009) pulled together over 100 experts from around the world working on a diversity of areas where technoethical inquiry is being applied. Following this, the first reader in Technoethics, *Technoethics and the Evolving Knowledge Society: Ethical Issues in Technological Design, Research, Development, and Innovation* (Luppicini, 2010), was published for use at the undergraduate and graduate level in a variety of courses that focus on technology and ethics in society. It explored a broad base of human processes and practices connected to technology embedded within social, political, and moral spheres of life. This text engaged students and researchers in critical debates connected to key ethical dimensions of a technological society. Its broad scope reinforced work appearing in the Handbook in an effort to highlight key topic areas of technoethical inquiry suitable for academic study. These publications helped set the stage for the academic journal that provides the main driving force for the field of Technoethics today.

In 2010, *International Journal of Technoethics* (Rocci Luppicini-Founding Editor-in-Chief) was launched to provide an ongoing forum for scholarly exchange among philosophers, researchers, social theorists, ethicists, historians, practitioners, and technologists working in areas of human activity affected by technological advancements and applications. With the strong support of IGI Global Publishing, the journal was assembled by its Editor-in-Chief and twelve associate editors, Allison Anderson (University of Plymouth), Keith Bauer (Marquette University), Josep Esquirol (University of Barcelona), Deb Gearthart (Troy University), Pablo Iannone (Central Connecticut State University), Mathias Klang (University of Lund), Andy Miah (University of the West of Scotland), Lynne Roberts (Curtin University of Technology), Neil Rowe (U.S. Naval Postgraduate School), Martin Ryder (Sun Microsystems), John Sullins III (Sonoma State University), Mary Thorseth (NTNU). The mission of the journal was as follows:

The mission of the International Journal of Technoethics (IJT) is to evolve technological relationships of humans with a focus on ethical implications for human life, social norms and values, education, work, politics, law, and ecological impact. This journal provides cutting edge analysis of technological innovations, research, developments policies, theories, and methodologies related to ethical aspects of technology in society. IJT publishes empirical research, theoretical studies, innovative methodologies, practical applications, case studies, and book reviews. IJT encourages submissions from philosophers, researchers, social theorists, ethicists, historians, practitioners, and technologists from all areas of human activity affected by advancing technology (International Journal of Technoethics, 2010).

The remarkable success of the journal can largely be attributed to unwavering publisher support, excellent associate editors and a large reviewer board of experts which expanded to over sixty members in its first year of publication. This present volume is based on a collection of articles derived from the inaugural year of the *International Journal of Technoethics*. It provides coverage of cutting edge work from a variety of areas where technoethical inquiry is currently being applied within the field of Technoethics.

OBJECTIVES OF THIS BOOK

What makes the chapters in this volume important rests on a number of factors including content adherence to methodological procedures, peer review standards, contribution to research knowledge about technology and ethics, and contribution to practice. As a book dedicated to scholarship emerging from the interdisciplinary field of Technoethics, the coverage in this volume is intended to be broad reaching in an effort to mirror the breadth of technological advancements and applications where ethical issues arise. The book covers a range of topic areas from computing to transhumanism. As a book intended to reflect the pragmatic orientation of Technoethics as an applied field of study, the topics covered are also intended to be of public interest and timely. The book addresses key areas of technoethical controversy from cyber-espionage to human implants.

As the founding editor-in-chief of the *International Journal of Technoethics* from which the contents of this volume are derived, a number of challenges were faced in deciding the scope of publication coverage. From a layperson's standpoint, technology touches almost every aspect of contemporary work and life in some way, not all of which warrants an ethical inquiry. To provide an ethical inquiry of all technology takes away the importance of such an inquiry in contributing unique insights into special cases which runs the risk of trivializing the field, not to mention wasting limited time and resources required to carry out such intense work. After all, the real world of technology is vast and advances quickly. It does not wait for academics to catch up with it. Therefore, the focus of Technoethics in the journal and this publication is on controversial technologies. It deals with all areas of work and life where technological development and application have raised serious ethical challenges and produced public debate. Although much of this scholarly work is rooted in academic theory and knowledge, the reader will notice that there is a decidingly pragmatic orientation to most of this work connecting academic knowledge to real life problems revolving around technology and its use in society.

In terms of readership consideration, this volume goes out to an audience as broad as the interdisciplinary base of scholars that contribute to the field of Technoethics. From cyberbullying to nuclear technology waste disposal, the contributor base and intended readership is eclectic and coming from various disciplines and fields. Because technology is designed, developed, and applied at so many levels of life and society one can expect that the readership will also come from different organizations and walks of life. This readership may include students, researchers, technologists, administrators, designers, instructors, etc. What binds this group together is the interest in technology and ethics which acts as the central organizing construct for delving into established theories and practices in an effort to understand and explain ethical controversies surrounding technology. Knowledge gained is intended to inform technology practices and leverage decision making to maximize the benefits of and minimize negative risks and consequences of technology.

ORGANIZATION OF THE BOOK

This volume deals with complex ethical issues and dilemmas within the field of Technoethics. It attempts to address a number pivotal questions arising in contemporary life revolving around some of the most controversial areas of ethics and technology: How are human thoughts, actions, and interactions mediated by technology? What is a moral mediator? What are the ethical implications of human-technological relations with respect to cultural objects and societal structures? What are the ethical implications of ubiquitous computing? How can the problems of an ethical judgment on science and technology be correctly approached? What ways of ethical thinking can guide new policies and laws that will protect human dignity in the advancing technological world? What ethical guidelines are relevant for safe-guarding online interaction and virtual life? What ethical guidelines are needed to deal with pervasive problems of online misconduct such as cyberbullying and cyberstalking? What ethical implications are there when dealing with human implantation? Does it make sense to consider the functional morality of robots? What measures can be taken to combat cyber-terrorism and ensure high standards of ethical journalism? What ethical considerations need to be made in the deployment of cyberweapons? These are some of the questions that this volume deals with.

In terms of the organization of this book, twenty-one chapters are divided into four sections in an effort to provide the reader with a logical flow writing organized according to a thematic scheme. Section 1: **Theoretical Perspectives** contains five chapters: Chapter 1, "*Material Cultures and Moral Mediators in Human Hybridization*" (Lorenzo Magnani), Chapter 2, "*The Significance of the Ethics of Respect*" (Josep M. Esquirol), Chapter 3, "*How Can the Problems of an Ethical Judgment on Science and Technology be Correctly Approached?*" (Evandro Agazzi), Chapter 4, "*Technology Traps: Who is Responsible?*" (Peter B. Crabb and Steven E. Stern), and Chapter 5, "*Ubiquitous Computing: Any Ethical Implications?*" (J. A. Quilici-Gonzalez, G. Kobayashi, M. C. Broens, and M. E. Q. Gonzalez).

Section 2: **Technoethics and the Digital Society** contains five chapters: Chapter 6, "*Identifying the Ethics of Emerging Information and Communication Technologies: An Essay on Issues, Concepts, and Method*" (Bernd Carsten Stahl et al.), Chapter 7, "*The Regulation of Gaze and Capture: New Media and the Image Economy*" (Yasmin Ibrahim), Chapter 8, "*Peer-to-Peer File-Sharing: Psychological Reactance and the Theory of Planned Behaviour*" (Peter Allen and Lynne Roberts), Chapter 9, "*An Exploratory Study of the Cyberbullying and Cyberstalking: Experiences and Factors Related to Victimization of Students at a Public Liberal Arts College*" (Ellen Kraft and Jinchang Wang), Chapter 10, "*Cyberbully-ing: A Sociological Approach*" (José Neves and Luzia de Oliveira Pinheiro).

Section 3: **The Ethical Side of Technological Applications** contains six chapters: Chapter 11, "*Reclaiming the Green Continent: Ecology, Globalization, and Policy and Decision in Latin America*" (Pablo Iannone), Chapter 12, "*The Ethics of Outsourcing Online Survey Research*" (Peter J. Allen and Lynne D. Roberts), Chapter 13, "*The Issues Related to Student Authentication in Distance Education*" (Deb Gearhart), Chapter 14, "*Amateur vs. Professionals Politics, Citizenship, and Science*" (Antonio Lafuente and Andoni Alonso), Chapter 15, "*The Ethics of Cyberweapons in Warfare*" (Neil C. Rowe), and Chapter 16, "*Not Just Software: Free Software and the (Techno) Political Action*" (Blanca Callén et al.).

Section 4: **New Trends in Technoethics** contains five chapters: Chapter 17, "*Shaping the Ethics of an Emergent Field: Scientists' and Policymakers' Representations of Nanotechnologies*" (Alison Anderson and Alan Petersen), Chapter 18, "*Transhumanism and Its Critics: Five Arguments against a Posthuman Future*" (Keith A. Bauer), Chapter 19, "*Human Implants: A Suggested Framework to Set Priorities*" (Laura Cabrera), Chapter 20, "*The Functional Morality of Robots*" (Linda Johansson), and Chapter 21,

"Cyber-Terrorism and Ethical Journalism: A Need for Rationalism" (Mahmoud Eid). A more detailed preview of each chapter is provided below.

How are human thoughts, actions, and interactions mediated by technology? What is a moral mediator? What are the ethical implications of human-technological relations with respect to cultural objects and societal structures? In Chapter 1, *"Material Cultures and Moral Mediators in Human Hybridization,"* Lorenzo Magnani explores the complex relation between material culture and distributed cognition while highlighting the importance of technological artifacts as moral mediators. This stimulating chapter contributes valuable insight on the role of moral mediators and the challenge of cultural isolation within key domains of human activity affected by advancing technology.

What does respect mean? What merits respect within contemporary society? How can an ethics of respect be useful as a guiding tool within our contemporary society shaped by science and technology? In Chapter 2, *"The Significance of the Ethics of Respect,"* Josep M. Esquirol investigates the conceptualization of respect and proposes an approach to the ethics of respect as a means of addressing current challenges faced by a society shaped by technology. By examining the notion of 'respect' at great lengths, the author attempts to show how it relates to an attentive gaze as the essence of respect. This thought-provoking chapter has promising applications within multiple fields including, ecology, medicine, education, and political science.

Does an ethical evaluation of science and technology make sense? There is a pervasive division in positions concerning whether or not an ethical evaluation of science and technology is appropriate. At one extreme end, some scholars believe that ethical judgments must not be introduced at all in the business of science and technology, while other scholars at the opposite extreme hold that ethical judgements are legitimate and should be mandatory in science and technology practice. In Chapter 3, *"How Can the Problems of an Ethical Judgment on Science and Technology be Correctly Approached?"* Evandro Agazzi examines existing arguments for and against the use of ethical judgments in science and technology in an effort to clarify the debate.

Technology draws people in like magpies to shiny bits of sparkling metal. As we all know, despite the 'bells and whistles' appeal of new technologies, they can also have a lasting negative impact on individuals, society, and the environment. These "technology traps" can be said to occur when individuals and societies become caught up with technologies and the harmful consequences produced by these technologies. In Chapter 4, *"Technology Traps: Who is Responsible?"* Peter Crabb and Steven Stern provide an insightful breakdown of five technology traps that they believe plague our current society. These are: incompetence, self-miscontrol, misbehavior, techno-centrism, and environmental degradation. The chapter discusses the ethical responsibility for these traps with respect to individual technology users, businesses, and government.

In this day and age, the once speculative idea of ubiquitous computing (information-processing capacity from computers available everywhere at any time, and integrated into everyday objects and activities) is a common reality that disappears into the background for many of us until, that is, there are reasons to question ubiquitous computing, and that is what is done in Chapter 5, *"Ubiquitous Computing: Any Ethical Implications?"* Key questions addressed include: What are the possible ethical implications ubiquitous computing systems in human perception/action? and how can the widespread application of ubiquitous computing systems affect the behaviour of individuals as embodied embedded agents? In this chapter, the authors provide an interdisciplinary perspective on the possible ethical implications of the presence of ubiquitous computing systems in human perception/action. The authors draw insightful contrasts for readers between traditional considerations of ethical issues and the Ecological Philosophy view concerning its possible consequences in the context of perception/action.

One of the most popular areas of Technoethics deals with the ethical issues of Information and Communication Technologies (ICTs). These issues are particularly salient in the public sphere where can have a profound impact on individual freedom, and happiness, and one's ability to lead a good life. This is partly why policy makers are so invested in discerning key ethical issues of ICTs and their consequences. The best way of creating ICT policy that is sensitive to ethical issues pertain to being proactive in addressing such issues at an early stage of the technology life cycle. To this end, Chapter 6, *"Identifying the Ethics of Emerging Information and Communication Technologies: An Essay on Issues, Concepts, and Method"* explores how knowledge of ethical aspects of emerging ICTs can be gained using a suggested methodology put forth by the chapter authors. This chapter makes a unique contribution by sketching out how a proper description of emerging ICTs can be used for an ethical analysis.

In recent years, the field of Technoethics has also begun delving into the study of the human identity and the body. The is largely due to the increasing importance of digital technology in the mediation in our identity along with the advancement of human enhancement technologies that allow us to alter aspects of our identity in significant ways that raise serious ethical questions. Chapter 7, *"The Regulation of Gaze and Capture: New Media and the Image Economy"* by Yasmin Ibrahim offers a novel perspective on this technoethical topic by focusing on how digital image capture has given rise to new forms of human gaze which has ethical, legal and social implications for societies. Yasmin Ibrahim reflects on the paradoxical state of this image economy where gaze, through mobile recording devices, can be both empowering (i.e., holding authorities accountable) and disempowering (i.e., invading privacy and enabling voyeurism). In response, this chapter offers a fresh perspective on how the digital image economy is creating new ways of at each other along with the countermeasures created to regulate image capture. The implications of this emerging digital image economy represent a serious ethical challenge for Internet users, regulators, and authorities that is only beginning to be understood within society.

Tackling a slightly different area of digital technology mediation, Chapter 8, *"Peer-to-Peer File-Sharing: Psychological Reactance and the Theory of Planned Behaviour"* by Peter Allen and Lynne Roberts presents an empirical study exploring a persisting trend in sharing and downloading media files over Peer-to-Peer (P2P) networks. Specifically, this research study draws on the Theory of Planned Behaviour (TPB) and examines whether or not psychological reactance could account for variance in individuals' intent to engage in, such behaviour. Interestingly enough, no support for psychological reactance as a predictor of P2P file downloading intent or behaviour is found. Rather, findings reveal that attitude, subjective norms, and perceived behavioural control were mediated by behavioural intent. Chapter interpretations offer a novel explanation with promising research potential for future work on human values and online misconduct.

Extending the discussion on technoethics and digital technology, the phenomenon of cyberbullying has risen to be one of the greatest fears of educators and parents around the globe when it comes to Internet use among children. On the one hand, the use of the Internet is becoming more and more embraced in educational settings to better prepare children for the real world and the digital knowledge economy that continually expanding. On the other hand, exposing children to the Internet also opens the door to new forms of exploitation and abuse that parents want to protect their children against. With this in mind, two chapters in this volume deal with the growing epidemic of cyerbullying. Chapter 9, *"An Exploratory Study of the Cyberbullying and Cyberstalking: Experiences and Factors Related to Victimization of Students at a Public Liberal Arts College"* by Ellen Kraft and Jinchang Wang. This chapter presents findings of a study on cyberbullying and cyberstalking experiences of students. The study found that college students under 25 years of age were experiencing and participating in cyberbullying at higher rates than older college students and that prior experience of cyberbullying in high school was a significant risk factor for cyberbullying and cyberstalking in college. Next, Chapter 10, "*Cyberbullying: A Sociological Approach*" by José Neves and Luzia de Oliveira Pinheiro takes a step back to look at cyberbullying through a sociological lens. In this insightful chapter, the authors conduct an exploratory study on cyberbullying among Portuguese university students. This chapter helps to clarify the relationship between bullying and cyberbullying and posit a unique model that helps explain the emerging nature of cyberbullying based on the theoretical contribution of Gregory Bateson. Both chapters make useful contributions to empirical research that advances knowledge on cyberbullying.

Beyond technoethical concerns that target individuals and groups, there are also technoethical considerations to address at the national level when technological innovation and economic development are at issue. Chapter 11, "*Reclaiming the Green Continent: Ecology, Globalization, and Policy and Decision in Latin America*" by Pablo Iannone addresses environmental concerns created by the impact of technology within economic activity. These macro level technoethical concerns faced by countries around the world create serious challenges to overcome and raise important questions to consider: How has technological and economic development in Latin America (and countries beyond Latin America) impacted ecological stability in ways that raise ethical challenges? What policy problems does the current state of technological and economic development in Latin America pose and what legalistic approaches and decision-making strategies have been used in addressing the situation? What lessons can be learned to advance ethical technological and economic development to help safeguard the environment for generations to come?

One of the consequences of increased Internet penetration over the last decade is that web surveying among researchers has become increasingly prevalent but are their ethical issues to consider. The answer is unmistakably yes. Chapter 12, "*The Ethics of Outsourcing Online Survey Research*" by Peter J. Allen and Lynne D. Roberts explores a trend in online research where academics and research students are outsourcing the design and/or hosting of their research to external service providers. This chapter a number of key ethical concerns including, possible threats to confidentiality and anonymity, the potential for loss of control over research data decision-making, and the reduced credibility of research. This chapter provides excellent recommendations on proper guidelines for academic institutions and researchers interested in outsourcing parts of their online research activity.

Technoethical inquiry is also pursued in higher education, especially when faced with ethical controversies surrounding the delivery of online courses and distance education programs with rely heavily on digital technology. Deb Gearhart's Chapter 13, "*The Issues Related to Student Authentication in Distance Education*" discusses current forms of student authentication and core technoethical issues related to student

authentication. It poses a number of questions that administrators of higher education are currently struggling with: Why is there a concern for student authentication in distance education and electronic assignment submissions? How do instructors know the student turning in the assignment is the student registered for the course? Will universities be forced to use biometric identification or is it unnecessary to go to such lengths?

Chapter 14, "*Amateur vs. Professionals: Politics, Citizenship, and Science*" by Antonio Lafuente and Andoni Alonso explores the growing public distrust in techno-scientific development since WWII. There is a growing concern that scientific and technological expertise is currently experiencing a crisis and that public trust concerning many aspects related to the techno-scientific development is waning. This chapter offers a fresh perspective on specific features of public doubt towards techno-scientific development today. In addition, the chapter provides valuable insights on how to make scientific and technological research more participative in spirit in an effort to win back public trust and reshape traditional ideas on science, technology, and progress to better adapt to public needs and interests.

It has been said that the next world war will be fought by pressing a few buttons rather than battling it out in the trenches. What kind of ethical standards can be applied to modern weaponry like cyberweapons which appear so different in form and function than traditional weapons? In Chapter 15, "*The Ethics of Cyberweapons in Warfare,*" Neil Rowe explores the ethical implications of using cyberweapons to attack computer data and other software during warfare. Insightful arguments are offered to treat cyberweapons more seriously since they have the potential to inflict harm like any other weapon. Assuming that unprovoked cyberattacks are illegal and unethical, does the same apply to cyber-counterattacks? This chapter raises valuable questions that provoke discussion.

Over the last decade, the free software movement has been a hot topic within economics, law, and political science as it pertains to discussions of democracy, equality, and intellectual property. As a result of this movement, society has begun to rethink the meaning of democratic participation along with the new technological forms of political action available to for political activists (aka techno-activism). In response to this movement, Chapter 16, "*Not Just Software: Free Software and the (Techno) Political Action*" explores the political challenge resulting from the free software movement from the standpoint of Hardt and Negri's (2000) theoretical work. This chapter helps discern key areas challenges and opportunities associated with techno-activism.

In a slightly different area, nanotechnology has raised new questions about issues of responsibility, accountability, and ownership: What do citizens know (and need to know) about the potential risks of nanotechnologies and their possible negative consequences? Which individuals (and groups) will be most affected by nanotechnology development? Who (or what organization) is most likely to control and benefit from various nanotechnology applications? Alison Anderson and Alan Petersen's Chapter 17, "*Shaping the Ethics of an Emergent Field: Scientists' and Policymakers' Representations of Nano-technologies,*" uses data from a UK-based research project, to help explain how scientists' and policymakers' positions on nanotechnologies have a very real impact on public opinion about ethical aspects of nanotech development.

In Chapter 18, "*Transhumanism and Its Critics: Five Arguments against a Posthuman Future*" by Keith Bauer deals with the topic of transhumanism and the current heated public debate about the acceptability of human enhancement technology. How much should individuals be able to alter themselves? Is there a limit to what can be considered human? This chapter provides an excellent background reading on the transhumanism movement that embraces the transformation of human nature through pharmacology, genetic manipulation, cybernetic modification, nanotechnology, and a variety of other technologies. In addition, the chapter presents and discusses a variety of arguments and counterarguments to transhumanism in an effort to clarify popular misunderstandings and shed light on what is core in this heated debate.

In Chapter 19, "*Human Implants: A Suggested Framework to Set Priorities,*" Laura Cabrera discusses one set of particularly controversial technologies which has the potential treat many human impairments but at the risk of reaching a stage beyond current human capacities and abilities. In this sense, human implants blur the line between therapy and enhancement creating new regulatory challenges in public health and public research funding. There is also the risk of further contributing to the existing 'technology-divide' and the inequalities that give unfair advantages to some over others. This chapter proposes closer scrutiny in dealing with human implants and need for a clear set of priorities when using human enhancement technologies.

In Chapter 20, "*The Functional Morality of Robots*," by Linda Johansson, the focus on technoethics turns from technologies for human enhancement to a special variety of technologies for human service that grew out of robotics. Once restricted to science fiction writings, robotics has evolved greatly over the last three decades, providing us with robots with increasingly sophisticated capacities and human uses in life and society. Given such complexity, what happens when negative consequences arise from robot actions? How should moral responsibility be assigned, if at all, to our robot creations?

The author in this chapter argues for the similar ascription of moral responsibility for robots and for humans based on a moral version of the Turing Test—a Moral Turing Test (MTT). That chapter takes the position that we should hold the robot morally responsible for actions and draws on anecdotal cases to illustrate.

In the final chapter, Chapter 21, "*Cyber-Terrorism and Ethical Journalism: A Need for Rationalism*," Mahmoud Eid tackles a very real fear that dominates current public forums and mass media broadcasts. Although terrorism has been a continual threat in traditional and contemporary societies, its recent evolution leveraged by new media technology and cyberspace has given rise to cyber-terrorism, a new form of terrorism with new ethical challenges to consider. This insightful chapter paper sheds light on the current state of cyber-terrorism by discussing four cyber-terrorism cases covered by the media that represent the most recent cyber-terrorist attacks on infrastructure and network systems in recent years. In an effort to improve the situation, the chapter suggests treating cyber-terrorists as rational actors with media goals, which need to be acknowledged by journalists in providing media coverage. The chapter draws on ideas from rationalism and game theory, along with major journalistic ethical principles to help provide guidance for effective media decision-making during times of cyber-terrorism.

Overall, this assembly of technoethical research studies provides a glimpse of selected work from a variety of areas where technoethical inquiry is employed. The breadth of topics covered attests to the ubiquitous nature of technological development, which drives technoethical considerations in life and society. At the same time, it must be noted that this volume presents only a selection of the many research areas currently pursued and yet to be pursued within the rapidly evolving field of Technoethics.

Rocci Luppicini
University of Ottawa, Canada

REFERENCES

Foucault, M. (1977). *Discipline and punish: The birth of the prison* (Sheridan, A., Trans.). New York, NY: Vintage.

Global, I. G. I. (2010). *International journal of technoethics*. Hershey, PA: IGI Global.

Luppicini, R. (2010). *Technoethics and the evolving knowledge society*. Hershey, PA: IGI Global. doi:10.4018/978-1-60566-952-6

Luppicini, R. (2011). *Technoethics and the future of nuclear energy in Canada*. Paper presented at the 2011 Value and Ethics Conference, Canadian Nuclear Safety Commission. Ottawa, Canada.

Luppicini, R., & Adell, R. (Eds.). (2009). *Handbook of research on technoethics* (*Vol. 1-2*). Hershey, PA: IGI Global.

Pierce, S. J. (1991). Subject areas, disciplines and the concept of authority. *Library & Information Science Research, 13*, 21–35.

Ziman, J. (2000). *Real science: What it is, and what it means*. Cambridge, UK: Cambridge University Press. doi:10.1017/CBO9780511541391

Section 1
Theoretical Perspectives

Chapter 1
Material Cultures and Moral Mediators in Human Hybridization

Lorenzo Magnani
University of Pavia, Italy

ABSTRACT

We already are hybrid humans, fruit of a kind of co-evolution of both our brains and the common, scientific, social, and moral knowledge we have produced by ourselves starting from the birth of material culture with our ancestors until the recent effects generated by the whole field of technological artifacts and of information and communication technologies (ICTs). We all are "constitutively" natural-born cyborgs, that is biotechnological hybrid minds. Our minds should not be considered to be located only in the head: human beings have solved their problems of survival and reproduction, "distributing" cognitive and ethical functions to external non-biological sources, props, and aids, which originate cultures. The paper also illustrates the interplay between cultures and distributed cognition and stresses the role of some technological artifacts as moral mediators. The second part of the paper is related to the analysis of the interplay between cultures, morality, and cognition and of some consequences concerning the problem of intercultural communication in the light of the role of moral mediators, docility, and cyberprivacy. Finally, I discuss some suggestions concerning the problem of what I call the moral principle of isolation of cultures, with respect to the effects of ICTs.

HYBRID HUMANS AND DISTRIBUTED COGNITION

Following Clark's conclusions on the relationships between humans and technology, especially information and communications technologies

DOI: 10.4018/978-1-4666-1773-5.ch001

(ICTs), we all are "constitutively" natural-born cyborgs–that is, biotechnologically hybrid minds (2003)[1]. Less and less are our minds considered to be in our heads: human beings have solved their problems of survival and reproduction by "distributing" cultures and cognitive functions to external non-biological sources, props, and aids. Our biological brains have delegated to external tools many activities that involve complex planning and elaborate assessments of consequences (p. 5). A simple example might be how the brain, when faced with multiplying large numbers, learns to act in concert with pen and paper, storing part of the process and the results outside itself. The same occurred when Greek geometers discovered new properties and theorems of geometry: they manipulated external diagrams to establish a kind of continuous cognitive negotiation with a suitable external support (like sand or a blackboard), to gain new important information and heuristic suggestions[2]. The use of external tools and artifacts is very common: cognitive skills and performances are so widespread that they become invisible, thus giving birth to something I have called "tacit templates" of behavior that blend "internal" and " external" cognitive aspects (Magnani, 2001a, chapter six).

New technologies will facilitate this process in a new way: on a daily basis, people are linked to non-biological, more-or-less intelligent machines and tools like cell phones, laptops, and medical prosthetics. Consequently, it becomes harder and harder to say where the world stops and the person begins. Clark contends that this line between biological self and technological world has always been flexible and that this fact has to be acknowledged both from the epistemological and the ontological points of view. Thus the study of the new anthropology of hybrid humans becomes important, and I would add that it is also critical for us to delineate and articulate the related ethical issues.

I certainly share Clark's enthusiasm in philosophically acknowledging our status as "cyborgs," but I would like to go further, to do more than just peer through the window of his book at the many cyberartifacts that render human creatures the consumers-cyborgs we are.

Our bodies and our "selves" are materially and cognitively "extended," meshed, that is, with external artifacts and objects, and this fact sets the stage for a variety of new philosophical and moral questions related to the role of cultures in our technological world. For example, because so many aspects of human beings are now simulated in or replaced by things in an external environment, new ontologies can be constituted – and Clark would agree with me. Pieces of information that can be carried in any physical medium are called "memes" by Dawkins (1989). They can "stay" in human brains or jump from brain to brain to objects, becoming configurations of artificial things that express meaning, like words written on a blackboard or data stored on a CD, icons and diagrams on a newspaper, configurations of external things that express meanings and cultural units like an obligatory route. They can also exist in natural objects endowed with informative significance – stars, for example, which offer navigational guidance. In my perspective the externalization of these chunks of information is described in the light of the cognitive delegation human beings concentrate in material objects and structures. Like memes, cultural units are distributed everywhere not only thanks to their dissemination in brains, but also thanks to their embodiment in various kinds of external materiality, in objects and artifacts of various type.

Beyond the supports of paper, telephone, and media, many human interactions are strongly mediated (and potentially recorded) through ICTs, for example the Internet. What about the concept of identity, so connected to the concept of freedom? At present identity has to be considered in a broad sense: the externally stored amount of data, information, images, and texts that concern us as individuals is enormous. This storage of information creates for each person a kind of external "data shadow" that, together with the biological body, forms a "cyborg" of both flesh and electronic data that identifies us or potentially identifies us. I contend that this complex new "information being" depicts new ontologies that in turn involve new moral problems. In turn these new ways of building intercultural relations tend depict uniform behaviors and habits because of the effect of their globalization. We can no longer apply old moral rules and old-fashioned arguments to beings that are at the same time biological (concrete) and virtual, situated in a three-dimensional local space but potentially "globally omnipresent" as information-packets. For instance, where we are located cybernetically is no longer simple to define, and the increase in telepresence technologies will further affect this point. It becomes clear that external, non biological resources contribute to our variable sense of who and what we are and what we can do[3].

MATERIAL CULTURE AND THE DISEMBODIMENT OF MIND

If, as Clark holds, the line between the biological self and the technological world is flexible and continually shifting, biological self and technological world are intertwined in "cyborgs" that present a variety of different cases and degrees. This story, related to the birth of hybrid humans is completely intertwined with the birth of culture, which is, intrinsically, immediately material and informational.

Let first of all consider the case of what I call tool-using humans (for instance related to clothing, shelters, etc.) (Magnani, 2007a, chapter three), appeared at least dating from the birth of the so-called material culture, when handaxes were constructed, so offering new cognitive chances to the co-evolution of the mind of some early humans, like the Neanderthals, These hominids already possessed isolated cognitive domains, Mithen (1996) calls different intelligences, probably endowed with different degree of fleeting consciousness about the thoughts and knowledge within each domain (natural history intelligence, technical intelligence, social intelligence). Unfortunately, when examined in light of its evolutionary history, the human mind is quite evidently limited as to the types of ideas it can hold and transmit between generations without material support.

It is extremely important to stress that material culture is not just the product of this massive cognitive chance but also cause of it. In this perspective we acknowledge that material artifacts are tools for thoughts as is language: tools for exploring, expanding, and manipulating our own minds. In this regard the evolution of culture is inextricably linked with the evolution of consciousness and thought.

Early human brain became a kind of universal and creative "intelligent" machine, extremely flexible so that we did no longer need different "separated" intelligent machines doing different jobs. A single one should suffice. As the engineering problem of producing various machines for various jobs is replaced by the office work of "programming" the Turing's universal machine to do these jobs, so the different intelligences very soon became integrated in a new universal device endowed with a high-level type of consciousness. This achievement is accomplished thanks to the birth of [material] culture. From this perspective the expansion of the minds is in the meantime a continuous process of disembodiment of the minds themselves into the cultural material world around them: the evolution of the mind is inextricably linked with the evolution of large, integrated, material cognitive/cultural systems.

Other more recent types of cyborgs appeared and others will appear: the ones we can call enhanced humans (related to the exploitation of prosthetics, pacemakers, artificial organs, etc.) and so-called medical cyborgs (fruit of IVF, cloning, genetic enhancement, etc.). We also have the cognitively enhanced cyborgs (using abacus, laptops, external cognitive representations in general, cell phones) and the super-cyborgs (endowed with stimulators implants, silicon chips transponders, etc.).

It is now clear that the biological brain's image of the body is protean and negotiable, an "outgoing construct" that changes as new technologies are added to our lives (Clark, 2003, p. 5). Take the human visual system, for example, where much of the database is left outside of the "head" and is accessed by outward-looking sensory apparatus (principally the eyes). As opportunistic cyborgs, we do not care whether information is held within the biological organism or stored in the external world, in, say a laptop or cell phone. And not only do new technologies expand our sense of self – they can even induce changes in the actual physical body: increased finger mobility has been observed among people under twenty-five as the result of their use of electronic game controllers and text messaging on cell phones (p. 86).

THE CO-EVOLUTION OF BRAINS AND CULTURES AND THE ROLE OF MORAL MEDIATORS

What I call semiotic brains (Magnani, 2007b) are brains that make up a series of signs and that are engaged in making or manifesting or reacting to a series of signs: through this semiotic activity they are at the same time engaged in "being minds" and so in thinking intelligently. An important effect of this semiotic activity of brains is a continuous process of disembodiment of mind that exhibits a new cognitive perspective on the mechanisms underling the semiotic emergence of cultures.

It is important to stress that in this semiotic activity of construction of artifacts, cognitive delegations to external materiality, and realization of what recently have been called "cognitive niches" (Toby and DeVore, 1987) human acts of cognition can add worth to or subtract value from an entity. In (Magnani, 2007a) I contend that revealing the similarities between people and things can help us to attribute to human beings the kind of worth that is now held by many highly valued non-human things. This process suggests a new perspective on ethical thinking: indeed, these objects and structures can mediate moral ideas and recalibrate the value of human beings by playing the role of what I call moral mediators.

What exactly is a moral mediator? I derived the concept of the moral mediator from that of the epistemic mediator, which I introduced in my previous research on abduction and creative and explanatory reasoning (Magnani, 2001). First of all, moral mediators can extend value from already prized things to human beings, as well as to other non-human things and even "non-things" like future people and animals. We are surrounded by human-made and artificial, entities, whether they are concrete objects like a hammer or a PC or abstractions like an institution or society; all of these things have the potential to serve as moral mediators. For this reason, I say it is critically important for current ethics to address not only the relationships among human beings, but also those between human and non-human entities. Moreover, by exploiting the concepts of "thinking through doing" and of manipulative abduction, we can see that a considerable part of moral action is performed in a tacit way, so to say, "through doing." Part of this "doing" can be considered a manipulation of the external world to build various moral mediators that function as enormous new sources of ethical information and knowledge. I call these schemes of action "templates of moral doing."

In the cases above, moral mediators are purposefully constructed to achieve particular ethical effects, but other aspects and cognitive roles of moral mediators are equally important: moral mediators are also beings, artifactual entities of various kind, objects, structures, that objectively, even beyond human beings' intentions, carry possible ethical or unethical consequences.

External moral mediators function as components of a memory system that crosses the boundary between person and environment. For instance, when a society moves an abused child into a foster home, an example I use in my book (Magnani, 2007a), it is seeking both to protect her and to reconfigure her social relationships; in this case, the new setting functions as a moral mediator that changes how she relates to the world – it can supply her with new emotions that bring positive moral and psychological effects and help her gain new perspectives on her past abuse and on adults in general. I contend these processes as "model-based" inferences, and indeed one way moral mediators transform moral tasks is by promoting further moral inferences in agents at the level of model-based abduction, a concept I introduced in my book on abductive reasoning (Magnani, 2001a). I use the term "model-based reasoning" to mean the constructing and manipulating of certain representations, not mainly sentential and/or formal, but mental and/or related to external mediators: obvious examples of model-based inferences include building and using visual representations, conducting thought experiments, and engaging in analogical reasoning. In this light, an emotional feeling also can be interpreted as a kind of model-based cognition. Of course, abductive reasoning – the process of reasoning to hypotheses – can be performed in a model-based way either internally or with the help of external mediators.

Moreover, I can use manipulation to alter my bodily experience of pain; I can, for example, follow the behavior template "control of sense data", during which I might shift – often unconsciously – the position of my body. Through manipulation I can also change my body's relationships with other humans and non-humans experiencing distress, as did Mother Theresa, whose rich, personal moral feeling and consideration of pain was certainly shaped by her physical proximity to starving and miserable people and by her manipulation of their bodies. In many people, moral training is often related to the spontaneous (and sometimes fortuitous) manipulations of both sense data and their own bodies, for these actions can build morality immediately and non-reflectively "through doing."

Technological artifacts serve as moral mediators in many situations, as is the case when certain machines affect privacy. For example the Internet mediates human interaction in a much more profound way than do traditional forms of communication like paper, the telephone, or the media, even going so far as to record interactions in many situations. The problem is that because the Internet mediates human identity, it has the power to affect human freedom. Thanks to the Internet, our identities today largely consist of externally stored amount of data, information, images, and texts that concern us as individuals, and the result is a "cyborg" of both flesh and electronic data that identifies us. In that, I contend that this complex new "information being" depicts new ontologies that in turn involve new moral problems. We can no longer apply old moral rules and old-fashioned arguments to beings that are simultaneously biological and virtual, situated in a three-dimensional local space yet "globally omnipresent" as information packets. Our cybernetic locations are no longer simple to define, and increasing telepresence technologies will exacerbate this effect, giving external, non-biological resources even greater powers to mediate ethical endowments such as those related to our sense of who and what we are and what we can do. These and other effects – of the Internet – almost all of which were unanticipated – are powerful motivators of our duty to construct new knowledge.

I believe that in the context of this abstract but ubiquitous technological presence, certain moral approaches that ethics has traditionally tended to disparage are worth a new look. Taking care of both people and external things through personal, particular acts – a moral orientation often associated with women – rather than relating to others through an impersonal, general concern about humanity has new appeal. The ethics of care does not consider the abstract "obligation" as essential; moreover, because it does not require that we impartially promote the interests of everyone alike, it allows us to focus on those who most need assistance.

In short, a considerable part of morality occurs in a implicit way, so to say, "through doing," and part of this "doing" features manipulating the external world in order to build various external "moral mediators" that can provide vast amounts of new information and knowledge, transform ethical features and effects, and sometimes, of course, generate unethical outcomes.

MATERIAL AND IMMATERIAL CULTURES

Taking advantage of the previous theoretical framework, resorting to the concept of distributed cognition and morality, and to the role of moral mediators, the second part of this paper provides their application to the analysis of the interplay between cultures (artifacts), morality, and cognition. In particular the study will deal with some consequences concerning the problem of inter-cultural communication, in the light of the role of moral mediators, docility, and cyberprivacy. Finally, I discuss some suggestions concerning the problem of what I call the moral principle of isolation of cultures, with respect to the effects of ICTs.

The tradition of studies on intercultural relations (Roth, 2001) distinguishes between material and immaterial cultures. Immaterial interactions would focus "on language, non-verbal expressions, and behaviors of the actors as well as on their perceptions, attitudes, and values" (p. 564). On the contrary, material culture refers to the people's material environment consisting in food, dwellings, furniture, and deals with social or territorial behaviors mainly related to intra-cultural aspects of national, regional, and cultural identities, but not to personal inter-cultural communications.

In the previous sections I have depicted a different perspective on material culture, taking advantage of some results coming form the area of embodied and distributed cognition. In this perspective every culture is material. There is not something "immaterial" (mental?) in terms of words, perceptions, or values, which we can distinguish from objects like hammers of laptops.

Beyond Cartesian dualism, I have illustrated that our – material – brains delegate meaningful cognitive (and ethical) roles to externalities and then tend to "adopt" what they have checked occurring outside, over there, in the external invented structure. Consequently, a large part of culture formation takes advantage of the exploitation of external representations and mediators.

My view about the disembodiment of mind certainly involves that the Mind/Body dualist perspective is less credible as well as Cartesian computationalism. Also the view that Mind is Computational independently of the physical (functionalism) is jeopardized. In my perspective on human cognition we no longer need Descartes dualism: we only have brains that make up large, integrated, material cognitive and cultural systems. The only problem seems "How meat knows": we can reverse the Cartesian motto and say "sum ergo cogito", it is "meat" that makes up external material cultures. In this perspective what we usually call mind simply consists in the union of both the changing neural configurations of brains together with those large, integrated, and material cultural and cognitive systems the brains themselves are continuously building.

Cultural Mediators: Artifacts and Cognition

Peirce's philosophical and semiotic motto "man is an external sign" is very clear about the materiality of mind and about the fact that the conscious self is a cluster actively embodied of flowing intelligible signs[4]. This semiotic perspective provides a goof framework in which we can depict a more satisfying and modern concept of culture (and of artifacts), that can better account for many aspects related to the impact of recent information and communication technologies (ICTs). Peirce says:

It is sufficient to say that there is no element whatever of man's consciousness which has not something corresponding to it in the word; and the reason is obvious. It is that the word or sign which man uses is the man himself. For, as the fact that every thought is a sign, taken in conjunction with the fact that life is a train of thoughts, proves that man is a sign; so, that every thought is an external sign, proves that man is an external sign. That is to say, the man and the external sign are identical, in the same sense in which the words homo and man are identical. Thus my language is the sum total of myself; fore the man is the thought. (Peirce, CP, 5.314)

We can exploit this fundamental philosophical argumentation to modernize the concept of "culture", with respect to the tradition of historical, sociological, and anthropological studies. It is by way of signs that we ourselves are semiotic processes – for example a more or less coherent cluster of narratives. If all thinking is in signs it is not true that thoughts are in us because we are in thoughts (Magnani, 2007b). This centrality of thoughts is the centrality of signs, and everywhere there are signs there are cultural units. External materialities, like laptops or brains can acquire cultural meanings and roles in so far as they are endowed with cognitive/semiotic delegations. One of the central property of signs is their reinterpretability. This occurs in a social process where signs are referred to material cultural objects. In this sense natural and artificial objects become what I propose to call cultural mediators[5].

Both trained neural networks in a human brain able to express cognitive skills, concepts, or emotions, and natural objects like stars, endowed with cognitive delegations, for example to help the navigation, become cultural units because they are inserted in a process of human cognitive signification, epistemic, moral, emotional, esthetic, economical, etc. The same happens in the case of material external artifacts, like for example a cell phone, a laptop, or other or another ICT. They are the effect of cognitive delegations that make them cultural units over there in the same time intertwined with human beings: we do not

have to forget that we already are semiotic and thus cultural processes, and in this sense, we are also partially defined by those external cultural units which continually affect us transforming humans in those cyborgs I have depicted in the previous sections.

It is clear that in this perspective the Peircian "person-sign" – that is culturally determined - is future-conditional, that is not fully formed in the present but depending on the future destiny of the concrete semiotic/cultural activity (future thoughts and experience of the community) in which s/he will be involved. If Peirce maintains that when we think we appear as a sign (Peirce, CP, 5.283) and, moreover, that everything is present to us is a phenomenal manifestation of ourselves, feelings, images, diagrams, conceptions, schemata, and other cultural representations are phenomenal manifestations that become available for interpretations and thus are guiding our actions in a positive or negative way. They become signs when we think and interpret them. It is well-know that for Peirce all semiotic experience is also providing a guide for action. Indeed the whole function of thought is to produce habits of action.

ARTIFACTS AND INTERCULTURAL COMMUNICATION

In the light of the considerations illustrated in the previous sections we can see every technology (and obviously ICTs, information and communication technologies, which are expressly built to carry information) as strictly intertwined with human beings through a continuous interplay of semiotic activities. In our era of increasing globalization ICT artifacts, like Internet, databases, wireless networks, etc. become crucial mediators of cross-cultural relationships between human beings and communities. I will treat this problem in this and in the following sections dealing with some effects of ICT technologies on the concept of human "docility", identity, and privacy and with respect to the properties of what I call moral mediators.

Clark correctly depicts a Nokia mobile phone as something that is "part of us," taken for granted, an object regarded as a kind of "prosthetic limb over which you wield full and flexible control, and on which you eventually come to automatically rely in formulating and carrying out your daily goals and projects" (Clark, 2003, p. 9). It is well-known that Heidegger distinguished between a tool's or artifact's being "ready-to-hand," like the hammer and the cell phone, and its being "present-at-hand." A ready-to-hand tool does not demand conscious reflection. "We can, in effect, 'see right through it,' concentrating only on the task (nailing the picture to the wall) [or writing a SMS message on a cell phone, we can add]. But, if things start to go wrong, we are still able to focus on the hammer [or on the cell phone], encountering it now as present-at-hand that requires our attention, that is, an object in its own right. We may inspect it, try using it in a new way, swap it for one with a smaller head, and so on" (Clark, 2003, p. 48). Using a tool becomes a continuous process of engagement, separation, and re-engagement. Just because "ready-to-hand," these tools are called "transparent" or "invisible" technologies[6.] Tools of this type express cultures which we call "implicit".

This brings me to the following point: okay, I also possess a Nec mobile phone and have, consequently, gained a new degree of "cyborgness." I am no longer only intertwined with classic tools like hammers, books, and watches, but I am also "wired" to a cell phone through which I work, I live, and I think. The problem is that our enthusiasm for information and communication technological advances may blind us to the inter-cultural and ethical aspects of the processes of engagement, separation, and re-engagement they make possible.

To heighten my awareness of such processes, I, as I use my cell phone and other tools yet to come, hope to acquire the moral knowledge necessary to maintain and even reinforce my identity, freedom, responsibility, and the ownership of my future; I would hope for the same for all other hybrid humans. I respect the new object or artifact that integrates its cognitive abilities with its users', but we must be mindful of the responsibilities technology brings so that it enhances rather than diminishes us. Moreover, does the cognitive value of the artifact count more than some basic biological cognitive abilities of the human body? What is the dignity of human beings, as special brain/body cultural "materials" with respect to the remaining externalized cultural objects and structures?

Everyone has experienced the difficulty and complexity of unsubscribing from some cyber service suppliers like cell phone companies or Internet providers. Such obstacles testify to the fact that even if they are effective tool-based cognitive extensions of our bodies, they also are tool-based economic institutions aiming to cast themselves as cognitively necessary and irreplaceable things. Because they satisfy market needs, which can be highly aggressive, they in some sense acquire more importance than the biological life itself.

As I have illustrated above, new artifacts become "ready-to-hand," but at what ethical and cultural cost? We must still be able to extricate, if we so choose, the technology that has appeared into our lives. Terminating a cell phone service contract, for example, should be an easy process without extended hassles or unexpected costs[7.] What way of ethical thinking fully explicates that right and will lead to new policies and laws that will protect human dignity in the future technological world? What "countercultural" strategies and cognitions I need if a sophisticated new neurophone (Clark, 2003, chapter one) is wired into my cochlear nerve as a direct electronic channel? Or how will one get rid of an "affective wearable" that monitors your stress levels and provides daily profiles and other data to you, but in the meantime is generating an intolerable information overload? (Picard, 1997, p. 236). You start to think you have another "self," and it feels as if you no longer own some of the information about yourself – that damn affective wearable also monitors all your frustrations and shows you an interpretive narrative on how things went. It is not simple to have the maturity necessary to deal with a kind of another "self", fruit of technology, that monitors and tells us another story about us. And certainly, scientific advances like the neurophone Clark describes and the "affective wearable" "will come first, and only later on the moral and legal rules." As I will better illustrate in the following section, the production of an appropriate counterculture is central to avoid the blindness to the dangerous ethical consequences of ICTs and other technologies.

Beyond simple cochlea implants and heart pacemakers other intrusions into the human body are currently tested or imagined. Warwick lists new super-cyborgs formed by human (or animal), machine brain/nervous system coupling (Warwick, 2003). Their diffusion will be able to produce new cultures, endowed with unexpected consequences. There are stimulator implants that counteract electronically the tremor effects associated with Parkinson's disease; implants that permit to transmit signals from brain of stroke victims to the computer to cause the cursor on the computer screen to move left, right, up and down (so spelling out words and making requests); silicon chips transponders surgically implanted in the upper left harm able to transmit unique identifying radio signals. In this last case it is also possible to install direct links with the nervous fibres in the arm, able to transmit and receive signals, that have permitted experiments on movement signals: experiments were made also on transmitting signals across the Internet directly from a human brain implant to a robot, to move its hand. Furthermore, extrasensory inputs sent to robots suitably sensing the world using ultrasonic sensors were also sent to human brains that were amazingly able to make sense of the signal.

Of course, as Warwick and Clark claim, these super-cyborgs can size and control of the process of evolution so that evolution is based entirely in technology rather than biology. Evolution will become even more than today –co-evolution, that is – from the viewpoint of human beings - the organism and the environment (disseminated by super-cyborgs) find a continuous mutual variation. The organism modifies its character in order to reach better fitness; however, the environment, and so cultures which develop in it, equally, are continuously changing and very sensitive to every modification. Within this complex system of changes, many organisms might fit the same environment (niche), which becomes highly sensible – and active - with regard to the organisms which live in it.

There is a profound tension between the biological and the cultures engendered by technological spheres of human hybrids, who are composed of a body plus cell phone, laptop, or the Internet, etc. Sometimes the two aspects can be reconciled by adjusting and redistributing various new cultural and ethical values, but the struggle is ongoing and the final results are unknowable: the outcome simply depends on the moral targets hybrid people identify and advocate. Do the cultural functions spontaneously engendered by a the cell phone count more than some preexistent cultural values related to the biological body "without" that artifacts, or "with" other old-fashioned artifacts? Is the new delegation of tasks to the cell phone, and the consequent cultural modifications, really compensated by new positive capabilities and chances, or does a biological body's lack of cognitive autonomy become intolerable at some point?

In my book Morality in a Technological World (Magnani, 2007a) I describe in details how the economic value of technological objects that are "grafted" onto human beings makes it dangerously easy to produces cultures where people are treated people as means, and it is well-known that the market economy is inherently inclined to regard human beings this way. In a market economy, qualities and worth of human beings – their intelligence, energies, work, and emotions, etc. – can be "arbitrarily" exploited and/or disregarded in favor of solely promoting the sales of artifacts, items which may or may not be that useful. Situations like these, of course, inevitably generate frustration. Central to this issue is the fact that many people are used to being considered things: they are, in Kantian terms, "treated as means (and only as means)." In the book I offer a way to recalibrate the cultural and ethical value of things so that "respecting people as things" becomes a positive way to regard them.

To give an example, imagine people who have used certain devices so much that some of their biological cognitive abilities have atrophied. Such people may yearn to be as respected as a cell phone – perhaps the expensive one of the future that I mentioned before, the direct electronic channel wired into my cochlear nerve that features a sophisticated processor, spectacular AI tools, and a direct Internet connection. In that cultural framework, the hybrid person at hand will feel herself dispossessed of the moral cognitive worth already attributed to nonbiological artifacts. It is very simple to imagine how this situation will be much more complicated by the appearance of future super-cyborgs endowed with huge extra memory, enhanced mathematical skills, extrasensory devices, and – why not - able to communicate "by thought" various signals. They will be more powerful than humans, with brain that are directly part human and part machine, so as the "epicentre of moral and ethical decision making will no longer be of purely human form, but rather it is a mixed human, machine base" (Warwick, 2003, p. 136).

Being cared for and valued is not always considered a human right, for instance collectives do not have moral (and legal) rules that mandate the protection and preservation of human beings' cognitive skill. As a result, we face a paradoxical situation that inverts Kant's thinking, one involving people who are not "sufficiently" or appropriately treated as means, as things. Yet people's biological cognitive skills deserve to be valued at least as much as a cell phone: human cognitive capacities warrant moral credit because it is thanks to them that things like cell phones were invented and built to begin with. In this way, human hybrids can reclaim "moral" recognition for being biological carriers of information, knowledge, know-how, autonomy, cultural traditions, etc., and gain the respect given to cognitive artifacts for being external cultural repositories: books, for example, PCs, or works of art. That human hybrid, who exhibits knowledge and capacity to reason and work, will expect to play a clear, autonomous, and morally recognized role at the level of his/her biological intellectual capacities.

What I have just illustrated will hold also in the case of the future super-cyborgs I depicted above, fruit of the most advanced ICTs revolution, just with slight modifications. Two moral problems will still be at stake: 1) the problem of the "equal" distribution among human beings/ brains of those sophisticated artificial endowments like extrasensory devices[8]; 2) the fact that super-cyborgs possess biotechnological cognitive skills deserves to be valued in a very balanced way: super cyborgs' "biological" cognitive capacities will have to be valued very much, not to consent the priority and the dominance of the artificial aspects, so determining cyborgs with intelligent prostheses but dull brains.

CULTURES, COUNTERCULTURES, AND DOCILE HUMANS

We have seen in the previous sections that material culture disembodies thoughts, that otherwise will soon disappear, without being transmitted to other human beings, and realizes a systematic semiotic delegation to the external environment forming the so-called cognitive niches. I contend that cultures are formed through semiotic anchorage of informational content to external material objects and structures. I have called this process as a kind of disembodiment of mind. We have also seen that unorganized brains organize themselves through a semiotic activity that is reified in the external cultural environment and then re-projected and reinterpreted through new configurations of neural networks and chemical processes. I also think the disembodiment of mind can nicely account for semiotic processes of creation of countercultures.

Material Cultures and Moral Mediators

We have said that through the mediation of the material culture the modern human mind can for example arrive to internally think the new meaning of animals and people at the same time, so generating a conceptual and cultural change. We can account for this process of disembodiment of our ancestors from a theoretical cognitive point of view.

- I maintain that cultural representations are external and internal. We can say that
  ○ external cultural representations are formed by external cultural materials that express (through reification) concepts and problems that are not necessarily present in the brain of some human beings;
  ○ internalized cultural representations are internal re-projections, a kind of recapitulations, (learning) of external representations in terms of neural patterns of activation in the brain. It is in this way that human beings take part in a culture or in a new culture. The representations can sometimes be "internally" manipulated like external objects and can originate new internal reconstructed representations through the neural activity of transformation and integration. It is at this level that a "countercultural" effect can be activated. When the fixation of external [new] cultural units - derived

from the interplay between the two levels - is reached, they can be in turn externalized to the aim of constituting new cultural devices open to a further possible diffusion.

In our technological world there is a huge expansion of private and public "objects" and "artifacts" that have gained a great importance in everyday life and for the self-definition of people, especially in industrialized societies. The global trade and the continuous exchange of commodities is one of the central aspects of our lives in the cyberage. Regional and national products have become available worldwide, and some of them have become international commodities, marketed and consumed globally.

I have illustrated how these artifacts play the role of "cultural mediators". Let us now describe some details of this effect of mediation, paying special attention to some ethical consequences. All artifacts embed a fragment of cultural knowledge and experience, and are the fruit of complicated cognitive delegations. These delegations explain, in the case above of the cell phone – explicitly related to ICTs – but also in the case of furniture or food, why artifacts can influence many communicative processes. Roth (2001, p. 567) illustrates some important cultural roles played by artifacts. Artifacts can be: 1) topics or themes of (intercultural) communication, which carries internationally the know-how about products; 2) material contexts that "wrap" each act of communication; 3) media for intercultural communication; 4) transferred and communicated across cultural boundaries, as merchandise; 5) entertainers of various relationships with humans, related to the available culture specificity; 6) used symbolically; 7) ways of overcoming the difficulties in interpreting foreign cultures.

Furthemore, artifacts play a spatial role in separating public and private spaces, workplaces, etc., like in the case of buildings and streets, chairs and table in houses and offices; they also have a personal dimension at the communication level, like in the case of clothes, utensils, ritual objects, fences, etc., and an actional dimension, in eating, working, celebrating, etc. These dimensions are usually related to standard roles the artifacts play, and only special interactions with humans can change these default characters. In the case of globalized artifacts it is through the cyclic process of internalization/externalization previously described that they can culturally acquire new ethnic, regional, or national ethical values and new identifications and meanings (Teuteberg, Neumann, and Wierlacher, 1997), in a process which sometimes is clearly characterized by a countercultural disposition, that can arise both at cognitive and emotional level (Lindner, 1997). In EU the controversies about Italian pasta, Dutch clogs, French champagne and German beer have demonstrated "the extent to which regional and national identities are tied to material cultures and local cultures are used as countercultures to globalization" (Roth, 2001, p. 573).

The insistence on the home country artifacts in the case of the emigrants demonstrates how values of objects can acquire new meanings and change their disposition once removed from their standard places; in other cases foreign objects and artifacts are often responsible of a kind of culture shock. The so-called countercultural effects of creolization (Howes, 1996) and localization (Lindner, 1997, Roth, 2001, p. 571) have affected the international cultural identity of goods like Coca-Cola, that certainly represents the symbol of globalization of products.

Similarly, in the case of new media and technical instruments which work at the level of worldwide transmission of information and/or at the level of global communicative networks, there is evidence (Bredin, 1996) that in their use (but also in the use of technological equipments like cell phones and laptops) there are significant cultural differences. In some cases the transfer of technology might not appreciate local values and it might also later on undermine those values

(Moss, 2005), so that a great part of the globe, as well as the majority of the world population, do not enjoy the fruits and benefits that information technologies are supposed to bring (Hongladarom, 2005). In other cases, some positive impacts have been experienced.

In this domain of the complex interaction between culture, technology and intercultural communication the literature of the so called Social Construction of Technology (SCOT) is also relevant (cf. Sismondo, 1993 and Winner, 1993). It is in this area studied that Latour's notions of the de-humanizing effect of technologies emerge and are based on the so-called "actor network theory" [9]. The actor network theory basically maintains that we should think of science, technology, and society as a field of human and non-human (material) agency. Human and non-human agents are associated with one another in networks, and they evolve together within these networks. Because the two aspects are equally important, neither can be reduced to the other: "An actor network is simultaneously an actor whose activity is networking heterogeneous elements and a network that is able to redefine and transform what is it made of [...]. The actor network is reducible neither to an actor alone nor to a network"[10].

A different but related perspective – one that, like Latour's, avoids anthropomorphic prioritization of human agency and addresses the dissolution of boundaries between things and people – is offered by Andrew Pickering in his writing on science-studies of post-humanism. He describes externalities (representations, artifacts, tools, etc.) as kinds of non-human agencies[11] that interact with a decentered human agency in a dialectic of "resistance" and "accommodation" called the mangle of practice[12]. The resistance is a failure to capture material agency in an intended form, while accommodation amounts to a reconfiguration of the apparatus that might find a way through its resistance. When human-and non-human agencies are brought together, as has often occurred in mathematics, natural sciences and technology throughout history, it is impossible to predict the results.

An example of a positive impact and of reinvention of roles of western technology in a developing country is given by the substantial role played by cell phones in ensuring, in the Republic of the Philippines, the success of the EDSA II people power revolution in 2001, which forced President Joseph Estrada to resign (Valdez, 2005). In this case technology was effectively used by civil society in raising new cultural consciousness of the Filipino people. During the height of the impeachment trial against president Estrada the total volume of the SMS text messages exchanged by Filipinos in a single day exceeded the total volume of text messages in the whole Europe. A similar event is of course unconceivable in western countries.

Another example of cross-cultural positive employment of technology is given by young women's exploitation of Internet booths in Indian villages to the aim of improving not only information and education but also effective economical growth in rural transformation (Krishnamurthy, 2005). Internet booths played a fundamental role in making those women able to overcome their personal and cultural borders.

Above I have introduced the concept of moral mediator[13]. A moral mediator is a cultural mediator where ethical aspects are crucial and the importance in potential intercultural relationships is central. What exactly is a moral mediator? Morality, is often performed in a tacit way, so to say, "through doing". Moreover, part of this "doing" can be seen as an activity of cultural manipulation of the external word for just building "moral mediators". They can be built in the aim of getting ethical effects, but they also consist in beings, entities, objects, structures, that objectively, beyond the human beings' intentionality, carry ethical or unethical consequences. Hence, a significant portion of manipulations is also devoted to building that vast new source of distributed information and knowledge that originates external moral mediators.

Moral mediators represent a kind of redistribution of the moral effort through managing objects and information in such a way that we can overcome the poverty and the unsatisfactory character of the moral options immediately represented or found internally (for example principles, prototypes, etc.). I also think that the analysis of moral mediators can help accounting for the mechanisms of the macroscopic and growing phenomenon of global moral actions and collective responsibilities resulting from the "invisible hand" of systemic interactions among several cultural agents at local level (Floridi and Sanders, 2003). A cultural object, like an Internet web page where some commodities are sold online, not only realizes an economical transaction but also carries ethical effects in so far as it implies certain customer's behaviors related to some policies and contraints.

Natural phenomena can also serve as external artifactual moral mediators: many external "natural" objects, animals for example, create opportunities for new ethical knowledge, as in the case of endangered species. Thanks to utilitarianism and environmentalism some animals have acquired the moral definition of "endangered": in turn people learnt something new by discovering – through those animals as moral mediators - how also human beings can be redefined as "endangered". Many external things that have been traditionally considered morally inert can be transformed into moral mediators. In general, we can use animals to identify previously unrecognized moral features of human beings or other living creatures, as we can do with the earth, or (non natural) cultural entities; we can also use cultural external "tools" like writing, narrative, ritual, and various kinds of pertinent institutions to reconfigure unsatisfactory social orders. Hence, not all moral tools are inside the head – many are shared and distributed in external objects and structures that function as ethical devices.

External moral mediators function as components of a memory system that crosses the boundary between person and environment. For example, they are able to transform the tasks involved in simple manipulations that promote in an agent further moral inferences. When an abused child is moved to a house to reconfigure her social relationships this new moral mediator can help her to experience new inferences (for instance new emotions concerning adults and new imageries about her past abuse).

Moreover, I can alter my bodily experience of pain through action by following the template control of sense data, as we previously outlined, that is through shifting – unconsciously – the position of my body and changing its relationships with other humans and non-humans experiencing distress. Mother Theresa's personal moral rich feeling and consideration of pain had been certainly shaped by her closeness to starving and miserable people and by her manipulation of their bodies. In many people, moral training is often related to these kinds of spontaneous (and "lucky") manipulations of their own bodies and sense data so that they build morality immediately and non-reflectively "through doing." It is obvious that these processes involve a cultural (often countercultural) redefinition of the role of bodies with respect to the received perspectives.

What is the suggestion we can get from the concept of moral mediator with respect to the problem of intercultural communication? I think that the main teaching regards the need to understand the "language of objects" of other cultures. Given the huge cognitive and emotional role played by things and external representations, it is through them we can increase the effects of commensurability even in the hardest cases of conflicting cultures. Let us illustrate the example of Islamic fundamentalists and Western capitalist culture, where a counterculture is activated, to the aim of reinterpreting capitalistic rules, transactions, and loans.

Islamic fundamentalists have resumed medieval objections to the charging of financial interest as part of a more extended attack on Western influences, and look for different ways of financing commerce and industry that in their eyes do less violence to Islamic society and countries. They consider international loans from Western governments and banks as basically exploitive, but expect to find and retain elements of capitalism within their domestic economies as tools for promoting development within the family: "So the medieval debate about the clever new forms of contract, aimed at circumventing the moral objection to interest, is being repeated in contemporary Islam, in the hope of squaring the needs of commerce with the traditional injunctions of the Sharĩ ya"(Jonsen and Toulmin, 1988, p. 310).

Here we see that using an old financial practice in a new context (modern Islam) generates problems; difficulties arise when international loans are made between countries with different cultures. The medieval conflict between "moral" investing and immoral money lending acquires new relevance. Simply applying a general principle against usury is not particularly productive, for it limits opportunities for commerce between Muslim nations and the rest of the world; instead, new ways of conducting business must be considered able to act as moral mediators of the puzzling situation. The underlying lesson here is that the concrete case – the seemingly irreconcilable conflict between cultures – takes agents beyond the reach of rules and compels them to take into account a particular set of circumstances – the fact that there are other commercial practices that are acceptable in Islamic business communities. In other cultural cases, similar situations can be found, when some abstract principles are not always universally "good" principles to use when deciding how (and whether) to treat particular cases, because their application can be techniques that can often be very useful but can have unacceptable negative side effects for both the children and their families. In the usury problem abstract rules must be suitably modified and mediated to fit particular circumstances.

Docile Humans Externalize Cultures and Artifacts

Following Simon's perspective, human beings first of all always and constitutively operate in a situation of "bounded rationality": human beings and other creatures do not behave optimally for their fitness, because they are not able to get knowledge and making inferences which would support optimization. Moreover, in order to survive, humans are "docile", in the sense that our fitness is enhanced by "the tendency to depend on suggestions, recommendations, persuasion, and information obtained through social channels as a major basis for choice" (Simon 1993, p. 156). In other words, we support our limited decision-making capabilities counting on external data obtained through the senses, from the social environment. The social context gives us the main data filter, available to increase individual fitness (Secchi, 2006).

The concept of "docility" is related to that of altruism, in the sense that one cannot be altruistic if s/he is not docile. In this perspective the intelligent altruist is the fittest. However, the most important element seems to be docility more than altruism, because docility is the condition of possibility of the emergence of altruism. In Simon's work docility is also related to the idea of "socializability", and certainly it is an aspect of both the human beings' continuous cognitive delegations to the external environment and to other social members.

The problem here is twofold. First, people delegate data acquisition to their experience and to the external cultural resources and individuals, as I have illustrated in the first sections of this paper. Second, people do trust others to learn. In (Magnani, 2006) I have illustrated how a big cortex, speech, rudimentary social settings, and primitive material culture furnished the conditions for the birth of the mind as a universal machine. I contended that a big cortex can provide an evolutionary advantage only in presence of a massive storage of meaningful information and knowledge on external supports that only an already developed small community of human beings can possess. If we consider high-level consciousness as related to a high-level organization of human cortex, its origins can be related to the active role of environmental, social, linguistic, and cultural aspects. It is in this sense that "docile" interaction lays on the very basis of our social (and neurological) development.

It is obvious that docility is related to the development of cultures, their availability, and to the quality of cross-cultural relationships. Of course the type of dissemination of cultures and their possible enhancement affect the chances human collectives have to exploit docility and so to increase their fitness. I guess the conflicts and lacks of dialogue between cultures, and the excessive normalization generated by globalization, can diminish the positive effects of docility. I strongly think research on these and similar aspects have to be established and encouraged.

Mediating Individual Privacy and Identity and the Principle of Cultural Isolation: The Role of ICT's

In chapter four of the already cited book (Magnani, 2007a) I have contended that knowledge has to be considered a duty. Of course the problem of its dissemination and distribution in cultures immediately arises. I also showed that from my examination of "knowledge as duty" considered to be a consequence of the current technological complexity of external things, a warning can be naturally made in the case of the problem of identity and cyberprivacy. I am now realizing that this warning has to be made not only at the micro-level of the individuals but also at the macro-level of cultures. I content that, if a lot of knowledge is incorporated in external artificial things through current ICTs (and we need knowledge to deal with external things – both natural and artificial), human beings are so intertwined with those external things that their "visibility" can be excessive and dangerous.

At present, identity has to be considered in a broad sense: the amount of data, information, images, and texts that concern us as individuals are enormous and are stored in external things/ means. This storage of information about human beings creates a kind of external "data shadow" for every human individual, that, together with the biological body, generates a kind of cyborg, also consisting of electronic data that identifies us or potentially identifies us. New moral ontologies are created: for example, a new human being is individuated, biologically "local" and cybernetically "global". In the cited book I have illustrated and discussed some ideas about the Panopticon effect as a metaphor of the mechanisms of large-scale social control that characterizes the modern world: as we have said, a detailed computational "shadow" of the person's private life can be built by storing collected pieces of information about people. I think we no longer can apply old moral rules and old-fashioned arguments to beings that are at the same time biological (concrete) and virtual, situated in a three-dimensional local space, but potentially "globally omnipresent" as information-packets. People have to be protected not only from being seen but also from feeling visible to avoid ostracism and stigmatization about minorities, to be protected from insult, to avoid becoming more conformist and conventional, and so to avoid the possibility of being oppressed.

I think something similar can be discussed and examined at the macro-level of cultures. The process of globalization jeopardizes local cultures from the point of view of their identity but also from the point of view, so to say, of their "privacy". I think cultures too need appropriate thresholds of isolation and self-protection. If the identity and the isolation of cultures are harmed beyond a certain degree, we have consequences for the specific freedom of the related affected collectives.

To make and example, surely at the micro-level of individuals the role of identity card and other tools for identifications have positive effects, for instance in terms of the enhancement of equality: we all have the identity card, then we are all citizens. Unfortunately we can reach negative outcomes in terms of repressive acts just made possible by the kind of "imprisonment" of subjectivity caused by the excessive identification policies, as Foucault magisterially described (Foucault, 1979, Kaboré, 2005). Similarly, globalization effects of ICTs can enhance local cultures, magnifying their identities, but they can also contaminate them in a way that generates the loss of isolation and so the loss of their role in the identification of the related collectives.

I contend that what I call the principle of isolation of cultures resorts to the protection against interference with the collectives' way of realizing and developing their interests, both in the sense of interests related to their practical objectives or merely intertwined with strands of their identity over time[14]. I also contend this protection has to be equilibrated with the need of promoting cyberdemocracy, which will be a real kind of counter-culture counterpoised to the negative effects of globalization (Cavalier, 2004; Barone and Magnani, 2006).

CONCLUSION

The main thesis of this paper is that the disembodiment of mind is a significant cognitive perspective able to unveil some basic features of the creation of cultures. Its fertility in explaining the interplay between internal and external levels of cognition is evident. I maintain that various aspects of culture formation could take advantage of the research on this interplay: for instance study on cultural mediators can provide a better understanding of the processes of intercultural communication.

I think the role of what I call "cultural and moral mediators" can be studied further also taking advantage of the research on the interplay between cultures and distributed cognition and appropriately stressing the problem of the co-evolution between brains and cultures. The final part of the paper aims at offering new suggestions related to the analysis of the interplay between cultures and cognition and of some consequences concerning the problem of intercultural communication in the light of the role of "moral mediators", docility, cyberprivacy, and the problem of isolation of cultures, with respect to the effects of ICTs. I think that because of the relationship between docility and culture, further research has to be promoted on the chances human collectives have to exploit docility and thus to increase their fitness, with respect to the role of inter-cultural communication. Furthermore, taking advantage of an analogy with research on cyberprivacy and identity, I contend that what I call the "principle of isolation" of cultures resorts to the protection against interference with the collectives' way of realizing and developing their interests, both in the sense of interests related to their practical objectives or merely intertwined with strands of their identity over time.

REFERENCES

Bardone, E., & Magnani, L. (2006). The Internet as a moral mediator. The quest for democracy. In *Computing, Philosophy, and Cognition* (pp. 131-145). London, College Publications.

Barlow, J. P. (1990). A declaration of the independence of Cyberspace. http://www.eff.org/~barlow/Declaration-Final.html

Bateson, G. (1972). *Steps toward and ecology of mind.* Novato, CA: Chandler.

Bredin, D. (1996). Transforming images: Communication technologies and cultural identity in Nishnawbe-Aski. In D. Howes (Ed.), *Cross-cultural consumption. Global markets, local realities* (pp. 161-177). London and New York: Routledge.

Bynum, T. W., & Rogerson, S. (Eds.). (2004). *Computer ethics and professional responsibility.* Malden, MA: Blackwell.

Callon, M. (1994). Four models for the dynamics of science. In S. Jasanoff, G.E. Markle, J.C. Petersen, and T.J. Pinch (Eds.), *Handbook of science and technology studies* (pp. 29-63), Los Angeles, CA: Sage.

Callon, M. (1997). Society in the making: the study of technology as a tool for sociological analysis. In W.E. Bjiker, T.P. Hughes, & T. Pinch (Eds.), *The social construction of technological systems* (pp. 83-106). Cambridge, MA: MIT Press.

Callon, M., & Latour, B. (1992). Don't throw the baby out with the bath school! A reply to Collins and Yearley. In A. Pickering (Ed.), *science as practice and culture* (pp. 343-368). Chicago and London: The University of Chicago Press.

Cavalier, R. (2004, June 2-5). Instantiating deliberative democracy. Project PICOLA. European Conference Computing and Philosophy (E-CAP2004_ITALY), Abstract, Pavia, Italy.

Clark, A. (2003). *Natural-born cyborgs. Minds, technologies, and the future of human intelligence.* Oxford and New York: Oxford University Press.

Dawkins, R. (1989). *The selfish gene.* Oxford: Oxford University Press.

Floridi, L., & Sanders, J. W. (2003). The method of abstraction. In M. Negrotti (Ed.), *Yearbook of the artificial. Nature, culture, and technology. Models in Contemporary Sciences* (pp. 177-220). Bern: Peter Lang.

Foucault, M. (1979). *Discipline and punish: The birth of the prison (1975)*. Translated by A. Sheridan. New York: Vintage Books.

Haraway, D. (1991). A Cyborg manifesto: Science, technology, and socialist-feminism in the late twentieth century. In D. Haraway, *Simians, cyborgs and women: The reinvention of nature* (pp. 149-181). New York: Routledge.

Hongladarom, S. (2005, January 7-9). The digital divide, epistemology and global justice. The 2nd Asia-Pacific Computing and Philosophy Conference, Chulalongkorn University, bangkok, Thailand.

Howes, D. (Ed.). (1996). *Cross-cultural consumption. Global markets, local realities*. London and New York: Routledge.

Hutchins, E. (1995). *Cognition in the Wild*. Cambridge, MA: MIT Press.

Johnson, D. G. (1994). *Computer ethics* (2nd ed.). Englewood Cliffs, NJ: Prentice Hall.

Jonsen, A. R., & Toulmin, S. (1988). *The abuse of casuistry. A history of moral reasoning*. Berkeley and Los Angeles: University of California Press.

Kaboré, B. (2005, May 29-30). Vie privée, identité et vol d'identité. *Technology and Changing Face of Humanity, Conference*. Canadian Jacques Maritain Association. The University of Western Ontario, Canada.

Krishnamurthy, S. (2005, January 7-9). Internet booths in villages of India. *The 2nd Asia-Pacific Computing and Philosophy Conference* (pp.1-28), Chulalongkorn University, Bangkok, Thailand.

Latour, B. (1987). *Science in action: How to follow scientists and engineers through society*. Cambridge, MA: Harvard University Press.

Latour, B. (1988). *The pasteurization of France*. Cambridge, MA: Harvard University Press.

Law, J. (1993). *Modernity, myth, and materialism*. Oxford: Blackwell.

Lindner, R. (1997). Global logo, local meaning. *Focaal, 30/31*, 193–200.

Magnani, L. (2001a). *Abduction, reason, and science. Processes of discovery and explanation*. New York, NY: Kluwer Academic/Plenum Publishers.

Magnani, L. (2001b). *Philosophy and Geometry. Theoretical and historical issues*. Dordrecht: Kluwer Academic Publishers.

Magnani, L. (2002). Epistemic mediators and model-based discovery in science. In L. Magnani & N.J. Nersessian (Eds.), *Model-based reasoning* (pp. 305-329).

Magnani, L. (2006). Mimetic minds, meaning formation through epistemic mediators and external representations. In A. Loula, R. Gudwin, & J. Queiroz (Eds.), *Artificial Cognition Systems* (pp. 327-357). Hershey, PA: Idea Group Inc.

Magnani, L. (2007a) *Morality in a technological world: Knowledge as a duty*. Cambridge: Cambridge University Press.

Magnani, L. (2007b). Semiotic brains and artificial minds: How brains make up material cognitive systems. In R. Gudwin & J. Queiroz (Eds.), *Semiotics and Intelligent Systems Development* (pp.1-41). Hershey, PA: Idea Group Inc.

Magnani, L., & Nersessian, N. J. (Eds.). (2002). *Model-based reasoning. Scientific Discovery, Technology, Values*. New York, NY: Kluwer Academic/Plenum Publishers.

Mithen, S. (1996). *The Prehistory of the Mind. A Search for the Origins of Art, Religion, and Science*. London: Thames and Hudson.

Moor, J. H. (1985). What is computer ethics? *Metaphilosophy, 16*(4), 266–275. doi:10.1111/j.1467-9973.1985.tb00173.x

Moor, J. H. (1997). Towards a theory of privacy in the information age. *Computers & Society*, *27*, 27–32. doi:10.1145/270858.270866

Moor, J. H., & Bynum, T. W. (Eds.). (2002). *Cyberphilosophy*. Maldem, MA: Blackwell.

Moss, J. (2005, January 7-9). Fixing the digital divide; sustaining or undermining local values? *The 2nd Asia-Pacific Computing and Philosophy Conference*, Chulalongkorn University, Bangkok, Thailand.

Norman, D. A. (1999). *The Invisible Computer*. Cambridge, MA: The MIT Press.

Peirce, C. S. (1931-1958) (CP). *Collected Papers*. In C. Hartshorne & P. Weiss (Eds.) (Vols. I-VI) & A.W. Burks (Ed.). (Vols. VII-VIII). Cambridge, MA: Harvard University Press.

Perkins, D. (2003). *King Arthur's round table. How collaborative conversations create smart organizations*. Chichester: Wiley.

Picard, R. W. (1997). *Affective computing*. Cambridge, MA: MIT Press.

Pickering, A. (1995). *The mangle of practice. Tome, agency, and science*. Chicago and London, The University of Chicago Press.

Roth, K. (2001). Material culture and intercultural communication. *International Journal of Intercultural Relations*, *25*, 563–580. doi:10.1016/S0147-1767(01)00023-2

Secchi, D. (2006). *A theory of docile society*. Submitted to Mind and Society.

Simon, H. (1993). Altruism and Economics. *The American Economic Review*, *83*(2), 156–161.

Sismondo, S. (1993). Some social constructions. *Social Studies of Science*, *23*, 515–553. doi:10.1177/030631279302300004

Tamura, T. (2005, January 7-9). Japanese feeling for privacy. The 2nd Asia-Pacific Computing and Philosophy Conference (pp. 88-93). Chulalongkorn University.

Teuteberg, H. J., Neumann, G., & Wierlacher, A. (Eds.). (1997). *Essen und kulturelle Identitä. Europäische Perspektiven*. Berlin: Akademie.

Tooby, J., & DeVore, I. (1987), The reconstruction of hominid behavioral evolution through strategic modeling. In W. G. Kinzey (Ed.), *Primate models of hominid behavior* (pp.183-237), Suny Press, Albany.

Valdez, V. J. (2005), Technology and civil society. *The 2nd Asia-Pacific Computing and Philosophy Conference*. Chulalongkorn University, Bangkok, Thailand, January 7-9, 2005.

Warwick, K. (2003). Cyborg morals, cyborg values, cyborg ethics. *Ethics and Information Technology*, *5*, 131–137. doi:10.1023/B:ETIN.0000006870.65865.cf

Weiser, M. (1991). The computer for the 21st Century. *Scientific American*, *9*, 99–110.

Winner, L. (1993). Upon opening the black box and finding it empty: Social constructivism and the philosophy of technology. *Science, Technology & Human Values*, *18*(3), 362–378. doi:10.1177/016224399301800306

ENDNOTES

[1] My enthusiasm for cyborgs echoes well-known 1990s discussion, including in Barlow's "A declaration of the independence of Cyberspace" (1996), who states "We will create a civilization of the Mind in Cyberspace", as well as in the foundational work of Haraway (1991), even if the concept of disembodiment – I will introduce in the fol-

lowing section - in the perspective of current cognitive research was not present.

2   I have devoted part of my research to analyzing the role of diagrams in mathematical thinking and geometrical discovery (Magnani, 2001b, Magnani, 2002).

3   A survey on new moral problems and ontologies caused by ICTs is given in Bynum and Rogerson, 2004, Johnson, 1994, Moor, 1985, 1997, Moor and Bynum, 2002.

4   Consciousness arises as "a sort of public spirit among the nerve cells" (Peirce, CP, 1.354).

5   I draw the concept of cultural mediator from that of epistemic mediator and of moral media-tor I have respectively introduced in Magnani, 2001a and 2007a. The cognitive anthropologist Hutchins (1995) already coined the expression "mediating structure" to refer to various external tools that can be built to cognitively help the activity of navigating in modern but also in "primitive" settings. Any written procedure is a simple example of a cultural mediator with possible various cognitive aims. Language, mental models, mathematical procedures, furniture, buildings, rules of logic, etc. are all mediating cultural mediators. Some of them, like traffic lights or supermarkets layouts, are also endowed with various specific mediating roles, economic, moral, legal, etc. and the contexts we arrange for one another's behavior. Of course cultural meditors are artifacts, institutions, ideas, and also various systems of social interaction, usually made existent and effective with the help of hybrid components: laws, habits, buildings, learned emotions, etc.

6   Weiser, 1991. On the so-called "invisible technologies" see Norman, 1999.

7   A human being may feel that while all people are mortal, one's subscription to the internet provider will never die. The "life" of these small external artificial things tend to overcome our own.

8   It is evident that already current human brains are provided in various degrees with external "natural" (teachers, parents, other human beings, etc.) and artificial cognitive mediators (books, schools, laptops, Internet access, etc.), because of biological differences and social inequalities. For more information about cognitive delegations to organizations, institutions, etc., see Perkins (2003).

9   This theory has been proposed by Callon, Latour himself, and Law (cf. Callon, 1994, 1997, Latour, 1987, 1988, Callon and Latour, 1992, and Law, 1993).

10 Callon, 1997, p. 93.

11 As a form of what Pickering calls "disciplinary agency," non-human agency also includes conceptual tools and representations – such as scientific theories and models or mathematical formalisms): "Scientific culture, then, appears as itself a wild kind of machine built from radical heterogeneous parts, a supercyborg, harnessing material and disciplinary agency in material and human performances, some of which lead out into the world of representation, of fact and theories" (Pickering, 1995, p. 145).

12 Cit., p. 17 and pp. 22-23.

13 Further details are illustrated in Magnani (2007a).

14 The modification of the concept and feeling of privacy induced by Internet in young Japanese people is illustrated in Tamura, 2005, who depict the new role in privacy of the "web diaries".

Chapter 2
The Significance of the Ethics of Respect

Josep M. Esquirol
University of Barcelona, Spain

ABSTRACT

In this paper, the author examines the idea of respect and makes this the cornerstone of a new approach to ethics that is particularly well suited to addressing the challenges society faces in an age shaped so profoundly by technology. The author uncovers a wealth of meaning in the notion of 'respect' and shows how this relates to the gaze. The attentive gaze is seen as the essence of respect. This thought-provoking analysis is presented in a straightforward way and is certainly open to further development and refinement in fields such as ecology, medicine, education and the promotion of civic-mindedness.

'An art which will not implant the faculty of sight [in the soul] for that exists already, but will set it straight when it has been turned in the wrong direction, and is looking away from the truth...'
(Plato, Republic, VII, 518d)

QUESTIONS

Three main questions are posed in this paper: what is *respect*? What merits respect? And why might the *ethics of respect* be a valuable approach for a time such as ours, shaped largely by science and technology?

There are words that explain and words that need explanation. There are also words that at the same time explain and need explanation; *respect* is such a word. In principle, the experience of respect for something or someone is not unusual or problematic: it is an altogether normal and straightforward phenomenon. Yet reflecting on the meaning of respect can turn out to be a very worthwhile endeavour. Despite being one of the most significant moral attitudes, the notion of respect has received little attention compared to the countless pages dedicated, for example, to love or to justice. As is the case for other important notions, the term's wealth of meaning makes defining its key concept more difficult; in response

DOI: 10.4018/978-1-4666-1773-5.ch002

to the broad and varied landscape before us, we must identify what is most essential. The position argued for here is that the essence of respect is determined by the *gaze*.

The second question formulated above reflects a common way of thinking about respect: it is believed and said that there are people and things that should be respected, that *deserve* respect. This expression alerts us to the fact that respect is an ethical attitude that links us directly to things, to the world. It is not my intention to resurrect outmoded forms of more or less naïve realism; after some of the lessons of modern philosophy, it is no longer possible to get around the centrality of the person as knowing subject. However, this does not preclude the possibility of exploring, as a number of contemporary approaches attempt to do, a philosophy that turns on the highly significant relationship between the self and the world. In a philosophy of this type, respect could play a crucial role given that it implies fundamental links between the self and the world – between the attitude of respect (on the part of the subject) and the person or thing that is the intentional object of that attitude. Reflecting on what it is that merits respect lead us to the notions of *harmony*, *fragility* and *secret*, and we see how, based on these ideas, it is possible to understand why there are things in the world that merit respect.

The third question is intended to draw attention to the fact that even if the need is not yet urgent, this is at least an opportune moment to promote an ethical system based on respect. No one disputes the fact that we are living in the age of science and technology, which are not only the driving forces for contemporary society but also ways of seeing and understanding the world and life. Indeed, even on the planetary scale, the *techno-scientific worldview* is gaining ever-greater hegemony. My objective is not to give respect a more significant role *within* the techno-scientific worldview, but rather to show that *respect is the key to a distinct worldview*. Moreover, if adopted together with the currently dominant worldview,

this new perspective would make us less one-dimensional and more balanced at a time when superficiality and imbalance are unmistakable ills afflicting our society.

EVERYDAY EXPRESSIONS

Philosophy frequently finds in familiar and colloquial turns of phrase not only a starting point for reflection but also clues that point to the essence of a particular term or concept. The word *respect* is part of our everyday speech; everyone uses it, knows what it means, and understands that respect for people and certain things is a good example of moral conduct. It is also one of the terms most frequently used in moral and political discourse and in ethical theories of all times. It comes up everywhere: 'respect for human dignity', 'respect for public things', 'respect for the environment', 'respect for the elderly', 'respect for oneself', 'respect for justice and freedom', 'respect for the law', 'respect for works of art', 'respect for animals and nature', 'respect for the sacred'…

Respect is an intentional relationship, an attitude towards someone or something. Given that we sometimes see respect as being based on a particular reason, we sometimes use the expression '*out of respect for…*' In the phrase 'out of respect for his age', for instance, we understand that age is the main reason for a certain kind of respect shown towards the person in question. We also find the expression '*respect of…*' used when we refer to the subject who adopts the attitude of respect, for example: 'the respect of students for their teacher' or 'earn the respect of everyone'.

Respect can be referred to as a kind of attitude – 'a respectful attitude' – or as a virtue – that ascribed to a respectful individual. Actions, particularly the use of language, may also be described as respectful. We speak of 'respectful language', as opposed to language that is coarse, immoderate, ill-mannered, or perhaps even worse, language used to express sarcasm or utter insults and offensive remarks. To speak respectfully of someone is to take care in our choice of words, avoiding terms that are too direct and using instead words and expressions that refer to or reach that person in a way that is considerate and measured. Words, in short, that maintain a certain 'respectful distance'.

With all of these different ways of using the word, however, it is not clear how respect should be defined. In the language of attitudes (in moral language) terms are not well-defined: like flexible materials, they are often stretched, or overlap and intertwine with other meanings. For example, when Marx asserts that 'the worker has a greater need of respect than of bread', we see that respect means something very close to recognition (including in the philosophical sense that Hegel had given the term). The worker wishes to be recognised as a subject instead of being treated merely as a source of labour power. It seems to me, however, that respect is something more than recognition: while respect presupposes recognition, recognition does not necessarily presuppose respect. The underlying idea may have been better expressed as: 'the worker has a greater need of recognition than of bread.'

In order to get at the core of the concept of respect we need to concentrate on situations in which it is equivalent to *attention*: to treat someone or something with respect means, for one thing, to treat that person or thing in an attentive way. In any dictionary we will find that the meaning of the word respect is similar or virtually equivalent to the meanings given for consideration, deference, attentiveness, regard… Consider the word *regard*, for instance: to hold someone in *regard* implies that the person in question is respected and granted a certain attention. In German, the word *Achtung* means both *respect* and *attention*. And here, in my view, lies the heart of the matter: in an attentive attitude. Specifically, in this book I argue that *the essence of respect is the attentive gaze*. Naturally, the role of the attentive gaze as a *condition* that makes respect possible will be analysed, and the reasons why *the essence of respect is the atten-*

tive gaze will also be examined. In the course of this inquiry we are bound to encounter some paradoxes: though respect arises from the attentive gaze, there are superficial forms of 'respect' which, when subjected to the attentive gaze and careful scrutiny, turn out to lack real substance. Obviously we do not end up respecting everything that we look at attentively, but *some of the things we manage to look at attentively are also things we end up respecting.*

ATTENTIVE GAZE, ETHICAL GAZE

'What is hardest of all? That which seems most simple: to see with your eyes what is before your eyes.' (Goethe)

There is something unusual, even paradoxical, about the way that we look at the world around us: the utter ease of looking contrasts with the difficulty of performing the same act well. If there is light, we just open our eyes and the things around us appear. In contrast, we must pay attention to become aware of certain aspects of reality and, in particular, to perceive things in a different way. Simply seeing, mere visual perception, involves virtually no effort (hence, for example, the success of television), but looking with care is harder: directing our gaze and concentrating on something involves an effort and can therefore be tiring. Moreover, many of the contexts in which we find ourselves lead us to take a less than thorough approach. Taken together with our personal energy-saving economy, this explains the fact that the attentive gaze is more uncommon than we might expect.

The fact that this movement of attention is anything but commonplace should be underlined. For the most part we tend to deal with people and things by operating in an automatic mode, acting in accordance with criteria that are usually adopted uncritically. Yet when we take this approach things are not really revealed to us, or it is only the surface of things that we see. In fact, the movement of attention is not only a means of recovering the other, whether a person or an object, it is also a way to regain ourselves. In the face of the acceptance and repetition of clichés, in the face of the effectiveness of certain ideological schemes we use to justify our opinions (as well as our actions or failure to act), attention emerges as the task that needs to be undertaken by the individual who *must* start anew, who recognises that he is subject to responsibility and that he is called upon to be himself (a theme at least as old as philosophy itself). Letting ourselves go with the flow is such an easy solution, and there are so many interests that want us to do just this, that an appeal to the self has a decisive role to play. And no one should deceive themselves into thinking that it is only the 'masses' that are manipulated by advertising slogans and ideological prejudices: intellectuals, politicians and scientists also repeat clichés, albeit sometimes dressed up in fancier rhetoric.

What is it that attention adds to the gaze to transform it in such a significant way? Why does the effort of directing our attention imply much more than a simple zoom effect? And, the key question: *why does attention make the gaze morally significant?*

It should be pointed out that the notion of *gaze* is used here in a broad sense which, while it includes the action of our eyes, also encompasses the 'mental gaze', which is equally important. Indeed, at times it is with our eyes shut that we see most clearly: 'Not all who see have opened their eyes, nor all who look, see.' (Gracián, 2003 p. 228).

Lowering or averting the gaze can also sometimes be an act of respect. Such cases are somewhat paradoxical in that *it is those who avert their gaze who see most*. The individual who averts his gaze does so because he has seen what there is to see in a particular situation. In contrast, the individual who continues to look has failed to grasp something, and his gaze becomes indiscreet, if not offensive. There are also those who fail to avert their gaze in such situations because they have not managed to look with due care and therefore fail to realise that a certain distancing is warranted out of respect. For averting the gaze is, in effect, a way of creating distance.

We may better understand the appropriateness of lowering our gaze in certain circumstances if we bear in mind that vision is the most direct and truest of our senses, reaching its object rapidly and without mediation. It can also be the most indiscreet of the senses, which is why there are occasions when averting our gaze is the right thing to do. This shows us that the attentive gaze is neither insistent nor indiscreet. On the contrary, *the attentive gaze knows how to look with discretion*. To look attentively is not to stare: it is rather to direct our gaze with care, without hurry, and with enough flexibility to be able to avert it when the situation requires.

In short, averting the gaze, in addition to showing us that the most lucid of gazes does not depend directly on our eyes, points to something even more important: *the ethical-moral dimension of the attentive gaze*. We begin to see that attentive gaze is synonymous with *ethical gaze*.

The relevance of speaking of an ethical gaze is also clear if we bear in mind that in interpersonal relationships the *ignorance* or *indifference* that one individual may show towards another already has a moral significance. Ignoring the other is precisely the opposite of taking him into account, paying attention to him, or showing consideration for him. In this sense attention is the first *movement* with ethical significance. Respect requires attention, and attention in turn implies moving closer, a process of approximation. 'Having treated someone attentively' means having treated them with respect. In practice, this may mean any number of things, but the common denominator is that we have looked with care; we have not remained indifferent; we have paid attention to the other person and directed our gaze at him for some moments.

As we make our way along our life paths, we cease to pay attention to what is peripheral, and what is not even perceived certainly cannot be the object of respect. Without looking, without paying attention, there are things of which I am unaware and things I may even end up stepping on. Ignorance is antithetical to respect. Hence the gaze and attention have both a cognitive and a moral dimension. This double nature is reflected, for example, in this interesting passage from *The Discourses* by Epitectus: 'But now when you have said: "To-morrow I will begin to attend", you must be told that you are saying this, "To-day I will be shameless, disregardful of time and place, mean; it will be in the power of others to give me pain; to-day I will be passionate and envious." See how many evil things you are permitting yourself to do. If it is good to use attention to-morrow, how much better is it to do so to-day! If to-morrow it is in your interest to attend, much more is it to-day, that you may be able to do so to-morrow also, and may not defer it again to the third day.' (Epictetus, 1952, pp. 243-244).

I am particularly interested in this passage because in it Epitectus establishes a very close link between attention and moral conduct. Paying attention ensures good conduct and happiness; when we cease to pay attention, the consequences are just the opposite. Moreover, Epitectus warns us how difficult it is to pay attention when we are no longer in the habit of doing so. For being attentive is a habit, a way of approaching life. Epitectus goes on to write: 'Why do you not maintain your attention constant? "To-day I choose to play." Well then, ought you not to play with attention?' (Epictetus, 1952, p. 243). This is a habit we should not get out of, one that can play a part in some of our everyday actions. Putting it off is a bad sign, not only because of the ills that lowering our guard may give rise to, but also because if we do not practise the habit it becomes increasingly difficult to regain.

If we were to seek precedents, we should note that the thesis that the ethical gaze is the attentive gaze was defended by Socrates,[1] the best teacher philosophy can refer to. The ethics of respect contains much that could be traced to Socrates. It differs in one important respect, however, from the moral intellectualism (at times somewhat abstract and elitist) that has been derived from Socratic thinking. The ethics of respect is not an intellectualist ethical system: paying attention puts us – as the words of Epitectus stress – in direct contact with the stuff of life. This is not a speculative approach to ethics, developed in an ivory tower or in the confines of academia, a system with little connection to real experience that must be adapted *a posteriori* to the real world; the ethics of respect and attention emerges from the very heart of life itself. In other words, the attention referred to here is not a concept drawn from any school of philosophy, but from the school of life. A good example of what I mean can be seen in Akira Kurosawa's film *Dersu Uzala,* inspired by the travel writings of Vladimir Klavdievich Arsenyev. The film's protagonist, Dersu, is an old hunter whose life is closely tied to the environment that surrounds him; he appears to be an integral part of the natural world. Dersu is hired as a guide by Arsenyev, the head of an expedition to explore the far reaches of Siberia. Over the course of the story, it becomes clear that Dersu's *gaze* is very different from that of the other explorers. It differs primarily in one way: it is an attentive gaze. When the members of the expedition look around them they see very different things. Dersu's gaze is richer than Arsenyev's: he sees more and he sees more deeply. As a result, Dersu can orient himself better, is more aware of the significance of even the smallest things, and is more capable of surviving in this extremely harsh land. But there is something even more important for our purposes. Precisely because Dersu's gaze is more attentive, it is more respectful: Dersu *respects because he sees.* His perceptiveness is simultaneously respect for people, animals and nature. Arsenyev learns from Dersu's way of looking at the world, and, thanks to Dersu, discovers other dimensions of nature and of life.

The ethics of respect, therefore, cannot involve a flight from the world of everyday problems. First, because the attentive gaze is at the service of orientation, and not merely at a theoretical level but in life. When we find ourselves in the middle of a forest we must look with care to see where we are and which way we need to go. Similarly, an attentive gaze is needed if we are to find our way in life. The second reason is that the attentive gaze connects us closely to the world. In no case is it an evasion of the world or a speculative way of looking at things from the height of some intellectual vantage point.

The individual who pays more attention is better oriented and shows greater respect.

SOCIETY DEPENDS ON RESPECT

Though not central to the matter at hand, at least not as it will progressively be defined here, it is worth noting briefly at this point the importance traditionally attributed to respect in its role as a cornerstone of our collective existence.

No one is likely to dispute that human society would be impossible without respect. Needless to say, none of us would be here now if, in general, sons and daughters had not respected their parents; if laws and customs had only been the object of mockery and disdain; if public places and institutions were not respected… In short, if no one respected anything or anyone else.

It is true that the objects of respect have changed over time and differ from culture to culture. There are some things that have fortunately ceased to be the object of respect, including certain violent religious practices involving sacrifice, and a long list of rights and privileges linked to a hierarchical conception of society that conferred respectability on some, based on their social class, while relegating the majority to low status and insignificance. In order to prevent these and many other abuses,

serious thought needs to be given to what 'merits' respect. Unfortunately, it is all too often the case that what should be respected is not, and what is respected should not be.

Without going into the question of what does or does not deserve respect, what can be said is that, though they do not necessarily share a particularly conservative mindset or a sense of nostalgia for days gone by, people see lack of respect as a sign that something is wrong in society. The certainty that without respect human society would be impossible appears to remain intact within us. This belief is so deeply rooted that it has also been transmitted to us in myth. One version of the myth of Prometheus is particularly relevant: it not only underlines the foundational character of respect, but also, in a way, gives it the same level of importance generally ascribed to technical capacity. And certainly it is clear that the city of men would not endure without technology, which finds its highest expression in the city itself (later I will present the technical dimension of the human condition under the concept of *cosmopoiesis*). The level of technical sophistication we have reached is such that it is difficult for us to imagine life without some fundamental elements of technology (houses, fire, the wheel and related developments, the basic plough and those that have followed it…). Indeed, we cannot even contemplate the possibility of getting by without much more recent advances such as electric light, household appliances, cars, computers… Which brings us back to the myth of Prometheus found in Plato's *Protagoras*. [320c-322d]. In Plato's dialogue, the sophist Protagoras recounts a version of the myth, which I summarise here: There was a time when only the gods existed. When the time came for animals and men to be brought into the light of day, Epimetheus was responsible for distributing talents and skills among them. He did this in such a way, however, that when he got to the human race he had already used up all the qualities that he had to distribute and did not know what to do. Then Prometheus, seeing man naked and unshod, stole technical skills (*technai*) and fire from the gods to offer to man. The result was quite impressive: men invented language, made houses and clothes, cultivated the fields… But time passed and men were still dispersed, which left them exposed to many dangers of the natural world. When they tried to live together, creating cities, they argued among themselves and attacked each other to such an extent that soon they were again dispersed and perishing. When Zeus saw this, he decided to intervene and grant man some of the qualities he still lacked: justice and respect: 'Zeus feared that the entire race would be exterminated, and so he sent Hermes to them, bearing reverence and justice [*aidos* and *dike*] to be the ordering principle of cities and the bonds of friendship and conciliation' (Plato, 1953, [322c], p. 147).

Respect, together with justice, is seen here as a prerequisite for the creation of cities (in other words, for human society); it has, then, a foundational character and is associated with the order that makes cities possible. In many ancient cultures, the city was conceived of as a small world, a *cosmion*, related in turn to another more transcendental order (the divine order). Men were understood to form part of a human order, which was in turn part of a transcendental order. This is where the sacred comes into play. We should bear in mind that the relationship between respect and the sacred is a fundamental one: the highest form of respect was that owed to the sacred. This primal relationship goes a long way towards explaining the difficulty of maintaining the significance of respect in a society like the one that exists now in the West, where any sense of the sacred has virtually been lost. Indeed, in the techno-scientific worldview, there appears to be no place for the sacred. In truth, this trend provides no grounds for optimism. On the contrary, our reaction, like that of Zeus, should be one of concern.

In many cultures, the link with the sacred was brought up-to-date as respect for that which is foundational, a 'bowing' before what came before as the source of life. This is always, to a large extent, the significance of respect for gods, ancestors and foundational texts (when they exist): the respectful relationship with that which is foundational is what ensures the continuity of the human world. This belief, as time-honoured as it is sensible, could continue to guide us in the contemporary world, albeit with a formulation that is more generic and open to subsequent refinement: *the order (the things) that we respect and serve is, at the same time, the order that serves us and makes the life we live possible.*

Here, above all to avoid mistaken or tendentious interpretations, I am not going to take the concept of the sacred as either a starting point or a core theme. The insistence that it is the attentive gaze that is essential to respect will have to be enough to reach, by another route, a point where we can recover, at least in part, the significance that the sacred had in other ages. An additional advantage of this approach is that the attentive gaze leads not only to the sacred, but also, in a very natural way, to closely related matters signposted by terms such as: modesty, moderation, shame, scruples, indulgence, consideration, etc.

So, for the moment I propose that the idea of respect, a quality esteemed by the gods, has an important place in the moral aptitude of human beings, and is as significant as love, mercy or egoism in other religious and philosophical systems.

THE OPPORTUNITY THAT THE ETHICS OF RESPECT PRESENTS

My appeal to the *opportunity that the ethics of respect represents for our age*, that is, to its advisability for the contemporary world, means simply that this attitude (which has always been part of human existence to one extent or another) could be of great value in addressing specific contemporary problems. More generally, the notion of respect can also help us get our bearings, providing us with a richer and deeper vision of the world and helping us live our lives in a fuller, more authentic way.

A greater presence of the attitude of respect, for example, might reasonably be expected to counteract two trends that are unfortunately widespread in our society: *indifference* and avidity for *possession* and *consumption*. Our age is one in which ease reigns supreme: being indifferent takes no effort; to be indifferent it is enough to do nothing. And, apart from the process of acquiring money, consumption is also easy: the powerful economic system currently in place seems to be an immense conspiracy designed to immerse us in effortless and unbridled consumption. The *movement* of respect contrasts with these dominant trends: while indifference is *maximum distance*, and possession and consumption imply the *elimination of all distance*, respect coincides precisely with proximity (an approximation that at the same time maintains a certain distance). The movements in question are not mutually exclusive: possession and distance also have and must have a place in human life. What is worrying is the *excess* of one type of movement and the relative absence of the other: contemporary society is characterised much more by indifference and consumption than by respect.

The relationship between the ethics of respect and science and technology is highlighted in the subtitle of this book because this is the age of technology, a time when techno-scientific power is shaping society, transforming our habitat and reconstructing our bodies. Genetic engineering, new sources of energy, the media revolution and the virtual world of computers, as well as the problems and dangers associated with genetic manipulation, environmental deterioration and the expansion of the cyber-world – such issues are the subject of conversations, information bulletins and press articles, school essays and disputes between experts. These concerns are a sign of the times. Technology shapes not only our lives but also our *vision* of life. The ethics of respect seeks to establish a dialogue with this vision of life.

As a result of techno-scientific development and related applications, a number of sectoral ethics have appeared in recent decades, including bioethics, ecological ethics and computer ethics, among others. The ethics of respect or of the attentive gaze is not another ethic of this type; it does not correspond to or seek to delimit a new field. Rather, it is an approach that should precede the ethics concerned with particular fields, and, with luck, one that will later be developed within the framework of each sectoral ethic. The outcome that would best reflect the soundness and potential of the approach would be for it to be applied in these sectoral ethics, not (as often happens) as an operating functional concept, but rather in all its density and as a core principle.

Moreover, a well-founded theory of respect will facilitate both the correction of arguments that are inappropriate or incorrect (and therefore weak and ineffective) and the support of sound analyses based on respect. An example of the first situation: many calls to respect nature are made in the name of the health and well-being of contemporary humans and future generations, but this is an inappropriate way to speak of the issue, for respect has nothing to do with calculating costs and benefits (Kolakowski, 1999, pp. 124-125). An example of the second situation: in the preamble to the 1948 Universal Declaration of Human Rights the word respect appears twice: it is made clear that the *main aim* of the declaration is to develop *respect* for rights and freedoms. In this case, clarifying the significance of respect and examining the concept in-depth could make a significant contribution towards achieving this aim.

The ethics of respect is a new development in the field of ethics: while respect has always been discussed, only Kant formulated an ethical system in which respect played a central role (and even he did so in a very particular way, which I will examine in due course). The debt that the ethics of respect owes to previous schools of thought must be acknowledged, though: I would stress the importance of Socratic philosophy (referred to already), Stoic and Kantian thought, and the personalism of authors such as Levinas and Ricoeur, among others. I will leave for a future work the dialogue that the ethics of respect could enter into with other contemporary discourses such as that of Hans Jonas and his principle of responsibility, or that of Jürgen Habermas and his discourse ethics. The application of the ethics of respect to specific problems and fields will also be considered on another occasion.

When Simone Weil wrote that 'looking is what saves us', she presupposed, naturally, that it was the attentive gaze that had this necessary and positive effect. That premise is my conviction.

Given that the attentive gaze arises from respect, almost everything I have to say could be summed up by paraphrasing the well-known words of Saint Augustine – 'love, and do what you like' – as follows: 'pay attention (look attentively), and do what you like.'

REFERENCES

Epitectus. (1952). *The Discourses of Epictetus* (G. Long trans.). Chicago: Encyclopaedia Britannica.

Gracián, B. (2003). *Oráculo manual y arte de la prudencia*. Madrid, Spain: Cátedra.

Kolakowski, L. (1999). *Freedom, Fame, Lying and Betrayal: Essays on Everyday Life* (pp. 124–125). London: Penguin Books.

Plato,. (1953). *The Dialogues of Plato (B. Jowett trans.)*. London: Oxford University Press.

ENDNOTE

[1] Socrates believed that virtue, *arete*, was grounded in knowledge, knowledge of oneself and knowledge of the truth about things. No one is deliberately bad: such conduct is the result of ignorance.

This work was previously published in International Journal of Technoethics, Volume 1, Issue 2, edited by Rocci Luppicini, pp. 1-9, copyright 2010 by IGI Publishing (an imprint of IGI Global).

Chapter 3

How Can the Problems of An Ethical Judgment on Science and Technology Be Correctly Approached?

Evandro Agazzi
Università Di Genova, Italy

ABSTRACT

Two opposite positions are currently dividing the field of discussion regarding the ethical evaluation of science and technology. On the one hand, many people maintain that such a judgment must not be introduced or, less radically, that it needs not be looked for; on the other hand, several scholars maintain that such a judgment is legitimate or, more radically, mandatory. Therefore, it is advisable to examine the arguments of both parties in order to see not so much which viewpoint is right but, perhaps, to what extent both might be right.

POSITION A

Let us first consider what reasons are proposed by those who, more or less strongly, deny the legitimacy of an ethical questioning of science and technology. We can summarize these reasons under the following headings:

DOI: 10.4018/978-1-4666-1773-5.ch003

More strongly:

1.1. Permitting that science (and also technology from a particular point of view) be subjected to moral judgment would jeopardize the *freedom of science*, which is a very significant part of the freedom of thinking. Therefore, such judgment *must not* be allowed for.

1.2. In addition, moral judgments could introduce interferences in the evaluation of scientific facts and theories and, in such a way, constitute serious dangers for the attainment of *scientific objectivity*. Therefore, in order to protect this capital requirement of scientific knowledge, such judgments *must not* be admitted.

Less strongly:

2.1. Even admitting that a moral evaluation of science as a whole could make sense, it is clear that science, having as its specific end the search for truth, is *good in itself*. Therefore, any additional ethical questioning is *not needed*.

2.2. Science is at the service of man, and this is again a morally positive connotation that makes any ethical questioning of it *superfluous*.

2.3. Admittedly, morally wrong *uses* of science are possible, but they are made by "other" agents and are not entailed by science (and technology) itself.

We can note that in points 1.1-1.2 science is considered essentially from a *cognitive* point of view, while in points 21-2.3 it is implicitly recognized that science has to do with *praxis*.

POSITION B

Coming now to the arguments of those who advocate the legitimacy of an ethical evaluation of science and technology, we can resume them under the following headings:

3.1. Science (and even more technology) is concretely *praxis-oriented* and, as a consequence, makes no exception to the fact that ethical considerations are pertinent and *legitimate* when human actions are considered.

3.2. In addition, moral judgments are *mandatory* because of the social *impacts* of science and technology, that may be beneficial or harmful to humans.

It is clear that these points lay stress on the *practical* aspects of science, much more than on its cognitive aspects.

We shall now outline a few comments on the above statements. Common to all of them is the idea that moral judgments aim at establishing, in the last analysis, what is *permitted* and what is not permitted, that is, they entail certain *limitations* of our freedom. This is undeniable and explains the concerns expressed in point 1.1 for it seems that, if we admit moral evaluation of science, we are led to accept that science *freedom* could be limited in the name of certain moral norms or principles. This limitation, however, is understood in this case as concerning the *cognitive aspect* of science and, as such, is interpreted as a limitation of the freedom of thinking and research. This interpretation is not fully arbitrary, since historical evidence shows that people have not been considered fully free to think, believe or investigate within a great deal of cultures: ideas, propositions and theories were condemned and *prohibited* for several reasons (mainly religious, ideological and political) and, inevitably, concrete persons or institutions were credited with the authority (and the power) of exerting this control and imposing these limitations. Therefore, *freedom of thinking* (including freedom of communicating and defending one's thoughts and ideas) is rightly considered as a fundamental conquest of Modernity, a conquest that, as usual, is never secured once for all, but must be constantly defended. Admitting moral judgments on science is therefore perceived as a subtle risk of reintroducing those prohibitions of scientific ideas and theories that, in the past, were mainly dictated by religious or ideological tenets, but could now reappear under the pretext of ethical concerns (in particular, there is the suspicion that certain "external" powers could take up the role of being the "censors" of science in the name of ethics). One must be aware, however, that freedom of thinking was not vindicated only as a consequence of modern *individualism*, that entailed a sphere of untouchable rights among which the right of thinking, of opinion and research were included, but also as the more substantial consciousness that moral judgments are *not pertinent* in the domain of cognition, in which the criteria for acceptance or rejection are not *good or evil*, but *true or false*. Therefore, if a statement or a theory are believed to be true (according to the truth criteria of a given domain of knowledge) they cannot be criticized or rejected for moral reasons, but only on the ground of arguments relying on the specific criteria of the said domain. In brief, there are no *morally prohibited truths*, because morality and ethics do not concern cognition, but *action*. As a consequence, that limitation of freedom that morality necessarily implies regards *freedom of action* and nothing else. Therefore, as far as one considers science *only* as a system of knowledge, it cannot be subjected to moral evaluations. The same is true of technology, to the extent that this is interpreted *only* as the invention of *efficacious tools and procedures*: their efficacy cannot be evaluated from a moral point of view, but is the matter of a strictly technological estimation, though, obviously, the different *use* of such efficient tools and procedures is of full moral relevance, since it regards *praxis*.

Coming now to the arguments advanced by those who consider legitimate or even mandatory a moral evaluation of science and technology, we can note that such people, implicitly or explicitly, attribute a *subordinate* role to the cognitive aspect of science (and even more of technology). Sure, such a role is not (and cannot be) totally ignored, but is seen as intrinsically influenced and *determined* by extra-cognitive factors. This view can be advocated within different intellectual contexts, which can be basically reduced to two. The first is typically expressed by the philosophical school of *pragmatism* that has been very influential es-

pecially in the Anglo-American culture. One of the most characteristic thesis of this school is that knowledge is intrinsically praxis-oriented and that, as a consequence, cognition is essentially a *problem-solving* activity, to which problems are posed, ultimately, by concrete practical needs though, in the course of the search for these solutions, several "subordinate" steps may occur in which purely theoretical and intellectual problems must be faced and solved. The second is expressed by those approaches that give a paramount importance to the *social dimension* of every human activity. These approaches can be rooted in certain specific philosophical doctrines (such as, e.g., Marxism) or in certain more general *socio-logistic* conceptions (such as the developments of "sociology of knowledge"). A blending of both approaches has taken place in recent years and, in particular, has largely influenced the philosophy of science and technology with different degrees of depth. For example, the so-called *post-empiricist* philosophy of science (whose most significant representatives are Hanson, Toulmin, Kuhn and Feyerabend) has stressed the social dependence of scientific theories, that goes from the *linguistic* dependence of their concepts to the more general dependence of their acceptance on the *paradigms* shared by the scientific community and even by the much broader world-views of particular cultures. Even more radical is the position held by the so-called *sociological interpretation* of science (advocated by authors such as Bernal, Bloor, Latour, Woolgar et al.). If one wants to point out the most significant difference between this position and the former, one could say that this second approach concentrates on the *concrete* way of doing science and lays particular stress on the variety of motivations, interests, conditionings that surround the scientific activity with the consequence of denying the appropriateness of that *idealized* image of science that is presented by those who consider it essentially as a cognitive enterprise. This entails not only a very strong consideration of those social, political and also ethical issues that are related with the conditions and consequences of doing science and using it, but also casts doubts on those cognitive qualities, such as objectivity, rigour, generality, that the "cognitivists" recognize as typical of science.

A Necessary Compatibilization of the Opposite Views

The reasons advanced by the two parties are rather convincing and we feel that both of them are right. However these reasons lead to very divergent conclusions as far as the legitimacy of a moral judgment on science and technology is concerned and we must understand why this is possible. The answer is not very difficult: the arguments proposed by the opposite parties are *sound* but *partial* or, to put it differently, they are right in what they *affirm* and are wrong in what they *deny* (such a situation is very common in a great variety of debates regarding complex issues). As a consequence, the rational attitude will consist in an effort for making them *compatible* and this will succeed if we are able to show that they are *complementary*, as we shall try to prove now.

The right point in position A consists in the defence of *freedom and objectivity* of science, provided that only the cognitive aspect of science is taken into consideration, and this aspect *must* be taken into a very serious consideration because science is indeed a system of reliable, rigorous and objective knowledge. The fact that this knowledge is never absolutely certain, that it can and must be submitted to critical scrutiny, that it can and must be revised if necessary, that it is never final are not objections against the fact that the *defining intrinsic end* of science is the acquisition of such a sound knowledge and, indeed, all criticisms and revisions are conceived in science as means for attaining this goal, that is, for securing a growth and an improvement of the body of scientific knowledge. From this point of view, science is only a *partial*, but very successful, way that mankind has found for pursuing the

search for truth. The risk that must be avoided is that of considering science as the *unique* way for searching truth, but this does not entail that, *within the specific and delimited domains* of scientific inquiry, only scientific criteria be admitted for judging whether the knowledge acquired is valid or not. This is why moral, political, religious, social judgments cannot concern the acceptance or rejection of the *contents* of science, as far as they are considered *within* their specific limits. Of course, if they are extrapolated in order to support or oppose certain views regarding other domains of research or activity, they are *ipso facto* legitimately questionable, but this because they are credited with a general validity that oversteps their genuine but restricted scientific validity.

The contents of science, however, must be *found* and this already implies that they are the result of some kind of *activity*; more precisely of the activity of human *research* that consists, as we have said, in the search for truth which is in itself a morally good end or value. One must note, however, that scientific research is not reducible to that particular "activity" that we could call *contemplation*: with very few exceptions, concrete *action* is needed for acquiring scientific knowledge and in such a way *ethics* legitimately comes into play since ethics specifically concerns the right and wrong of human *actions* in general. This is immediately evident in the case of the experimental sciences, but is much more general since the "scientific work" in every sector relies upon many *conditions*, is concretely performed in view of certain *objectives*, can have several *consequences*, can be applied in several *uses*, and these facts are all the matter of moral evaluation. In conclusion, freedom of scientific and technological research, and their objectivity, must be defended as far as their cognitive aspect is concerned, but this does not entail that *whatever ways and means* for doing this research be acceptable since this concerns the rightness of human actions, a domain in which no privileged fields of exemption from ethical appreciation exist, unless we affirm that science is *the absolute value*, but this is obviously a (very debatable) *axiological* tenet and not a scientific statement, from which an (equally debatable) *ethical* corollary is deduced.

The right points in position B are essentially related to the fact that science and technology are also particular and very important systems of concrete human activities that are motivated, supported, conditioned, by many factors of individual and social nature, and have in turn very significant effects on the life of individuals and society, bringing about deep modifications in the conditions of existence of humans that are not necessarily or automatically *for the best*. If we speak of "the best" we implicitly refer to some *good* with respect to which it is possible to make progress but also to have regression. Moreover, this good is hardly identifiable with a single precise condition, end, ideal, but is rather articulated in a series of particular more precise goods that we can call *values* and that inspire and motivate human actions. The complication derives from the fact that the "best" satisfaction of one value can often result in a serious decrease in the satisfaction of other values: in other words, *conflicts of values* are a well-known and often dramatic fact of life. Examples of such conflicts are easy to mention: an economically successful activity can sometimes be performed at the price of social injustice or have social injustice as a consequence; a politically able strategy can sometimes be repugnant from a moral point of view; the absolute respect for such military values as discipline and obedience to orders can bring to perpetrate atrocities against innocent people; unrestricted promotion of welfare in few countries can increase poverty in many other countries. Coming to our matter, the growth of scientific and technological knowledge can produce (not "as such", but owing to the complex network of relations in which scientific and technological activities are embedded) serious damages in the satisfaction of other values (in particular, of moral values).

The consideration of these facts shows why those who advocate a moral evaluation of science and technology "are right" but at the same time it indicates when they are no longer right. This happens when moral criteria (as well as other extra-scientific criteria) are adopted for discriminating what is scientifically *true* or at least admissible as a tentative hypothesis. Admitting such an intrusion would amount to jeopardizing a fundamental *value*, the value of the search for true knowledge, and this is no less unjustified than jeopardizing social justice or the survival of mankind because the search for truth is one of the most fundamental needs and rights of human beings. Moreover, such an attitude would undermine the progress of mankind in general because, after all, science and technology have provided humans with a great deal of *reliable knowledge and reliable know-how* in numberless domains, and it would amount to a real loss of *wisdom* to deprive humans of the *confidence* in these conquests of their history.

An Axiological View of Scientific Activity

We are approaching the solution of our problem. The correct way of attaining a *compatibilization* of the opposite position is that of considering them within an *axiological view* of scientific activity, a view, to be sure, that should be adopted regarding any sort of human activity. It must be recognized that *values* are all those *goods* or *ideals* that humans consider as *worthy being pursued* because they *give a sense* to their existence. Depending on his or her personal *history* (that includes also a great deal of social elements) every human being tries to find a sense to his *Life* and determines, more or less consciously, what is *valuable* for him: pleasure, wealth, power, glory, health, beauty, friendship, love, honesty, courage, solidarity, altruism, and many other values can easily be mentioned and normally every person also has an order of priority among these values, in the sense of feeling what is *more valuable* for her in general. In every concrete *situation*, however, several conflicting values usually appear, and the person must face the problem of "applying" her "hierarchy of values" in this situation. A strict application of the "general" hierarchy is seldom adopted because every value is accompanied by a particular "weight" in the particular situation. Therefore, the spontaneous and "wise" choice consists in trying to satisfy the most relevant values without completely sacrificing the other values. This "compatibilization" has therefore the characteristic of an *optimisation*, that is, of a choice in which no value is *absolutized* to such an extent as to completely sacrifice the other values but all are respected in a more or less limited measure. In short, any human activity must be embedded in the whole of *human life* and evaluated in the light of the *different values* that provide a *sense* to life. This means, in particular, that science and technology are *de facto*, but also *de jure*, submitted to *value judgments* the most prominent of which is the *specific* value judgment regarding their truth and reliability, but which is not sufficient to give *full sense* to science and technology. Saying that it is not sufficient does not mean that it is not *necessary*, and here lies the root of the *complementarity* of which we have spoken. We must be able to give a sense to science and technology not by distorting their nature, but by affirming that their "doing" must be sensitive to several other values.

A Systems-Theoretic Model for the Complementarity of Value-Criteria

What we have said until now is rather general and considers science and technology essentially as individual activities. This perspective, however, is too restricted since science and technology are also, and even more significantly, *social* activities. This is already true in a rather limited sense, that is, in the sense that scientific and technological research are concretely performed within their respective *communities*, but is also true in a more general sense, that is, in the sense that they are

performed inside the global *social context*. This can be affirmed also for the cognitive aspects of science and technology, in which the originality and creativity of particularly gifted individuals is indispensable for securing progress and making significant breakthroughs, but in which the availability of commonly accepted back-ground knowledge, the critical comparison of ideas, the mutual checking of empirical results and experimental outcomes is no less essential. This, however, is more evident if we consider the *practical* aspects of science and technology, which are strictly related with the different needs of society and have concrete impacts on its life.

In order to offer a significant portrayal of this situation, the author of the present paper has proposed for many years a "model" or "approach" inspired by *general systems theory*. According to this systemic model, society is considered as a great complex *system* resulting from a great variety of *subsystems*. In every system, as is well-known, the satisfactory "functioning" of the global system is secured by the correct "functioning" of its subsystems, which interact reciprocally and through their interactions permit the conservation of their own integrity and that of the global system as well. Whereas in set-theory the fundamental relation is that of *membership* between the *elements* and the *set* ($e \in S$), in systems-theory the fundamental relation is that between a *system* and its *subsystems*, a relation, moreover, that is (in general) *functional* in a sense different from the usual mathematical one since it expresses the idea of a particular *action* capable of producing certain effects. In set-theory a set can be in turn an element of another set; similarly, in systems-theory a system is usually a subsystem of other systems and this fact is often expressed by saying that any system is embedded in its *environment*, in the sense of entertaining mutual relations with it.

There is a rather large variety of systems: for our purposes we restrict our attention to those that can be "characterized" by one or more *specific functions* that can be symbolically represented by one or more *essential variables.* Any such system tends to preserve its integrity, in the sense of securing its "good functioning", that is, of maintaining the value of its essential variables within a certain *critical interval.* This can be said to constitute the *specific goal* of the system concerned. Of our interest are only *open* systems (that is, those that can exchange with their environment information, matter, and energy), that are in addition *adaptive* (that is, that can secure their integrity and functioning by modifying their internal structure). Biological organs and organisms are typical examples of open adaptive systems, that are normally able to show a *homeostatic* behaviour (that is, to recover the conditions for their correct functioning despite different kinds of environmental perturbations, and thanks to their internal mechanisms). The notion of equilibrium is typical of statics; in the case of homeostasis it must be noted that it expresses the idea of a *dynamic equilibrium,* in the sense that it does not correspond to a recovery of a previous fixed state, but to the attainment of a new state in which the correct functioning is again possible. We can call *intentional systems* those that are able to *envisage their specific goals* and also to partially modify them, such that their functioning can be qualified as a system of *actions.* It could seem that human individuals are good examples of intentional systems but this would not be appropriate since it is impossible to define a list of "specifically human actions" because every man can perform a great variety of actions each of which can inscribe him as an agent of a particular system. In this way we are led to our final step, that is, to the consideration of the *social systems* that can be schematically characterized as *open, adaptive, intentional systems* whose functioning consists of the *actions* of several individuals.

In the case of any social system we can speak again of its specific goals, essential variables, exchange with its environment, taking these characterizations in an *ideal-typical sense,* that is, not as though the agents of one such system do nothing else than performing its specific activity,

but in the sense that we restrict our attention to this activity and consider the conditions of its well functioning and the interrelation of this activity with the other systems (mostly social, but not necessarily only social). Referring to our previous characterization of the notion of value, we can also say that every social system is characterized by the pursuit of a particular *specific value.* At this point it is not difficult to mention a few important social systems: the political system, the educational system, the industrial system, the economic system, the administrative system, the legal system, the communication system, the moral system, the religious system and also the *scientific system* and the *technological system.* They are all subsystems of the overall *social system,* understood as the system represented by a given society, which constitutes the *environment* (or, better, a part of the environment) of any social subsystem. The social system itself, however, is related with other systems, some of them being again "social" (such as the international organizations) and some being non-social (such as the energetic system, or the biological system).

Considering now the interactions between systems, we can suitably summarize them, in the case of every system, under the familiar heading of *outputs* and *inputs,* where the outputs obviously indicate all the kinds of "influences" that a given system exerts on other systems of its environment, and the inputs obviously indicate the "influences" it receives from its environment. In particular, the inputs can be usefully distinguished in *requests, oppositions and supports* that induce stimulations on the behaviour of the system (which is "adaptive", as we have said). This simple scheme helps us better understand the dynamics of systems functioning: not only the *internal* functioning of a system can be oriented in a certain direction by some inputs "coming in" from its environment, but it can often happen that a particular result of its internal functioning, "going out" into the environment, produces as reaction a response in the form of requests, oppositions or support, coming from one or more other systems of the environment (this is the well-known *feedback loop*) which determines a reorientation of the internal functioning of the original system in order to keep its essential variables within their critical interval. In this way the internal functioning of a system evolves in virtue of three distinct factors: its specific structure, the direct inputs from the environment, the indirect effect of its internal functioning "filtered" through the feedback with the environment. It is easy to see, therefore, that the *good functioning* of any subsystem needs the satisfaction of these three conditions, that is, not only that its specific internal way of operating remains "good", but also that its "response" to the external inputs be "adequate" (in the sense of responding to demands, of reducing possible oppositions and gaining as much support as possible), both in the case of "spontaneous" inputs from the environment and in the case of those inputs that are the consequence of a feedback produced by the action of the subsystem itself.

We have now enough elements to tackle our specific problem by divesting it of the negative flavour of undue "interference" from external powers. Let us start with a simple example: The industrial system can send to the scientific and technological systems a "request" for some innovation and this amounts to a "support" for certain investigations in both fields. The results of such research can be profitably applied in industrial production but, for example, produce negative consequences at the social level (entailing the dismissal of certain activities and the related unemployment), or produce negative impacts on the natural environment. These facts can easily produce "oppositions" against the particular scientific and technological activities involved, but this does not automatically imply a blocking of these two systems: scientific and technological research will probably be stimulated to find different means for satisfying the industrial needs and avoid at the same time some of the negative consequences, while the industrial system will

be stimulated to find means for avoiding other consequences, and the political system can be stimulated to provide similar means from its side. The final result of these various feedbacks should (ideally) be a situation of dynamic equilibrium in which the goals of the different systems concerned could be "optimally" satisfied, that is, satisfied in a measure that is not "maximal" for any one of them, but "acceptable" for all of them.

The situation in which the *moral system* is concerned is quite similar. Let us consider a project of a biological research from which significant advancements in biological knowledge are expected and also useful applications in the medical domain, but plans experiments on humans for attaining these results. The *ends* of this research are morally good, but the *means* envisaged are morally *questionable* and possible oppositions can come from the moral system not regarding the ends, but the means (that obviously need *action*). The feedback effect can be of different kinds: it can lead to looking for a way of attaining the same results without experimenting on humans; it can lead to the elaboration of detailed strategies for experimenting on humans under morally acceptable conditions (indeed, there are well-elaborated ethical codes regarding clinical experiments, for instance). Moreover, ethical objections usually depend on the kind and the force of the ethical principles applied, so that it may happen that the planed research be considered as morally legitimate under the consideration of certain specific conditions and according to certain moral doctrines. Other moral issues could emerge from taking into account other borderline conditions or possible consequences of the envisaged enterprise. Whatever the *solution* of the moral problems could be, it is clear that it is, on the one hand, *specifically moral* and, on the other hand, concerns a *specifically scientific* project and the correct solution could never be found by distorting the correct scientific pattern of the issue (for example, by denying that the project is scientifically sound, if it is sound, or by modifying it in a scientifically inconsistent way in order to avoid moral objections), nor by trying to mask the real moral issues at stake by introducing morally irrelevant elements of judgment. The correct solution shall consist in taking the moral objections as *constraints* of the scientific action, a way of thinking that is absolutely normal in any systemic and decision-theoretic reasoning: we are normally prepared to plan our "rational" actions under the consideration of many constraints (usually financial, legal, energetic, technical, "material" in a broad sense) and it is only a matter of consistency, within a systemic approach, to consider also other constraints coming from other systems, including the moral system.

The Merging of the Axiological and Systemic Approach

If we remember that every social system has been characterized by the pursuit of a particular *value*, our systemic approach amounts to recognizing that *the whole* of the social values must be taken into consideration and respected also in the functioning of the scientific and technological systems. This will become easier if every social system is really *open* and *adaptive*, that is, if it maintains that dynamic equilibrium that depends on the various feedbacks it entertains with the other systems. This condition holds also for ethics, whose specific goal is that of finding norms for the *concrete actions* of humans, in the concrete historical situation that, in particular, is deeply shaped by the advancements of science and technology (that also modify the self-understanding of man on which morality is ultimately based). Therefore, the real difficulty is not that of avoiding *limitations of freedom*: indeed, the progress of mankind has constantly been characterized by the affirmation of new kinds of freedom, but at the same time by the determination of legitimate limitations of the *freedom of action*. The fundamental requirement is that these limitations become more and more *freely accepted*, and this has to do with two factors: a reaffirmation of the sense of *moral responsibility*, and the (very difficult) elaboration of a *public ethics* in which the *moral conscience* of the individuals could cope with a sound public *ethos*. This is obviously a long-term effort, that involves the education of the new generations, the preservation of what is vital in the *tradition* and the openness to *new views*. The risk we must avoid is that of having a science and technology insensitive to the moral dimension of life, and a morality incapable to cope with the inedited situations produced by the advancements of science and technology. Why this risk must be avoided is simply the consequence of something we have already mentioned: every human activity must be in accordance with the global *sense of life* and this is essential not only for any single individual, but also for those *systems* in which the concrete individuals are performing their most specific activity, because, after all, any person cannot be simply a scientist, a politician, a teacher, a medical doctor, a financial operator, but is necessarily a full *human person* and, as such, has the right (and the duty) of satisfying all the values that give a sense to her life and to the life of the other humans.

This work was previously published in International Journal of Technoethics, Volume 1, Issue 2, edited by Rocci Luppicini, pp. 10-18, copyright 2010 by IGI Publishing (an imprint of IGI Global).

Chapter 4
Technology Traps:
Who Is Responsible?

Peter B. Crabb
The Pennsylvania State University at Hazleton, USA

Steven E. Stern
University of Pittsburgh at Johnstown, USA

ABSTRACT

Technologies can have harmful effects on users' psychological health, on society, and on the environment. "Technology traps" arise when users and societies become stuck with technologies and the harmful consequences produced by these technologies. In this paper, the authors describe five technology traps: incompetence, self-miscontrol, misbehavior, techno-centrism, and environmental degradation. The authors then examine the share of ethical responsibility for these traps among end-users, businesses, and government.

TECHNOLOGY TRAPS: WHO IS RESPONSIBLE?

Technologies are often ambivalent to the well-being of users and society. Despite the many benefits modern technologies have conferred on the human species, there are also costs in the form of undesirable or unexpected consequences (Ellul, 1954, 1964; Perrow, 1984; Sarason, 1984; Tenner, 1996). When societies adopt technologies that produce undesirable consequences that are

difficult to separate from the benefits, situations arise that resemble what Platt (1973) called *social traps*: "traps formally like a fish trap, where men or organizations or whole societies get themselves started in some direction or some set of relationships that later prove to be unpleasant or lethal and that they see no easy way to back out of or avoid" (p. 641). In this article, we examine a subspecies of social traps we call *technology traps*, characterized by the use of technologies that provide immediate benefits but that pose unavoidable longer-term costs to the well-being of individual users, society, and the planet. We

DOI: 10.4018/978-1-4666-1773-5.ch004

describe five technology traps that plague modern society and then examine the issue of attributing responsibility for these traps.

To illustrate what we mean by technology traps, we consider cellular or mobile telephones. The perceived benefits of cell phones (mobility, immediate communication access) are accompanied by numerous costs. Cell phones cause disruptive ringing and intrusive conversations in public and in the workplace (Monk et al., 2004); they can increase the risk of having a motor vehicle accident by more than 500% (Violanti, 1998); among teenagers, they can promote addictive behavior (Baldacci, 2006), codependency (Gross, 1999), disruptions in schools (Chaker, 2007), and assault, robbery, and homicide (Leo, 2006); they have been used for taking privacy-invasive "upskirting" and "downblousing" photographs (Gostomski, 2005); they have been used to detonate roadside bombs in war zones (Cloud, 2005); they have led to the demise of the public pay telephone, thus reducing telephone access for people who do not use cell phones (Maurstad, 2003); and cell phone technology mars landscapes with unattractive transmitter towers (Brunsman, 2006) that kill millions of birds annually (Woodall, 2002). As long as cell phones are considered "standard equipment," individuals and society will be stuck with these undesirable side-effects. That is the essential character of technology traps.

FIVE TECHNOLOGY TRAPS

The Incompetence Trap

When technologies do what people could do themselves, there is little or no opportunity or incentive for people to learn and maintain the skills that the technologies embody. Thus, such technologies can "deskill" users, rob them of manual and cognitive skills, erode self-efficacy (i.e., beliefs that one can successfully perform

a task), and increase dependence on tools and technical experts (Kipnis, 1991).

Everyday life is filled with technologies that take over skills that people could master themselves. For example, alarm clocks automate the task of awakening at a target time, with the result that users feel incompetent at self-awakening and are completely dependent on the devices (Crabb, 2003). Use of automatic cameras similarly robs people of opportunities to develop photographic skills, and routine use of ready-to-eat foods prevents people from learning how to cook (Stern & Kipnis, 1993).

The transfer of skills and self-efficacy from person to machine has a variety of costs. The routine use of electronic calculators to solve math problems results in more negative moods, decreased motivation, and more negative attitudes toward math than doing math problems with paper and pencil (Stern, Alderfer, & Cienkowski, 1998). In industrial settings, automation often creates conditions that are less satisfying and more tedious than skilled manual work (Blauner, 1964; Chadwick-Jones, 1969; Persson et al., 2003).

Technical knowledge and skills themselves become trivialized by automated technologies that only require that users know the proper sequence of pushing buttons (Fromm, 1955; Shaffer, 1981; Skinner, 1986). People do not understand how everyday technologies work (Bandura, 1995), and all that is required is that they know how to use the device and when it is time to throw it away.

The Self-Miscontrol Trap

Modern automated technologies make it unnecessary and often undesirable for human users to exercise control over their own behavior. One consequence of this is that users may experience a failure of self-control when their behavior is controlled by technological devices rather than by social norms, considerations of health, or even laws (Carver & Scheier, 1981).

Many technologies elicit failures of self-control that strongly resemble addictions. College teachers are acutely aware of students' addiction to cell phones: students have great difficulty keeping their hands and eyes off their phones, and the first thing they do when classes let out is make calls or check for messages. Internet addiction also appears to be widespread (Young, 2004), and may sometimes involve compulsive sexual addiction (Stern & Handel, 2001). Other technologies that promote addictive behavior include television (McIlwraith et al., 1991), remote control devices (Ferguson, 1994), stereos and digital audio players (Florentine et al., 1998), and even motor vehicles (Reser, 1980).

Multitasking–performing more than one technological operation at the same time–is an extreme failure of self-control that has become routine as consumer toolkits expand in size. While doing homework, students simultaneously listen to music, watch television, surf the Internet, email, and text-message (Aratani, 2007). Not only does talking on cell phones while driving increase the risk of accident, but compact disk players, onboard computers, GPS systems, and even televisions o compete for drivers' attention and self control, with potentially tragic consequences.

The Misbehavior Trap

Many technologies encourage intentional behavior that conflicts with established social norms, rules, and laws (Crabb, 1996a; Marx, 1994). Email encourages hostile *flaming* (Kiesler, Siegel, & McGuire, 1984). The Internet makes it possible for 24/7 deployment of computer viruses, spam, and fraudulent scams (Furnell, 2002). Video cameras encourage voyeurism and exhibitionism (Crabb, 1996b). Caller ID makes "telephone stalking" possible (Case, 2000). Misbehavior in the form of aggression is also facilitated by many technologies. The mere presence of weapons has been found to arouse thoughts of violence (Berkowitz, 1993).

Ownership of guns is positively correlated with homicide rates (Duggan, 2001), and aggressive fantasies almost always include thoughts about weapons (Crabb, 2000, 2005). Weapons themselves play a significant role in structuring aggressive thoughts and motivating violent behavior. Even technologies that are not intended to be used for aggressive purposes nonetheless can be used as weapons: motor vehicles are commonly used as instruments of aggression (James & Nahl, 2000), and the Internet and text messaging can facilitate teenage bullying (Harmon, 2004) as well as hate crimes (Glaser, Dixit, & Green, 2002).

The Techno-Centrism Trap

Because modern technologies reliably perform tasks with a minimum of effort and skill, people come to trust, depend on, and even have affection for technologies (Dzindolet, Pierce, Beck, & Dawe, 2002; LaFrance, 1996; Muir, 1994; Skitka, Mosier, & Burdick, 2000).

Excessive positive regard for technologies can inadvertently lead to the erosion of trust and regard for other people (Kipnis, 1984; Stern, 1999; Stern, Mullennix, & Wilson, 2002) and can create a culture in which technology is valued above all else. Excessive trust of technologies and distrust of humans is epitomized by surveillance technologies. The very presence of surveillance cameras and computer monitoring systems unambiguously signals an absence of trust, and the activity of surveillance itself induces distrust of those who are under surveillance (Strickland, 1958). As businesses increase monitoring of employees and customers and governments expand surveillance of citizens, the predictable outcome will be greater distrust, prompting a spiral of yet more surveillance and other measures of social control.

The Environmental Degradation Trap

Technologies since the dawn of the Industrial Revolution have spawned all of the environmental problems of our time: pollution of the air, water, and soil, global warming, depletion of the ozone layer, deforestation, species extinction, and human overpopulation. Coupled with the ideologies and practice of capitalism and unlimited growth, continuing dependence on unsustainable technologies is fouling the planetary nest and risking unprecedented global catastrophe.

At the level of individual behavior, the convenience offered by many technologies often obscures inefficiencies and other environmental harms. Technologies that use remote control devices, such as televisions, stereos, and garage door openers, are always "on" so that they may be ready to receive commands, yet these technologies give no indication that they are consuming electricity. As a result, they waste as much as 10% of all electricity consumed (European Commission, 2005). To generate that extra electricity, enormous amounts of greenhouse gases and nuclear waste must be produced.

Attempts to mitigate obvious technology-induced environmental problems typically use more technology. One such "technofix" is waste recycling programs, which consume more energy and generate more pollution than if the recycled materials were simply discarded in landfills (Crabb, 1992). Rather than addressing the primary problem of overproduction and overconsumption of nonessential products (e.g., billions of plastic bottles of Coca-Cola), recycling serves as a pseudopalliative that institutionalizes polluting practices and entraps society in an unsustainable way of life.

Awareness of the adverse impacts of technological activities on the environment is itself subject to entrapment. Many children spend their young lives isolated indoors with the technologies of child-rearing: television, video games, and the Internet (Louv, 2005). Those technologies offer contrived experiences that divert attention away from the natural world. As "screen time" replaces "green time," children will fail to develop an understanding and appreciation of the natural en-

vironment. As adults, they will probably not care about the harmful impact of their technological activities on the quality of their own lives and the lives of future generations.

WHO IS RESPONSIBLE?

The five technology traps we have described by no means exhaust the myriad troubles humans can get into with technology. Our point has been to suggest that the use of many technologies can result in more or less intractable harms to individual psychological functioning, to society, and to the planet. We suggest that these harms are predictable and avoidable, and therefore that they constitute violations of ethical conduct. But who is responsible for this unethical behavior?

End-users obviously share a portion of responsibility for the harms caused by their technological activities insofar as those activities are voluntary. However, there are two respects in which everyday technological activities of users are *not* wholly voluntary.

First, technologies themselves can *compel* people to use them. By virtue of their design and function, technologies exert control over users' motivational processes. One can conceive of cell phones, for example, as reinforcement machines that periodically make users feel good when they receive calls or text messages. Those good feelings ensure the phone will be used again and again, often to compulsive extremes. In this way, much of the technological activity seen today is largely involuntary and parasitically feeds on basic human psychological mechanisms. It would be less accurate to claim that end-users freely choose to do what they do with their various gadgets, and more accurate to acknowledge the coercive structuration of users' behavior by the technological milieu.

Second, modern technological devices are not natural features of the landscape in which the human species evolved, but rather are human-made objects that are "arbitrary" to the natural world (Ellul, 1954/1964). Decisions to design, manufacture, and market technological devices are made in executive suites of corporations and implemented by engineers and product designers. The very appearance of technologies in the home, at work, and in public spaces is not under the control of end-users. In many instances end-users have no choice but to use the technologies that are imposed on them. In a very real sense, industry not only manufactures the technologies that people use, but also the social norms that govern people's lives.

For these reasons, we conclude that end-users bear only a small portion of responsibility for the harms produced by their own technological activities. End-users may be considered responsible when they know that they can choose not to use harmful technologies but they intentionally use them anyway, for example, when driving a motor vehicle "just for fun." This leaves two other possible sources of responsibility for technology traps: businesses and government.

Businesses not only design, manufacture, and market technologies; they profit from them. The first responsibility of businesses is to produce an acceptable return on owners' investments. However, if the pursuit of profits results in harm to customers, society, or the environment, then businesses should be held accountable for violating their ethical responsibilities to "do no harm" (Carroll, 1991). Of course, businesses would have to be aware that their technological products cause harm, which they may not be unless customer complaints or lawsuits reach a threshold that threatens profitability. Ideally, producers of technologies should perform "safety research" that would detect potential harms before technologies are released to the marketplace. If a technology is found to have harmful effects, businesses would be obliged to redesign the product or abandon it altogether. In the absence of such checks, businesses that produce harmful technologies fail to live up to their ethical responsibilities to society.

Because it is unlikely that technology producers will voluntarily perform costly safety research (Bakan, 2004), government should take a leading role in encouraging product testing for potentially harmful effects. This is especially important in light of the complex and enduring nature of technology traps. Platt (1973) advocated just such a super-ordinate authority to alleviate social traps. Gate-keeping government agencies should either mandate safety research by technology producers or conduct such research itself (Hogan, 1983). In the U.S., Congress's Office of Technology Assessment (OTA) played this role (Saxe & Dougherty, 1985) for 23 years before funding for the OTA was discontinued by a Republican-controlled Congress in 1995 (Office of Technology Assessment, 1996). It seems clear that government leadership on assessing potential harms of technologies would serve as an appropriate corrective to the ethical blindness that can afflict businesses as they pursue profitability.

CONCLUSION

In this paper we have described the phenomenon of technology traps. The burden of ethical responsibility for these technology traps generally rests with businesses that produce harmful technologies, and also with government when it fails to assess and regulate such technologies. Whether businesses and government will accept responsibility for technological harm remains to be seen. History shows that societies are not incapable of making poor choices about how to manage their way of life (Diamond, 2005).

REFERENCES

Aranti, L. (2007, February 26). Teens can multi-task, but what are costs? *Washington Post*, p. A1.

Bakan, J. (2004). *The Corporation*. New York: Free Press.

Baldacci, A. (2006, July 12). Lost connection: Is technology isolating us? *Chicago Sun-Times*.

Bandura, S. (1995). *Self-Efficacy in Changing Societies*. New York: Cambridge University Press.

Berkowitz, L. (1964). *Aggression*. Philadelphia, PA: Temple University Press.

Blauner, R. (1964). *Alienation and Freedom*. Chicago: University of Chicago Press.

Brunsman, B. J. (2006, July 13). Ugly or not, cell phone tower likely coming to Pierce Park. *Cincinnati Inquirer*.

Carroll, A. B. (1991, July-August). The pyramid of corporate social responsibility: Toward the moral management of organizational stakeholders. *Business Horizons, 34*, 39–48. doi:10.1016/0007-6813(91)90005-G

Carver, C. S., & Scheier, M. F. (1981). *Attention and Self-Regulation*. New York: Springer Verlag.

Case, D. O. (2000). Stalking, monitoring and profiling: A typography and case studies of harmful uses of Caller ID. *New Media & Society, 2*, 67–84. doi:10.1177/14614440022225715

Chadwick-Jones, J. K. (1969). *Automation and Behavior: A Social Psychological Study*. London: Wiley.

Chaker, A. M. (2004, January 24). Schools move to stop spread of 'cyberbullying'. *Pittsburgh Post-Gazette*.

Cloud, D. S. (2005, June 22). The struggle for Iraq: Insurgents. *New York Times*, pp. A1, A10.

Crabb, P. B. (1992). Effective control of energy-depleting behavior. *The American Psychologist, 47*, 815–816. doi:10.1037/0003-066X.47.6.815

Crabb, P. B. (1996a). Answering machines take the 'answering' out of telephone interactions. *Journal of Social Behavior and Personality, 11*, 387–397.

Crabb, P. B. (1996b). Video camcorders and civil inattention. *Journal of Social Behavior and Personality, 11*, 805–816.

Crabb, P. B. (2000). The material culture of homicidal fantasies. *Aggressive Behavior, 26*, 225–234. doi:10.1002/(SICI)1098-2337(2000)26:3<225::AID-AB2>3.0.CO;2-R

Crabb, P. B. (2003). Technology and self-regulation: The case of alarm clock use. *Social Behavior and Personality, 31*, 343–348. doi:10.2224/sbp.2003.31.4.343

Crabb, P. B. (2005). The material culture of suicidal fantasies. *The Journal of Psychology, 139*, 211–220. doi:10.3200/JRLP.139.3.211-220

Diamond, J. (2005). *Collapse: How Societies Choose to Fail or Succeed*. New York: Penguin.

Duggan, M. (2001). More guns, more crime. *The Journal of Political Economy, 109*, 1086–1114. doi:10.1086/322833

Dzindolet, M. T., Pierce, L. G., Beck, H. P., & Dawe, L. A. (2002). The perceived utility of human and automated aids in a visual detection task. *Human Factors, 44*, 79–94. doi:10.1518/0018720024494856

Ellul, J. (1954, 1964). *The Technological Society*. New York: Vintage Books.

European Commission. (2005). *EU Stand-By Initiative*. European Union.

Ferguson, D. A. (1994). Measurement of mundane TV behaviors: Remote control device flipping frequency. *Journal of Broadcasting & Electronic Media, 38*, 35–47.

Florentine, M., Hunter, W., Robinson, M., Ballou, M., & Buus, S. (1998). On the behavioural characteristics of loud-music listening. *Ear and Hearing, 19,* 420–428. doi:10.1097/00003446-199812000-00003

Fromm, E. (1955). *The Sane Society.* New York: Holt, Rinehart and Winston.

Furnell, S. (2002). *Cybercrime.* Boston: Addison-Wesley.

Glaser, J., Dixit, J., & Green, D. P. (2002). Studying hate crimes with the Internet: What makes racists advocate racial violence? *The Journal of Social Issues, 58,* 75–90. doi:10.1111/1540-4560.00255

Gostomski, C. (2005, November 13). Ironing out the kinks. *Morning Call,* p. A32.

Gross, J. (1999, November 5). A long-distance tether home. *New York Times,* pp. B1, B10.

Harmon, A. (2004, August 26). Internet gives teenage bullies weapons to wound from afar. *New York Times,* p. A1.

Hogan, T. P. (1983). Psychology and the technological revolution. *Canadian Psychology, 24,* 235–241. doi:10.1037/h0080747

James, L., & Nahl, D. (2000). *Road Rage and Aggressive Driving.* Amherst, NY: Prometheus.

Kiesler, S., Siegel, J., & McGuire, T. W. (1984). Social psychological aspects of computer mediated communication. *The American Psychologist, 39,* 1123–1134. doi:10.1037/0003-066X.39.10.1123

Kipnis, D. (1984). Technology, power, and control. *Research in the Sociology of Organizations, 3,* 125–156.

Kipnis, D. (1991). The technological perspective. *Psychological Science, 2,* 62–69. doi:10.1111/j.1467-9280.1991.tb00101.x

LaFrance, M. (1996). Why we trust computers too much. *Technology Studies, 3,* 163–178.

Leo, A. (2006, July 26). Teen killed over cell phone dispute. *Connecticut Post.*

Louv, R. (2005). *Last Child in the Woods.* Chapel Hill, NC: Algonquin.

Marx, G. T. (1994). New telecommunications technologies require new manners. *Telecommunications Policy, 18,* 538–551. doi:10.1016/0308-5961(94)90064-7

Maurstad, T. (2003, April 12). Callers seek less privacy, opt for cell phones instead of stalls. *Dallas Morning News.*

McIlwraith, R., Jacobite, R. S., Kubey, R., & Alexander, A. (1991). Television addiction: Theories and data behind the ubiquitous metaphor. *The American Behavioral Scientist, 35,* 104–121. doi:10.1177/0002764291035002003

Monk, A., Carroll, J., Parker, S., & Blythe, M. (2004). Why are mobile phones annoying? *Behaviour & Information Technology, 23,* 33–41. doi:10.1080/01449290310001638496

Muir, B. M. (1994). Trust in automation: Part I. Theoretical issues in the study of trust and human intervention in automated systems. *Ergonomics, 37,* 1905–1922. doi:10.1080/00140139408964957

Office of Technology Assessment. (1996). *OTA Archive* (On-line). Retrieved from http//www.access.gpo.gov/ota/

Perrow, C. (1984). *Normal Accidents.* New York: Basic Books.

Persson, R., Garde, A. H., Hansen, A. M., Orbaek, P., & Ohlsson, K. (2003). The influence of production systems on self-reported arousal, sleepiness, physical exertion and fatigue consequences of increasing mechanization. *Stress and Health, 19,* 163–171. doi:10.1002/smi.967

Platt, J. (1973). Social traps. *The American Psychologist, 28,* 641–651. doi:10.1037/h0035723

Reser, J. P. (1980). Automobile addiction: real or imagined? *Man-Environment Systems, 10,* 279–287.

Sarason, S. (1984). If it can be studied or developed, should it be? *The American Psychologist, 39,* 477–485. doi:10.1037/0003-066X.39.5.477

Saxe, L., & Dougherty, D. (1985). Technology assessment and Congressional use of social psychology: Making complexity understandable. *Applied Social Psychology Annual, 6,* 255–280.

Shaffer, L. S. (1981). The growth and limits of recipe knowledge. *Journal of Mind and Behavior, 2,* 71–83.

Skinner, B. F. (1986). What is wrong with daily life in the Western world? *The American Psychologist, 41,* 568–574. doi:10.1037/0003-066X.41.5.568

Skitka, L. J., Mosier, K., & Burdick, M. (2000). Accountability and automation bias. *International Journal of Human-Computer Studies, 52,* 701–717. doi:10.1006/ijhc.1999.0349

Stern, S. E. (1999). Effects of technology on attributions of performance and employee evaluation. *Journal of Applied Social Psychology, 29,* 786–794. doi:10.1111/j.1559-1816.1999.tb02024.x

Stern, S. E., Alderfer, R. R., & Cienkowski, H. A. (1998). From brain to pencil to calculator: An exploratory test of the effect of technological evolution on attitudes. *Journal of Social Behavior and Personality, 13,* 503–516.

Stern, S. E., & Handel, A. D. (2001). Sexuality and mass media: The historical context of psychology's reaction to sexuality on the Internet. *Journal of Sex Research, 38,* 283–291. doi:10.1080/00224490109552099

Stern, S. E., & Kipnis, D. (1993). Technology in everyday life and perceptions of competence. *Journal of Applied Social Psychology, 23,* 1892–1902. doi:10.1111/j.1559-1816.1993.tb01071.x

Stern, S. E., Mullennix, J. W., & Wilson, S. J. (2002). Effects of perceived disability on persuasiveness of computer-synthesized speech. *The Journal of Applied Psychology, 87,* 411–417. doi:10.1037/0021-9010.87.2.411

Strickland, L. H. (1958). Surveillance and trust. *Journal of Personality, 26,* 201–215. doi:10.1111/j.1467-6494.1958.tb01580.x

Tenner, E. (1996). *Why Things Bite Back.* New York: Knopf.

Violanti, J. M. (1998). Cellular phones and fatal traffic accidents. *Accident; Analysis and Prevention, 30,* 519–524.

Woodall, P. (2002, November 25). Cell phone towers can be deadly magnet for birds. *Sun Herald,* p. A1.

Young, K. S. (2004). Internet addiction: A new clinical phenomenon and its consequences. *The American Behavioral Scientist, 48,* 402–415. doi:10.1177/0002764204270278

Chapter 5
Ubiquitous Computing:
Any Ethical Implications?

J. A. Quilici-Gonzalez
Federal University of ABC, Brazil

G. Kobayashi
Federal University of ABC, Brazil

M. C. Broens
University of São Paulo State, Brazil

M. E. Q. Gonzalez
University of São Paulo State, Brazil

ABSTRACT

In this article, the authors investigate, from an interdisciplinary perspective, possible ethical implications of the presence of ubiquitous computing systems in human perception/action. The term ubiquitous computing is used to characterize information-processing capacity from computers that are available everywhere and all the time, integrated into everyday objects and activities. The contrast in approach to aspects of ubiquitous computing between traditional considerations of ethical issues and the Ecological Philosophy view concerning its possible consequences in the context of perception/action are the underlying themes of this paper. The focus is on an analysis of how the generalized dissemination of microprocessors in embedded systems, commanded by a ubiquitous computing system, can affect the behaviour of people considered as embodied embedded agents.

INTRODUCTION

The generalized dissemination of sensors, cameras and other technological tools, used by ubiquitous computing systems, has introduced a new aspect into human perception and action. Thus, for

example, the presence of cameras on roads and in airports immediately induces an awareness of the speed of the vehicle or the checking of illicit objects in our suitcases. Are these unusual cases of induced behaviour that could change our patterns of perception/action? This kind of question is investigated in an emergent research area known as *technoethics*.

DOI: 10.4018/978-1-4666-1773-5.ch005

Technoethics is an interdisciplinary field of investigation concerned with ethical aspects of technology. Since the 1970's, after Mario Bunge introduced the term *technoethics* in his article *Towards a Technoethics,* there have been several characterizations of this area (Bunge, 1977; Galvan, 2003; Lupiccini, 2008) focusing on ethical issues related to the possible consequences of technological development on human society and the environment. For the present article, Lupiccini's (2008) definition of *technoethics* is of special relevance:

Technoethics is defined as an interdisciplinary field concerned with all ethical aspects of technology within a society shaped by technology. It deals with human processes and practices connected to technology which are embedded within social, political, and moral spheres of life. It also examines social policies and interventions occurring in response to issues generated by technology development and use. (p. 4)

The above definition, in common with the majority of other available definitions, expresses aspects of an interdisciplinary field concerned with the analysis of problems related to rapid technological development, during which new tools have been incorporated into human social life, bringing about previously unknown social behaviour, in a society "shaped by technology".

Since it is not possible to establish a necessary parallelism between technological and moral progress, it seems crucial to investigate whether contemporary technical advancements are ethically acceptable. Would new ethical standards be needed in order to evaluate new emergent patterns of social behaviour, or are traditional ethical principles adequate to accomplish such an evaluation? In other words, could technoethics help to improve the traditional field of applied ethics? We are only just beginning to investigate possible answers to this type of question formulated in the expansive field of technoethics. A central question to be ad-

dressed in this article is: What could be the impact of the long-term existence of ubiquitous computing, of which we are not immediately aware, in our everyday life? Possible ethical implications of the presence of ubiquitous computing systems in human perception/action constitute the focus of the present analysis.

The term *ubiquitous computing* is used here to characterize information-processing capacity from computers that is available everywhere and all the time, integrated into everyday objects and activities.

The dissemination of ubiquitous computing, in which the information-processing power of computers is distributed in countless, intelligent, devices imperceptible to an inattentive observer, is growing apace: small passive tags help to detect the circulation of books and commodities in libraries or convenience stores; intelligent badges can open doors or tollgates, adjust the room temperature of offices, help in the location of people, and operate various electronic devices, amongst other things. Even though information concerning the habits of individuals can normally be accessed on personal computers via manual processes, this information, when widely available, can be used for different purposes, including those which put personal privacy at risk.

In this paper, we examine the question of how the generalized dissemination of microprocessors in embedded devices, controlled by a ubiquitous computing system, can affect the perception/action of people considered as rational and autonomous agents. Initially, we reflect on aspects of ubiquitous computing from the perspective of traditional ethics. This perspective is then contrasted with the Ecological Philosophical view, concerning possible consequences in the context of perception/action.

Ubiquitous Computing

The concept of *ubiquitous computing* was first coined by Mark Weiser (1991), when he was chief technology officer at Xerox's Palo Alto Research Center. He wrote an article, "The Computer for the 21st Century", where he envisions a future in which computers disappear from our environment and from our sight but are still present, interacting seamlessly with us, providing services and resources for our activities, although we are not aware of using them. According to Weiser (1991):

Specialized elements of hardware and software, connected by wires, radio waves and infrared radiation, will be so ubiquitous that no one will notice their presence. The most profound technologies are those that disappear. They weave themselves into the fabric of everyday life until they are indistinguishable from it. (p. 94)

He exemplifies "ubiquitous" in the case of writing or "literacy technology", where written information is present all around us, from newspapers to candy wrappers; we can use it without active attention, but it is difficult to imagine modern life without it. Literacy technology empowers us: we can walk around a city without becoming lost because we can read street names and city maps, we can find places, we can choose products and we can use them, there is an "interaction" between us and the written information.

Characterized in this way, ubiquity not only means availability of written material but also requires our ability in reading and using the information and, equally important, the interpretation of the context of environment (place and time). If you can only read in English and you visit a Chinese city, for example, the ubiquity is lost in that environment because you cannot read Chinese characters. Some graphic symbols are universal and can retain ubiquity capabilities in different places, but usually they are very limited.

Writing is a technology that has developed over centuries of evolution and perfection, and its simplicity and precision are difficult to match. Although there are sayings such as "A picture is worth a thousand words", could anyone imagine a picture representing, precisely, "I will wait for you in front of the main train station at 6 o'clock tomorrow"? Context is very important for ubiquity, as some information and its importance depends on place and time or surrounding conditions. There is no sense in placing a street's nameplate inside a room, for example, even if the house is located on that street.

More than 17 years after the publication of Mark Weiser's article, computing is far from being ubiquitous in a sense of ease of use. As he stresses, the need for active focus and attention in using present-day computers reveals the contrast between the "ubiquitous paradigm" and the "desktop paradigm" that is still around us. However, computers are becoming closer to us: palmtops, smartphones and iPhones are all items we now carry with us. Although becoming easier to use, they are restricted to more educated or tech-savvy people. Cheaper microprocessors are embedded in home appliances to make them more functional and efficient, but more options means that these appliances need more information from their users, often making them more difficult to use than previous versions without processors. Videocassette recorder (VCR) timer programming for recording is an emblematic case of a function seldom employed due to difficulty of use. Regardless of these examples, we can see computing becoming slowly but surely ubiquitous.

The spread of ubiquitous computing in everyday life starts to raise privacy and security concerns amongst its users and society in general. Thus, for example, the apparently innocent use of identification tags, as shown in Figure 1, may afford control that is not perceived by customers. When fully deployed, ubiquitous computing means that we will be surrounded and interrogated by intelligent devices that will gather all available information from us, and from our environment.

Sensing and collecting information is a core function of ubiquitous computers, as they need information to communicate with us, prepare services based on our past preferences, adapt

Figure 1. Electronic identification system

RFID - Radio Frequency Identification

Electronic Identification System through digital information exchange by radio frequency. The RFID has three components:

Transponder (known as RF TAG)
Antenna
Transceptor (Reader / Writer)

services from changing conditions, and so on. All these personal data will not necessarily be ours or will be controlled by us, but will necessarily be distributed to certain external agents or service providers if you want a good and seamless service. Although this may be fearsome and painful to some people, others don't mind, and some even like it if in exchange they receive better and more personalized services. Figure 2 provides a schematic view of the main components of ubiquitous systems.

Recent popularization of the Internet, due to cheap personal computers and availability of affordable broadband digital communications, has made it easier than ever for an individual to connect and distribute personal writings, audios and videos worldwide. This phenomenon is the opposite of privacy, because the objective is to expose oneself to the widest possible audience. So, the same ubiquitous computing technology that raises privacy concerns can be used for the opposite purpose. In this sense, it would seem, at first glance, that ubiquitous computing is a neutral technological tool. However, a careful examination of the possible consequences of integrating this technology into our everyday life may reveal transformations in our social interactions and our corresponding moral conduct and ethics.

Figure 2. Elements of ubiquitous systems

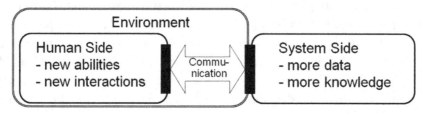

In what follows, possible ethical consequences of deploying ubiquitous computing in everyday life are going to be considered from distinct paradigms.

ETHICAL CONSEQUENCES OF UBIQUITOUS COMPUTING

Nowadays, in the so-called *technological societies*, there is a tendency to make reality a spectacle of itself, stimulating exhibitionist behaviour of social or private agents. To exit anonymity, by means of public exposure of CVs and personal profiles on social websites, for example, can be associated with a successful career and steps in the direction of personal and professional recognition. Also, the ease of access and abundance of images registered by ubiquitous cameras can supply rich material for the study of social customs, or for the sentimental recording of happy moments experienced by anonymous personalities.

In this context, in what way can the impact of ubiquitous computing on peoples' behaviour be evaluated? Several answers could be given to this question, depending on the perspectives adopted.

According to the supporters of deontological ethics (Kant, 1783), duty, and not the consequence of an act, must govern the choices and decisions of a person. For example, an observer, who saw a person running away, when interrogated by a bandit running in the direction taken by his victim, should not avoid the duty of always telling the truth. From this perspective, ubiquitous computing could be seen as an external tool able to help with the preservation of the common good.

Utilitarian ethics (Bentham, 1907), on the other hand, asserts that "any action…must be approved or rejected as a function of its tendency to augment or diminish the happiness of the party whose interest is in question". Thus, from a utilitarian perspective, the consequences of usages of ubiquitous computing should be investigated according to the following question: Would it augment or diminish the contentment of people involved with it? If the second alternative applies, then its use should be strictly regulated, and so on.

In the same vein, Pascal (1963) argues that actions should be performed in order to increase collective benefit: cooperative habits created by societies should attend fundamental needs, avoiding the worst of social consequences, such as civil war.

Customary Ethics

In several fragments of his *Pensées* (Pascal, 1963, pp. 575-576), Blaise Pascal (1623-1662) stresses a distinction between principles that govern the development of geometric and mechanistic knowledge and those regulating human conduct. The first are abstract self-evident principles, not too numerous, that when methodically applied help to obtain certainties. In contrast, principles regulating conduct are easily perceived by means of our senses, are almost infinitely numerous and do not always follow rules of inference. *Principles of geometry and arithmetic allow the construction of mechanical tools that may facilitate human life, helping with the improvement of common happiness*. One example of this possibility is the famous *calculating machine*, built by Pascal in 1650, that constituted the first mechanistic model capable of manipulating the four arithmetical operations.

In contrast, principles concerning social organization cannot be expressed with the same efficacy in the domain of human conduct; they cannot always guarantee the facilitation of human social life. Many times, they can neither help with collective happiness nor prevent what he considered the greatest of all evils – the civil war. In his *Pensées*, Pascal (1963) stresses that:

The licentious tell men of orderly lives that they stray from nature's path, while they themselves follow it; as people in a ship think those who move are on the shore. On all sides the language is similar. We must have a fixed point in order to judge. The harbour decides for those who are in a ship; but where shall we find a harbour in morality? (p. 547)

It is undeniable, on one hand, that human society is governed by certain rules that allow the regulation of action. On the other hand, given that many actions cannot be regulated by universal rules, and given also the impossibility of establishing rational procedures necessary for harmonious collective conduct, rules of collective action should emerge from *customs*.

According to Pascal (1963), customs and habits cannot be dissociated. Habits result from the embodiment of ways of acting (fragment 252) – shaping body movements and dispositions – and direct conduct. When a habit is considered socially successful, it can shape a collective pattern of action that, in turn, gives rise to a *custom*. This will be reproduced until it can be substituted by another custom considered more appropriate to the social dynamics in question. Thus, customs result from embodied habits; new habits are created when social dynamics require them.

Hence, we can now go on to investigate whether ubiquitous computation might interfere in this process of constitution of customs from shared habits, and if so, how.

Since the emergence of the first human communities, the habitual behaviour of agents in everyday situations in public spaces is generally observed in a casual and inattentive way. The explicit observation of conduct is only common in specific circumstances, such as public events and learning situations. Furthermore, in many cultures ostentatious observation of strange behaviour in common situations is interpreted as offensive or threatening. Considering, as we have seen, that customary behaviour arises from shared cultural habits incorporated by agents, the question arises: How are agents going to constitute new collective patterns of conduct while they are the targets of vigilant observation?

This question is especially relevant on an ethical level due to the dynamics of that which we consider to be socially desirable/undesirable or moral/immoral over the course of time. Conduct at first considered a threat to public order sometimes reveals valuable sources of rejuvenation of that order, without which society would collapse. Some socially acceptable habits are later shown to be damaging and unhealthy. Values taken to be universal are often re-evaluated when unforeseen circumstances arise.

In short, the plasticity of the social dynamic seems to result from a complex interplay of adjustments between habits of agents that, in some way, breaks expectations and violates accepted standards of conduct and those habits which place value on established wisdom. It is possible that the generalized implementation of ubiquitous computing could interfere in the process of adjustment and renewal of collective habits, due to the establishment of surveillance and control practices.

Furthermore, we can recall the characterization of principles of conduct suggested by Pascal (1963): Principles regulating conduct are easily perceived by means of our senses, they are almost infinitely numerous and do not always follow rules of inference. One of the main principles is that successful social practices are shared by *imitation*. Imitation is achieved through learning – a progressive adjustment of conduct by trial and error – and by a tacit confidence in the agent whose conduct is being imitated. Ubiquitous computing could profoundly alter observation practices linked to learning and to the establishment of the necessary trust between agents that allows imitation. If this occurs, customs established because of mutual trust could disappear.

As we shall see later, in connection with the role of the relation perception/action, Ecological Philosophy can help us to investigate possible implications of ubiquitous computing on agents.

Normative Utilitarian Ethics

According to Bentham's (1907) moral philosophy, the validity of an action should be measured by the result it produces in the lives of people affected by it. Hence, one can say that its ethics are utilitarian, or consequentialist, or teleological. "... Ethics at large may be defined, the art of directing men's actions to the production of the greatest possible quantity of happiness, on the part of those whose interest is in view," (Bentham, 1907). According to Bentham, the dissemination of ubiquitous computing could be evaluated by the impact caused on peoples' behaviour, ruled by a principle of utility:

By the principle of utility is meant that principle which approves or disapproves of every action whatsoever, according to the tendency which it appears to have to augment or diminish the happiness of the party whose interest is in question: or, what is the same thing in other words, to promote or to oppose that happiness (Bentham, 1907).

In any case, although ubiquitous computing may be invisible to the common citizen, by, for example, using a radio frequency identification device (RFID), he/she must be aware of its presence and his/her behaviour may therefore show some influence of the reduction in privacy.

Those who contravene the law may need to take extra care not to be identified. The common citizen may stop engaging in minor antisocial acts because the anonymity, which previously assured impunity, is no longer possible. It is highly likely that information on the common citizen will become available to unauthorized businesses or persons. Ubiquitous computing may simultaneously generate new risks and benefits. Nevertheless, as with other technologies, ubiquitous computing may receive the tacit approval of the silent majority, because the immediate benefits offset the possibility of damaging effects occurring in the long term.

Perhaps one of the possible objections to this line of reasoning relates to the nature of the technology involved: the technology is perceived as neutral, and it is left to its usage to determine whether the outcome is good or bad! Concerning utilitarianism, Rawls (2005) criticizes classical utilitarianism – understood as the philosophy that tries to maximize the total amount of happiness in society – as much as its modern version – which tries to optimize the average level of happiness in society. He asserts that the principles of social justice that steer human actions might be elaborated by persons who are theoretically well-informed about society's dilemmas, but ignorant of their own positions in society and of the actual issues involved. In such a situation, according to Rawls, people don't seek to maximize the total quantity of happiness, but instead to maximize the well-being of the least favored sectors of society.

Normative Deontological Ethics

Kant (1785) supported the notion that every ethical dilemma should be decided according to universally applicable principles or by "explicit imperatives" of the type "I am never to act otherwise than so that I could also will that my maxim should become a universal law" (Kant, 1785), regardless of the consequences arising from such decision. This means, for example, that nobody should lie or steal, because a universally applicable law could not result from such actions. A justification for this stance is the respect with which all persons should be treated, since for Kant human relations cannot be alienating or, similarly, people should not be treated as things. What attributes moral value to an action is not the result obtained, but the motivating cause of that action. Therefore, another of his maxims states:

... Man and generally any rational being exists as an end in himself, not merely as a means to be arbitrarily used by this or that will, but in all his

actions, whether they concern himself or other rational beings, must be always regarded at the same time as an end (Kant, 1785).

Considering that the laws that govern a community were created by its members, it would be contradictory to use a rational being as the means to a greater end, since there is no greater end than the rational being itself.

Apparently, a small proportion of people base their behaviour on deontological ethics. But for these persons a possible loss of privacy or increased self-indulgence does not influence their life decisions, because these decisions would be the same in adverse situations. The probability that ubiquitous computing will permit the tracking of people and the control of their actions might perhaps force them to respect the law. However, for Kant, an action only possesses moral value when we fulfill our duties without the need for coercion. On the other hand, however, it should be remembered that in certain cases the loss of privacy could result in a threat to personal or collective security. Perhaps those who support deontological ethics might be forced to modify some of their customs, not because they consider them morally unacceptable, but because public exposure might cause damage to their material wealth or their anonymity.

Applied Ethics

Another line of reasoning is inspired by Foucault (1995), who suggests that power may be diffused in various forms (even though many of them may be controlled by the State) and that descriptions of power are not expressed purely in negative terms. Foucault refers to one of Bentham´s works to describe how a prisoner of Panopticon sees the control tower but never knows who is observing him and from where, creating a situation in which an invisible control power is exercised over him. The Panopticon is a structure whose design allows a vigilant observer to see the prisoners or residents without being seen himself, constituting: "A new mode of obtaining power of mind over mind, in a quantity hitherto without example" (Bentham, 1995). As described by Foucault (1995):

Bentham's Panopticon is the architectural figure of this composition. We know the principle on which it was based: at the periphery, an annular building; at the centre, a tower; this tower is pierced with wide windows that open onto the inner side of the ring; the peripheric building is divided into cells, each of which extends the whole width of the building; they have two windows, one on the inside, corresponding to the windows of the tower; the other, on the outside, allows the light to cross the cell from one end to the other. All that is needed, then, is to place a supervisor in a central tower and to shut up in each cell a madman, a patient, a condemned man, a worker or a schoolboy. By the effect of backlighting, one can observe from the tower, standing out precisely against the light, the small captive shadows in the cells of the periphery. They are like so many cages, so many small theatres, in which each actor is alone, perfectly individualized and constantly visible. The panoptic mechanism arranges spatial unities that make it possible to see constantly and to recognize immediately. In short, it reverses the principle of the dungeon; or rather of its three functions - to enclose, to deprive of light and to hide - it preserves only the first and eliminates the other two. Full lighting and the eye of a supervisor capture better than darkness, which ultimately protected. Visibility is a trap. (pp. 199-200)

Although Foucault´s discourse on the Panopticon affirms that "it is in fact a figure of political technology that may and must be detached from any specific use" (Foucault, 1995, p. 205), a possible analogy with the effects of ubiquitous computation is immediately obvious, in that the dissemination of RFID, sensors, cameras, transponders, etc. helps to create the conditions for this kind of system. However, this system does not exert its control based only on its repressive capability. The system shows positivity in its ability to discipline in order to become more productive. In this sense, "panopticism is the general principle of a new 'political anatomy' whose object and end are not the relations of sovereignty but the relations of discipline" (Foucault, 1995, p. 208). And in discovering and exploring the potentialities of its subjects, in optimizing its productive capacity using scientific methods, science is no longer seen as neutral, because it is an operational part of the system or, in the best case, because much of what is presented as a universal scientific truth is, in reality, an expression of contingent historical forces.

From Foucault's detailed studies of laws and disciplinary institutions, it can be concluded that mechanisms of control and conditioning already existed long before the advent of ubiquitous computing. Although, according to this line of reasoning, science apparently does not play a neutral role, ubiquitous computing in particular does not alter Foucault's rationale, and the principle that care for others is a prerequisite for ethical conduct.

Normative Ethics of Virtues

Does technology drive history? To what extent? Without us noticing, or in a consensual way? In any case, one of the points that interest us here is the possible threat to privacy, which in turn depends on what we understand by liberty and wellbeing. The notion of liberty might be based on an absence of undesirable restrictions, but might also be based on the concept of autonomy, in which people voluntarily (in other words, with reasonable knowledge of the circumstances) accept certain restrictions in exchange for a common wellbeing. In other words, human beings might feel themselves to be more free acting in accordance with consensually approved moral or governmental norms, with the exercise of their

intellectual and moral virtues. Thus, for example, during a debate the consensual establishment of a norm discouraging anyone from monopolizing the discussion could transmit a greater sensation of freedom to those involved. In the same way, stricter road safety rules or the use of cameras at dangerous junctions could encourage careless drivers to become more responsible, creating a sensation of less danger and greater wellbeing in the community. In other words, in a democratic society ubiquitous computing could contribute to democratically established autonomy.

It is a fact that ubiquitous computing is spreading rapidly and inexorably. The way each society will react depends on the way in which its institutions are organized, and the nature of the State (democratic or totalitarian) or, equivalently, the degree of development of its social capital (Putnam, 1993). Democratic societies should stimulate the positive aspects and put in place safeguards against any detrimental outcomes. How? The positive side is that which improves peoples' quality of life (for example, those with heart pacemakers would be warned when they enter areas of high magnetic fields; nobody would waste time looking for a place to park at the airport or the shopping centre; personal identification would be simplified; elderly people with memory problems would not get lost in the street; nobody would cross a red traffic light without receiving an audible warning signal; criminal acts would be more easily solved or prevented, given a register of those present at the scene of the crime, etc.). The negative side is essentially the threat to personal privacy. How can a democratic society protect itself from this danger? Encoding all collected information, in such a way that its secrecy is safeguarded and access to it is only allowed for a competent authority (as occurs with access to bank accounts in democratic societies) may be one way. In societies that are undemocratic, totalitarian, or dictatorial, ubiquitous computing gives even greater power to their repressive policing institutions, making them still more efficient and oppressive.

Ubiquitous Computing: An Approach from the Ecological Philosophy Perspective

To conclude this paper, an alternative approach to the problem of adequacy of utensils to human action is proposed based upon Ecological Philosophy (Gibson, 1986; Large, 2003). In contrast to Philosophy of Ecology, which would focus on virtues or utilitarian consequences of ubiquitous computing, Ecological Philosophy's center of attention is the intrinsic *natural* relation between organism and environment in the context of perception/action. From this perspective, the impact of ubiquitous computing is evaluated not in terms of its merits, but mainly in accordance with the dynamics of *affordances* available to organisms.

Affordances, as defined by Gibson (1986) constitute meaningful information specifying unambiguous (non-mediated) opportunities for action. This characterization of affordances as information *directly* perceived by organisms, without any (representational) mediation, constitutes an apparent focus of interest for contemporary computation and robotics, as can be noticed, for example, in Murphy's (2000) words:

What makes Gibson so interesting to roboticists is that an affordance is directly perceivable. Direct perception means that the sensing process doesn't require memory, inference, or interpretation. This means minimal computation, which usually translates to very rapid execution times (near instantaneous) on a computer or robot. (p. 86)

Even though Murphy's focus in the concept of *affordance* may be troublesome, given Gibson's effort to distinguish his Ecological Psychology from Physics on the basis of a systemic non-mechanistic perspective, the above quotation is relevant to the present analysis of ubiquitous computing. The main issue here is that *affordances* are directly perceivable, and as Murphy stresses, direct percep-

tion doesn't require interpretation. In Murphy's terms this means 'minimal computation'.

As indicated previously, 'minimal computation', understood in a sense of 'ease of use', is fundamental to the paradigm of ubiquitous computing. Although contemporary computing is far from being ubiquitous in this sense, it is exploring and already altering – directly our indirectly – the domain of *affordances* available for humans. A problem with this exploration is that it seems to be growing in a non-systemic perspective. However, as Gibson has shown, *affordances* should be properly understood from a systemic perspective that conceives (potential) organisms in straight *unified* relation with the environment. The presupposition of a systemic order, constitutive of the informational tissue of *affordances*, is grounded in Gibson's theory of perception-action, according to which organisms and environment develop mutually in such a unified way that one supports the other reciprocally.

Gibson's principle of *mutuality*, according to which organisms and environment co-evolve, characterizes a systemic view: Each animal (including, of course, humans) has its own system of locomotion that constrains its relationships with other animals, plants and inorganic things, dynamically shaping its own surroundings. Even though locomotion is common to all animals, it varies amongst them in many ways, populating the environment with a rich diversity of *affordances* (Gibson, 1986). It is from this systemic way of understanding the organism/environment interaction that explorations of ubiquitous computing may constitute a source of apprehension. In this context, ethical questions concerning possible consequences of ubiquitous computing may be reformulated as: What are the consequences of the dissemination of generalized sensors, cameras, amongst other technological tools, in human perception and action? In what way, in the long run, might they alter basic human habits developed from a straightforward systemic relation with the environment?

To illustrate the topic under discussion here, imagine a group of wild dogs that suddenly have to interact with human vehicles. In order to survive in this condition, they are forced to adjust their natural perception of depth and locomotion. Also, as natural hunters, wild dogs have to grasp new (negative) *affordances* related to the speed of cars, motorbikes and various other types of vehicles. As these *affordances* do not exist in isolation, but constitute complex systems that constrain relationships with other animals, plants and so on, changes in some of them may produce great transformations in the dynamics of habit formation, re-shaping their perception/action.

In the human context, applying Gibson's principle of mutuality, environment and agents have to be conceived as complementary in perception/action. The existence, for example, of a ladder with steps that are proportional to the length of the legs of a person *affords* a natural way for somebody to go upstairs. The presence of a window in a room *affords* the possibilities of fresh air, privacy and personal safety, among others. The possibility of action inherent in objects perceived by humans and other animals, as described by Gibson's notion of *affordance,* is sufficiently clear when applied to objects that can be visually perceived. But how could *affordances* of the virtual environment be characterized? How can we address the case of ubiquitous computing, in which the functionality of electronic devices is invisible to an inattentive agent? The term *technological affordance* shall be applied here to characterize the potential availability of sensors, cameras and other technological tools including virtual (not immediately accessible) realities in which human perception has to be adjusted in order to allow actions to spontaneously occur. This notion requires improvement, but it seems adequate to distinguish, for example, the *affordance* of a chair to a tired person from the *technological affordance* of a hidden camera that would allow him/her to identify someone walking outside the house.

There are several studies in robotics (Murphy, 2000; Rome et al., 2008) that expand the original formulation of the concept of affordance in order to model the system robot/environment. In this system, robot and environment are not described as distinct entities, but as complementary: Robots' actions are oriented towards the insinuating functionality of self-organizing objects that are part of their perceptual layout. In the case of humans, an analogous scenario can be considered in which the social environment acquires a certain dynamics with the inclusion of ubiquitous computing and virtual space. In this new scenario, humans would re-orientate their perceptual universe as a function of *technological affordances* created by dynamic self-organizing electronic artifacts, especially the invisible devices of ubiquitous computing.

The question to be considered here is: What could be the possible consequences of this re-orientation? In other words: Could the generalized use of microprocessors, cameras and intelligent sensors widespread in our environment drastically change the *affordances* available to our everyday routine? If so, what are the implications for the dynamics of our perception/action? These questions open up a new debate, which has not been addressed by traditional considerations of ethical issues in ubiquitous computing. One of the contributions of this paper is to nourish this debate from an Ecological Philosophical perspective. In the classic, top-down, normative ethic scheme the consequences of the adoption of ubiquitous computing may create ethical dilemmas with predominantly epistemological implications and consequent need of reformulation of some of its tenets. In contrast, in the more bottom-up descriptive patterns of perception/action behind Ecological Philosophy, predominantly ontological implications are at issue, underlying survival dilemmas.

FINAL COMMENTS

We suggest that, on the negative side, ubiquitous computing could impose a supposedly preventative form of social surveillance, of the kind 'mind over mind' proposed by Bentham. The principle underlying such surveillance is that people act differently when they know that they are being watched, and this condition tends to inhibit behaviour that might be considered undesirable. Hence new *affordances* directly related to mistrust would be developed, which would alter spontaneous habits of actions based on mutual confidence.

Of course, as pointed out, context is very important for ubiquity, as some information and its relevance depends on place and time or surrounding conditions. By changing long-term *affordances* that have existed on the basis of trust in a systemic way, ubiquitous computing could alter the context in which humans identify and recognize themselves as partners and members of a community. As Rennie (2008) suggests in his editorial of the special issue of Scientific American dedicated to the debate on *The future of privacy*:

What should concern us most is not whether the changing state of privacy is making us more or less safe or happy. It is whether, as Bentham predicted, it subjects us to a new 'power of mind over mind'. Does uncertainty about whether someone is observing us, exploiting our secrets or even stealing our identity cause us to preemptively sacrifice our freedom to be and act as we would wish? When privacy disappears, do we first respond by hiding from ourselves? (p. 4)

In the same way that large glass structures disorientate birds, or that high-speed vehicles may become dangerous artifacts to dogs because of their notion of depth, it interests us here to inquire into the consequences of innovations brought about by ubiquitous computing and virtual reality. Could these innovations reduce our autonomy, or could they help us to perform difficult cognitive activities or even exhaustive physical tasks? In both cases, the possible ethical implications concerning the increase or diminishment of autonomy seem to be at the heart of the issue.

The above debate is only an open gate designed to initiate a line of reflection whose ultimate direction remains uncertain. Its clearer definition will to a large extent depend on the feedback which society itself will provide.

ACKNOWLEDGMENT

We would like to thank the Federal University of ABC, UNESP – University of Sao Paulo State and CNPq for supporting this research, and Dr. Andrew George Allen for English revision of the paper.

REFERENCES

Bentham, J. (1907). *An introduction to the principles of morals and legislation*. Chicago: Library of Economics and Liberty. Retrieved November 3, 2009, from http://www.econlib.org/library/Bentham/bnthPML18.htm

Bentham, J. (1995). *The panopticon writings*. London: Verso. Retrieved October 16, 2009, from http://cartome.org/panopticon.htm

Bunge, M. (1977). Towards a technoethics. *The Monist, 60*(1), 96–107.

Foucault, M. (1995). *Discipline and punish: the birth of the prison*. New York: Vintage Books.

Galván, J. M. (2003). On technoethics. *IEEE Robotics & Automation Magazine, 10*(4), 58–63.

Gibson, J. J. (1986). *The ecological approach to visual perception*. Boston: Houghton-Miffin.

Kant, E. (1785). *Fundamental principles of the metaphysic of morals*. (T. K. Abbott, Trans.). Retrieved October 13, 2009, from http://www.gutenberg.org/dirs/etext04/ikfpm10.txt

Large, D. (2003). *The ecological philosophy*. Newcastle upon Tyne, UK: Newcastle Philosophy Society. Retrieved June 15, 2008, from http://www.newphilsoc.org.uk/Ecological/DavidLarge.PDF

Luppicini, R. (2008). The emerging field of technoethics. In Luppicini, R., & Adell, R. (Eds.), *Handbook of Research on Technoethics* (pp. 1–18). Hershey, PA: IGI Global.

Murphy, R. R. (2000). *Introduction to AI robotics*. Cambridge, MA: MIT Press.

Pascal, B. (1963). Pensées. In B. Pascal (Ed.), *Œuvres Complètes*. Paris: Éditions du Seuil. Retrieved October 23, 2009, from http://www.ccel.org/ccel/pascal/pensees.txt

Putnam, R. D. (1993). *Making democracy work: civic traditions in modern Italy*. Princeton, NJ: Princeton University Press.

Rawls, J. (2005). *A theory of justice*. Cambridge, MA: Harvard University Press.

Rennie, J. (2008, September). Here in the fishbowl. *Scientific American.*

Rome, E., Hertzberg, J., & Dorffner, G. (Eds.). (2008). *Towards affordance-based robot control*. Heidelberg, Germany: Springer Verlag. doi:10.1007/978-3-540-77915-5

Weiser, M. (1991, September). The computer for the 21st century. *Scientific American*, 94–104. doi:10.1038/scientificamerican0991-94

This work was previously published in International Journal of Technoethics, Volume 1, Issue 3, edited by Rocci Luppicini, pp. 11-23, copyright 2010 by IGI Publishing (an imprint of IGI Global).

Section 2
Technoethics and the Digital Society

Chapter 6
Identifying the Ethics of Emerging Information and Communication Technologies:
An Essay on Issues, Concepts and Method

Bernd Carsten Stahl
De Montfort University, UK

Jeroen van den Hoven
Delft University of Technology, The Netherlands

Richard Heersmink
Delft University of Technology, The Netherlands

Kutoma J. Wakunuma
De Montfort University, UK

Philippe Goujon
Facultés Universitaires Notre-Dame de la Paix, Belgium

Veikko Ikonen
VTT (Technical Research Centre of Finland), Finland

Catherine Flick
Facultés Universitaires Notre-Dame de la Paix, Belgium

Michael Rader
Karlsruhe Institute of Technology, Germany

ABSTRACT

Ethical issues of information and communication technologies (ICTs) are important because they can have significant effects on human liberty, happiness, and people's ability to lead a good life. They are also of functional interest because they can determine whether technologies are used and whether their positive potential can unfold. For these reasons, policy makers are interested in finding out what these issues are and how they can be addressed. The best way of creating ICT policy that is sensitive to ethical issues pertain to being proactive in addressing such issues at an early stage of the technology life cycle. The present paper uses this position as a starting point and discusses how knowledge of ethical aspects of emerging ICTs can be gained. It develops a methodology that goes beyond established futures methodologies to cater for the difficult nature of ethical issues. The authors outline how the description of emerging ICTs can be used for an ethical analysis.

DOI: 10.4018/978-1-4666-1773-5.ch006

INTRODUCTION

If we knew the consequences of novel technologies, then we would be in a better position to leverage or address them. Expected and unexpected positive results could be supported and strengthened while problems could be avoided or mitigated. An important aspect of the consequences of technologies is related to moral perceptions and ethical norms. In the area of information and communication technologies (ICTs), prominent examples of such issues are those of privacy, intellectual property, security and access. But how can we know these consequences?

This question is of central importance to policy makers who wish to be proactive in addressing moral and ethical issues. Despite its importance, it is an exceptionally difficult question to answer. The combination of uncertainty of the future, conceptual issues surrounding the very term "technology", the potential infinity of issues and the problems of contextualising abstract issues combine to render ethics of emerging technologies all but intractable. And yet, giving up in the face of these problems is no viable solution either. Not exploring ethics of emerging technologies constitutes one possible choice in dealing with them. And this is arguably the worst possible choice. It is arguably the worst choice because leaving potential ethical issues of emerging technologies unattended to does not make the problems go away but may only exacerbate them when the technologies finally come to fruition. Therefore, finding ways of trying to deal with them even though they may not be conclusive helps to initiate and potentially find a solution to for some if not all ethical problems.

This leaves scholars with an interest in ethics and emerging ICTs in the position of having to come up with workable solutions to finding out what possible issues may be, knowing full well that any result they produce may be more than fallible. While there has been some attention to the problem of ethics of emerging technologies

(Sollie & Düwell, 2009), there is little in terms of practical guidance on how to identify emerging technologies and the ethical issues they raise. The present paper outlines a methodological approach that fills this gap in knowledge and allows a robust, transparent and rigorous method of identifying the ethics of emerging ICTs. It starts out by describing how the technologies themselves can be identified. This includes a discussion of the different problems such future oriented research faces. On the basis of the exploration of these issues, the paper then presents the different steps of the suggested methodology. This leads to the question of the ethics analysis of the emerging ICTs. The conclusion will reflect on the limitations of this approach and further research.

While the paper concentrates on information and communication technologies, it is of relevance to other aspects of the field of technoethics. Where technoethics is the interdisciplinary field that addresses moral and ethical concerns arising due to the social use of technologies, questions of emerging technologies and possible policy responses are relevant. In addition, the field of ICT is increasingly linked to most other socially relevant technologies such as nanotechnology or biotechnology to the point where many scholars speak of the convergence of technologies. An indication of this increasing interlinking was the recent 2009 conference of the Society for Technology and Philosophy which was dedicated to the topic of these converging technologies (see: http://www.utwente.nl/ceptes/spt2009/). Conceptual and methodological questions arising from ICTs are thus a core concern that the novel field of technoethics needs to come to grips with.

The paper presents and justifies the choices made by the consortium of the ETICA project, a European research project funded under the 7th Framework Programme. (For more details on the project see www.etica-project.eu) It explains the way in which the members of this project have come to a conclusion on these difficult problems. This does not imply that the solutions and methodological choices discussed here are the only ones possible. Despite the provenance from a particular research project, the paper addresses the general issue of methodology in ethics in technology and thereby makes an important contribution to the discourse on ethics in technology, specifically ICTs. It represents a contribution to epistemology and methodology in technoethics. It is important to note, however, that the epistemological and methodological problems discussed here are not merely theoretical but of primary importance of practice. Technology policy that wants to be informed by research needs to be able to rely on acceptable methodologies.

QUESTIONS IN THE IDENTIFICATION OF EMERGING ICTS

From an ethical perspective it is desirable to have an accurate description of the situation in which ethical issues are to be evaluated. This is true for most, if not all, ethical perspectives, including utilitarian consequentialism, Kantian deontology or Aristotelian virtue ethics but also for other approaches such as ethics of care or postmodern ethics. Much ethical debate is predicated on the assumption that all relevant aspects are known or at least could be known. In practice this is often not the case. The problem of uncertainty of ethical evaluation becomes inevitable when ethics is applied to something that is fundamentally uncertain. This is the case for future occurrences. The issue of uncertainty may be the most important reason why ethics is often weak when it is charged with evaluating future developments, including future developments in technology (Sollie, 2007). This section outlines the most important problems that research on ethics of emerging ICTs will face. These include conceptual issues, epistemological problems and the problem of ubiquity of ethical issues.

Conceptual Problems

All of the individual terms in "ethics of emerging information and communication technologies" can raise problems that need to be spelled out in order to ensure that the eventual methodology can be appropriate.

Emergence

The term "emergence" has a long history in philosophy and can be found in a number of other disciplines. Very briefly, it can be understood as a counterpoint to linear and predictable developments. Emergent phenomena are not easily predictable but develop from the interaction of components of a system.

Given this position, it is almost a contradiction in terms to do research to determine emerging technologies. They defy easy recognition by definition. There are, however, differences in certainty of knowledge about emerging issues that are related to the temporal frame in which they are investigated. We therefore concentrate on the time frame of 10 to 15 years. According to the European Commission's own view, funding for current research projects should lead to technologies on the market in approximately this time scale. Such technologies are currently being researched and developed and one can therefore say that they must be in a state of emergence that is relatively stable. This does not mean, however, that one can unambiguously describe them at present, which is partly caused by the nature of the concept of technology.

Technology

It is not the purpose of this paper to engage in the general philosophy of technology (Dusek, 2006; Olsen, Pedersen, & Hendricks, 2009). Characteristics of technology that one can typically find include a basis in structured thought, temporal stability and reproducibility, and a reflection in artefacts which may (but do not have to be) of a physical nature. Technologies are typically developed for specific ends. This raises the question of the relationship between technology and application. It is easily conceivable that a particular technological artefact can raise different ethical issues depending on their context and application of use but also on their conception and representation. This issue will be referred to again below.

An important issue related to the concept of technology is the question of interpretive flexibility. Interpretive flexibility denotes the property of technology of being constituted by use. It is a position that is opposed to technological determinism, which holds that technology has an observer-independent reality and will have clear and predetermined uses and applications. Proponents of interpretive flexibility argue that technology is not fixed but will develop during perception and use. The tenets of interpretive flexibility are widely recognised in science and technology studies where different positions such as social study of technology (SST) or the social construction of technology hold such views (Bijker, 1997; Grint & Woolgar, 1997; Howcroft, Mitev, & Wilson, 2004) and also in related fields such as Actor Network Theory (Latour, 2007; Law & Hassard, 1999). Some scholars distinguish between interpretive and interpretative flexibility with the former referring to the epistemological aspect of the social construction of technology and the latter being a stronger position that sees the construction as ontologically constitutive of technology (Cadili & Whitley, 2005).

Such questions are important for the overall theoretical background of the project because they rule out the possibility that there is one definitive answer to the question which are emerging technologies. There is a direct link between emergence and interpretive flexibility. Interpretive flexibility is a function of social interaction and pertains to particular discourses. That means that a technology may emerge in one context even though it may well be established elsewhere. It

also means that the same underlying artefact can emerge into different technologies in terms of usage and application. Interpretive flexibility is connected to the social meaning of a technology, which requires researchers to avoid the technical determinist position and to consider the political and social framing of technological meaning.

From a methodological point of view it means that a plurality of viewpoints needs to be considered and that there is no guarantee that expert views are going to be the dominant or correct ones above all since expert discourses are framed by their field of expertise. This is relevant for the present paper because in an initial step it will rely on published work on emerging technologies in order to identify and categorise these. It will thus draw on different discourses, many of which originate with authors considered "experts" in their domain but this expert status does not guarantee that the findings will be correct or complete.

ICT

This paper concentrates on information and communication technologies, mostly in order to limit the field of enquiry. There is, however, no clear and unambiguous definition of ICT. The terms "information" and "communication" are as complex as "technology". Concentrating on ICT does rule out a substantial number of potential technologies but it leaves a large number. In addition, one can observe initiatives to realise the convergence of ICT with other technologies, notably biotechnology, nanotechnology, and cognitive technologies (also called NBIC technologies).

Rather than attempting to provide a comprehensive definition, one can choose to be open to a range of views and technologies that project members or respondents perceive to be in the area of ICT. A pragmatic solution for a project that is funded by a European research programme is to define as "ICT" all those projects that are funded under the ICT calls. This does not rule out that there are technologies being funded elsewhere, including the European research Framework Programme that would fall under the definition of ICT.

Here the question is not only what ICTs are going to emerge but, more importantly, which ethical issues they raise. This requires a view of the concepts of ethics, and arguably of the closely related concept of morality.

Ethics and Morality

Moral philosophy has a long history and the range of possible meanings and theories of ethics is impressive. Again, there are diverse and long-standing discourses that the present paper needs to be aware of but that it will not bring to a conclusion. Ethics is related to questions of duty, justice, utility and many others. For Ricoeur, ethics is defined as the aim of a good life with and for the other, in just institutions (Ricoeur, 1990). Using Ricoeur's position, ethics of ICT could pertain to the question of the relationship between ICT and the good life, the impact of ICT on interpersonal relationships, or the question of the influence of ICT on justice and institutions.

Another way to address the question of how ethics and ICT may be related is to distinguish between "ethics" and "morality". One possible way of defining the terms would be to say that ethics is a philosophical discipline that deals with morality, i.e., with implicit and/or explicit rules of moral human behaviour. Such rules deal with the respect/disrespect human owe to each other (or other (living) beings). This allows the distinction of the positive and observable fact of social morality from the justification and evaluation of morality (Velasquez, 2001). To put it differently, the distinction of ethics and morality allows a clearer view of another way of dividing up moral philosophy, namely as descriptive and normative ethics, which is often complemented by adding meta-ethics. Doing research on ethics of emerging ICT application could comprise all three of these aspects. It could be descriptive and try to capture moral perceptions, it could be normative

in exploring theoretical questions and giving justifications of moral norms and values or it could engage in abstract theoretical considerations of ethical theories and addressing the condition of ethical issues determination and resolution. To some degree the ETICA project will touch on all of these issues but it is important to note that they raise fundamentally different theoretical and methodological challenges. The present paper will concentrate only on the methodology of identification and ethical evaluation of emerging ICTs.

Epistemological Problems

There is no simple methodological algorithm to follow in order to achieve the aims of a foresight project, mostly because of the epistemological problem of understanding the future. The main question that needs to be asked of any method or approach is whether it contributes to the aim of providing a plausible account of possible futures.

Given the social nature of perceptions and uses of technology, one can say that the reliance on multiple methods, sources and approaches is desirable to overcome blind spots of any one method, source or approach. This includes a wide net of information sources that goes beyond conventional wisdom and includes what Callon (2009) calls "hybrid forums" by which he means local and non-authorised knowledge (or "experts in the wild") that supplements and in many cases exceeds official expertise. Support of this idea of the inclusion of non-expert and a wide range of stakeholders to understand technology and its development comes from other quarters as well. It is central to the idea of participative technology assessment (Joss & Belucci, 2002; Genus & Coles, 2005; Joss, 2002; Stephan, Wütscher, Decker, & Ladikas, 2004). From the perspective of the ETICA project such a participative approach would have the advantage of being able to address not only issues of local knowledge and expertise but also of overcoming the question of what counts as "emerging" ICTs. Emergence could be observed in the interplay between different stakeholder groups.

The problem of a wide participative approach is that the scope of the project is too wide (ICTs in general) to allow a reasonable way of identifying all fields in which such technologies may emerge. Such participative research would also require large amounts of resources to undertake a generalised participative investigation of all emerging ICTs. Such a more general participative approach to ethical issues of emerging ICTs and appropriate policy and governance arrangements would be a desirable next step. There is also the problem of how to cover the entire range of positions and views. Methods to achieve this aim are still very much at the experimental stage

It will nevertheless be important to allow a range of voices to be heard to complement the different sources used by the various work packages to validate the findings and to provide a "reality check" of the different aspects of the project.

Ubiquity of Ethical Issues

A further problem worth noting, arising from the epistemological uncertainty of the future, is that there is a potential infinity of ethical issues that arise from each technology. Each of the potentially infinite number of technologies can be used in a similarly infinite number of context and for an infinite number of applications. Each of those can easily lead to a large number of possible ethical problems. It seems fundamentally impossible to capture all of these and even more difficult to evaluate all of them.

One possible way forward would be to try to become more concrete, by providing examples or applications of technologies which can then be evaluated. This is the approach used by scenario analysis. It would be interesting to do this but it is clearly impossible to do it for all emerging ICTs and all applications. Choosing a select number of examples to give an indication of ethical issues is likely to inject the researchers' bias into the further analysis.

Table 1 outlines the main problems scholars interested in the ethics of emerging ICTs face.

THE METHODOLOGY OF IDENTIFYING EMERGING ICTS

Having now outlined the problems faced by scholars who wish to investigate ethical issues

Table 1. Core Problem Areas of identifying and evaluating emerging ICTs

Problem	Description
Concept "ethics of emerging ICTs"	Lack of clarity of all constituent terms, i.e.: • Emergence • Information • Technology • Ethics and morality
Scientific justification of the methodology used to identify emerging ICTs	• Uncertainty of the future • Purpose of investigations of futures studies • Sources of knowledge about the future • Justification of chosen sources over others • Justification of timeframe (short, medium or long term?) in which to identify emerging ICTs
Reproducible and scientifically acceptable link between emerging ICTs and ethical issues	• Potential infinity of ethical issues arising from technologies • Avoidance of bias in capturing ethical issues
Practical issues	• Workload • Delimitation and distribution of work • Knowing when to stop the identification and justification of such a decision

of emerging ICTs and the main aim of such an investigation, the current section discusses a way of achieving this aim.

Scope of the Investigation

The question of an appropriate methodology is closely linked to the truth claims that the researchers aim to generate from their research. It is therefore important to discuss the scope and limitations of the investigations. We need to underline that we do not claim to know the future and that we do not pretend to be able to achieve certainty about future developments. This then raises the questions of which claims are raised and what is the contribution of such research.

In answering this question, we follow Cuhls (2003) who uses the term of "foresight" instead of "forecasting" in order to underline the difference between one-dimensional and multi-dimensional views of the future. In this sense, we describe here a foresight method that aims to provide a more detailed picture of ethical issues of emerging ICTs with a view to coming to a better understanding of what will be required of decision makers in order to ensure that future challenges are met. The aim is not to describe the one and only real future but to come to an understanding of different possible futures. On the basis of a better understanding of

possible futures, a selection is made of which one is either desirable or most important to consider for other reasons (Figure 1).

This understanding of possible futures and the development of means to determine which ones are in need of particular attention then allows concentrating on particular items and issues, which can be investigated in more depth. On the basis of this focus, governance arrangements and other policy advice can then be produced.

The aim of foresight activities is not to describe one true future but some or all of the following (Cuhls, 2003, p. 98):

- To enlarge the choice of opportunities, to set priorities and to assess impacts and chances
- To prospect for the impacts of current research and technology policy
- To ascertain new needs, new demands and new possibilities as well as new ideas
- To focus selectively on economic, technological, social and ecological areas as well as to start monitoring and detailed research in these fields
- To define desirable and undesirable futures and
- To start and stimulate continuous discussion processes.

Figure 1. Selection of future option (adapted from Cuhls, 2003)

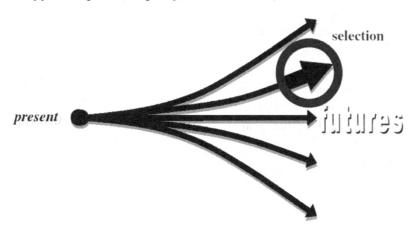

This understanding of the aims of foresight fits well with the ETICA project. It renders the entire project feasible because it underlines that there is no claim to a correct description of the future but only one to a plausible investigation of possible options and outcomes. This raises the question of how such a claim to a plausible description of possible futures can be validated: the question of methodology.

Identification of Emerging Technologies

The method described here is based on the idea that the closest one can come to identifying emerging ICTs is to capture the discourse (or probably better: discourses) on future ICTs that currently exist. This can be done in a bottom-up manner in the sense that the futures described in the literature are initially collected without much editorial control and are categorised according to criteria that are useful for the further development of the project (see section on analytical grid below). This approach is akin to the Grounded Theory approach in social sciences (Charmaz, 2007; Corbin & Strauss, 2008; Glaser & Strauss, 1999; Strauss & Corbin, 1997), which aims to refrain from an a priori theoretical framing of the research subject and concentrate on themes emerging from the data. While such a completely unprejudiced development of description of phenomena is probably impossible, the suggested method aims to follow this descriptive and bottom-up approach for the identification stage. Some of the major findings arising from this approach are quite predictable. However, the overall picture that emerges is less predictable and is also likely to underline details that may be as important or even more important than the headline technologies. The critical evaluation of this approach will then be undertaken in the two later stages. The following section provides a more detailed description of how this approach will be implemented.

Choice of Data Sources

There is a rich literature on emerging technologies produced by futures researchers and foresight institutes. Such research, if of interest and relevant to the problem, has to contend with the difficulty that it is often driven by market interests and reproduces existing hype cycles. We therefore used this type of literature to compile a list of frequently named emerging ICTs as a benchmark but sought different sources of information to come to an understanding of emerging ICTs and their ethical issues.

It was decided to rely simultaneously on two interrelated but different discourses. One of these is the official governments' view of emerging ICTs as reflected by governmental research and funding strategies such as those of the European Commission and the National Science Foundation. These are contrasted with documents authored by established research institutions such as Ofcom and ISTAG as well as private organisations such as Microsoft or Siemens. Combining these two types of sources (see Figure 2) develops an understanding of expected futures by organisations that are in a position to substantially influence these developments.

Figure 2. Sources of analysis

The delimitation of data sources (suggested in Figure 2) is justified by the fact it will give a good view of what is intended and envisaged by organisations that are in a position to enforce their view of the world. It should not be misunderstood as aiming at a true or verifiable prediction of the future. What it can do is to aim to provide plausible possible futures to enrich discourses concerning desirable futures and possible ways to get there. In order to spawn such discourses, thought needs to be given to what aspects of the sources need to be analysed and in what way, so that the outcome of analysis is of relevance and produces novel insights.

After accepting the principal delimitation of sources to be analysed, a more detailed question is *which criteria documents must fulfil in order to be included in the data analysis*. The following criteria outline in our opinion the most important aspects of the source documents.

- Explicit attention to the core characteristics of technologies

The "core characteristics" are those that allow the technology to have an influence on the way humans interact with the world.

- Length and breadth of vision

Documents need to have the required temporal horizon (at least 10 to 15 years into the future) as well as a wide understanding of technology.

- Complementarity of sources

The different sources need to complement each other in order to avoid blind spots. That means that sources from a range of national, disciplinary and other backgrounds need to be considered if they are available.

In addition to these theoretically motivated criteria, texts also need to fulfil the practical criterion that the researchers have the language capacity required to analyse them.

Analytical Grid

The next step was to define the characteristics of technologies that are of interest for ethical analysis. Given the broad range of items described in the literature, ranging from large socio-technical systems that have the possibility of affecting almost everyone in most situations to very detailed ideas about particular items, it was decided to distinguish between technologies (high level socio-technical systems), application examples (the use of technologies for particular purposes) and artefacts (smaller scale technical items to be used for various purposes). This distinction proved useful but difficult to agree on in many instances, so that relationships between entities were added to the principles of analysis of the text.

For all of these items (technologies, application examples and artefacts) certain characteristics were of interest. These include social impact, critical issues (i.e., ethical and legal questions), capabilities and constraints. Figure 3 shows the principle of this data analysis.

During the data analysis it became clear that there was going to be a large number of technologies, application examples and artefacts that could be identified. In order to render these manageable and to facilitate ethical analysis and subsequent evaluation, it was decided to group the findings into general high level technologies. Given that an initial idea of the data analysis was to collect "vignettes" of technologies, i.e. illustrative examples for the purpose of rendering them less abstract, the name chosen for the high level description of the technologies was "meta-vignettes". This is meant to illustrate the essence of a technology, the way in which it changes the way the technology affects the way humans interact with the world.

Figure 3. Categories of data analysis (analytical grid)

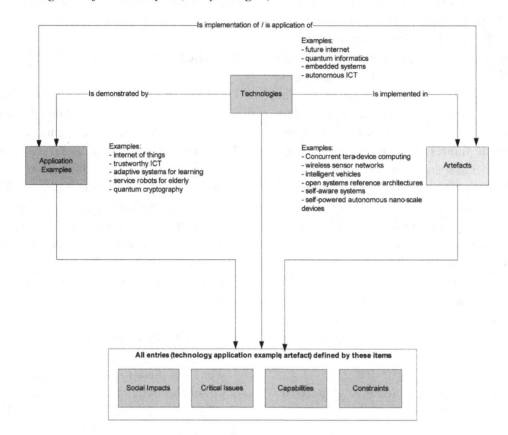

The analytical grid proved helpful in indicating which of the analysed items were related and thereby pointing to the most pertinent ones. It provided the basis for the identification of top level technologies for which meta-vignettes were developed. For each of these top level technologies, the meta-vignette was constructed on the basis of the data derived from the analysis of discourses but also drawing on additional data. The structure of the meta-vignettes was:

- Technology Name
- History and Definitions (from discourse analysis and other sources)
- Defining Features ("essence" of technology, how does it change the way we interact with the world)
- Application Areas / Examples
- Relation to other Technologies

- Critical Issues (ethical, social, legal and related issues as described in the discourse)
- References

Validation of Findings The method just described provides a transparent and justifiable way of identifying emerging ICTs for the purpose of foresight, as described earlier. It can nevertheless have blind spots because it relies on interrelated discourses by governments and research institutions. It was therefore decided to use several methods to ensure that the list of technologies was reasonable. These consisted of a set of focus groups with technology users, a survey of technology development project leaders, and a cross-check with an amalgamated list of technologies from current futures research. Having now described the way emerging ICTs could be identified, the next question is how the ethical issues they raise can be identified.

METHODOLOGY OF ETHICAL ANALYSIS

When looking at emerging technologies, an important question is whether ethical principles or theories are applicable. Moor (2008), for example, suggests that we need better ethics for emerging technologies. From a methodological perspective, this exacerbates the difficulties of the investigation. Not only do the researchers have to contend with the uncertainties of future technologies, but also with future ethics. This raises the question of the choice and justification of the ethical approach taken. Just as most technologies have a potential infinity of possible applications and thus a potential infinity of moral problems, there is now a huge number of ethical evaluations to contend with. One possible approach would be to decide on a particular ethical approach that is widely accepted, such as the mid-level ethical principles generally used in biomedical ethics (Beauchamp & Childress, 2008). This would leave open the question of the relationship to other ethical views and might lead to blind spots where the chosen ethical theory is not well developed.

The present project therefore decided to take a pluralist approach that allows a number of different voices to be heard. This plurality, while running the risk of inconsistency, has the advantage of covering a broad range of issues and views and offering different interpretations. It was therefore decided to concentrate on the discourse of ICT ethics and, in the first instance, extract this field's views on the ethics of the emerging technologies. The chosen approach for ethical analysis thus mirrors the approach used in the technology identification part in that it relies on published work and thereby seeks to minimise injecting the researchers' biases into the analysis. This section first defines the field and then describes how it

has been analysed to allow the identification of ethical issues.

Computer and Information Ethics

Computer and information ethics can be understood as that branch of applied ethics which studies and analyzes social and ethical impacts of ICT (Bynum, 2008). The more specific term 'computer ethics', coined by Walter Maner in the 1970's, refers to applying normative theories such as utilitarianism, Kantianism, or virtue ethics to particular ethical cases that involve computer systems or networks. Computer ethics is also used to refer to professional ethics for computer professionals such as codes for conduct that can be used as guidelines for an ethical case. In 1985, Jim Moor (1985) and Deborah Johnson (1985) published seminal papers that helped define the field. From then on, it has been recognized as an established field in applied ethics, with its own journals, conferences, research centers and professional organizations. Recently, computer ethics is related to information ethics, a more general field which includes computer ethics, media ethics, library ethics, and bioinformation ethics (Brey & Soraker, 2009). For contemporary overviews of the field, see Floridi (2010); Tavani and Himma (2008); and Van den Hoven and Weckert (2008).

The field of computer ethics is also institutionalized inside ethics, e.g. in the International Society for Ethics of Information Technology (INSEIT) and outside applied ethics for example in several working groups of organizations for IT professionals such as the Association for Computing Machinery (ACM), International Federation for Information Processing (IFIP) and national professional organizations across the globe.

Overview of Computer and Information Ethics

Scholars in computer and information ethics present their work in a limited number of academic journals and conferences. These journals and conferences are selected according to our experience and expertise in the field, and according to the descriptions on their website. Having established the criteria of demarcation of the field of computer and information ethics, an extensive overview is constructed. This overview, or dataset, contains references, abstracts and keywords of articles published in 12 journals and 3 conference proceedings in the field of computer and information ethics between 2003 and 2009. We acknowledge that we do not claim we are making an overview of the entire field, but it is fair to say that the dataset of abstracts largely covers what has been written on computer and information ethics in the last 7 years.

As mentioned before, computer ethics emerged in the 1980s. However, we have restricted ourselves to publications from the last 7 years, because ethical issues in relation to emerging ICTs are mainly published in that period of time. Before 2003 emerging ICTs was not really an issue and not much has been published on the topic at hand before that time. The first conference devoted to emerging ICTs was the Sixth International Conference of Computer Ethics: Philosophical Enquiry (CEPE) 2005; named 'Ethics of New Information Technology'. From then on, ethics of emerging ICTs gained attention in academic literature and conferences.

The following 6 journals publish explicitly and exclusively on computer and information ethics and are referenced in the dataset.

- *Ethics and Information Technology* (Publisher: Springer). Indexed from 2009 Volume (11) Issue 4 till 2003 Volume (5) Issue 1.
- *Information, Communication and Society* (Publisher: Taylor and Francis). Indexed from 2009 Volume (12) Issue 7 till 2003 Volume (6) Issue 1.
- *International Review of Information Ethics* (Publisher: International Center for

Information Ethics). Indexed from 2009 Volume (11) till 2004 Volume (1), which is everything published in this journal.
- *Journal of Information, Communication & Ethics in Society* (Publisher: Emerald). Indexed from 2009 volume (7) issue 4 till 2003 Volume (1) Issue 1, which is everything published in this journal.
- *Journal of Information Ethics* (Publisher: Springer). Indexed from 2009 (18) issue 1 till 2006 (15) issue 1, no abstracts available after 2006.
- *The Ethicomp Journal* (Publisher: Center for Computing and Social Responsibility). Indexed from 2008 Volume (3) Issue 2 till 2004 Volume (1) Issue 1, which is everything published in this journal.

Due to the convergence of ICT with other technologies such as biotechnology, nanotechnology and cognitive science, we have also included abstracts from journals which cover the phenomenon of converging technologies. Furthermore, articles on computer and information ethics are not exclusively published in the above mentioned journals, but in other journals as well. We have identified 6 journals that are relevant and leading in the adjacent fields. However, note that from these journals only the abstracts of articles related to ICT have been used for the dataset.

- *AI & Society* (Publisher: Springer). Indexed from 2009 Volume (24) Issue 4 till 2003 Volume (17) Issue 1.
- *Behavior and Information Technology* (Publisher: Taylor and Francis). Indexed from 2009 Volume (28) Issue 6 till 2003 Volume (22) Issue 1.
- *Nanoethics* (Publisher: Springer). Indexed from 2009 Volume (3) Issue 2 till 2007 Volume (1) Issue 1, which is everything published in this journal.
- *Neuroethics* (Publisher: Springer). Indexed from 2009 Volume (2) Issue 3 till 2008

Volume (1) Issue 1, which is everything published in this journal.

- *New Media & Society* (Publisher: SAGE). Indexed from 2009 Volume (11) Issue6 till 2003 Volume (5) Issue 1.
- *Science and Engineering Ethics* (Publisher: Springer). Indexed from 2009 Volume (15) Issue 3 till 2003 Volume (9) Issue 1.

There are several conferences (partly) devoted to computer and information ethics. These conferences have proceedings in which conference papers are published. The below conference proceedings have been used for the dataset. However, in case of the proceedings of the SPT 2009 conference, only the abstracts from the 'Philosophy and Ethics of Information Technology' track have been collected.

- Computer Ethics Philosophical Enquiry (CEPE) 2005 & 2007
- Society for Philosophy and Technology (SPT) 2009

In total, 1038 references, abstracts and keywords have been collected from the above presented academic journals and conference proceedings. The abstracts are categorized under certain headings. The initial idea was to categorize the abstracts under ethical values such as 'privacy', 'autonomy', 'freedom', 'trust' and so forth. However, during the meta-analysis of the literature it became clear that not every abstract can be categorized under one or more particular ethical values as they are articulated in the literature. For example, an abstract of an article on Emmanuel Levinas' perspective on virtual reality cannot be categorized in an obvious way under a particular ethical value. For this reason, we also included headings like 'virtual reality', 'ubiquitous computing,' 'culture', 'policy' and several others as well. Furthermore, some abstracts do not in any obvious or straightforward sense fit under any heading. For these abstracts we have included

the heading: 'miscellaneous'. Thus, we started out with categorizing the abstracts under ethical values and added new categories on the basis of a bottom-up approach. One of the reasons for constructing this dataset of abstracts is because it makes searching for literature on ethics of emerging ICTs much easier and efficient. When interested in ethical issues of ambient intelligence (AmI), one merely has to use the search function of Word and one can quickly scan the dataset for relevant literature on that topic at hand. However, the dataset also serves a second purpose, which is outlined in the next section.

Bibliometrical Analysis

After having constructed the dataset of abstracts, it is analyzed with VOSviewer, which is a computer program for bibliometrical analyses developed to construct thesauri, terminology frequency lists and visual maps of the co-occurrence of key terms in a dataset. The program is designed by Nees Jan Van Eck and Ludo Waltman (N. J van Eck & Waltman, 2009; Van Eck & Waltman, 2006; Van Eck, Waltman, & van den Berg, 2005). VOSviewer makes visible which ethical concepts are used in relation to which (emerging) ICTs in the academic literature on computer and information ethics (Heersmink, van den Hoven, Nees J. van Eck, & van den Berg, 2011). For example, if the concepts AmI, privacy, and autonomy often co-occur in the same abstracts, VOSviewer will put these concepts close to each other in the visual map. So it makes visible syntactic proximity relations between key concepts. The basic idea of this type of analysis is that it very quickly shows which ethical issues or concepts are mentioned in relation to which emerging ICTs. One can e.g., click on a particular concept in the map and see which concepts are related to it. However, please keep in mind that the application of this computer tool is merely a *heuristic* for signaling which ethical concepts are used in the literature of computer and information ethics in relation to certain emerging ICTs. For the sake of convenience we left out most of the technical aspects of the program, but for those who are interested in the practical implementation of the statistics can visit: http://www.vosviewer.com/.

Identifying Ethical Issues

The identification of emerging technologies is condensed in what we called meta-vignettes. These are encyclopedia-like articles that describe essential characteristics of the technology as well as a number of application examples. The meta-vignettes are ethically analyzed in the following way. First, the defining features of the technology are ethically analyzed. In case of AmI, for example, these defining features are: (1) embeddedness and invisibility of the sensors and computational devices, (2) interconnectedness of the sensors and computational devices, (3) the AmI system is adaptive, that is, the system adapts to its circumstances, (4) the system is personalized, tailored to the needs of its users, (5) the system is anticipatory, that is, it can anticipate its users needs and desires, and (6) the system is context-aware, it can recognize specific users and its situational context and can adjust to the user or context. These defining features have ethical consequences. To give one example: if a user delegates decisions to an anticipatory AmI system, it reduces the amount of autonomy and freedom a person has, which is seen by (some) ethicists as undesirable. All the defining features of the emerging technology and their consequences are analyzed from an ethical point of view.

Second, the application examples of the emerging ICT as described in the meta-vignettes are ethically analyzed. Take AmI, this technology can be applied in basically every societal field such as healthcare, households, workplace and transportation, to name a few. Several examples in certain application areas will be analyzed.

It is important to note that during the ethical analysis of the defining features and application examples we draw from existing literature on ethics of (emerging) ICTs. A significant amount of work has already been done on ethics of emerging ICTs in existing literature. We have a dataset of 1038 abstracts on computer and information ethics from 12 leading journals and 3 central conference proceedings published in the last 7 years. This is a rich and elaborate source to draw from and covers a large area of what has been written on computer and information ethics, including ethics of emerging ICTs. If we are analyzing an emerging technology, robotics for example, we search in the overview for abstracts on this topic, which is relatively easy because all the abstracts are categorized under relevant headings and all the keywords are indexed. If there are abstracts on this topic, we collect the accompanying article and extract the relevant ethical issues from the article and incorporate it in our ethical analysis.

Furthermore, the ethical analysis is pluralistic in nature, which means that we make use of – depending on each technology - different normative ethical positions to analyze the technology. This means that the articulation and formulation of the ethical aspects and problems of emerging ICTs is not limited by a particular normative ethical framework or meta-ethical position, but is instead described from different normative ethical positions (van den Hoven, 2010). As indicated in the introduction to this section, the analysis is not wedded *a priori* to, e.g., a Kantian, (rule or act) utilitarian, or a virtue ethics perspective, nor does it cast problems exclusively in terms of rights, or obligations, responsibilities, emotions, risks, fiduciary duties, human dignity, etc. These perspectives and their associated terminology can and are invoked when and where appropriate. Moreover, Tjsalling Swierstra and Arie Rip (2007) have argued that moral debates on new and emerging science and technology follow certain patterns. They refer to this as NEST-ethics (new and emerging science and technology ethics). Debates usually start with consequentialist arguments followed by Kantian arguments, justice arguments and virtue ethics arguments. Thus, moral debates on emerging science and technology are pluralistic in nature. This implies that if one wants to capture the most salient ethical issues of emerging ICTs, one must adhere to a pluralistic approach, which is much richer in content and covers a wider spectrum of ethical issues.

Third, we employ the bibliometrical analysis to assess whether we have discussed the most important ethical values, ethical considerations or problems during the analysis of the meta-vignette. When analysing a meta-vignette on, e.g., AmI, we will look for the concept 'AmI' in the visual map and see which ethical concepts are close to it and therefore associated with it by many authors in our overview of computer and information ethics. This method tells us which ethical concepts or ethical values have been used in the academic literature on computer and information ethics in relation to AmI. During the ethical analysis of AmI, it is important that we at least take into account the ethical concepts which are closest to it. The visual map of concepts gives us information we may have overlooked during the ethical analysis of the defining features and application examples.

And finally, the ethical analysis ends with a concluding discussion in which the three previous sections are discussed and evaluated. So, the ethical analysis of the emerging ICTs has the following structure: (1) discussion of defining features, (2) discussion of application examples, (3) bibliometrical analysis, and (4) concluding discussion.

CONCLUSION AND REFLECTION

The present paper has described a series of steps that allow scholars to identify emerging technologies and develop an ethical analysis of these technologies. It is meant to contribute to the debate on how societies can deal with the opportunities and problems arising from new technologies.

The research does not stop at the identification of ethical issues. In the project that developed the

methodology described here a subsequent step after identifying emerging ICTs and their ethical issues will be to explore and evaluate these from several angles including gender, law, philosophy and technology assessment. This further analysis aims to provide an evaluation and ranking of the most important technologies that policy makers need to be aware of. The final step of the project will then be an analysis of governance arrangements that are currently used to address ethics in ICT with a view to identifying suitable ways forward. On the basis of the earlier list of ethically significant technologies, the ETICA project will explore how foreseeable issues can be addressed. This analysis will be used to inform policy advice to be given to policy makers on a European, national and industry level. Figure 4 gives an outline of all steps to be taken in the project.

Following the steps outline here provides an academically justified way of doing research on ethics of emerging ICTs and providing policy advice to decision makers. Providing policy advice requires openness on the limitations of the approach. In this case, many of the limitations are linked to the epistemic uncertainty concerning the future. The way to address this in the method presented here is to rely on and analyse in depth several discourses: The political and funding-related discourse on future ICT, the scientific discourse, and the discourse in ICT ethics. We have argued that these contain a plausible claim to our best estimate of the technical future. However, we concede that they may also be wrong. In addition there may be other discourses which are more informed about particular technical or socio-technical developments that are not covered here. Furthermore, the reliance on discourses implies that we rely heavily on experts, understood as the individuals who gain reputation in particular discourses. As indicated earlier, there is no guarantee that these experts are right. In terms of democratic policy advice, the chosen approach is also somewhat elitist in that it gives relatively little weight to views of the population.

Figure 4. Graphical representation of all project steps

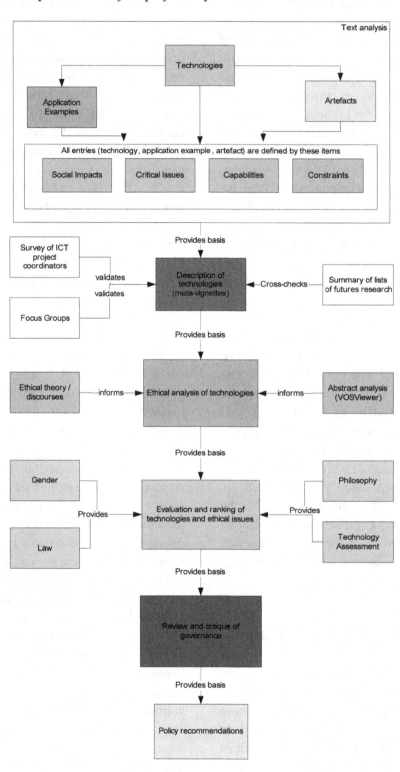

Given all of these limitations, it is clear that we do not claim to have found and described the only way of assessing future ICT developments and their ethical consequences. In fact, there are a number of alternative approaches to the same problem, some of them taken in related projects. We believe that exchange between these projects using different methods and approaches will contribute to a better understanding and thereby eventually to a better and hopefully more democratic way of dealing with emerging ICTs.

ACKNOWLEDGMENT

This paper is based on work that was undertaken in the research project, *Ethical Issues of Emerging ICT Applications* (ETICA) (GA no 230318) funded by the European 7th Framework Programme.

REFERENCES

Beauchamp, T. L., & Childress, J. F. (2008). *Principles of Biomedical Ethics* (6th ed.). New York: OUP.

Bijker, W. E. (1997). *Of Bicycles, Bakelites, and Bulbs: Toward a Theory of Sociotechnical Change.* Cambridge, MA: MIT Press.

Brey, P., & Soraker, J. H. (2009). Philosophy of Computing and Information Technology. In Gabbay, D. M., Meijers, A. W., Woods, J., & Thagard, P. (Eds.), *Philosophy of Technology and Engineering Sciences* (*Vol. 9*, pp. 1341–1408). New York: North Holland. doi:10.1016/B978-0-444-51667-1.50051-3

Bynum, T. (2008). *Computer and Information Ethics.* Retrieved December 4, 2008, from http://plato.stanford.edu/entries/ethics-computer/

Cadili, S., & Whitley, E. A. (2005). On the interpretative flexibility of hosted ERP systems. *The Journal of Strategic Information Systems, 14*(2), 167–195. doi:10.1016/j.jsis.2005.04.006

Callon, M., Lascoumes, P., & Barthe, Y. (2009). *Acting in an Uncertain World: An Essay on Technical Democracy.* Cambridge, MA: MIT Press.

Charmaz, A. B. A. K. (2007). *The SAGE Handbook of Grounded Theory.* Thousand Oaks, CA: Sage Ltd.

Corbin, J., & Strauss, A. (2008). *Basics of Qualitative Research: Techniques and Procedures for Developing Grounded Theory* (3rd ed.). Thousand Oaks, CA: Sage.

Cuhls, K. (2003). From forecasting to foresight processes - new participative foresight activities in Germany. *Journal of Forecasting, 22*(2-3), 93–111..doi:10.1002/for.848

Dusek, V. (2006). *Philosophy of Technology: an Introduction.* New York: Wiley Blackwell.

Floridi, L. (Ed.). (2010). *The Cambridge Handbook of Information and Computer Ethics.* Cambridge, UK: Cambridge University Press.

Genus, A., & Coles, A. (2005). On Constructive Technology Assessment and Limitations on Public Participation in Technology Assessment. *Technology Analysis and Strategic Management, 17*(4), 433–443..doi:10.1080/09537320500357251

Glaser, B. G., & Strauss, A. L. (1999). *Discovery of Grounded Theory: Strategies for Qualitative Research.* Piscataway, NJ: AldineTransaction.

Grint, K., & Woolgar, S. (1997). *The Machine at Work: Technology, Work and Organization.* New York: Polity Press.

Heersmink, R., van den Hoven, J., van Eck, N. J., & van den Berg, J. (2011). A Bibliometrical Study of Computer and Information Ethics. *Ethics and Information Technology.*

Himma, K. E., & Tavani, H. T. (Eds.). (2008). *The Handbook of Information and Computer Ethics*. New York: Wiley. doi:10.1002/9780470281819

Howcroft, D., Mitev, N., & Wilson, M. (2004). What We May Learn from the Social Shaping of Technology Approach. In Mingers, J., & Willcocks, L. P. (Eds.), *Social Theory and Philosophy for Information Systems* (pp. 329–371). New York: Wiley.

Johnson, D. G. (1985). *Computer Ethics* (1st ed.). Upper Saddle River, NJ: Prentice Hall.

Joss, S. (2002). Toward the Public Sphere--Reflections on the Development of Participatory Technology Assessment. *Bulletin of Science, Technology & Society*, *22*(3), 220–231.. doi:10.1177/02767602022003006

Joss, S., & Belucci, S. (Eds.). (2002). *Participatory Technology Assessment: European Perspectives*. London: University of Westminster, Centre for the Study of Democracy.

Latour, B. (2007). *Reassembling the Social: An Introduction to Actor-Network-Theory*. Oxford, UK: OUP.

Law, J., & Hassard, J. (1999). *Actor Network Theory and After*. New York: Wiley Blackwell.

Moor, J. H. (1985). What is computer ethics. *Metaphilosophy*, *16*(4), 266–275. doi:10.1111/j.1467-9973.1985.tb00173.x

Moor, J. H. (2008). Why we need better ethics for emerging technologies. In Hoven, J. V. D., & Weckert, J. (Eds.), *Information Technology and Moral Philosophy* (pp. 26–39). Cambridge, UK: Cambridge University Press. doi:10.1017/CBO9780511498725.003

Olsen, J. B., Pedersen, S. A., & Hendricks, V. F. (2009). *A Companion to the Philosophy of Technology*. New York: Wiley Blackwell. doi:10.1002/9781444310795

Ricoeur, P. (1990). *Soi-même comme un autre*. Paris: Seuil.

Sollie, P. (2007). Ethics, technology development and uncertainty: an outline for any future ethics of technology. *Journal of Information. Communication & Ethics in Society*, *5*(4), 293–306. doi:10.1108/14779960710846155

Sollie, P., & Düwell, M. (Eds.). (2009). *Evaluating New Technologies: Methodological Problems for the Ethical Assessment of Technology Developments*. New York: Springer.

Stephan, S., Wütscher, F., Decker, M., & Ladikas, M. (2004). *Bridges Between Science, Society and Policy: Technology Assessment - Methods and Impacts*. New York: Springer.

Strauss, A. C., & Corbin, J. (1997). *Grounded Theory in Practice*. Thousand Oaks, CA: Sage Publications, Inc.

Swierstra, T., & Rip, A. (2007). Nano-ethics as NEST-ethics: Patterns of Moral Argumentation About New and Emerging Science and Technology. *NanoEthics*, *1*(1), 3–20..doi:10.1007/s11569-007-0005-8

van den Hoven, J. (2010). The use of normative theories in computer ethics. In Floridi, E. B. L. (Ed.), *The Cambridge Handbook of Information and Computer Ethics*. Cambridge, UK: Cambridge University Press.

van den Hoven, J., & Weckert, J. (2008). *Information Technology and Moral Philosophy* (1st ed.). Cambridge, UK: Cambridge University Press. doi:10.1017/CBO9780511498725

Van Eck, N. J., & Waltman, L. (2006). VOS: a new method for visualizing similarities between objects. In *Proceedings of the 30th Annual Conference of the German Classification Society, Studies in Classification, Data Analysis, and Knowledge Organization* (pp. 299-306).

Van Eck, N. J., & Waltman, L. (2009). Software survey: VOSviewer, a computer program for bibliometric mapping. *Scientometrics*, 1–16.

Van Eck, N. J., Waltman, L., & van den Berg, J. (2005). A novel algorithm for visualizing concept associations. In *Proceedings of the Database and Expert Systems Applications, Advances in Data Analysis, Sixteenth International Workshop* (pp. 405-409).

Velasquez, M. G. (2001). *Business Ethics: Concepts and Cases* (5th ed.). Upper Saddle River, NJ: Pearson Education.

This work was previously published in International Journal of Technoethics, Volume 1, Issue 4, edited by Rocci Luppicini, pp. 20-38, copyright 2010 by IGI Publishing (an imprint of IGI Global).

Chapter 7
The Regulation of Gaze and Capture:
New Media and the Image Economy

Yasmin Ibrahim
University of London, UK

ABSTRACT

The increasing use of the body for embedding technology as well as the convergence of multiple features in mobile telephony have made image capture an important phenomenon that presents new ways to capture events and their constructs, which cast new forms of gaze into everyday life. The ways in which one captures and gazes has increasing ethical, legal and social implications for societies. The civilian gaze through mobile recording devices can be empowering in terms of holding authorities accountable, but it can equally debilitate societies by transgressing privacy and enabling new forms of voyeurism and deviance. In recognition of this, many governments and authorities are restricting the ways in which we capture and upload images. This paper looks at how this image economy is creating new ways of looking and how the new rules are, for different reasons, seeking to curb this architecture of capture.

INTRODUCTION

The increasing convergence of technologies and ability to make connections with the wider world to communicate, upload and download images through mobile telephony is creating new ways to connect with people and create content. The convergence of technologies, the ubiquitous use of mobile phones and the increasing ability for users to express themselves both discursively and through images have created new information and exchange economies. The ability to create content and to contribute to media event construction through visual and discursive content has given rise to discourses about citizen empowerment and the rise of citizen journalism. This has inspired a proliferation of academic writing that has been

DOI: 10.4018/978-1-4666-1773-5.ch007

assessing how these user practices - whether it be blogging or creating videos and images - are leading to new forms of journalistic practices and networks as well as new forms of consumption which often blur the boundaries between public and private realms (See Black, 1997; Friedland, 2003; Haas, 2007). The conjoining of the private and public spheres is a resonant strand of the new media environments. The new media environment can be defined as one that includes the internet, the content of the World Wide Web, as well as a multitude of applications, features and modes of communication (synchronous, asynchronous, and one-to-one as well as one-to-many) available on these interactive platforms and which can be made available and accessible on mobile technologies through convergence. The ability of mobile users of telephony to connect with public platforms with ease and without restraint constructs a postmodern culture of making connections not just through voice telephony but also discursive modes such as text or emoticons and perhaps even new forms of collectively understood languages and moving and still images.

The ability of people to capture images on the move and to exchange them through mobile telephony or to make them available in public platforms such as the internet has established new forms of production and consumption economies, but these new forms of image capture and exchange have had moral, ethical and legal implications for society, too. Beyond raising the spectre of voyeurism and creating new forms of aesthetics, the notion of capture and new forms of gaze enabled through convergent mobile technologies is never complete in our accelerated modernity. Whilst non-consensual photography is not a new phenomenon, with the advent of new technologies and convergence, the means of capturing and distributing such images have become more sophisticated and instantaneous (Kelley, 2007). This paper explores the notion of looking in our post-surveillance society, as surveillance through convergent technologies becomes an

open-ended exercise where looking is not just one-dimensional and moves beyond the Foucauldian notion of surveillance as a form of discipline. In post-modernity the politics of looking becomes multi-dimensional, non-uniform and can lead to unexpected consequences.

With the increased embedding of video recording functions in mobile telephony the act of looking becomes complex in the post-surveillance network where CCTV cameras coexist with mobile bodies which can record images and events on the move. Unlike surveillance equipment installed by governments and authorities these provide new opportunities and risks which can both empower and debilitate society. I argue that mobile telephony conjoins other mechanisms of looking and tracing data in a surveillance society to form a surveillance economy that can create new forms of voyeurism, aesthetics, as well as vulnerabilities which will reframe certain forms of image capture and consumption of these images as deviance in society. In tandem with this, authorities in different parts of the world are enacting new ways to control the ways in which people capture, upload, download, consume, exchange and archive images.

Mobile technology, with its image capture and recording functions, is also enabling mobile bodies to become witnesses to events in unexpected ways. Bearing witness through mobile telephony and through images crafts new ways to understand and construct events. The valorization of image in such an economy seeks to construct images as an ontological reality of an event. Images have had an uneasy relationship with the real throughout human history. Both in the history of art and in our critical appraisal of photography as a measure of the real, our unease with delegating truth or validity to images remains contested despite increasing use of images to communicate narratives in our sound bite culture where the communication of news is increasingly dependent on the image. Both popular culture and the popularisation of the news and news-making implicate the image as a salient feature of our postmodern consciousness where 'to see is to believe'.

The relevance of the image in new media environments invokes the need to comprehend both ethical and legal concerns in different cultures and societies. Whilst older laws such as libel, copyright infringement, intellectual property rights or privacy laws have been employed by governments to deal with image-related deviance in societies, the moral and ethical dimensions of human and technological interactions are much more tenuous to discern and address. David Resnick (2007) defines ethics (or morals) as rules which people apply in distinguishing between right or wrong. These become norms of conduct to discern between acceptable and unacceptable behaviour. Resnick points out that whilst people recognise some common ethical norms there may be differences in the ways in which people apply and interpret or balance these norms which in turn may be shaped by both individual life experiences and values. Laws and ethics are not the same as the latter can be broader and informal and may provide the basis or premise to enact laws (Resnick, 2007). For example, whilst adult pornography and its dissemination on the Internet may not be illegal in a country it might nevertheless be considered as unethical by individuals and communities.

In tandem with this, the ethical and moral considerations of non-stop capture are much more difficult to ascertain. Where an image is both legally and ethically deviant and where a law can address this deviance or regulate it, the ethical dimension becomes subsumed by the legal imperative. On the other hand, where an image (whether its capture, dissemination or consumption) does not constitute legal deviance but if it nevertheless raises ethical issues or transgresses taboos or moral boundaries of a society, the ethical dimension becomes much more problematic. The embedding of mobile technologies in our everyday lives and the convergence on various features and applications in such technologies which enable the ease of capture and dissemination implicate and

entwine technology as an entity in these moral dialogues and dilemmas as well as social and legal processes. Rocci Luppicini (2009, pp. 6-7) locates such enquiries within the field of technoethics which he defines as one that is 'concerned with all ethical aspects of technology within a society shaped by technology. Thus technoethics is not only confined to human practices and processes of technology but embedded within wider social, political and moral spheres of life where policy debates, interventions, critical discourses on responsibility as well as consensual ways to resolve issues related to technology shape the field' (2009, p. 7). The enquiry into the social, ethical and legal consequences of ubiquitous capture of images falls within this ambit where societies have to resolve new ethical and moral crises.

The paper considers the ubiquitous capture of image through the entrenched literature on surveillance and through the domestication of technologies in everyday life. In assessing its pervasiveness it analyses the ways in which it is being regulated by societies and evaluates the ethical challenges of the image economy.

THE PERVASIVENESS OF WATCHING

In post-modernity the idea of being watched and captured through technology constructs a society where watching is both about power and subjectivity. The act of watching non-stop and recording the movement of bodies for social control and disciplining hence creates a surveillance society where watching is not without the emergence of data which can be coded, stored and retrieved. David Lyon (2001b, p. 2) defines surveillance as 'any collection and processing of personal data, whether identifiable or not, for the purposes of influencing or managing those whose data have been garnered.' Watching in post-modernity is not uniform nor is it simply one-sided but becomes a complex mix of phenomena where watching is justified under national and public security whilst increasingly questioned by interest groups and civil society organizations as a phenomenon which undoubtedly erodes human rights and privacy. With the convergence of various technologies in the mobile phone, new forms of gaze are enabled where mobile recording technologies can challenge spaces of power and authority but not in a concerted or uniform manner compared with institutional or state power.

Lyon contends that surveillance in post-modernity has veered away from the coordinated and centralized machinery of the panopticon advanced by Foucauldian perspectives or the 'Big Brother watching' scenario of George Orwell. Gandy (1998) similarly asserts that surveillance is not unilateral or totalising as the panopticon metaphor suggests. Surveillance in post-modernity is more networked and rhizomatic - as conceived by Gilles Deleuze and Pierre-Félix Guattari - where it represents an assemblage. Social-technical developments and the increased embedding of information and communication technologies in our everyday lives create, assemble and conjoin data with individuals and groups in complex ways (Lyon, 2001a).

Torin Monahan (2006, pp. 515-516), in tracing the decentralization and privatization of surveillance in modern society, points out that a crisis in capital accumulation in the mid-1970s has intensified a shift from mass production to flexible production regimes. This shift, according to Monahan, is evident in the organizational decentralisation which has in turn led to the development of new mechanisms of social control to regulate bodies. But, more importantly, it has led to the privatization of spaces whilst sustaining the act of surveillance. The dramatic increase in fortified enclaves such as gated communities, shopping malls and business centres have reinforced the surveillance of public life whilst sacrificing civic accountability and civil liberties. Monahan asserts that telecommunications and other infrastructure distribute access to goods and services unevenly,

on the one hand, but facilitate the collection of data and surveillance of the public on a mass scale on the other.

Beyond the capturing of images, the surveillance society is also one in which there is a non-stop creation, collection and processing of personal data. As Felix Stalder (2002) postulates, our physical bodies are 'shadowed by an increasingly comprehensive 'data body'' and at times this data body can precede us instead of following us and as such our data may already be available to an institution before we offer it. Social control in the surveillance society happens through an access to large data-sets of personal information. Stalder contends that outside of the home it becomes increasingly difficult to avoid entering into relationships that produce electronic data.

The increasing ability of states and governments to capture citizens in public places and trace people's movements and behaviour through digital and economic transactions highlights the role of surveillance as an intrinsic component of modern governance and statecraft. In line with this governments are spending increasing amounts of money on expanding the architecture of surveillance in public buildings and spaces, especially in urban centres. The global surveillance industry was estimated to be worth $1 trillion in 2006, covering a wide array of goods and services from military equipment through high-street CCTV to smart cards (cf., Wood & Ball, 2006). According to Privacy International's 2007 report, £500 million was spent in the UK from 1996-2006 to expand the surveillance industry and the country presently has an estimated 4.2 million cameras installed in public spaces. This works out to one for every fourteen people and a person can be captured on over 300 cameras each day (Wood & Ball, 2006). London is often credited with having the most extensive CCTV network, with an estimated 500,000 cameras making up the "Ring of Steel" that dates to the early 1990s (Klein, 2008).

Similar investments have been made in other countries. According to Professor Neil Rees, the

Chairman of Victoria Law Reform Commission in Australia, 'Much of the growth in surveillance had occurred since the 2001 terror attacks in the US' (cf., Herald Sun, 2009). He asserts that the public cannot escape the gaze of surveillance cameras and 'the chances your image or another identifying feature have been captured during the course of the day is almost a certainty, whether you walk, go by a car, taxi or public transport, your image has been captured by one of the many cameras operating in Melbourne's Central Business District'. (cf., Herald Sun, 2009). However, the act of watching and capturing in post-modernity do not just happen with closed-circuit television but through a host of other devices and platforms where the act of watching becomes complicated. Internet mapping tools such as Google Street View, global positioning systems, invasive X-ray machines that see through clothes, and facial recognition technology can make watching a more complex activity which may be entangled with social control, discipline, deviance and new forms of voyeurism. These new forms of technology dismember the body, coding its various parts through iris scans, fingerprints, and DNA profiling. Also, these technologies can capture and create data in spaces on the internet which people may consider as private. The convergence of technologies and the ability to use the internet to publish and publicise private images make watching an open-ended endeavour in post-modernity where moving bodies are not only captured through technology but have themselves the potential to capture spaces, events and people on the move.

The centralization and privatization of surveillance, the co-ordinated and well-orchestrated collection and capture of public data, the ability to create data through everyday transactions, along with the co-existence of unorganized and civilian counter-sites of gaze through mobile telephony and other mobile recording devices are defining features in the economy of gaze. The pervasive act of watching in post-modernity becomes a dialectical enterprise where contrasting and contradictory forces can co-exist and interface in unexpected ways. It is through this paradigm that this paper situates the ability to capture and gaze on the move through mobile telephony and its connection with the World Wide Web which enables private moments to be put on a public space.

ARCHITECTURE OF GAZE

The use of camera phones has been rising inexorably in many countries. Unit sales rose from 3 million in 2001 to 500 million in 2006 worldwide and global camera phone handset revenue is predicted to grow to over $120 billion by 2011 with one-third of the world's population anticipated to own a camera phone (Taylor, 2007). According to a 2005 study by research firm InfoTrends, camera phones are expected to account for 89% of all mobile phone handsets shipped in 2009 and the primary factors driving this rise are improvements in imaging functions (i.e. image sensors, zoom, and auto-focus); rapid declines in prices for this functionality; higher-speed wireless bandwidth; and easier-to-use handsets, services, and peripherals (Business Wire, 2005). The study predicts that the total number of images captured on camera phones will reach 227 billion by 2009, exceeding the number of photos taken on digital still cameras and film cameras combined.

Our ability to hold those in power accountable through counter-sites of gaze has been evident in many instances where the civilian gaze has clamoured for accountability and has exposed abuse and injustice. From the Rodney King incident to the natural disasters of the Indian Ocean tsunami and Hurricane Katrina to the Saffron revolution in Burma and uprisings in Tibet, the camera phone has provided new ways to construct and gaze at events. The need to capture and share events as they happen has invited much scholarship on this front (See Stelmaszewska et al., 2006; Kindberg et al., 2005; Okabe, 2004). Capturing and sharing photographs enables one to partake in an event and to form communion through this act of bearing witness. Since the advent of camera phones the civilian gaze has become an intrinsic part of event construction and institutional and mainstream media have capitalised on this phenomenon to invite images taken from mobile recording devices to be published and broadcast on mainstream media platforms. The now-famous picture of the ripped-apart bus in Tavistock Square during the 7/7 bombings in London was sent to the BBC website within 45 minutes of the bombing and used on the front page of two national newspapers (Bristow, 2005). Following the incident more than 300 emails containing an average of three images and about 30 video clips were sent to the BBC and some clips were on air only 20 minutes after being received by rolling news channels (The Guardian, 2005). Similarly, Scotland Yard, after an appeal for public help, received more than 250 emails containing footage and photos of the devastation underground (The Guardian, 2005).

Images captured by civilians have become a definitive part of event construction and news-making in the digital age. In view of this news organizations are exploring new ways in which they can incorporate people's ability to capture and create content on the move. The practice of 'crowd sourcing' is quickly becoming part of the political economy of news-making. For example, Reuters is reportedly working on a tool to monitor the microblogging service Twitter for mentions of newsworthy keywords whilst Associated Press has agreed to buy content from user-generated site www.nowpublic.com (The Guardian, 2009).

The ability of civilians to capture images at unexpected moments when the media is not available has brought forth an important social force to post-modernity where watching could both be pervasive and unexpected. Beyond CCTV footage, the civilian body embedded with recording equipment such as mobile phones can capture events and this narrates post-modernity as having the capacity to gaze and capture non-stop. Humanity's need

to partake in events by capturing images and by sharing them with friends and strangers has often been unproblematically categorised as a form of citizen journalism. This categorisation is seen as a form of empowerment where citizens can publish their own content and conjoin it with institutional media. Whilst these civilian contributions can provide new vantage points when events happen and can equally hold those in power accountable or challenge the official account of events, they can also simply satisfy the human need to partake in national or tragic events or to form communion with wider humanity. Nevertheless, the categorisation of civilian participation through the act of capturing images has made the act of event capture a phenomenon that cannot be completed. Unseen footages can emerge to thwart official narration of events and in the process question the validity of these official accounts. During the 2009 protests against the G20 summit held in London, where bystander Ian Tomlinson died shortly after being pushed to the ground by a policeman, the police force was perceived to be heavy-handed in its treatment of protestors, and in the subsequent controversy the emergence of video footage taken by civilians cast new doubts on the sequence of events. The Ian Tomlinson incident showed that the act of gazing at an event is often incomplete. New images and vantage points often thwart our ability to construct coherent narratives. As the video evidence mounts in this case the act of watching becomes an open-ended phenomenon and is malleable to an almost infinite array of constructions.

Camera phones are seen to have changed the ways in which news is reported, with civilians being co-opted into creating content and widening news coverage through their gaze. Camera phones and their potential for image creation have also created new forms of social capital where images are exchanged to maintain relationships and to share experiences with friends and wider society. They lead to new forms of visibilities where anything from everyday mundane activities to the unusual can be posted on a public platform like the internet, inviting both the gaze of the known and unknown. Whilst the act of capturing events and uploading them and publishing them on personal websites or media websites has been associated with citizen journalism leading to the rise of the consumer-producer and discourses of empowerment, there are concerns that mobile recording features in mobile telephones can transgress privacy, create new forms of deviance and be disruptive for authorities trying to maintain law and order in many countries.

CONSTRUCTION OF DEVIANCE AND IMAGE CAPTURE

With the proliferation of camera phones there have been concerns about new forms of deviance that have emerged through the embedding of this technology in people's everyday lives. Various governments are exploring new ways to curb and control behaviour that is deemed as predatory or can potentially cause harm or offence to the wider public. The different types of regulations governing the use of camera phones reflect the different range of concerns that have emerged. In many places such as health clubs, leisure centres and swimming pools camera phones are banned due to the fear that they will encourage voyeurism and sexually deviant behaviour. Similarly, camera phones are off-limits in bathhouses in Japan, a country where these devices are fast replacing standard cameras. The construction of camera phone use as deviant is emerging through certain resonant strands: the transgression of privacy; the outrage to modesty; their use in spaces or places where they are perceived as obstructing law and order or breaking protocols and values associated with a space; and where they are seen as breaking the moral or societal norms of a society. Photography in public spaces and of iconic landmarks in a post-9/11 world is also increasingly associated with terrorism and often an innocent act of cap-

ture may be prohibited on the grounds of national security. Also, the construction of mobile phone use as deviance is intimately allied to the economy of distribution, publication and accessibility. The potential of private images to transcend into the public platforms of the internet to facilitate a wider or potentially global audience raises various legal and ethical dimensions in this architecture of gaze as images can be taken out of context and viewed without an understanding of the image or its origins. This portends the emergence of new forms of vulnerabilities and voyeurism where the capture may not be limited to holding those in power accountable but may extend to removing boundaries between private and public, resulting in a process that makes anything and everything visible with those responsible being only dimly aware of the profound consequences.

The consumption of pornography and violent images often invoke moral dilemmas in society. The infamous images of torture which emerged from Abu Ghraib were a case in point and these created a moral backlash against America. America on its part feared that it would incite further violence against its soldiers. In the case of Abu Ghraib whilst the images were made legally available through court ruling in 2004, further images have been leaked to news stations and websites through confidential sources. Thus news agencies and websites functioned to publicise the unseen aspects of the torture when extra images emerged in 2006 (USA Today, 2006). In 2009, US President Barack Obama blocked the release of up to 2,000 images of alleged abuse at American prisons in Iraq and Afghanistan fearing this might inflame anti-American sentiments (Spillius, 2009).

In 2005 another scandal broke when it emerged that American GIs were sending pictures of dead Iraqis to a website called NowThatsFuckedUp.com in exchange for naked pictures of other people's girlfriends (Brown, 2005; Harkin, 2006). These 'trophy photos', though not a consequence of new technology, are able to enter new exchange economies by means of digital cameras and the internet (Hartman, 2005). With sites such as MySpace and YouTube becoming a repository for gruesome images of war shot by American soldiers in Iraq and Afghanistan, these images can be made available to the wider public for consumption. Additionally, specialist sites such as Ogrish use sophisticated programmes to monitor Jihadi websites to provide their customers with a vast archive of images of death and dismemberment. Ogrish claims to receive between 125,000 and 200,000 unique hits on its website and on a major news day it can rise to 250,000 (Harkin, 2006). In response the American army has been demanding that its soldiers stop posting video clips on the web. However, before the issue several soldiers had already been demoted or fined for posting the images on their blogs and commanders in Iraq also issued rules on what can be posted on soldiers' blogs (Hartman, 2005). Whilst these rules addressed only soldier owned and maintained websites and were purely concerned with security issues the rules did not cover matters of prurience. Hartman 2005 points out that such acts would be covered under a US military law which prohibits conduct 'unbecoming an officer and gentleman' and secondly it would also be a contravention of the Geneva Convention which upholds the respect for the remains of those who have died as a result of hostilities. Whilst trophy pictures of war are not a new phenomenon in themselves a digital economy makes it possible to access, disseminate and consume on demand with a mouse click the gory and the salacious as entertainment whilst enabling a global spectacle into distant spaces well marked off from the rest of humanity as in the case of Abu Ghraib. This image economy is then double-edged where the visibility can raise awareness of the abuse while fuelling prurient behaviour.

Another behaviour that has caused concerns the world over is the phenomenon of 'upskirting' and 'downblousing' where photographs are taken, often on a mobile-phone camera, of an unsuspecting woman's thighs or cleavage. Different countries have responded to this phenomenon by either invoking existing laws to cover this behaviour or enacting new ones which would specifically address it. In the UK, if the person photographed is in a place where there is reasonable expectation of privacy then the behaviour can be charged under the Sexual Offences Act 2003 and a person convicted under this act may be placed on the Sex Offenders Register (Saner, 2009) or it could also be dealt with under the offence of 'outraging public decency'. In contrast, the state of Oklahoma enacted two new laws to deal with this behaviour. The state took a decision to change its laws in 2007 to make it illegal for anyone to photograph another person without their consent for 'prurient, lewd or lascivious purposes'. In Japan, where upskirting is considered to be rife, authorities have imposed a rule that all mobile phones, when used to take still or video footage, make a sound which cannot be turned off. Like Japan, the US is considering forcing manufacturers to produce camera phones that issue audible warnings each time an image is captured with the Camera Phone Predator Alert Act proposed in Jan 2009. Many parts of Australia forbid upskirt and downblouse photography and the Victoria Law Commission introduced the Upskirting laws in 2007 which cover both photographing as well as distributing such images. Similarly, Germany passed a law in 2004 which prohibits the photographing of persons in their apartments or other protected areas (such as changing rooms) and publication and distribution of such photographs on the internet (Privacy International, 2007, p. 3).

This phenomenon of capturing people's body parts without their consent has also created a whole distribution economy where new sites have been created to make available these images. Pornographic moblog (mobile blogging) websites have sprouted on the internet where photographs are used without people's knowledge. This trading, exchange and publication makes the public vulnerable to being captured, commodified and traded without their knowledge or consent.

In 2004 a Sydney resident was fined 500 Australian dollars for using his mobile phone to take photos of topless women sunbathing at Coogee Beach. The incident set off wider debates about whether mobile phone advertisements were inadvertently promoting voyeurism in their marketing campaigns and this raised calls for governments and courts to promote responsible mobile phone use (See Abood, 2004). In July 2004 the Australian Computer Society released its policy on mobile camera phones including a recommendation for the development of responsible guidelines by manufacturers, retailers and promoters of this technology to be distributed with all phone cameras sold and to accompany advertising (Abood, 2004). Victoria and Western Australia now have surveillance devices legislation that restricts how photographs of private activity may be taken or used. These states are extending their listening devices legislation to cover surveillance devices. A main aspect of the Victorian legislation limits a person's ability to 'knowingly communicate or publish a record or report of a private conversation or private activity that has been made as a direct or indirect result of the use of a device' (McLeod, 2003). This means that whilst private activity may be recorded by one of the parties the recording nevertheless cannot be published without the consent of all parties. In March 2003 the Italian information commissioner, the watchdog that oversees the ways in which companies and individuals use data they collect about other people, issued regulations concerning what people can and can't do with mobile phones. The rules allow images of people to be snapped for personal use but require that images be kept safe and users are legally obliged to tell people if the image they have taken of them will appear online (BBC News, 2003). The Italian watchdog is concerned that users will abuse the ease with which snaps can be taken with phones.

In the United States some states have adopted statutes prohibiting the use of video surveillance for voyeuristic purposes and to this end anti-video voyeurism legislation was passed by the US Congress in 2004. The Video Voyeurism Prevention Act prohibits knowingly videotaping, photographing, filming or recording by any means or by broadcasting an image of a private area of a person without that individual's consent, under circumstances in which the person has a reasonable expectation of privacy (Privacy International, 2007, p. 2). The act prohibits photographing and videotaping a naked person without his or her consent in any place where there can be a 'reasonable expectation of privacy' and punishment can include fines of up to $100,000 or up to a year in prison or both (Sullivan, 2004). The act was initially introduced in 2000 before the appearance of camera phones in the US and the original enactment focused mainly on privacy infringements using hidden video cameras. Unlike Washington and Louisiana, other states' criminal codes still do not protect a person's privacy while they are in public places. State laws are primarily geared toward prosecuting 'peeping toms' who spy on people in their homes rather than in public places. Before the Video Voyeurism Prevention Act, previous laws did not prohibit activities like taking a picture of up a woman's skirt when the woman was in a public place (Sullivan, 2004).

Ethical and moral questions were also raised when crowds at the Vatican used their camera phones to photograph Pope John Paul II's body during his lying in state ceremony. The photographing or filming of a dead pope is a sensitive issue after Pius XII's personal doctor, Riccardo Galeazzi-Lisi, sold sensationalistic photographs of the dying and dead Pope to the media in 1958 (Winterman, 2005). Although taking pictures or filming a dying pope is banned, taking pictures of a pope after death may be allowed if the Vatican deems that is not improper or contradictory to its sacred rites. When Pope John Paul was lying in state the public was not disallowed from taking pictures as the pontiff's body was prepared and dressed investments (Winterman, 2005). From religious and theological perspectives, the capture of certain images can be deemed as deviance or transgressing sacred taboos. In other instances, the need to govern photography has also been dictated by rules imposed within certain spaces such as courts. In the UK, 19-year-old Shaun Nash was sentenced to 6 months for using his mobile to take photographs during a friend's court trial, forcing the trial to be aborted as there is a general ruling that mobile phones cannot be used in court. In America photography in public places is protected under the First Amendment. However recent cases show that rules are unknown or misapplied leading to photojournalists and amateur cameramen being harassed or handcuffed for taking pictures in security-sensitive mass transit hubs such as train stations (Rushmann, 2009).

According to the Pentagon Force Protection Agency in the US Federal regulations ban photography on the entire 280 acres of the Pentagon Reservation, including the Pentagon building and the Metro station. However, the ban is 'just a deterrent if something was to happen' (cf., Rushmann, 2009). With the World Trade Centre attacks in 2001, photography of public places and particularly iconic landmarks is viewed with much suspicion. According to Chris Dunn, associate legal director for the New York Civil Liberties Union, 'no law prohibits photography in subway stations unless special equipment like extra lighting is used and that there is widespread belief that cameras are 'suspicious and unlawful'' (cf., Rushmann, 2009).

In South Korea, where there were 3 million camera phones in use in 2003 (Associated Press, 2003), camera phones enable the highlighting and construction of social deviance. Here the connection to the act of capturing and the ability to invite public gaze and censure through the internet and particularly through blogging sites is a significant feature. When a young woman refused to clean up the excrement of her pet dog in the subway despite requests from fellow travellers it led to her public censure. A witness took photos of the incident and posted it on a popular website. Net users became interested in the story, clamoured for more information on the woman, and nicknamed her the 'dog poop girl'. The incident then became national news in South Korea (Krim, 2005). The subsequent public pressure and intrusion into the girl's private life was seen as justifiable and a means of holding her to account for her socially unacceptable behaviour.

In some countries the camera phone has been perceived as catalyst in eroding strict moral codes between men and women. In Jakarta, some religious leaders have blamed mobile phones for facilitating illicit relationships and sexual deviance. According to 2004 research carried out at the Widya Mandala Catholic University in Surabaya in Indonesia, 25 percent of teenagers had exchanged pornographic images via Multimedia Messages Services (MMS) (Naommy, 2004). In Saudi Arabia a ban was imposed on camera phones in 2002 on the basis that the phones were a challenge to the social rules which women have to abide by. There were fears that women's pictures could be taken without their knowledge and published on the Internet (Lettice, 2004). Saudi Arabia's Grand Mufti, Sheikh Abdul Aziz al-Sheikh, had ruled in September 2004 that camera phones are not acceptable as 'some of the girls have had their photos taken by the mobile cameras, and that such practices have led to extreme moral damage to the modesty and chastity of the girls that were involved' (cf., Lettice, 2004). The remark by the Mufti is thought to be prompted by a public outcry to the circulation of a video of rape captured on a camera phone in July 2004. The ban was eventually lifted by the authorities in late 2004 however the ban did not discourage the public from acquiring these phones illegally, highlighting their popularity. Strict societal norms and moral codes are also prompting other communities to ban the use of camera phones by their community members. The ultra-Orthodox Jewish or Haredi communities in Jerusalem are requiring their members to use 'Kosher' mobile phones which cannot receive or send text messages, browse the internet or take photographs as these activities are considered 'immodest' amongst Haredis. As in Saudi Arabia, all photos of women are forbidden (Chernofsky, 2008)

Beyond what is considered sexual deviance, camera phones are also associated with industrial espionage, and some companies in Asia have restricted the use of camera phones at key factories and research centres (Noammy, 2004). In South Korea, for example, Samsung Electronics has banned camera phones in its semiconductor and research facilities (Associated Press, 2003). Other trades and industries are also wary of camera phones eating into their profits. In Japan, bookstores are vigilant about consumers photographing magazines and journals without purchasing them. Japan's magazine publishers association is mailing out 34,000 posters to bookstores asking patrons not to use camera phones to shoot pages from periodicals, although it is not a copyright violation to take pictures for private consumption (Associated Press, 2003). Similarly, schools and education institutions are banning camera phones in many parts of the world as they fear that students may use them to photograph tests and cheat in examinations.

In France the notion of citizen journalism has been restricted with the French Constitutional Council approving a law that criminalizes the filming or broadcasting of acts of violence by people other than professional journalists. The law could lead to the imprisonment of eyewitnesses who film acts of violence, and anyone publishing such images, e.g. on a website, faces up to five years in prison and a fine of 75,000 euros (Sayer, 2007). According to the authorities the main objective behind the legislation is to target the practice of 'happy slapping' in which a violent attack is filmed by an accomplice typically with a camera phone for the amusement of the attacker's friends. Critics of the law feel it will discourage

people from filming police violence and will lead to difficulties in interpreting the law. According to Reporters without Borders (RSF), it imposes a deliberate distinction between professional journalists and citizens even though the public has a longer history of highlighting human rights abuses than the press (Sage, 2007).

On 16 February in the UK, section 76 of the Counter-Terrorism Act 2008 came into effect and allows for the arrest, fining and imprisonment for up to 10 years of anyone who takes pictures of police officers. Whilst the act does not explicitly mention photography, its anti-terrorism adverts and its emphasis that 'it's illegal to gather or publish information about police or armed forces that is likely to be useful' for terrorist activity indirectly casts photography as a negative or deviant activity. In Singapore, the government introduced a Public Order Act in March 2009 which gives police additional powers to deal with public order offences but more importantly it provides an extra clause on filming where the police can prohibit the public from filming, communicating or exhibiting films of activities which are deemed illegal or detrimental to law and order (Ramesh, 2009).

The perceived need to impose standards on images has led to the regulation of the capture and dissemination of images. The European Commission (EC) is considering means to make websites and mobile phone services that feature video images to conform to minimum standards on areas such as advertising, hate speech and the protection of children (Sherwin, 2006). The rules proposed under the Television without Frontiers directive seeks to extend the definition of broadcasting to cover services such as video-on-demand or mobile phone clips. There is increasing unease over the proposal as critics point out that such extenuating standards should not be imposed on amateur videos or images created by consumers and that criminal law in member states is sufficient to deal with material that might incite hate or cause harm to children. The issue of what constitutes online broadcasting becomes crucial in enacting new regulations. Presently in the UK, the government's definition of broadcasting covers feature films, sports events, situation comedies, documentaries, children's programmes and original drama but excludes personal websites and sites where people upload and exchange video images. The proposal mooted by the EC is also opposed by Ofcom, the UK's independent regulator of communications industries, which feels that the proposed directive could stifle new multimedia businesses in Europe.

Other regulations such as the enactment of national norms and the imposition of cultural codes are also regulating the image economy. A case in point is China's censorship of the Internet and video portal sites within this platform. Freedom House, a US-based think tank conducting research on democracy and political freedom, has expressed concern over China's further restrictions in April 2009 to increase censorship in video-sharing websites (Freedom House, 2009). The regulations were issued after China's blocking of the video-sharing website YouTube after the site released a video that allegedly showed Tibetans being beaten by Chinese forces. The regulations issued by the State Administration of Radio, Film and TV include a ban on videos and shows which depict torture or distort Chinese culture or history. Videos that 'hurt the feelings of the public' or 'disparage' security forces are also banned. In particular the regulation addresses 'netizen reporters' who in the past have revealed to the Chinese public incidents of police brutality, the melamine scandal, and issues of corruption surrounding the aftermath of the 2008 Sichuan earthquake. Additionally, the Chinese government since 2007 has required that all domestic video-sharing websites to be state-owned except for prominent pre-existing sites and reportedly closed these in 2008 to conduct 'self-inspection'. During national or sensitive events (e.g., the Beijing Olympics or protests in Tibet) the authorities have also been known to block international sites.

ETHICAL CONCERNS AND THE IMAGE ECONOMY

The need to enact new rules, laws and legislation to regulate the use of mobile recording devices in various societies and countries reveals the nature of ethical concerns in indigenous societies. In appropriating technologies and embedding them into our everyday lives societies go through a process of negotiation of what is acceptable or unacceptable to a community. Different communities can enact different rules to safeguard and protect their norms and values. In these processes of negotiation, new laws will have to balance existing safeguards on privacy and human freedoms whilst addressing the social and ethical concerns of surveillance, data mining, and child pornography amongst others. Existing social and political ideologies, relationships, and norms along with secular and religious ideals will continue to mediate the image economy. Many of the ethical concerns raised by mobile recording devices cannot be fully addressed by legislation and members of a community may agree consensually on appropriate methods to curb their use and the dissemination of images taken by such devices.

In societies, whether liberal or conservative, the enactment of new rules and regulations have tended to reflect the ethical concerns of the immediate physical context and how these are maintained or eroded by the existing power relationships. The different forms of legislation and discourses also reflect the unexpected range of phenomena that have emerged. The ongoing struggle with the unexpected becomes a dominant aspect of the image economy where consequences may not be immediate but imminently dilemmatic for societies. Whist the physical spaces will be governed through territorially bounded legislation it will remain challenging to comprehend new phenomena or practices that can evolve on virtual platforms and impact on offline societies.

The saturation of images in our mediated world becomes a double-edged sword where images can provide both a form of human connection as well as become tools of exploitation where boundaries of human privacy and decency can be constantly eroded through the act of capture and gaze. The way in which we divulge information on social networks and publish images on public domains constructs us as 'complicit risk communities' (Ibrahim, 2009) where publishing and divulging private details constitute both a form of social capital in building networks as well as risk that can create an environment where various fraudulent activities can take place. The ethical dimension of self-exposure is then dialectical, invoking a post-risk society scenario where risk is embraced as a necessary element in constructing identities and forming human communion. The image economy can reconfigure the private act of sharing between two people when it is hosted on a global platform such as the internet where a multitude of processes can co-exist, giving rise to new forms of gaze. The disembedding of images from the context of origin and their uploading on public platforms often reduce them to content repositories flattening significant moments of history and assembling them among private and amateur home videos. Images of suffering, war and strife become interspersed with offerings of popular culture making consumption an ethically problematic process in post-modernity.

CONCLUSION

The image economy that has emerged with new recording and capturing facilities on mobile phones has increasingly raised new forms of visibility into both everyday events and those played out on the national media. The new vantage points created by mobile telephony have provided new opportunities and vulnerabilities as well as new forms of empowerment and deviance. This paper argues that this new image economy in many ways conjoins with the mechanisms of the surveillance society and in the process presents new ways of looking and gazing and disseminating still and moving images to a wider audience via SMS and the Internet. The categorisation of this mode of capture as 'civilian journalism' often reduces the complex social phenomenon that prompts people to capture, share and archive images. The need for communion during catastrophic events and equally the potential to capture both the everyday and the extraordinary creates a ubiquitous civilian eye that is recording events when one least expects it and which in the process can moot challenges to official narratives of events or augment the media eye when important events occur. This civilian gaze makes the notion of an event incomplete as new images can re-narrate events and scramble the coherence of previous narratives. The unexpected challenges it moots to entrenched sources of power in society in challenging and documenting abuse, on the one hand, and the rise of new forms of deviance on the other has prompted many societies to control this architecture of gaze. This paper outlined new types of regulations and norms which seek to regulate this image economy. While these rules and norms are still evolving the ubiquitous capture and dissemination of images will pose more challenges and will continue to mediate the notion of a surveillance society where watching will happen both by those in power but also by mobile bodies in an un-coordinated and disorganised manner, creating unexpected consequences.

REFERENCES

Black, J. (Ed.). (1997). *Mixed News: The Public/Civic/Communitarian Journalism Debate*. Mahwah, NJ: Lawrence Erlbaum.

Bristow, J. (2005, July 12). Moving Images. *Spiked*. Retrieved June 15, 2009, from http://www.spiked-onlein.com/index.php?site/article/865/

Brown, A. (2008, September 28) The New Pornography of War. *The Guardian.* Retrieved December 12, 2009, from http://www.guardian.co.uk/world/2005/sep/28/afghanistan.comment

Camera Phones Incite Bad Behaviour. (2003, September 7). *Associated Press.* Retrieved June 19, 2009, from http://www.wired.com/print/culture/lifestyle/news/2003/07/59582

Chernofsky, E. (2008, October 16). Is that Cellphone Kosher? *BBC News.* Retrieved July 6, 2009, from http://newsbbc.co.uk/go/pr/fr/-/1/hi/world/middle_east/7636021.stm

Crowdsourcing. (2009, July 12). *The Guardian.* Retrieved July 13, 2009, from http://www.guardian.co.uk/technology/crowdsourcing

Deleuze, G., & Guattari, F. (1987). *A Thousand Plateaus.* Minneapolis, MN: University of Minnesota.

Forsberg, B. (2005, May 23). *Restrictions placed on Camera Phones, More Places say they may violate Privacy, Security.* San Francisco, CA: SFGate. Retrieved July 19, 2009, from http://www.sfgate.com/cgi-bin/article.cgi?f=/c/a/2005/05/23/BUG7KCSLRE1.DTL

Freedom House Dismayed by new regulations, increasing censorship on video-sharing websites. (2009, April 2). Washington, DC: Freedom House. Retrieved July 15, 2009, from http://www.ifex.org/china/2009/04/03/freedom_house_dismayed_by_new_regulations/

Friedland, L. (2003). *Public Journalism: Past and Future.* Dayton, Ohio: Kettering Foundation Press.

Furtive Phone Photography Spurs Ban. (2003, April 4). *BBC News.* Retrieved June 19, 2009 from http://newsvotebbc.co.uk/mapps/pagetools/print/news.bbc.co.uk/1/hi/technology/2916353.stm

Gandy, O. (1998). Coming to Terms with the Panoptic Sort. In Lyon, D., & Zureik, E. (Eds.), *Computers, Surveillance and Privacy.* Minneapolis, MN: Minnesota University Press.

Haas, T. (2007). *The Pursuit of Public Journalism: Theory, Practice and Criticism.* New York: Routledge.

Hartman, B. (2005, September 28). Did Troops Trade Photos of War Dead for Porn? *ABC News.* Retrieved July 13, 2009, from http://abcnews.go.com/Technology/IraqCoverage/story?id=1166772&page=1

Ibrahim, Y. (2009). The New Risk Communities: Social Networking Sites and Risk. *International Journal of Media and Cultural Politics, 4*(2), 245–253. doi:10.1386/macp.4.2.245_3

InfoTrends/CAP Ventures Releases Worldwide Mobile Imaging Study Results. Study Projects Nearly 900 Million Camera Phone Shipments Worldwide by 2009. (2005, January 10). *Business Wire.* Retrieved July 3, 2009, from http://www.businesswire.com/portal/site/google/index.jsp?ndmViewId=news_view&newsId=20050110005831&newsLang=en

Kelley, B. (2007). Criminalisation: Applying a Living Standard Analysis to Non-Consensual Photography and Distribution. *QUT Law and Justice Journal, 2*(7), 464–476.

Kindberg, T., Spasojevic, M., Fleck, R., & Sellen, A. (2005, April 2-7). *I Saw This and Thought of You: Some Social Uses of Camera Phones.* Paper Presented at CHI '05, Portland, OR.

Klein, A. (2008, February 11). Police Go Live Monitoring D.C. Crime Cameras. *The Washington Post.* Retrieved July 1, 2009, from http://www.washingtonpost.com/wp-dyn/content/article/2008/02/10/AR2008021002726_pf.html

Krim, J. (2007, July 7). Subway Fracas Escalates Into Test of the Internet's Power to Shame. *The Washington Post*. Retrieved July 2, 2009, from http://www.washingtonpost.com/wpdyn/content/article/2005/07/06/AR2005070601953.html?referrer=emailarticle

Latest Abu Ghraib Pictures Threaten to Inflame Anger in Iraq. (2006, February 16) *USA Today*. Retrieved July 12, 2009, from http://www.usatoday.com/news/world/iraq/2006-02-16-prison-abuse_x.htm

Lettice, R. (2004, November 10). Saudi ministers urge removal of camera phone ban. *The Register*. Retrieved July 5, 2009, from http://www.theregister.co.uk/2004/11/10/saudi_camera_phone_ban/

Luppicini, R. (2009). Technoethical Inquiry: From Technological Systems to Society. *Global Media Journal - Canadian Edition, 2*(1), 5-21.

Lyon, D. (2001, November 21). *Terrorism and Surveillance, Security, Freedom and Justice After September 11 2001*. Retrieved July 16, 2004, from http://privacy.openflows.org/lyon_paper.html

McLeod, C. (2003, August). Sneaky Cameras. *Press Council News, 15*(3). Retrieved June 19, 2009, from http://www.presscouncil.org.au/pesite/apcnews/aug03/cameras.html

Monahan, T. (2006). Counter-Surveillance as Political Intervention. *Social Semiotics, 16*(4), 515–624. doi:10.1080/10350330601019769

Noammy, P. C. (2004, March 2). Cameraphones and Worries Over Possible Misuse. *The Jakarta Post*. Retrieved July 3, 2009, from http://www.thejakartapost.com/print/108533

Okabe, D. (2004). *Emergent Social Practices, Situations and Relations through Everyday Camera Phone Use*. Paper Presented at the International Conference on Mobile Communication, Seoul, Korea.

Ramesh, S. (2009, March 23) Public Order Act Introduced to Examine New Realities in Managing Security. *Channel NewsAsia*. Retrieved December 12, 2009, from http://www.channelnewsasia.com/stories/singaporelocalnews/view/417146/1/.html

Resnik, D. B. (2007). *What is Ethics in Research & Why is It Important?* Retrieved December 29, 2009, from http://www.niehs.nih.gov/research/resources/bioethics/whatis.cfm

Rushmann, A. (2009). Photographers Tangle with Vague Rules in Transit Hubs. *The New Media & the Law, 33*(2), 34. Retrieved July 16, 2009, from http://www.rcfp.org/news/mag/33-2/photographers_tangle_with_vague_rules_in_transithubs

Sage, A. (2009, March 3). Happy Slapping Film Ban Will Gag Citizen Journalists. *The Times*. Retrieved July 5, 2009, from http://www.mail-archive.com/sustainablelorgbiofuel@sustainablelists.org/msg69077.html

Saner, E. (2009, February 25). I Felt Completely Violated. *The Guardian*. Retrieved June 16, 2009, from http://www.guardian.co.uk/lifestyle/2009/feb/25/women-upskirting/print

Sayer, P. (2006, June 3). France Bans Citizen Journalists from Reporting Violence. *Infoworld.com*. Retrieved June 15, 2009, from http://www.infoworld.com/print/27840

Sherwin, A. (2006, October 17). Amateur Blogger 'Video Bloggers' Under Threat From EU Broadcast Rules. *The Times*. Retrieved July 15, 2009, from http://www.timesonline.co.uk/tol/news/world/europe/article603123.ece?print=yes&ra

Sherwood, J. (2009, January 28). US Considers Audible Warnings for Cameraphones 'Attention! Possible Voyeur Taking Pictures!' *The Register*. Retrieved July 6, 2009, from http://www.rehardware.co.uk/2009/01/28/cameraphone_alert_bill/print.html

Spillius, A. (2009, May 14). Barack Obama Attempts to Block Alleged Torture Photos. *The Daily Telegraph*. Retrieved July 13, 2009, from http://www.telegraph.co.uk/news/worldnews/northamerica/usa/barackobama/5320559/Barack-Obama-attempts-to-block-alleged-torture-photos.html

Stalder, F. (2002, September). Privacy is not the Antidote to Surveillance, *Surveillance & Society*, *1*(1), 120–124. Retrieved April 16, 2007 from http://felix.openflows.com/html/priv_surv.html.

Stelmaszewska, H., Fields, B., & Blandford, A. (2006). Camera Phone Use in Social Context. In *Proceedings of HCI 2006* (Vol. 2).

Sullivan, M. (2004, July 23). Law May Curb Cell Phone Camera Use. *PC World*. Retrieved June 19, 2009, from http://www.pcworld.com/printable/article/id,117035/printable.html

Taylor, C. (2007, July 2). 1/3 of world population to have camera phones by 2011, firm says. *Electronic News*. Retrieved July 3, 2009, from http://www.allbusiness.com/electronics/computer-electronics/6365632-1.html

Victorian Law Reform Commission Investigates Surveillance Cameras. (2009, March 30). *Herald Sun*. Retrieved June 19, 2009, from http://www.news.com.au/heraldsun/story/0,21985,25265948-661,000.html

Video Surveillance. (2007, December 18). *Privacy International*. Retrieved June 15, 2009, from http://www.privacyinternational.org/article.shtml?cmd%5B347%5D=x-347-559088

Winterman, D. (2005, April 7). Snapping the Dead Pope on a Camera Phone. *BBC News*. Retrieved July 2, 2009, from http://news.bbc.co.uk/1/hi/magazine/4415947.stm

Wood, D., & Ball, K. (Eds.). (2006, September). A Report on the Surveillance Society. London: Surveillance Studies Network.

This work was previously published in International Journal of Technoethics, Volume 1, Issue 3, edited by Rocci Luppicini, pp. 49-63, copyright 2010 by IGI Publishing (an imprint of IGI Global).

Chapter 8

Peer-to-Peer File-Sharing:
Psychological Reactance and the Theory of Planned Behaviour

Peter J. Allen
Curtin University, Australia

Katherine L. Shepherd
Curtin University, Australia

Lynne D. Roberts
Curtin University, Australia

ABSTRACT

Despite persistent government and industry efforts to stop the sharing and downloading of media such as files over peer-to-peer (P2P) networks, this activity shows no sign of abating. This research investigated whether psychological reactance could account for variance in the intent to engage in, and the extent of such behaviour beyond that accounted for by the standard Theory of Planned Behaviour (TPB) variables. No support for psychological reactance as a predictor of P2P file downloading intent or behaviour was found in this paper. However, the results did indicate that attitude, subjective norms, and perceived behavioural control each accounted for significant variance in P2P file downloading behaviour, and that these relationships were fully mediated by behavioural intent. These findings are consistent with, and provide strong support for, the use of the TPB within this domain.

INTRODUCTION

The downloading and sharing of copyright protected entertainment media (e.g., music files and motion pictures) and software over peer-to-peer (P2P) networks is widely practised, illegal, and

arguably unethical. Despite its clear illegality, and persistent industry efforts to curb its prevalence (Alexander, 2002; Allen, 2008), public attitudes towards the ethics of copyright infringing behaviour on P2P networks vary widely. Altschuller and Benbunan-Fich (2009) liken public attitudes to illegal downloading to reactions to the prohibition of alcohol in the US in the 1920s, arguing that

DOI: 10.4018/978-1-4666-1773-5.ch008

"society seems to be repelling its own behavioral guidelines" (p. 49), with a growing disconnect between perceptions of the illegality of the behaviour and ethical beliefs about, and engagement in, the behaviour. Presented with a scenario on illegal downloading to discuss, approximately half of the students in Altschuller and Benbunan-Fich's research felt such downloading was wrong, yet the majority condoned the behaviour. A commonly expressed view amongst students who download is that illegal downloading is a harmless act that does not negatively impact on musicians or the music industry (Levin, Dato-on, & Rhee, 2004; Tappan, 2006). Even when illegal downloading is perceived to be 'wrong', individuals may still engage in it (Tappan, 2006), with only a weak relationship found between the perceived ethics of illegal downloading and intention to download (Lysonsky & Durvusula, 2008). This ambivalence is also echoed in the range of views held by workers in the entertainment industries. For example, Madden (2004) conducted a survey of 2,793 musicians, songwriters and music publishers, reporting that approximately a quarter stated that file-sharing was bad for artists due to breach of copyright, approximately a third that file-sharing was not bad for artists as it helped promote and distribute their work, and a further third agreeing with both points of view. Only one in twenty reported that illegal downloading had hurt (and not helped) their careers.

How can we make sense of this disconnect between perceptions of the legality and ethics of P2P file-sharing, and its practise? The field of technoethics provides a focus on the ethical considerations associated with technological change (Lupiccini, 2009) and provides an appropriate lens through which to view online copyright infringing behaviour. A key question within technoethics is how to "deal with Internet abuse and misuse such as piracy" (Lupiccini, 2009, p. 9). This question is central to this paper, which is focused on predictors of P2P file-sharing behaviour. In this article we begin by providing an overview of the extent of

P2P file-sharing, and current efforts to curb this behaviour. The concept of psychological reactance is then introduced as a possible explanation for the ineffectiveness of government and industry efforts to stop the sharing and downloading of copyrighted content over P2P networks. The results of our study testing whether psychological reactance is a useful predictor of P2P file-sharing (beyond already established predictors) are presented, and the implications of the findings discussed.

BACKGROUND

Internet penetration has increased rapidly over the last decade, with recent Pew Internet and American Life data indicating that almost three quarters of American adults regularly access the internet from home (Horrigan, 2009). Of these, nearly 90% connect at broadband speeds. Data from the Australian Bureau of Statistics (2009), the UK Office for National Statistics (2009) and the OECD's Directorate for Science, Technology and Industry (2009) reveal that broadband Internet penetration levels are similarly high in Australia, the UK, and many other industrialised nations.

Commensurate with this increase in broadband penetration has been an increase in the popularity of P2P file-sharing. Indeed, the ability to download large files (e.g., music files) from P2P networks has been recognised as one of the key motivators behind Internet users' transitioning from dial-up to broadband connections (Hellweg, 2003; Mulligan, Card, Laszio, & Peach, 2003). During the first half of 2004, CacheLogic estimated that, at any given time, around 8 million people were connected to the four main file-sharing networks (A. Parker, 2004). By the end of 2004, as much as 60 percent of all Internet traffic was P2P, mainly on the BitTorrent and eDonkey networks (A. Parker, 2005; Thompson, 2005). Survey data collected by Entertainment Media Research (2007) and network traffic analyses by iPoque (Schulze & Mochalski, 2009) offer no reason to suggest that the popularity of P2P has declined in more recent years. Currently, BitTorrent is the most popular P2P protocol, and accounts for as much as 80% of all P2P traffic in some regions of the world (Schulze & Mochalski, 2009).

Although P2P technologies like BitTorrent are both "capable of substantial non-infringing uses"-(to quote Circuit Judge Thomas' written opinion for *MGM v. Grokster* in the United States Court of Appeals for the Ninth Circuit, 2004, 19 August, p. 11737), and are indeed used for many legal purposes (e.g., for Free Software distribution; sharing public-domain and Creative Commons licensed material etc.), they are primarily being used in ways that infringe on copyrights. In *MGM v. Grokster* the plaintiffs alleged that over 70 percent of the files exchanged through P2P networks infringe on their copyrights, and another 20 percent infringe on copyrights held by others. Circuit Judge Thomas did not dispute this claim. Neither did US Supreme Court Justice Souter who, in that Court's June 2005 opinion on *MGM v. Grokster*, wrote that "the vast majority of users' downloads [on the FastTrack and Gnutella P2P networks] are acts of infringement", and that "the probable scope of [this] copyright infringement is staggering" (p. 5). A recent independent sampling of content on the BitTorrent Mainline DHT (distributed hash tables) network suggested that up to 99% of it was copyright-infringing (Felten, 2010).

To reduce the extent of online copyright infringement and to stem losses that, according to some estimates, amount to billions of dollars annually (e.g., Castro, Bennett, & Andes, 2009; International Federation of the Phonographic Industry [IFPI], 2008; Siwek, 2007), members of the content publishing (e.g., music, film and software) industries have employed numerous deterrence-based strategies (Allen, 2008). These strategies, which have thus far met with limited success, have included court actions, the use of DRM (digital rights management) software and other 'anti-piracy' technologies, and educational campaigns aimed at dissuading people from engaging P2P file-sharing and other forms of digital copyright infringement.

d'Astous, Colbert, and Montpetit (2005) recently investigated the effectiveness of three arguments commonly used in campaigns developed to dissuade people from sharing music files online: "(1) stressing the negative personal consequences of pirating music, (2) stressing the negative consequences for the artists, and (3) stressing the unethical nature of this behavior" (p. 289). Their participants completed questionnaires, which were identical except for a portion of the introduction that served as their experimental manipulation. To emphasise the negative personal consequences of online music sharing, the introduction stressed that fines and legal prosecution were possible consequences of engaging in this behaviour. To stress negative consequences for artists, participants were informed that music piracy results in loss of income and job insecurity for artists. The claim that music piracy is unethical was emphasised in the final condition. Their control introduction made no reference to either the consequences or ethics of music piracy.

d'Astous and colleagues (2005) hypothesised that stressing the negative personal consequences and unethical nature of music piracy would influence participants' attitude toward this behaviour. They further predicted that stressing the negative consequences for the artists would influence subjective norms, and lessen participants' intent to engage in music piracy. These hypotheses were not supported, leading d'Astous and colleagues to argue that the persuasive nature of the 'anti-piracy' messages they presented to participants may have led to feelings of manipulation and, as a consequence, their rejection. They went on to suggest that such persuasion may be viewed as a threat to "attitudinal freedom" (p. 308), and that people may react to such threats by maintaining their current attitudes and behaviours. That is, they may disregard the anti-piracy messages, and continue their current P2P file downloading behaviour. Such a response can be understood in the context of psychological reactance theory.

PSYCHOLOGICAL REACTANCE

Psychological reactance theory rests on the notion of free behaviours: the set of behaviours that an individual has the "relevant physical and psychological abilities to engage in" (Brehm, 1966, p. 4), either now, or in the near future. When free behaviours are threatened, a sense of reactance is induced, and efforts are made to restore the threatened freedom (Brehm & Brehm, 1981).

Brehm and Brehm (1981) note four essential characteristics of behavioural freedoms: knowledge that the freedom exists; competence to exercise the freedom; the strength with which a freedom is held; and absolute versus conditional freedoms. Downloading files over P2P networks may be regarded as a free behaviour that meets the first three of these characteristics. Prior experience, the knowledge that many others also engage in the behaviour, and access to the required technology, mean millions of people worldwide "know" that they are able to download music, movies and software over P2P networks, and through experience have demonstrated the competence to do so. A belief widely held by Internet users is that what is available on the Internet is free to take (Beuscart, 2005). The more strongly a person believes this, the less likely they may be to relinquish this freedom. P2P file downloading may best be conceptualised as a conditional freedom, where engaging in the behaviour is conditional on the individual's ability to access P2P networks.

Once a freedom is established, it is open to threat or elimination. "Any force on the individual that makes it more difficult for him or her to exercise the freedom" (Brehm & Brehm, 1981, p. 30) is considered a threat. Commands, persuasive arguments and threats of punishment may all be perceived as threats. These social influence techniques are commonly used in efforts to prevent unauthorised file-sharing. It is therefore possible that these methods are not having the intended effect (i.e., stopping people from downloading), but rather, are eliciting a reactance response in people.

Reactance is the emotional state elicited in an individual when they believe that a free behaviour is threatened or blocked (Brehm & Brehm, 1981). Reactance has two direct effects. Usually, a person experiencing reactance will fight to restore the threatened/blocked free behaviour (Brehm, 1966). It may also magnify the appeal of the threatened/blocked free behaviour, increasing the individual's motivation to continue the behaviour. Originally conceived as being situation specific, psychological reactance is now considered to be a personality trait and, as such, can be applied to a wide range of everyday behaviours and measured as an individual differences variable (Hong & Faedda, 1996). That is, an individual who reacts strongly to the blocking of one free behaviour is likely to also react strongly to the blocking of other free behaviours.

Psychological reactance has been used to explain the ineffectiveness of persuasive messages, particularly those related to health behaviours (Dillard & Shen, 2005). For example, Bensley and Wu (1991) investigated the effects of low- and high-threat persuasive messages on levels of alcohol consumption in college students, and found that students receiving high-threats (messages recommending abstinence) indicated greater intent to consume alcohol than those receiving low-threats (messages recommending controlled drinking). To our knowledge, psychological reactance has not yet been considered in the context of 'anti-piracy' campaigns.

The Theory of Planned Behaviour

The Theory of Planned Behaviour (TPB) is the framework used in the current study to examine factors involved in downloading media over P2P networks. The TPB is an extension of Fishbein and Ajzen's (1975) Theory of Reasoned Action (TRA), which proposed that behaviour is best predicted by intent, which is - in turn - best predicted by a combination of attitude (or "the degree to which a person has a favorable or unfavorable evaluation or appraisal of the behavior in question") and subjective norms (or "the perceived social pressure to perform or not to perform the behavior"; Ajzen, 1991, p. 188).

The TPB builds on the TRA, and extends its predictive utility to behaviours that are not under complete volitional control, by including an additional variable, perceived behavioural control (PBC). PBC, defined as "peoples' perception of the ease or difficulty of performing the behaviour of interest" (Ajzen, 1991, p. 183), influences behaviour directly, and also indirectly through its influence on intent (Ajzen, 2002). This variable is particularly important when examining file-sharing over P2P networks. In order to perform this behaviour people must not only have attitude and subjective norms conducive to the behaviour, but also have the skills and resources required to successfully perform it (e.g., access to a computer and internet connection; the knowledge required to access P2P networks and find desired files etc.).

The TPB has been useful in predicting a wide range of intentions and actions, including speeding and other traffic offences (D. Parker, Manstead, Stradling, Reason, & Baxter, 1992; D. Parker, Stradling, & Manstead, 1996), substance use (Orbell, Blair, Sherlock, & Conner, 2001; Petraitis, Flay, & Miller, 1995), condom use and other safe sex behaviours (Fishbein et al., 2001; Jemmott, Jemmott, Fong, & McCaffree, 1999; Sutton, McVey, & Glanz, 1999), cancer screening attendance (Sheeran & Orbell, 2000), wildlife hunting (Hrubes & Ajzen, 2001), recycling (Tonglet, Phillips, & Read, 2004), public transport use (Bamberg, Ajzen, & Schmidt, 2003), and "dishonest" behaviours like shoplifting and cheating on exams (Beck & Ajzen, 1991; Tonglet, 2002). It has also been used in efforts to explain a range of computer-based and online behaviours, including searching for and purchasing goods over the internet (George, 2002; Shim, Eastlick, Lotz, & Warrington, 2001), illegal software downloading and sharing (aka. software piracy; Chang, 1998; Fukukawa, 2002; Lau, 2003; Limayem, Khalifa, & Chin, 1999; Lin, Hsu, Kuo, & Sun, 1999; Loch & Conger, 1996; Peace, Galletta, & Thong, 2003; Seale, Polakowski, & Schneider, 1998), and online file-sharing (Kwong & Lee, 2002; LaRose, Lai, Lange, Love, & Wu, 2005).

One of the strengths of the TPB is that "other relevant theoretical variables" (d'Astous et al. 2005, p. 293) can be added to the model, with the aim of increasing its overall predictive utility. Recent research has applied the TPB to the behaviour of downloading music from the Internet, and has investigated the effect of adding additional variables to the model.

Using the TPB to investigate online music piracy in a student sample, d'Astous and colleagues (2005) found that 47% of the variance in behavioural intent was accounted for using attitude, subjective norms and PBC. They then added a further three variables to the model: past behaviour; personal consequences (perceived negative personal consequences that may arise from online music sharing); and, ethical predispositions. They found significant positive relationships between past behaviour and behavioural intent, and significant negative relationships between attitude, and both personal consequences and ethical predispositions. This extended model explained 62% of variance in behavioural intent. Past behaviour was found to be the strongest predictor of behavioural intent.

In a similar study, Cronan and Al-Rafee (2008) added moral obligation ("the feeling of guilt or the personal obligation to perform or not perform a behaviour", p. 532) and past piracy behaviour to the basic TPB model. This adapted model explained 71% of variance in behavioural intent in the sample. Evaluation of the variables in the basic TPB model found that people with a favourable attitude towards digital piracy and those with higher perceived behavioural control had greater intent to engage in digital piracy. Subjective norms had a positive relationship with behavioural intent, but this relationship was not found to be statistically significant (Cronan & Al-Rafee, 2008). As noted by Armitage and Conner (2001), subjective norms is often the weakest of the TPB variables.

Like d'Astous and colleagues (2005), past piracy behaviour was the variable found to have the greatest effect on behavioural intent in Cronan and Al-Rafee (2008). The results indicated that people who had downloaded more frequently in the past showed greater intent to engage in digital piracy in the future. The positive relationship between moral obligation and behavioural intent was the second strongest, and indicated that people with higher moral obligations had lower intent to pirate digital material (Cronan & Al-Rafee, 2008).

Summary and Hypotheses

Despite government and industry efforts to stop the illegal sharing and downloading of media files over P2P networks, this activity shows no signs of abating (Allen, 2008). It may be that these efforts are failing because they threaten behavioural freedoms. According to psychological reactance theory, when behavioural freedoms are threatened, we fight to restore them. In the case of file-sharing over P2P networks, this may involve continuing (and perhaps escalating) past downloading activities. The current study asked whether psychological reactance could account for variance in the intent to, and extent of, downloading over P2P networks, beyond that accounted for by the basic TPB variables. It was hypothesised that:

H1: After controlling age and gender, attitude, subjective norms, perceived behavioural control and psychological reactance will collectively and uniquely account for a significant amount of the variance in intent to download media over P2P networks.

H2: After controlling age and gender, attitude, subjective norms, perceived behavioural control and psychological reactance will collectively and uniquely account for a significant amount of variance in the behaviour of downloading media over P2P networks.

H3: After controlling age and gender, the relationships between attitude and behaviour (H3a), and between subjective norms and behaviour (H3b) will be fully mediated by intent.

H4: After controlling age and gender, the relationships between perceived behavioural control and behaviour (H4a), and between psychological reactance and behaviour (H4b) will be partially mediated by intent.

METHOD

Research Design

This was a cross-sectional, correlational study examining the predictors of downloading media over P2P networks.

Participants

A convenience sample of 174 adults (aged 18+) was recruited via advertisements posted on university noticeboards and websites, and email snowballing techniques. All participants indicated that they had downloaded music, movies or television programs over a P2P network (such as Bit-Torrent) in the past, and were aware that sharing files over P2P networks is actively discouraged by copyright holders.

Fifty-seven percent of participants were male (n = 99), 41% were female (n = 72), and 2% did not specify a gender. They ranged in age from 18 to 56 years (M = 25.61, SD = 6.49). Most participants were engaged in full time employment (54%), with 34% working part time or casually, and 10% were not employed (2% unspecified). Fifty percent of participants were not students, 38% studied full time, and 10% studied part time (2% unspecified). The majority of participants resided in Australia (88%), with the remaining residing in the USA (5%), the UK (3%), and Singapore (2%; with 2% unspecified). Ninety-six percent of participants downloaded media using a broadband Internet connection, and only 1% used a dial-up connection. Three percent of participants did not report their Internet connection type.

Prior to recruiting participants, this study was reviewed and approved by the Human Research Ethics Committee (HREC) at Curtin University in Perth, Western Australia. Participants were treated in accordance with the Australian National Health and Medical Research Council's (2007) statement on ethical conduct in human research. No compensation was provided for participation, however participants were offered the opportunity to enter a prize draw as a token of our appreciation.

Apparatus and Measures

An online questionnaire was constructed to measure the TPB variables and psychological reactance, and to collect demographic information from participants.

Attitude, subjective norms, perceived behavioural control and intent. Permission was obtained from Timothy Paul Cronan (personal communication, April 22, 2008) to modify and use his digital piracy attitude (4 items), subjective norms (3 items), perceived behavioural control (5 items) and intent (3 items) measures (Cronan & Al-Rafee, 2008). The attitude measure uses 7-point semantic differential scales, whilst the remaining three measures are 7-point Likert scales. Cronan and Al-Rafee reported adequate levels of internal consistency for all four measures (Cronbach's α = .91 for attitude; .76 for subjective norms; .94 for perceived behavioural control; and .98 for intent), and provided evidence for the convergent and discriminant validity of each.

Several modifications were made to the Cronan and Al-Rafee (2008) measures prior to their use in the current research. First, it was felt that the term "pirate digital media", which is used throughout

the measures, was too negatively loaded, and it was thus replaced with "download media". Second, two questions were slightly reworded so they could be answered on a scale ranging from "strongly disagree" to "strongly agree" (rather than "very difficult" to "very easy" and "not care" to "disapprove"). Third, the three questions measuring intent were modified to ask about participants' intentions "over the next three months", instead of "in the near future". Fourth, an additional item (adapted from Peace, Galletta, & Thong, 2003) was added to the subjective norms measure in an effort to increase its content validity. Finally, two of the original subjective norms items were deleted after principal axis factoring (PAF) with varimax rotation. The first ("when considering downloading media, I wish to do what people who are important to me do") was deleted because it did not load onto any of the factors extracted during the PAF. The second ("if I download media, then most people who are important to me would approve") was deleted because it loaded higher on the 'attitude' factor than it did on 'subjective norms'. The final set of 14 modified Cronan and Al-Rafee items and their final factor loadings are presented in Table 1, along with Cronbach's alpha for each measure.

Behaviour. Participants were asked how many songs, television programs and movies they had downloaded in the month prior to completing the survey. A month was chosen as an appropriate timeframe given that most Internet plans are provided on a monthly basis, and it was expected that people would be able to accurately report on their downloading behaviour over this period.

An inspection of the raw data showed that although many people had downloaded music in the past month ($n = 133$), fewer had downloaded television programs ($n = 94$), and fewer still had downloaded movies ($n = 80$). Therefore, the responses given on the three individual measures of downloading behaviour were totalled to provide a single score. Scores ranged from 0 to 3025, and were substantially positively skewed.

Table 1. Final factorlLoadings (from principal axis factoring with varimax rotation) for the modified Cronan and Al-Rafee (2008) items, and Cronbach's Alpha for each factor

	Factor			
	PBC	Intent	Attitudes	SN
For me to download media, it would be very easy	.904			
I have the resources necessary to download media	.776			
If I wanted to, I could easily download media	.766			
I can find digital media to download if I want to	.573			
I believe that I have the ability to download media	.421			
I think that downloading music, movies or television programs is:				
Foolish – Wise			.717	
Favourable – Unfavourable[a]			.707	
Good – Bad[a]			.689	
Harmful – Beneficial			.561	
I will make an effort to download media in the next three months		.848		
I will try to download media in the next three months		.841		
I intend to download media in the next three months	.400	.645		
Most people who are important to me would look down on me if I downloaded media[a]				.793
Most people who are important to me think that I should <u>not</u> download media[a]				.784
Cronbach's alpha	.83	.91	.78	.79

Note. Factor loadings <.30 are not shown. The attitudes items were presented as 7-point semantic differential scales; all other items used a 7-point response scale from 1 = "strongly disagree" to 7 = "strongly agree". [a] Item responses required reverse coding prior to analysis. PBC = Perceived Behavioural Control. SN = Subjective Norms.

Consequently, this variable was logarithmically transformed prior to data analysis.

The decision to use a measure of past, rather than future behaviour was made due to the sensitive nature of the topic being investigated (an illegal behaviour), and a need to protect participant anonymity. (Follow-up measures of behaviour would have required collecting personally identifiable data from participants.) Our use of past behaviour as a proxy for future behaviour is consistent with a sizable body of TPB research, and recognises that past behaviour is generally considered to be the best predictor of future behaviour (Ajzen, 2002).

Psychological Reactance. The Hong Psychological Reactance Scale (HPRS; Hong & Faedda, 1996) is composed of 11 statements (e.g., "I consider advice from others to be an intrusion"), to which participants respond on a 5-point scale from "strongly disagree" to "strongly agree". Hong and Faedda reported a Cronbach's alpha of .77 for the measure, and provided evidence for its convergent and discriminant validity. Cronbach's alpha for the HPRS was .82 in the current study.

Research using the HPRS has found it to contain four correlated factors (e.g., Shen & Dillard, 2005; Thomas, Donnell, & Buboltz, 2001). However, principal axis factoring with varimax rotation on the current data identified just two factors. After evaluating the psychometric properties of the scale, Shen and Dillard concluded that it was "theoretically and empirically justifiable" (p. 80) to use a single score, obtained by totalling the responses to each item on the scale. This was the approach taken in the current study.

Demographics. Participants were asked to specify their gender, age, employment and student status, Internet connection type, and country of residence.

Procedure

Following HREC approval, the online questionnaire was constructed at QuestionPro (http://www.questionpro.com/), a commercial web survey host located in the United States. As per the recommendations of Allen and Roberts (2010) it was 'sandwiched' between an information page and a debriefing page, both of which were hosted on our University's web server.

Potential participants were initially directed to the information page. Those choosing to take part in the study indicated consent by clicking a link at the bottom of this page, which automatically

directed them to the questionnaire on the Question-Pro website. After completing the questionnaire, participants were automatically re-directed back to a debriefing page on the University's website. This page gave participants an opportunity to enter a prize draw for an AU$50 iTunes or Amazon.com gift voucher. The questionnaire and debriefing page were set up such that it was impossible for the researchers to link the identifiers that participants provided when entering the prize draw back to specific questionnaire responses. The questionnaire was available for a period of approximately two months between July and September 2008.

RESULTS

To test the first hypothesis, hierarchical multiple regression analysis (MRA) was used. On step 1 of the hierarchical MRA, age and gender (the control variables) accounted for 10% of variance in intent, $R^2 = .100$, adjusted $R^2 = .090$, $F (2, 167) = 9.33$, $p < .001$. On step 2, attitude, subjective norms, perceived behavioural control and psychological reactance accounted for an additional 33.6% of the variance in intent, $\Delta R^2 = .336$, $\Delta F (4, 163) =$

Table 2. Regression coefficients (with associated confidence intervals and standard errors) and squared semi-partial correlations (sr²) for each predictor on each step of a hierarchical MRA predicting intention to download media over P2P networks

	B [95% CI]	Std. Error B	β	sr^2
Step 1				
Age	-.194 [-.295, -.093]s***	.051	-.280	.078
Gender	-1.638 [-2.957, -.319]*	.668	-.181	.032
Step 2				
Age	-.124 [-.208, -.039]**	.043	-.179	.029
Gender	-.004 [-1.142, 1.13]	.576	.000	.000
Attitude	.259 [.144,.374]***	.058	.279	.068
SN	.277 [.047,.507]*	.116	.150	.020
PBC	.389 [.264,.515]***	.064	.401	.129
Reactance	.040 [-.038,.119]	.040	.061	.003

Note. CI = confidence interval. PBC = Perceived Behavioural Control. SN = Subjective Norms. * $p < .05$. ** $p < .01$. *** $p < .001$.

24.34, $p < .001$. In combination, the six predictors accounted for a substantial 43.6% of the variance in intent, $R^2 = .436$, adjusted $R^2 = .416$, $F (6, 163) = 21.07$, $p < .001$. As can be seen in Table 2, all variables except gender and psychological reactance accounted for unique variance in intent on the final step of the hierarchical MRA.

Hypotheses 2 though 4 were tested using a second hierarchical MRA, with (the logarithmic transformation of) behaviour as the dependent variable. On step 1 of the hierarchical MRA, age and gender accounted for 14.8% of the variance in behaviour, $R^2 = .148$, adjusted $R^2 = .138$, $F (2, 167) = 14.51$, $p < .001$. On step 2, attitude, subjective norms, perceived behavioural control and psychological reactance accounted for an additional 16.4% of the variance in behaviour, $\Delta R^2 = .164$, $\Delta F (4, 163) = 9.73$, $p < .001$. As shown in

Table 3, all predictors except psychological reactance were statistically significant (at $\alpha = .05$) on step 2. On step 3 of the hierarchical MRA, intent accounted for a further 12.8% of the variance in behaviour, $\Delta R^2 = .128$, $\Delta F (1, 162) = 37.13$, $p < .001$. As shown in Table 2, the TPB predictors (attitude, subjective norms and perceived behavioural control), which were statistically significant on step 2, dropped to non-significance after inclusion of intent in the regression model on step 3. In combination, the seven predictors accounted for a sizable 44.1% of the variance in behaviour, $R^2 = .441$, adjusted $R^2 = .416$, $F (7, 162) = 18.22$, $p < .001$ (Figure 1).

The results are graphically depicted as a path model in Figure 1.

Table 3. Regression coefficients (with associated confidence intervals and standard errors) and squared semi-partial correlations (sr^2) for each predictor on each step of a hierarchical MRA predicting the behaviour of downloading media over P2P networks

	B [95% CI]	Std. Error B	β	sr^2
Step 1				
Age	-.035 [-.052, -.019]***	.008	-.312	.096
Gender	-.388 [-.599, -.177]***	.107	-.261	.067
Step 2				
Age	-.030 [-.045, -.015]***	.008	-.263	.063
Gender	-.238 [-.445, -.032]*	.105	-.160	.022
Attitude	.035 [.014,.056]**	.011	.227	.045
SN	.052 [.011,.094]*	.021	.172	.026
PBC	.031 [.008,.053]**	.012	.192	.030
Reactance	.003 [-.012,.017]	.007	.024	.001
Step 3				
Age	-.020 [-.034, -.006]**	.007	-.177	.027
Gender	-.238 [-.425, -.051]*	.095	-.160	.022
Attitudes	.014 [-.006,.034]	.010	.094	.007
SN	.031 [-.008,.069]	.019	.100	.008
PBC	.000 [-.023,.023]	.012	.000	.000
Reactance	.000 [-.014,.013]	.007	-.005	.000
Intent	.078 [.053,.104]***	.013	.477	.128

Note. CI = confidence interval. PBC = Perceived Behavioural Control. SN = Subjective Norms. * $p < .05$. ** $p < .01$. *** $p < .001$.

Figure 1. Path model depicting the standardised regression coefficients (β) for the TPB model of P2P downloading behavior (* p <.05. *** p <.001)

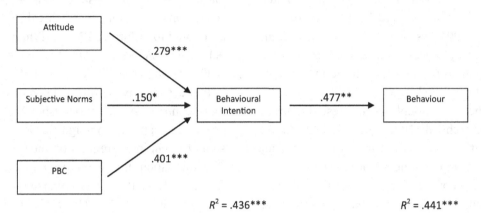

DISCUSSION

The main aim of this research was to investigate whether psychological reactance could account for variance in the intent to, and extent of, downloading media over P2P networks, beyond that accounted for by the standard TPB variables. It did not. However, the results do provide considerable support for the TPB, and its utility for predicting file-sharing intent and behaviour. As can be seen in Table 2, attitude, subjective norms and PBC each accounted for unique variance in intent, as predicted in hypothesis 1. Furthermore, each of these variables accounted for unique variance in P2P file downloading behaviour on step 2 of our second hierarchical MRA, as predicted in hypothesis 2; but dropped to non-significance after the inclusion of intent on step 3 (see Table 3). This is consistent with hypothesis 3, and indicates that the relationships between attitude and behaviour and between subjective norms and behaviour are fully mediated by intent (Baron & Kenny, 1986). However, it is not consistent with hypothesis 4, which predicted that the relationship between PBC and behaviour would be only partially mediated by intent. Instead, the relationship between these two variables was fully mediated by intent. In combination, our predictor variables accounted for 43.6% of the variance in intent, and 44.1%

of the variance in behaviour. These figures are consistent with those reported by d'Astous and colleagues (2005), who used the TPB to predict music piracy intent, and with Armitage and Conner's (2001) meta-analysis of 185 TPB studies. The results of the current study provide support for the use of TPB in explaining P2P file-sharing behaviour.

The lack of relationship between psychological reactance and downloading behaviour was an unexpected result, considering psychological reactance has previously been used to account for the ineffectiveness of persuasive attempts to change behaviour (Shen & Dillard, 2007). There are several possible reasons for the lack of relationship between psychological reactance and P2P downloading behaviour. The most obvious reason is that psychological reactance does not play a role in downloading behaviour. Alternatively, it may be that while psychological reactance does not differentiate between individuals in terms of downloading extent, it may differentiate between those who stop downloading and those who continue with this behaviour. This is a possible direction for future research. Finally, it is possible that while trait psychological reactance (as measured in this research) does not contribute to the prediction of P2P downloading, situation specific (state) psychological reactance (Brehm, 1966) may. This provides a possible area for further research, where state reactance may be elicited by exposing groups of participants who engage in P2P downloading to different hypothetical deterrents (e.g., the threat of prosecution, or the impact of downloading on copyright holders) prior to measuring reactance, and its effects on behaviour.

A further possible direction for future research is extending the range of age groups included. For ethical reasons the current research was limited to people aged 18 years and over. However, evidence suggests that people much younger than this are engaging in file sharing (e.g., Lenhart & Madden, 2005; Quantum Market Research, 2003), and the effect of age on reactance may be an interesting area for future research. Further, this study relied on recruiting participants who engage in P2P downloading; an illegal behaviour. In order to access this 'hidden' population, snowballing was used to recruit participants. While widely used for recruiting participants who engage in deviant behaviour, snowballing can result in samples that are not representative of the population, limiting the generalisability of results (Atkinson & Flint, 2001; Biernacki & Waldorf, 1981; van Meter, 1990).

While TPB was able to explain almost half of the variance in P2P downloading behaviour, this still leaves more than half the variance in downloading behaviour unexplained. There are methodological limitations to this research that may have affected the amount of variance explained. First, past P2P downloading behaviour was measured and used as a proxy for future P2P downloading behaviour. While past behaviour is the best indicator of future behaviour (Ajzen, 2002) it is possible that the use of this retrospective measure did not adequately capture the intended variable. While from a methodological perspective a longitudinal study would be preferred for this type of research, there are ethical considerations associated with obtaining identifying information from participants who are asked about illegal activities (Roberts & Indermaur, 2003), and

identifiers would be required to track participants over time. Second, the measurement of subjective norms in this study was less than optimal. While four items measuring subjective norms were included in the questionnaire, following factor analysis, two items were removed. While the two items provided an internally consistent measure that was weakly predictive of P2P downloading behaviour, further work is required to extend the range of items to cover all aspects of the subjective norms construct. As recommended by previous authors (Armitage & Conner, 2001; d'Astous et al., 2005) the measurement of subjective norms should be a focus of future research. However, it is unlikely that attending to these methodological limitations will account for all of the unexplained variance, and future research is needed to identify other factors predictive of P2P file-sharing behaviour.

From a technoethics perspective, it is important that we develop an understanding of the factors that influence P2P file-sharing behaviour in order to develop appropriate responses. One promising area for future research is to build on the work by d'Astous and colleagues examining the influence of moral obligation. Recent research (Wingrove, Korpas, & Weisz, 2010) has highlighted that students view file-sharing differently from shoplifting a CD. Endorsement of deterrence, social influence, personal morality, and obligation to obey the law as reasons for complying with laws was lower for illegal music downloading and file-sharing than for shoplifting. Deterrence, personal morality, and obligation were all significant predictors of recent downloading. Wingrove and colleagues note that young people may not support laws relating to downloading and sharing music, and without this support efforts to reduce the extent of online copyright infringement are unlikely to succeed.

In summary, the results of this study indicate that psychological reactance is not a significant predictor of downloading media using P2P networks. However, the results provide strong support for the TPB model in explaining this behaviour.

Attitude, subjective norms and perceived behavioural control were found to significantly predict P2P downloading behaviour, with their effect on behaviour fully mediated by behavioural intent.

REFERENCES

Ajzen, I. (1991). The theory of planned behavior. *Organizational Behavior and Human Decision Making Processes, 50*, 179–211.. doi:10.1016/0749-5978(91)90020-T

Ajzen, I. (2002). Residual effects of past on later behavior: Habituation and reasoned action perspectives. *Personality and Social Psychology Review, 6*, 107–122.. doi:10.1207/S15327957PSPR0602_02

Alexander, P. J. (2002). Peer-to-peer file sharing: The case of the music industry. *Review of Industrial Organization, 20*, 151–162. doi:10.1023/A:1013819218792

Allen, P. J. (2008). Rip, mix, burn … sue … *ad infinitum*: The effects of deterrence vs. voluntary cooperation on non-commercial online copyright infringing behaviour. *First Monday, 13*(9). Retrieved from http://firstmonday.org/htbin/cgiwrap/bin/ojs/index.php/fm/article/view/2073/2025.

Allen, P. J., & Roberts, L. D. (2010). The ethics of outsourcing online survey research. *International Journal of Technoethics, 1*, 35-48.

Altschuller, S., & Benbunan-Fich, R. (2009). Is music downloading the new prohibition? What students reveal through an ethical dilemma. *Ethics and Information Technology, 11*, 49–56.. doi:10.1007/s10676-008-9179-1

Armitage, C. J., & Conner, M. (2001). Efficacy of the theory of planned behaviour: A meta-analytic review. *The British Journal of Social Psychology, 40*, 471–499.. doi:10.1348/014466601164939

Atkinson, R., & Flint, J. (2001). Accessing hidden and hard-to-reach populations: Snowball research strategies. *Social Research Update, 33*. Retrieved from http://sru.soc.surrey.ac.uk/sru33.html

Australian Bureau of Statistics. (2009). *Household use of information technology, Australia, 2008-09*. Retrieved from http://www.abs.gov.au/Ausstats/abs@.nsf/mf/8146.0

Bamberg, S., Ajzen, I., & Schmidt, P. (2003). Choice of travel mode in the theory of planned behavior: The roles of past behavior, habit and reasoned action. *Basic and Applied Social Psychology, 25*, 175–187.. doi:10.1207/S15324834BASP2503_01

Baron, R. M., & Kenny, D. A. (1986). The moderator-mediator variable distinction in social psychological research: Conceptual, strategic, and statistical considerations. *Journal of Personality and Social Psychology, 51*, 1173–1182.. doi:10.1037/0022-3514.51.6.1173

Beck, L., & Ajzen, I. (1991). Predicting dishonest actions using the theory of planned behavior. *Journal of Research in Personality, 25*, 285–301.. doi:10.1016/0092-6566(91)90021-H

Bensley, L. S., & Wu, R. (1991). The role of psychological reactance in drinking following alcohol prevention messages. *Journal of Applied Social Psychology, 21*, 1111–1124.. doi:10.1111/j.1559-1816.1991.tb00461.x

Biernacki, P., & Waldorf, D. (1981). Snowball sampling: Problems and techniques of chain referral sampling. *Sociological Methods & Research, 10*, 141–163.

Brehm, J. W. (1966). *A theory of psychological reactance*. New York: Academic Press.

Brehm, S. S., & Brehm, J. W. (1981). *Psychological reactance: A theory of freedom and control*. New York: Academic Press.

Castro, D., Bennett, R., & Andes, C. (2009). *Steal these policies: Strategies for reducing digital piracy*. Retrieved from http://www.itif.org/files/2009-12-15.DigitalPiracy.pdf

Chang, M. K. (1998). Predicting unethical behavior: A comparison of the theory of reasoned action and the theory of planned behavior. *Journal of Business Ethics, 17*, 1825–1834.. doi:10.1023/A:1005721401993

Cronan, T. P., & Al-Rafee, S. (2008). Factors that influence the intention to pirate software and media. *Journal of Business Ethics, 78*, 527–545.. doi:10.1007/s10551-007-9366-8

d'Astous, A., Colbert, F., & Montpetit, D. (2005). Music piracy on the web: How effective are anti-piracy arguments? Evidence from the theory of planned behaviour. *Journal of Consumer Policy, 28*, 289–310.. doi:10.1007/s10603-005-8489-5

Dillard, J. P., & Shen, L. J. (2005). On the nature of reactance and its role in persuasive health communication. *Communication Monographs, 72*, 144–168.. doi:10.1080/03637750500111815

Directorate for Science, Technology and Industry, Organisation for Economic Co-Operation and Development. (2009). *OECD key ICT indicators*. Retrieved September 20, 2009, from http://www.oecd.org/sti/ICTindicators

Entertainment Media Research (in association with Olswang). (2007). *The 2007 digital music survey*. Retrieved from http://www.entertainment-mediaresearch.com/reports/EMR_Digital_Music_Survey2007.pdf

Felten, E. (2010, January 29). *Census of files available via BitTorrent*. Retrieved from http://www.freedom-to-tinker.com/blog/felten/census-files-available-bittorrent

Fishbein, M., & Ajzen, I. (1975). *Belief, attitude, intention and behavior: An introduction to theory and research*. Reading, MA: Addison-Wesley.

Fishbein, M., Hennessy, M., Kamb, M., Bolan, G. A., Hoxworth, T., Iatesta, M., & Zenilman, J. M. (2001). Using intervention theory to model factors influencing behavior change: Project RESPECT. *Evaluation & the Health Professions, 24*, 363–384.. doi:10.1177/01632780122034966

Fukukawa, K. (2002). Developing a framework for ethically questionable behavior in consumption. *Journal of Business Ethics, 41*, 99–119.. doi:10.1023/A:1021354323586

George, J. F. (2002). Influences on the intent to make Internet purchases. *Internet Research, 12*, 165–180.. doi:10.1108/10662240210422521

Hellweg, E. (2003, September 10). The Kazaa conundrum. *CNN Money*. Retrieved from http://money.cnn.com/2003/09/10/technology/techinvestor/hellweg/index.htm

Hong, S.-M., & Faedda, A. (1996). Refinement of the Hong Psychological Reactance Scale. *Educational and Psychological Measurement, 56*, 173–182.. doi:10.1177/0013164496056001014

Horrigan, J. (2009, June). *Home broadband adoption 2009: Broadband adoption increases, but monthly prices do too*. Washington, DC: Pew Internet & American Life Project. Retrieved from http://pewinternet.org/Reports/2009/10-Home-Broadband-Adoption-2009.aspx

Hrubes, D., & Ajzen, I. (2001). Predicting hunting intentions and behavior: An application of the theory of planned behavior. *Leisure Sciences, 23*, 165–178.. doi:10.1080/014904001316896855

International Federation of the Phonographic Industry. (2008). *IFPI digital music report 2008*. Retrieved from http://www.ifpi.org/content/library/DMR2008.pdf

Jemmott, J. B., Jemmott, L. S., Fong, G. T., & McCaffree, K. (1999). Reducing HIV risk associated sexual behavior among African American adolescents: Testing the generality of intervention effects. *American Journal of Community Psychology, 27*, 161–187.. doi:10.1007/BF02503158

Kwong, T. C. H., & Lee, M. K. O. (2002, January). *Behavioral intention model for the exchange mode internet music piracy.* Paper presented at the 35th Hawaii International Conference of System Sciences, Maui, HI.

LaRose, R., Lai, Y. J., Lange, R., Love, B., & Wu, Y. (2005). Sharing or piracy? An exploration of downloading behavior. *Journal of Computer-Mediated Communication, 11*, 1–21.. doi:10.1111/j.1083-6101.2006.tb00301.x

Lau, E. K. W. (2003). An empirical study of software piracy. *Business Ethics (Oxford, England), 12*, 233–245.. doi:10.1111/1467-8608.00323

Lenhart, A., & Madden, M. (2005, November 2). *Teen content creators and consumers.* Washington, DC: Pew Internet & American Life Project. Retrieved from http://www.pewinternet. org/Reports/2005/Teen-Content-Creators-and-Consumers.aspx

Levin, A. M., Dato-on, M. C., & Rhee, K. (2004). Money for nothing and hits for free: The ethics of downloading music from peer-to- peer web sites. *Journal of Marketing Theory and Practice, 12*, 48–60.

Limayem, M., Khalifa, M., & Chin, W. W. (1999, December). *Factors motivating software piracy: A longitudinal study.* Paper presented at 20th International Conference on Information Systems, Charlotte, NC.

Lin, T.-C., Hsu, M. H., Kuo, F.-Y., & Sun, P.-C. (1999, January). *An intention model-based study of software piracy.* Paper presented at 32nd Hawaii International Conference on System Sciences, Maui, HI.

Loch, K. D., & Conger, S. (1996). Evaluating ethical decision making and computer use. *Communications of the ACM, 39*(7), 74–83.. doi:10.1145/233977.233999

Luppicini, R. (2009). The emerging field for technoethics. In Luppicini, R., & Adell, R. (Eds.), *Handbook of research on technoethics* (pp. 1–19). Hershey, PA: IGI Global.

Lysonski, S., & Durvasula, S. (2008). Digital piracy of MP3s: Consumer and ethical predispositions. *Journal of Consumer Marketing, 25*, 167–178.. doi:10.1108/07363760810870662

Madden, M. (2004). *Artists, musicians and the Internet.* Washington, DC: Pew Internet & American Life Project. Retrieved from http://www. pewinternet.org/Reports/2004/Artists-Musicians-and-the-Internet.aspx

Mulligan, M., Card, D., Laszio, J., & Peach, A. (2003). *European broadband strategies: Reducing subscriber churn and adding consumer value with digital music services.* New York: Jupiter Research.

National Health and Medical Research Council. (2007). *National statement on ethical conduct in human research.* Retrieved from http://www. nhmrc.gov.au/publications/synopses/e72syn.htm

Office for National Statistics. (2009, August 28). *Internet access: Households and individuals.* Retrieved from http://www.statistics.gov.uk/pdfdir/iahi0809.pdf

Opinion of the Supreme Court of the United States for Metro-Goldwyn-Mayer Studios Inc. *et al.* (2005, June 27). Retrieved from http://www.eff. org/IP/P2P/MGM_v_Grokster/04-480.pdf

Opinion of the United States Court of Appeals for the Ninth Circuit for Metro-Goldwyn-Mayer Studios Inc. *et al.* (2004, August 19). Retrieved from http://www.eff.org/IP/P2P/MGM_v_ Grokster/20040819_mgm_v_grokster_decision. pdf

Orbell, S., Blair, C., Sherlock, K., & Conner, M. (2001). The theory of planned behavior and ecstasy use: Roles for habit and perceived control over taking versus obtaining substances. *Journal of Applied Social Psychology, 31,* 31–47.. doi:10.1111/j.1559-1816.2001.tb02480.x

Parker, A. (2004). *The true picture of peer-to-peer filesharing.* Retrieved from http://web.archive. org/web/20041022013828/www.cachelogic.com/ research/index.php

Parker, A. (2005). *P2P in 2005.* Retrieved from http://web.archive.org/web/20060808053516/ http://www.cachelogic.com/research/p2p2005. php

Parker, D., Manstead, A. S. R., Stradling, S. G., Reason, J. T., & Baxter, J. S. (1992). Intention to commit driving violations: An application of the theory of planned behavior. *The Journal of Applied Psychology, 77,* 94–101.. doi:10.1037/0021-9010.77.1.94

Parker, D., Stradling, S. G., & Manstead, A. S. R. (1996). Modifying beliefs and attitudes to exceeding the speed limit: An intervention study based on the theory of planned behavior. *Journal of Applied Social Psychology, 26,* 1–19.. doi:10.1111/j.1559-1816.1996.tb01835.x

Peace, G., Galletta, D. F., & Thong, J. Y. L. (2003). Software piracy in the workplace: A model and empirical test. *Journal of Management Information Systems, 20,* 153–177. Retrieved from http://www.jmis-web.org/.

Petraitis, J., Flay, B. R., & Miller, T. Q. (1995). Reviewing theories of adolescent substance use: Organizing pieces of the puzzle. *Psychological Bulletin, 117,* 67–86.. doi:10.1037/0033-2909.117.1.67

Quantum Market Research. (2003, July). *Understanding CD burning and Internet file sharing and its impact on the Australian music industry: Key quantitative findings prepared for ARIA* (Project No. 23006). Retrieved from http://www.aria. com.au/pages/documents/AriaIllegalMusicResearchReport_Summary.pdf

Roberts, L. D., & Indermaur, D. (2003). Signed consent forms in criminological research: Protection for researchers and ethics committees but a threat to research participants? *Psychiatry, Psychology and Law, 10,* 289–299.. doi:10.1375/ pplt.2003.10.2.289

Schulze, H., & Mochalski, K. (2009). *Internet study 2008/2009.* Retrieved from http://www. ipoque.com/resources/internet-studies

Seale, D. A., Polakowski, M., & Schneider, S. (1998). It's not really theft! Personal and workplace ethics that enable software piracy. *Behaviour & Information Technology, 17,* 27–40.. doi:10.1080/014492998119652

Sheeran, P., & Orbell, S. (2000). Using implementation intentions to increase attendance for cervical cancer screening. *Health Psychology, 19,* 283–289.. doi:10.1037/0278-6133.19.3.283

Shen, L., & Dillard, J. P. (2007). Reactance proneness assessment. In Reynolds, R. A., Woods, R., & Baker, J. D. (Eds.), *Electronic surveys and measurements* (pp. 323–329). Hershey, PA: IGI Global.

Shen, L. J., & Dillard, J. P. (2005). Psychometric properties of the Hong Psychological Reactance Scale. *Journal of Personality Assessment, 85,* 74–81.. doi:10.1207/s15327752jpa8501_07

Shim, S., Eastlick, M. A., Lotz, S. L., & Warrington, P. (2001). An online prepurchase intentions model: The role of intention to search. *Journal of Retailing, 77,* 397–416.. doi:10.1016/S0022-4359(01)00051-3

Siwek, S. E. (2007). *The true cost of copyright industry piracy to the U.S. economy* (IPI Policy Report No. 189). Retrieved from http://www.ipi.org/IPI/IPIPublications.nsf/PublicationLookupFullText/23F5FF3E9D8AA7978625736900 5B0C79

Sutton, S., McVey, D., & Glanz, A. (1999). A comparative test of the theory of reasoned action and the theory of planned behavior in the prediction of condom use intentions in a national sample of English young people. *Health Psychology, 18,* 72–81.. doi:10.1037/0278-6133.18.1.72

Tappan, T. N. (2006). The road more travelled: Illegal digital downloading. *Tennessee's Business, 15*(1), 20–23.

Thomas, A., Donnell, A. J., & Buboltz, W. C., Jr. (2001). The Hong Psychological Reactance Scale: A confirmatory factor analysis. *Management and Evaluation in Counseling and Development, 34,* 2-13. Retrieved from http://mec.sagepub.com/

Thompson, C. (2005, January). The BitTorrent effect. *WIRED Magazine, 13*(1), 150-153, 178-179.

Tonglet, M. (2002). Consumer misbehavior: An exploratory study of shoplifting. *Journal of Consumer Behaviour, 1,* 336–354.. doi:10.1002/cb.79

Tonglet, M., Phillips, P. S., & Read, A. D. (2004). Using the theory of planned behaviour to investigate the determinants of recycling behaviour: A case study from Brixworth, UK. *Resources, Conservation and Recycling, 41,* 191–214.. doi:10.1016/j.resconrec.2003.11.001

van Meter, K. M. (1990). Methodological and design issues: Techniques for assessing the representatives of snowball samples. In Lambert, E. Y. (Ed.), *The collection and interpretation of data from hidden populations (NIDA Research Monograph 98)* (pp. 31–43). Rockville, MD: National Institute on Drug Abuse, US Department of Health and Human Services.

Wingrove, T., Korpas, A. L., & Weisz, V. (2010). Why were millions of people not obeying the law? Motivational influences on non-compliance with the law in the case of music piracy. *Psychology, Crime & Law.*. doi:10.1080/10683160903179526

This work was previously published in International Journal of Technoethics, Volume 1, Issue 4, edited by Rocci Luppicini, pp. 49-64, copyright 2010 by IGI Publishing (an imprint of IGI Global).

Chapter 9
An Exploratory Study of the Cyberbullying and Cyberstalking Experiences and Factors Related to Victimization of Students at a Public Liberal Arts College

Ellen M. Kraft
Richard Stockton College of New Jersey, USA

Jinchang Wang
Richard Stockton College of New Jersey, USA

ABSTRACT

This article shows the results of a study of the cyberbullying and cyberstalking experiences of students at a public liberal arts college. A survey was administered online to sophomores, juniors, seniors, and graduate students at the college. The prevalence rates were 10% for cyberbullying and 9% for cyber-stalking, shown in the sample of 471 respondents. Traditional college students under 25 years of age were experiencing and participating in cyberbullying at higher rates than older college students. Prior experience as a victim of cyberbullying in high school was a significant risk factor for cyberbullying and cyberstalking in college, which implies that students' roles in cyberbullying are maintained from high school to college. The majority of college students are handling cyberbullying incidents themselves rather than utilizing campus resources, but two-thirds of respondents would be more likely to consider reporting an incident if there was a central e-mail address available for reporting incidents.

DOI: 10.4018/978-1-4666-1773-5.ch009

INTRODUCTION

The Millennial generation's view of technology is different from prior generations who did not grow up with the Internet. According to research by the Pew Internet and Life, the Millennial generation is the first generation to "view social networking sites, YouTube.com, Google, and the Wikipedia not as astonishing innovations of the digital era, but as everyday parts of their social lives and their search for understanding" (Keeter & Taylor, 2009). "The millennial generation's view of technology is different from prior generations who did not use the Internet while they were growing up. Technoethics is a field that "recognizes technology as an intricate part of societal development which fosters change and new ethical considerations to address" (Luppicini, 2008, pp. 2). Ethical considerations arise when new norms of how people interact with technology are being established such as in the case of the Millennial generation using the Internet for socializing and viewing the Internet as part of their everyday life. Web 2.0 technologies are shaping how college students socialize on the Internet and raise the technoethical issue of what content they perceive as normal to see on the Internet. They also are faced with the technoethical dilemma of deciding what content they want to post online.

Cyberbullying can occur when content that is posted online is offensive to others. There are several research studies published that document that cyberbullying is currently a problem for middle school and high school students (Beran & Li, 2005; Patchin & Hinduja, 2006; Shariff, 2008; Ybarra & Mitchell, 2007). Students are now coming to college having experienced cyberbullying in high school. Cyberbullying offenders in high school may be graduating to more serious forms of online harassment such as cyberstalking in college. There is limited empirical research about cyberbullying and cyberstalking of college students although there have been many anecdotal incidents documented in the literature

(Dickerson, 2005; Pepitone, 2006; Rogerson, 2002; Schweitzer, 2005; Kraft, 2010).

College students using the Internet for socializing need to consider the technoethical issues of the opportunities to access information about others and have an extended social network online versus the risks of having their privacy and security compromised (Caruso & Solaway, 2008). However, students are often unaware or indifferent to privacy and risks on the Internet (Caruso & Solaway, 2008). Having the freedom to post content on the Internet and meet new people without seeing them in person places college students at risk for cyberbullying and cyberstalking.

Further research is needed to document the problem of cyberbullying and cyberstalking among college students. This study will explore the following issues:

1. What is the prevalence rate of cyberbullying and cyberstalking at a public liberal arts college?
2. What types of cyberbullying and cyberstalking incidents have students experienced?
3. What is the impact of cyberbullying?
4. Are there factors such as demographics or experiences with cyberbullying in high school that would place students at risk for being victims of cyberbullying in college?
5. How would students choose to report an incident of cyberbullying or cyberstalking?

WHAT IS CYBERBULLYING?

There is no precise, universal definition of cyberbullying (Szoka & Thierer, 2008). Educators, lawyers, law enforcement, and researchers have conceptualized cyberbullying based on established definitions of traditional in person bullying and online behaviors (Belsey, 2010; Patchin & Hinduja, 2006; Willard, 2007). Canadian school teacher Bill Belsey defined cyberbullying as "The use of information and communication technologies to support deliberate, repeated, and hostile behavior by an individual or group that is intended to harm others" (Belsey, 2010). This definition conveys the concepts from the definition of traditional bullying being a form of repeated intentional abuse against a victim from an individual or group of individuals (Campbell, 2005; Olewus, 2001).

The National Crime Prevention Council states on its website that cyberbullying "happens when teens use the Internet, cell phones, or other devices to send or post text or images intended to hurt or embarrass another person" (National Crime Prevention Council, 2010). Examples of cyberbullying behaviors are listed on the website. These behaviors include "teens pretending they are other people online to trick others, spreading lies and rumors about victims, tricking people into revealing personal information, sending or forwarding mean text messages, and posting pictures of victims without their consent" (NCPC, 2010). The National Crime Prevention Council does not specify that the act of cyberbullying must be repeated as required by the definition of in person bullying or Mr. Belsey's definition of cyberbullying.

The examples of cyberbullying behaviors on the National Crime Prevention website are similar to examples that Nancy Willard, an attorney and the Director of the Center for Safe and Responsible Internet Use has identified to support her definition of cyberbullying. The forms of cyberbullying behaviors identified by Willard (2007) are listed in Table 1 (Willard, 2007, pp. 1-2). Willard (2007) defines cyberbullying as "being cruel to others by sending or posting harmful material or engaging in other forms of social aggression using the Internet or other digital technologies" (Willard, 2007, pp. 1).

The types of in person bullying aggressive behavior can be physical such as hitting pushing or shoving; verbal which includes name calling and threats, or psychological which includes spreading rumors and exclusion (Nansel et al., 2001). The online behaviors identified by Willard (2007) as forms of cyberbullying are similar to in person verbal and psychological bullying behaviors. Instead of calling a victim names to their face or spreading rumors in person with peers, these activities are done online through e-mail, text messages, instant messages, and website postings. Exclusion from in person socializing is parallel to excluding someone from an online group. Physical attacks are filmed and uploaded to a website as part of a new trend known as "Happy Slapping" (Saunders, 2006). Happy Slapping is a form of cyberbullying that begins with physical bullying and is extended online by posting a video of the incident.

Attorney Parry Aftab defines cyberbullying as "when a child, preteen, or teen is tormented, threatened, harassed, humiliated, embarrassed, or otherwise targeted by another child, preteen or teen

Table 1. Forms of cyberbullying behaviors defined by Nancy Williard (Willard, 2007, pp. 1-2)

Form of Cyberbullying	Definition
Flaming	Online fights with nasty or vulgar language.
Harassment	Repeatedly sending nasty mean and insulting messages.
Denigration	Online gossip or rumors intended to damage a person's reputation.
Impersonation	Pretending to be someone else online and posting material to get that person in trouble.
Outing	Sharing someone's secrets or embarrassing information or images online.
Trickery	Talking someone into revealing secrets or embarrassing information, then sharing it online.
Exclusion	Intentionally and cruelly excluding someone from an online group.
Cyberstalking	Repeated, intense harassment and denigration that includes threats or creates significant fear.

using the Internet, interactive and digital technologies or mobile phones" (Aftab, 2010a) Ms. Aftab believes that cyberbullying is "usually not a one time communication" (Aftab, 2010a), however, she also states that there are circumstances that cyberbullying can be a one time incident "such as death threat or a credible threat of serious bodily harm" (Aftab, 2010a). Although Mr. Belsey in his definition states that cyberbullying is intended to harm others, Ms. Aftab believes that some cases cyberbullying may be accidental (Aftab, 2010b). In other cases victims or their friends retaliate against bullies and cyberbullies online, but feel justified in the cyberbullying acts (Aftab, 2010b; Shariff, 2008; Willard, 2007) because they were hurt by the bully. In her definition Ms. Aftab states that cyberbullying is "an act that occurs among minors" (Aftab, 2010a). She considers the incident to be cyber-harassment or cyberstalking (Aftab, 2010b) not cyberbullying if adults are involved.

Although Ms. Aftab defines cyberbullying as occurring only in childhood and adolescence, researchers have documented that bullying occurs in childhood, adolescence, college, and during adulthood (Chappel et al., 2006). Workplace bullying is a form of bullying that occurs among adults in the workplace that is similar to verbal and relational bullying (Harvey, Treadway, Heames, & Duke, 2009).

The definition of bullying includes adults. Anecdotal evidence of online behaviors of college students are similar to those specified by Willard and the National Crime Prevention Council. We have decided to conceptualize cyberbullying as occurring when someone uses technology such as e-mail, cell phones, web cameras, or pagers to offend or embarrass others.

This definition considers college students as being able to participate in cyberbullying as analogous to adults participate in bullying. The definition is open ended to allow for subjects to report one time incidents of cyberbullying and accidental incidents of cyberbullying. It incor-

porates newer technologies such as cell phones and web cameras.

CYBERBULLYING MANIFESTS ITSELF AT COLLEGES

One of the first highly publicized online harassment incidents occurred in 1995 when Jinsong Hu was expelled from the Ph.D. program at California Institute of Technology for harassing another student by e-mail who was his former girlfriend (Harson, 1995). The problem of online harassment of college students has progressed since the mid 1990's. The primary complaint from students and faculty at the early part of the 21st century was harassing e-mail messages, followed by cyberstalking, hacking, mail bombs, viruses, and hijacking (Rogerson, 2002). Dickerson (2005) reported law school students engaging in cyberbullying behaviors similar to adolescents. The law school students attacked other students, faculty, and administrators on web sites and in chat rooms based on physical appearance, perceived sexual orientation, and intellectual capabilities (Dickerson, 2005). They also bragged about drug and alcohol use, made sexually explicit statements, and posted inappropriate pictures taken on campus (Dickerson, 2005).

In 2004 the website Facebook.com was founded. College students revealed pictures and personal information when they created profiles on this site. In October 2005, a Fisher College student was expelled for a Facebook.com post about a campus police officer, saying the officer "loves to antagonize students and needs to be eliminated" (Schweitzer, 2005). In February 2006, four Syracuse University freshmen were placed on disciplinary probation for their harassing posts about a graduate student who was teaching a course (Pepitone, 2006).

The examples reviewed show that cyberbullying does continue from adolescence into the college years. The anonymity of the Internet coupled with students' inherent nature to want to take risks on the Internet leads them to participate in social misconduct (Workman, 2008) such as cyberbullying and cyberstalking. Electronic communication lacks non verbal cues such as facial expressions and tone of voice (EPACT, 2005). Students also have lowered inhibitions when using the Internet due to the anonymous environment of the Internet (Workman, 2008). The unique environment of the virtual world with its lack of non verbal cues and lowered inhibition of users causes college students to say things that they would not say in person (Beran & Li, 2005; Patchin & Hinduja, 2006). The lack of discretion in posting content can place them at risk of posting content that could jeopardize their reputation or the reputation of others. The content they post online can also place them at risk for cyberbullying of cyberstalking.

Online College Gossip Web Sites

Juicycampus.com was an online college gossip web site that started in October, 2007 and expanded to 500 campuses by October 2008. There were derogatory comments posted on the site about "physical appearance, ethnicity, race, and implied sexual experiences of students" (Kraft, 2010). Many students harassed by those comments felt being "humiliated, maligned, and having their reputation tarnished" (Kraft, 2010). Juicycampus.com became a major source of controversy on campuses across the United States as a result of the content of the posts. Students were dividend in their reaction to the site. Some students enjoyed visiting the site to read the gossip while other students were offended by the explicit and derogatory posts on the site. Students complained to campus administrators; however, administrators had no control about the site's content since it was not actually affiliated with any college (Young, 2008). Many administrators thought that students should simply ignore the site so it would eventually have to close if it did not have an audience (Young, 2008). Students decided to take action themselves against Juicycampus.com by complaining to advertisers, creating groups on Facebook.com to protest the site, creating websites to addresses issues about Internet speech, writing editorials in their college newspaper and posting comments directly on Juicycampus.com (Kraft, 2010). Students and parents reported serious incidents of cyberstalking that occurred as a result of Juicycampus.com to their state Attorney General's office.

Although many of the posts on Juicycampus. com were not true, some were. Victims of posts that were true were ostracized on campus. In cases where the in person harassment on campus was so intense victims had to leave campus or drop out of school (McNiff & Varney, 2008). Other victims of the posts felt angry, cried, felt betrayal, and suffered from depression (McNiff & Varney, 2008). Much to the relief of college administrators, the web site closed in February 4, 2009 due to financial difficulties. However, the traffic to Juicycampus. com was immediately purchased by Collegeacb. com. Collegeacb.com and CampusGossip.com are sites where students continue to post gossip during the 2009-2010 academic year.

Studies about Online Harassment of College Students

A 2002 study of 339 undergraduate students at the University of New Hampshire revealed that approximately 10% of the participants received "repeated messages that threatened, insulted, or harassed" (Finn, 2004, p. 474) through e-mail or instant messages. More than half of the respondents received unwanted pornographic messages or pictures (Finn, 2004). The messages were from strangers, acquaintances, and significant others. Only 6.8% of the students who were harassed online reported the incidents. The reasons the respondents cited for not reporting the incidents were that they did not consider the problem serious enough to report (37.5%), ignored the message (19.5%), did not know who to report it to (12.5%), or handled the problem by themselves (19.5%) (Finn, 2004). Respondents who said they had reported the harassment were more likely to have received the e-mail from strangers and received pornography (Finn, 2004).

A 2004 Rochester Institute of Technology study revealed that 17% of students were harassed online and 8% were threatened (McQuade, 2007). Another study found that one-third of 235 undergraduates' experienced online harassment (Spitzberg & Hoobler, 2002). A more recent study by the Massachusetts Aggression Reduction Center (MARC) found that 8% of respondents were cyberbullied by instant messages and 3% admitted to cyberbullying while in college (Englander, Muldowney, & McCoy, 2009).

The studies of the prevalence of online harassment at colleges ranged from 8%-33%. The variation is due to the definition of online harassment used by the researchers and the respondents sampled. The majority of the students do not report harassment incidents. Student's perceive harassment from strangers to be more serious than harassment from people they know (Finn, 2004).

CYBERSTALKING AT COLLEGES AND UNIVERSITIES

Cyberbullying can escalate into cyberstalking. The U.S. Department of Justice defines cyberstalking as the "the use of the Internet, e-mail, or other electronic communications devices to stalk another person" (U.S. Department of Justice, 2000). Cyberstalking is a repeated harassment through electronic communication that causes the victim to fear for his/her safety (U.S. Department of Justice, 2000). Victims of cyberstalking are at risk of physical stalking and physical harm or homicide (United States Department of Justice, 2000). The intensity of the fear and anxiety of cyberstalking is similar to that of stalking in the physical world (Finn, 2004). As of December 2009, 47 states have laws that include electronic forms of communica-

tion within stalking or harassment laws (National Conference of State Legislators, 2010).

Cyberstalking behaviors are not well defined. Bocij (2003) initially identified cyberstalking behaviors based on an analysis of 25 cyberstalking cases published on the Internet (Bocij, 2003). Subsequent research from a study of 169 respondents revealed the most commonly reported cyberstalking behaviors were online threats, posting rumors online, damaging a victim's computer by sending a virus, attempting to monitor the victim's actions by inserting a Trojan horse on the victim's computer, and attempting to access confidential information on a victim's computer such as credit card numbers (Bocij, 2003). The respondents from the study also reported that in some instances others were encouraged to harass them (Bocij, 2003).

The National Center for Victims of Crime states that "Cyberstalking takes many forms such as: threatening or obscene e-mail; spamming; live chat harassment or flaming (online verbal abuse); leaving improper messages on message boards or in guest books; sending electronic viruses; sending unsolicited e-mail; tracing another person's computer and Internet activity, and electronic identity theft" (National Center for Victims of Crime, 2010).

Research by Finn (2004) and the U.S. Department of Justice consider mass repeated or unwanted e-mails to be cyberstalking. Finn (2004) identified that mass email that floods a victim's e-mail account is cyberstalking (Finn, 2004). The National Center for Victims of Crime defines spamming in the context of cyberstalking as "the stalker sends a victim a magnitude of junk e-mail" (National Center for Victims of Crime, 2010).

Cyberstalking is becoming an increasingly noticeable problem at American colleges and universities (Boyer, 2006; Lee, 1998; Olsen, 2001). College students allow themselves to be vulnerable to cyberstalking online that can place them at risk for stalking in the real world by posting personal information such as their last name, cell phone number, or address (Caruso & Salaway, 2008). They do not exercise the same caution when communicating with strangers online as they would in person.

A study of 302 undergraduate and graduate students found that 13% of the students were victims of cyberstalking (Paullet, Rota, & Swan, 2009). The study found with statistical significance that students who were victims of cyberstalking were more likely to receive harassment by e-mail and social networking sites (Paullet et al., 2009). This study shows the importance of students protecting themselves with privacy settings to reduce the likelihood of experiencing cyberstalking when using social networking sites.

Colleges and universities vary in their responses to the problem of cyberstalking. Virginia Polytechnic Institute and State University defines cyberstalking on its website as "an escalation of online harassment where an individual "follows" another around the Internet. This may include sending emails and IM's, showing up in chat rooms, newsgroups and/or websites when the victim is using them" (Virginia Polytechnic Institute and State University, 2010). Some colleges and universities, in addition to defining terms such as e-mail harassment and cyberstalking (Virginia Polytechnic Institute and State University, 2010), state in their computer acceptable use policies the consequences of online harassment (Read, 2006). Larger universities have central offices for handling complaints and providing support services to victims. The University of Maryland at College Park has Project NEThics (Project NEThics, 2010) that has a central office responsible for handling violations of the university's acceptable use policy (Carlson, 2002). The staff provides information about computer use policies as well as contacts for helping victims of harassment. The office maintains a file for each complaint received. Most cases are handled directly by a staff member. In cases of repeat offenders the office staff may have to contact disciplinary offices on campus or the police.

METHOD

The purpose of this study was to determine, at a public liberal arts college, the prevalence rate of cyberbullying and cyberstalking. The researchers wanted to learn about the types of cyberbullying and cyberstalking incidents students had experienced. The impact of the cyberbullying incidents on victims, and how students would choose to report incidents of cyberbullying or cyberstalking. The investigators wanted to determine if victims of cyberbullying and cyberstalking had a demographic profile and if prior experience as a victim or perpetrator of cyberbullying in high school was a risk factor for victims.

A survey instrument was used to collect the data for the study. It was approved by Richard Stockton College of New Jersey's IRB for Human Subjects committee. The format of the survey was designed by the authors with Zoomerang's online survey tool. There were 69 questions in the survey. The Zoomerang survey tool has a skip logic design feature that allows the survey to administer questions based on answers to previous questions. Most respondents did not have to answer all of 69 questions. Five of the 69 questions were open-ended. The other questions were multiple choice questions.

The definitions of cyberbullying and cyberstalking were given in the survey along with examples. Respondents were given the following definition of cyberstalking, "Cyberstalking is a repeated harassment through the Internet, e-mail, or other electronic communication that causes the victim to fear for their safety (U.S. Department of Justice, 2000). Technology is used to stalk the victim with the intention of annoying, alarming, or threatening the victim" (U.S. Department of Justice, 2000). Examples of cyberstalking were given in a bulleted list. This list was adapted from research conducted by Bocij (2003), Finn (2004), U.S. Department of Justice (2000), The National Center for Victims of Crime (2010), and Williard (2007). The definition of cyberbullying was given to respondents as, "Cyberbullying occurs when someone uses technology such as e-mail, cell phones, web cameras, or pagers to offend or embarrass others." Respondents were provided with examples of cyberbullying that were adapted from research conducted by Aftab (2010 b.), Dickerson, (2005) and Willard (2007) as well as anecdotal evidence seen by the researchers at Juicycampus.com (Kraft, 2010).

The survey was administered online from October 26, 2008 to November 15, 2008. It was sent through e-mails to all sophomores, juniors, seniors and graduate students at the public liberal arts college. Freshmen were not considered in this survey because they did not have sufficient college experience yet. As an incentive for student participation in the study there was a lottery for a $50 gift certificate for Amazon.com. It took students about 30-45 minutes to complete the survey. A total of 5,806 surveys were sent out, and 471 complete surveys were returned.

The majority of the respondents in this study were female (76%) college students. Having a high percentage of female subjects is consistent with the research finding that females are more likely to respond to an invitation to participate in an online survey (Patchin & Hinduja, 2006). The distribution of respondents' races was 83% white, 5% African American, 4% Asian, 4% Hispanic, and 1% biracial. Most of the participants were traditional age (under age 25) (80%) and full time students (89%). The participants lived in a variety of settings such as on campus (34%), off campus by themselves (9%), off campus with roommates (13%), living with parents (34%), or living with other family members (6%).

DATA AND ANALYSIS

Prevalence and Severity Rate

The prevalence rates were 10% for cyberbullying and 9% for cyberstalking, shown in the sample of

471 respondents. The cyberbullying prevalence rate, 10%, was similar to the rate of e-mail or instant messaging harassment reported in the University of New Hampshire study (Finn, 2004), but slightly higher than the 8% rate reported by the study at the Massachusetts Aggression Reduction Center (Englander, 2009). Both cyberbullying and cyberstalking prevalence rates in this study were lower than those reported in the University of Rochester study (McQuade, 2007) and the study by Spitzberg & Hoobler (2002). In our sample 28% of the victims were cyberbullied once, 50% were cyberbullied 2-5 times, 9% were cyberbullied 6-10 times, and 13% were cyberbullied more than 10 times. Beran and Li (2007) report that most of their subjects say that they have been cyberbullied once or twice, however, still consider these incidents to be cyberbullying as victims may under report cyberbullying (Beran & Li, 2007).

About half of the 471 respondents had ever heard of college students' cyberbullying (48%) or cyberstalking (50%) other people, 48% of the respondents had ever heard about college students being cyberbullied, and 47% had ever heard of college students being cyberstalked. When asked if cyberbullying was a problem for college students, 57% of the respondents said yes.

Type of Cyberbullying Incidents

Forty-six respondents said they had experienced cyberbullying. They were asked further questions in the survey about the type of incident, its impact, the relationship of the person that had offended them, if the victim told anyone about the incident, and if the victim had sought help from anyone on campus. Table 2 shows the types of cyberbullying incidents reported by the students in the survey, which are sorted in descending order according to the frequency of occurrences. The focus of prior research about online harassment involving college students was on using e-mails and instant messages (Finn 2004; Englander 2009) to harass others. The results in this study indicate that cell

Table 2. Types of cyberbullying incidents experienced by victims

Type of cyberbullying incident	n=46
Text messaging	43%
Received harassing cell phone calls	39%
Instant messages	37%
e-mail	35%
Posts to Facebook.com	22%
Received unwanted pornography	15%
Other, please specify	13%
Racist, sexist, anti-religious, or homophobic comments	11%
Phony profile	11%
Attacked in a chat room	11%
Embarrassing pictures posted to the web	9%
Posts on social networking sites	7%
Posts to JuicyCampus.com	2%

Table 3. Themes of cyberbullying

Did any of the cyberbullying incidents involve	n=46
Being called a slut	50%
Accusations damaging to reputation	35%
Sexism	35%
Offensive comments about appearance	30%
Negative comments about intelligence	28%
Offensive comments about weight	20%
Accusations about being a homosexual	20%
Other, please specify	17%
Racism	9%
Anti-Semitism	7%
Other anti-religious comments	4%

Impact of Cyberbullying Experiences on Victims

Table 4 lists the emotions experienced by the victims, ranked according to the percentage of victims who had the feelings. The most common emotions experienced by the victims included anger, frustration, feeling upset, hurt, humiliated, distressed, and sad. These feelings were consistent with the results of the studies of Beran and Li (2005) and Patchin & Hinduja (2006) that the most common feelings for victims of adolescent cyberbullying were anger, sadness, frustration, and fear. According to research done by Beran and Li (2005) and Patchin and Hinduja (2006), victims of adolescent cyberbullying suffered more serious effects such as clinical depression, fear of going to school, and declining school performance; a few even committed suicide. In this study, respondents reported similar effects such as depression, grades dropping, and suicidal thoughts. In their responses to the open ended questions victims reported feeling stressed about the incidents, annoyed, and being afraid or scared. Since 20 of the 46 cyberbullying victims claimed to be cyberstalking victims, the findings about cyberbullying are consistent with the definition of cyberstalking given by U.S. Department of Justice (2000) that

phone calls, text messages, and web postings are becoming more frequently used media for cyberbullying.

Most of the victims reported that they knew their offenders. The relationship of the victim to the offender was ex-boyfriend/girlfriend (28%), other students at their college or university (26%), and students from other colleges/universities (26%). This result is consistent with the past finding that ex-intimates are a primary perpetrator of cyberstalking (Bocji, 2003). Only 37% of the victims did not know who their perpetrators were.

The most common theme of the cyberbullying incidents was calling the victim a slut, which was related to about 50% of incidents in the cyberbullying victim sample. Table 3 shows the percentage of victims reporting each theme of cyberbullying sorted in descending order. The top five themes of cyberbullying involved are being called a slut, accusations damaging to the victim's reputation, sexism, offensive comments about appearance, and negative comments about intelligence.

Table 4. Emotions experienced by victims of cyberbullying

Emotions	n=46
Anger	72%
Frustration	63%
Upset	52%
Felt Hurt	48%
Humiliated	39%
Distressed	37%
Sadness	35%
None of these emotions	15%
Depression	15%
Other, please specify	7%
Experienced suicidal thoughts	2%

characterizes cyberstalking to have the intention of annoying, alarming, or causing the victims to fear for their safety (U.S. Department of Justice, 2000). The length of time of the effect of a cyberbullying incident on a victim varied. Twenty-four percent of victims in this study experienced a short term effects of less than a day, 22% said the incident affected them for up to one week, and 13% reported the incident affected them for as long as one month. Long term effects lasting one to three months were reported by 7% of the victims, effects lasting four to six months were reported by 11% of the victims, and effects lasting seven to twelve months were reported by 11% of the victims.

Characteristics of Students Experiencing Cyberbullying in College Age

In this study, students in two age groups, over age 25 and age 25 and under, were compared based on their cyberbullying and cyberstalking experiences. There were 92 respondents who were older than 25 years old and were placed the "over 25 sample". The remaining 379 respondents were placed in the "25 and younger sample".

The researchers hypothesized that there would be differences between the two groups with their demographics, past cyberbullying experiences in high school, as well as their use of social networking sites. Statistical hypothesis testing was used to evaluate the significance of the percent differences for a response between the two groups. The null hypothesis for a factor, social networking usage, for example, is that the two age groups have the same percentage of students who visit social networking sites. The p-value was calculated by using the method for statistical inference for the difference of two sample proportions with different sample sizes. The null hypothesis is rejected if the p-value is less than 0.05. Rejecting the null hypothesis implies that a significant difference exists between the two groups.

Table 5 compares the responses to questions about demographics, cyberbullying experiences, and social networking site usage of the "25 and younger" and "over 25" age groups. It is statistically significant (p=0.031) that more students in the "25 and younger" sample (11%) experienced cyberbullying victimization within the past year than students in the "over 25" sample (5%). This result shows that younger students tend to be cyberbullied in college. The two age groups did not show significant differences in the proportion of students who experienced cyberstalking victimization.

The reasons why younger students were more likely to be cyberbullied can also be found in Table 5. There are six other factors with p-values less than 0.05 showing that the proportions of the two age groups are significantly different for the following factors:

1. Being a full-time student (96% for "25 and younger" versus 46% for "over 25")
2. Living on campus (41% for "25 and younger" versus 3% for "over 25")
3. Experiencing cyberbullying in high school (18% for "25 and younger" versus 4% for "over 25")

Table 5. Over Age 25 sample versus Age 25 and younger sample

Factor	Over Age 25 Sample (n=92)	Age 25 and Under Sample (n=379)	p-value	Is Percent Difference Significant?
Female	71% (65)	77% (291)	0.249	No
Transfer Student	13% (12)	15% (55)	0.613	No
Full-Time	46% (35)	96% (364)	**<0.001**	**Yes**
Live on Campus	3% (3)	41% (159)	**<0.001**	**Yes**
White Race	87% (80)	82% (309)	0.214	No
Experienced Cyberbullying in College	5% (5)	11% (41)	0.031	Yes
Experienced Cyberstalking in College	8% (7)	9% (34)	0.754	No
Experienced Cyberbullying in High School	4% (4)	18% (67)	**<0.001**	**Yes**
Participated in Cyberbullying in High School	1% (1)	6% (24)	**0.002**	**Yes**
Have a Social Networking Account	49% (39)	88% (335)	**<0.001**	**Yes**
Visit a Social Networking Account 14+ Times per Week	13% (6)	35% (117)	**<0.001**	**Yes**

4. Participating in cyberbullying in high school (6% for "25 and younger" versus 1% for "over 25")
5. Having a social networking account (88% for "25 and younger" versus 49% for "over 25")
6. Visiting a social networking account 14+ times a week (35% for "25 and younger" versus 13% for "over 25")

These six factors provide possible interpretations about why younger students were more likely to be cyberbullied. For example, older students may have family responsibilities so that they do not live on campus and do not have much time to spend visiting social networking sites; therefore, they have less risk of being cyberbullied than the younger students.

It is likely that cyberbullying behaviors continue from high school to college. At the time when the students currently over age 25 were in high school, cyberbullying did not exist or just started. So, fewer college students over age 25 have experienced and participated in cyberbullying while in high school, and it is reasonable that fewer older college students were harassed in college than the younger students.

Victims of Cyberbullying

The "regular sample" refers to the sample with all 471 participants. Of the 471 respondents, there were 46 students that reported cyberbullying victimization in college who are classified as being part of the "victim sample". Table 6 compares the responses of the sample of the 46 victims to the sample of 471 uncharacterized students in the "regular sample". Table 6 compares the responses to questions about demographics, cyberbullying experiences, and social networking site usage of the "regular sample" and the "victim sample".

There are four p-values less than 0.05 in Table 6, each of which is associated a potential risk factor for being a victim of college cyberbullying. The four risk factors show what characteristics of students place them at risk to be victims in cyberbullying in college. The four risk factors are:

1. Full time students are more likely to experience cyberbullying victimization, since there

Table 6. Regular sample versus cyberbullying victims sample

Factor	Regular Sample (n=471)	Victims of Cyberbullying (n=46)	p-value	Is Percent Difference Significant?
Age 25 or Younger	80% (379)	89% (41)	**0.070**	at (p<0.10)
Female	76% (356)	83% (38)	0.234	No
Transfer Student	14% (67)	19% (9)	0.326	No
Full-Time	89% (421)	95% (44)	**0.049**	Yes
Live on Campus	34% (159)	40% (19)	0.427	No
White Race	83% (389)	91% (42)	0.079	at (p<0.10)
Experienced Cyberstalking in College	9% (41)	57% (26)	<0.001	Yes
Experienced Cyberbullying in High School	15% (71)	41% (19)	<0.001	Yes
Participated in Cyberbullying in High School	5% (25)	15% (7)	<0.001	Yes
Have a Social Networking Account	81% (380)	85% (39)	0.472	No
Visit a Social Networking Account 14+ Times per Week	23% (123)	36% (14)	0.076	at (p<0.10)

are a higher proportion of victims that are full time students (p=0.049) compared to the overall sample. This result is consistent with the results addressed in the previous section where a greater proportion of students from the "25 and under" group were full-time students and also victims of cyberbullying.

2. Cyberstalking is closely correlated with cyberbullying (p<0.001). Fifty seven percent of students that had been cyberbullied were also being cyberstalked compared to 9% of the survey respondents reporting that they were cyberstalked.

3. Victims in high school tend to be victims in college (p<0.001). That is, the cyberbullying role of victim tends to extend from high school to college. Victims who experienced cyberbullying in high school may not have learned how to protect themselves online and are still experiencing cyberbullying in college.

4. A greater percentage of college students experiencing cyberbullying victimization reported being cyberbullying offenders in high school (p<0.001). This discovery looks interesting. It is possible that offenders in

high school may be victims of revenge from their targets while in college.

Past research of cyberbullying and traditional bullying indicated that cyberbullying was an extension of in school bullying (Beran & Li, 2007). Students who used to be bullies or victims in elementary school would maintain the same roles in high school and college (Chapell et al., 2006). Research about students who were bullied in college by traditional methods found that there a correlation between having been bullied in college and having been bullied in high school (Chapell et al., 2006). The results of our study suggest that roles in cyberbullying are maintained over time similar to roles in traditional bullying.

In addition to the four risk-factors with p-values less than 0.05, there were three factors with p-values between 0.05 and 0.1 that can be called "risk factors with some significance". These factors are being age 25 or younger (p<0.070), of the white race (p<0.079), and visiting a social network account more than 14 times per week (p<0.076). The finding that a greater percentage of victims were younger than 25 years old, compared to regular students (p=0.07) is consistent with the result discussed in the previous section that age could be a risk factor for experiencing cyberbullying. Note that the proportion of respondents having a social networking account from both groups was not significantly (p=0.472) different. This implies that having a social networking account was not a risk-factor for being cyberbullied; but highly frequent visits to a social networking account would increase the stake of being cyberbullied.

Victims of Cyberstalking

Table 7 compares the responses of the 41 victims of cyberstalking which is called "cyberstalking victim sample" with the responses of the sample of 471 uncharacterized students which is called the "regular student sample". The table shows the proportions of the "regular student sample" versus the proportions of the "cyberstalking victim sample" in terms of demographic factors, history of cyberbullying experience, and use of social networking accounts.

There are three p-values in Table 7 that are less than 0.05, indicating significant differences between the cyberstalking victims and regular students. These factors are that a significantly higher percentage of students in the "cyberstalk-

ing victim sample" reported they experienced cyberbullying in college (p<0.001), experienced cyberbullying in high school (p< 0.001), and visited a social networking account more than 14 times per week (p<0.001) than students from the "regular sample".

The finding that a greater percentage of the respondents from the cyberstalking victims sample had experienced cyberbullying victimization in high school and college, compared to the respondents from the regular student sample, shows the significant correlation between cyberbullying and cyberstalking. The exact reasons why there is a greater percentage of cyberstalking victims having cyberbullying experience in high school require further research to investigate. In the prior section it was proposed that roles in cyberbullying may be maintained over time similar to the roles in traditional bullying. The intensity of victimization in cyberspace could escalate from high school to college. Hence, the victims of cyberbullying in high school may be experiencing cyberstalking as a more serious form of victimization in college.

The next finding was that a greater percentage of cyberstalking victims visited the social networking accounts fourteen times or more in

Table 7. Regular sample vs. cyberstalking victim sample

Factor	Regular Sample (n=471)	Victims of Cyberstalking (n=41)	p-value	Is Percent Difference Significant?
Age 25 or Younger	80% (379)	83% (34)	0.626	No
Female	76% (356)	80% (33)	0.541	No
Transfer Student	14% (67)	17% (7)	0.622	No
Full-Time	89% (421)	95% (30)	0.105	No
Live on Campus	34% (159)	34% (14)	1.000	No
White Race	83% (389)	82% (34)	0.873	No
Experienced Cyberbullying in College	9% (41)	63% (26)	<0.001	**Yes**
Experienced Cyberbullying in High School	15% (71)	41% (17)	0.001	**Yes**
Participated in Cyberbullying in High School	5% (25)	15% (6)	0.078	**At (p<0.10)**
Have Social Networking Account	81% (380)	85% (35)	0.495	No
Visited Social Networking Account 14+ Times per Week	23% (123)	49% (17)	0.001	**Yes**

a week, compared to regular students. This finding implies a positive relationship exists between the frequency of visiting the social networking accounts and likelihood of being cyberstalked.

In addition to the above three risk factors with p-values less than 0.05, the proportion of cyberstalking victims that participated in cyberbullying in high school has a p-value=0.078 which can be called a "risk factor with some significance". The proportion difference between the samples on this factor calls attention to a possible area for future research. This finding implies that cyberbullying offenders in high school are more likely to be cyberstalking victims in college, compared to regular students.

Victims' Reporting Incidents

This study shows that 20% of cyberbullying victims did not tell any one about the incident. Most victims of cyberbullying said that someone helped them cope with the cyberbullying problems, who was their friend (72%), parent (39%), significant other (30%), brother or sister (20%), or same age relative (11%). Less than 10% of respondents sought help from the campus resources such as a professor (9%), the counseling center (7%), college administrator (4%), campus police (2%), and computer services (2%). The primary reason respondents gave for not seeking help from anyone on campus was that they handled the problem themselves (60%). Other reasons cited were they did not think the incident was serious enough to report (22%), they did not know whom to report it to (18%), and they did not think the college would do anything about it (18%).

In the open ended questions respondents reported a couple of ways that they handled the incidents by themselves. These measures included blocking messages, changing e-mail address, and changing phone numbers. Some respondents said that talking with friends helped them solve the problem.

All of the respondents were asked how they would prefer to report a cyberbullying or cyberstalking incident. Over half (52%) of the respondents would send e-mails to a central email address, 21% would report it to an office on campus designated to handle cyberbullying and cyberstalking incidents, and 13% would call an anonymous hotline. Only 8% of respondents said they would report the incident to campus police and fewer students would report the incident to other campus resources such as computer center (3%), a professor (2%), or the counseling center (1%). Students said that they would be more likely to report the incident if a central e-mail address was available specially for handling cyberbullying or cyberstalking incidents.

DISCUSSION

The Sample

The sample in this study was taken from one public liberal arts college. The findings are for cyberbullying and cyberstalking incidents at this particular liberal art college, which are not supposed to be generalized to all college and university students. In addition, the sample was a convenience sample because it was composed of the students who chose to finish the survey. Such a convenience sample may have some features that are different from the population. The sample in this study, for example, was represented by 76% of female students. Therefore, not all the findings are necessarily representative of the entire student body.

The questions a respondent received during the survey varied based on their answers. Respondents who reported cyberbullying were asked considerably more questions. There was an incentive of winning a $50 gift certificate for Amazon.com for taking the survey. It is possible that respondents may have underreported cyberbullying to answer fewer questions or not read the questions carefully so as to complete the survey quickly and be eligible to win the gift certificate.

The length of the survey could have influenced the results since it was extensive, especially for subjects who reported cyberbullying. The subjects may have become tired during the survey and not answered the questions carefully or gave fewer details in the open ended questions.

There were up to five open ended questions in the survey to collect qualitative measures of students' cyberbullying and cyberstalking experiences. Answers to these questions were discussed briefly in the research findings and could facilitate further analysis.

Definition of Cyberbullying and Cyberstalking

In the survey, the definitions of cyberbullying and cyberstalking were provided, and victims of cyberbullying and cyberstalking were asked to describe their experiences. It was found that victims of cyberstalking provided more detailed descriptions of their experiences than the victims of cyberbullying. There were 26 respondents who reported both cyberbullying and cyberstalking experience, of which 15 students reported the same incident for both cyberbullying and cyberstalking in the open ended question. That phenomenon can be addressed by the research result of the Finn (2004) who believed that college students do not understand the term cyberstalking. It may also be caused by the complication that an incident started with cyberbullying might have escalated to cyberstalking. On the other hand, there were 26 participants in the study who seemed to understand the terms cyberbullying and cyberstalking well. They either provided proper and different examples for their cyberbullying and cyberstalking experience, or clearly identified only a cyberbullying or cyberstalking incident.

Future Research

Some other sampling methods than the convenience sampling could be utilized to improve the sample's representativeness. A survey could include students from several colleges and universities to extend its representativeness.

Further research is needed to explore how the Millennial generation defines cyberbullying and cyberstalking behaviors. Since students view the Internet as part of their daily life (Keeter & Taylor) they may have different ideas of what is considered normal behavior online. Their vernacular speech on the Internet may be perceived differently by other generations. Students' understanding of the definitions of cyberbullying and cyberstalking could be investigated so as to make the survey results more accurate.

The correlation between cyberbullying in high school and cyberbullying in college could be further studied. A detailed profile of the college cyberbullying could be established to help preventing it from happening.

CONCLUDING COMMENTS

This study has found that cyberbullying does not end in high school. In fact, participating in cyberbullying and being victims of cyberbullying in high school were significant risk-factors for later experiencing cyberbullying in college. A possible explanation is that students' roles in cyberbullying are maintained from high school to college similar to their roles in traditional bullying being maintained over time (Chapell, 2006). This study has also found that college students are experiencing cyberbullying predominately with calls and text messages from cell phones. The study by Finn (2004) did not find significant differences in age, race, class standing or residence for differences in online harassment (Finn, 2004). This study discovered correlations between cyberbullying experience and some factors like age, race, and social networking account access in a liberal arts college.

This study shows that college students are primarily handling cyberbullying incidents by themselves by blocking messages, and changing email addresses or cell phone numbers. They are seeking help from friends, parents, siblings, and significant others to cope with cyberbullying and cyberstalking incidents instead of using campus resources.

The majority of respondents in this study reported that they would like to report incidents of cyberbullying and cyberstalking stalking to a central e-mail address and almost two-thirds of the respondents said they would be more likely to consider reporting an incident if this resource was available. This is an important message for colleges and universities. Having a central e-mail address, which is low in cost and easy to implement, seems to be an effective measure of helping students handle cyberbullying incidents.

REFERENCES

Aftab, P. (2010 a). *Stop Cyberbullying: What is cyberbullying, exactly?* Retrieved February 8, 2010, from http://www.stopcyberbullying.org/what_is_cyberbullying_exactly.html

Aftab, P. (2010 b). *Stop Cyberbullying: Why do kids cyberbully each other?* Retrieved February 8, 2010, from http://www.stopcyberbullying.org/why_do_kids_cyberbully_each_other.html

Belsey, B. (2010). *Always on, always aware.* Retrieved April 30, 2010, from http://www.cyberbullying.org

Beran, T., & Li, Q. (2005). Cyberharassment: A study of a new method for an old behavior. *Journal of Educational Computing Research, 32*(3), 265–277. doi:10.2190/8YQM-B04H-PG4D-BLLH

Beran, T., & Li, Q. (2007). The relationship between cyberbullying and school bullying. *Journal of Student Wellbeing, 1*(2), 15–33.

Bocij, P. (2003). Victims of cyberstalking: An exploratory study of harassment perpetrated via the Internet. *First Monday, 8*(10). Retrieved January 30, 2010, from http://firstmonday.org/htbin/cgiwrap/bin/ojs/index.php/fm/article/view/1086/1006

Boyer, M. (2006, August 22). Colleges work to combat cyberstalking. *Fox News.* Retrieved January 14, 2010, from http://www.foxnews.com/story/0,2933,209395,00.html?sPage=fnc.college101

Campbell, M. (2005). Cyberbullying: An older problem in a new guise? *Australian Journal of Guidance & Counselling, 15*(1), 68–76. doi:10.1375/ajgc.15.1.68

Carlson, S. (2002, June 7). Trending the Net: Computer discipline offices offer a human touch when investigating student complaints. *The Chronicle of Higher Education, 35.*

Carruso, J. B., & Salaway, G. (2008, October). *The ECAR Study of Undergraduate Students and Information Technology, 2008.* Retrieved May 18, 2010, from http://net.educause.edu/ir/library/pdf/ERS0808/RS/ERS0808w.pdf

Chapell, M. S., Hasselman, S. L., Kitchin, T., Lomon, S. N., MacIver, K. W., & Sarullo, P. L. (2006). Bullying in elementary school, high school, and college. *Adolescence, 41*(164), 633–648.

Dickerson, D. (2005). Cyberbullies on campus. *Toledo Law Review, 37*(1). Retrieved January 14, 2010, from http://law.utoledo.edu/students/lawreview/volumes/v37n1/Dickerson.htm

ECPAT International. (2005). *Violence in Cyberspace against children*. Retrieved February 10, 2006, from http://www.ecpat.net/eng/publications/Cyberspace/PDF/ECPAT_Cyberspace_2005-ENG.pdf

Englander, E., Muldowney, A. M., & McCoy, M. (2009). Cyberbullying and information exposure: User-generated content in post secondary education. *International Journal of Contemporary Sociology*, *46*(2), 213–230.

Finn, J. (2004). A survey of online harassment at a university campus. *Journal of Interpersonal Violence*, *19*(4), 468–483. doi:10.1177/0886260503262083

Harson, A. (1995, November 25). Student's expulsion over e-mail raises concern. *Los Angels Times*. Retrieved December 11, 2007, from http://mr.caltech.edu/media/time.html

Harvey, M., Treadway, D., Heames, J. T., & Duke, A. (2009). Bullying in the 21st century global organization: An ethical perspective. *Journal of Business Ethics*, *85*, 27–40. doi:10.1007/s10551-008-9746-8

Keeter, S., & Taylor, P. (2009). The Millenials. *Pew Internet Research*. Retrieved May 20, 2010, from http://pewresearch.org/pubs/1437/millennials-profile

Kraft, E. M. (2010). Juicycampus.com: How was this business model culpable to encouraging harassment on college campuses? In Shariff, S., & Churchill, A. (Eds.), *Truths and myths of cyber-bullying: International perspectives on stakeholder responsibility and children's safety* (pp. 65–103). New York: Peter Lang Publishing.

Lee, R. (1998). Romantic and electronic stalking in a college context. *The College of William and Mary Journal of Women and the Law*, 373-409.

Luppicini, R. (2008). The emerging field of Technoethics. In Luppicini, R., & Adell, R. (Eds.), *Handbook of Research on Technoethics* (pp. 1–18). Hershey, PA: IGI Global.

McNiff, E., & Varney, A. (2008, May 14). College Gossip Crackdown: Chelsea Gorman Speaks Out: Juicy Campus' Cruel Online Postings Prompt Government Investigation. *ABC News*. Retrieved May 20, 2010, from http://abcnews.go.com/2020/Story?id=4849927&page=1

McQuade, S. (2007). We Must Educate Young People About Cybercrime Before They Start College. *Chronicle of Higher Education, 53*(14), B29. Retrieved January 13, 2010, from http://chronicle.com/article/We-Must-Educate-Young-People/23514/

Nansel, T., Overpeck, M., Pila, R., Ruan, W., Simmon-Morton, B., & Scheidt, P. (2001). Bullying behaviors among U.S. youth: Prevalence and association with psychosocial adjustment. *Journal of the American Medical Association*, *285*(16), 2094–2100. doi:10.1001/jama.285.16.2094

National Center for Victims of Crime. (2010). *Cyberstalking*. Retrieved May 20, 2010, from http://www.ncvc.org/ncvc/main.aspx?dbName=DocumentViewer&DocumentID=32458

National Conference of State Legislators. (2010). *State Electronic Harassment or "Cyberstalking" Laws*. Retrieved April 20, 2010, from http://www.ncsl.org/default.aspx?tabid=13495

National Crime Prevention Council. Cyberbullying FAQ for Teens. Retrieved May 18, 2010, from http://www.ncpc.org/topics/cyberbullying/cyberbullying-faq-for-teens.

Olewus, D. (2001). Peer harassment: A critical analysis and some important issues (introduction). In Juvonen, J., & Graham, S. (Eds.), *Peer harassment in school: The plight of the vulnerable and victimized* (pp. 3–20). New York: Guildford Press.

Olsen, F. (2001). Michigan deactivates Internet program linked in several stalking incidents. *The Chronicle of Higher Education, 47*(7), 34.

Patchin, J. W., & Hinduja, S. (2006). Bullies move beyond the schoolyard, - A preliminary look at cyberbullying. *Youth Violence and Juvenile Justice, 4*(2), 148–169. doi:10.1177/1541204006286288

Paullet, K. L., Rota, D. R., & Swan, T. T. (2009). Cyberstalking: An exploratory study of students at a mid-Atlantic university. *Issues in Information Systems, 10*(2), 640–648.

Pepitone, J. (2006, February 8). Kicked in the face: Freshmen claim Judicial Affairs threatened expulsion for creation of Facebook group critical of TA. *The Daily Orange*. Retrieved January 13, 2010, from http://www.dailyorange. com/media/paper522/news/2006/02/08/News/ Kicked.In.The.Face.Freshmen.Claim.Judicial. Affairs.Threatened.Expulsion.For.Crea-1603618. shtml?norewrite

Project NEThics. (2009). Retrieved January 24, 2010, from http://www.nethics.umd.edu/

Read, B. (2006, January 20). Think Before You Share Students' online socializing can have unintended consequences. *The Chronicle of Higher Education, 52*(20), A38. Retrieved January 14, 2010 from http://www.usi.edu/stl/vpsa/forms/ ThinkBeforeYouShare.pdf.

Rogerson, S. (2000). Computer based harassment on college campuses. *Student Affairs online: The Online Magazine about Technology and Student Affairs, 1*(1). Retrieved December 12, 2007, from www.studentaffairs.com/ejournal/Spring_2000/ article5.hml

Sauders, R. (2005). Happy slapping: transatlantic contagion or home-grown, mass-mediated nihilism? *The London Consortium Static, 1*. Retrieved April 30, 2010, from http://static.londonconsortium.com/issue01/saunders_happyslapping.pdf

Schweitzer, S. (2005, October 6) Fisher College expels student over website entries. *Boston Globe*. Retrieved January 13, 2010, from http://www.boston.com/news/local/articles/2005/10/06/fisher_college_expels_student_over_website_entries/

Shariff, S. (2008). *Cyber-bullying: Issues and solutions for the school, the classroom and the home*. New York: Routledge.

Spitzberg, B. H., & Hoobler, G. (2002). Cyberstalking and the technologies of interpersonal terrorism. *New Media & Society, 4*, 71–92. doi:10.1177/14614440222226271

Szoka, B., & Thierer, A. (2009, June). Cyberbullying legislation: Why education is preferable to regulation. *The Progress and Freedom Foundation, 16*(12). Retrieved April 29, 2010, from http://www.pff.org/issues-pubs/pops/2009/ pop16.12-cyberbullying-education-better-than-regulation.pdf

United States Department of Justice. (2000). *The Electronic Frontier: The challenge of unlawful conduct involving use of the Internet. Report of the President's working group on unlawful conduct on the Internet*. Retrieved May 19, 2010, from http://www.justice.gov/criminal/cybercrime/ unlawful.htm

Virginia Polytechnic Institute and State University. (2010). *Cyberstalking/Online Harassment @ Virginia Tech*. Retrieved January 31, 2010, from http://www.stopabuse.vt.edu/cyberstalking.php

Willard, N. (2007). *Educator's Guide to Cyberbullying and Cyberthreats. Center for Safe and Responsible use of the Internet*. Retrieved December 16, 2009, from http://cyberbully.org/ cyberbully/docs/cbcteducator.pdf

Workman, T. (2008, October). How Digital Culture Shapes Student's Minds. The Real Impact of Virtual Worlds. *The Chronicle of Higher Education, 55*(4).

Ybarra, M., & Mitchell, K. (2007). Prevalence and Frequency of Internet Harassment Investigation: Implications for Adolescent Health. *The Journal of Adolescent Health*, *41*(2), 189–195. doi:10.1016/j.jadohealth.2007.03.005

Young, J. (2008b, March 28). How to Combat a Campus-Gossip Web Site (and Why You Shouldn't). *Chronicle of Higher Education*. Retrieved May 19, 2010, from http://chronicle.com/weekly/v54/i29/29a01602.htm

This work was previously published in International Journal of Technoethics, Volume 1, Issue 4, edited by Rocci Luppicini, pp. 74-91, copyright 2010 by IGI Publishing (an imprint of IGI Global).

Chapter 10
Cyberbullying:
A Sociological Approach

José Pinheiro Neves
University of Minho, Portugal

Luzia de Oliveira Pinheiro
University of Minho, Portugal

ABSTRACT

Cyberbullying has become a major social concern because it raises questions about technoethics. It has been the subject of research, information and prevention activities for different groups to protect against the misuse of technology, and because of that, this paper is based on an exploratory study about the sociological phenomenon of cyberbullying among Portuguese university students. The paper stresses the connection between the concepts of bullying and cyberbullying while promoting a flexible epistemological model that highlights the emerging nature of these phenomena based on the theoretical contribution of Gregory Bateson. In the end, the authors present the main conclusions of the empirical study.

CYBERBULLYING: A SOCIOLOGICAL APPROACH

The cyberbullying has become a major social concern because raises questions about the ethical use of technology. In recent years, has been the subject of research and information and prevention activities for different groups such as governmental and non-governmental organizations, schools and parents' associations to protect against

DOI: 10.4018/978-1-4666-1773-5.ch010

the misuse of technology. This issue has become so important that the media also understood the importance of encouraging debate about it. Based on its magnitude, in the present work, our goal is to describe the phenomenon and present some results of an empirical study (Pinheiro, 2009).

On the Definition of Bullying

Before characterizing the phenomenon of cyberbullying, we will make a short description on bullying, distinguishing it from other situations of violence. Then we will draw attention to some characteristic features of cyberbullying.

Although bullying exists long ago as a social phenomenon, it only started to be investigated in the 70s by Dan Olweus, a professor at University of Bergen in Norway (Abrapia, 2006). He found that bullying was not natural or typical in the development of a child but something that could cause suicide (quoted in Pereira, 1997). However, the institutions were not interested on that subject until when, in the 80's, three young boys aged between 10 and 14 committed suicide in Norway (Abrapia, 2006). Then, the first anti-bullying campaign was conducted in Norway in 1993: the National Campaign Anti-Bullying. Simplifying, school bullying is a term that refers to all acts of violence and aggressive behaviour that are intentional and repetitive. This means that all acts of violence deliberated and systematic, with the purpose to tarnishing the image of others, are considered bullying (Abrapia, 2006; McCarthy, Sheehan, Wilkie, & Wilkie, 1996, p. 50). Although this phenomenon is more expressive in public schools it also happens in the particular ones. The physical space where it happens more often is the playground (Cortellazzo, 2006). According to Dan Olweus, bullying has three key features (DeVoe, Kaffenberger, & Chandler, 2005):

- It is an aggressive and harmful behaviour;
- A behaviour carried out repeatedly;
- A behaviour that occurs in a relationship where there is a discrepancy of power between peers.

This somewhat simple definition does not include the various dimensions of the phenomenon. In truth, "the investigation of bullying is further complicated by the complex dynamics of bullying scenarios and the developmental context for social development in which bullying plays a role" (DeVoe, Kaffenberger, & Chandler, 2005). For example, the conceptual separation between the social relations of violence and aggression that arise in human interactions spontaneously and the type associated with bullying are not yet very clear. "Further, aggression among youth often serves varied purposes for children at different stages of development" (DeVoe, Kaffenberger and Chandler, 2005). (DeVoe, Kaffenberger, & Chandler, 2005). Therefore, it is necessary to make some clarifications, based on the existing literature. For the first feature we should know what is the type and degree of negativity and aggression. The definition of bullying, according to some authors, is a complex task, which goes beyond the mere physical and verbal aggression: it also covers psychological focused behaviours, for example manipulation. In a way, there will be an interaction that approaches the social aspects of the relation (Ericson, 2001). According to most authors, there are two types of direct bullying: physical bullying associated to physical aggression and verbal bullying based on insults and humiliation. However, according to some authors, another type of bullying is appearing in school: the social bullying by denying integration in groups and activities (Wikipedia, 2009). In Figure 1 we can perceive what kinds of aggression are associated with the three forms of bullying practice:

Repetitive. In the first place, as argued by Adams (quoted in Cortellazzo, 2006, p. 1), European Commissioner for Combating Bullying, this problem is not just an accidental conflict, but a repeated situation. It should present, therefore, a characteristic that differentiates bullying from a traditional dispute between peers, more or less serious. Therefore we know that this is a case of bullying while the disagreement among peers is in fact continuous (Carvalho, Lima, & Matos, 2001). The continued disagreement is easily visible as we will see over days, weeks, months and years, the same peers in consecutive disagreements (Abrapia, 2006). Throughout this time, we found that one of the peer's attacks and the other takes the

Figure 1. Forms of bullying more common

Physical
- Agress (punch, kick, push...)
- Break, steal or extort belongings
- Steal and extort money

Verbal
- Ofend and insult
- Put "names" (big nose, cow...)
- Count jokes and provoke
- Launch rumours
- Threaten

Psychological
- Imitate and pursue
- Humiliate and discriminate
- Ignore and do not speak
- Exclude and isolate
- Intimidate and dominate

role of victim, and can at some point try to defend himself against the aggressor, but never managing to talk him out of it for a long time (Abrapia, 2006).

Between peers. Hawkins, Pepler, and Craig (2001) found that peers were present in 88 percent of bullying episodes. Thus, bullying frequently involves the support of peers within the school community and is often not an isolated event between two individuals. Thus, bullying frequently involves the support of peers within the school community and is often not an isolated event between two individuals. To be more precise, when the bullying happens, we usually have a victim and some peers around her.

Reversal roles. Thirdly, this continuity supported for the peer gives its author (the aggressor in this case) a sense of power and to the victim the image of "bad guy" (Abrapia, 2006; McCarthy, Sheehan, Wilkie, & Wilkie, 1996), or, in other words, provoking the circumstance (which is not true, as the instigator

of the situation is the perpetrator). This is based on the logic of reversal roles between the aggressor and the victim, resulting in misjudgements of the situation by adults (see Palacios & Rego, 2006, p. 2). Thus, in most cases where the victim denounces the offender to an adult, it replied that it just happened "because you did something," placing the responsibility of the situation on the victim and protecting the aggressor (Palacios & Rego, 2006, p. 2). When it does, the aggressor have literally the way open to continue to practice bullying and the victim is, and will continue to be the victim of the aggressor, the victim of indifference and insensitivity of adults who could help (Palacios & Rego, 2006, p. 2). And suffer doubly with it: on the one hand, suffers with the bullying infringed by the aggressor and on the other hand feel indifference and lack of assistance from the adults who could help but didn't. This can cause several depressions to the victim and lead to suicide, only for lack of help (Pinheiro, 2007). On the other hand, the aggressor, enjoying an additive sense of power and impunity, takes advantage of being seen as a victim and because of that continues to humiliate their peers.

In fact, according to other authors, bullying behaviour emerges from the will of strength and power, becoming a popular person, bullying colleagues, showing them his superiority and terrorizing them (McCarthy, Sheehan, Wilkie, & Wilkie, 1996, p. 54). In other words, it becomes a repetitive situation that may be associated with an additive behaviour.

Indirect bullying – Cyberbullying. Bored to practice bullying always the same way the bullie looks for new ways to do it. So, curious, he decides to try out new technologies to practice bullying because they are easy to access and use the know-how.

In summary, bullying is a social phenomenon whose complexity can only be understood through the concepts of social theory. Some authors thought that the main aim of social sciences should be trying to understand the characteristics of links in its multiple and interdisciplinary nature (Latour, 2005; Bateson, 1955, 1989).

CHARACTERIZATION OF CYBERBULLYING

Let us now see how, starting from the previous reflection, we characterize the emerging phenomenon of Cyberbullying. It will be convenient to make here a slight reflection on the definition of cyberbullying. Some people understand this phenomenon merely as the extension of school bullying. However, cyberbullying is something more complex and therefore is not limited simply to that.

Nowadays, much of cyberbullying phenomena become popular as harassment, psychological pressure, verbal abuse, threats, theft of personal data and image manipulation through new technologies, especially computer with Internet access.

This phenomenon has expanded throughout the world and quickly the media wake up to it. Increasingly well known to us, cyberbullying, name by which this issue is known in the U.S. and the UK is already the focus of studies and campaigns to prevent and combat it (Wikipedia, 2007).

How did happen. However, contrary to popular belief, this phenomenon did not start with cell phone, much less the Internet. The cyberbullying, according to information obtained through the empirical part, have emerged from the social conjecture to the way we know it now. Chronologically, we can distinguish a gradual evolution of cyberbullying in three stages, each divided according to the technological resources employed in its practice.

We started by describing the genealogy of cyberbullying. In the first stage (1), the pre-cyberbullying that was when the cyberbullying appeared and began to take form. This term (pre) is appropriate to the fact that at this stage, the technological resources used still can not be completely known by the prefix "cyber", which is understandable since they are a photocopying and telephone. It was with a photocopying we reproduced and distributed many false images and text and / or insulting stories about the victims and the telephone was used to spend hours making anonymous calls to all the colleagues with whom he wanted to "enjoy".

But as the technologies are constantly developing, this phenomenon has evolved, entering the second stage (2): the cyberbullying. Adopting the name and the form for which it is known today. This fact arises with the emergence of mobile phones. With the 1st generation of mobile phones, cyberbullying starts happening through text messages. Fast and low cost, SMS are used to spread offensive stories quickly, and resulting in numerous waves of laughter through the corridors of classrooms where the victims went. Subsequently, with the mobile phones advance and with that starts emerging on the market the 2nd generation of mobile phones, equipped with camera. It was at this point that we began to prepare the ground for the third stage but the transition was not done yet. So, equipped with cameras, the cyberbullies began taking pictures to their victims as a hobby, usually during and after they are attacked. The photos then were used to show on the cell phone, because sending multimedia messages is more expensive than the text messages. The solution was for share the images on the Internet. However, there were few people who had access to them. Over time and with a few technological advances, the Internet turns into something well known to our young people.

With the expansion of the Internet to schools entered the third stage (3) of this phenomenon, which now assumes the name of digital bullying.

Figure 2. Evolution of the phenomenon: the 3 stages

```
Stage 1
Pre-cyberbullying
      Photocopying
      Telephone

Stage 2
Cyberbullying
      Mobile phones (1ˢᵗ and 2ⁿᵈ generation)

Stage 3
Digital bullying
      Mobile phones (3ʳᵈ generation)
      Internet
```

This designation is appropriate because it begins to be consummate principally through digital technologies such as the Internet. At this time, the photographs taken with mobile phones and digital cameras are now posted and distributed by e-mail. They also are created fake profiles with these photos. In the midst of this, mobile phones have a new development and there is the 3rd generation, with mobile phones equipped with a camcorder. This is where the bullying took the contours for which is today know it.

In Figure 2 we can have a best view of this development:

Basic definition. Once explained the emergence of the phenomenon under study, is now time to define it. We already know that cyberbullying had developmental periods and that is practiced with the new technologies, but what is it exactly? Bill Belsey (2005), professor in Cochrane, Alberta, who we think to have been the first person to use the term, defines cyberbullying as a variant of traditional bullying. Later, cyberbullying has been defined by the use of communication technologies and information to denigrate, humiliate and / or defame a person or a group of people.

Currently practiced by email, phone, pager, personal websites, text messages, multimedia messages and videos, that the cyberbullying out mainly on the Internet contributed to it transformation into a global problem more complex than traditional bullying (Wikipedia, 2007).

Problems. However we have to note that not all persons identifying this phenomenon as cyberbullying, for what, for some it can be considered cyberbullying, for others it may be a simple case of defamation.

Therefore, it is appropriate give a slight reflection on the definition of cyberbullying. Some people understand this phenomenon merely as the continuation of school bullying, however, cyberbullying is something more complex and therefore is not simply limited to this (Bateson, 1989).

We conclude that the diffusion of defamatory messages and images and / or false about one or more individuals can be considered cyberbullying. But this raises some questions, specifically whether all occurrences would be cyberbullying. Vamos então analisar esta questão. Let us examine this question. If we use an image found on Google or some other site with a photo of our profile, so as not to be recognized, this is not cyberbullying. It's having a false identity. However, it is cyberbullying if the image in question was used intentionally to humiliate and / or defame the person who that image belongs. Finally, it should explain how we can distinguish cyberbullying of crimes such as defamation. The answer is not simple. The cyberbullying are all acts premeditated and intentional, having or not to aware of the real extent of such an act on the victim (Belsey, 2005). Once on the Internet the characteristic of continuity does not equate, because if is not totally eliminated, it is continuous, so there don't needs to be repeated by the same person (Mitchell, 2007).

According to legal data in Portugal, defamation has the same characteristics, except that is something discontinuous.. However, defamation on the Internet can be understood as cyberbullying.

Ways and degrees of intensity of Cyberbullying.

After having defined the object of study we will analyze it by the features it presents. Analyzing, we observe that the cyberbullying have multiple characters (different from the bullying at school), specifically the graph (1), concerning about the use of the image, the verbal (2), referring to the use of language and the psychological (3), regarding the diffusion of false data about the victim.

Analyzed the characteristics of cyberbullying and after the study of different types of cases found through the empirical work done, we can point to various levels of occurrence, namely three, depending of the type of case. The first level (1) is one in which only occurs cyberbullying. Only happens in the Internet and is practiced by insults, obscene messages, sexual comments and / or harassment by an exchange of e-mail and creating false profiles, usually several. The main characteristic of this type of defamation is that it is practiced spontaneously, with the only intention to humiliate the victim and to harass them. The second level (2) is the bullying more cyberbullying where the second is a continuation of the first. Not satisfied, the bullies using the new technologies, specifically the mobile phones and the Internet, for an innovation sending some text messages with stories about the victim. This type of behaviour is characterized by happen consciously in order to frighten the victim and to enjoy seeing the reaction of the victim. Finally, the third level (3) is one in which resort to bullying to practice cyberbullying. Similar to the previous level but different, this type has two variations that are called "light" and "heavy." The "light" is one in which to make a "mockery", rather than simply

take occasional photos, bullies attacks the victim in order to take these pictures and then allocated that pictures on multimedia messages or the Internet. On the other hand, we have the "heavy" when, as in the previous case, a victim is chosen but without the intention of taking pictures, but to film all aggression. In other words, in the "hard" version of cyberbullying type 3, a group of people reunited to harm anyone on purpose to be filmed and posted on Youtube almost like a "trophy." We have here an example of the phenomenon of "happy slap", much appreciated in the U.S.

Having defined the types of cyberbullying that we may find ourselves, it's time to look into the characteristics of those who practice it. The cyberbullies is the practitioner of cyberbullying, is distinguished into two groups: the accidental cyberbullies (1) and addicts (2). The accidental cyberbullies (1), are characterized by being those who use new technologies or to play (in a pejorative way) with a person or as a form of revenge. They are thus who, for example, creates a false personal page, exchange intimate images of someone with they group and expose stories in blogs. The cases of revenge following the end of a relationship are regularly like a police source said. But what distinguishes this type of addictive cyberbullying is that the accidental cyberbullies fails the notion of the effect of his act on the victim. In fact, the idea here is to be something now, passenger and with not other intentions than to "play" with the person in that moment. Then we have the most serious level, the addict cyberbullies (2). These are those who practice cyberbullying because its gives pleasure. This type of cyberbullying could be started by practice cyberbullying to try and see how it is, but sometime have experienced some kind of good feeling from this practice, and it became a habit. This type of cyberbullies runs personal pages as predators and as sexual predators, choose a victim, and pursue it until near exhaustion (Neves, 2008). Unlike predators, the addict cyberbullies do not look for physical pleasure, but for the psychological, as the feeling of control.

The face to face relation and the mediated relation. In addition, gradually contributing to this is the fact that, contrary to what occurs when practicing bullying at school, on the Internet the face to face interaction does not equate, so we ended up doing things we would not do in a face to face interaction. New technologies facilitate the same to process a blur between reality and imagination. We often hear someone say, *"is on the Internet, does not matter."* And we feel a transcendent freedom when plunged into the network. They are only *avatars* and *nicknames*. We can give free rein to imagination and not repress any kind of behaviour. We can insult someone in a virtual community without fear. After all, the worst scenario is to see our account disable, but what matters if it gave us a great pleasure insult that individual? We can always create a new account. We are free to do it. The truth is that the cyberbullies, the ones who practice cyberbullying, feel they will never be identified. Consequently the promise of anonymity offered by the Internet is a great engine for spreading this type of violence. However the promise of anonymity is not true, for is just that: a promise. All of us when we use the Internet are subjects of identification (each computer, each phone has a unique identification number). Furthermore, all things share on the Internet are impossible to be removed because they are exposed to an infinite audience, whose ability to absorb, transmit, share and change information is invaluable, which can lead cyberbullies to satisfaction (Correa, 2008).

THE NEED FOR A NEW EPISTEMOLOGY IN THE STUDY OF CYBERBULLYING

Decided to study an emerging phenomenon with the use of the Internet and new technologies, we found in the theories of new media a starting point, since it seeks to describe the network of relations in space and time with the condition that an entity that provides communication is the actor.

Focusing on the study of cyberbullying as an emerging phenomenon with the use of new technologies and covers communication processes, then we draw it to the need to formulate a new epistemology in the field of communication studies. This should then be characterized by the insertion of new media studies in the field of communication according to triad technology / communication / society and the link between theory and practice.

In this sense we can highlight the empirical observation and correlation as key elements in the study of phenomena of new media, as is advocated Röhl (2005, p. 420), William Mitchell (in Correa, 2008), Neil Postman (in Correa, 2008) and Muniz Sodré (in Correa, 2008), since the production of knowledge in the new media equate in real life, making the immateriality of cyberspace and assigning the same condition of space electronic flow of communication and sociability in an logic, of neo-tribalism (Rabot, 2009). Several authors, inspired by the tradition of interpretive social sciences, such as José Luis Braga (2007) defend the premise that the production of knowledge in this field can not be similar to that used in the natural sciences, because it is necessary to interpret and create meaning. Since the communicational phenomena are not things in themselves closed and should be observed and studied on a case (Correa, 2008). Therefore, it becomes clear that it is through the association of meanings that we can produce knowledge. Therefore, it is now possible to delineate, with greater conceptual clarity, the epistemological model to follow in the study of phenomena of new media (Martins, 2006; Miranda, 2002; Neves, 2006).

In this sense, according to Braga (2007), the epistemological model suggested in these cases should be characterized by:

- The study of individual cases,
- The phenomena clues not immediately evident,
- For the distinction between essential and accidental signs,
- The link between the evidence and selected,
- For the derivation of inferences

That's because the study of the phenomena of the new media is based on the triad situation empirical / theoretical / research problems. Being fruitful the union of knowledge gained through all areas of science, shaping them for the benefit of ongoing research, because communication is a process of cultural development. After all, as argued by Lev Manovitch (2003), social networking is polychronic and multidirectional.

THE CONTRIBUTION OF GREGORY BATESON: THE META-LANGUAGE AND THE MEDIATED RELATION

Thus, it seemed appropriate to study the open question of research using the perspectives that are at the borders between sociology and the areas like animal biology, along the lines suggested by Bateson. As Bateson very well realised, the human and animal communication goes beyond verbosity and writing, as it is surrounded by gestures, facial and bodily expressions, tone of voice, melodies and vocal expressions different, the so-called meta-language or meta-communication. Thus, according to Bateson (1955), the meta-language is fundamental to understanding the real meaning of the action of another. Without her, we would lose an important part of the message. You could not understand a phrase like "You're so crazy"

is ironic in the sense of humiliation or just a joke (Baptista, 2004). Carrying Bateson's theory for the study of cyberbullying, which we see fit as there is a great lack of meta-communication through the use of new technologies compared to existing meta-communication regarding the face to face interaction, as in school bullying. Now if, as argued by Gregory Bateson (1955), the meta-language is necessary to understanding the true intentions of the human interaction, it means that in case of interaction through new technologies, we will be more difficult to interpret the action of other, since we are not face to face interacting. When we not do that, we didn't observe the body language of others (in case of video calling you can not see the other as a whole, for example, the position of the feet, hands ticks, etc.) and many cases do not hear the tone (in case you hear the tone that we are subject to this being distorted), so that the meta-language is limited, so the interpretation of the action of another is partial too. In this regard, Bateson (1955) helps us understand why cyberbullying happens in some cases: misinterpretation of the meaning of the actions of another. Using the tables of interaction proposed by Bateson, highlights the ambiguity in communication between humans, then advocating the adoption of an interdisciplinary perspective including social psychology and sociology of communication.

RESULTS OF THE EMPIRICAL STUDY ON YOUNG PORTUGUESE UNIVERSITY

Given that emergent phenomena are difficult to study, we adopted a research strategy combining qualitative and quantitative techniques that included observation, focus groups, interviews and investigation. Thus, in this study, whose aim is to explore and define the characteristics of cyberbullying in Portugal we have studied the behaviour of university students in terms of information, attitudes and beliefs. In this sense, the central question that arose in our study was to understand this new dependency as being a continuation of a typical phenomenon in human societies: the daily violence of social relations, which have additive effects. This was confirmed during the practical part, they were combined qualitative and quantitative techniques. We can see that despite the intensive use of new technologies, the majority of people show reduced levels of information about the problem (cyberbullying), about which many people had only vaguely heard on television. Despite the knowledge of the subject does not reveal directly to the type of use made of the Internet, the type of use is directly linked to the number of hours spent online per week. The longer we spend by week on the Internet, the greater the potential to come across cases of cyberbullying, which, because of the limited information that brings about the phenomenon, we can simply ignore by not knowing that it is cyberbullying. However, if we take into account the beliefs of our young people with regard to cyberbullying, imagine at the outset that ever practice something like this and that if faced with a case of these and knew identify, denounce the situation and try to help the victim. But is not the case: our young people actually show very good intentions (high levels of beliefs about the subject) but with regard to practical action it is not confirmed.

According to research, university students tend to think one thing and doing another in relation to cyberbullying, showing that there is great ambiguity in how the phenomenon is viewed and practiced. The attitudes of young people, contrary to what would wait, are not consistent with their beliefs.

In short, the investigation led us to the following main conclusions:

- The university students have little information about the subject;
- Have attitudes of sympathy toward the bully behaviour;
- However, have very critical beliefs about cyberbullying showing ambiguity thus how they face the phenomenon.

One can perhaps say that agree with what essentially characterizes modern society: an increase of the ambiguity and its fleeting and ambiguous nature.

CLOSING REMARKS

We left open the need for further studies on this subject without falling into an empirical linear and simplistic characterization, based on an approach that makes his genealogy and characterization of new patterns of (inter) human action. Some issues: the extent to which the form of cyberbullying does not oblige us to revise the classical categories of sociology that are based on the physical relation of face to face? The fact that many of these situations involve a contact that is mediated and simultaneously, without the presence of the physical body, can lead us to revise the schemes proposed by the classical scholars of the interaction as Erving Goffman (1986). Perhaps the use of the work of Gregory Bateson (1989), as mentioned above, is helpful in attempting to rethink the border areas between our animal heritage and ambiguous characteristics of human violence in the cyber society.

REFERENCES

Abrapia. (2006). *Programa de redução do comportamento agressivo entre estudantes*. Retrieved February 19, 2007, from http://www.bullying.com.br/Bconceituacao21.htm

Baptista, C. (2004). *A fragilidade da experiência: Erving Goffman e os quadros da interacção*. Unpublished doctoral dissertation, Universidade Nova de Lisboa, Portugal.

Bateson, G. (1955). A Theory of Play and Fantasy. In *A.P.A. Psychiatric Research Reports, II*, 177–193.

Bateson, G. (1989). *Metadiálogos*. Lisboa, Portugal: Gradiva.

Belsey, B. (2005). *Cyberbullying: An emerging threat to the "always on" generation*. Retrieved January 16, 2007, from http://www.cyberbullying. ca/pdf/feature_dec2005.pdf

Bourhis, R., & Leyens, J.-P. (1994). *Stéréotypes, discrimination et relations intergroupes*. Brussels, Belgium: Mardaga Editores.

Brabham, D. C. (2008). *Review of a book: Organized networks: media theory, creative labour, new institutions*. Retrieved November 24, 2008, from http://rccs.usfca.edu/bookinfo. asp?ReviewID=535&BookID=288

Braga, J. L. (2007). *Comunicação, disciplina indiciária*. Paper presented at the GT "Epistemologia da Comunicação," Anais do XVI Encontro da Compós, Curitiba, Brasil.

Carvalhosa, S., Lima, L., & Matos, M. (2001). *Bullying - a provocação/vitimação entre pares no contexto escolar português*. Retrieved March 8, 2007, from http://www.scielo.oces.mtces.pt/ pdf/asp/v19n4/v19n4a04.pdf

Corrêa, E. S. (2008). Reflexões para uma epistemologia da comunicação digital. *Observatório, 4*, 307-320. Retrieved October 10, 2008, from http://obs.obercom.pt/index.php/obs/article/ view/116/142

Cortellazzi, L. (2006). *Bullying: humilhar, intimidar, ofender, agredir*. Retrieved March 26, 2007, from http://www.eep.br/noticias/docs/ bullying.pdf

Davis, R. A. (2001). *What is Internet addiction?* Retrieved March 12, 2009, from http://www. internetaddiction.ca/internet_addiction.htm

DeVoe, J. F., Kaffenberger, S., & Chandler, K. (2005). Student Reports of Bullying. Results of 2001 *School Crime Supplement to the National Crime Victimization Survey*. Washington, DC: US National Center for Education Statistics. Retrieved November 26, 2009, from http://nces. ed.gov/pubs2005/2005310.pdf

Ericson, N. (2001). *Addressing the Problem of Juvenile Bullying*. Washington, DC: U.S. Government Printing Office.

Goffman, E. (1986). *Frame Analysis: An Essay on the Organization of Experience*. New York: Northeastern Press.

Goldberg, I. (1999). *Internet addiction disorder*. Retrieved December 14, 2008, from http://www. uml.edu/student-services/counseling/internet/ netdisorder.html

Hawkins, D. L., Pepler, D. J., & Craig, W. M. (2001). Naturalistic Observations of Peer Interventions. In *Social Development*. Retrieved January 29, 2009, from http://www3. interscience.wiley.com/journal/119028433/ abstract?CRETRY=1&SRETRY=0

Latour, B. (2005). *Reassembling the Social: an Introduction to Actor-Network-Theory*. Oxford, UK: Clarendon.

Manovitch, L. (2003). New Media from Borges to HTML. In Wardrip-Fruin, N., & Montfort, N. (Eds.), *The New Media Reader*. Cambridge, MA: The MIT Press.

Martins, M. L. (2006). A nova erótica interactiva. In *Revista de Comunicação e Linguagens (No. 37)*. Braga, Portugal: ICS.

McCarthy, P., Sheehan, M., Wilkie, S., & Wilkie, W. (1996). *Bullying: causes, costs and cures*. Brisbane, Australia: Beyond Bullying Association Inc.

Miranda, J. B. (2002). *Teoria da Cultura*. Lisbon, Portugal: Século XXI.

Morais, T. (2007). *Cyberbullying em crescendo.* Retrieved May 31, 2008, from http://www.miudos-segurosna.net/artigos/2007-04-04.html

Neves, J. P. (2006). *O apelo do objecto técnico.* Oporto, Portugal: Campo das Letras.

Neves, J. P. (2008). *Algumas considerações provisórias acerca das redes sociais na Internet e o conceito de dependência.* Retrieved November 2, 2008, from http://www.socialsoftware.blogspot.com

Olweus, D. (1991). Bully/victim problems among schoolchildren: basic facts and effects of school based intervention program. In Pether, D., & Rubin, K. (Eds.), *The development and treatment of childhood aggression.* Hillsdale, NJ: Erlbaum.

Palácios, M., & Rego, S. (2006). Bullying: mais uma epidemia invisível? Retrieved April 5, 2007, from http://www.scielo.br/pdf/rbem/v30n1/v30n1a01.pdf

Pinheiro, L. (2007). *Bullying: o perfil da vítima.* Retrieved October 12, 2008, from http://sites.google.com/site/bullyingemportugal/

Pinheiro, L. (2009). *Cyberbullying em Portugal: uma perspectiva sociológica.* Braga, Portugal: Universidade do Minho. Retrieved December 12, 2009, from http://repositorium.sdum.uminho.pt/bitstream/1822/9870/1/tese.pdf

Rabot, J.-M. (2009). Os videojogos: entre a absorção labiríntica e a sociedade. In *SOPCOM/LUSOCOM* (pp. 432-445). Retrieved May 13, 2009, from http://conferencias.ulusofona.pt/index.php/sopcom_iberico/sopcom_iberico09/paper/viewFile/463/462

Rohle, T. (2005). Power, reason, closure: critical perspectives on new media theory. *New Media & Society, 7*(3), 403–422. doi:10.1177/1461444805052283

Shapira, N., Goldsmith, T., Keck, P., Szabo, S., Lazoritz, M., Gold, M., & Stein, D. (2003). Problematic Internet use: proposed classification and diagnostic criteria. *Depression & Anxiety, 17,* 207-216. Retrieved December 27, 2008, from http://www3.interscience.wiley.com/journal/104539090/abstract

Wikipedia. (2009). *Bullying.* Retrieved November 26, 2009, from http://pt.wikipedia.org/wiki/Bullying

Young, K. S., & Rodgers, R. C. (1998). *Internet addiction: personality traits associated with its development.* Retrieved December 18, 2008, from http://netaddiction.com/articles/personality-correlates.htm

This work was previously published in International Journal of Technoethics, Volume 1, Issue 3, edited by Rocci Luppicini, pp. 24-34, copyright 2010 by IGI Publishing (an imprint of IGI Global).

Section 3
The Ethical Side of
Technological Applications

Chapter 11
Reclaiming the Green Continent:
Ecology, Globalization, and Policy and Decision in Latin America

A. Pablo Iannone
Central Connecticut State University, USA

ABSTRACT

This essay examines Latin American technological development and its connections with regional economic development, ecological deterioration, political freedoms' fluctuations, and globalization processes—understood as the spreading interconnectedness of business, science, technology, politics, and culture through large regions or the entirety of the world. The essay investigates how policy and decision issues resulting from Latin American technological development and its correlates can be plausibly addressed and argues for several theses, most notably, that in dealing with the issues, national legislation and international treaties have attained and are likely to attain their purposes only to a limited extent and in a mixed manner; that less legislation-dependent procedures evidence greater effectiveness and political feasibility; and that some globalization processes help fuel the environmental issues, while others help facilitate their resolution. The essay provides some concrete examples of how the issues can be soundly addressed.

INTRODUCTION

During the late nineteenth and early twentieth century, many saw Latin America as a land of promise. The Green Continent, as the Colombian historian and educator Germán Arciniegas called

DOI: 10.4018/978-1-4666-1773-5.ch011

it, attracted millions of immigrants who expected it soon to develop its technology—communications, transportation, and energy availability—, thereby promoting economic development and the growth and amenities of its cities (Arciniegas, 1944, p. vii and p. 223; Iannone, 1999, pp. 120-121). Some—Arciniegas among them—also hoped that such developments would lead to the demise of Latin American dictatorships (Rother, 1999, passim.).

Technological development came to pass in some Latin American regions. Its expected economic and political results, however, have been mixed, and its surprises many. Accordingly, I will ask: To what extent and in what ways has technological development led to economic development in Latin America? What other changes have accompanied Latin American technological and economic development, especially, concerning ecological stability? How are these changes related to processes of globalization, (which I will understand as the spreading interconnectedness of business, science, technology, politics, and culture through large regions or the entirety of the world)? What policy and decision problems does the current situation pose? How helpful are legalistic approaches in addressing these problems? Does soundly addressing them call for a shift away from an exclusive or primary focus on legislation and treaties? What alternative and plausible approaches are there? What are the prospects for ethics and sociopolitical philosophy in dealing with these problems?

Since ethics and sociopolitical philosophy have no purpose in isolation of the concrete problems that call for it, I will first describe, in some detail, cases of development in Latin America, the environmental problems and issues they pose, and the role globalization processes play in them. Then, with these cases in mind, I will argue for seven theses: First, in dealing with environmental issues like those described, national legislation and international treaties have attained and are likely to attain their purposes only to a limited extent and in a mixed manner. Second, such legislation has not been and, unless current circumstances change, is unlikely to be soundly implemented in the foreseeable future. Third, in at least some of the Latin American cases discussed, implementation shortcomings result from lax enforcement, lack of commitment—especially concerning who is going to foot the bill—and lack of human

resources. Fourth, past uses of less legislation-dependent procedures, as well as current policy making developments, evidence the greater effectiveness and political feasibility of non-confrontational and non-adversarial approaches. Fifth, the philosophical and political approach the present essay adopts is better suited for dealing with the issues and offers a chance of cementing social and environmental arrangements along morally acceptable lines. Sixth: This approach also offers prospects of a bright future for ethics and sociopolitical philosophy in contributing to deal with environmental problems and issues in Latin America and elsewhere. Seventh: some globalization processes, say, competition for global or regional markets, play a role leading to environmental issues in Latin America and arguably elsewhere; but other globalization processes, say, global communications through high speed communication networks, play a substantial role in facilitating local resistance, negotiation and organization strategies used to defend ecological and social concerns, and assert individual freedoms.

LATIN AMERICAN DEVELOPMENT, POLITICS AND ECOLOGY; SOME SALIENT FACTS

Latin American problems and issues associated with technological developments significantly concern the tensions between risks, benefits, individual rights, and practical constraints involved in deforestation practices, pesticide use, the development of genetically modified organisms, urban waste disposal, energy production, and population change policies. I will describe their salient features in some detail next.

The Transamazonic Highway System

The most conspicuous example of gigantic highway construction in Latin America is the transamazonic highway system. It runs across Brazil's

Amazon jungle and merges into the Transoceanic Highway, projected to end in the state of Acre and from there connect with the Peruvian ports of the Pacific (Departamento Nacional de Infra-Estrutura de Transporte, 2001, passim.). Its construction was part of "operation Amazon," a series of legislative acts and decrees aimed at developing, occupying, and integrating Amazonia into the rest of Brazil (Mahar, 1976, p. 358). However, rather than coming to be hand-in-hand with political freedoms, it was instituted and seen well on its way by the military governments which came to power in 1964 and lasted until the late 1970s (Black, 1993, pp.1-2). It also had significant ecological consequences, to which I turn next.

Amazonian development, its ecological consequences, and the policy and decision problems they pose, display seven salient features. First, the largest river system irrigating Amazonia is the Amazon River system, which contains one fifth of all the fresh water in the planet (Roberts, 2003, p.132). Second, the scope of the Amazon region varies depending on whether its definition is based on types of rainforest plants or on climatological conditions, not to mention the fact that the governments of the countries reached by the Amazon River basin—Brazil and Venezuela—define the region differently; but, in any case, it covers between 1.4 and 2.3 million square miles or roughly an area as large as the continental US minus Texas and Ohio (Roberts, 2003, p. 132). Third, Amazonia is not uniform, but varies depending on differences in rainfall, temperature, and soil composition in its various habitats—e.g., upland well drained forest constitute about 85% of Amazonia, flood plains of Andean silt-carrying rivers constitute about 6% (Bates, 2001, passim; Roberts, 2003, pp. 132-3). Fourth, Amazonia includes the largest tropical rainforest on earth, estimated to be home to between 1 and 2 million species (about one in every five life forms on the planet) most of which have not been identified (Roberts, 2003, p.132,). Fifth, given current

Amazonian development, it is estimated that one of these species goes extinct each hour (i.e., five hundred to one thousand times the natural extinction rate) and that 273,000 square miles or 10 to 15 percent of the Amazon region (a highly controverted estimate) has already been deforested (Roberts, 2003, pp.132 and 138). Sixth, the extinction of species is worrisome not just because of loss of opportunity to acquire new biological knowledge, or find new cures for diseases, but because their diversity ensures, while their loss threatens the stability of the entire network of Amazonic ecosystems (Ferrier, 2002, p.331). Seventh, deforestation of Amazonia is worrisome because the Amazonic rain forest significantly regulates weather patterns on large regions of the continent—arguably on the entire planet—and consequently, its substantial disappearance poses a risk to agriculture, hence to human life, as we know them (Laurance, 2004, passim., Laurance, 2001, passim.).

Pesticides

The Township of Almolaga, in the Western highlands of Guatemala, produces vegetables sold in Mexico and Central America. Water resources are abundant, but the available cultivable land is limited. Hence, in order to increase their crops' yield, Almolaga's farmers make intensive use of synthetic pesticides. They display little or no cautiousness in using them. In conjunction with these farming practices, researchers have noticed significant occurrences of anemia, congenital malformations, cancer, respiratory illnesses and still births in the area's population. They have also noticed widespread infectious and parasitic diseases as well as nutritional deficiencies which, they hypothesize, may be hightened by excessive pesticide use (Arbona, 1998, pp.47 and 55-60), a correlation which is not unusual in a number of Latin American countries whose exports of fruits and vegetables are increasing and casual pesticide use is frequent (Arbona, 1998, p.54; Frank, 2002, p. B5; Pallister, 1999, p.13; Roberts, 2003, pp.66-67; Wright, 1990, passim.). As for Guatemala, the US Food and Drug Administration regularly detains shipments of its produce because their pesticide content fails to be in accordance with import regulations. This is no surprise: the AVANCSO, the Guatemalan association for the advance of social science, reported in 1994 that 53 percent of the producers of non-traditional crops failed to follow the specified intervals of pesticide application and 41 percent of the pesticides being used were restricted, no longer sold, or not allowed in food (AVANCSO, 1994, p.1). Since the US is not the main foreign market for these Guatemalan farmers, however, and Mexico and Central America have less stringent import regulations, the casual use of the said pesticides has continued (Arbona, 1998, pp.54-55 and 62). The unusually high rates of anemia, congenital malformations, cancer, respiratory illnesses and still births continue as well.

Genetically Modified Organisms

Genetic engineers have endowed traditional crops (wheat, corn, rice, and soybeans) with genes which make the crops resist disease and herbicides, and exercise pesticide functions (Haughton A. J. 2003, p.1863 and 1875; Moffatt, 1999, p370). Around the turn of the millenium, they focused their attention on other crops, most notably potatoes, in an effort to emulate, for Latin America's tastes and climates, the US doubling in potato yields since the 1950s. Initial results were attained in 1999 at the Research Institute of Genetic Engineering and Molecular Biology, in Buenos Aires, where 16 transgenic lines were created coded for resistance to various viral, fungal, and bacterial diseases. They began to be tested in Brazil and Chile soon thereafter. The same approach has been applied to cassava, palms and bananas (Moffat, 1999, p.370). These crops, like their forerunners, have raised a range

of questions concerning their safety to humans and their effects on bees and other invertebrates whose populations are detrimentally affected by the said pesticide functions and without which a great variety of crops would suffer because, e.g., without enough bees (which pollinate one or more cultivars of >66% of the world's 1,500 crop species and are directly or indirectly essential for an estimated 15–30% of food production), they could not be pollinated (Haughton A. J. 2003, passim.; Kearns, C.A., 1998, passim.; Kremen, 2002, passim.; McGregor, 1976, passim.; Roubik 1995, passim.).

Urban Wastes

Three out of every four Latin American residents (380 million out of Latin America's total population of 507 million residents) lived in an urban environment around the year 2000 (CEPAL, 2000, p.2). The region includes 52 cities with populations over 1 million and four megacities: Rio de Janeiro with 12.5 million, Buenos Aires with a metropolitan area population of 13 million, Sâo Paulo with a metropolitan area population of 22 million, and Mexico city, one of the largest cities on earth, whose metropolitan area population equals 25.6 million (United Nations Research Institute for Social Development, 2005, p.60). Behind them, Lima, Bogotá, Santiago de Chile, Caracas, Belo Horizonte, Guadalajara, Porto Alegre, Monterrey, Recife, and Salvador have 3 million each (Roberts, 2003, 93). These enormous population concentrations cause equally enormous ecological pressures which issue into unsafe drinking water, untreated sewage, air pollution, solid waste dumping, contaminated soils, and what not. Estimates concerning the consequences of these pollutants vary, but one 1994 CEPAL publication attributed 80% of illnesses and one-third of deaths in the region to contaminated water (Rico, 2000, in Roberts (2003), p. 99.; CEPAL, 1994, passim.).

Energy

Since the 1970s, Latin America has been one of the most active regions in the world concerning dam construction. In 1982, the largest hydroelectric project on earth, the Itaipú Dam, was completed on the Paraná River, in Paraguay. It could generate 12,600 megawatts, and provides power primarily to Brazil. Another significant project, the Balbinas Dam, flooded a huge section of the Amazon rainforest, leading to some of the ecological and population consequences discussed below. In addition, the Paraguay-Paraná Hidrovía is a proposal to convert 3,400 km of the Paraguay and Paraná River system of South America into an industrial shipping channel. The project, which has been called "the backbone" of Mercosur, the Southern cone Common Market, is part of a broader plan to expand agribusiness and mining activities. It could have irreversible impacts on the world's largest wetlands, the Brazilian Pantanal, and other valuable ecosystems in Bolivia, Paraguay, and Argentina (Bonetto, 1990, pp.1-3; Cummings, 1995, pp.151-160; Fearnside, 1996, pp.615-648; Hall, 1994, pp.1793-1809).

In the 1990s, ENDESA, the largest private company in Chile, began constructing six hydroelectric dams on the Biobío river, which flows from the Andes, through gorges and forests of Araucaria pine, to the Pacific Ocean. Over one million people use the Biobío for drinking and irrigation water, recreation, and fisheries. The first of those dams, Pangue, was already completed in 1996 (NASA, 2008, passim.). ENDESA also announced it planned to move ahead with construction of the largest of the Biobío dams, called Ralco. Ralco would be a 155 meter-high dam with a 3,400 hectare reservoir, which would displace more than 600 people, including 400 Pehuenche Indians. The upper Biobío, where the Ralco dam is planned, is home to the Pehuenche group of the Mapuche Indians, the last group of Mapuche who continue their traditional lifestyle. The dam would flood over 70 km of the river valley, inundating the richly diverse forest and its wildlife. Environmental and indigenous rights groups have opposed the project on the grounds that it would cause large scale destruction and that projections of Chile's future energy requirements indicate that the energy it would produce would not be needed. Critics of Ralco also said that construction would violate the new Chilean Environmental and Indigenous Peoples Laws and prior agreements between ENDESA and the World Bank (CIEL, 2004, passim.; Usher, 1997, pp.133-170).

Population

During the past three decades, millions of individuals in Latin America have migrated from rural areas to the big cities and from one country to another, typically running away from poverty and going where there were jobs. Notable among these migrations is that related to the development of Amazonia, which created a boom fever in the last decades of the 20th century. The first move towards developing Amazonia traces back to the building of the new capital, Brasilia, by the Juscelino Kubitschek administration (1956-61) in the state of Goias. The pace quickened with the construction of the previously mentioned Transamazonic Highway. During the mid 1970s, the government began offering incentives for clearance of the rain forest and tax shelters to major corporations. The offers drew large numbers of individuals from the Northeast and Southeast who helped clear the land and start small farming operations. Also, a free-trade zone was created in Manaus, a city which had decayed when its rubber industry had lost markets to synthetic-rubber and its byproducts. As a result, the population of Manaus grew exponentially to more than 1,000,000. Ranching, logging, and public and private mining ventures also were undertaken, accompanied by infrastructure projects to build roads, bridges, and dams, at an increasing pace since the 1980s (Black, 1993).

As previously discussed, huge electric dams were built covering millions of acres of forest with water and providing electricity to whole sections of the jungle. An area the size of Belgium was cut or burned down—with the concomitant enormous release of smoke into the atmosphere— for the sake of growing cocoa and raising cattle.

In the process, various Native American tribes—Yanomani, the Nambi-kwara, the Kayapo, the Uru-Eu-Wau-Wau, and the Xingu—were uprooted. It is estimated that only about 200,000 of Brazil's indigenous tribal peoples have survived, with perhaps 50,000 of them still living deep in the rain forest. And, as previously discussed, many lives were lost to malaria, yellow fever, typhus, diarrhea and other diseases. Further, within ten years after this experiment started, much of the Transamazonic highway had been washed away by torrential rains, or taken back by the jungle. The small-farm concentrations were practically empty, some totally abandoned. The soils, leached by tropical rains, stopped producing crops. Since the soil is often so infertile, farmers and corporations have earned more from tax write-offs than from anything cultivated. Forest clearance incentives were revoked in 1987, in response to international pressures, but land speculation continues. Some farmers returned to the cities looking for work. Others proceeded to search for gold, and were joined by additional migrants from the cities, further into the jungle where over one million miners are estimated to have staked claims, digging holes, clearing more forest, dredging rivers and pouring mercury into them, while leading Brazil to become the world's third largest gold producer. On the other hand, by the 1980s, many peasants had become an itinerant labor force, primarily located in instant slum towns on the margins of the land they had cleared (Boccaccio, 2008, passim.). This process has continued to expand leading to conflicts between neighboring countries. One such conflict is that between Argentina and Uruguay, concerning the Scandinavian paper mill opera-

tions on the shores of the Uruguay river shared by both countries but, according to Argentina's claim before the International Court of Justice, in violation the countries' accords. Another is a related conflict between the same countries concerning the imminent plans by British and Australian capitals through the Río Tinto Company to build a port terminal in the La Agraciada area to export tons of iron and coal from Brazil (Colonna, 2008, pp.1-2).

The above cases give ample evidence of the wide range and complex nature of ecology related developments facing Latin America and the role globalization plays in them. Let us now turn to an examination of the problems they pose and issues they prompt, and the contributions ethics and socio-political philosophy can make to deal with them.

ENVIRONMENTAL ISSUES AND GLOBALIZATION

Environmental issues characteristically involve sharp differences of opinions or conflicts of demands about ecological concerns and their apparent, or real, conflicts with economic, political, technological, and cultural concerns, together with what people do to uphold their opinions or satisfy their demands (Iannone, 1994, pp. 1-12). Some of those involved in issues concerning the previously described cases have charged that globalization is the culprit, while others deny it, and still others argue that it is part of the solution, though the latter often disagree about how much, if anything, can be done to govern globalization processes towards a solution. There are those who hail the globally integrative forces affecting Latin America as a way out of widespread poverty, legal and political sectarianism, cultural stagnation, and long-standing oppression of traditionally disenfranchised groups—say, the poor living in Brazil's favelas or Argentina's Villa Miserias.

Others argue that those globally integrative forces are regionally, locally, and even globally disintegrative and a sure way to economic and political dependence, cultural decadence, loss of national identity, and the destruction of traditionally disenfranchised groups—say, the previously mensioned Amazonian groups and the Chilean remaining traditionally living Mapuches (Vargas Lloza, 2001, passim.). Let us next turn to how these conflicts should be addressed.

What Role for Legalistic Approaches?

The history of international environmental treaties since the 1970s offers more evidence of hopes and wishes than of actual commitments. Though it has shown some progress, it is full of false starts and backtracking. For example, environmental concerns clashed with other concerns at 1974 and 1984 and 1992 international meetings and, once again in 1994 (Iannone, 1999, pp. 56-57). This is not to say that the treaties are unnecessary. Yet, they are merely opening moves in a policy making process that, as I will further argue, can hardly succeed along exclusively legalistic lines. In fact, this is exactly what the Kyoto Treaty indicates when it refers to flexibility in the execution timeframe for attaining its goals as the first commitment period. (United Nations, 1998, art. 6 and 7).

Can legalistic approaches at the national level help? They could, but are undermined by enforcement and implementation failures. Consider the following case: regulations of Argentine national parks are, like those of U.S. national parks, quite comprehensive and strict. However, out of twenty-one species of mammals, five species of birds, and one reptile species that became extinct in Argentine national parks, many of them became extinct after the areas became national parks (Rapoport, 1990, p. 33). This did not merely result from enforcement failures. Lack of human resources also contributed. In 1990, there were ten thousand endangered species in Argentina and, in order to address each species' predicament soundly, many studies were needed. But Argentina then had only about eight hundred ecologists (counting biologists, agronomists, veterinarians, and related professionals), and only a few of them worked on conservation and genetic resources. That is, the human resources were not available to carry out the studies required by the environmental protection task faced. (Rapoport, 1990, p. 33). Argentina's predicament is likely to be shared by Latin American countries which count with even less resources. At any rate, the discussion so far supports this essay's first three theses: First, in dealing with environmental issues like those described, national legislation and international treaties have attained and are likely to attain their purposes only to a limited extent and in a mixed manner. Second, such legislation has not been and, unless current circumstances change, is unlikely to be soundly implemented in the foreseeable future. Third, in at least some of the Latin American cases discussed, implementation shortcomings result from lax enforcement, lack of commitment—especially concerning who is going to foot the bill—and lack of human resources.

As previously indicated, to say this is not to say that environmental laws and treaties are unnecessary or that environmental safety is unimportant. It is just that environmental laws and treaties are only a first and partial move in dealing with environmental issues. Besides, the environmental issues involved and the alternative environmental policy-making options about them are not merely legal or organizational, but are also moral issues because they and the policies and decisions meant to address them affect or are likely to affect people's lives and society at large in significant ways. Accordingly, as indicated at the essay's outset, in addition to relying on the environmental policy making literature, this essay approaches the problems against the backdrop of contributions that ethics and sociopolitical philosophy can make to the resolution of the problems. Let us next turn to this.

ETHICS, SOCIOPOLITICAL PHILOSOPHY, AND ENVIRONMENTAL POLICY MAKING

A Brief Discussion of Traditional Philosophical Approaches

Traditional philosophical approaches to policy making have focused either primarily on consequences, especially along the lines of utilitarianism (Mill, 1998, passim.; Smart, 1973, passim.), or primarily on rights (Waldron, 1984, passim.), or primarily on character (Crisp,1997, passim.). Accordingly, they have respectively asked either "What will be likely to bring about the greatest favorable balance of desirable over undesirable consequences for all affected?" or "Would any rights be violated which take priority in the circumstances?" or "Would people develop a better character in the circumstances?"

The question arises: Should the overriding concern of the above approaches be the consequences for humans, the rights of humans, or the personal development of humans, or should non-human individuals, species or ecosystems as a whole sometimes take precedence over the former? This has led to the controversy between conservationism and preservationism—a controversy which is itself a version of the wider anthropocentrism v. non-anthropocentrism controversy. Anthropocentrism holds that whenever the interest of humans and the good of non-humans conflict, the interest of humans always takes precedence, while non-anthropocentrism holds that the interest of humans does not always take precedence over the good of non-humans. Hence conservationism holds that whenever conflicts arise between some interest of humans—e.g., to discharge hot water from a paper mill into a stream at regular intervals—and the conservation of non-humans—e.g., the conservation of the stream's fish whose survival is endangered by the stream's resulting increase in temperature—, the conservation of the latter takes precedence if, and only if it can be shown to constitute a resource for humans and, further, to satisfy an even greater human interest, say, that of fishermen. By contrast, preservationism holds that the environment and its components should be preserved for their own sake. On this view, many accommodations between humans and non-humans are possible; but, if non-humans are endangered by plans aimed at satisfying human interests, the interests of humans do not necessarily take precedence. A range of views, from ecocentrism, which invariably gives precedence to non-humans (sometimes considering humans even a plague), to other, less extreme positions, have been advanced.

One could defend anthropocentrism by arguing that, in practice, preservationism is hardly an alternative, because what is good for non-humans must be invariably decided by humans. But preservationists counter that, even if humans must do this job, from a preservationism's standpoint, they should ask questions such as "Should what is good for the non-humans likely to be affected by human activities in this case—say, for fish likely to be affected by humans mixing mercury into a stream in the process of searching for gold—take precedence over the interests of these humans?" and these questions are simply irrelevant from anthropocentric standpoints like conservationism.

Yet, once conservationism takes seriously both humans' need to preserve the biota, and the latter's need for biodiversity, preservationism's injunctions tend to converge with those of conservationism. Accordingly, in those cases described at the outset, considerations focused on individual or collective consequences, individual rights, and personal development, whether conservationist or preservationist, arguably tend to enjoin convergent conclusions—Latin American development should proceed so as to help bring the poor out of poverty while at the same time preserving ecological stability, hence species diversity, and respecting individual rights.

The question however remains How do we get from here to there? And the philosophical theories previously mentioned do not address it, focusing instead merely or primarily on consequences to seek, rights to respect, or character to develop. A different ethical approach is needed—one that I have called philosophy as diplomacy and, as I argued in detail elsewhere (Iannone, 1994, pp. 55-86), takes discovery and invention, judgment and decision, reason and choice, ends and means to be closely interconnected with each other and with action in the policy making process. Let us next turn to this.

ENVIRONMENTAL POLICY ASSESSMENT: ECONOMICS, ETHICS AND SOCIOPOLITICAL PHILOSOPHY, AND WORLD REALITIES

One question guiding much environmental policy assessment has been How much environmental deterioration is too much? In this regard, even anthropocentric thinkers differ regarding what environmental factors should be the focus of concern—Only those constituting a risk to human health or general well-being? Also those undermining human satisfaction of preferences? Or also those diminishing of persons and their liberties? In addition, they also differ about how the factors of concern should be assessed—merely through economic assessment methods, or though entirely different approaches?

Virtues and Excesses of Quantification in Environmental Policy Assessment

During the 1950s and 1960s, environmental policy makers and economists tended to agree that the environmental focus of concern about environmental matters had to do with spillover damage of market activities to unconsenting third parties. This however excluded aesthetic and ethical preferences about, for example, the fact that, as a result of deforestation, large sections of Amazonia had become deserts and entire social groups were being decimated, on the grounds that these aesthetic and ethical preferences were intrinsically unquantifiable.

In the 1970s, however, economists began to replace the notion of physical spillover with that of transaction or bargaining cost in evaluating the efficiency of a project or a policy, specifically, of a project or policy concerning pollution. The focus was thereby widened to cover any unpriced benefit or cost—i.e., anything a person may be willing to pay for—even if markets do not typically price it correctly or at all. To be sure, its critics have cautioned against mindless quantification (for those not willing to pay for pollution prevention or abatement may do so simply because they are too poor to pay for it). Yet, it is as easy to be mindless without looking at numbers. Whatever method of analysis, policy makers need information and tools that will allow them to examine more explicitly and precisely, whether quantitatively or qualitatively, what those affected by environmental policy value, and how this value can be determined.

One suggestion to improve willingness to pay is that cut-off points resulting from willingness-to-pay—i.e., what persons are willing to pay for what they value—could be assessed in bundles on the assumption of the substitution principle, according to which, the bundles' components can always be substituted. That is, they are not in lexicographic order so that, for example, a certain amount of pollution abatement would take precedence over all else. Yet, it is controversial whether such substitutions apply to all environmental deterioration levels, no matter how high, on the grounds that their victims, present or future, could always receive other goods or services instead.

It is also controversial whether willingness-to-pay, even when thus improved, is a morally or even logically appropriate criterion to apply when dealing with environmental problems. One reason to think that it is not, is that it places individuals in the role of mere consumers or bidders. Instead, the argument goes, the question should place them in a different role, say, that of a citizen or a trustee of one's own and others' health, and of all other things that matter to people's lives. On this view, what should be determined is not what individuals would be willing to pay for their health and other things they value, but what they would exchange their health or these other things for—i.e., a willingness-to-sell criterion should be used. This would imply the said individuals have property rights to an environment they value.

Is this sufficient? It may, only if the individuals making the value judgments are powerful and resourceful enough not to have to sell at all or settle for a significantly lower selling price than they would want. Yet, whatever assessment method is used, at budget allocation time, there often is less money available than needed to cover everything people want preserved—which creates conflicts and issues. And the approaches just discussed are too far removed from policy making reality to be of much help in dealing with the said conflicts and issues. This is a reason why the conflicts and issues should addressed by also including non-economic considerations. (Iannone, 2005, passim). How? I will next turn to this.

A More Flexible Approach

I will proceed in accordance with two guiding hypotheses. One is The Range Hypothesis, according to which there is a range of policy and decision problems with the following characteristics: At one extreme, individual rights carry much more weight in dealing with problems because, for example, natural rights are significantly and unequivocally at stake in those problems. At the other extreme, consequences carry the most weight because, for example, the very existence and well-being of a reasonably good society are at stake. In between, rights and consequences have less

decisive weight, though, fortunately, they often reinforce each other. Sometimes, however, they appear to conflict with each other, constituting hard cases to deal with. All along the range of problems, pragmatic considerations set limits to the alternatives that would otherwise have served to address the problems (Iannone, 1987, p. 6; Iannone, 1989, p. 6, Iannone1994, p. 11).

The second hypothesis is The Balance Hypothesis, according to which there is a range of policy and decision problems with the following characteristics: At one extreme, the search for feasible and effective policies through a reliance on meaningful dialogue and the use of reason carries much more weight than any other consideration; time and other constrains make the search possible. At the other extreme, the need to deal with the social facts posing policy and decision problems (e. g., with public acquiescence or the insensitivity of influential people concerning ecologically or socially disastrous environmental practices) carries more weight than any other consideration. Meaningful dialogue and the use of reason are not dominant in these circumstances, which involve a clear and immediate threat to the very existence and well-being of one or more communities or societies. In between, the search for policies and decisions through reliance on reason and meaningful dialogue, and the pressing need to deal with the problems, have less decisive weight, though, fortunately, they often reinforce each other. Sometimes, however, they appear to conflict with each other, constituting hard cases to deal with. All along, pragmatic considerations set limits to (1) the extent to which the cases can be emphasized, and (2) the procedures suited for realistically attending to them (Iannone, 1994, p. 11).

The previously discussed Latin American cases of ecological concern typically involve conflicting considerations, say, individual rights of some peasants versus those of others and the stability of their community or society. And the two hypotheses just mentioned help address the questions: How should the relative weights of competing considerations be addressed? And even when this matter, and which overall goals should be sought, is settled in the current circumstances, how should we get from here to there, given that there is controversy and even confrontation about all these things? Taken together, then, the hypotheses just formulated treat as morally and politically crucial a range of social decision procedures—from strictly non-adversarial ones such as discussion of merits and negotiation, which rely only on reason and meaningful dialogue; through primarily non-adversarial ones such as bargaining, voting, mediation, arbitration, consensus building and compromise; to adversarial but non-confrontational ones such as policy insulation, manipulation, side-stepping, boycotts and suing; to thoroughly confrontational adversarial procedures such as striking and combat, where reason and meaningful dialogue take a back seat. Depending on how pressing and conflictive the circumstances are, each one of these procedures constitutes a politically viable and morally preferable way of dealing with problems and issues. For exaggerating the role of reason, or that of unreason in the issues, can only undermine morality, paralyze politics, and further destabilize tenuous situations such as those involved in the previously discussed Latin American cases concerning ecology. In seeking how to apply the balanced approach just outlined, let us examine and assess some social decision procedures which have been prominently used in dealing with environmental and related problems in Latin America.

ENVIRONMENTAL PROBLEMS AND ISSUES AND SOCIAL DECISION PROCEDURES

A procedure which caught the imagination of some commentators and, to some extent, seemed to reach success in Brazil in the late 1980s was the empate. It was a nonviolent adversarial approach used by Chico Mendes and other tappers to save Amazonian Rainforest areas scheduled for logging in order to make room for ranching concerns. Whenever Mendes and other tappers and union leaders learned where future logging was planned, they went to the site and had a calm discussion with the loggers indicating how cutting the trees threatened the loggers' future. The loggers typically abandoned their chainsaws behind and left while the tappers destroyed their camp. Eventually two of Brazil's largest ranchers left the area (Newton and Dillingham, 1993, pp. 145-146). Yet, this social decision procedure worked so long as the situation did not become predominantly confrontational. Eventually, the ranchers were so enraged that the situation did become confrontational making the empate ineffective—in fact leading to some ranchers' goons killing Chico Mendes, and to further logging (Iannone, 1999, pp. 69-70). It is then crucial to ask concerning the application of available decision procedures: Is this social decision procedure justified in the situation? Is the situation primarily a controversy or primarily a confrontation? What other social decision procedures are likely to be not merely effective but morally justified in the circumstances?

It should be mentioned that, though exclusively legalistic approaches have limited effectiveness, they do give negotiation and bargaining power to environmentalists who, for example, learn to use the legal challenge process to win commitments from a variety of institutions, often in the form of negotiated settlements to the dispute. Yet, the settlements are parasitic on legal challenges, that is, on adversarial approaches to dealing with environmental noncompliance and, when enforcement is lax or when environmental legislation is weaker (or absent) and its implementation limited, there is less, or no, legal leverage for negotiating similar settlements. Further, another—and crucial—limitation is that the said challenges typically occur after the fact, when environmental damage has already occurred, or momentum towards environmental damage has already been built. This is a significant reason for seeking still other—less legislation-dependent and, in general, less adversarial, proactive—approaches.

The preceding discussion supports our next two theses: Fourth, past uses of less legislation-dependent procedures, as well as current policy making developments, evidence the greater effectiveness and political feasibility of non-confrontational and non-adversarial approaches. Fifth, the philosophical and political approach the present essay adopts is better suited for dealing with the issues and offers a chance of cementing social and environmental arrangements along morally acceptable lines.

To be sure, this essay's proposed approach will not eliminate the fact that most currently significant environmental policy and decision problems in Latin America (and, for that matter, elsewhere) involve social conflict. But, as evidenced in the previous discussion and further exemplified below, dealing with this fact along the lines of this essay's approach points to a less wide-eyed and less divisive process. Our sixth thesis follows: This approach also offers prospects of a bright future for ethics and sociopolitical philosophy in contributing to deal with environmental problems and issues in Latin America and elsewhere. That is, ethics and sociopolitical philosophy, through the approach I have previously outlined, can help address environmental problems and issues. In doing so, attention should be turned to such social decision procedures as negotiation, bargaining, mediation, consensus building, and various forms of convention settling. What additional procedures incorporate them? I will address this next.

ENVIRONMENTAL MANAGEMENT PARTNERSHIPS

One—though by no means the only—helpful non-adversarial procedure is to form environmen-

tal management partnerships between affected institutions and local communities concerned with their environment, with making a living in it—say, by engaging in agriculture, mining, or nearby fishing—, and with dwelling in it. There is a precedent for this type of approach in the United States finance of community development. An outstanding US example is that of the Local Initiatives Support Corporation (LISC), which currently administers a wide range of programs that help address urban and rural environmental problems (Iannone, 2007). Other such partnerships have been developed locally and globally with the specific goal of dealing with environmental issues. One is the International Council for Local Environmental Initiatives (I.C.L.E.I.) or its associated Campaña Ciudades por la Protección Climática (C.C.P.).

Environmental management partnerships are different from, say, the Nature Conservancy, which addresses environmental problems primarily by purchasing natural areas for conservation and preservation purposes. By contrast, while environmental management partnerships can, they need not involve any purchase, the commitment of resources being worked out between interested institutions and communities. This increases flexibility—a good thing given that resources are typically scarce.

Can however these partnerships be sufficiently effective given the enormous pressures from global firms and countries to carry out planned developments? They can do their part, though, as indicated, treaties and legislation are necessary, and other social decision procedures and arrangements may be required at times. But environmental management partnerships are not merely helpful in dealing with environmental problems and issues. They are necessary. Even governments need them and other bottom-up approaches because governments cannot address environmental problems and issues by themselves (Christoff, 2005, pp. 301-302; Clapp, 2005, pp. 275-277).

GLOBALIZATION'S ROLE IN DEALING WITH ENVIRONMENTAL PROBLEMS AND ISSUES

Globalization's role concerning environmental issues is mixed. Some globalization processes (e.g., competition for global or regional markets) contribute to creating the issues, while other globalization processes (e.g., global communications through internet use) contribute to form and develop organizations which help soundly address them. The I.C.L.E.I. and its truly global C.C.P. network, for example, benefit immensily form global communication (I.C.L.E.I., 2008, passim.). So do aboriginal groups who can and do organize resistance or negotiation strategies through information sharing, email messages requesting action, cross-border and even wider coordination, and the like (Roberts, 2003, p. 178). From this and the essay's previous discussions, our last thesis follows: some globalization processes, say, competition for global or regional markets, play a role leading to environmental issues in Latin America and arguably elsewhere; but other globalization processes, say, the growth of global communications through high speed communication networks, play a substantial role in facilitating local resistance, negotiation, and organization strategies used to defend ecological and social concerns, and assert individual freedoms.

The short list of environmental management and related organizations just provided is by no means exhaustive. Yet, it offers a somewhat detailed idea of the models suitable to the approach suggested in this essay, and of their moral justifiability—which involves their ecological, economic, political, and cultural feasibility and effectiveness (Iannone, 1994, passim.; and Iannone, 1999, passim.). The arrangements thus worked out are likely to be more effective and morally sounder than adversarial approaches. For they will tend to prevent or curb environmental deterioration significantly long before it reaches the point of no return. Such approaches would help us all,

Latin Americans and non-Latin Americans, deal more intelligently with environmental issues, thus surviving ourselves and the consequences of our often misdirected policies in these ecologically and socially crucial times.

REFERENCES

Arbona, S. I. (1998, Jan.). Commercial Agriculture and Agrochemicals in Almolonga, Guatemala. *Geographical Review, 88*(1), 47–63. doi:10.2307/215871

Arciniegas, G. (1944). *The Green Continent.* New York: Alfred A. Knopf.

AVANCSO. (1994). *Impacto ecológico de los cultivos hortícolas no-tradicionales en el altiplano de Guatemala.* Guatemala, Instituto AVANCSO.

Bates, J. M., & Demos, T. C. (2001, Sep.). Do We Need to Devalue Amazonia and Other Large Tropical Forests? *Diversity & Distributions, 7*(5), 249–255. doi:10.1046/j.1366-9516.2001.00112.x

Black, J. K. (March 1st, 1993). Limits of Boom-and-Bust Development: Challenge of the Amazon. *USAToday, 121*(2574), 34, 3p, 3 bw.

Boccaccio, A. (2008). *Where Madness Follows.* Retrieved January 18, 2009 from www.boccacciophoto.com/amazongold/.

Bonetto, A. A., & Wais, I. R. (1990). Powerful Paraná. *The Geographical Magazine, 62*(3), 1–3.

CEPAL-United Nations Economic Commission on Latin America and the Caribbean (November 2000), Cepal News.

Christoff, P. (2005). Green Governance and the Green State: Capacity Building as a Political Project. In R. Paehlke & D. Torgerson (Eds.), *Managing Leviathan* (pp. 289-310). Ontario, CA: Broadview Press Ltd.

CIEL-The Center for International Environmental Law. (2004). *CIEL Helps Protect the Rights of Indigenous Communities Displaced by the Ralco Dam along the Upper BioBio River in Southern Chile.* Retrieved January 18, 2009 from http://ciel.org/Tae/Ralco_Aug04.html.

Clapp, J. (2005). Responses to Environmental Threats in an Age of Globalization. In R. Paehlke & D. Torgerson Eds.), *Managing Leviathan* (pp. 271-288). Ontario, CA: Broadview Press Ltd.

Colonna, L. (2008). Nuevo foco de conflicto con Uruguay. *LANACION.com.* Retrieved January 18, 2009 from http://www.lanacion.com.ar/politica/nota.asp?nota_id=988139&origen=premium

Cook-Deegan, R. M. (1994). *The Gene Wars: Science, Politics, and the Human Genome.* New York: Norton.

Crisp, R., & Slote, M. A. (1997). *Virtue Ethics.* Oxford and New York: Oxford University Press.

Cummings, B. J. (1995). Dam the Rivers; Damn the People: Hydroelectric Development and Resistance in Amazonian Brazil. *GeoJournal, 35*(2), 151–160. doi:10.1007/BF00814061

Departamento Nacional de Infra-Estrutura de Transporte. (2001). Retrieved January 18, 2009 from https://gestao.dnit.gov.br/menu/rodovias/mapas.

Fearnside, P., & Barbosa, R. I. (1996). Political Benefits as Barriers to Assessment of Environmental Costs in Brazil's Amazonian Development Planning: The Example of the Jatapu Dam in Roraima. *Environmental Management, 20*(5), 615–630. doi:10.1007/BF01204135

Fearnside, P., & Barbosa, R. I. (1996). The Cotingo Dam as a Test of Brazil's System for Evaluating Proposed Developments in Amazonia. *Environmental Management, 20*(5), 615–648. doi:10.1007/BF01204135

Ferrier, S. (2002, April). Mapping Spatial Pattern in Biodiversity for Regional Conservation Planning: Where to from Here? *Systematic Biology, 51*(2), 331–363. doi:10.1080/10635150252899806

Frank, D. (June 4, 2002). Our Fruit, Their Labor and Global Reality. *The Washington Post* (p. B5).

Hall, A. (1994). Grassroots Action for Resettlement Planning: Brazil and Beyond. *World Development, 22*(12), 1793–1809. doi:10.1016/0305-750X(94)90174-0

Haughton, A. J., Champion, G. T., Hawes, C., Heard, M. S., Brooks, D. R., & Bohan, D. A., et al. (2003, Nov. 29). Invertebrate Responses to the Management of Genetically Modified Herbicide-Tolerant and Conventional Spring Crops. II. Within-Field Epigeal and Aerial Arthropods. *Philosophical Transactions Biological Sciences, 358* (1439), 1863-1877.

Iannone, A. P. (1987). *Contemporary Moral Controversies in Technology.* London and New York: Oxford University Press.

Iannone, A. P. (1989). *Contemporary Moral Controversies in Business.* London and New York: Oxford University Press.

Iannone, A. P. (1994). *Philosophy as Diplomacy. Essays in Ethics and Policy Making* Atlantic Highlands, NJ and Anherst, NY: Humanities Press and Humanity Books. Atlantic Highlands, NJ: Humanities Press.

Iannone, A. P. (1999). *Philosophical Ecologies: Essays in Philosophy, Ecology, and Human Life.* Atlantic Highlands, NJ and Anherst, NY: Humanities Press and Humanity Books.

Iannone, A. P. (2005). Pollution entry. In C. Mitcham (Ed.), *Encyclopedia of Science, Technology, and Ethics.* New York: Macmillan.

Iannone, A. P. (2008). *Papeles del gobierno, los mercados, y la cultura cívica en programas de desarrollo comunitario estadounidenses.* Publication of the School of Administrative and Economic Sciences. Lima, Perú: Universidad Inca Garcilaso de la Vega.

I.C.L.E.I. (2008). *Local Governments fro Sustainability.* Retrieved January 18, 2009 from http://www.iclei.org/index.php?id=iclei-home&no_cache=1.

Kearns, C. A., Inouye, D. W., & Waser, N. M. (1998). Endangered Mutualisms: The Conservation of Plant-Pollinator Interactions. *Annual Review of Ecology and Systematics, 29,* 83–112. doi:10.1146/annurev.ecolsys.29.1.83

Kremen, C., Williams, N. M., & Thorp, R. W. (2002, December 24). Crop Pollination from Native Bees at Risk from Agricultural Intensification. *Proceedings of the National Academy of Sciences of the United States, 99*(26), 16812–16816. doi:10.1073/pnas.262413599

Laurance, W. F. (Mar. 29, 2004). Forest-Climate Interactions in Fragmented Tropical Landscapes. *Philosophical Transactions: Biological Sciences, 359*(1443), Tropical Forests and Global Atmospheric Change, 345-352.

Laurance, W. F., Cochrane, M. A., Bergen, S., Fearnside, P. M., Delamônica, P., & Barber, C. (2001, Jan. 19). The Future of the Brazilian Amazon. *Science. New Series, 291*(5503), 438–439.

Mahar, D. J. (1976, August). Fiscal Incentives for Regional Development: A Case Study of the Western Amazon Basin. *Journal of Interamerican Studies and World Affairs, 18*(3), 357–378. doi:10.2307/174962

McGregor, S. E. (1976). *Insect Pollination of Cultivated Crop Plants.* Washington, D.C.: U.S. Department of Agriculture–Agricultural Research Service.

Mill, J. S. (1998). *Utilitarianism.* Oxford and New York: Oxford University Press.

Moffat, A. S. (1999, July 16). Crop Engineering Goes South. *Science, 287,* 370–371. doi:10.1126/science.285.5426.370

NASA. (2008). *Visible Earth, A Catalog of NASA Images and Animations of Our Home Planet.* Washington D.C.: NASA. Retrieved on January 18, 2009 from http://visibleearth.nasa.gov/view_rec.php?id=16728.

Newton, L. H., & Dillingham, C. K. (1993). *Watershed.* Belmont, CA: Wadsworth.

Orrego Silva, J. P. (1997). In Defence of the Biobío River. In A. D. Usher (Ed.), *Dams as Aid: A Political Economy of Nordic Development Thinking* (pp. 153-170). London: Routledge.

Pallister, M. (March 2, 1999). Banana Workers Toil in a Pear-Shaped World. *The Herald* (Glasgow), p. 13.

Rapoport, E. H. (1990, November-December). Vida en Extinción. *Ciencia Hoy, 2*(10), 33.

Rico, M. N. (2000). *Desarrollo sustentable, Manejo de recursos de agua y género.* Paper presented at the 2000 Conference of the Latin American Studies Association, Miami, FL. Cited in Roberts (2003), p. 99.

Roberts, J. T., & Thanos, N. D. (2003). *Trouble in Paradise: Globalization and Environmental Crises in Latin America.* New York and London: Routledge.

Rother, L. (December 5, 1999). German Arciniegas, 98, Critic Of Latin American Dictators. *The New York Times.* Retrieved January 18, 2009 from http://query.nytimes.com/gst/fullpage.html?res=9A02EED8153EF936A35751C1A96F958260&st=cse&sq=German+Arciniegas%2C+98%2C+Critic+of+Latin+American+Dictators&scp=1.

Roubik, D. W. (1995). *Pollination of Cultivated Plants in the Tropics.* Rome: Food Agric. Org. U.N.

Smart, J. J. C., & Williams, B. (1973). *Utilitarianism: For and Against.* Cambridge, England: Cambridge University Press.

United Nations. (1998). *Kyoto Protocol to the United Nations Convention on Climate Change.* New York: United Nations. Retrieved January 18, 2009 from http://unfccc.int/resource/docs/convkp/kpeng.pdf United Nations Research Institute for Social Development-UNRISD (1995). States of Disarray: The Social Effect of Globalization. London: UNRISD.

Usher, A. D. (1997), Kvaener's Game. In A.D. Usher (Ed.), *Dams as Aid: A Political Economy of Nordic Development Thinking* (pp. 133-152). London: Routledge.

Vargas Lloza, M. (2001, February). The Culture of Liberty. *Foreign Policy, 122,* 66–71.

Waldron, J. (1984). *Theories of Rights.* Oxford and New York: Oxford University Press.

Wallerstein, I. M. (1974, 1989). *The Modern World-System.* San Diego: Academic Press.

Wright, A. (1990). *The Death of Ramon Gonzalez: The Modern Agricultural Dilemma.* Austin, TX: University Press.

This work was previously published in International Journal of Technoethics, Volume 1, Issue 1, edited by Rocci Luppicini, pp. 45-59, copyright 2010 by IGI Publishing (an imprint of IGI Global).

Chapter 12
The Ethics of Outsourcing Online Survey Research

Peter J. Allen
Curtin Health Innovation Research Institute, Australia

Lynne D. Roberts
Curtin Health Innovation Research Institute, Australia

ABSTRACT

The increasing level of Internet penetration over the last decade has made web surveying a viable option for data collection in academic research. Software tools and services have been developed to facilitate the development and deployment of web surveys. Many academics and research students are outsourcing the design and/or hosting of their web surveys to external service providers, yet ethical issues associated with this use have received limited attention in academic literature. In this article, the authors focus on specific ethical concerns associated with the outsourcing of web surveys with particular reference to external commercial web survey service providers. These include threats to confidentiality and anonymity, the potential for loss of control over decisions about research data, and the reduced credibility of research. Suggested guidelines for academic institutions and researchers in relation to outsourcing aspects of web-based survey research are provided.

INTRODUCTION

Recent Pew Internet and American Life survey data indicate almost three quarters of American adults regularly access the Internet from home (Horrigan, 2009). The vast majority of these connections are at broadband speeds. Data from the Australian Bureau of Statistics (2008), the UK Office for National Statistics (2009) and the OECD's Directorate for Science, Technology and Industry (2009) reveal that Internet penetration levels are similarly high in Australia, the UK, and many other industrialised nations.

As Internet penetration has risen, researchers have increasingly moved their data collection ef-

DOI: 10.4018/978-1-4666-1773-5.ch012

forts 'online' (Lee, Fielding, & Blank, 2008; Reips, 2007; Skitka & Sargis, 2006). These efforts have variously involved online interviewing (Hewson, 2007; O'Connor, Madge, Shaw, & Wellens, 2008), observation and other non-reactive methods (Janetzko, 2008; Robinson, 2001), experimentation (Birnbaum, 2007; Reips, 2007) and web surveying (Best & Krueger, 2008; Reips, 2008). Of these online data collection methods, web surveying is currently dominant (Reips, 2008), is continuing to grow in popularity (Lee et al., 2008)[1], is the online method most frequently reviewed by Human Research Ethics Committees (HRECs; Buchanan & Hvizdak, 2009) and thus is the primary focus of this paper.

The growing use of web surveying merits attention to the possible impacts of the technology on research participants. Such ethical considerations are situated within the emerging scholarship on technoethics. Technoethics provides a focus on the ethical considerations associated with technological change (Luppicini, 2009). Within the broad field of technoethics, Internet ethics and cyber ethics have been identified as key areas (Luppicini, 2009) with major questions including "What are the ethical responsibilities of Internet researchers to research participants?" (p. 10) and "What are the ethical responsibilities of Internet researchers to protect the identity and confidentiality of data derived from the Internet?" (p. 10). We begin this article by providing an overview of web surveying, including the tools and services that have emerged facilitate the development and deployment of web surveys. We provide evidence to suggest that commercial web survey hosts are widely used by academic researchers, yet the ethical issues associated with this use have received only limited attention in the academic literature. The main body of this article provides a focus on specific ethical concerns associated with outsourcing aspects of the web surveying process, with particular reference to external commercial web survey hosts. These include threats to confidenti-

ality and anonymity associated with breaches of data protection and the potential loss of control over decisions about the data. Further, the possible impact of externally hosting academic surveys on response rates and responding is examined in terms of online privacy concern and the perceived credibility of research. This article concludes with some suggested guidelines for institutions and researchers in relation to the outsourcing of aspects of academic research utilising web surveys.

Web Surveying

Web surveying typically involves administering a series of questionnaire items of varying types (e.g., rating scales, fixed-choice, open-ended etc.) over the world-wide-web, and can offer a number of advantages over paper and telephone based surveying methods. Such advantages include, but are not limited to, timely access to large samples (Skitka & Sargis, 2006) that are often more diverse and 'representative' than traditional samples (Gosling, Vazire, Srivastava, & John, 2004); access to samples that would otherwise be prohibitively costly or difficult to achieve (e.g., Hildebrandt, Langenbucher, Carr, Sanjuan, & Park's, 2006) large sample of anabolic steroid users); reduced social desirability and experimenter expectancy effects (Hewson & Laurent, 2008); and the ability to easily randomize and impose conditional logic on the presentation of survey items and stimuli (Best & Krueger, 2004).

The topics that have been investigated using web surveying are diverse, and a full review is beyond the scope of this paper. However, a small sample might include studies typical of Skitka and Sargis's (2006) three broad categories of web-based research: translational, phenomenological and novel.

Translational studies are those that investigate traditional topics using methods and measures developed offline, and adapted for use on the web. Such adaptation is primarily to capitalize on the efficiencies and global reach afforded by the web. For example, Oliver John, Sam Gosling and colleagues have used online variants of the Big Five Inventory (BFI; see John, Naumann, & Soto, 2008) to collect large volumes of self-report questionnaire data used in a series of investigations into the psychometric properties of the measure, as well as the characteristics and correlates of the 'big five' personality factors more broadly (e.g., Rentfrow, Gosling, & Potter, 2008; Robins, Tracy, Trzesniewski, Gosling, & Potter, 2002; Robins, Tracy, Trzesniewski, Potter, & Gosling, 2001; Soto, John, Gosling, & Potter, 2008; Srivastava, John, Gosling, & Potter, 2003). Sample sizes in these studies have ranged from 100,000 to over 600,000 participants (in the case of Rentfrow et al., 2008). Many additional examples of ongoing translational survey research are indexed on websites like Hanover College's *Psychological Research on the Net*[2] and the *Web Survey List*[3], hosted at the University of Zurich.

Skitka and Sargis's (2006) second category of web-based research, phenomenological, is also well represented on *Psychological Research on the Net* and the *Web Survey List*. Phenomenological web-based research is focused on the nature of Internet behavior itself, and includes examples such as McFarlane, Bull, and Rietmeijer's (2002) study of young adults' online sex seeking behavior, as well as various investigations into 'Internet addiction' (e.g., Greenfield, 1999; Whang, Lee, & Chang, 2003).

Finally, Skitka and Sargis (2006) identified a third category of web-based research, which they referred to as novel. Novel web-based research capitalizes on unique features of the Internet to ask questions that would be methodologically difficult, if not impossible, to address offline. As an example of novel web-based research employing survey methods, Skitka and Sargis cite Vazire and Gosling (2004), who examined the nature and accuracy of personality impressions derived from viewing personal websites.

Web Surveying Tools and Hosting

As the popularity of web surveying has increased, many software tools have been built to facilitate their development and deployment (Kaczmirek, 2008). These tools typically reduce (and often completely eliminate) the specialised programming knowledge that researchers would otherwise require to create and maintain a custom-built online surveying instrument, and can vary greatly in terms of their feature sets, flexibility, usability and cost to the end-user. These tools also vary in the extent to which they require the researcher to outsource aspects of the research (e.g., survey hosting, data collection, storage etc.) to an external service provider.

SurveyMonkey.com Corporation[4] (hereafter *SurveyMonkey*) is one such service provider. It is a commercial venture that provides subscribers with access to a proprietary, browser-based survey editor, which can be used to build and deploy surveys containing a common range of question types (e.g., fixed-choice, open-ended etc.). Surveys constructed with the *SurveyMonkey* editor, as well as the data they are used to collect, are hosted on the company's secure web-servers. In other words, researchers using *SurveyMonkey* are essentially outsourcing survey formatting, data collection and storage (at least in the short term) to the company.

Although it is a current market leader, *SurveyMonkey* is but one of literally dozens (and probably hundreds) of companies to which survey hosting and data storage can be outsourced. For more exhaustive reviews and evaluations of some of the available alternatives, the reader is directed to Crawford (2002), Beiderniki and Kerschbaumer (2007), Gordon (2002), Wright (2005), Sue and Ritter (2007) and Gaiser and Schreiner (2009). Gaiser and Schreiner, in particular, provide useful guidelines for evaluating commercial web survey hosts based on costs, ease of use, output viewing options and technical support. Many of the more popular outsourcing options are also indexed in the University of Ljubljana's *WebSM*[5] resource, where they are referred to as "hosted solutions".

Rather than outsourcing, many researchers prefer to, are required to, and/or have the facilities to, host web surveys internally, or 'in-house'. In other words, to host them on web-servers owned and/or managed by the researcher's home institution. In some instances, these surveys will be hand-coded by or for the researcher; in others, they will be developed using standard web authoring software (e.g., *Adobe Dreamweaver*[6], *Microsoft Expression Web*[7] etc.), or more specialised survey development applications like *Opinio*[8] and *Lime Survey*[9].

Lime Survey is an example of a widely used open-source web application that can be installed on any web-server running MySQL and PHP. *Lime Survey* surveys and databases are typically hosted on the installation web-server. Like *SurveyMonkey*, *Lime Survey* can be used to build and deploy surveys containing a common range of question types. Unlike users of *SurveyMonkey* (and users of closed-source applications such as *Opinio*) users of *Lime Survey* are free to modify and add to its current feature set, a practice that is encouraged amongst open-source software developers. For a more comprehensive review of open-source surveying options, the reader is referred to Baker (2007). On *WebSM*, both closed- and open-source web surveying applications suitable for building and hosting surveys in-house can located by browsing for software that runs "on user's server".

Universities vary in both the types of software used to develop web surveys, whether surveys are hosted internally or externally, and the policies and procedures surrounding their use. For example, at our institution, Curtin University of Technology, both *SurveyMonkey* and *Lime Survey* are currently being used, along with a range of other tools that are hosted both on- and off-site. To determine whether or not this was common practise, we examined each of the studies employing online

survey methods listed on Hanover College's *Psychological Research on the Net* website on 19 September 2009 that had been added in the three months from 20 June to 19 September 2009. *Psychological Research on the Net* was selected because of its size, popularity, and exclusive focus on ethical academic research (the requirements for listing a study on the site include providing information about the researchers, affiliations, and ethics review processes).

Of the 66 studies meeting our criteria, 35 had chief investigators (CIs) with affiliations at United States universities or colleges, and 23 had CIs with United Kingdom affiliations. The remaining studies were Australian (4), Canadian (1), Irish (1), Singaporean (1) and Swiss (1).

Consistent with Buchanan and Hvizdak (2009), who found that just 24% of the United States Human Research Ethics Committee (HREC) representatives they surveyed worked at institutions with "specific tool[s] to use for online surveys" (p. 40), only 17 (i.e., 26%) of the 66 surveys we examined were hosted on web-servers owned and operated by the CI's institution, or another academic institution with which the CI was affiliated. Of the remaining 49 surveys, 47 were hosted off-site (see Table 1), and we were unable to draw any conclusions about the final two. Excluding the five surveys hosted on personally owned web servers, the off-site surveys we looked at were exclusively hosted by commercial service providers, primarily *SurveyMonkey*.

These findings suggest considerable variation across institutions and researchers, with the majority outsourcing major aspects of the web surveying process to commercial service providers. Such outsourcing can offer a number of advantages to academic researchers. First, it is typically quicker and easier to use existing products for survey design and deployment, than to develop systems internally. Ease of use may be of particular concern to academics supervising student research projects with short time-lines, or

Table 1. Hosting locations of 47 online surveys listed at 'Psychological Research on the Net' in the three months to 19 September 2009 and not hosted on the CI's Institution's web-servers

Host	Website address	N
SurveyMonkey	http://surveymonkey.com	27
Psych Data	https://psychdata.com	5
Qualtrics	http://qualtrics.com	2
Survey Gizmo	http://surveygizmo.com	2
Bristol Online Surveys	http://survey.bris.ac.uk	2
Globalpark/Unipark	http://unipark.info	2
Formsite	http://formsite.com	1
QuestionPro	http://questionpro.com	1
Researcher's Personal Web Server	n/a	5
Total		**47**

utilising online surveys in their teaching (Gaiser & Schreiner, 2009). Second, outsourcing usually eliminates the need for sophisticated technical knowledge, including the need to maintain a web-server and databases (Kaczmirek, 2008). Furthermore, large commercial providers can usually offer researchers guaranteed 'up-time', a regular backup schedule, and high levels of data security (Kaczmirek, 2008), often at a considerably lower cost than deploying and maintaining a comparable service in-house (Gaiser & Schreiner, 2009; Kaczmirek, 2008). On the surface, these advantages make the outsourcing of web surveys an attractive option for many researchers. However, outsourcing also raises a number of significant ethical concerns.

ETHICAL ISSUES ASSOCIATED WITH OUTSOURCING

In the previous section, we noted the popularity of outsourcing significant aspects of the web surveying process to external (and typically commercial) service providers. Such outsourcing can offer many advantages, but also raises a number of ethical concerns, particularly when service providers are selected and used by researchers on a seemingly case-by-case, ad-hoc basis[10]. In this section we examine ethical issues associated with outsourcing, focusing on two key areas. First, we outline potential threats to anonymity and confidentiality associated with both data protection methods and the collection of IP addresses. Then we examine the potential impact of the perceived credibility of a data collection website on response rates and the accuracy of reporting. While recognising that each discipline has their own set of ethical guidelines, in our discussion of these issues we refer to the American Psychological Association's Ethical Guidelines (APA, 2002). These guidelines, in common with most other sets of ethical guidelines, are based on the principles of beneficence and nonmaleficence, fidelity and responsibility, integrity, justice and respect for the rights and dignity of individuals.

Data Protection: Threats to Anonymity and Confidentiality

The protection of data at all stages of the research process, from initial data collection through to storage, is vital to ensuring the confidentiality and anonymity of research participants. With online research, data protection moves beyond the traditional methods for protection of paper documents to cover the protection of digital data. The potential for intentional malicious damage to online surveys is not simply a theoretical risk. Online surveys have been hacked (see Andrews, Nonnecke, & Preece, 2003, for details of how their online survey was hacked twice and infected with a virus) highlighting the need to ensure a high level of data protection. As noted by the American Psychological Association Policy and Planning Board (2009) "issues of protecting participant privacy in Internet transmission and computer storage are paramount but challenging" (p. 458).

The data protection measures employed need to increase with the increasing sensitivity of the data collected. Barchard and Williams (2008) recommended researchers of highly sensitive topics go beyond basic security measures and refer to the security standards in the computing industry, such as those provided by the Payment Card Industry Standards Council[11], for the most up-to-date advice on data protection. The American Psychological Association's Board of Scientific Affairs' Advisory Group go further, recommending that where acceptable protections cannot be put in place, alternatives to Internet research should be used (Kraut, Olson, Banaji, Bruckman, Cohen, & Couper, 2004).

The outsourced hosting of surveys is associated with additional layers of threats to data protection over those shared by all web surveys. While many commercial web survey hosting services may employ high level data protection measures that are consistent with industry standards[12], a major concern is that the researcher does not have complete control over who can, and cannot, access the research data. A second area of concern with the external hosting of web surveys is the additional risks associated with the transmission of data from the host to the researcher.

External hosting services also vary in their data protection policies and practices. Further highlighting the potential for breaches of data security, Buchanan and Hvizdak (2009) reported that more than a third of their Human Research Ethics Committee representative survey respondents did not, as part of the ethics review process, consider the security and privacy policies of external service providers. As Buchanan and Hvizdak noted (2009), "until each tool is vetted and its privacy policies and data security policies understood, we cannot be 100% certain how security, content and privacy are instantiated within the individual tools" (p. 46).

Collection of IP Addresses: A Threat to Anonymity

A further threat to participant anonymity is the collection of IP addresses. A unique Internet Protocol (IP) address is assigned to a computer each time it connects to the Internet. Banks of IP addresses are allocated to organisations and Internet Service Providers (ISPs) through five regional Internet registries: AfriNIC servicing the Africa region, APNIC (Asia Pacific), LACNIC (Latin America and the Caribbean), American Registry for Internet Numbers (ARIN) and RIPE NCC covering Europe, the Middle East and parts of Central Asia. In some circumstances it is possible to trace the location of a specific computer from an IP address. This may be done through one of the regional registries, along with the records of the ISP originally allocated the address of interest (Barchard & Williams, 2008).

While it is possible to use IP addresses and cookies to identify/track use on individual computers (Charlesworth, 2008), it is difficult to make a definitive link from an IP address to a specific individual. An IP address only identifies a computer, not a user (Nosek, Banaji, & Greenwald, 2002). Furthermore, many ISPs use dynamic IP allocation, whereby an IP address is assigned to a computer for the duration of the session only (Nosek et al, 2002), meaning that over a course of a day several computers may have been assigned the same IP address. Furthermore, a computer may be used by multiple users (e.g., a computer located in a public library) and/or a single account may be used by multiple family members (Hewson, Yule, Laurent, & Vogel, 2003).

However, the uniqueness of IP addresses, when used in combination with time and date information, means they should be treated in survey research as potential identifiers. Preferably, IP addresses should not be recorded as part of a survey (Nosek et al., 2002). When using an external survey provider, the option of not recording IP addresses may not be possible. Where a commercial survey provider automatically captures IP addresses, it is recommended that they be deleted as soon as possible, preferably before saving the data file to the researcher's computer (Barchard & Williams, 2008; Benfield & Szlemko, 2006). However, the external survey provider is likely to retain IP information, regardless of whether or not the researcher deletes it, posing an ongoing threat to confidentiality and anonymity. For example, the *SurveyMonkey* Privacy Policy[13] states:

As is true of most Web sites, we gather certain information automatically and store it in log files. This information includes internet protocol (IP) addresses, browser type, internet service provider (ISP), referring/exit pages, operating system, date/ time stamp, and clickstream data.

We use this information, which does not identify individual users, to analyze trends, to administer the site, to track users' movements around the site and to gather demographic information about our user base as a whole.

We do not link this automatically-collected data to personally identifiable information

However, that such data is not generally linked does not mean it will never be linked. Later in the *SurveyMonkey* Privacy Policy under 'Legal Disclosure' it is stated that:

We reserve the right to disclose your personally identifiable information as required by law and when we believe that disclosure is necessary to protect our rights and/or to comply with a judicial proceeding, court order, or legal process served on our Web site

This effectively means that control over the decision of whether or not to disclose research data to legal authorities may be taken out of the hands of the researcher and his/her institution. This

may be a particular issue for researchers conducting surveys on criminal behaviour, where there have been cases of off-line research data being subpoenaed or research suspended over concerns about being able to maintain confidentiality (Roberts & Indermaur, 2003). In line with the APA's recommendations on informed consent (APA, 2002), research participants must be informed of the limits of confidentiality.

The Impact of Credibility of Site on Response Rates and Accuracy of Reporting

Ethical issues also arise in relation to public perceptions of the credibility of surveys hosted at non-academic domains. The external hosting of an academic web survey risks diluting public perceptions' of the academic nature of the research. In addition to academic researchers, commercial, non-profit and media organisations, and members of the lay-public also use web surveys to collect data. For example, Couper (2000) refers to 'web surveys as entertainment', which includes collections of non-scientific surveys or polls and media 'question of the day' polls. Some potential research participants may be unable to differentiate between academic research surveys and other commercial surveys, potentially affecting the credibility of academic surveys housed by commercial survey providers (Binik, Mah, & Kiesler, 1999; Fricker & Schonlau, 2002). Some external hosting services routinely use banner advertisements on survey pages, further blurring the distinction between academic and commercial data collection. This highlights the need for researchers to clearly delineate their work as 'academic research' that has ethical approval from the relevant HRECs/IRBs.

Suggested ways of strengthening the perceived links between research and academic instiutions include posting researchers' photographs and links to researchers' home pages on the survey site (Binik et al., 1999). Peden and Flashinski

(2004) examined psychology research websites for evidence of institutional affiliation. Only 22% of 22 websites housing psychology surveys and experiments reviewed in early 2002 contained an active link to a university website, although 88% identified institutional affiliations. Further, only a minority of sites (31%) stated that the research had been granted ethical approval by a HREC/IRB, with even fewer (27%) actually providing contact details for the approving body.

The perceived credibility of a survey domain may affect both willingness to participate in research and the candidacy of responding. While Internet users vary in their levels of concern about online privacy, the majority do express some concern about disclosing personal information online. For example, of 1,482 US residents surveyed as part of an online survey about Internet use, 53.7% reported being 'very concerned' and 27.1% 'somewhat concerned' about security on the Internet, where security was defined to include privacy, confidentiality and identity issues (O'Neil, 2001). Further, online privacy concern may vary by domain. Home Internet users vary in the degree to which they find website privacy statements from corporations and government institutions credible (Turow & Hennessy, 2007). While the proportion of Internet users who trust commercial online survey providers or universities has not been established, the percentage of 1,200 adult home Internet users surveyed who trusted an institution to protect their information online and not disclose it without their consent varied by institutional type, from 4% for major advertisers to 25% for makers of privacy protection software (Turow & Hennessy, 2007).

The presence of online privacy policies on websites has limited impact on perceptions of privacy risk (Myerscough, Lowe, & Alpert, 2006). Further, the majority of Internet users do not systematically read online privacy notices. Based on survey responses from a stratified random sample of 2,468 U.S. adults from the Harris Poll

Online panel, Milne and Culnan (2004) reported that 17.3% of respondents stated they never read privacy notices on websites. Of those who did report reading privacy notices, less than five percent reported always reading them. As Binik et al. (1999) suggest, "researchers should not assume that a promise of anonymity or non-anonymity is always viewed as such by participants" (pp. 85-86).

Where individuals have online privacy concerns, the majority take actions to protect their privacy (Paine, Reips, Steiger, Joinson, & Buchanan, 2007). While protective measures are largely based around hardware and software (e.g., firewalls, use of antivirus software etc.), almost 10% of Paine and colleagues' survey respondents volunteered that they were careful about the information they revealed online. Experimental research suggests that online survey responding is sensitive to, and responses may be affected by, privacy concerns. Joinson, Paine, Buchanan, and Reips (2008) manipulated level of privacy concern in online surveys, demonstrating that the use of an 'I prefer not to say' option is sensitive to both priming and manipulation of privacy concern.

Online privacy concern may also affect the candidacy of survey responses. While early research into the computer administration of measures suggested that this mode of administration reduced socially desirable responding and increased the candidacy of responses (Feigelson & Dwight, 2000), more recent research has failed to find differences between various modes of administration (e.g., Bates & Cox, 2008; Uriell & Dudley, 2009). Respondent concerns over web survey data security have the potential to reverse any positive effects on social desirability responding (Couper, 2000).

Perceptions of confidentiality and anonymity of survey responses can affect responding to survey questions deemed sensitive by the respondent. A meta-analysis of research conducted into the effect of confidentiality assurances in offline research indicated that confidentiality assurances can improve responding to sensitive questions (Singer, 2004; Singer, Von Thurn, & Miller, 1995). More recent research has suggested that perceptions of anonymity have a greater effect than assurances of confidentiality on preparedness to reveal sensitive information (Ong & Weiss, 2000).

In addition to the impact of the immediate environment, Binik et al. (1999) suggest that online cues and the survey interface may impact on perceptions of anonymity. Perceptions of anonymity and security of survey responses influence intention to respond to online surveys (Rogelberg, Spitzmueller, Little, & Reeve, 2006) and accuracy of reporting. Uriell and Dudley's (2009) survey of enlisted US navy personnel found that web survey respondents were significantly more likely than pen-and-paper survey respondents to think that others could access their survey responses and that their survey responses would be linked with identifying and personal information. Accuracy of responses was positively correlated with perceived anonymity and confidentiality of survey responses. Participants' concern over the potential identifiability of data from web surveys suggests that researchers need to make explicit how anonymity will be maintained (Chizawsky, Estabrooks, & Sales, 2009).

The history of privacy violations online creates an atmosphere unconducive to building a relationship of trust between respondents and researchers (Cho & LaRose, 1999). This distrust may be magnified where commercial survey providers are utilised for data collection. Research in offline settings has demonstrated that the perceived legitimacy and authority of researchers is influential in the decision to participate in research (Groves, Cialdini, & Couper, 1992) with higher responses rates for university sponsored research (Fox, Crask, & Kim, 1998). The internal hosting of web surveys on education domains may increase the credibility of research and hence response rates (Cho & LaRose, 1999), as well as the candidness of responding.

HOSTING ON-SITE

Researchers may seek to avoid or address some of the ethical concerns associated with outsourcing by simply moving their web surveying on-site. This can seem particularly tempting to those researchers with a reasonable degree of IT savvy and administrator level access to a web server. We do not wish to imply that the outsourcing of academic web survey development and hosting is necessarily inferior to developing and hosting surveys internally. Indeed, while internal development and hosting increases the transparency of research (Buchanan & Hvizdak, 2009) and strengthens the identification of the research with the university, it can also raise a raft of new concerns. For example, are procedures in place to ensure that the both the surveying application *and* the software and services on which it relies (e.g., the web server, database server, web application framework etc.) are appropriately maintained (i.e., regularly updated/patched, backed-up etc.)? How are 'default' security and privacy policies set, and reviewed? Who has administrator level access to the web server, and are these people appropriately qualified? How are access rights and user accounts managed? Can users edit and/ or view each other's surveys or data? If so, how is confidentiality managed? These issues are largely beyond the scope of this paper, but illustrate that the decision about whether to outsource or not is a challenging one, and should not be made lightly. With this in mind, in the final section of this paper, we offer a series of suggestions to those readers needing to make such a decision.

GUIDELINES

First and foremost, we recommend that each university develop a coordinated, institution-wide approach to online surveying, rather than relying on ad-hoc decisions by individual researchers, and the duplication of systems and services that such decisions often result in. We recommend the development of this approach involve representatives from the university HREC/IRB, legal department and IT department, in addition to academics from a range of disciplines who are experienced in conducting online research. A set of clearly stated policies and procedures for conducing web surveying should also be developed. As part of a coordinated, institution-wide approach, a university may choose to provide and support internal survey development and hosting and/or to provide a short-list of 'approved' external services for survey development and hosting. Each of these options will be briefly explored below.

In our view, the greatest protection to research participants is offered where the university provides and supports the development and hosting of online surveys, and the online surveying facilities are managed and maintained by staff skilled in IT security and familiar with the ethical and legal requirements that researchers are bound by in their geographic regions and professional disciplines. Such facilities can be based on an open source software package like *Lime Survey*, or a proprietary solution such as *Opinio*. Larger institutions may also consider the option of developing a customised surveying package in-house, rather than depending on code developed or maintained by outsiders.

However, we recognise that is not always possible to harness the resources necessary to provide surveying facilities in-house. This may be particularly the case for smaller or specialised institutions, or institutions were there is little demand for web surveying. Where this is the case, we would recommend that representatives from the university HREC, legal department, IT department and active research academics examine the terms of use and security provisions of a range of widely used commercial survey providers with the aim of providing a short list of acceptable providers. In recognition of the rapidly changing

field, it is recommended that this list of preferred providers be reviewed on an annual basis. Where necessary for the specifics of their research project, individual students/researchers can present a case for utilising another survey organisation, and this can be assessed on a case-by-case basis.

Where the decision is made to outsource the hosting of a survey, we recommend that the survey content, hosted on the commercial site, is 'sandwiched' between an information sheet and debriefing page, both hosted on a university server. This will strengthen perceptions of the association between the research and the university. It also allows for the collection of identifying information for purposes such as informed consent or entry into a prize draw to occur on the university server. This separation of collecting survey information on the commercial survey provider's server and identifying information on a university server provides an additional layer of protection for participants (Barchard & Williams, 2008).

Where a university has not developed a coordinated, institution-wide approach to online surveying, individual researchers may need to make their own decisions about outsourcing aspects of their web survey research. In our own research and supervision of research students we have successfully used both internally hosted surveys developed using an open source software package and surveys externally hosted on commercial web surveying sites. These choices were largely influenced by the technical skills and experience of the researchers/students and duration of the projects, with those with limited IT skills and a limited data collection period being directed towards external survey companies where the researcher requires few technical skills to be able to 'create' their on-line survey. In choosing between external providers, particular consideration should be given to data protection and privacy policies, privacy certification, and hardware and software configurations.

CONCLUSION

The use of web surveying in academic research is a relatively new phenomenon, and occurs within a rapidly changing environment characterized by technological innovation. New modes of data collection are likely to evolve, enabled by technological change (Tourangeau, 2004). While the principles underlying ethical research remain the same, the application of these principles to new methodologies such as web surveying lags behind their introduction. In this article we have outlined some of the ethical issues associated with outsourcing aspects of web surveying at the current point in time. While we have provided suggested guidelines in relation to the outsourcing (or otherwise) of web surveys, researchers will need to keep abreast of both social and technological changes in the field, including both standards for data protection and evolving interpretations of ethical codes.

REFERENCES

American Psychological Association. (2002). *Ethical principles of psychologists and code of conduct*. Retrieved from http://www.apa.org/ethics/code2002.pdf

American Psychological Association Policy and Planning Board. (2009). How technology changes everything (and nothing) in psychology: 2008 annual report of the APA Policy and Planning Board. *The American Psychologist, 64*, 454–463. doi:10.1037/a0015888

Andrews, D., Nonnecke, B., & Preece, J. (2003). Electronic survey methodology: A case study in reaching hard-to-involve Internet users. *International Journal of Human-Computer Interaction, 16*, 185–210. doi:10.1207/S15327590IJHC1602_04

Australian Bureau of Statistics. (2008). *Household use of information technology, Australia, 2007-08* (Catalogue Number 8146.0). Canberra, Australia: Author. Retrieved from http://www.abs.gov.au/Ausstats/abs@.nsf/mf/8146.0

Baker, J. D. (2007). Open source survey software. In Reynolds, R. A., Woods, R., & Baker, J. D. (Eds.), *Handbook of research on electronic surveys and measurements* (pp. 273–275). Hershey, PA: IGI Global.

Barchard, K. A., & Williams, J. (2008). Practical advice for conducting ethical online experiments and questionnaires for United States psychologists. *Behavior Research Methods, 40*, 1111–1128. doi:10.3758/BRM.40.4.1111

Bates, S. C., & Cox, J. M. (2008). The impact of computer versus paper-pencil survey, and individual versus group administration, on self-reports of sensitive behaviors. *Computers in Human Behavior, 24*, 903–916. doi:10.1016/j.chb.2007.02.021

Beiderniki, G., & Kerschbaumer, A. (2007). Comparison of online survey tools. In Reynolds, R. A., Woods, R., & Baker, J. D. (Eds.), *Handbook of research on electronic surveys and measurements* (pp. 264–272). Hershey, PA: IGI Global.

Benfield, J. A., & Szlemko, W. J. (2006). Internet-based data collection: Promises and realities. *Journal of Research Practice, 2*, 1–15.

Best, S. J., & Krueger, B. S. (2004). *Internet data collection*. Thousand Oaks, CA: Sage.

Best, S. J., & Krueger, B. S. (2008). Internet survey design. In Fielding, N., Lee, R. M., & Blank, G. (Eds.), *The SAGE handbook of online research methods* (pp. 217–235). London: Sage.

Binik, Y. M., Mah, K., & Kiesler, S. (1999). Ethical issues in conducting sex research on the Internet. *Journal of Sex Research, 36*, 82–90. doi:10.1080/00224499909551971

Birnbaum, M. H. (2007). Designing online experiments. In Joinson, A., McKenna, K., Postmes, T., & Reips, U.-D. (Eds.), *The Oxford handbook of Internet psychology* (pp. 391–403). New York: Oxford University Press.

Buchanan, E. A., & Hvizdak, E. E. (2009). Online survey tools: Ethical and methodological concerns of Human Research Ethics Committees. *Journal of Empirical Research on Human Research Ethics; JERHRE, 4,* 37–48. doi:10.1525/jer.2009.4.2.37

Charlesworth, A. (2008). Understanding and managing legal issues in Internet research. In Fielding, N., Lee, R. M., & Blank, G. (Eds.), *The SAGE handbook of online research methods* (pp. 42–57). London: Sage.

Chizawsky, L. L. K., Estabrooks, C. A., & Sales, A. E. (in press). The feasibility of web-based surveys as a data collection tool: A process evaluation. *Applied Nursing Research.*

Cho, H., & LaRose, R. (1999). Privacy issues in Internet surveys. *Social Science Computer Review, 17,* 421–434. doi:10.1177/089443939901700402

Couper, M. P. (2000). Web surveys: A review of issues and approaches. *Public Opinion Quarterly, 64,* 464–494. doi:10.1086/318641

Crawford, S. (2002). Evaluation of web survey data collection systems. *Field Methods, 14,* 307–321.

Directorate for Science, Technology and Industry, Organisation for Economic Co-Operation and Development. (2009). *OECD key ICT indicators.* Retrieved September 20, 2009, from http://www.oecd.org/sti/ICTindicators

Ess, C. (2007). Internet research ethics. In Joinson, A., McKenna, K., Postmes, T., & Reips, U.-D. (Eds.), *The Oxford handbook of Internet psychology* (pp. 487–502). New York: Oxford University Press.

Ess, C., & the The AIOR Ethics Working Committee. (2002). *Ethical decision making and Internet research: Recommendations from the AOIR ethics working committee.* Retrieved August 31, 2009, from http://www.aoir.org/reports/ethics.pdf

Evans, J. R., & Mathur, A. (2005). The value of online surveys. *Internet Research, 15,* 195–219. doi:10.1108/10662240510590360

Feigelson, M. E., & Dwight, S. A. (2000). Can asking questions by computer improve the candidness of responding? A meta-analytic perspective. *Consulting Psychology Journal: Practice and Research, 52,* 248–255. doi:10.1037/1061-4087.52.4.248

Fox, R. J., Crask, M. R., & Kim, J. (1988). Mail survey response rate: A meta-analysis of selected techniques for inducing response. *Public Opinion Quarterly, 52,* 467–491. doi:10.1086/269125

Fricker, R. D. Jr, & Schonlau, M. (2002). Advantages and disadvantages of Internet research surveys: Evidence from the literature. *Field Methods, 14,* 347–367. doi:10.1177/152582202237725

Gaiser, T. J., & Schreiner, A. E. (2009). *A guide to conducting online research.* London: Sage.

Gordon, A. (2002). Product review: SurveyMonkey.com—Web-based survey and evaluation system. *The Internet and Higher Education, 5,* 83–87. Retrieved from http://www.SurveyMonkey.com. doi:10.1016/S1096-7516(02)00061-1

Gosling, S. D., Vazire, S., Srivastava, S., & John, O. P. (2004). Should we trust web-based studies? A comparative analysis of six preconceptions about Internet questionnaires. *The American Psychologist, 59,* 93–104. doi:10.1037/0003-066X.59.2.93

Greenfield, D. N. (1999). Psychological characteristics of compulsive Internet use: A preliminary analysis. *Cyberpsychology & Behavior, 2,* 403–412. doi:10.1089/cpb.1999.2.403

Groves, R. M., Cialdini, R. B., & Couper, M. P. (1992). Understanding the decision to participate in a survey. *Public Opinion Quarterly, 56*, 475–495. doi:10.1086/269338

Hewson, C. (2007). Gathering data on the Internet: Qualitative approaches and possibilities for mixed methods research. In Joinson, A., McKenna, K., Postmes, T., & Reips, U.-D. (Eds.), *The Oxford handbook of Internet psychology* (pp. 405–428). New York: Oxford University Press.

Hewson, C., & Laurent, D. (2008). Research design and tools for Internet research. In Fielding, N., Lee, R. M., & Blank, G. (Eds.), *The SAGE handbook of online research methods* (pp. 58–78). London: Sage.

Hewson, C., Yule, P., Laurent, D., & Vogel, C. (2003). *Internet research methods: A practical guide for the social and behavioural sciences*. London: Sage.

Hildebrandt, T., Langenbucher, J., Carr, S., Sanjuan, P., & Park, S. (2006). Predicting intentions for long-term anabolic-androgenic steroid use among men: A covariance structure model. *Psychology of Addictive Behaviors, 20*, 234–240. doi:10.1037/0893-164X.20.3.234

Horrigan, J. (2009, June). *Home broadband adoption 2009: Broadband adoption increases, but monthly prices do too*. Washington, DC: Pew Internet & American Life Project. Retrieved from http://pewinternet.org/Reports/2009/10-Home-Broadband-Adoption-2009.aspx

Jenetzko, D. (2008). Nonreactive data collection on the Internet. In Fielding, N., Lee, R. M., & Blank, G. (Eds.), *The SAGE handbook of online research methods* (pp. 161–173). London: Sage.

John, O. P., Naumann, L. P., & Soto, C. J. (2008). Paradigm shift to the integrative big-five trait taxonomy: History, measurement, and conceptual Issues. In John, O. P., Robins, R. W., & Pervin, L. A. (Eds.), *Handbook of personality: Theory and research* (3rd ed., pp. 114–158). New York: Guilford Press.

Joinson, A. N., Paine, C., Buchanan, T., & Reips, U.-D. (2008). Measuring self-disclosure online: Blurring and non-response to sensitive items in web-based surveys. *Computers in Human Behavior, 24*, 2158–2171. doi:10.1016/j.chb.2007.10.005

Kaczmirek, L. (2008). Internet survey software tools. In Fielding, N., Lee, R. M., & Blank, G. (Eds.), *The SAGE handbook of online research methods* (pp. 236–254). London: Sage.

Keller, H. E., & Lee, S. (2003). Ethical issues surrounding human participants research using the Internet. *Ethics & Behavior, 13*, 211–219. doi:10.1207/S15327019EB1303_01

Kraut, R., Olson, J., Banaji, M., Bruckman, A., Cohen, J., & Couper, M. (2004). Psychological research online: Report of the Board of Scientific Affairs' Advisory Group on the conduct of research on the Internet. *The American Psychologist, 59*, 105–117. doi:10.1037/0003-066X.59.2.105

Lee, R. M., Fielding, N., & Blank, G. (2008). The Internet as a research medium: An editorial introduction to 'The Sage Handbook of Online Research Methods. In Fielding, N., Lee, R. M., & Blank, G. (Eds.), *The SAGE handbook of online research methods* (pp. 3–20). London: Sage.

Luppicini, R. (2009). The emerging field for technoethics. In Luppicini, R., & Adell, R. (Eds.), *Handbook of research on technoethics* (pp. 1–19). Hershey, PA: IGI Global.

McFarlane, M., Bull, S. S., & Rietmeijer, C. A. (2002). Young adults on the Internet: Risk behaviors for sexually transmitted diseases and HIV. *The Journal of Adolescent Health, 31*, 11–16. doi:10.1016/S1054-139X(02)00373-7

Milne, G. R., & Culnan, M. J. (2004). Strategies for reducing online privacy risks: Why consumers read (or don't read) online privacy notices. *Journal of Interactive Marketing, 18*(3), 15–29. doi:10.1002/dir.20009

Myerscough, S., Lowe, B., & Alpert, F. (2006). Willingness to provide personal information online: The role of perceived privacy risk, privacy statements and brand strength. *Journal of Website Promotion, 2*, 115–139. doi:10.1080/15533610802104182

Nosek, B. A., Banaji, M. R., & Greenwald, A. G. (2002). E-research: Ethics, security, design and control in psychological research on the Internet. *The Journal of Social Issues, 58*, 161–176. doi:10.1111/1540-4560.00254

O'Connor, H., Madge, C., Shaw, R., & Wellens, J. (2008). Internet-based interviewing. In Fielding, N., Lee, R. M., & Blank, G. (Eds.), *The SAGE handbook of online research methods* (pp. 271–289). London: Sage.

O'Neil, D. (2001). Analysis of Internet users' level of online privacy concern. *Social Science Computer Review, 19*, 17–31. doi:10.1177/089443930101900103

Office for National Statistics. (2009, August 28). *Internet access: Households and individuals.* Retrieved from http://www.statistics.gov.uk/pdfdir/iahi0809.pdf

Ong, A. D., & Weiss, D. J. (2000). The impact of anonymity on responses to sensitive questions. *Journal of Applied Social Psychology, 30*, 1691–1708. doi:10.1111/j.1559-1816.2000.tb02462.x

Paine, C., Reips, U.-D., Stieger, S., Joinson, A., & Buchanan, T. (2007). Internet users' perceptions of 'privacy concerns' and 'privacy actions'. *International Journal of Human-Computer Studies, 65*, 526–536. doi:10.1016/j.ijhcs.2006.12.001

Peden, B. F., & Flashinski, D. P. (2004). Virtual research ethics: A content analysis of surveys and experiments online. In Buchanan, E. (Ed.), *Readings in virtual research ethics: Issues and controversies* (pp. 1–26). Hershy, PA: IGI Global.

Reips, U.-D. (2007). The methodology of Internet-based experiments. In Joinson, A., McKenna, K., Postmes, T., & Reips, U.-D. (Eds.), *The Oxford handbook of Internet psychology* (pp. 373–390). New York: Oxford University Press.

Reips, U.-D. (2008). How Internet-mediated research changes science. In A. Barak (Ed.), *Psychological aspects of cyberspace: Theory, research, applications* (pp. 268-294). Cambridge, UK: Cambridge University Press. Retrieved from http://gsb.haifa.ac.il/~sheizaf/cyberpsych/12-Reips.pdf

Rentfrow, P. J., Gosling, S. D., & Potter, J. (2008). A theory of the emergence, persistence, and expression of geographic variation in psychological characteristics. *Perspectives on Psychological Science, 3*, 339–369. doi:10.1111/j.1745-6924.2008.00084.x

Roberts, L., & Indermaur, D. (2003). Signed consent forms in criminological research: Protection for researchers and ethics committees but a threat to research participants? *Psychiatry, Psychology and Law, 10*, 289–299. doi:10.1375/pplt.2003.10.2.289

Robins, R. W., Tracy, J. L., Trzesniewski, K., Gosling, S. D., & Potter, J. (2002). Global self-esteem across the life span. *Psychology and Aging, 17*, 423–434. doi:10.1037/0882-7974.17.3.423

Robins, R. W., Tracy, J. L., Trzesniewski, K., Potter, J., & Gosling, S. D. (2001). Personality correlates of self-esteem. *Journal of Research in Personality, 35,* 463–482. doi:10.1006/jrpe.2001.2324

Robinson, K. M. (2001). Unsolicited narratives from the Internet: A rich source of qualitative data. *Qualitative Health Research, 11,* 706–714. doi:10.1177/104973201129119398

Rogelberg, S. C., Spitzmueller, C., Little, I., & Reeve, C. L. (2006). Understanding response behavior to an online special topics organizational satisfaction survey. *Personnel Psychology, 59,* 903–923. doi:10.1111/j.1744-6570.2006.00058.x

Singer, E. (2004). Confidentiality, risk perception and survey participation. *Chance, 17*(3), 31–35.

Singer, E., Von Thurn, D. R., & Miller, E. R. (1995). Confidentiality assurances and response: A quantitative review of the experimental literature. *Public Opinion Quarterly, 59,* 66–77. doi:10.1086/269458

Skitka, L. J., & Sargis, E. G. (2006). The Internet as psychological laboratory. *Annual Review of Psychology, 57,* 529–555. doi:10.1146/annurev.psych.57.102904.190048

Soto, C. J., John, O. P., Gosling, S. D., & Potter, J. (2008). The developmental psychometrics of big five self-reports: Acquiescence, factor structure, coherence, and differentiation from ages 10 to 20. *Journal of Personality and Social Psychology, 94,* 718–737. doi:10.1037/0022-3514.94.4.718

Srivastava, S., John, O. P., Gosling, S. D., & Potter, J. (2003). Development of personality in early and middle adulthood: Set like plaster or persistent change? *Journal of Personality and Social Psychology, 84,* 1041–1053. doi:10.1037/0022-3514.84.5.1041

Sue, V. M., & Ritter, L. A. (2007). *Conducting online surveys.* Thousand Oaks, CA: Sage.

Tourangeau, R. (2004). Survey research and societal change. *Annual Review of Psychology, 55,* 775–801. doi:10.1146/annurev.psych.55.090902.142040

Turow, J., & Hennessy, M. (2007). Internet privacy and institutional trust: Insights from a national survey. *New Media & Society, 9,* 300–318. doi:10.1177/1461444807072219

Uriell, Z. A., & Dudley, C. M. (2009). Sensitive topics: Are there modal differences? *Computers in Human Behavior, 25,* 76–87. doi:10.1016/j.chb.2008.06.007

Whang, L. S.-M., Lee, S., & Chang, G. (2003). Internet over-users' psychological profiles: A behavior sampling analysis on Internet addiction. *Cyberpsychology & Behavior, 6,* 143–150. doi:10.1089/109493103321640338

Wright, K. B. (2005). Researching Internet-based populations: Advantages and disadvantages of online survey research, online questionnaire authoring software packages, and web survey services. *Journal of Computer-Mediated Communication, 10*(3). Retrieved from http://jcmc.indiana.edu/vol10/issue3/wright.html.

ENDNOTES

[1] A recent *Google Scholar* search by Lee et al. (2008) indicated that the number of social science articles with 'web survey', 'Internet survey' or 'online survey' in their titles increased from 4 in 1994 to 1146 in 2006.

[2] http://psych.hanover.edu/Research/expon-net.html

[3] http://genpsylab-wexlist.unizh.ch/browse.cfm?action=browse&modus=survey

[4] http://surveymonkey.com/

[5] WebSM (http://websm.org/) allows users to search through 350+ web surveying appli-

cations and services on characteristics like cost to the user, availability of source code (i.e., closed vs. open source), and whether or not the user's surveys and data are hosted on the vendor's, or user's own web-server.

6   http://www.adobe.com/products/dream-weaver/

7   http://www.microsoft.com/expression/

8   http://www.objectplanet.com/opinio/; a proprietary application developed and distributed by Object Planet Inc.

9   http://www.limesurvey.org/

10   This paper focuses solely on ethical issues associated with outsourcing web surveys. That is, the use of commercial survey hosting services for academic surveys. For a more general discussion of online research ethics please see Ess (2007) and Ess and the AIOR

Ethics Working Committee (2002). Our focus on the ethical issues associated with a specific online methodology and context is consistent with Ess's (2007) claim that "research ethics is intimately interwoven with the specific methodology/ies used in a given project" (p. 495).

11   See https://www.pcisecuritystandards.org/security_standards/pci_dss.shtml

12   For example, *SurveyMonkey* is a licensee of the TRUSTe Privacy Program, complies with the EU Safe Harbor framework and employs Secure Socket Layer (SSL) technology to encrypt sensitive information.

13   http://www.surveymonkey.com/Monkey_Privacy.aspx (last accessed on 21 September 2009).

This work was previously published in International Journal of Technoethics, Volume 1, Issue 3, edited by Rocci Luppicini, pp. 35-48, copyright 2010 by IGI Publishing (an imprint of IGI Global).

Chapter 13
The Issues Related To Student Authentication in Distance Education

Deb Gearhart
Troy University, USA

ABSTRACT

As long as there has been distance education there has been the question, 'how do you know the student turning in the work is the student registered for the course?' As technology has been improving distance education course delivery, online education has been growing in leaps and bounds. The most recent Sloan-C report stated that in the U. S. alone there were almost 3.9 million students taking at least one online course during the fall of 2007 term (Allen and Seaman, 2008). Legislators took a hard look at the issue of student authentication in distance education with the passage of the Higher Education Opportunity Act of 2008. This paper reviews the issues related to student authentication and reviews the current forms of student authentication, reviewing one institution's answer to student authentication in its online programs.

BACKGROUND

To understand the issues related to student authentication a little history on distance education and an understanding of biometrics is needed as background. Distance education in the United States has been around for about 125 years. Educators have been trying to provide educational experiences to meet the needs of underserved students. Starting with the print based medium, know for many years as correspondence study, institutions have met the needs of learners around the country. Other media followed including radio, television, audio and video recordings, audio and video conferencing, computer mediated instruction and with the introduction of the Internet, what is now known at online learning (Wang & Gearhart, 2006).

DOI: 10.4018/978-1-4666-1773-5.ch013

One of the issues that has been around as long as there has been distance education is the issue that the student registered for the course is the student doing the work, student authentication. Why the concern for student authentication in distance education? Primarily because not all students are ethical and some do cheat. Over the years students have found ways to cheat on assignments and exams. Students have had other students do work for them and turn it in as their own; students have plagiarized papers, students will cheat on exams. Studies have shown that cheating is on the rise. McCabe and Trevino (2002) noted that cheating reported on nine campuses grew from 26% in 1963 to 52% in 1993. Gearhart (2007) discussed an additional replication of the study in 2001 noting that 72.8% of the students reported cheating. Part of the disconnect with cheating involves students' own perceptions of their own roles in a course. Craig, et. al. (2008) reported in their study that 87% of the students felt it was important to submit their own work, yet the studies on student cheating continue to grow. Students will comment it is important to do their own work, to not cheat, however, especailly in the case of online learning, where students do not directly see the consequences of their actions find it does no harm to cheat (Gearhart, 2007).

Distance education administrators have been dealing with the issue of student authentication for many years. One way, which is the emphasis of this paper, is dealing with academic integrity of an online course through the use of a proctored exam. Proctored exams have been a means for academic integrity for many years. Distance education programs have used human proctors and a complex proctor approval process to ensure academic integrity of student coursework. However, finding and approving human proctors is not an easy task. In this day and age of technology integration, use of technology for student authentication has become more prominent. The next few sections of this paper explain the forms of authentication and how they can be used with technology and in higher education to set up the case study of one institution's resolution to this issue.

AN INTRODUCTION TO BIOMETRICS

Fingerprints are the ridge and valley patterns on the tips of the fingers and are the oldest and most accepted form of biometrics. Ancient kings and queens sealed letters and authenticated them with fingerprints in the wax thousands of years ago. Over hundred years ago, in the US and in Europe fingerprints were used for identification. In all this time, no two fingerprints have been found to be the same. They are truly unique to each individual (Upendra, Singh, Kumar, and Verma, 2007). Upendra, Singh, Kumar, and Verma (2007) explain how online fingerprint systems work. During the registration process a reference biometric template of the fingerprint is stored in a database. Then when the authentication process, when the user is being verified, the biometric template is reviewed and used to match at the established threshold.

According to Crews, Jr. (2003) authentication is now commonplace in society with face recognition cameras found in airports, city streets, among other public places. Other forms of biometric authentication have developed. Langenderfer and Linnhoff (2005) describe the biological traits used for authentication purposes including fingerprints, face, palm, hand geometry, hand vein pattern, fingernail bed, iris, retina, body odor, skin reflection, ear shape, teeth, and DNA; while voice, lip motion, signature, gait, and keystroke dynamics have been used as behavioral measures. Many of the technologies are beneficial for security reasons. Crews (2003), however, is concerned about the point at which such technology goes beyond voluntary to becoming an invasion of privacy to the point where a potential loss of fourth amendment protections cab occur. Will we be forced to mandatory biometric identification? These issues that loom within society are also issues related to higher education. Most affected in higher education is distance education. There has always been concern that the student taking a distance course is the student completing the assessments to the course. The issues of authentication are part of academic integrity.

The concept of academic integrity notes that students who uphold a high standard of academic integrity maintain that the work they complete is authentic (Academic Integrity, 2009). Academic integrity means that work completed in assignments is the students' won – not plagiarized, copied, or is misuse of content from the Internet; that students follow their own code of honor.

UNDERSTANDING HOW BIOMETRIC SYSTEMS WORK

Langenderfer and Linnhoff (2005) explain the two stages of operation to verify identity in a biometric system, which are enrollment and authentication. Enrollment is the stage where the biometric data is obtained and stored. The authentication stage makes identification and verification possible.

Mason (2007) developed three characteristics of authentication: reliability, integrity and usability. Looking at reliability, there should be evidence that records are created and captured as part of the process and used for future authentication. Integrity of the authentication is protected from unauthorized alteration. Usability demonstrates the authentication process is easily retrieved, presented and interpreted correctly. Mason also noted that standards and best practices should be a guide in selection authentication formats. Be sure to document the policies and procedures related to authentication and develop and document decision-making criteria related to authentication.

Why go to such lengths to provide authentication? Why isn't using an ID and password good enough? That question was addressed in an article by Abram (2004). Abram discussed the sheer number of IDs and passwords we use in today's society, for work, for banking, for online shopping, to name a few. It is getting hard to track so many IDs and passwords and to come up with unique passwords that can not be easily determined by knowing the user. Among solutions presented by Abram include smartcards, Shibboleth, bar codes and radio frequency identification tags (RFID) and biometrics.

In distance education programs, the "why use authentication" goes to address the issue of whether the student taking a distance education course is the student doing the course assessment. This issue has gone as far as to be included in the Higher Education Opportunity Act of 2008 which includes: '(ii) the agency or association requires an institution that offers distance education or correspondence education to have processes through which the institution establishes that the student who registers in a distance education or correspondence education course or program is the same student who participates in and completes the program and receives the academic credit;'" (HEOA, 2008 Part H—Program Integrity).

The questions to be addressed with biometric student authentication include: How do you ensure online testing integrity for your distance education program? Is the student who is taking the test the student who is registered for the course? Is there someone else in the room assisting the student? Is the student copying or sharing the exam? Is the student using notes or an open book, when it is not permitted for the exam? Is the student using the Internet to find answers?

The goals of using student authentication are to prevent cheating in online assessments, to provide flexibility to students who are using distance education because they cannot attend a facility or go to a facility for course assessments; and to meet or exceed the requirements for regional accreditation and federal regulation.

AUTHENTICATION NEEDS IN HIGHER EDUCATION

The library is a common user of remote authentication. There has been an increased demand for off-site library access; particularly to meet the demand of distance learning programs. In one case study the Obvia Corporation developed the remote data access (RDA) server. The RDA server provides a two tier authentication system, which first authenticates each user and then passes the information on to the database providers. Authentication is anonymous; the database providers are not given the true identity of the library patron. Each remote user's information is stored in a singly user directory. This means that each use's access information is stored just once. This removes the need to enter each user's information into each separate database account or vendor's system. Another advantage of the Obvia RDA sever was if the university Web system was down remote users could still access the subscription databases (Eckley, 1999).

Another area in higher education where there is a great need for student authentication is in financial aid. One solution provided by Pearson Government Solutions is STAN, the Student Authentication Network. STAN was developed to provide an electronic signature capability for federal student loans. Pearson worked with the Office of Federal Student Aid (FSA) to reengineer the student loan system from the personal identification number (PIN) infrastructure to develop STAN to be web based, available 24/7, meeting current legislation and providing faster loan processing.

Another form of digital signature, used for requesting academic transcripts, is known as Public Key Infrastructure (PKI) technology. PKI technology enables the placement of an electronic signature on a digital file which assures the recipient that the digital file has not been altered and originates from a verifiable party (Black & Mohr, 2004). Students will authenticate themselves to the registrar's secure transcript system using a known user ID and password. Once authenticated, a report is generated containing the academic information for each student. The secure transcript allocation server uses the student information to create a digitally singed document, in PDF format, that is delivered to the end user either on a Web browser to be downloaded on the student's computer.

ISSUES RELATED TO THE FUNCTION OF BIOMETRICS

Fratto (2003) discussed issues related to the use of biometrics including such problems as the effect of environmental conditions on the biometric devices. Dirt, smudges and humidity can affect fingerprint readers and iris scanners. Additional conditions affecting iris scanners are glasses and contact lenses. Another environmental condition has to do with the power sources for the hardware and software and the compatibility with organizational network systems. There is also the issue of false acceptance and false rejection rates. False acceptance rates occur when the user is being incorrectly accepted and false rejection rates occur when the device incorrectly rejects a user. There are enrollment issues, the user must be on a local computer for enrollment which prohibits an ease of use for remote authentication.

Fratto (2003) provides a checklist of questions to ask before implementing a biometric system for authentication:

- Does the device suit the environment?
- Is there power source nearby?
- Is the reader-to-PC interface supported on the PC?
- Are authentication thresholds configurable?
- Does the device provide the extra protection of "liveness" testing?
- Are there anti-replay features to help thwart electronic resubmission of biometrics?

As authentication becomes more important, policymakers also want a say in the matter, as authentication impacts privacy. One view of lessening online anonymity would make it more difficult to cause problems for online security but that does impact privacy. Crews, Jr. (2007) note that we need at all times to identify ourselves and validate the identity of others. Although this resource was geared to the private sector is equally being looked at in higher education, particularly for distance education.

THE TROY UNIVERSITY AUTHENTICATION PROJECT

Troy University, founded in 1887, is a university of 30,000 students with a global reach, including four campuses in Alabama, sites across the country and internationally. The outreach arm of Troy University is Global Campus. Global Campus is comprised of the national and international teaching sites and the eCampus, the online delivery branch of Troy University. Even before the passage of the HEOA, Troy University was working to provide a flexible alternative for online learners to be authenticated for course exams and to provide for program integrity.

McCabe and Pavela (2000) commented that they have long researched and demonstrated that institutions with a traditional academic honor code have lower rates of academic dishonesty than institutions without such codes. Troy University has such an honor code. The number one violation of the Troy University Standards of Conduct found in the Oracle, the student handbook is:

1. Dishonesty, such as cheating, plagiarism or knowingly furnishing false information to the University, faculty or other officers or employees of the University. (See Appendix A)

However, even with honor codes, online learners often do not have the same connection to the university that traditional students do and do not receive the emphasis on the honor code as campus students would.

Maramark and Maline (1993) concluded that institutions must take a proactive stance on cheating and improve the climate for academic integrity. That is what Troy University eCampus has done with the implementation of a new Proctoring Policy. The policy states:

POLICY REQUIREMENTS

The policy requires the student to use one of the following four options:

1. Individually purchase and use the Securexam Remote Proctor (SERP) device;
2. Use a third party certified testing center, such as Sylvan or Prometrics;
3. Use an approved Military Education Office testing office; or
4. Use a designated Troy University testing center located at a Troy University campus or teaching location.

Students with extenuating circumstances restricting them from complying with one of the four options can contact the eCampus Assistant Director for Testing for assistance. Troy University AOP 8-19-08-01. (See Appendix B)

As mentioned earlier, Troy University is dealing with the issues of authenticating distance learning students for means of assessment. The Troy University eCampus has worked with the colleges of the university to adopt a more stringent proctoring policy, above, which includes the use of the Securexam remote proctor. Troy University worked with Software Secure to develop the Securexam Remote Proctor device to provide the means of student authentication for the online students at Troy University. The remote proctor requires both picture identification and a fingerprint scan for authentication to access online exams through the University learning management system. The Troy University learning management system interfaces with the server at Software Secure where the demographic information on the students, the name, picture, fingerprint and captured video are stored. The fingerprint is stored in a mathematical algorithm. When a student logs into an exam they first are verified by the information stored on the Software Secure server. The remote proctor device captures real-time video and audio during the exam. The video component of the remote proctor device is designed to display a view of the entire room. The device is designed to have the system detect suspicious behavior, limiting the need for constant monitoring by a human proctor. The video has a motion detection filter; limiting the amount of video uploaded for review and the audio component has a high gain microphone to record audio in the room where the exam is taken. The administration and grading of the exam is all conducted through the learning management system. The faculty member's role in the process is to set the test environment parameters and to review suspicious video.

Troy University is in the implementation stage of the device, starting first with the graduate programs. The device will eventually be used in all online programs at Troy University. The Troy University online programs have a global reach. The remote proctor has been successfully used outside the United States. The advantages of the remote proctor for global use mean a timely distribution of course assessments and security for the assessments along with authentic identification of the student. The cost to the student is less than $200 per unit and can be purchased with financial aid. Once the proctoring policy is implemented for an online program, the student will be able to use throughout the program.

Kitahara and Westfall (2007) note that by creating computer-based accountability, Troy University is taking a proactive approach to ensuring online academic quality while making the online programs

available to students, worldwide, creating the proper framework for maintaining the highest standards of academic integrity and fairness. They go on to comment that although many academics are excited by the potential for the technology to suppress cheating, ethical issues remain, particularly a concern of intrusion of the lives the online learners. However, policies have been established to cover these types of concerns, including a privacy policy.

RECOMMENDATIONS

How best then can distance educators provide student authentication in their courses?

First, carefully review the types of biometric authentications and select the best form of authentication to meet the needs of the program. Discussed in this paper were issues related to different forms of biometrics. Consider the environmental related issues, use the suggested checksheet and follow standards and best practices. Be sure the student population can easily access and use the form of authentication selected. Second, consider costs of implementation and costs to students. As well there will be costs involved for training both faculty and students. Third, have in place policies and procedures related to the implementation of student authentication.

What the Securexam remote proctor device has provided for the Troy University eCampus is a form of student authentication to ensure test integrity. It alleviates the concerns of educators, of accrediting agencies, of providers of financial aid and tuition assistance, and concerns about dealing with students in a global educational arena.

REFERENCES

Abram, S. (2004). IP authentication and passwords – on life support and NOT expected to make it. *Information Outlook, 8*(8). Retrieved from ProQuest Educational Journals.

Academic Integrity. (2009). Retrieved March 1, 2009 from http://demo.flvs.net/webdav/navbar/integrity.htm.

Allen, E. I., & Seaman, J. (2008) Staying the course: online education in the United States, 2008. *The Sloan Consortium*. Retrieved from http://www.sloan-c.org 11/13/2008.

Black, T., & Mohr, J. (2004). Are we ready for another change? Digital signatures can change how we handle the academic record. *College and University, 80*(1). Retrieved from ProQuest Educational Journals.

Craig, A., Goold, A., Coldwell, J., & Mustard, J. (2008). Perceptions of roles and responsibilities in online learning: a case study. *Interdisciplinary Journal of E-Learning and Learning Objects V4.*

Crews, C. W., Jr. (2003). Monitoring biometric technologies in a free society. *USA Today, 132,* 2698. Retrieved from ProQuest Educational Journals.

Crews, C. W., Jr. (2007). Cybersecurity and Authentication: the marketplace role in rethinking anonymity – before regulators intervene. *Springer Science and Business Media, 20*. Retrieved from ProQuest Educational Journals.

Eckley, T. (1999). Remote Authentication: the Obvia solution. *Library Computing, 18*(2). Retrieved from ProQuest Educational Journals. eCampus Proctoring Policy (2008). Retrieved from http://www.troy.edu/academics/aop/documents/AOP_08-19-08-01.pdf April 14, 2009.

Fratto, M. (2003). Are biometrics the answer? *Network Computing, 14*(3). Retrieved from ProQuest Educational Journals.

Gearhart, D. (2009). Preparing students for ethical use of technology: a case study for distance education. In U. Demiray & R. C. Sharma (Eds.), *Ethical Practices and Implications in Distance Learning*. Hershey, PA: Information Science Reference.

Kitahara, R. T., & Westfall, F. (2007). Promoting academic integrity in online distance learning courses. *MERLOT Journal of Online Learning and Teaching, 3*(2).

Langenderfer, J., & Linnhoff, S. (2005). The emergence of biometrics and its effect on consumers. *The Journal of Consumer Affairs, 39*(2). Retrieved from ProQuest Educational Journals.

Maramark, S., & Maline, M. B. (1993). *Academic dishonesty among students: issues in education.* Washington, DC: Office of Educational Research and Improvement. Eric Document reproduction service no. ED360903.

Mason, S. (2007). Authentic digital records: laying the foundation of evidence. *The Information Management Journal*. Retrieved from ProQuest Educational Journals.

McCabe, D., & Pavela, G. (2000). Some good news about academic integrity. *Change, 32*(5). Retrieved from ProQuest Educational Journals.

Pearson Government Solutions. (2006). *Enabling a paperless student loan process using electronic signatures*. Retrieved from ProQuest Educational Journals.

The Oracle. (2008). Retrieved from http://www.troy.edu/studentservices/oracle/2008-2009_Oracle.pdf April 14, 2009.

Upendra, K., Singh, S., Kumar, V., & Verma, H. K. (2007). Online fingerprint verification. *Journal of Medical Engineering & Technology, 31*(1). Retrieved from ProQuest Educational Journals.

Wang, H., & Gearhart, D. L. (2006). *Designing and developing web-based instruction*. Upper Saddle River, NJ: Pearson Merrill Prentice Hall.

APPENDIX A: TROY UNIVERSITY STANDARDS OF CONDUCT FROM THE ORACLE, THE STUDENT HANDBOOK

Misconduct Defined

By enrollment at the University, a student or organization neither relinquishes rights nor escapes responsibilities of local, state, or federal laws and regulations. The "STANDARDS OF CONDUCT" are applicable to behavior of students and organizations on and off the university campus if that behavior is deemed to be incompatible with the educational environment and mission of the university.

A student or organization may be disciplined, up to and including suspension and expulsion, and is deemed in violation of the "STANDARDS OF CONDUCT", for the commission of or the attempt to commit any of the following offenses:

1. Dishonesty, such as cheating, plagiarism or knowingly furnishing false information to the University, faculty or other officers or employees of the University.
2. Forgery, alteration or misuse of university documents, records or identification.
3. Issuance of a worthless check made payable to Troy University.
4. Actual or threatened physical abuse, threat of violence, intimidation, hazing, harassment, or any other act that endangers the health or safety of any person.
5. Destruction, damage, or misuse of university property, public, or private.
6. Theft, attempted theft, burglary, attempted burglary, accessory to these acts, and/or possession of stolen property.
7. Unauthorized manufacture, sale, delivery, use, or possession of any drug or drug paraphernalia defined as illegal under local, state, or federal law.
8. The unlawful possession, use, or distribution of alcoholic beverages, public drunkenness, driving under the influence, or the public display of alcoholic beverages and the use or display of such in public areas of the residence halls and all other public areas of the campus.
9. Participation in any form of gambling.
10. Use, possession, or distribution of firearms, bows, illegal knives, fireworks, any incendiary, or any type of explosive device or material. Only duly-constituted law enforcement officers may possess firearms on campus.
11. Disorderly conduct, including rioting, inciting to riot, assembling to riot, raiding, inciting to raid, and assembling to raid university properties.
12. Lewd, indecent, obscene behavior or expression.
13. Trespassing or unauthorized entry to or use of university facilities.
14. Unauthorized use or attempted use of any services belonging to or provided by the University, including but not limited to, computer, telephone, cable television, copying facilities, or any other such service.
15. Unauthorized possession of a key to any university facility.
16. Interference with the use of or access to university facilities, obstruction or disruption of teaching, research, administration, service, disciplinary procedures, or other activities on university property by either university or non-university person or groups.

17. Failure to promptly comply with directions of university officials or law enforcement officers acting in the performance of their duties as such officials and officers.

18. Entering false fire alarms, or bomb threats, tampering with fire extinguishers, alarms, or other safety or fire-fighting equipment.

19. Any activity which creates a mentally abusive, oppressive, or harmful situation for another is a violation. Use of the mail, telephone, computer and electronic messages, or any other means of communication to insult, threaten, or demean another is prohibited.

20. Conviction of any misdemeanor or felony that adversely affects the educational environment of the University.

21. Violation of any university policies or regulations as published or referred to in the Student Handbook, including, but not limited to, those governing the time, place and manner of public expression; the registration of student organizations; the use of university facilities; occupation and visitation of residence halls and other housing owned or controlled by the university; and the use and parking of motor vehicles on the campus.

22. Conduct in violation of public law, federal and state statutes, local ordinances, or university regulations or policies whether or not specified in detail, that adversely affects the student's suitability as a member of the academic community and regardless of whether such conduct has resulted in a conviction under a statute of ordinance.

23. Any other activity or conduct not specifically stated herein that impairs or endangers any person, property, or the educational environment of the University.

Source: The Oracle. (2008). pages 43-44.

APPENDIX B: AOP-8-19-08-01 ECAMPUS PROCTORING POLICY

Introduction

TROY eCampus implemented a more stringent proctoring policy beginning August 2008 which will improve the validity of claims related to student authentication and enforcement of the instructor's requirement for a standardized testing condition.

Policy Requirements

The policy requires the student to use one of the following four options:

1. Individually purchase and use the Securexam Remote Proctor (SERP) device;
2. Use a third party certified testing center, such as Sylvan or Prometrics;
3. Use an approved Military Education Office testing office; or
4. Use a designated Troy University testing center located at a Troy University campus or teaching location.

Students with extenuating circumstances restricting them from complying with one of the four options can contact the eCampus Assistant Director for Testing for assistance.

Implementation

The policy implementation is incrementally by degree programs beginning August 2008. A demonstration of student identity authentication will be required for every student, every course, once the policy is fully implemented. The SERP device is available for purchase through MBS. Options three and four are available contingent upon the ability of the organization to accommodate students. TROY Global Campus will charge a nominal fee per exam for examinations proctored at teaching sites used to provide funding to support testing centers. Each Alabama campus will provide a fee-based proctoring solution. Students choosing to use any other options listed above are responsible for paying any fee(s) related to proctoring services. eCampus supports requiring a proctored exam be required for each course, each student, as approved by the appropriate academic dean. Course examinations must be deliverable through Blackboard examination module unless exempted by the appropriate academic dean. Questions related to this policy should be directed to the Director, eCampus.

Approved By: Academic Steering Committee, August 19, 2008 OPR: Dr. Earl Ingram Source: http://www.troy.edu/academics/aop/documents/AOP_08-19-08-01.pdf

This work was previously published in International Journal of Technoethics, Volume 1, Issue 1, edited by Rocci Luppicini, pp. 60-69, copyright 2010 by IGI Publishing (an imprint of IGI Global).

Chapter 14

Amateur vs. Professionals:
Politics, Citizenship and Science

Andoni Alonso
Universidad de Extremadura, Spain

Antonio Lafuente
Instituto de Historia, CSIC, Spain

ABSTRACT

Scientific and technological expertise is currently experiencing a crisis. The public shows a growing distrust in many aspects related to the techno-scientific development. The birth of that suspicion begins after World War II but has transformed in the past few decades. In this paper, the authors examine how that doubt has specific features in the present moment. Also, there is a reaction to propose another way to make scientific and technological research where there is a more participative spirit. These changes reshape traditional ideas on science, technology and progress. Amateur efforts in science and technology maybe are opening the possibility of a change for these activities and information technology seems to support these efforts. If these can be considered, a consistent trend is difficult to predict.

DISTRUST KNOWLEDGE

2nd World War showed what unleashed scientific and technological development could produce. Reactions among intellectuals, scientists and technicians produced at least some more cautionary approach to this endeavor. Pughwash movement, environmentalists, STS activism, consumer's associations and academic work among others count

DOI: 10.4018/978-1-4666-1773-5.ch014

as more reflexive ways to deal with something that improved human condition but at the same time threatened the existence of human species itself. Conviction that progress does not happen spontaneously become more and more accepted. But last decades have changed in an important way. Take for instance the pertinence of STS studies. In 1994 Ivan Illich, one of the most important thinkers in this field, suggested that STS programs had no reason any longer. The rationale for that claim was based in different arguments.

First activism abandoned STS a long ago. Every university, college or higher education institution had a STS program already so there was little room for activism since STS was transformed into an academic question (Duden, 2003). Main goal for STS also was achieved; there is a general distrust for Science and Technology among the public but at the same time the idea we do not have more opportunities than those given by Science and Technology themselves. Illich characterized for foreseeing future scenarios such as education and lack of proportion in our technological society. And some facts seem to support his claims. An interesting survey made by the European Union (Euro barometer) showed how Europeans distrust biotechnology in a significant degree: 54% of Europeans consider that those technologies will not improve their lives. Also about 90% of the Europeans believe that we are about to confront a deep environmental crisis and we are feeding the problem with present consumption system. There is a vast array of technologies that create concern among the public: reproduction technologies, bioengineering and genetic modified organism, pollutants, nanotechnologies, relaunched nuclear energy programs and so on. There is a diffused and general idea that we will confront new problems according to the emergence of new technologies. So progress and wellbeing is not something that happens automatically. But somehow it seems effortless to fight against those facts. The same way there is something as a diffuse environmental worry everywhere also there is the conviction that science and technological advancements do not translate into a promising future.

Experts are under suspicion, many cases have revealed a lack of honesty or accuracy and science and technologies are seen more a more as the first place where problems take place. Chernobyl for instance is one of these paradigmatic cases in the public mentality. The idea that nuclear risks could be managed vanished in 1986. Chernobyl polluted more than Nagasaki and Hiroshima bombs together and the core of one of the af-fected reactor was about to melt (Burlakova & Naidich, 2006). Experts do not agree on the final result on that accident but it seems that almost all Western Europe received radiation, from Sweden to Spain. So if 1989 was the end of communism (the demolition of the Berlin Wall), before general public experienced how certain catastrophic claims made by supposedly amateur experts such as ecologists, could become true. Facts developed in a frantic way around the Ukrainian nuclear power plant. Each new coming from the extinct URSS showed a madness dealing with potentially one of the biggest civil accident in history. Even today experts contradict about how dangerous has been and how to measure the amount of victims. After Chernobyl, things changed.

Expertise has its inner problems; an expert can be well trained and credited inside labs but nothing guarantees the same qualification outside the lab, in the middle of public and political life. Lack of confidence grows when more and more experts become part of corporations and groups of interest (something that Rachel Carson tried to fight in the far sixties). Public manifests its worries about the lack of information and a growing distrust on governments and experts. One recent case is the A flu virus and all the campaigns and discussions. According to statistical sources 80% of Europeans manifests do not trust either in governments or in experts. It is an old dispute how to achieve objectivity and if experts are the real source for such. Sometimes fights among different opinions transform expert's report in part of the problem. As a result the distance among the technological elite and lay people grows. For instance, a number of world meetings dealing with the global climate change have transformed scientific data into bitter wars among experts, environmental groups, companies and so on. For instance, Kyoto, Johannesburg and Rio do Janeiro meetings are evidences of that struggle. Scientists, politicians, activists, journalists etc., take part on discussing the evidence of the climate change; journals, articles, data etc. Scientific theories do not relay in a balanced and calm discussions. Many times arguments are accusation of fraud or vested interests or hidden political agendas. There are parties that fight each other in the media or in political terms. Therefore it is extremely difficult to consider science only as something done in labs, isolated from society completely. Wall labs become diffuse; inside and outside merge. Somehow the impression is as if a global experiment is being carried out where we are part of that experiment. So it is easily understandable why so many people want to take part in its design. If this is true there is another consequence that follows: traditional split among nature and culture becomes more and more difficult: where ends one and begins the other. Nature used to be the place for objectivity and culture for opinion and human action. And this is another question that makes present science and technology more difficult to deal with. Science is culture somehow because implement also human action.

Experts and scientists are under attack but this does not mean to dismiss expertise as a whole. Transforming science and technology in a matter of polls of opinion does not help to clarify present situation. Techno-phobia and science-phobia do not lead anywhere; both activities are human and we need them to survive in this world. Then, that would be a dangerous path that leads to conflicts or, what is known as "scientific wars". Maybe the most representative case of those science wars is evolution. As it is widely known, Darwin's theory is not accepted in the US. According to Gallup only 35% of American population considers evolution as a contrasted and valid scientific theory. Against evolution there is a pure ideological proposal -intelligent design- framed as an alternative. What is interesting is how this proposal acquired notoriety via the mass media. Michael Behe, a well-known creationist was able to publish in prestigious newspapers such as *New York Times* and *US Today* (Behe, 2007). Both newspapers did not pay any attention to traditional and respected institutions of American science such as the Na-

tional Academy of Science and The American Association for the Advancement of Science. Both institutions manifested their support to Darwin's theories due to the huge amount of evidences and dismissed creationist point of view just because the lack of any proof. Tolerance, political correctness and open-minded positions do not translate so easily into science and technology where there exist hard facts. As supposedly senator Moynihan stated: *Everyone is entitled to his own opinion, but not his own facts.*

Intelligent design against evolution presents, according to some researches similarities with the global warming debate. In this battle there are skeptics that consider the theory of the global climate change as something without any evidence or experimental support. Also according to opponents this theory is a major threat for the economy and foreign policy. Again Moynihan's statement fits here. Even the debate adopts low profile ideological discourses: defenders of the global climate change are the foreign agents that try to destroy US as a superpower. This reminds Bill Gates' dictum comparing hackers as the new communists. They appear experts with no previous background starting a bitter discussion against basic evidences supporting the global climate change. Steve McIntyre's case is very symptomatic. McIntyre became a notorious figure on climate-change studies publishing even at the Wall Street Journal, a newspaper that paid no attention to that up to the moment. McIntyre's paper tried to show how models for the increase of temperature were full of wrong data so there would not support evidence for a warming up. Immediately politicians entered into the dispute. Senator James Inhofe recruited McIntyre and invites him to a deliver a paper at the Marshall Institute (a foundation supported by the petrol corporation ExxonMobil) and, according to the *Financial Times*, became a major scientist of that discipline. Other politicians entered in the dispute; congressman Joe Barton demanded Michael Mann (the main source attacked by McIntyre and one of the most relevant scientist in this field) explanations about methods, measures and data. Scientific community -*Nature,* the AAAS the NAS- defended Mann and supported the evidence of a rapid warming. Pseudo-scientific and expertise dictums against evidence are all around. One interesting case is but at the same time there are rapid changes on the question if there is or not a global climate change caused by human activities. Suddenly acceptance of that issue becomes opportunities for new business such as geo-engineering or nuclear produced energy. Therefore different sectors that denied global climate warming are using that incontrovertible fact as a way to advance new possibilities. Then experts seem to move from a place to another and public's trust decreases. Scientific and technical consensus moves from labs and higher education institutions towards media coverage. The invisible academy is somehow gone and those ethical principles inherent to scientific practice -as Thomas Merton underlined- seem to vanish in most cases.

MONEY AND EXPERTISE

Big companies and corporations are funding scientific and technological research. For the first time in history, private money is taking over research and public funds are under. According to some statistics funds from private sectors into scholarly research has grown an 800%. Young researchers must work for low wages and big workloads: there is a proletarization of science. Effects of that fact are important. Results sometimes contradict private expectations. As a result 15% of scientists accept to have modified findings in order to fit sponsor's requirements (Martison, Anderson, & De Vries, 2005). Somehow this is not a new fact but has adopted an intricate shape. For instance, scientific media coverage transforms into news simple communiqués by experts paid by pharmaceutical companies. Also there has been a flourishing of institutions, foundations and re-

search centers that are funded by private interests. They offer reports trying to fight back other reports given by activists, against what they call "junk science". As Rampton and Stauber (2001) put it: "*Junk science* first emerged in the courtroom as a disparaging term for the paid expert witnesses that attorneys hire to testify on behalf of their clients. In many cases, of course, an expert witness is unnecessary. If one person shoots another in front of witnesses, you don't need a rocket scientist to know who is responsible. During the twentieth century, however, courts expanded the system of tort law under which personal-injury lawsuits are filed in order to cover cases in which proof of causation is somewhat more complicated. Many of these cases require a scientist's testimony particularly when the injury in question comes from environmental or toxic causes-for example, cancer in army veterans subjected to radiation from atomic bomb tests; asbestos-related mesothelioma; Reyes Syndrome caused by taking aspirin; or the link between swine flu vaccinations and Guillain-Barre Syndrome. By expanding the system of tort law, courts made it possible for people injured through these sorts of causes to collect damages from the companies responsible". Then environmental associations, consumer's groups and alike are considered as lacking accuracy or excess on their positions. In fact it is necessary to collect these organizations that present themselves as non-profit organizations but they are not. Scientists have organized themselves and as a result there is a web place called "Integrity in Science" that tries to clarify these suspicious ties among industry and scientific research. Some of the hot topics that this site underlies are for instance: pharmaceuticals, tobacco or chemical industry. But also this organization manifests its fears the increasing ties among industries and researches that lead to hide results, mistrusts on evaluating new substances and procedures and so on.

Some branches of research are more vulnerable to this new situation and also to new procedures. Medicine and private interests are transforming reliability on experts and tests. Conflicts on interests are in the media and threaten the system as a whole. Daniel Haley qualifies this conflicts as authentic "drug wars" and R Horton, editor of the most prestigious journals in medicine, *The Lancet*, accuses The Drug and Food Administration (FDA) of malpractice. The FDA was for sure one of the most respectable and powerful authority on the approval of new procedures and medicaments. There are other ways to corrupt expertise; big investment companies pay researchers to know beforehand if a new product will work. Later these companies trade in the stock market. According to the media there are 26 cases of fraudulent information concerning new medicaments. But estimations suggest about 60.000 bio-doctors informing groups like Wachowia Securities, UBS and alike. This fraudulent knowledge goes beyond corruption; they jeopardize the test system as a whole because protocols are not followed. Real medicaments and placebos are used for tests and researchers should not know if a patient is being treated with which one. Also to assure effectiveness, different hospitals take part in the trial and number of individuals accessing data tends to be small. Those who sell information do not respect those basic protocols and corrupt the whole system that protects future users.

LAYPERSON'S REVOLT

There are many cases of scientific fraud and technological malpractice. There is possible to identify particular persons behind them but somehow the problem seems to go deeper. Maybe what happens is that free market and private initiative is corrupting the system, maybe there is something structural about how things go wrongly. It is possible to pile up more cases but what is needed is some reaction from the public. Science and technology are human essential activities required for our survival therefore they have a political and ethical element that should be considered seriously. Being

so important the public should adopt the position of techno-citizens: individuals that enter into the public debate about science and technology. This is an old idea repeated many times in history but never achieved. Illich suggested that this idea has failed; STS was one of the most important efforts to reach that goal through education. But somehow STS transformed into a simple part of academic curricula losing the activist or political element. But maybe it is important to look around and try to identify what in fact can be qualified as a public intervention in science and technology design. Maybe amateur science and technology can offer a response about how it is possible to see things from other perspectives. Against free market and profit there has been other ways to make science and technology in the last decades. Beginning with free software there has been a tendency to consider knowledge in a complete different perspective. Instead of privatization, quick profit and commoditization of knowledge there has been a bet for sharing, collaboration and freedom to distribute. Interestingly enough this movement represents vast amount of resources, volunteering, and money. It has been a silent revolution, completely unexpected that can change many aspects of our society.

How big this change is can be estimated with some basic data: SETI project uses more than five million particular computers around the world to analyze radio signals from outer space. Free software GNU/Linux operating system required the cooperation of more than 100,000 developers. Now there are more than 20,000.000 registered users (but some free software pieces like Mozilla Firefox is becoming the most used web browser). There is a strong volunteering movement that only in European Community is a 20% of population (this goes for all kind of NGOs). A classical study on this rise of the amateurs show interesting facts (Ledbeater & Miller, 2004): in UK there are 6 million people involved in environmental activities, 4.500 independent archeologists work in different research projects, the Royal Horticultural Society alone counts with 350.000 volunteers. There are about 23 million volunteers working in different areas and the sum of time devoted is about 90 million hours whose value is about 45 billion euros. Another interesting fact is what is known as "blogsphere". There are millions of all kinds of blogs ranging from political issues to scientific and technological ones. Of course there is a wide range of quality but what is interesting about them is how the create communities. Kevin Kelly, former editor of Wired Magazine, points out some basic features for that blogsphere and its political consequences. Social web has promoted an active user instead of passive ones that traditional mass-media produce. Also sharing has become an intrinsic value for these social networks on-line. Internet technologies promote easiness to publish, transmit, collaborate and share. The web does not explain by itself these growing social movements of all kind especially in technology and science. Previous movements like environmental groups or science activists like Pugwash were the social awareness from the sixties. What the social web has added is the easiness and quick speed to organize, inform, share and distribute. For sure this is a side effect of this technological system, impossible to predict. In this sense something has emerged, what specialists like Christopher Allen denominates as "social software". There is a set of software tools that associate certain practices and goals that help amateur efforts. 40% of the Internet flux is commercial but there is a big 60% left ranging very varied activities. Again, blogging has become a frequent activity; there are more than 50 million and about a 30% of American net users access regularly some of them (this is about 49.5 million persons only in US). Reason for that success could be explained for the social nature of blogs. They create communities instead of shaping public opinion. Also there is a new economy behind that fact; the gift economy. Reward is not money but recognition and visibility, that is, to find a place inside different communities. That is the reason to develop free software but at the same time to spend time, effort and intelligence to set up and update a blog. Also this non-money profit reason explains how blogs can create public opinion and favor citizen's activism.

Adding both elements, the activist movements from sixties and seventies and the use of social software, it is possible to analyze important cases such as the AIDS social intervention. Consumer's activism, environmental groups and wild life associations showed distrust in science and technology in that time. But they approached to science and technology knowledge. The reason is obvious; there was an ongoing debate and it was necessary to take part on it. The question is now how to discuss with experts and scientists and try to underline the social and political factors in technology and science. As said above, pharmaceuticals and biomedical industry are one of the places where distrust on experts is more common. And somehow AIDS activism transformed into a counter-balance to that fact. Also AIDS activism has become a paradigmatic model for other associations that fight for patient's rights. According to Epstein, the AIDS case shows something new in medical history: "credibility struggles" among doctors, researchers, patients, organizations...; "What difference has it made to have activists involved in issues of AIDS research and drug development? How has biomedical research been reconfigured as a result? Examples prove to be numerous: The arguments of AIDS activists have been published in scientific journals and presented at formal scientific conferences. Their publications have created new pathways for the dissemination of medical information. Their pressure has caused the prestigious journals to release findings faster to the press. Their voice and vote on review committees have helped determine which studies receive funding. Their efforts have led to changes in the very definition of "AIDS" to incorporate the HIV-related conditions that affect women. Their interventions have led to the establishment of new mechanisms for regulating drugs, such as expanded access and accelerated approval. Their arguments have brought about shifts in the balance of power between competing visions of how clinical trials should be conducted. Their close scrutiny has encouraged basic scientists to move compounds more rapidly into clinical trials. And their networking has brought different communities of scientists into cooperative relationships with one another, thereby changing patterns of informal communication within science" (Epstein, 2004, p. 338-339). This is a clear example how amateurs enter into the expertise domain. The basic component was the concern of suffering people (patients and families) that allowed an organization that grew with time. Organization of civil society influenced experts and knowledge was the product of all the agents.

AIDS began in the pre-internet era but somehow it proposed a model that changed patient-expert system. The Internet has been able to favor other associations like for instance the Brain Talk community. This web site gathers 300 different groups of neurological patients and about 200,000 regular users. They engage in discussing, symptoms, therapy practices, how to identify new pathological signs, side effects of different treatments... Some technical journals such as PlosMedicine consider that these communities can be understood as a promising resource: "I have also learned that an online group like the BrainTalk Communities epilepsy group is not only much smarter than any single patient, but is also smarter, or at least more comprehensive, than many physicians—even many medical specialists. While some postings do contain erroneous material, online groups of patients who share an illness engage in a continuous process of self-correction, challenging questionable statements and addressing misperceptions as they occur. And while no single resource, including physicians, should be considered the last word in medical knowledge, the consensus opinion arrived at by patient groups is usually quite excellent. And if more expert clinicians offered to consult informally with the online support groups devoted to their medical specialties—as I now do—we could help group members make information and opinion shared in these groups even better" (Hoch & Ferguson, 2005). Hoch and Ferguson noted that only 6% of posts were inaccurate, old fashioned or simply wrong. The reason for that accuracy is the continuous effort made by the community itself checking and correcting. There are two different sides that should be mentioned. First communities like Brain Talk generate a valuable knowledge able to be used. This is the creation of a gift economy against the present trend of privatization and patenting. These "volunteers" continuously test personal experiences, side effects and success of therapies so their knowledge would be used by the bio-industry. Second clinicians change their role with patients. According to Hoch & Ferguson (Hoch & Ferguson, 2005) there is something new, something that can be named as "expert patients". Patients become then normal persons with the right to be correctly informed, self-organized and able to engage in a real discussion with specialists and clinicians. This goes beyond the usual stories about Internet as the preferred place for hypochondriacs and gives some hope to correct a system that has become corrupt in some practices. According to Ferguson: The medical world view of the 20th century did not recognize the legitimacy of lay medical competence and autonomy. Its metrics, research methods, and cultural vocabulary are poorly suited to studying this emerging field. Something akin to a major system upgrade in our thinking is needed, a new cultural operating system for health care in which e-patients can be recognized as a valuable new type of renewable resource—managing much of their own care, providing care for others, helping professionals improve the quality of their services, and participating in collaborations between patients and professionals. Given the recognition and support they deserve these new medical colleagues may help us find sustainable solutions to the seemingly intractable problems that now plague all modern systems (Ferguson, 2004, pp. 1148-1149).

AND NOW WHAT?

Surprisingly there are two contradictory currents in knowledge production living together. One tries to privatize under patents, copyright laws and other devices that production. On the other side there is a tendency to open knowledge and allow it to circulate and improve. First one obeys to a free market logic relaying on knowledge as a scarce resource. It requires investment and practices not always legally or ethically acceptable. One of the results is a growing distrust in companies, governments and knowledge elites. Some of the cases analyzed before show why that system somehow is in crisis. Some critics claim that the patenting legal system goes against innovation because has transformed into something different of what it was supposed to be. According to Ruichard Stallman software patents harm the public good in an unfair way: "Software patents don't cover programs or code; they cover ideas (methods, techniques, features, algorithms, etc.). Developing a large program entails combining thousands of ideas, and even if a few of them are new, the rest needs must have come from other software the developer has seen. If each of these ideas could be patented by someone, every large program would likely infringe hundreds of patents. Developing a large program means laying oneself open to hundreds of potential lawsuits. Software patents are menaces to software developers, and to the users, who can also be sued" (Stallman, 2005). As a corollary, only big companies can survive this limiting patent system. Instead of favoring innovation favor economic and legal battles leaving aside the public good that science and technology should pursue. More and more profit is the ultimate goal and public good a secondary target.

On the other hand, as technology always does, there is a crisis about old procedures and mentalities because they are confronting new scenarios. It is interesting to note how previous practices like activism have found a very useful tool in information technologies. New technologies allow sharing and spreading knowledge at a very cheap price. But this is only one aspect. Collective knowledge is able to surpass private resources: communities know more than individuals. Some of the cases mentioned before show that fact. Hierarchical organization of knowledge does not resist other possibilities where individuals organize themselves and create communities of knowledge. There are paradigmatic cases like Wikipedia, GNU/Linux, Open access scientific knowledge etc. Economic foundations for these communities of knowledge are the gift economy. Contributing to a specific community has the sense of being part of that community, have a reputation and having the basic idea that finally there will be a general good for everybody but also for each individual. But this is not something completely new. Apart from being a practice among other peoples and cultures, Western civilization has practiced the gift economy along its history. For instance, science worked with this basic assumption for many centuries. Things have change only in the last fifty or sixty years. So what self organized amateurs show is how things can be made in another fashion. And technology favors this new way of producing knowledge. But these two factors alone do not guarantee a real or rapid change on how things are done. Right now these two opposite tendencies are rivals. What will be the final result it is unclear but there is a window for hope.

REFERENCES

Allen, C. (2004). *Tracing the Evolution of Social Software Evolution.* Retrieved September 9, 2009 from http://www.lifewithalacrity.com/2004/10/tracing_the_evo.html

Behe, M. (2007). Design for Life. *New York Times.*

Burlakova, E. B., & Naidich, V. I. (2006). *20 years after the Chernobyl accident: past, present and future*. New York: Nova Sciencia.

Carlat, D. (2007). Diagnosis, Conflict of Interest. *New York Times*. Retrieved September 6, 2009 from http://www.nytimes.com/2007/06/13/opinion/13carlat.htmlEpstein, S. (2004). *Impure Science AIDS, Activism, and the Politics of Knowledge*. Berkeley, CA: University of California Press.

Duden, B. (2003). *Ivan Illich. Beyond Medical Nemesis (1976): The Search for Modernity's Disembodiment of "I" and "You."* Paper presented at the Bremen Symposium "Ivan Illich zum Abschied". Retrieved September 9, 2009 from http://www.pudel.uni-bremen.de/pdf/Iv_tra_b.pdf

Ferguson, T. (2004). The first generation of e-patients. *British Medical Journal, 328*, 1148–1149. doi:10.1136/bmj.328.7449.1148

Hoch, D., & Ferguson, T. (2005). What I've Learned from E-Patients. *PLoS Medicine, 2*(8). doi:10.1371/journal.pmed.0020206

Horton, R. (2004). Vioxx, the implosion of Merck, and aftershocks at the FDA. *The Lancet, 364*, 1995-1996. *Integrity in Science*. (n.d.). Retrieved September 6, 2009 from http://www.cspinet.org/integrity

Lafuente, A. (n.d.). *El megachute tecnológico*. Retrieved September 6, 2009 from http://weblogs.madrimasd.org/tecnocidanos/archive/2008/01/20/82705.aspx

Ledbeater, C., & Miller, P. (2004). *The Pro-Am Revolution: How enthusiasts are cha..nging our economy and society*. London: Demos. Martison, B. M., Anderson, M. S., & De Vries, R. (2005). Scientists behaving badly. *Nature, 435*, 737–738.

McYntire, S. (2005). *Environmental Science and Technology*. Retrieved September 9, 2009 from http://www.climateaudit.org/?p=333

Rampton, S., & Stauber, J. (2001). *Trust Us, We're Experts! How Industry Manipulates Science and Gambles with Your Future*. New York: Tarcher/Putnam.

Stallman, R. (2005). *Bill Gates and other communists*. Retrieved September 6, 2009 from http://news.cnet.com/Bill-Gates-and-other-communists/2010-1071_3-5576230.html

This work was previously published in International Journal of Technoethics, Volume 1, Issue 2, edited by Rocci Luppicini, pp. 37-45, copyright 2010 by IGI Publishing (an imprint of IGI Global).

Chapter 15
The Ethics of Cyberweapons in Warfare

Neil C. Rowe
U.S. Naval Postgraduate School, USA

ABSTRACT

The author discusses the ethical issues of using cyberweapons, software that attacks data and other software during warfare. Many people assume these are relatively benign weapons, but we argue that they can create serious harms like any weapon. He defines cyberweapons and describes them in general terms, and survey their status as per the laws of war. He then discusses the unreliability of cyberweapons, the problem of collateral damage, and the associated problems of damage assessment, maintenance of secrecy, and mounting cyber-counterattacks. He examines some possibilities for creating more ethical cyberweapons and discusses the alternative of cyber-blockades. He concludes that cyberattacks should generally be outlawed by international agreement.

INTRODUCTION

Cyberweapons are software used to attack other software or data within computer systems (Bayles, 2001). We distinguish cyberweapons and cyberattacks (attacks using cyberweapons) from "information warfare", a more general term that includes propaganda, electronic surveillance,

cyber-espionage, and defensive information operations (Jones, Kovacich, & Luzwick, 2002). That is, we will focus on "network attack" and not "network exploitation" or "network defense".

Like conventional weapons, cyberweapons can be used against a variety of targets in a variety of circumstances with a wide range of lethality (White Wolf Security, 2009). Often cyberweapons exploit flaws or errors in software. Proponents have cited these as "clean" weapons that are safer than conventional weapons since they do not dam-

DOI: 10.4018/978-1-4666-1773-5.ch015

age physical objects (Libicki, 2007). Furthermore, unlike chemical, biological, and nuclear weapons, people have no visceral fear of cyberweapons for reasons like health consequences. But maybe they should. All weapons can have serious harms by virtue of their being weapons. The public is unaware of the degree to which they depend on computer systems and the information they store, and thus weapons targeting them can have many unforeseen consequences. For instance, targeting a country's Internet service providers can prevent goods from being delivered, and cause people to starve or die from lack of necessary medical supplies.

There are several schools of ethics. In this article we will follow a pragmatic approach derived from utilitarian ethics in which we argue that a technology is unethical if it has a significant net harm to world society ("negative utilitarianism"). We would also like to derive ethical principles of using cyberweapons, so we will follow "rule utilitarianism". Such principles can then be codified in laws of warfare. However, we do not need an elaborate ethical foundation here because most of the ethical issues with cyberattacks seem similarly problematic under any ethical framework.

THE STATE OF THE ART IN CYBERWEAPONS

Military organizations have noted the success of amateur attackers ("hackers") in damaging computer systems, and have hoped to use these techniques or "exploits" for military advantage, much as they seek a wide variety of ways to gain advantage in warfare (Denning, 1999). Many of these techniques exploit flaws in software. Certain kinds of errors such as failure to check for buffer overflows in loops or failure to properly label data on Web sites can lead to granting of unauthorized special privileges to users of a system. Cyberweapons are programs that package a set of such exploits against a computer system and its data. Cyberweapons can be launched or controlled either externally, from another computer or the Internet, or internally, by spies and saboteurs (Knapp & Boulton, 2007).

Cyberattackers can use their access and privileges to destroy the data and software on a computer system or network, but that is pretty obvious and tells the victim they have been attacked. Cyberattackers can modify the data on a victim system to impede military operations, but that requires a good deal of contextual knowledge about the data. So a better goal for cyberweapons is to take control of a system without the knowledge of the system's owner so it can be used for the attacker's purposes. This technology is called "rootkits" (Kuhnhauser, 2004). Sets of such remotely controlled computers can be used to create "botnets", networks of slave computers under the control of a single user (Bailey et al., 2009). Hacker botnets have been used to earn money by sending spam or phishing email from the slave computers, have been used for denial-of-service attacks against organizations the attacker does not like, have been used for blackmail of organizations by threatening malicious mischief, and have been used for espionage. Botnets developed for military purposes could stop an adversary's military organization from communicating or defending itself.

Cyberweapons can be an innocent-looking software module. Running them to see what they do is not easy because many require passwords to run and their effects may be very subtle. Thus it is difficult to identify cyberweapons within a computer system. Cyberweapons are easy to transport because they are just bit patterns that can be easily copied, or they can even wander autonomously as mobile "agents" (Ceruti, 2001). And when they have served their purpose, they can be deleted. This makes it considerably harder to police cyberweapons than nuclear, chemical, and biological weapons. Nonetheless, traces of a cyberattack will be visible on the victim's computers and networks, and range of methods of "computer forensics" (Mandia & Prosise, 2003) can analyze these traces.

Cyberweapons can attack many kinds of military targets. An obvious one is an adversary's "command and control", their communications and electronic mail, because these are essential to organizing a defense. Since command-and-control tools are distributed across many machines, there are many potential entry points for an attack. Weapons-controlling and vehicle-controlling software are also desirable targets of cyberweapons, but they are harder to attack because they are carefully protected and often (especially for weapons) do not use networks much. Logistics and supply could be targeted, but effects would not be immediate, and surprise is a key element of cyberattack effectiveness. Managerial support for the military could be targeted, because its protections tend to be less, but again the effects would not be immediate, and troops can fight without managers. Public relations (like Web sites) might be a good target, because public perception is so much a part of winning a war, but the damage would only be psychological.

Cyberattacks may be coupled to conventional military attacks, and this may enhance the effectiveness of both. For instance, China claims sovereignty over the island of Taiwan, but Taiwan has formidable defenses and the support of the U.S. Navy. If China were to attack, they would need all the resources they could muster, and a simultaneous cyberattack could be very helpful considering the heavy reliance of the U.S. Navy on software and digital data.

Cyberattacks can also target a country's important civilian infrastructure such as its Internet sites, its financial services sector, its power grid, or even the common software it uses. The Department of Homeland Security in the United States studies this kind of threat. Attacks on nonmilitary targets are generally outlawed by the international warfare conventions, with exceptions for strong military necessity. They are not guaranteed to succeed because there is considerably less centralization in the civilian sector than there is in military organizations, and it can be hard to hit enough targets to achieve the effect of a conventional military attack. They are thus not the first choice of military commanders because the commanders' biggest concern is preventing counterattacks, and they will get them unless they primarily target a country's military. Terrorists might be more likely to choose civilian targets for cyberattacks because terrorist organizations are hard to find and track. Nonetheless, a terrorist organization needs to do public relations for recruitment, needs to acknowledge attacks to gain a public-relations benefit, and needs to maintain a communications network, and this provides a start in tracking them down.

Cyberweapons development has been reported in several major countries in the last few years. Most reports have focused on China which has ambitious goals for military operations in cyberspace, but other countries with software expertise such as Russia have also been mentioned. The United States military does not like to lag technologically behind anyone; recent announcement of a U.S. Air Force "Cyberspace Command" (24th Air Force Command) suggests the United States is now investigating these weapons in secret work. Cyberweapons need not be confined to advanced countries, however, because the technology for developing them does not require much capital investment. It does require expertise in software, which limits their development in countries with poor educational systems. Cyberweapons do not currently seem to be an interest of terrorist groups. They could be (Verton, 2003), but it seems unlikely in the near future since most groups today are anti-technology or, like Al Qaeda, forced to avoid technology to avoid being tracked.

LAW FOR CYBERATTACKS

Cyberattacks using cyberweapons are activities that would classified as crimes in their victim countries if done by ordinary citizens. Necessarily they involve trespassing; to be effective they must employ fraud and vandalism; and often they must also involve espionage, sabotage, and virtual assaults. In many cases they violate international war conventions as well (Arquilla, 1999). While enforcement of international laws of war has been inconsistent, enforcement has been increasingly successful in recent years, so they should be taken seriously.

A particularly troubling issue with cyberattacks is their frequent use of identity deceptions of various kinds, such as by the concealed modifications of an operating system done by rootkits, or the masquerading as legitimate users to gain access. This brings cyberattacks often close to perfidy, a war crime outlawed by international law. Perfidy is attackers masquerading as a legitimate civilian activity, such as soldiers pretending to be Red Cross workers. Perfidy is considered unacceptable in war because it blurs the distinction between combatants and noncombatants, and encourages attacks on civilians. It is certainly fair for combatants to use camouflage. But an operating system is essential to use a computer, so compromising it and turning it into a computer-virus delivery tool is like putting a poison in a community's water system. The argument for perfidy is strongest for the critical parts of an operating system for enforcing access controls, the "kernel", since everyone relies on them and there is no legitimate reason to tamper with them. Other possible candidates for perfidy are tamperings with the key networking software such as routers and as TCP/IP protocols since they are essential for many cyberspace activities.

If someone damages a computer or data, the owner of the computer or data can sue the attacker in civil legal proceedings in many countries. This may apply to cyberattacks. If the victims are suf-ficiently widespread within a country, the country as a whole may be able to sue the attacker, even if it is another country, using international tort law. Cyberattacks also can be unethical even if legal. Much literature over the years has addressed the ethics of warfare (Walzer, 1977; Nardin, 1998) and many of the ideas extend to cyberweapons. Unethical behavior can be punished by activities like cyber-blockades as discussed below.

A possible analogy to cyberweapons are biological weapons, weapons that cause illness and disease (Lederberg, 1999). These have been banned by international convention because they affect military and civilian personnel equally and are difficult to target exclusively to military personnel. Targeting is difficult because biological agents can spread unpredictably due to wind, contacts, and normal biological processes. Perhaps the best analogy to cyberweapons is that of biological warfare against crops (Whitby, 2002), banned by the Biological and Toxin Weapons Convention of 1972. Crops are necessary resources that everyone in society needs, and are societal infrastructure. Attacking them is akin to terrorism.

Analogously, cyberwarfare does not target military personnel directly but only their software and data. But usually cyberattacks will be effective against any computer with the same type of vulnerable software. Military organizations use mostly software that is also used by civilians. So civilian computers could also suffer from military cyberattacks; in fact, they are usually more vulnerable because their countermeasures are not as good. If an attack on a military target goes astray, or if an attack propagates from a military target, civilian computers can easily be damaged. Or it may be tempting for a nation with cyberweapons to deliberately attack civilian computers and networks to cripple the economy of a target country, even though this violates international law. The Allies in World War II deliberately targeted civilian centers with bombing because they thought it would end the war more quickly.

RELIABILITY AND EFFECTIVENESS

One important difference between cyberattacks and conventional military attacks is in the reliability and effectiveness of the attack. If you fire a bullet at a target, it is highly likely to arrive there. If you execute cyberattack software against a cyber target, it is much less likely to work. For one thing, software-based systems can fail in many more ways than a bullet (Neumann, 1995). For another, the attack design itself may be faulty, the attack may not be able to find the target, or the target may not be vulnerable to the attack because assumptions made about it are no longer valid. Computers and software can be precise and highly controllable tools, so why cannot cyberweapons be made precise and controllable too?

Some of the reason is the nature of warfare. To defend yourself, you need to hide and harden your assets. Military computers and software are known targets of adversaries, and governments try to limit their use to authorized personnel by passwords, encryption, enumerated access rights, and other access controls. Military systems are often on special networks behind layers of firewalls, or left unconnected to networks as in the case of weapons systems. System configurations like IP addresses can be changed periodically to foil overly specific attacks, and decoy machines and "honeypots" (attack-data gathering machines) can divert an adversary and collect data about them. Network and system logging can track who is using systems and how, so abnormal usage can be caught quickly. Targeting is not as precise as is believed with conventional weapons anyway, as discussed in (Bissett, 2004). So cyberweapons are likely to be unreliable, and "surgical strikes" are unlikely in cyberspace.

A contributing factor is that cyberweapons are new, and new weapons have high error rates and low reliability (Dunnigan, 2003). This is because new technology is usually complex and many things can go wrong. Software technology in particular permits implementation of very com-

plex mechanisms. An exacerbating factor is that cyberweapons are poorly understood by military commanders since few have expertise in software. This means that commanders will tend to use cyberweapons, more than regular weapons, against the wrong targets in the wrong circumstances to achieve the wrong goals.

Will cyberweapons improve in reliability and effectiveness with time? It is unlikely, as software in general is not getting any more reliable (Neumann, 1995). More specifically, cyberattacks depend on the novelty of their methods and secrecy to enforce it (as we discuss below). There are a limited number of attack methods and they generally can be used only once. So attackers will chronically suffer from inability to practice their attacks, and this will hurt their effectiveness.

THE RISK OF COLLATERAL DAMAGE IN CYBERSPACE

"Collateral damage" or accidental harm to civilians is a key issue in both ethics and laws of warfare. Unfortunately, it is quite possible for cyberattacks aimed at military targets to accidentally hit civilian targets due to their unreliability and uncontrollability. One factor is that it can be hard to distinguish a military computer from a civilian computer. The localization of the target in physical space and identification from its appearance that help so much in conventional warfare have no counterpart in cyberspace. Cyberspace addresses can be spoofed so one site can masquerade as another. Military organizations often use the same operating systems, bookkeeping, word-processing, and presentation software as businesses because it saves money (Jones, Kovacich, & Luzwick, 2002), so examining the software may not indicate a military system. Most military files and data look just like files and data from any large civilian business, since most of both are undecipherable without knowing a good deal of specific jargon. (Some specialized sites can be more easily recognized, such as those controlling power plants, but they are well protected.) Within a military site, it may be hard to distinguish information about humanitarian activities such as hospitals and disaster relief from warfare information, so there could be intrasite collateral damage too; on a battlefield, it is easy to distinguish a tank from a Red Cross truck. Although many military computers have military network names and addresses, they could be camouflaged with a civilian name or address to reduce the chances of an adversary finding it (although it is harder in the U.S. where military site names all end in ".mil"). A clever adversary might also camouflage a civilian computer as a military one to provoke an adversary to attack it in the hope of provoking international outrage.

Secondly, because of the difficulty of reaching military targets for a network-based attack or management of an internal attack, it is tempting to use other systems as "stepping stones" which the cyberattack subverts in a chain to reach the target machines. It is appealing to use civilian machines as stepping stones because many (like home computers) have minimal security. Damage to the stepping stones will occur in setting up communications. This kind of activity is trespassing and is illegal in most countries (Himma, 2004).

Thirdly, even if a civilian computer is not initially attacked, an attack may spread to it. Some cyberattacks use computer viruses and worms that can propagate from one computer to another. Most other cyberattacks have some ability to spread from their original targets because targeting mistakes can be made or defensive surprises may occur. And some attacks like denial-of-service ones require propagation to work. But propagation abilities also make it easier for attacks to spread from military machines to civilian machines. The ubiquity of the Windows operating system and much of the same software on both military and civilian machines facilitates attack spread.

Fourthly, technologically developed countries provide the best targets for cyberweapons because they have so many things to attack. But cyber-weapons require considerable technical expertise to develop, and such expertise is only readily available in the most technologically developed countries. This means an attack by a less technologically developed country is more likely to go astray and attack civilians, or perhaps be more likely to be deliberately targeted to do so because civilians are easier targets.

DAMAGE ASSESSMENT

An issue exacerbating the collateral damage problem with cyberweapons is the difficulty of determining what they did. When aircraft bomb a target, much damage can be seen from the air. With cyberweapons, the damage is not directly visible, which makes it more persistent and costly. Attacks may also cause much indirect damage because of interdependencies that may not be obvious at first (Borg, 2005). Attacks may also fail for a host of unforeseen reasons; (Libicki, 2007) likens information warfare to introducing noise into a military organization, and the organization may or may not succeed at handling it.

This has important consequences for both the victim and the attacker. It may be hard for the victim to know if they have been attacked. The effects of an attack may be subtle, as when a worm slows down normal operations without changing anything else. Then the harm may persist for a long time because no one realizes anything is wrong. Or the effects may be time-delayed, as when a virus in a defender's weapons system causes it to fail only during combat. Then it may be difficult to find the cause, the harm will also persist until it is found, and repair may be costly. It would be foolish for an attacker to use an attack known to antivirus, antiworm, or antispyware tools, so we can assume such tools will be useless in finding or repairing damage from such attacks. While there are techniques for "system restoration" from backup storage media (Dorf & Johnson, 2007), they are time-consuming and require expertise, and may not be able to restore important data unless backup has been highly diligent. And the original vulnerabilities that enabled the attack need to be found and fixed ("patched") to prevent new attacks of the same kind, something that requires research and knowledgeable systems personnel. Less advanced countries may not have anyone with the necessary skills to do these things, leading to long-persistent damage much like that of landmines and chemical toxins that get into the water supply.

For the attacker, it may be very hard to know if their cyberattack had an effect. They may overcompensate by launching an unnecessarily powerful attack to be sure of an effect, or they may attack repeatedly unnecessarily. They may attack unnecessarily many kinds of software or data, and they may do unnecessarily drastic modifications to it. Unnecessarily strong attacks that are deep may be unnecessarily difficult to repair, and unnecessarily strong attacks that are broad run a higher risk of collateral damage to civilians. Unnecessarily strong attacks are particularly a danger for cyber-counterattacks, as we will discuss, because an adversary is anticipating counterattacks.

SECRECY OF CYBERWEAPONS

As mentioned, most cyberattacks exploit bugs or flaws in software. If the victims knew of these, they would have fixed them. So secrecy of attack methods is essential to the success of most cyberweapons.

This secrecy by itself can be unethical. Secrecy makes it harder for victim countries to figure out what happened to them. Standard attack-intelligence resources like Computer Emergency Response Teams (CERTs) collect information about known vulnerabilities, but cannot provide much help for cyberattacks used in warfare because the vulnerabilities will likely be new. This exacerbates the problem of diagnosis and repair discussed above. Also, misinformation

about poorly-understood attacks may spread far in a crisis, creating overreaction and panic in the victim country. Misunderstanding can lead to scapegoating of innocent countries or groups, much as terrorist acts tend to be blamed on a country's known adversaries. It will be essential for information-security experts to provide dispassionate technical analysis of what has occurred, perhaps with neutral experts from an international agency.

Secrecy also has negative consequences for the society that uses it (Bok, 1986). It encourages those who know the secrets to think they are better than those that do not, and permits those responsible for foolish attacks to avoid blame. Secret weapons are harder to test, since testing cannot be done publicly, and without adequate testing it is more likely that they will fail or cause collateral damage. An especially important consequence of the necessary secrecy of cyberweapons is that they can only be used effectively once (Ranum, 2004). Once they are used and they create some military effect, computer-forensics methods can usually figure out what happened. Then a solution – fixing a bug, disabling software, turning off a utility, or blacklisting a site – can often be found in a day or so, and often a good solution will prevent similar attacks of the same type as well. This means that cyberweapons provide a poor return on investment, since exploitable flaws in software require considerable work to find. They are like a type of bomb that can only be used once anywhere in the world and never any bomb of that type again. It appears ethically unjustifiable for a society to spend resources on developing cyberweapons when there are so many other more useful things they could spend money on.

CYBER-COUNTERATTACKS

International law prohibits attacks on other countries unless a country is attacked first (Walzer, 1977). Countries must agree to this in signing the United Nations charter; in the United States, the charter was a treaty approved by the U.S. Senate, and thus has the same force as any other law of the U.S. So unprovoked cyberattacks are clearly illegal and unethical. But what about cyber-counterattacks?

It is more difficult to prove responsibility for a cyberattack than for a conventional attack, since it is hard to trace from where it came. The apparent source may be "spoofed" by illicit modification of source-identification data, the apparent source may just be a "stepping-stone" as discussed earlier, and networks sites do not always keep good records. Even if we can trace an attack, the evidence is highly technical. This makes it hard to justify a counterattack to world public opinion.

In addition, a serious technical problem of cyber-counterattacks is the preparation and experimentation time necessary to set up good ones. If the cyber-counterattacks are from within a system, time is needed to establish a foothold on that system and station attack software on it. It will be unlikely that an attacker will succumb to the same attack they themselves launched – they should have plenty of time to harden their systems against it. In fact, an attacker should take special pains to harden their systems against all attacks, since counterattacks are sanctioned by international law. A smart attacker could even terminate all their network connections to the rest of the world for a time after an attack to markedly reduce the chances of an externally launched counterattack or exploitation of an internally launched one. Or they could put all their operating systems into hardware to prevent modification by Trojan horses and other exploits. So it will not be easy to launch a successful counterattack, and some considerable number of tries by the counterattacker with many methods may be necessary to find one that works, if one can be found at all.

These issues create problems for the laws of war, because the legitimacy of a counterattack in conventional warfare is established by its immediacy after the attack, its being of the same type as the attack, and its proportionality to the magnitude of the attack (Gardam, 2004). Legitimate counterattacks cannot wait years (such as the claim that the 2001 attack on the New York World Trade Center was a response to the U.S.-Iraq war of 1991), cannot use some quite different technology (as the introduction of poison gas by the Germans in 1915), and cannot be considerably larger. Counterattacks that violate these criteria must be classified as new attacks and are therefore illegal and unethical (Fotion and Elfstrom, 1986).

One way to facilitate counterattacks is to station counterattack software in advance of attack, and channels to communicate with it like those of botnets, on computer systems of adversaries just in the chance there might be hostilities which could use it. Then they might be invoked quickly. Such capabilities could deter an adversary attack in the first place, if the adversary knows or cares about those capabilities (deterrence does not always work well as a military strategy). However, designing counterattacks that will work when needed is not easy. Just because they worked in the laboratory against fixed targets does not provide much confidence they will work during warfare, a problem that occurs in testing much new military technology. Computer systems are installing new protections all the time, so possible attack methods can become obsolete without warning. That means that the older an attack is, the less likely it is to work. Counterattack software is identical to attack software, so it is just as criminal to use in most countries, and just as hard to test in realistic warfare conditions. Furthermore, a hasty counterattack may harm the counterattacker more than the attacker because it reveals counterattacker cyberweapons to the attacker and allows them to test how they can be defeated, information that they might not be able to obtain otherwise.

A way to reduce counterattack obsolescence is to use a broader "strategic" counterattack rather than a tactical one. An example would be modifying all the code for a networking protocol used by an adversary by modifying the source for that code in a repository. If all adversary military systems download their code from there, all could be infected from a single source, and the code could function normally until the counterattack. Such methods would be high on the scale of perfidy. But there are difficult practical problems. Adversaries that contemplate attacking other countries will set a high priority on protecting their frequently used software and will use hashes (pseudorandom data reductions) regularly to check for modifications to it. Most software is updated regularly, so the counterattacker would need to repeatedly modify the code with each update. Most updates come directly from software companies and not a military repository, and it would be hard for counterattackers to reach all these sources, and even harder to modify code in transmission. A broad strategic attack is easier to diagnose than a tactical (limited) one because there will be many malfunctioning systems simultaneously; this provides good data for identifying the type of attack and its software locus, so such attacks can be fixed more quickly than those that attack just one system. Finally, a broad counterattack based in common software risks more collateral damage to noncombat functions of computer systems than a more targeted counterattack.

Not all cyber-counterattacks require preparation. Those launched across the Internet can be mounted more easily at any time. Defending against such attacks is, however, the primary focus of the network intrusion-prevention systems which defend most of our network sites, which are kept updated with the latest known attacks. It is difficult, though not impossible, to invent a new attack that will succeed against these formidable defenses. A country could try to "stockpile" new such attacks in the interests of its defense, but the effort to find such attacks might quickly be wasted as countermeasures are independently discovered as discussed above. What attacks that do succeed in circumventing the first level of defenses may succumb to second levels of defenses that note anomalous behavior, so they are unlikely to

succeed for long once they start attacking. For instance, systematic search for the computers on a local-area network is necessary for precisely targeted attacks, but such searching is obvious to network packet monitoring since normal usage rarely does it. So network-based attacks are quite unreliable, and military commanders dislike unreliable technology. Thus it appears that cyber-counterattacks are infeasible.

DESIGNING ETHICAL CYBERWEAPONS

Despite the issues raised here, countries will likely continue to develop cyberweapons. Can such weapons be designed and used more ethically? We believe they can, since ethical discriminations can be made today among different kinds of weapons. For instance among nuclear weapons, neutron bombs are arguably less ethical than hydrogen bombs of the same explosive power when civilians are at risk because they harm humans disproportionately (Johnson, 1984).

Since controllability is a serious concern with cyberweapons, ethical weapons should use a variety of methods to ensure focused targeting. Propagation via viruses and worms should be minimized. Attacks should focus on a limited set of important targets which should be clearly identified and confirmed during the attack using more than their Internet address. Important civilian systems such as commercial infrastructure should clearly identify themselves as civilian so attacks can know to avoid them.

Ethical attacks should also be easily stoppable. If an adversary surrenders, it is unethical as well as against international law to continue attacking and causing damage. This means that all attacks should be under quick control via some mechanism such as an emergency channel so that they can be halted if necessary. This may be difficult with automated attacks, and the effects of any attack will likely impede communication. But it is important.

Identification of the attacker ("attribution") should also be a key feature of ethical attacks, much as how uniforms to identify military personnel in warfare. Acting as a soldier while not wearing a uniform is outlawed by international law. So some data associated with a cyberattack should identify who is responsible for an attack. One way is to add a digital signature to data or a program (Mel & Baker, 2000). Several technologies to do this are available, and the best-known is encryption with a private key of a public-private key pair of a hash of the contents. Using a hash means that the public key confirms that the contents were not modified after they were signed. Responsible attackers will find signatures useful because they prove they are responsible for an attack and prevent scapegoating of others. Unattributed attacks are not very useful anyway since attacks are usually a way to force a country to do something, and the victim cannot know what to do unless they know who has attacked them. Signatures also permit the attacker to recognize their own signature on already-attacked systems and avoid reattacking them. Public keys for attack signatures could be kept with international organizations like the United Nations as a form of "key escrow" like that proposed for backup on encrypted systems.

Not everyone agrees that attacks should be attributable. (Robb, 2009) argues that cyberattacks will be ineffective unless that have deniability, like some instances of "special operations" using commandos. But if he is right, then all effective cyberattacks are forms of terrorism.

A weakness of signatures is that they might be recognized by defenders and enable them to realize they are being attacked, which might matter with the more subtle attacks. But it will not be easy to recognize attack signatures because many programs today have signatures as a security measure. Also, since they are a function of the contents, their bits will differ when attached to different files or data. However, if it is important that a signature be concealed, steganography can be used by the attacker (Wayner, 2002). This is a class of techniques for concealing data inside innocent-looking other data, like concealing code messages in the least-significant bits of pictures.

Since damage persistence is a key problem with cyberweapons, it would be more ethical to use weapons whose damage is easily repairable at the end of hostilities. This is more possible in cyberspace than in conventional warfare. For instance, an attack could encrypt important parts of a victim's system so that they cannot be used until the attacker supplies a key to undo (decrypt) them. Since encryption and decryption do not lose any information, the attack would be completely reversible. This would be an ethical alternative whenever it is impossible for a victim to restore a system from backup. Similarly, an attack could withhold important messages (like orders or email) from a victim. If the attacker saves those messages, they could be supplied to the victim at the cessation of hostilities, thereby reversing the attack. In both cases, there may be some damage from denial of timely access to data, but this can be minimized if the target systems are chosen carefully.

OTHER CYBER-MEASURES

There are many alternatives to the use of cyberweapons such as negotiation and conventional weapons. Even within the cyberspace realm, there are nonviolent alternatives. Publicizing a cyberattack may elicit sympathy and support for a victim country, and may make a counterattack unnecessary; if it cannot do so, a counterattack is probably inadvisable. "Cyber-blockades" may also be effective responses to cyberattacks. Much as with methods to impede financing of terrorists (Biersteker & Eckert, 2008), countries can block or disable Internet connections (particularly banking transactions) of the offending country. Traditional blockades and sanctions do not always work, but countries depend so much on their Internet connections that cyber-blockades could be more effective than physical blockades. There are alternatives to banks, but there is only one Internet.

CONCLUSION

Most coverage of cyberweapons has been relatively neutral, referring to cyberweapons as inevitable new weapons technology that can be employed much like any other. Our argument here is that this cyberweapons have a variety of unique problems that impede their effectiveness and ethicality, and that "cyber-pacifism" should be encouraged. Cyberweapons are less reliable and less controllable weapons than conventional ones, much like biological weapons, and thus a poor choice in warfare. They disproportionately threaten civilians and harm the society that develops and uses them. It is hard to figure out what is happening when cyberweapons are used due to secrecy and the inherent difficulty of analyzing cyberspace, and their employment for counterattacks seems particularly challenging. While some ways of using cyberweapons are better than others, there are currently insufficient incentives to use them ethically. Their use should be outlawed.

ACKNOWLEDGMENT

The views expressed are those of the author and do not represent those of any part of the U.S. Government.

REFERENCES

Arquilla, J. (1999). Ethics and information warfare. In Z. Khalilzad, J. White, & A. Marsall (Eds.), *Strategic appraisal: the changing role of information in warfare* (pp. 379-401). Rand Corporation, Santa Monica, CA, USA.

Bailey, M., Cooke, E., Jahanian, F., Xu, Y., & Karir, M. (2009, March). A survey of botnet technology and defenses. *Proc. Conf. for Homeland Security: Cybersecurity Applications and Technology.*

Bayles, W. (2001). Network attack. *Parameters. US Army War College Quarterly, 31,* 44–58.

Berman, P. (2002). The globalization of jurisdiction. *University of Pennsylvania Law Review, 151*(2), 311–545. doi:10.2307/3312952

Biersteker, T., & Eckert, S. (2008). *Countering the financing of terrorism.* London: Routledge.

Bissett, A. (2004). High technology war and 'surgical strikes'. *Computers & Society, 32*(7), 4.

Bok, S. (1986). *Secrets.* Oxford, UK: Oxford University Press.

Borg, S. (2005, November-December). Economically complex cyberattacks. *IEEE Security and Privacy, 3*(6), 64–67. doi:10.1109/MSP.2005.146

Ceruti, M. (2001, March). Mobile agents in network-centric warfare. *Proc. 5th International Symposium on Autonomous Decentralized Systems* (pp. 243-246).

Denning, D. (1999). *Information Warfare and Security.* Boston, MA: Addison-Wesley.

Denning, D. (2007). The ethics of cyber conflict. In K. Himma, & H. Tavani (Eds.), *Information and computer ethics.* New York: Wiley.

Dorf, J., & Johnson, M. (2007). Restoration component of business continuity planning. In H. Tipton, & M. Krause (Eds.), *Information security management handbook* (6th ed.) (pp. 645-1654). CRC Press.

Dunnigan, J. (2003). *How to make war. (4th ed.).* New York: Quill.

Fotion, N., & Elfstrom, G. (1986). *Military ethics: guidelines for peace and war.* Boston: Routledge and Kegan Paul.

Gardam, J. (2004). *Necessity, proportionality, and the use of force by states*. Cambridge, UK: Cambridge University Press.

Gutman, R., & Rieff, D. (1999). *Crimes of war: what the public should know*. New York: Norton

Himma, K. (2004). The ethics of tracing hacker attacks through the machines of innocent persons. *International Journal of Information Ethics, 2*(11), 1–13.

Hollis, D. (2007). New tools, new rules: international law and information operations. In G. David, & T. McKeldin (Eds.), *The message of war: information, influence, and perception in armed conflict*. Temple University Legal Studies Research Paper No. 2007-15, Philadelphia, PA, USA.

ICRC (International Committee of the Red Cross). (2007). *International humanitarian law – treaties and documents*. Retrieved December 1, 2007 from www.icrc.org/icl.nsf.

Jensen, E. (2003). Unexpected consequences from knock-on effects: a different standard for computer network operations? *American University International Law Review, 18*, 1145–1188.

Johnson, J. (1984). *Can modern war be just?* New Haven: Yale University Press.

Jones, A., Kovacich, G., & Luzwick, P. (2002). *Global information warfare*. Boca Raton, FL: CRC Press.

Knapp, K., & Boulton, W. (2007). Ten information warfare trends. In L. Janczewski & A. Colarik (Eds.), *Cyber Warfare and Cyber Terrorism* (pp. 17-25). Hershey, PA, USA: IGI Global.

Kuhnhauser, W. (2004, January). Root kits: an operating systems viewpoint. *ACM SIGOPS Operating Systems Review, 38*(1), 12–23. doi:10.1145/974104.974105

Lederberg, J. (Ed.). (1999). *Biological weapons: limiting the threat*. Cambridge, MA: MIT Press.

Libicki, M. (2007). *Conquest in cyberspace: national security and information warfare*. New York: Cambridge University Press.

Mandia, K., & Prosise, C. (2003). *Incident response and computer forensics*. New York: McGraw-Hill / Osborne.

Mel, H., & Baker, D. (2000). *Cryptography decrypted* (5th ed.). Boston, MA: Addison-Wesley Professional.

Molander, R., & Siang, S. (1998, Fall). The legitimization of strategic information warfare: ethical considerations. *AAAS Professional Ethics Report, 11*(4). Retrieved November 23, 2005 from www.aaas.org/spp/sfrl/sfrl.htm.

Nardin, T. (Ed.). (1998). *The ethics of war and peace*. Princeton, NJ: Princeton University Press.

Neumann, P. (1995). *Computer related risks*. Reading, MA: ACM Press.

Ranum, M. (2004). *The myth of homeland security*. Indianapolis, IN: Wiley.

Robb, J. (2007). *The U.S. and cyberwarfare*. Retrieved February 6, 2009 from globalguerrillas.typepad.com/globalguerrillas/2007/12/the-us-and-cyber.html.

Schmitt, M. (2002). Wired warfare: computer network attack and *jus in bello*. *International Review of the Red Cross, 84*(846), 365–399.

Verton, D. (2003). *Black ice: the invisible threat of cyber-terrorism*. New York: McGraw-Hill Osborne Media.

Walzer, D. (1977). *Just and unjust wars: a moral argument with historical illustrations*. New York: Basic Books.

Wayner, P. (2002). *Disappearing cryptography: information hiding: steganography and watermarking.* San Francisco, CA: Morgan Kaufmann.

Westwood, C. (1997). *The future is not what it used to be: conflict in the information age.* Fairbairn, ACT, Australia: Air Power Studies Center.

Whitby, S. (2002). *Biological warfare against crops.* Houndmills, UK: Palgrave.

White Wolf Security. *Offensive operations in cyberspace.* Retrieved February 6, 2009 from www.whitewolfsecurity.com/publications/offensive_ops.php.

This work was previously published in International Journal of Technoethics, Volume 1, Issue 1, edited by Rocci Luppicini, pp. 20-31, copyright 2010 by IGI Publishing (an imprint of IGI Global).

Chapter 16
Not Just Software:
Free Software and the (Techno) Political Action

Blanca Callén
Universitat Autònoma de Barcelona, Spain

Daniel López
Universitat Oberta de Catalunya, Spain

Miquel Doménech
Universitat Autònoma de Barcelona, Spain

Francisco Tirado
Universitat Autònoma de Barcelona, Spain

ABSTRACT

The practice of developing and creating Free Software has been the centre of attention for studies related to economics, knowledge production, laws and the intellectual property framework. However, the practice that constitutes the initiative of Free Software also means a call to rethink current forms of political action and the in-depth meaning of what is understood as "political". This constitutes the field which has been called techno-activism. Along these lines, the authors propose a particular reading of the political challenge that is Free Software from the standpoint of Hardt and Negri's (2000) theoretical work. The authors put forward various contributions -regarding the organization, the agents and the form of political action- that they consider to pose a crisis for traditional proposals and urge society to renew its way of relating to information, the raw material upon which the current exercise of government and practices of techno-activist resistance rest.

"We have to write a new generalised oath to the sciences as a whole, as all wise men have responsibilities of creation. They may swear it or not, it is their free choice. The one that writes it will open a new millennium." (Michel Serres, 1994)

DOI: 10.4018/978-1-4666-1773-5.ch016

INTRODUCTION: FREE SOFTWARE AS A POLITICAL PRACTICE

The main transformation caused by the massive implementation of Internet in our day-to-day lives has not been, precisely, in the field of information transfer. We have to look for it, to the contrary, in the field of imaginary (Flichy, 2001). Internet is above all a promise: of freedom and cooperation (Lévy, 1995). And if there is a paradigmatic practice of such a promise, it is the search for and promotion of Free Software. "Free" not because we wish for something for nothing (in relation to a price, a value or a measure), but because we are dealing with a particular concept of freedom in virtual environments. Hence the concept of "Free Software" refers to the irrevocable right to run, copy, distribute, study, modify and improve such software. A right which materializes in four specific practices: a) the freedom to run a program for any conceivable purpose; b) the freedom to study how the program works and adapt it to the needs of any user; c) the freedom to redistribute copies of the program and in this way help others; and d) the freedom to improve the program and put these improvements within reach of all and every community.

If we look back at the decade of the sixties, the moment when the computing phenomenon began, we can see that the concept of "Free Software" did not exist. Simply put: all software was free. Computer programs and their source codes (codes written by programmers and which are essential if we wish to know the internal functioning of the program) circulated freely among Internet users, who at the time were limited to small groups of academics and researchers. Developments were taken advantage of and reused by others, who improved them and, once again made them available to the rest. This way, a specific work became a group benefit and a tacit community of cooperation was set up which permanently generated innovation. The Unix project, the first multi-user and multi-task operating system which was based on respecting open code (source), was the paradigm of this logic.

The appearance of personal computers changed the situation. Private companies appeared which developed software and marketed licences to use it. Concealing the source code meant that other companies or programmers were prevented from knowing how it worked, the participation of users in its innovation and development was eliminated and all other uses other than simply running the program were prohibited. At the same time the user was forced to pay for updates or improvements, an activity which remained firmly in the hands of the company alone. Nowadays, most software that is used and distributed is of this type.

The Free Software movement is a reaction against this situation and vindicates the conditions under which telematics was born. In the extract below from the manifesto which Richard Stallman prepared to publicise his project we can see these pretensions clearly:

"I consider that the golden rule requires that if I like a program I must share it with other people who like it. Software sellers want to divide the users and conquer them, making each user agree not to share with others. I refuse to break solidarity with other users in this way. The fundamental act of friendship among programmers is the sharing of programs; marketing arrangements now typically used essentially forbid programmers to treat others as friends. By working on and using GNU rather than proprietary programs, we can be hospitable to everyone and obey the law. In addition, GNU serves as an example to inspire and a banner to rally others to join us in sharing. Once GNU is written, everyone will be able to obtain good system software free, just like air. Complete system sources will be available to everyone. As a result, a user who needs changes in the system will always be free to make them himself, or hire any available programmer or company to make them for him. Users will no longer be at the mercy of one programmer or company which owns the sources and is in sole position to make changes. Finally, the overhead of considering who owns the system software and what one is or is not entitled to do with it will be lifted" (http://www.gnu.org/gnu/manifesto.html).

Many authors (Rullani, 2005; González-Barahona, 2004) have centred their work on analysing how the Free Software movement forms a challenge and essentially economic confrontation with the large computer corporations. But we can see from the above that the movement is much more than just this. It recovers the promise of freedom and cooperation that Internet once meant and in its day-to-day practices and ways of doing things amounts to a phenomenon of political action. Free Software is computing and economics, of course, but above all it is politics. The use of Free Software refers to carrying out practices which challenge the politics and control operations of the very phenomenon of globalisation.

In fact, in this article we will show that the practices associated with Free Software mean a renovation of traditional political action. A renovation which is characterised by: a) putting information and communication technologies at the centre of such action and b) constituting a potential that challenges and answers the new forms of political control that appear with the phenomenon of globalisation. We have called this aforementioned renovation techno-activism. To understand the complex challenge that Free Software means to recent forms of control and power we refer to the work of Hardt and Negri (2000) on the political condition of our immediate present.

The Deployment of Imperial Bio-Politics

The literature on the phenomenon of globalisation is extensive. Nevertheless, there is something lacking in it: there are hardly any studies on the political condition of the same. And much less any analysis that shows the connection between said condition and the growth of technologies of information and communication. In 2000, Michael Hardt and Antonio Negri published a work entitled *Empire* which attempted to put a clear delimited face to the political dimension of globalisation.

Empire describes a global form of sovereignty. This is not based on borders or fixed barriers. Neither does its activity refer to any metropolis nor is dominant class, its domination decentralised and de-territorialized. For the same reason, there is no identity linked to the power centre which is unitary and a basic point of reference. The concept of Empire refers to hybrid identities, flexible hierarchies and plural exchanges by means of adaptable command networks. But the most important thing is that it attempts to give rise to an action which not only governs a territory and a population but also lays down the conditions to create reality. That is, Empire creates the world in which it lives itself. Therefore, it is a concept which describes a governing action which is, above all, ontological. The most remarkable effect of such an operation is shown in the area of life. Empire not only regulates human interaction, it aspires to a direct government of human nature, a total domination of social and biological life. In this sense, in the Empire the creation of value and wealth are connected with bio-political production. And this takes its form in the paradigmatic rationality of government. As the authors admit, their proposal develops, to its greatest extent, the notion of bio-politics put forward decades before by Michel Foucault (1976).

Bio-politics is a notion developed by the author to describe the programme or rationality of government that emerges with the liberal project. This possesses two differentiated but narrowly linked dimensions. On the one hand it refers to acting on the body as a machine. In this sense it points to the development of a disciplined order and the emergence of a normalization society (Michel Foucault, 1975). And on the other hand, it refers to acting on the body as a species, which is the production of truth regimes which allow for the government of human populations. The most paradigmatic example put forward by the author is sexuality (Michel Foucault, 1976). Hence, in the bio-politics of Empire the first aspect loses relevance in favour of the management or government of human multitudes.

Given the above, we should not make the mistake of thinking that this new form of sovereignty or rationality is imposed and exercised by means of macro cultural processes or states which are on a higher level than our day-to-day life. On the contrary, if there is anything interesting and novel about the notion of Empire it is, precisely, the lack of distinction between the micro and macro dimensions of reality. In fact, there would be no difference at all. Day-to-day life refers to small groups, practices and relationships that do not hold a lesser extension than any other formation which is, a priori, much larger, such as, the city, the state or the family. Given that the object of Empire's action is social life in its entirety, it refers, actually, to an operation, which nests or manifests itself in a multitude of small practices and formations which extend everywhere. But, what does such a practice or operation consist of? Of something very simple: in the deployment of a continuum with three completely dependent but differentiated phases. Firstly we have the inclusive phase. Any aspect of social life is taken without differentiation, and a homogenous homothetic space is created. This will be a common space for communication. In this space all people, things and relationships are equal.

Secondly we have the differential phase. In this phase differences are highlighted as long as they are in the exclusively cultural field. If such differences refer only to a cultural dimension then they are therefore contingent, variable and in short, not transcendent. All references to differences of an ontological, political, economic nature etc are eliminated. Lastly, we have the administration of such differences: they are managed, ordered and therefore controlled. As Hardt and Negri (2000, p. 242) point out, one of the novelties that Empire contributes is that it is based on a permanent state of exception. Differences are administered by means of intervention which is always exceptional, even when it always happens. The establishment

of this state of exception means that there are no codes or fixed guidelines for this management. They are established depending on the area of differences which are to be controlled. The criteria are, therefore, never the same. They vary: neither do we know the guidelines on variation nor the criteria on which such variation is fixed in a clear regulation.

Obviously, the sequence described above may be found in other administration and management practices prior to the establishment of the Empire. But the novelty of this *modus operandi* is its global dimension: in extension, as we have mentioned, it affects the whole planet; and in intension, it refers to any aspect of our social lives. We are dealing with total bio-politics!

The Empire Feeds on the Multitude

But Empire is only one of the terms of a relationship; on the other side we have the Multitude. Here we are dealing with a choice between one or the other. We do not have an Empire or a Multitude. No way! We have an Empire and a Multitude: a set. And we have a fear, a fear of the threat that the Multitude poses. Because this set, although it may sound paradoxical, is not a dichotomy. We are not offered two terms which look one another in the eye. Empire is a practice or operation which is defined by and thanks to the Multitude, to its exploitation and, at any moment, the Multitude might overwhelm it. But, what exactly is the Multitude?

Firstly it is a name for the imminent, for that moment when people are liberated from transcendence and recognise that reality is something produced by themselves. Secondly, it is the name of this productive action. The Multitude is always creative and in movement. Multitude and working class is not the same. The latter is limited by the point of view of production and by that of social cooperation (it refers to some producers, workers who share a space, a consciousness...). When we speak of the exploitation of the Multitude by the Empire we are speaking about the exploitation of the cooperation of singularities, not the exploitation of individuals, of their work or their cooperation. The set of singularities that make up this group, the networks of these networks, is exploited... In the exercise of this exploitation there is no generation of individuals, all identical and equal. Empire deals with a more basic exploitation, which does not demand the constitution of a great apparatus which, while exploiting, also generates individuality. Hardt and Negri distance themselves from the Marxist notion of modern exploitation: the exploitation of individuals or agents. When Marx speaks of this exploitation he is speaking of industrial and objective production, not of cooperation. Thirdly the Multitude is, in Nietzschean concepts, the willingness of power, it expands, and it overwhelms its own frontiers, its own irruption or emergence. And above all, it acquires body, it becomes flesh, it expresses itself materially: in certain social movements, practices of resistance... Fourthly, the multitude is an event, irruption of the unexpected or contingent in the ordered space of the Empire. And additionally, in spite of what we might imagine, the multitude does not speak of multiplicity. A multiplicity is the sum, no more, of various elements, for example, we could enumerate red.. and car... and 35 and... a... and the white book... and... This is a multiplicity. But in the multitude there is a unity or plan which groups all of these elements together. This plan has to do with creation, with the fact that out of all these elements something appears which groups them together in a very novel way.

But above all, the Multitude, just like the Empire, is an operation, but not one of capture or exploitation. The important thing about the Multitude is that, as we have seen, it brings together singularities. Singular is that which we do not share, that which makes us unique, irreducible... And the multitude allows the singular to co-operate or work together. How is this possible? Thanks to the appearance of a middle ground in which such singularities meet, in this third space they share

something and a meeting take places. This space is a transformation; it is much more than the forms of each singularity. This meeting on something is novelty, creation, and the surprise which nests in the Multitude. Therefore, co-functioning, and a certain trans-formation are the moments of this. Hence, the Multitude is more than multiplicity: a meeting which respects singularity, but which also contributes the value of novelty and creation. This value is desired and exploited by the imperial form.

And, precisely, information is a field of play on which the Empire-Multitude tension is played out with special interest. On this field, as we will show below, a practice which we have called techno-activism is defined and manages to renovate traditional political action.

Techno-Activism: The Renovation of Political Action

As we have mentioned above, the appearance of personal computers transformed an initial situation of complete cooperation into one of absolute competition. Suddenly, the world of information was commercialised and access to goods which up till then had been free, collective and unlimited was capitalised. Justifying such action on certain patent laws, what is known as Corporative, Proprietary or Private Software arose. With it came a blocking of creative processes and cooperation, the exploitation of what had once been the fruit of an entire community, the restriction of global benefits which had before been open and the appearance and privilege of certain owners above that of a great mass of users and consumers. The constant creation which had arisen previously from a Network (albeit small) of endless, unrepresentable and self-organized cooperation of singularities; now by means of a profitable operation facilitated by property laws and restrictive patents became a scarce resource owned by a few: just a few corporations (with time, basically just one monopoly: Microsoft) that subsumed what was social in capital in order to administer it. And in such a way that the only freedom left was that of the choice, in exchange for money, of running one product or another. With this panorama as a historical backdrop, the GNU project ("*GNU is Not Unix*") and the Free Software movement appeared in 1984, promoted by Richard Stallman, with the aim of creating an operating system completely based on open code.

Then a space for work and cooperative practices opened up in which people could relate to others without giving up their singularity and where the sharing of such a heterogeneity of experiences and knowledge fostered the emergence of creativity. Forms of work that continued in Free Software project development. Hence from an unexpected error of software programming, from pure immanence and chance, came the occasion to join together, to sum, cooperate, transform; to operate, in short, as "Multitude". In this way Free Software becomes an unlimited, free and public good which arises out of group creativity and cooperation. And in this operation of planetary cooperation it is impossible to point to a central or proprietary command. A representation. So that in this self-organised "Multitude" there is no law, no contract, no rules that articulate it further than itself and its own action. The simple freedom of choice mentioned above is replaced by freedom of action. And to achieve this, this type of Software is articulated in terms of Copyleft licence, which in the form of the GPL licence (General Public Licence), acts as an "infrastructure of free excess" (Holmes, 2003) favouring development, growth and circulation freely. Ensuring its survival and expansion at the same time as protecting it from capture and domination by intellectual property, patent and copyright laws. It protects it without limiting it, preserving its use rather than its ownership, guaranteeing its liberties rather than restricting them, and ensures its growth thanks to the circulation of knowledge, favouring contagion and the constant sum of forces.

But in spite of this there are attempts to impose control and regulation upon this creative practice.

A clear example is the attempt to create an European regulation on software patents. This tried to prohibit the use of patented ideas or codes even if they had been "discovered" or created by means other than those registered. Such a regulation may be conceptualised as a constitutive practice of what we have referred to as imperial operations. Firstly it is presented as something absolutely inclusive, in extension and intension: its aim covers social life as a totality, as a whole. And, secondly, it is formulated in order to govern, and at the same time, to become the only possible condition for the emergence of this social reality. In the terms of Hardt and Negri, we are facing bio-political actions based on the management of information.

However, the Free Software movement may be understood as a multitude which overwhelms such operations as the above. To do so it is essential to establish a global group network of cooperative work. A network which is governed by common benefit and interest. Where something is given (time, work, etc...) and shared in order to produce a third distinct inaugural space (in the form of the software itself, in the program, but also in the social network in which it arises) which will allow a relationship between those involved. A space to connect, transform and then generate novelty. Hence, from each of the singularities that make up this multitude a totality is generated which materializes in something as immaterial as software. This is the expression of a meeting that causes, among other things, two great social effects that are worth mentioning. Firstly the redefinition of meanings and the reopening of certain political debates on the notions of "public", "free" or "ownership". And secondly, it shows that the hegemonic regulations and practices that rule us are contingent, are open to change and may be repoliticised.

Therefore, Free Software is something more than just a program or a grammar describing sequences of instructions open to the public. It constitutes an exercise in disaffection which enables the creation of other worlds of experiences

–a non-state public sphere as an author such as Virno (2003) would say- that are considered inappropriate and cannot be appropriated by means of these Imperial operations which are patent, proprietary software or Copyright licences. Free Software is, above all, an affirmative action which blocks cooption and appropriation of its productive forces by networks of intellectual property thanks, precisely to the permanent public circulation of the same. And it is possible to understand this as an auto-institutive practice of lines of flight which seek to diffract some of the dominant bio-political logic. In other words, the political merit and the novelty of the GNU/Linux system lies especially in the socio-technical mechanisms which are brought into play by its development and use, which are able to generate conflict and force which can repoliticise the field of information and communication.

We have called this action techno-activism. This concept brings together these "multitude" operations which overwhelm what is deployed by the Empire in its exercise of global political domination. But we argue that it possesses a characteristic which differentiates it from other possible resistance and protest operations: information. We are facing actions or operations which are deployed in and from the management of information and communication technology. For this reason we believe that the Free Software movement is a paradigm of techno-activism. It possesses the power to redefine some of the traditional dimensions of political action (Callén, 2006). Let us look at some of the most important.

The Appearance of New Organizational Figures

Free Software projects allow knowledge and functionality to be articulated with an ease that would otherwise be difficult to achieve. It deals with generating a common production thanks to the deployment of an open network structure which is distributed where a productive tension between what is common (projects, tools, products, etc.) and what is singular (materials, time, spaces, knowledge and skills, etc.) arises. But this tension, rather than being a problem is seen as the condition which enables the emergence of the aforementioned common work. Each participant or local community functions as a node connected to other nodes in the network and whose work points to particular local conditions, while also being immersed in global action and production of group knowledge. In such a way that the singularity of each locality is not denied or annulled to foster a supposed final unity, but rather is reinforced by feedback with the return of the collective product in which it has been partially involved. This type of work breaks with the notion of centre-periphery, or hierarchy, command or status; because each part which is involved is equivalent to the rest (in an epistemological sense) but such equality comes from, precisely, the difference, the specific nature and irreducible singularity of each part. Hence the traditional distinction between developer-producer-active subject and user-receiver- passive object is diluted in favour of a network of political agents with distributed co-responsibilities.

Redefinition of Agents and Political Subjects

The above organizational system means, also, the definition of a new political subject. The idea of an identity which is closed, homogenous and stable in terms of its attitudes and commitments, as a form of privileged organization for political action which aspires to generate lasting effects in space and time is replaced by one of agencies which articulate "one with another" to achieve specific aims. They do not renounce at any time their own singularity. They connect and operate thanks to the "between", to that preposition which gives them meaning (Whithead, 1925). The "between" keeps them separate and distinct, but at the same time links them. It allows a constitutive, creative difference to arise, which allows groups to include, simultaneously, what is common and what is multiple. Techno-activism exploits the possibilities of action thrown up by group articulation (Laclau & Mouffe, 1985; Mouffe, 1992; Haraway, 1991, 1992). It shows us that the networked, hybrid, partial, and unnecessary connections between singularities are viable and that, by means of such collective work, can generate wide-ranging effects.

Techno-activism and the Free Software movement are good examples of this, and vindicate what some authors have called "post-identity politics" (Mouffe, 1992; Haraway, 1995). This points to the fact that the fragmentation, incompleteness and plurality of emerging identities does not necessarily mean a loss in political capacity. Quite the opposite, by betting on partial or temporary identifications which articulate and connect us momentarily in common socio-technical projects means accepting cooperation and co-functioning between the heterogeneity of human -and non-human- singularities as the central productive element of political action.

Rejection of Teleological Action

Techno-activism shows us that there are other organizational forms which produce political effects and other subjects which are susceptible to engaging in political action. And as a consequence, it also redefines the notion of political action itself.

The classical concept of political action (Laclau & Mouffe, 1985) calls for deployment and engagement in teleological action programmes which are shared by a group. At the same time it calls for the need to establish a regulatory dimension in this action which should guide its development, ensuring proper compliance and equal engagement on the part of all those involved. Against this notion, techno-activism assumes that a new political subject, articulated in organizations which are not strictly hierarchical, does not aspire to the above. On the contrary, their objective is diffraction (Haraway, 1992). This means irruption,

transformation, and decomposition, opening up the status quo in a multitude of differentiated possibilities, even if this should be based on a miniscule feature or characteristic.

We argued above that techno-activism possesses the potential to reinvent the field of political action. This does not mean that its project is assured success and triumph. It simply implies that there is a new promise in our reality. Its success depends on all of us. And especially on the relationship that we establish with this atom that constructs, day by day, such reality: information. Our future depends on the contract we enter into with it.

CONCLUSION: THE INFORMATIONAL CONTRACT

Many centuries ago the growth of cities and nation-states forced us to rethink the basis of human relations. It was the era of the social contract. Two decades ago, ecological problems and environmental disasters led the philosopher Michel Serres to propose to the United Nations the need to think in-depth about our relationship with nature. He put forward to the world the need for a natural contract. Along similar lines the Free Software movement, in particular, and what we have called more generally techno-activism, point in the direction of a reflection on our relationship with information. They point to the possibility of an Information contract.

Contract is a word which comes from Latin and means "rope". Contracts are the ropes which connect, unite and tie up the conditions for a more convenient life. Just like the social and natural contracts the Information contract aspires to lay down the conditions for a more liveable world. By considering the practices and ways of life which tell us, precisely, of how what is given *may* be another distinct thing. We consider there are three great issues on its agenda.

Firstly it would redefine the notion of technology itself. Habitual political practices usually use a completely "technocratic" concept of the political-technological relationship. This understands that the former is merely a set of values and projects which the latter materializes as a mere tool at its service, drive belt which does not produce any distortion and represents a true picture. In the face of this concept, it is possible to vindicate an image of technology as a poetic and creative dimension, a mediator (Latour, 1999, 2002). Constitutive of what we are constituted by what we do. In fact, "what we call "technologies are the ways of ordering our world" (Winner, 1987).

The Information contract shows us that we have always been faced by a process of mutual domestication between the human and the technological the result of which erases all traces of any fiction about independent and alien origins. Technology is incorporated into our routines and everyday habits, of course, but these are also transformed and adapted by the artefacts which surround us.

The second issue deals with a set of principles which recognise that information allows us to establish connections between absolutely heterogeneous entities, which are multiple and different from each other (between humans and non- humans, machines and organisms, lay persons and experts, physical things and virtual things, local and global…). Such hybridisation frees us from the modern dichotomies which have so marked our knowledge and social practice. Here we are referring to the individual-group, masculine-feminine, human-technological, culture-nature tensions, etc. The mixture, the absence of clear limits, rather than a problem of functioning, would operate as a preventative mechanism against totalitarian temptations. As Haraway (1991, p. 254) argues:

"The cyborg is our ontology, it provides us with our politics…" "its struggle is against perfect contamination, against the single code which translates all meanings perfectly. It insists on noise and supports pollution, taking delight in the illegitimate fusions of animal and machine"

Lastly we would recognise that our relationship with information, as in the political proposal of Free Software, produces constitutive affirmative potential that is, it allows groups, proposals and ideas to emerge, which, in their creative character, pose a challenge to the market's regulatory operations and the global economy. Creation is subversion, a challenge and a transformation of the status quo. But it should not be understood as an anti-power operation or reactive contra-power, but rather it talks of overwhelming power. In the same way we should not think that the Information contract rejects technology, the law or the global situation… No way! Its proposals are simpler: our relationship with information allows for the creation of and generation of more liveable worlds from within the limits marked by the aforementioned.

In its desiderata, the Information contract states that it does not promise utopia, something unreachable, a brave new world. It simply argues that social change and transformation do not depend on State power or globality, or on thinking of the future as a promise (communist perspective) nor a disaster (post-modern Apocalypse perspective). It depends, although it may seem somewhat insignificant, on understanding the creative potential of our everyday relationship with information. And the experience of Free Software is a good example of this.

REFERENCES

Callén, B. (2006). *Tecnología…política hecha por otros medios. Una comprensión del tecnoactivismo desde Riereta.net*. Universitat Autònoma de Barcelona, Proyecto de investigación para doctorado.

Foucault, M. (1975). *Vigilar y Castigar*. Madrid: Siglo XXI.

Foucault, M. (1976). *Historia de la sexualidad: La voluntad de saber*. Madrid: Siglo XXI.

González-Barahona, J. M. (2004). El software como servicio. O de cómo producir programas libres y no morir en el intento. En V. Matellán et al. (Eds.), *Sobre Free Software. Compilación de ensayos sobre Free Software. Grupo de Sistemas y Comunicaciones*. Madrid: Universidad Rey Juan Carlos.

González-Barahona, J. M. (2004). La imparcialidad de los estados y la industria del software. En V. Matellán et al. (Eds.), *Sobre Free Software. Compilación de ensayos sobre Free Software. Grupo de Sistemas y Comunicaciones*. Madrid: Universidad Rey Juan Carlos.

González-Barahona, J. M. (2004). Free Software, monopolios y otras yerbas. En V. Matellán et al. (Eds.), *Sobre Free Software. Compilación de ensayos sobre Free Software. Grupo de Sistemas y Comunicaciones*. Madrid: Universidad Rey Juan Carlos.

Haraway, D. (1991). *Ciencia, Cyborg y mujeres. La reinvención de la naturaleza*. Madrid: Ediciones Cátedra.

Haraway, D. (1992). Las promesas de los monstruos: Una política regeneradora para otros inapropiados/bles. *Política y Sociedad, 30,* 121–163.

Hardt, M., & Negri, A. (2000). *Imperio*. Barcelona: Paidós.

Holmes, B. (2003). *Vers une scission dans l'Empire*? Retrieved from http://infos.samizdat.net/article.php3?id_article=211

Laclau, E., & Mouffe, C. (1985). *Hegemonía y estrategia socialista: Hacia una radicalización de la democracia*. Madrid: Siglo XXI editores.

Latour, B. (1999). *La esperanza de Pandora*. Barcelona: Gedisa.

Latour, B. (2002). Morality and Technology: the end of the means. *Theory, Culture & Society, 19*(5-6), 247–260. doi:10.1177/026327602761899246

Levy, P. (1995). *Qué es lo virtual?* Barcelona: Paidós.

Mouffe, C. (1992). Feminism, citizenship and radical democratic politics. En J. Butler & J. Scott (Eds.), *Feminist theorize the political* (pp. 369-384).New York: Routledge.

Rullani, E. (2005). Capitalismo cognitivo: ¿Un déjà-vu? En O. Blondeau et al. (Eds.), *Capitalismo cognitivo, propiedad intelectual y creación colectiva*. Madrid: Traficantes de sueños.

Serres, M. (1994). *Atlas*. Madrid: Cátedra.

Virno, P. (1994). *Virtuosismo y revolución, la acción política en la época del desencanto*. Madrid: Traficantes de Sueños.

Webgrafía (n.d.). Retrieved from http://www.gnu.org/gnu/manifesto.html

Whitehead, A. N. (1925). *Process and reality*. New York: Free Press.

Winner, L. (1987). *La Ballena y el reactor: Una búsqueda de los límites en la era de la alta tecnología*. Barcelona: Gedisa.

This work was previously published in International Journal of Technoethics, Volume 1, Issue 2, edited by Rocci Luppicini, pp. 27-36, copyright 2010 by IGI Publishing (an imprint of IGI Global).

Section 4
New Trends in Technoethics

Chapter 17
Shaping the Ethics of an Emergent Field:
Scientists' and Policymakers' Representations of Nanotechnologies

Alison Anderson
University of Plymouth, UK

Alan Petersen
Monash University, Australia

ABSTRACT

Nanotechnologies present significant new challenges for the study of technoethics. While they are surrounded by high expectations there is considerable uncertainty about their impact. Discussions about their likely ethical implications have often assumed that ethical issues and standpoints are relatively clear. The commonly held narrow utilitarian conception of benefits versus risks tends to overlook broader issues concerning the operation of power in problem definition, unimagined or unknown effects, and accountability. Drawing upon data from a recent UK-based study, this article examines how scientists' and policymakers' representations of nanotechnologies contribute to shaping thinking about the 'ethics' of this field. It suggests that their particular framing of the field is likely to constrain debate on a range of important matters in need of urgent deliberation, including the direction of current research efforts and whether the investments in particular lines of research are likely to bring about the promised economic and social benefits or have deleterious impacts. Overall, the study found that most of the respondents were optimistic about the perceived benefits of nanotechnologies and sought to distance their work from wider non-technical questions. Scientists and policymakers, it is argued, need to reflect much more upon their own assumptions and consider how these may influence the trajectory of technology development and public responses.

DOI: 10.4018/978-1-4666-1773-5.ch017

INTRODUCTION

New and emergent technologies invariably give rise to questions about their 'risks' and 'ethics'. This is no less the case with nanotechnologies. Hailed by their proponents as constituting the next Industrial Revolution, nanotechnologies are seen as poised to revolutionize almost every sector of industry. Notoriously difficult to define 'nanotechnology' involves the design and manipulation of material at the atomic or molecular level. However, among scientists, it is generally agreed that nanotechnology is neither a new nor a single technology; hence, the generally preferred pluralized term (Kjølberg & Wickson, 2007; Wood et al., 2007). The definitional ambiguity and multiplicity of the technologies poses a considerable challenge for those concerned with understanding their ethical implications. Assessing the implications of any technology or spectrum of technologies assumes that there exists some level of agreement among stakeholders about the nature of the technologies and their applications. According to a common conceptualization, the potentiality and novelty of nanotechnologies is seen to arise from their future convergence with other technologies, including biotechnologies, digital technologies and neurotechnologies. As the Royal Society and Royal Academy acknowledged, in their much cited 2004 report, *Nanoscience and Nanotechnologies: Opportunities and Uncertainties*, 'convergence probably presents some of the biggest uncertainties [about nanotechnologies], with respect to what is genuinely plausible and when new technologies might actually come into use' (RS/RAE, 2004: 54). Since the nature and timing of this convergence cannot be foreseen, one cannot be certain about the implications of nanotechnologies in the future. Nanotechnologies are surrounded by considerable expectations about what they will deliver but these expectations may not be fulfilled (at least within envisaged timelines) for a range of reasons - economic, political and social. The more radical visions of nanotechnologies (both utopian and dystopian) which shape many current debates deny the long term, incremental and unpredictable nature of most technology innovations (Wood et al., 2008). Technologies are likely to develop in directions unimagined by scientists or to be taken up and employed by 'users' in unanticipated ways. However, despite these definitional ambiguities and uncertainties, discussions about the ethical or likely ethical implications of nanotechnologies have often proceeded as though ethical issues and standpoints are relatively clear. Views range from those who confidently proclaim that nanotechnologies raise no novel ethical questions to those who see the implications as being potentially profound – often reflecting commentators' different experiences and evaluations of past technology developments.

As key actors and stakeholders in the process of nanotechnology development, scientists and science policymakers play a major role in establishing the social definition of nanotechnologies, including their 'benefits' and 'risks'. Together, they develop the knowledge and the framework of expectations that shape future policy and action. In turn, the question of how nanotechnologies are publically represented shapes their future – the research and roles in which they will be engaged - and thus they can be seen to have a vested interest in particular portrayals of this field. They contribute significantly to the ethical framing of nanotechnologies through the particular visions that they bring to this field and through the ways they articulate the relationship between technologies and society in their publications and other forums. As cultural histories of science and technology reveal, technologies are always developed with particular users and uses in mind, albeit this may not always be explicit in research programs or policy decisions (Hård & Jamison, 2005). Given their social standing as producers of knowledge and their privileged access to the media and other public forums, scientists are strategically positioned to impose their definitions of the nature and significance of technologies. Likewise, policymakers play a key role in shaping the trajectory of technology development through their decisions affecting funding of research and the regulatory environment. However, scientists' and policymakers' current conceptualisations of nanotechnologies have been little researched to date.

Drawing upon data from a recent (and, to our knowledge, first) UK-based study involving surveys and interviews with scientists and policymakers who are involved in the nanotechnology field as researchers (of the science or of the toxicological and environmental impacts of technologies) or funders of research, respectively, this article examines how these actors' representations of nanotechnologies contribute to shaping thinking about the 'ethics' of this field. Specifically, it examines their representations of the nature, benefits and risks of nanotechnologies during a period in which the technologies have a low but growing public visibility. It is suggested that their particular framing of the field – their highlighting of certain issues and their neglect of others - is likely to restrict debate on a range of important matters urgently in need of deliberation, including the direction of current research efforts and whether the investments in particular lines of research are likely to deliver the promised economic and social benefits or have detrimental effects. Based on this analysis, in the conclusion we offer some observations for the developing field of nanoethics.

NANOETHICS

In recent years, 'nanoethics' has rapidly grown as an area of academic study, evidenced by the launch of a journal of the same name and a growing number of books on this topic over recent years (e.g. Allhoff et al., 2007; Allhoff & Lin, 2006; Allhoff & Lin, 2008; Bennett-Woods, 2008; Hunt & Mehta, 2006; Preston, 2006; Schummer & Baird, 2006). One of the key issues preoccupying policymakers,

ethicists, social and natural scientists alike has been how best and when to engage publics in discussions about nanotechnologies, including their various applications and implications. For many scientists and policymakers who are keen to exploit the potential of nanotechnologies, fears about a potential GM style backlash and the resulting decline in public confidence and trust has contributed to efforts to engage publics early on. Such anxieties have contributed towards funding bodies (such as the US National Science Foundation (NSF) and the European Parliament's sixth and seventh framework programmes) allocating budgets for research into social and ethical issues in this area (see Kjølberg & Wickson, 2007). Also there have been limited attempts to develop corporate social responsibility in this area (see Lee & Jose, 2008). In particular, concerns have been raised about privacy, surveillance, human enhancement and issues of justice and equity (see Hunt & Mehta, 2006). However, identifying specific ethical issues is itself a matter of controversy (Allhoff et al., 2007). One of the key challenges in assessing the 'ethics' of nanotechnologies is that technologies are expected to have a wide range of applications each of which is likely to have its own array of benefits and risks (see Anderson et al., 2009). The very definition of nanotechnologies involves ethical and political dimensions; it can influence what is deemed significant and what is ignored, affecting policy decisions, public concerns and research funding developments (UNESCO, 2006).

In Grunwald's (2005) view, which is widely held, nanotechnologies pose few completely new ethical questions that have not previously been raised in relation to other emergent technologies. A corollary is that nanotechnology governance may then involve the utilization of the same regulatory mechanisms used for other technologies; for example the establishment of protocols to protect privacy, regulations to minimize physical harms, acknowledgement of rights to access, and so on. However, nanotechnologies may be seen as distinctive in their complex, trans-disciplinary nature, and in the potential to lead to novel outcomes as both 'enabling' and 'disruptive' technologies (see Ach & Siep, 2006). As with biotechnologies, some applications involve control over life (in terms of nanomedicine), but nanotechnologies have an incredibly diverse array of applications stemming from many different scientific disciplines resulting in everyday consumer products. There are already a range of products on the market containing engineered nanoparticles including: sunscreens; cosmetics; golf balls; tennis rackets; textiles; computer hard drives; and paints. Indeed at the time of writing, according to the Project on Emerging Technologies inventory of nanotechnology-based products, there are over 800 products located in 21 countries around the world (Woodrow Wilson, 2009). Despite this, as experts themselves acknowledge (e.g. RS/RAE, 2004), there is considerable lack of knowledge about the potential effects of nanoparticles on human health and the environment. Increasing numbers of people are likely to come into contact with nanotechnologies in the course of everyday life, but they generally lack awareness that such products involve the use of nanomaterials (Sparrow, 2009).

In their 2004 report, the Royal Society and Royal Academy of Engineering emphasised the challenges in assessing the implications of nanotechnologies because of their 'upstream' nature. They are 'upstream' in a number of senses. Firstly, many of the significant decisions about funding and R&D infrastructure have yet to occur and therefore require broad public debate. Secondly, as mentioned, the social and ethical implications are hypothetical at present and depend upon how technologies converge in the future. And, thirdly, public awareness of nanotechnologies is currently low and thus publics' views are potentially open to various influences (RS/RAE, 2004: 64). Despite acknowledgement by these major science organisations of the need for increased public dialogue and debate during the technologies' emergent phase, however, thus far discussion about the so-

cial and ethical implications of nanotechnologies has tended to be couched in a narrow utilitarian framework of cost-benefit analysis which overlooks wider issues of unforeseen/unknown effects, the exercise of power in problem definition and accountability (Kurma & Besley, 2008; Petersen et al., 2007; Wilsdon & Willis, 2004). This approach assumes that identified problems can simply be dealt with through further research and enhanced regulatory procedures, thereby downplaying the complexities and uncertainties of nanotechnologies and the involvement of vested interests in certain 'framings' of issues (Anderson et al., 2008). Scientists and science policymakers thus far have not reflected on how their own particular framing of the field may shape how information is communicated and how publics may understand and respond to issues. This failure to reflect on their own assumptions, we suggest, may not only work against publics' deep understanding of the issues but may ultimately undermine trust in science.

THE STUDY

Our study aimed to explore how science and science policymakers portray the future applications of nanotechnologies as applied to medicine and environmental sustainability through surveys (involving a combination of multiple and fixed choice questions) and in-depth, semi-structured interviews. These two areas of nanotechnology application are expected to be significant and are those which are seen by many commentators to pose the most immediate risks to health and community wellbeing. Questionnaires explored views on nanotechnologies, benefits and risks, timelines for applications in the above fields, and self-rating of knowledge and of risks. Some questions allowed more open-ended responses; for example, 'what do you believe is driving government policy?' The interviews explored issues raised in the questionnaires in more depth (e.g. 'In the survey you mentioned that....Do you still agree with this answer?') and allowed respondents scope to raise issues not covered elsewhere in the questionnaire or interview. To date, there has been very little research into the views of scientists and policymakers working in the nanotech field employing mixed methods. Most studies have been based upon questionnaire surveys alone, which are useful in providing a broad insight (e.g. McGinn, 2008) but are limited in providing in-depth understanding of perspectives. The semi-structured interviews allowed us scope to explore respondents' views in depth, which we believe is important given the complex and uncertain nature of the issues. In the first instance, respondents were contacted through an international conference, 'Environmental Effects of Nanoparticles and Nanomaterials', sponsored by a number of UK government organisations and funding bodies and held in London in 2006. A colleague from our university's science faculty who helped organise this event assisted us in gaining access to respondents. Hard copies of the questionnaire were distributed to all conference delegates and email versions were sent to all non-attendees listed on the conference programme, resulting in a total of 75 individuals in all. Of these, responses were elicited from 39 people representing a response rate of 52%. In addition to this, an electronic version of the questionnaire was subsequently distributed to the Chemistry Innovation Knowledge Transfer Network (CIKTN) which resulted in a further 30 responses, and one further response was gained from a researcher/analyst for an advocacy group involved in public engagement activities. In total, then, responses were elicited from 70 scientists and science policymakers working in the nano-technologies field. Most were scientists, relatively new to the area (5 years or less experience of working with nanotechnologies), and the majority (51 of the 70) were based in the UK (see Petersen and Anderson, 2007 and Anderson et al. 2009 for further details). In addition to the survey, in-depth interviews were conducted with a sub-sample of 20 individuals who agreed to discuss their

responses in greater detail. Given that the sample was relatively small and most participants were quite new to the field the interpretation of the findings should be viewed with some caution. Also, given the recruitment methods described above, it needs to be borne in mind that the sample was likely to be skewed towards those with an interest in nanoparticle risk and toxicity. Nevertheless, this study represents one of the first surveys of scientists' and policymakers' attitudes towards nanotechnologies to have been conducted in the UK and provides an interesting insight into the representations of these individuals at an early stage of the technologies' development.

FINDINGS

Optimism

Overall there was considerable optimism among our respondents about the perceived benefits of nanotechnologies. When asked in the question-naire, 'Are there particular applications which are/will be especially beneficial?' 55 of 63 (ie 87 per cent) answered in the affirmative. The majority (53) were able to cite specific benefits in a number of areas. For example, our survey responses included: 'disease prevention and cure, energy independence, homeland security, measuring environmental pollutants and change in ecosystems'; 'Energy: improved solar cells, energy storage and transmission, solid state lighting, energy generation...'; 'drugs, pigments, chemical reactions'; 'sensors, medical applications, general reduction of chemical usage'; 'environmental remediation, industrial lubricants, self-cleaning glass'. This optimism was strongly evident in the interviews, with one policymaker commenting:

I'm very optimistic, I think, that this is a technology which is going places. I think there's a lot of concerted effort around the world to make sure that the implication work keeps up with ap-

plication work and that, you know, not too many things happen or products are developed and put into the market without due consideration of the implications.... We've just got to hope that, you know, something doesn't happen, an incident, you know, to turn public opinion against, you know, nanotechnology and generally brand the area as, you know, something similar to GM. (Science policy advisor, hazard/risk assessment policy development)

On the other hand, virtually all (69) acknowledged that risks were associated with nanotechnologies. When we asked them whether they thought there were applications that were 'especially risky' of those who responded (60 out of 70), 52 or 87 per cent responded 'yes'. Most of these responses tended to cluster around the risks of inhalation or ingestion of nanoparticles through the manufacturing process or consumption of products containing nanomaterials (including sunscreens; aerosols; foods; medical implants; cosmetics; fuel additives and the remediation of ground water). This emphasis is not altogether surprising given the background of the sample and their interests in these fields. As would be expected, their perceptions of risk reflected their position within the science production/consumption/assessment cycle. Those working in the field of risk assessment tended to have particularly strong views on the nature and challenges of determining risk.

Explicit references to ethical issues, as in the following quote, however, were rare:

... the potential benefits in this area of use of nanotechnology will be so big that there will be a lot of pressure on the use of it I think because if we can treat cancer before then, I think we will do it.... There's an area here where we might come into some ethical considerations about whether it should be used or not used.... There is this consideration about OK in this that we may be damaging some things in the environment so you

put human health above the environmental health, and I want to underline really that this could raise some difficult questions about should we use the technology before it's actually, before the side effects are known? (Scientist, environmental risk assessment)

Respondents, in the main, expressed strong confidence in the management or regulation of risks. For example, another scientist, despite stating that there could be public anxiety over nanotechnology in food production, responded:

The benefits will outweigh the risks because I mean we're in a situation where governments are aware that this is an emerging technology, therefore everything is in place to be able to, with accumulated knowledge, assess risk in the appropriate way and so I think that any risks should be well managed and the benefits will definitely outweigh the risks. We're in a good position and I think there's innumerable possibilities for this sort of technology and materials. (Scientist, environment and fisheries)

A similar view was:

I think the potential benefits outweigh the risks... my view is that everything we do you have to manage the risk successfully, then I think the benefits outweigh the risks. (Scientist, physical chemist)

Given the focus of the study, on the representation of nanotechnologies rather than ethical implications, it is perhaps not surprising that ethical issues were rarely raised by respondents. However, as most questions focused on views on 'benefits' and 'risks', and respondents had scope to raise any ethical concerns that they may have had, in both the surveys and the interviews, it is surprising how infrequently such issues were raised. It should be noted, too, that this study occurred in the aftermath of a period of intensive media coverage of nanotechnology-related issues

(Anderson, et al., 2005) and the much publicized and discussed Royal Society and Royal Academy of Engineering report, which included reference to a range of social and ethical questions and concerns which surrounded nanotechnologies.

Conceptions of Risk

In both the questionnaires and the interviews we were careful not to impose any definition of 'benefit' or 'risk'. We hoped that conceptions of these would be revealed in the responses. Although, as mentioned, most respondents were optimistic about the future of nanotechnologies, most did acknowledge risks although, as these latter two comments reveal, in the main, the benefits were seen to outweigh the risks. Risks were seen as both biophysical *and* social risks. The former included, for example, 'unknown properties of known elements and compounds', 'limited knowledge of behaviour of manufactured nanoparticles in the environment', 'direct human exposure via the lung', 'dermal exposure via broken skin', 'release of nanoparticles during their production'. Interestingly, however, a number of respondents mentioned *without prompting* that *social responses* posed a risk. In their questionnaire response to 'what are these risks?' (following the question 'Do you see any risks associated with nanotechnologies?', with a tick box 'yes'/ 'no' response), one noted:

Public misunderstanding of nanotechnologies, leading to general mistrust in the media, withdrawal of funding for nanotechnologies, and a knock-on effect for UK scientific R&D and the UK economy. (Scientist, surface science)

A similar response was:

Irrational overhyping of the benefits and risks. Evidence-based decision making should be key. Media, politicians, seekers of grant money can all

cause problems. (Scientist, colloid and interface science)

An economic policy manager with a background in chemistry responded to the same question:

Misunderstanding of the science by the general public. An outcry similar to that seen for genetic modification. (Policymaker, economic policies)

For a prominent academic who had been involved in developing companies in the area:

The biggest risk is a witch-hunt mentality by pressure groups that are unwilling to engage in finding out the facts! (Scientist, engineering science)

References to 'public misunderstanding' and 'irrational overhyping', in the two first comments, would seem to reflect adherence to a deficit model of public understanding, whereby supposed public 'ignorance' and adverse reaction is seen to require more or better 'education' – a position which has been explicitly rejected by the Royal Society and Royal Academy of Engineering (2004: 66). Further, the last comments also reflect this position (e.g. reference to 'finding out the facts') and, in addition, would seem to dismiss pressure groups' concerns as illegitimate. Although comments such as these were not majority views among our respondents they do highlight worries that some scientists have about public responses that have been voiced elsewhere, such as in science reports (RS/RAE, 2004: Chapter 6).

Policy Drivers

To gain further insight into scientists' and policymakers' perceptions of the factors shaping the development of nanotechnologies and consequently the context of their own work, we asked them what they see as 'driving' government policy. The survey and interview responses revealed that economic factors and the striving for 'market advantage' as well as political factors were seen as significant influences. A typical response from a scientist was: 'If you look at government as a whole...I think it is short-sighted economical benefitsthat is really driving it.' (Scientist, PhD student, nanotechnology risk assessment). As another scientist explained:

Nano is now used on the high streets and we have the ipod nano and all these kind of things, so it's entered the common psyche and therefore if it's in the common psyche it's of interest to governments, because at the end of the day people vote and so in terms of international prestige there is effectively a race on now in terms of how much nanotechnology your country can develop, because of the obvious advantages of having nanochips, nanobatteries, nanofuel cells etc and the huge market advantage that would give your companies if your country developed them. (Scientist, junior research fellow, electro-chemistry of nanomaterials)

Indeed, most of our respondents saw the knowledge-based economy as powering government policy in this area. For example:

If we have the technology to do something then we hold the key to that technology. Therefore we can make money out of our knowledge and understanding... to develop hi-tech, high-value companies, if you like, that perhaps produce very little mess-wise but have a lot of value because what they're producing is what the rest of the world wants... one of the saving goals for the West is to develop a high-value, high-tech economy as opposed to mass manufacturing. (Scientist, synthesis of nanomaterials)

The sustainability agenda was seen by most of our respondents as influencing the agenda and contributing to the attractiveness of nanotechnology development, suggesting the importance of the wider political context. For example, a science policy advisor stated:

That is a major driver these days for policy and so if nanotechnologies are likely to lead to greater sustainability then clearly, you know, our policy would be very much to drive those forward, encourage those developments. That's the reason why, you know, [department's name] actually got involved in the benefits study because, you know, we're an environmental department and concerned about sustainability, so it seemed that we should do a bit more than just, you know, concentrate on the hazards and risks, but try and do a little bit to see how benefits to the environment could accrue through the use of nanotechnologies. (Science policy advisor, hazard/risk assessment policy development)

These 'drivers' of innovations were mostly presented in a matter-of-fact rather than in a critical way. There were few references to the implications of such imperatives. For example, there was little reference to resulting divisions between communities and nations arising from uneven development or uptake of technologies – a concern that has been raised by ethicists and social scientists in recent years (e.g. Hunt, 2006). One of our respondents did however mention a potential nano-divide arising from this economic 'driver':

For our Western countries it's only further progress in technology which can maintain the high standard of living which we have here with respect to other countries... and that's why nanotechnology's one of those areas which can have a lot of benefits, especially if you're thinking about the energy area, you know, we are very dependent on energy... the problem is maybe the divide between the countries who are not able to invest now later will increase (Scientist, Head, research centre, materials science)

Are Nanotechnologies Novel?

Proponents of nanotechnologies emphasise the novelty of nanotechnologies. It is these novel qualities that are seem to provide the expected innovations – the creation of super-hard, ultra-light materials, new capabilities (e.g. in drug delivery, energy storage), miniaturisation of components (e.g. in computers), and so on – that will deliver substantial economic and social benefits in the future. However, some doubts have been expressed about these claims to novelty. Indeed, the Royal Society and Royal Academy of Engineering question this claim, in their 2004 report, where it is noted that 'nanoscience and nanotechnologies are not new' and that scientists have been working with molecules at the nanoscale for decades, for example in computing and chemistry (RS-RAE, 2004: 5). Further, as mentioned, uncertainties surround the expected applications since these will be reliant on the merging of nanotechnologies with other technologies and how and when this will occur is unknown. Since the veracity of these claims to novelty is likely to influence decisions affecting policies and programs that will affect communities and entire societies they should be open to critical scrutiny.

There is evidence to suggest that some existing technologies have been 're-branded' by scientists as 'nanotechnologies', to help gain a public profile for their work and to help secure funding in what is seen as an increasingly lucrative area of research. Some of the scientists we spoke to informed us of this fact, 'off the record'. An interesting observation on the 're-branding' of research and the role of the media in giving visibility to the field was provided by a research fellow working in the field of electrochemistry, in their questionnaire response:

The word 'nano' is to government policy what 'micro' was twenty years ago (think '--chip', '--processor', '--sensor'. There is a lot of hype and 'potential' opportunities - things that grab any government's eye, especially when the media put the buzz words into the public domain and common psyche, but there is also a lot of investment and job creation opportunities.... (Scientist, junior research fellow, electro-chemistry of nanomaterials)

The question of how the technologies are portrayed by scientists during the early phase of their public visibility – as 'beneficial', 'novel', 'revolutionary', and so on - is very likely to shape subsequent responses to them by the media, publics, and policymakers. That there may be vested interests involved in the promotion of particular views of nanotechnologies was rarely mentioned by our respondents. Comments revealed little evident reflection on the dangers of presenting an (overly) optimistic view – a 'positive spin' - on the potentialities of nanotechnologies. The following, cynical view, expressed by one of our respondents, was unusual:

They're not going to choose people, especially as the big companies hold so much sway over them, they're not going to go and then court a load of scientists who have the opposite view. They, they're going to go and find the scientists that think that everything's wonderful and then use them as the example of why nanotechnology holds no worries for us in the future... When we find things that come up against what's politically expedient it's very easy to write a few scientists off as cranks. Look at the way... the global warming people were treated... like twenty years ago, thirty years ago, just fringe idiots. (Scientist, environmental microbiologist)

In fact, there was a perception among the scientists that the benefits of nanotechnologies had not been publicized very much in the UK and the emphasis had largely been on the risks. For example, one respondent, who worked at the interface of science and policy, stated:

... I think that the benefits associated with the applications in medical and public health have probably not been promoted terribly widely within the UK, or at least I haven't seen an awful lot of easy, well-communicated pieces of information and I think there's a lot about managing the risks of these technologies that is about understanding benefits as well as risks and I think it would be timely to see some of those benefits being described a bit more ... the energy agenda is very big and is set, I think, to grow, particularly in the context of climate change and nano has a big part to play in that (Scientist, environmental regulation)

For our respondents, then, nanotechnologies were mostly viewed in an uncritical, embracing way. The scientists and policymakers surveyed and interviewed tended to adopt a narrow conception of the ethical dimensions of nanotechnologies, neglecting to mention 'downsides' of developments apart from bio-physical risks and adverse social responses. Their comments revealed that their main concern was with the public acceptance of the technologies. Such findings are in line with other surveys of nanotechnology scientists in the US which suggest that those working in the field typically display some sensitivity towards ethics when directly questioned about the ethical implications of their work, and accepting the general principle of ethical responsibility, but tending to view themselves as relatively uninformed about such matters (Berne, 2006; McGinn, 2008). For example, McGinn found that only 16 per cent (167) of his sample of nanoscientists strongly agreed that 'there are significant ethical issues related to NT' (2008: 104). However, the majority (76 per cent) strongly agreed with the proposition that 'when a nanotechnology researcher has good reason to believe that her/his work will be applied in society so as to pose a risk of significant harm to human beings' they have an ethical responsibility to alert pertinent authorities to the potential dangers (2008: 114). Similarly, Berne (2004) found that her respondents tended to draw a clear line between

scientific discovery (their own scientific work) and the application of scientific knowledge (over which they feel relatively powerless). Indeed they tended to view scientific areas other than their own as having the most ethical dilemmas. Such responses suggest that scientists are either 'ethically blind'- perhaps due to a trained incapacity to recognise the ethical dimensions of their work – or seek to distance their work from its broader (non-technical) implications, perhaps because they do not wish to confront the uncomfortable truth that their work is inherently value laden. The latter seems likely given the self representation of science as 'objective' and 'value-free'.

CONCLUSION

The question of how scientists and policymakers represent nanotechnologies is a profoundly 'ethical' one since it has the potential to shape thinking and action at many levels. An overly optimistic view of the technical capabilities may strongly influence research agendas and funding decisions and lead to the downplaying of potential implications, such as the creation of socio-economic divisions and investment in areas of dubious public benefit. With the current public visibility of nanotechnologies being low but growing there is a real opportunity to address social and ethical issues at an early stage in the research and development process. In light of concerns about the potential for a crisis in public confidence in science to occur (e.g. House of Lords Select Committee on Science and Technology (2000)), increasing emphasis has been placed upon engaging publics during the early stages of technology development, particularly in the UK. However it is questionable as to how far efforts to move public engagement 'upstream' have genuinely opened up wide-ranging debate about the implications of nanotechnology among a diverse range of publics (see Anderson et al., 2009; Petersen et al., 2008). Given the complexity of the science, coupled with low public awareness of nanotechnologies and their potential applications and impacts, it is difficult to see how knowledge can be built completely from the bottom-up (Wood et al., 2008). Nevertheless, analyses of 'risk' need to be conducted in an inclusive and transparent way. A preliminary study in the US suggests that industry and university scientists are the most trusted sources of information for the public (Scheufele et al., 2007). As key authoritative voices in the nanotechnology debate, industry and scientists play a significant role in the framing of issues, particularly in relation to the benefits and risks of technologies. Together with policymakers they have a responsibility to ensure that publics are informed about the nature and potential diverse impacts of innovations in the nanotechnologies field.

Nanotech therefore raises crucial issues of responsibility, accountability and ownership. Key questions that need to be asked include: What do people need to know about the potential dangers of nanotechnologies? Who will be most affected by developments? Who is likely to own and control the technologies? Who is likely to benefit and who is most likely to be disadvantaged by particular innovations? And crucially, as Lewenstein points out, who should decide what becomes defined as a social and ethical issue in the first place? (Lewenstein, 2006) It is essential to recognize that many social actors are involved in shaping nanotechnologies – not just scientists and policymakers but also industry, regulators, NGOs, citizens and the media (Johnson, 2007; Schummer, 2004). Science and technology exist within a social context and the power to define what may be viewed as a 'social and ethical' issue is critical (Lewenstein, 2006). Efforts to separate social and ethical issues from 'pure scientific' ones are problematic as they are likely to obscure the way in which power operates across a broad range of areas (Anderson et al., 2008). Thus, as Lewenstein observes, '… we should be wary of the attempt to draw boundaries between (social

and ethical) issues and technical ones.' (2006:214) As Johnson argues:

Issues of distributive justice are fundamental to ethics and the field of nanoethics should be focused not just on how the benefits of nanotechnology get distributed but also whether resources should be put into the development of nanotechnology. The issue of distributive justice is not just a matter of who will benefit the most from the development of nanotechnology and who will be made worse off. It is also a matter of what problems can be solved with nanotechnology and what other problems need solving. (2007: 29)

Thus far, however, debate about the overall direction and broad implications of nanotechnology R&D has been limited and undertaken in a sustained way mostly by groups that are considered marginal to the policy agenda-setting area; principally NGOs. Where concerns have been voiced by influential actors, these have focused largely on bio-physical risks; namely, harms posed by manufactured nanoparticles (e.g. DEFRA, 2007). We contend that there is a need to broaden the terms of debate about nanotechnologies to include questioning the assumptions of scientists, policymakers, and other key players (e.g. business groups), whose views are often taken for granted in discussions about public engagement and dialogue. If scientists and policymakers are serious about broadening the agenda for debate about nanotechnologies they need to remain open to the possibility that the representations that prevail may not always be ones that accord with their own interests.

ACKNOWLEDGMENT

The authors gratefully acknowledge the support of the British Academy who funded this research (grant no: SG-44284) and Dr Rachel Torr, who provided the research assistance.

REFERENCES

Ach, J. S., & Siep, L. (Eds.). (2006). *Nano-bio-ethics. Ethical dimensions of nanobiotechnology.* Münster: NoE Nano2Life.

Allhoff, F., & Lin, P. (2006). What's so special about nanotechnology and nanoethics? *The International Journal of Applied Philosophy, 20*(2), 179–190.

Allhoff, F., & Lin, P. (Eds.). (2008). *Nanotechnology and society: Current and emerging issues.* Dordrecht: Springer.

Allhoff, F., Lin, P., Moor, J., & Weckert, J. (2007). *Nanoethics: The social and ethical dimensions of nanotechnology.* Hoboken, NJ: Wiley.

Anderson, A., Allan, S., Petersen, A., & Wilkinson, C. (2008). Nanoethics: News media and the shaping of public agendas. In R. Luppicini & R. Adell (Ed.), *Handbook of research on technoethics* (pp. 373-90). Hershey, New York: Idea Group Publishing.

Anderson, A., Petersen, A., Wilkinson, C., & Allan, S. (2005). The framing of nanotechnologies in the British newspaper press. *Science Communication, 27*(2), 200–220. doi:10.1177/1075547005281472

Anderson, A., Petersen, A., Wilkinson, C., & Allan, S. (2009). *Nanotechnology, risk and communication.* Houndmills: Palgrave Macmillan.

Bennett-Woods, D. (2008). *Nanotechnology, ethics and society.* Florida: CRC.

Berne, R. W. (2006). *Nanotalk: Conversations with scientists and engineers about ethics, meaning, and belief in the development of nanotechnology.* Mahwah, NJ: Lawrence Erlbaum Associates.

Department for Environment. Food and Rural Affairs (DEFRA) (2007). *Characterising the potential risks posed by engineered nanoparticles, Second government research report.* London: DE-FRA. Retrieved May 5, 2009, from: http://www.defra.gov.uk/environment/nanotech/research/pdf/

Grunwald, A. (2005). Nanotechnology – a new field of ethical inquiry? *Science and Engineering Ethics, 11*(2), 187–201. doi:10.1007/s11948-005-0041-0

Hård, M., & Jamison, A. (2005). *Hubris and hybrids: A cultural history of technology and science.* New York: Routledge.

House of Lords Select Committee on Science and Technology. (2000). *Science and society: Third report.* London: HMSO.

Hunt, G. (2006). The global ethics of nanotechnology. In G. Hunt & M. Mehta (Ed.), *Nanotechnology: Risk, ethics and law* (pp. 183-95). London: Earthscan.

Hunt, G., & Mehta, M. (Eds.). (2006). *Nanotechnology: Risk, ethics and law.* London: Earthscan.

Johnson, D. G. (2007). Ethics and technology "in the making": An essay on the challenge of nanoethics. *NanoEthics, 1*(1), 21–30. doi:10.1007/s11569-007-0006-7

Kjølberg, K. L., & Wickson, F. (2007). Social and ethical interactions with nano: Mapping the early literature. *NanoEthics, 1*(2), 89–104. doi:10.1007/s11569-007-0011-x

Kuzma, J., & Besley, J. (2008). Ethics of risk analysis and regulatory review: From bio- to nanotechnology. *NanoEthics, 2*(2), 149–162. doi:10.1007/s11569-008-0035-x

Lee, R., & Jose, P. D. (2008). Self interest, self restraint and corporate responsibility for nanotechnologies: Emerging dilemmas for modern managers. *Technology Analysis and Strategic Management, 20*(1), 113–125. doi:10.1080/09537320701726775

Lewenstein, B. V. (2006). What counts as a social and ethical issue in nanotechnology? In J. Schummer & D. Baird (Ed.), *Nanotechnology challenges: Implications for philosophy, ethics and society* (pp. 201-16). London: World Scientific.

McGinn, R. (2008). Ethics and nanotechnology: Views of nanotechnology researchers. *Nano-Ethics*, *2*(2), 101–131. doi:10.1007/s11569-008-0040-0

Mnyusiwalla, A., Daar, A. S., & Singer, P. A. (2003). Mind the gap: Science and ethics in nanotechnology. *Nanotechnology*, *14*, R9–R13. doi:10.1088/0957-4484/14/3/201

Petersen, A., & Anderson, A. (2007). A question of balance or blind faith?: Scientists' and science policymakers' representations of the benefits and risks of nanotechnologies. *NanoEthics*, *1*(3), 243–256. doi:10.1007/s11569-007-0021-8

Petersen, A., Anderson, A., Allan, S., & Wilkinson, C. (2008). Opening the black box: Scientists' views on the role of the news media in the nanotechnology debate. *Public Understanding of Science*. Published 1ˢᵗ October via Online First.

Petersen, A., Anderson, A., Wilkinson, C., & Allan, S. (2007). Nanotechnologies, risk and society *Health Risk & Society*, *9*(2), 117–124. doi:10.1080/13698570701306765

Retrieved April 17, 2009, from: http://pus.sage-pub.com/cgi/rapidpdf/0963662507084202v1, Preston, C. (2006). The promise and threat of nanotechnology: Can environmental ethics guide us? In J. Schummer & D. Baird (Ed.), *Nanotechnology challenges: Implications for philosophy, ethics and society* (pp. 217-48). London: World Scientific.

Royal Society and Royal Academy of Engineering RS/RAE. (2004). *Nanoscience and nanotechnologies: Opportunities and uncertainties report*. London: Royal Society.

Scheufele, D. A., Corley, E. A., Dunwoody, S., Shih, T., Hillback, E., & Guston, D. (2007). Scientists worry about some risks more than the public. *Nature Nanotechnology*, *2*(12), 732–734. doi:10.1038/nnano.2007.392

Schummer, J. (2004). Social and ethical implications of nanotechnology: Meanings, interest groups and social dynamics. *Hyle*, *8*(2), 56–87.

Schummer, J., & Baird, D. (Eds.). (2006). *Nanotechnology challenges: Implications for philosophy, ethics and society*. London: World Scientific.

Sparrow, R. (2009). The social impacts of nanotechnology: An ethical and political analysis. *Journal of Bioethical Inquiry*, *6*(1), 13–23. doi:10.1007/s11673-009-9139-4

UNESCO. (2006). *The ethics and politics of nanotechnology*. Paris: UNESCO. Retrieved April 17, 2009, from: http://unesdoc.unesco.org/images/0014/001459/145951e.pdf

Wilsdon, J., & Willis, R. (2004). *See-through science: Why public engagement needs to move upstream*. London: Demos.

Wood, S., Geldart, A., & Jones, R. (2008). Crystallizing the nanotechnology debate. *Technology Analysis and Strategic Management*, *20*(1), 13–27. doi:10.1080/09537320701726320

Wood, S., Jones, R., & Geldart, A. (2007). *Nanotechnology, from the science to the social: The social, ethical and economic aspects of the debate*. Swindon: Economic and Social Research Council. Retrieved May 16, 2008, from: http://www.esrcsocietytoday.ac.uk/ESRCInfoCentre/Images/ESRC_Nano07_tcm6-18918.pdf

Woodrow Wilson Project on Emerging Technologies. (2009). *Consumer products: An inventory of nanotechnology-based consumer products currently on the market*. Retrieved April 17, 2009, from: http://www.nanotechproject.org/inventories/consumer/

This work was previously published in International Journal of Technoethics, Volume 1, Issue 1, edited by Rocci Luppicini, pp. 32-44, copyright 2010 by IGI Publishing (an imprint of IGI Global).

Chapter 18
Transhumanism and Its Critics:
Five Arguments against a Posthuman Future

Keith A. Bauer
Jefferson College of Health Sciences, USA

ABSTRACT

Transhumanism is a social, technological, political, and philosophical movement that advocates the transformation of human nature by means of pharmacology, genetic manipulation, cybernetic modification, nanotechnology, and a host of other technologies. The aim of this movement is to increase physical and sensory abilities, augment intelligence and memory, and extend lifespan. After providing some background on transhumanism, its philosophical heritage, and its goals, the author looks at three arguments against transhumanism, arguing that they are unpersuasive and should be rejected. This paper presents two arguments against transhumanism that have merit. The first argument is an argument from justice that addresses the distribution of benefits and burdens for funding, developing, and employing enhancement technology. The second argument examines a significant assumption held by many transhumanists, namely, that there is an essential "human nature" that can be transcended.

INTRODUCTION: TECHNOETHICS AND TRANSHUMANISM

Technoethics is an intellectually broad and multi-professional field of study that is intentionally unrestricted to the examination of just one kind of technology, a singular profession, or particular ethical issue. Technoethicists are interested in the plethora of overlapping ethical and social issues found in, for example, computer ethics, engineering ethics, military ethics, bioethics, environmental ethics, nanoethics, and neuroethics. More generally, technoethicists are eager to explore the ever-changing relationships among humans and technology (e.g., ethical implications for life, social norms and values, education and work, politics and law, and the environment) that no one field of applied ethics can capture (Luppicini & Adell, 2008).

DOI: 10.4018/978-1-4666-1773-5.ch018

Specialization, of course, has its merits, but can lead to disparate and isolated silos of inquiry. This is particularly true when dealing with a highly faceted subject such as transhumanism. As a movement, transhumanism is "ecumenical," transcending professional affiliations and encompassing the broad and diverse use of technology. Transhumanists fully understand that we are in a new era of technologic convergence that will change human life as we know it. Technoethicists understand this as well (Roco & Bainbridge, 2002). For these reasons, the field of technoethics—its diversity of topics, disciplines, and research methodologies—is well situated to explore transhumanism as it should be explored.

The Values and Goals of Transhumanism

For transhumanists, science and technology are the stepping stones to a world where we will be stronger, smarter, disease free and possibly immortal. By means of science and technology, we will have the freedom to become more than human. In the future, we will be able to change and shape our own natures at will, to transcend ourselves physically, mentally, and emotionally. Through the power of science and technology, the choice to be or not to be human will be ours. This possible future may seem absurd to many, but for transhumanists it is their *raison de être* (Harris, 2007).

There are good reasons for transhumanists to be optimistic. For one thing, governments around the globe are investing billions of dollars to research the commercial, medical, and military applications of nanotechnology (Roco & Bainbridge, 2002). As of today, we are using nano-particles to make our clothes stain resistant, camouflage soldiers, and more importantly to identify and to treat some cancers. In the future, transhumanists expect nanobots to inhabit our bodies, continuously repairing damaged cells, tissues and organs,

as well as keeping our arteries free of plaque. A second reason for optimism is that biotech companies and governments have been working feverishly to develop genetic tests and therapies for various ailments, which could eventually lead to the rise of genetic enhancements (Stock, 2002). Third, the use of information and communication technology continues to grow exponentially. In medicine, implantable microchips and biosensors are now being used as prostheses for quadriplegics, allowing them to type and send email by means of electrical impulses transmitted directly from their brains to their computers (Viseu, 2003; Bauer, 2007). One day, it may be possible to have cell phone-like devices implanted within your skull. Transhumanists see a day when no cell phone is ever misplaced.

Contrary to the claims of its detractors, transhumanism is not a form of racial eugenics. In fact, transhumanists are categorically opposed to pseudoscience, racism, and authoritarianism. Second, transhumanism is not a religious movement or cult. Most transhumanists are non-theistic. Third, transhumanism is not a political movement in the narrow sense. Transhumanists range across the entire spectrum of political views. Rather, transhumanism is a broad movement that affirms the possibility and desirability of fundamentally altering the human condition through applied reason, especially by using technology to slow, if not eliminate, aging and to enhance human intellectual, physical, and psychological capacities (Bostrom, 2005).

Transhumanism's intellectual lineage is rooted in *humanism*, a naturalistic philosophy that rejects all supernaturalism and relies primarily upon reason, science, and technology to understand and improve the human condition (Herrick, 2005). Transhumanists are like humanists to the extent that they value and employ reason, science, and technology. Unlike humanists, transhumanists are not satisfied with the mere perfection of man; they strive to transcend humanity's physical and cognitive limitations in order to become *posthuman*. Strictly speaking, then, a transhuman is a transitional human taking the first steps towards becoming posthuman? A posthuman is a human descendant who has been augmented to such a degree as to be no longer a human, that is, no longer a member of the species *Homo sapiens*. As a posthuman, you would be smarter than any human genius. Your body, assuming you had one, would not be susceptible to disease and would not deteriorate with age. You would have a greatly expanded capacity to feel emotions and to experience pleasure, love, and artistic beauty. You would not need to feel tired, bored, or irritated about petty things. In short, transhumanists want to create a world that allows individuals to live longer, happier, and smarter lives where humans and posthumans peacefully coexist.

Some of the underlying beliefs and values governing the transhumanist movement include a pragmatic, "it can be done" attitude," respect for diversity, as well as moral consideration for the well-being of all sentient beings. Most importantly, transhumanists think citizens should have the option to enhance themselves so long as they do so in a thoughtful and informed manner. For transhumanists, "morphological freedom" requires citizens to assume associated responsibilities (Hughes, 2004). It is for this reason that transhumanists believe there should be continuous efforts to improve understanding and critical thinking by means of research, public debate, and a willingness to reexamine assumptions. If this approach is taken, there is, at least for transhumanists, neither hubris nor moral wrongdoing when "tampering with nature." By making its goals explicit and public, the transhumanist movement is in a better position to identify and use ethically appropriate means to achieve their goals as well as minimize the risk of unwanted consequences. Transhumanists want to take a rational, prudent, and ethically appropriate approach to choreographing our evolution as a species. The alternative is to let our species change by means of natural selection, which is random, haphazard, and willy-nilly. For transhumanists, it is simply irrational to leave our futures to chance.

THE ETHICAL CHALLENGE

The goal of becoming posthuman poses novel ethical challenges that are both disturbing and exhilarating, depending on your point of view. As Leon Kass (1971) remarked nearly 40 years ago when discussing the future of genetic manipulation, "engineering the engineer seems to differ in kind from engineering his engine" (p. 780). As we gradually move from designing our environments to designing the designers, it is important to see that our increasing ability to control our own evolution is not merely a technological development; it is the beginning of a philosophical sea change in which "human nature" becomes a product of our intelligent and purposeful designs. For transhumanists, our nature will be neither the result of random mutations nor a gift from God that is complete and static.

As would be expected, critics have very little good to say about the transhumanist enterprise. Some claim that, since it is impossible for transhumanists to overcome the daunting scientific and technologic obstacles that stand in their way, transhumanism is, at its worst, a quixotic fantasy. For these critics, transhumanism is not a threat. Other critics, however, have quite a different perspective on transhumanism (Hook, 2004; Fukuyama, 2002). For these critics, transhumanism is a dangerous, hubristic, ungodly, unnatural, and unethical campaign that will decimate, if not entirely eliminate, the human race if left unchecked.[1]

THREE BAD ARGUMENTS AGAINST TRANSHUMANISM

For the sake of our discussion, let us assume the technologic and scientific feasibility of the transhumanist movement. The question for us, then, is not "Can it be done?" but instead "Should it be done?" When answering "no" to the latter question, what justifications or arguments do anti-transhumanists employ and how do they measure up to critical evaluation? In what follows, I examine three such arguments against transhumanism and conclude that they are unconvincing and should be rejected.

Playing God Argument

A very popular argument against transhumanism is the "playing God" argument. According to this argument, transhumanism's goal to transform human nature is an arrogant and misguided attempt to usurp God's power by working against his master plan for his creation, namely, nature, including human nature. Depending on one's theological commitments, what is sometimes assumed by this objection is that moral law, what we ought and ought not do, has been woven into the fabric of our nature, and can be discovered by reason in the same manner that reason discovers the physical laws of nature. Thus, by trying to transcend human nature, what God has created, transhumanists are acting contrary to nature and violating God's moral laws for us. To illustrate, take the case of human reproduction: Because intercourse between a man and a woman *is* the god-given and, thereby, natural manner for reproduction, then intercourse *should* be for reproduction. Therefore, since the use of prophylactics and non-coital means of reproduction (e.g., artificial insemination by donor) interfere with God's designs, their use constitutes ethical wrongdoing.

One problem with the "playing God" argument is that it fails to address the fact that unfettered nature, God's creation, can be brutal, terrifying, and deadly. If, however, we accept the argument in its current form, it would be morally wrong to try to cure cancer, morally wrong to limit the spread of HIV by advocating the use of condoms,

and morally wrong to genetically modify crops to increase yield to feed the starving. At this point, however, transhumanism's critics often claim that this is not what they mean by "playing God." We should do these things, they explain, because we are created in God's imagine and, thereby, endowed with reason and freedom of will. Therefore, when we use our God-given intellect to solve problems, such as developing a cure for cancer, our interference with nature is itself something natural and consistent with God's plan.

The issue, then, is not whether we interfere with nature, but rather, whether our interference is consistent with God's goodness and his plan for us. But even on this interpretation of the "playing god" argument, it still remains necessary to determine God's plan for his creation. But is knowledge of God's plan really possible, assuming there is a God? What kind of knowledge are we talking about and how do we come to know it? These are serious epistemological hurdles that must be overcome, if the "playing God" argument is to carry any weight. Furthermore, is it not an act of hubris and arrogance to think such knowledge is obtainable by us? Is it not the case that those who advance the playing god argument are "playing God" themselves when they claim to know the mind of God? Assuming there is a God with a plan, and the use of our reason is God given, maybe it is the transhumanists who are properly using their intellect in pursuit of morally appropriate ends, not its detractors. How is one to know? Strictly speaking, we cannot know, which means that those who oppose transhumanism on theistic grounds do so without an epistemologically privileged vantage point.

This brings us to the fundamental problem with the "playing God" argument, which is that it requires us to grant the existence of a creator God, who remains actively involved with his creation. This, however, is a leap of faith that many are unwilling to make. For agnostics and atheists, the "playing God" objection, for obvious reasons, lacks persuasive force. This is true even for some theists who believe in a creator god, but one who is disinterested and uninvolved with his creation. These theists, who are known as Deists, think of God as an impersonal first cause or explanation for how there is something rather than nothing.[2] But would this mean the "playing God" argument would have merit, if, in some possible world, everyone had the same understanding of god? No, it would not. In addition to being an anathema to pluralistic, democratic societies everywhere, it would not because the flaw of the "playing God" argument is not that some people believe in a particular God and others do not. It's not about the numbers. Rather, the Achilles' heel of the argument is that it is based on one's faith in God, and faith, in addition to being optional, does not require a rational justification. If one's faith in God *required* a rational justification, it simply would not be faith.[3]

As many throughout history have concluded, the mysterious footpath of faith begins where the road of reason ends. If this much is accepted, then the "playing God" argument is not, in the strict sense, a moral argument at all, but an assertion of one's faith in God, which requires no justification whatsoever, making the charge of "playing God" more indicative of colliding worldviews rather than a rationally justified argument against transhumanism.

It's Not Normal Argument

The lynchpin for the second argument opposing transhumanism is the belief that the concept "normal," in addition to its descriptive function about what *is* the case, also has an ethical function of prescribing what *should* be the case.[4] For instance, take the "normal life span" for human beings. In the late 1800s, a normal life span for a man was around 50 years, but now hovers in the late 70s in the early 21st century. Also, take the case of IVF. Prior to 1978, there were no "test tube" babies (Sutcliffe, 2002). Today, however, IVF is commonplace among couples wishing to have children. It is obvious that the average human life span and the means to reproduce are not what they used to be.

These examples above illustrate that "normal" is a protean concept whose meaning changes over time.[5] This, however, is exactly what opponents of transhumanism fail to recognize when they argue, for example, that genetic therapy is ethically acceptable because its purpose is to re-establish "normal" species functioning, whereas enhancement is deemed ethically wrong, because its purpose is to exceed the "normal" function of our species (Daniels, 1985). The problem with that line of reasoning is that the distinction between "therapy" and "enhancement" depends on our acceptance of an abstract, hypothetical, yet fluid, point called "normal health."[6] Getting people to normal health is considered therapy whereas taking them beyond the point of normal health is considered enhancement, for example, using psychotropic medications to alleviate serious depression versus using the same drugs to create a friendlier and more pleasant personality. But if everyone had enhanced personalities, this would be the new normal. This means that those who lacked chemically modified personalities would require therapy, not enhancement, in order achieve "normal species functioning" and "normal health." Therefore, when transhumanists "violate" what is "normal" about human nature, they are not violating biological necessities of our species or some immutable essence. What transhumanists are doing is re-constructing already socially constructed and relative value judgments and expectations for our species.

Slippery Slope Argument

A third argument commonly used against transhumanism is the "slippery slope" argument. One version of this argument claims that *when we allow X, we also allow Y.* For example, granting permission for the cloning of individual human cells is granting permission to clone complete human beings. One problem with this logic is the assumption that there is a *necessary connection* between the cloning of human cells and the cloning of human beings. There are, no doubt, similarities between the two types of cloning, and it is *possible* the cloning of individual human cells could lead to the cloning of human beings. But similarity and possibility are not sameness and necessity. This means, then, that allowing for the cloning of human cells does not entail the cloning of complete humans. If the cloning of human cells happened to lead to the cloning of human beings, this would be a matter of contingency, not logical necessity.

A second version of the slippery slope argument is less about logic and more about a pessimistic disposition toward the unknown. For example, some critics fear that an unbounded transhumanism will lead to the creation of a master race. They point out that the military has for decades pursued the creation of the super-soldier, who will be created by means of biochemicals, bioelectronics, and DNA manipulation. These augmented soldiers will be faster, stronger, fatigue resistant, less fearful and anxious, and possibly equipped with integrated weaponry. But why, the critics ask, would these enhanced humans take orders from their non-augmented leaders? Their answer is that they would not. Confident in their pessimism, these critics of transhumanism are sure that 2.0 humans will become a new sort of dominant caste, who will force weaker 1.0 humans into servitude or possibly extinction. This could happen, but it's not inevitable that it will. In this version of the slippery slope, humanity's barbaric and ignoble features are highlighted to the exclusion of its civilized and noble aspects. For the critics, a realized transhumanist agenda is synonymous with apocalypse. But this is a myopic perspective, driven by fear of the unknown, which sees every new day as Armageddon.

A third problem with the slippery slope argument is that it often involves a skewed conception of our moral agency, which assumes we are incapable of making subtle moral distinctions and associated moral judgments. In this version of the argument, human beings are capable of only making ham-fisted moral decisions based on all or nothing thinking. On this view, it's not that human beings are bad; they are just not all that smart. If this were the case, the slippery slope argument would make some sense. This, however, is not the case, at least not for most rational persons.

The truth is that if we elect to do so, we can make fine moral distinctions. When it comes to ethical decision making, the slippery slope need not be a slope all, but rather a staircase: When we take the first step, we need not simultaneously take the last step. On each step we are free to pause, reflect, and decide if we should continue, stop, or reverse our course. This characterization of ethical decision making is consistent with transhumanism's commitment to the responsible use of science and technology, robust education, and informed public discourse, which serve as breaks against uncontrolled downward slides. Therefore, as we take steps to develop genetic therapies for various diseases, for example, it is not inevitable that we will end up with a Nazi-like eugenics program or some other retched state of affairs.

When faced with the aforementioned criticisms, anti-transhumanists might reluctantly concede that their slippery slope argument(s) is not as good as they initially thought, but still maintain that transhumanism's aim to become posthuman is ethically defective and should be rejected. For the anti-transhumanist, it turns out that there is no need to show that transhumanism's first steps at the top of the slope will end at the bottom of the slope, because the bottom is where transhumanism begins in the first place. This tactic, however, does nothing to advance the anti-transhumanist agenda. It fails because a dislike for transhumanism is a matter of opinion or aesthetic judgment; it's not an argument, not even a fallacious one.

TWO COMPELLING ARGUMENTS AGAINST TRANSHUMANISM

Three arguments against transhumanism have been found unpersuasive for various reasons.[7] In what follows, I discuss two arguments against transhumanism that do have persuasive force and should give us pause about the transhumanist agenda. The first argument, the justice argument, addresses the potentially inequitable distribution of benefits and burdens that could result from transhumanism's goal to fund, research, develop, and employ various technologies for the purpose of achieving physical and mental enhancements. The second argument, the problem of human nature, identifies a significant assumption held by many transhumanists, namely, a belief in an essential human nature.

Justice Argument

My aim here is not to advocate for a particular conception of justice and subsequently point out how the transhumanist project will lead to an unjust or just society. My objective, rather, is to make explicit how any claim that transhumanism is just or unjust presupposes some understanding of what justice is. Since transhumanists and anti-transhumanists often hold very different conceptions of justice, it is important to know whether objections against transhumanism are about transhumanism's goals per se or more about what justice requires of transhumanism.[8]

For some critics of transhumanism, justice or its absence is about a future where the human race will divide along the lines of biological haves and have-nots.[9] People with enough money will be able to augment their cognitive and physical attributes as they see fit, while those without financial means will be left to bank on the genetic and social lotteries. The upper classes will utilize cloning, designer organ replacement, and genetic therapy to ward off disease, dysfunction, and death, while the majority of humanity will continue to

suffer them. If the aforementioned scenario seems farfetched, just look at the current allocation of healthcare services here and abroad. With this in mind, it's not at all difficult to envision a future where the wealthy and politically connected not only posses the means to send their children to the best schools, but also have the means to make their children smarter, faster, better looking, and longer living. What chance would a poor, uneducated, and un-enhanced child have against such *uber* children?

For our purposes, justice will be generally understood to be about *rights* and *duties*. Therefore, when we speak of justice in the context of transhumanism, we are talking about the criteria or conditions necessary for having a right or claim to enhancement technology and the obligations or duties society has to provide such technology. Thus, before meaningfully discussing whether transhumanism will affect an unjust allocation of enhancement technology, we must go above and beyond general talk about rights and duties and stipulate specific criteria for distinguishing legitimate from illegitimate claims to augmentation. For example, a just allocation of enhancement technology occurs when individuals use their own money to augment themselves. On this view of just allocation, the poor, who cannot buy enhancements, are simply unfortunate; their rights have not been violated because they have no right, claim or entitlement to enhancement technology and society has no duty to provide it to them. On the other hand, being a citizen of a state and simply wanting enhancements may be all that is required to have a right to enhancement technology, depending on the particular conception of justice one holds.

I don't want to suggest transhumanists are oblivious to the potential justice issues morphological freedom invites. They are not. The fact is most transhumanists fully recognize that a society with great disparities in its distribution of social goods such as education, decent healthcare, and gainful employment is a society that will be hard pressed to be more than nominally democratic. If the cost of morphological freedom is the further loss of equal opportunity and the weakening of democratic institutions, it is doubtful that most transhumanists, if they wish to remain consistent with their values, would be willing to pay such a price. With that said, the justice argument still has merit. The value of the justice argument is that it requires both critics and advocates of transhumanism to be clear about their own conceptions of justice. When it comes to considerations of justice, it is important to know whether transhumanists and anti-transhumanists are speaking the same language. What is required from both sides is an understanding of what rights and obligations are in force, how they are acquired, and to whom they apply.

Human Nature Argument

There are various ways to conceptualize human nature. One such way is known as reductionism, which is the view that overt complexity can be broken into its constituent parts (analysis), and, in turn, can explain the same complexity by the parts (Sarkar, 1998). As a method of science, reductionism is firmly established and works very well for explaining and predicting the function of simple systems such as chemical reactions and the motion of planets. Reductionism, however, does not always work well when trying to understand highly complex and emergent systems such as human nature.

The reductionism argument against transhumanism involves the charge that transhumanists have a distorted vision of human nature in which the complexity of human nature, talents, and disabilities are reducible to our biology. As critics correctly point out, the error of biological reductionism is that it fails to appreciate how human beings are not just biological beings, but rather bio-psycho-social beings. On this latter view, complex systems such as human nature are inherently irreducible to mere biology and

require a holistic approach to understand them. What this means, then, is that since human nature is a complex of bio-psycho-social elements, the modification or augmentation of human biology alone would not necessarily make us posthuman. In short, if we accept the anti-reductionist position, then biology is not constitutive of human nature and, therefore, not our destiny, be it a posthuman destiny or otherwise.

It seems reasonable to think that there is an essential human nature and that it is an irreducible complex of bio-psycho-social elements. It is also reasonable to believe that most clear-thinking transhumanists share this view. But what if we push anti-reductionism to its extreme limit (Horst, 2007), push it to a point where what we call "human nature" is simply a way of speaking that makes sense, but does not refer to anything that exists?[10] Andy Clark (2003) takes this very position and argues there is no essential human nature. For him and other like-minded individuals, the concept "human nature" simply refers to disparate biological, technological, mechanical, and cognitive processes that work together.

Clark's view is similar to the holistic bio-psycho-social approach discussed above to the extent that it does not reduce human nature to biology. His approach, however, is radically different because "human nature" has only nominal existence and a linguistic function. According to Clark:

There is no self, if by self we mean some central cognitive essence that makes me who and what I am. In its place there is just the "soft self": a rough-and-tumble, control-sharing coalition of processes—some neural, some bodily, some technological (p. 138).

For Clark, there is no essential self or human nature that can be overcome by means of technological enhancement. But if we grant Clark's thesis, then what exactly does it mean to be transhuman and posthuman? How can one transcend what does not exist? Clark's answer is that we are natural-born cyborgs, who, from the beginning have used technology to enhance and augment ourselves, from the use of animal skins to stay warm to the use of computers to store information well beyond what our brains can hold. To put it in existential terms, being human is to be engaged in a project of self transcendence in which the emphasis is on the "how" of being human rather than on the "what" of being human.

If we accept the radical anti-reductionist thesis of no essential human nature, then the basic tenet of transhumanism that there is a human nature to transcend is exploded. With that said, I don't want to suggest that Clark's view on human nature is the correct view; I merely want to make the point that transhumanism must make certain assumptions about human nature that are not universally accepted. Moreover, the nonexistence of an essential human nature does not mean that transhumanism is impossible and the movement defunct. It means, rather, that transhumanism is only an expression and intensification of those "coalition of processes" that we call "human nature," not an actually transcendence of it.

CONCLUSION

My approach in this paper has been intentionally one sided, focusing only on arguments against transhumanism. I have not evaluated any positive arguments for transhumanism. This is important to keep in mind, because a rejection of anti-transhumanist arguments does not mean the movement has passed the ethics smell test and gets a "green light" to proceed. Arguments for transhumanism are required and like those against transhumanism they run the spectrum of very good to very bad. Any final judgment about the ethical permissibility or impermissibility of transhumanism should include a careful assessment of those arguments as well (Jordon, 2006).

With that said, the transhumanism movement has *prima facie* many appealing features that go beyond its vision for the future, namely, the underlying values that support its vision: personal autonomy, social responsibility, respect for all sentient life, curiosity, democracy, the use of reason, critical thinking, public discourse, and so on. In addition, even if we reject the reality of an essential human nature, transhumanism still makes sense because as "human beings" we are always in a state of perpetual change and of self-overcoming, whether it is by the creation of a written language, the production of a highly engineered running shoe, or the implantation of an artificial heart.

REFERENCES

Bauer, K. (2007). Wired patients: Implantable microchips and biosensors in patient care. *Cambridge Quarterly of Healthcare Ethics, 16*(3), 281–290. doi:10.1017/S0963180107070314

Bostrom, N. (2005). A history of transhumanist thought. *Journal of Evolution and Technology, 14*(1).

Clark, A. (2003). *Natural-Born Cyborgs: Minds, Technologies, and the Future of Human Intelligence*. Oxford, UK: Oxford University Press.

Daniels, N. (1985). *Just Healthcare: Studies in Philosophy & Health Policy*. Cambridge, UK: Cambridge University Press.

Fukuyama, F. (2002). *Our Posthuman Future: Consequences of the Biotechnology Revolution*. New York: St. Martin's Press.

Harris, J. (2007). *Enhancing Evolution: The Ethical Case for Making Better People*. Princeton, NJ: Princeton University Press.

Herrick, J. (2005). *Humanism: An Introduction*. Amherst, NY: Prometheus Books.

Hook, C. (2004). *Transhumanism and posthumanism. Encyclopedia of Bioethics*. New York: Macmillan Press.

Horst, S. (2007). *Beyond Reduction: Philosophy of Mind and Post-reductionist Philosophy of Science*. Oxford, UK: Oxford University Press.

Hughes, J. (2004). *Citizen Cyborg: Why Democratic Societies Must Respond to the Redesigned Human of the Future*. Boulder, CO: Westview Press.

Jordon, G. (2006). Apologia for transhumanist religion. *Journal of Evolution and Technology*, *15*(1).

Kass, L. (1971). The new biology: What price relieving man's estate? *Science*, *174*, 780. doi:10.1126/science.174.4011.779

Luppicini, R., & Adell, R. (2008). *Handbook of Research on Technoethics*. Hershey, PA: Information Science Reference.

Marx, K. (1993). *Grundrisse: Foundations of the Critique of political Economy*. New York: Penguin Books Ltd.

Nozick, R. (2003). *Anarchy, State, and Utopia*. Oxford, UK: Blackwell Publishing Ltd.

Orr, J. (1934). *English Deism: Its Roots and Its Fruits*. Grand Rapids, MI: Eerdmans Press.

Rawls, J. (1993). *A Theory of Justice*. Cambridge, MA: Harvard University Press.

Roco, M. C., & Bainbridge, W. S. (2002). *Converging Technologies for Improving Human Performance* (NSF/DOC-Sponsored Report). Retrieved September 29, 2009, from http://www.wtec.org/ConvergingTechnologies/Report/NBIC_report.pdf

Sarkar, S. (1998). *Genetics and Reductionism*. Cambridge, UK: Cambridge University Press.

Stock, G. (2002). *Redesigning Humans: Choosing Our Genes, Changing Our Future*. Orlando, FL: Houghton Mifflin Company.

Sutcliffe, A. (2002). *IVF Children: The First Generation: Assisted Reproduction and Child Development*. Nashville, TN: Parthenon Publishing Group.

Viseu, A. (2003). Simulation and augmentation: Issues of wearable computers. *Ethics and Information Technology*, *5*, 17–26. doi:10.1023/A:1024928320234

ENDNOTES

[1] This assumes the transhumanist's project is scientifically and technologically feasible. Recall, however, that not all critics think this is the case. For them, "serious" anti-transhumanists are, too, poking at windmills.

[2] According to John Orr (*English Deism: Its Roots and Its Fruits*. Eerdmans, 1934, pp. 13), "...theists taught that god remained actively interested in and operative in the world which he had made, whereas the Deist maintained that God endowed the world at creation with self-sustaining and self-acting powers and then abandoned it to the operation of these powers acting as second causes.

[3] Although faith and reason are different from each other, it would be an error to conclude that they are mutually exclusive. Justifications or reasons can be given for one's faith in god, but they are not necessary. Moreover, even when one's faith is supported by reasons, faith in god for most people precedes their reasons for faith. In other words, people do not typically go through some kind of decision procedure and conclude that it is rational to have faith in god. There are, for example, notable exceptions such as Pascal and William James.

4   This "secular" argument is similar to the "playing god" argument because the terms "normal" and "natural" have descriptive and prescriptive features. In the context of the present argument, however, the concept "nature," when used as a synonym for "normal," refers to the totality of forces explored by science, not a world created by god endowed with meaning and purpose.

5   Whether these changes are random or the result of conscious social construction and social control is beyond the scope of this paper.

6   For example, most people in developed countries do not see childhood immunizations as a kind of human enhancement, but they are.

7   To conclude they are "unpersuasive" is to say simply that the reasons for rejecting them are better than the reasons for accepting them. From this, however, we should not erroneously infer that transhumanism gets the equivalent of a moral "green light." Arguments in support of transhumanism are still required.

8   Different theories of justice include, for example, Libertarianism (Robert Nozick, *Anarchy, State, and Utopia*, Blackwell Publishing Ltd, 2003), Egalitarianism (John Rawls, *A Theory of Justice*, Harvard University Press, 2005), and Marxism (*Grundrisse: Foundations of the Critique of political Economy*, Penguin Books Ltd, 1993).

9   As I mentioned previously, the objection here is not so much about the ethics of enhancement, but how enhancement technology will be "fairly" or "justly" distributed.

10   For example, when we speak of "dragons," this term has meaning, but does not refer to anything real beyond a linguistic reality.

Chapter 19
Human Implants:
A Suggested Framework to Set Priorities

Laura Cabrera
Charles Sturt University, Australia

ABSTRACT

Human implants are among the technology applications that deserve to be carefully assessed as they have the potential to help us treating many devastating human conditions, but also to assist us reaching a stage beyond current human capacities and abilities. Such a development would introduce many challenges for society, governments, and the individual. Human implants can blur the line that lies between what is acknowledged as therapy and enhancement. The lack of a clear distinction between therapy and enhancement will confront governments with new regulatory challenges in public health and funding technology research. This brings to the fore issues of justice, such as how to close instead of widen the 'technology-divide' and how to define priorities for funding, distributing, and using human implants. Given the potential impact that new and improved human implants can have for the individual and for society, a better understanding on the direction and reasons for developing such applications is needed to handle them in a wiser way. One way of assisting such a development is by rethinking our priorities when using technology for human enhancement applications.

INTRODUCTION

One of the most interesting areas of technology is human implants. This is because these applications can be used not only for treating certain medical conditions in order to bring someone back to the 'medical norm'[1], but more importantly because

they can be used to take people beyond it, namely enhancing human performance and cognition. Even if we accept that most technologies have enhancing capabilities, human implants are among the technology applications that can take enhancement to a different degree not seen before. This will confront governments with new challenges for developing policies and regulations related to public health and public funding involving tech-

DOI: 10.4018/978-1-4666-1773-5.ch019

nology usage. Moreover, it puts more urgency on moving the therapy-enhancement debate – which is seen as highly controversial (Coenen et al., 2009; Roco & Bainbridge, 2002)—to a space in which political decisions can be shaped and taken. In this regard technoethics, 'as an interdisciplinary field concerned with all ethical aspects of technology within a society shaped by technology' (Luppicini & Adell, 2008), plays a key role.

There are three main reasons for technoethics playing such an important role in the use, development and funding of certain technological applications, such as human implants. The first one is connected to the fact that human implants are an area in which technology is incorporated (merged in a way) with the individual in question, raising many ethical concerns. The second reason has to do with the social, cultural, political and economical forces embedded in our ethical reflections behind the choice, development and/ or funding of certain kind of human implant over other possibilities. The last reason considered here, deals with the fact that human implants are no longer used only for so called medical purposes, but they are envisioned to be used for entertainment, the military and even helping an individual to attain capabilities beyond the current range human capabilities (i.e., technological posthuman).

This paper will argue for an approach that does not rely on the idea that therapy and enhancement are mutually exclusive concepts or as if any distinction could be made between them—ideas that have generated the ongoing therapy-enhancement debate. Instead, it argues for a different approach, an approach that acknowledges that if a distinction is needed for policy making purposes, it needs to be a dynamic and context dependent one. Such an approach could allow us to reach a consensus on how to prioritize the development, distribution and applications of human implants. Moreover, it will seem to respond in a better way to social changes, the plurality of societies and adapt to the context of the usage of a given implant.

Human Applications: Implants

An implant is a prosthesis, in other words, it is an engineered technological device used to restore bodily functions, replace missing biological structures and more recently to augment, add, or enhance human functions or capacities. Therefore, implants are a good example of a technology application in which the distinction (if any) between therapy and enhancement has become blurrier and blurrier. For example, a neuro-implant can have a therapeutic value, such as enabling a blind individual to see within the medical norm, which in most cases is based on species-typical features. However, the same technology can be used for designing a neuro-implant that enables an individual that is already considered to have a 'normal' range of vision to see beyond that 'normal' range, i.e. infrared vision. Thus, in this later case most people would agree that the implant was used for enhancement purposes and not just therapy.

Currently, there is a large variety of human implants available, from artificial limbs to implanted drug-delivery systems and brain-machine interfaces. Human implants are obviously not a new issue; however, with new technologies (such as nanotechnology or neurotechnology) they will most certainly have tremendous improvements –such as improved efficiency, biocompatibility, and strength—and changes, such as becoming smaller and more active (Greenemeier, 2008; Hodgins et al., 2008; Shipman, 2008; Simonite, 2007). Connected to the issue of becoming more active, it can be said that implants have become more than just passive applications, take for instance the neuro-implant built by researchers at Brown University which helps paralyzed people manipulate objects using only their brains. In this example, the implant has to be able to translate and decode information in ways that previous implants didn't.[2]

Moreover, there are also the kind of implants that so far just entertain the thoughts of some people, such as many transhumanists, i.e., Raymond Kurzweil, Eric Drexler, and Nick Bostrom, which supposedly will make us think faster, multitask better, record and play back thoughts, back up our minds (up-load), dream feelings, interchange between sensory reality and virtual reality seamlessly, and enable us to reach a stage beyond current human capacities and abilities: a so called stage of 'posthumanity'.

Enhancement: Beyond Therapy?

Before getting into the issue of posthumanity, I think is worth mentioning human enhancement, because according to the literature it is by enhancing human performance and cognition that the stage of posthumanity will be reached. The debate on the distinction between therapy and enhancement is definitely not a new one. Thus it is safe to say that issues related to enhancement have been widely discussed, and have had increasing attention over the last decade in many fields such as genetics, pharmacology and neuroscience; and different contexts from cosmetic surgery to technologies that aim to merge with the human body (Coenen et al., 2009; Greely, 2005; Kass, 2003; Parens, 2006).

In the literature the most common definition of therapy is based on the idea that therapy is only concerned with restoring or preserving species-typical levels of functioning (Daniels, 1992). Consequently, enhancement has been understood generally as those interventions to augment the capacities, characteristics and performances of the human body viewed as the normal features of members of our species (Daniels, 1992, 2008; Kass, 2003; Wolbring, 2005, 2008). However, this distinction is not free of ambivalences and has been the target of a debate that until now has not reached any substantial conclusions.

Within the debate some people maintain that it is possible to draw a line between therapy and enhancement, and that such a line should be drawn because the distinction is needed to inform ethical debate (DeGrazia, 2005; Fukuyama, 2002; Kass,

2003; Sandel, 2004). Others, on the other hand, argued that such a line cannot be sustained or that is blurry at best (Harris, 2007). Considering that the possible criteria against which either therapy or enhancement are generally contrasted – such as a health standard, non-disease states, and normal or natural states – are context dependent and subjective, the later view seems to be supported. It is therefore plausible to say that, on the one hand a serious injury or a chronic disease might be a clear point of departure from a standard of health; however there are cases that defy classification. On the other hand the concept of what 'normal' or 'natural' means in our current society seems to be more and more malleable. There seems to be no clear boundary anymore between what is normal and what is pathological. In addition what seems normal or natural for someone now, might have been something unthinkable for another human a couple of centuries ago, particularly since technology has been redefining the norm and changing social and individual expectations (Kass, 2003; Wolbring, 2008).

To complicate the issue even more, there are areas with no controversy at all, where enhancement is not even perceived as such (i.e., the case of vaccines, which in a certain degree enhance our immune systems). Thus, in practice we are left with no clear reference point to discriminate between therapy and enhancement, and to discriminate between the appropriate and the inappropriate kind of enhancement interventions. Moreover, the term enhancement has been regarded as abstract and imprecise. Does enhancing a human function means increasing or improving the function's quantity or quality? Or does it mean bringing a function or condition out more fully, rather than altering it qualitatively?

Moreover, we don't need to think about so-called enhancement uses of implants to find pressing ethical issues to be analyzed. The case of the cochlear implant is a good example. Generally speaking, the cochlear implant is considered to be an implant that aims to bring hearing within the range of 'normal' hearing. However, the implant has being seen for some groups of people as ethnic cleansing and as a device that confronts the experience of being disabled (Hockenberry, 2001; Barry, 1991).

There is also the case of implants that by restoring human functions end up giving competitive advantages over the species typical features, for example the cases of Oscar Pistorious and Aimee Mullins. South African Oscar Pistorius and Aimee Mullins are both double-leg amputees that have challenged the widely held conception in which having an impairment was a disadvantage, and have even proved that artificial legs can be more interesting that having 'normal human legs' (Smith & Morra, 2006).[3] These issues shed some light on how problematic the debate on human implants could turn out to be, making even more urgent the need for technoethics.

Posthumanity

Current research into human implants, which range from medical, military and even entertainment (ASTR, 2006; Coenen et al., 2009; Roco & Bainbridge, 2002), makes it plausible to think that implants are not only being designed to restore to a medical norm, but also, that they are being directly designed for going beyond certain known human limits, and this is generally understood as human enhancement. When someone uses a human enhancement application that leads to a capacity that greatly exceeds "the maximum attainable by any current human being without recourse to new technological means" (Bostrom, 2008, p. 1), it is argued that he or she has attained a new mode of being. This new mode of being is what some people, such as Nick Bostrom, defined as posthumanity.

Considering that there are different understandings of posthumanity such as the one suggested by Katherine Hayles (1999), it is important clarifying a couple of things. First, in this paper I will be using the term posthumanity meaning technological

posthumanity, particularly Bostrom's definition (2008), in which a posthuman is a human being who has attained through *technology* at least one posthuman capacity–being intellectual, physical or psychological. And second, I will not be taken the extreme version of technological posthumanity suggested by Francis Fukuyama (2002), who has argued that a posthuman is a technological creature in which the biological human part has become obsolete.

Taking into account, that the posthuman stage requires going 'beyond certain human limits', and that enhancement is also closely related with transcending certain limits; it seems plausible to argue that technological enhancements, such as those brought forward by human implants, are a path to reach posthumanity. Nonetheless, even if such a technological state has something valuable to offer, as some people have argued (Bostrom, 2008; Kurzweil, 2005), there are many reasons to be cautious about it, particularly when only a small number of individuals will benefit from it. Hence, among the many ethical issues that human implants bring to the fore, I am focused in this paper with those related to social justice.

WHY A DIFFERENT APPROACH?

The most recurrent concern about social justice and enhancement procedures is along the lines that the worst outcomes of enhancement come from the fact that enhancement technologies might not be available to everyone, causing unjust distribution (Daniels, 2008). Enhancement procedures alone will not lead to unjust results, but rather injustice will come about if it happens to be an unjust distributive scheme. So even though justice arguments regarding the usage of technology are not new, there are a couple of reasons that have motivated the suggestion for a new approach focused on social justice, regarding the development, distribution and usage of human implants, particularly those with the potential to bring about posthumanity.

Firstly, because justice is among the most important virtues of social institutions (Rawls, 1971), and social institutions in this case are essential to ensure the development, distribution and legislation of human implants. Social institutions are also essential to broaden the discussion concerning human enhancement and posthumanity beyond the academia and techno-progressive groups of people.

Secondly, implants are not a kind of unlimited resource. The materials used for these application can be limited (that is to say not many of them are available in nature or are very expensive to produce/manufacture/develop and as such are limited only to those with the acquisitive power to pay for them). Furthermore people might need to be trained not only on how to develop them but also on how to insert, apply and even use these implants, which means that at the beginning human resources with this knowledge will also be limited to a few people in some geographical areas.

Finally, new technologies have had a historical tendency to exclude. Here, is worth pointing out that is not technology per se which excludes, but rather the economic and political institutions in which is embedded. They tend to exclude those who do not have the economical, political or social power to buy, develop or use them. And the same line of thought seems to be applicable in the case of human implants. In this regard, defenders of enhancement and posthumanity have claimed that there is no reason to think that enhancement applications of technology will be unevenly distributed. And in some cases some people have argued that given that all new technologies present this tendency there is no reason to worry in particular about human implants. Nonetheless, in the case of human enhancement applications that have the potential to bring about posthumanity, it seems plausible to argue that there is something substantially different compare with other technologies. A skewed distribution of human implants could exacerbate not only feelings of discrimination (Fukuyama, 2002; Habermas, 2003), envy or anxiety (de Botton, 2005), but it could also create a division far greater and meaningful than the so called 'digital divide'[4], namely a capability divide. Human implants used for reaching a posthuman stage could bring an ontological leap in the already segregate distribution of capabilities, as posthumanity implies the attainment of at least one atypical human capability.

Now that I have stated why justice is an important consideration when dealing with the development, distribution and usage of human implants, we still have to delineate what should count as just and unjust.

WHAT KIND OF JUSTICE?

When thinking about human implants, particularly those used for enhancement, we need to delineate what are the parameters to decide what justice requires from us. Hence, we need to start asking ourselves on what grounds we want our justice concerns to be based. There are distinct views of what constitutes distributive justice, depending on the criterion used: need, effort, equality of something, or a combination.

When talking about justice, and especially about distributive justice, is common to think about the theory of one of the most well-know American philosophers, John Rawls, author of the book *A theory of justice* (1971). According to Rawls, society is responsible for the distribution of the primary social goods conforming to the principles of justice that would be accepted in the social contract. In this regard people with extravagant preferences are responsible for addressing their own unhappiness with life and have no claims of justice on us (Rawls, 1971). Rawls' approach also endorses a difference principle, which allows for inequalities as long as they work to make those who are worst off as well off as possible, compared to alternative measures and without undercutting equality of opportunity.

In this paper I am interested in this idea of equality of opportunity, which has been further developed by Amartya Sen and Martha Nussbaum. In contrast with Rawl's approach which focuses on primary social goods, Sen and Nussbaum focus on a sufficient set of capabilities (i.e., not necessarily equality in all capabilities).

A capability is an exercisable or accessible opportunity or option needed to function as a cooperative member of society (Nussbaum, 2008; Nussbaum & Sen, 1993). It is because capabilities are so fundamental in what we can do or be, that I believe that they are a good start to base our justice concerns regarding human enhancement. However, given that we live in pluralistic societies we cannot commit ourselves "to pursue equality of capabilities, but only assuring that individual's capability sets are nor distinctly worse than those of others" (Daniels, 2008, p. 68). Here I am referring to a capability set (or opportunities for functioning) following Amartya Sen's neo-Aristotelian primary use of the notion of capability, as to indicate a space within which comparisons of quality of life can most fruitfully be made. In this regard the basic political principles are focused on promoting capabilities and not actual functioning, in order to leave to individuals the choice to pursue or not the relevant function, as Martha Nussbaum (2008) has suggested.

If there is something that really defined us as humans (and differentiate us from trees and rocks), then there must be ways to secure that we all enjoy of those basic human capabilities. If that is the case, then failure in meeting these basic capabilities is a problem of justice (Nussbaum, 2008). Here is worth stressing that I am not arguing that we should all have two legs to move from point A to B, that is to say I am not arguing for the attainment of 'normal' features, but rather for the attainment of the basic set of capabilities that would allows us to perform within the range that has so far defined the human, for instance that we all have the capability to get from point A to B if so wanted.

An approach based on capabilities does not per se ensure that justice will be met, as Nussbaum and Sen have highlighted, it will also be needed a kind of "overlapping consensus", as used by John Rawls, among people who otherwise have very diverse comprehensive conceptions of the good (Nussbaum, 2008). Only when such deliberation has been accomplished, regarding the kind of capabilities that should count as basic, that the approach can be sensitive to pluralism and cultural difference, and focus in promoting those capabilities that are really needed and not just desired.

THE SUGGESTED APPROACH

After the abovementioned considerations, it seems plausible to argue that a more just way to handle human implants—research, development and distribution—can be reached by prioritizing those implants that promote equality of opportunity within a society, particularly, opportunity to live a valuable life.

The suggested approach considers the following:

(i) Firstly, the need to develop tools that allows us to prioritize between cases in which the controversy does not lie in an application being seen or not as unacceptable.

(ii) Secondly, the need for guidelines connected not so much on whether a certain application is seen as therapy or as an enhancement, but instead connected to the kind of values and opportunities that certain human implants bring forward.

(iii) Thirdly, given that for policy making purposes a distinction between therapy and enhancement might be needed, a 'dynamic' border is considered. By 'dynamic' I mean that it does not support an absolute distinction between therapy and enhancement, but rather it supports a distinction that acknowledges that the concepts are context dependent (relative) and overlapping. So in contrast with the current debate I am not arguing that there is an absolute and universal distinction between the concepts, or that we cannot draw a distinction. Instead, I am taking the nature of the conflict to help set a dynamic boundary that allows policy making to move forward.

(iv) Finally, the approach considers that the distribution of human capabilities can be represented in a Gaussian distribution curve (often known as the normal distribution curve, see Fig 1). In such a 'normal human capability distribution curve' the mean, that is to say the average of the distribution curve for certain capabilities, moves depending on variables such as time, country, age, gender and so on (depending on the considered human capability); and the standard deviation (σ), which is a measure of the distribution of the values of a certain multiset of values, represents the distribution of a certain human capability for a certain group (Figure 1).

As a result of these considerations, the suggested approach argues that priority should be given to anyone whose capabilities 'C' are below one standard deviation from the curve's mean ($C<-1\sigma$). Here, it is worth mentioning that they would be given the opportunity to reach at least levels that are within one standard deviation from the curve's mean ($-1\sigma < C < \mu$), but in case the individual considers that he or she can still lead a valuable life even with those differences, they will not be made to fit the 'normal' parameters at the time, as long as they are given the opportunity to make this informed decision. The previous idea takes into consideration the views from people with impairments, who sometimes do not think they want to fit any species-typical norm as long as their opportunities to lead a valuable life are met (i.e. the case of deaf people). In other words, not meeting certain species-typical features does not make the individual necessarily worst-off per se, but rather in most cases the fact that socio-political structures do not provide those individuals with a fair range of life opportunities, is what makes them being worst-off.

Once we have handled the priority cases, the suggested approach argues that attention should be given next to those cases in which C is below the curve's mean ($C < \mu$), then, to cases in which C is between the curve's mean and 1 standard deviation ($\mu <C<1\sigma$) and so on.

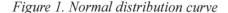

Figure 1. Normal distribution curve

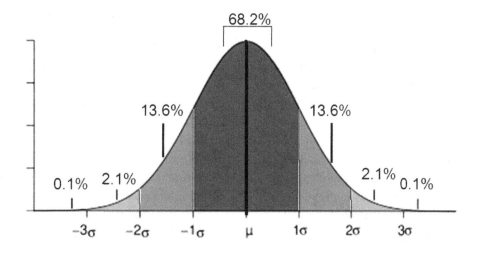

Taking into account that the curve's mean for a certain human capability could differ for different human features in different societies or groups, certain applications might be prioritized for a certain society and not for another. However, considering the way in which human capabilities are distributed within a certain society, it is plausible to say that the further away from one standard deviation the feature is (>1σ), the more societies are likely to agree that those cases should not count as priority cases. The reason for not prioritizing human implants that bring capabilities beyond the basic set of capabilities is that the kind of justice defended here requires that we focus first on those implants that would help us reach the basic set of capabilities.

By using these parameters a better distribution of human implants among society could be attained, rather than remaining concentrated in small powerful groups. Consequently, only when most of the population have access to certain implants (regardless of whether they choose to use it or not), society can shift the curve's parameters for that certain capability, and new implants can begin to be used (e.g., implants that are aimed at attaining features that in the past were seen as above μ).

The reason for considering intervals based on standard deviations is that such kinds of intervals still include sets of values for a certain capability (among a group of people, society or humankind), that a certain percentage of the members within that group still share (of course the more standards deviations from μ, the less members of that group will present that capability). The idea allows changes to the human condition provided that most people can actually enjoy such changes. So even if posthumanity becomes a widely spread human desire, the approach ensures that only when most members of the still human species can attain such posthuman capacities, will the technology that makes possible these capacities be allowed. Therefore, it hopes to prevent exacerbation of social divides that could arise from an unfair distribution.

The approach also acknowledges that what a 'normal' human capability is considered to be is not absolute; taking a more flexible view on the limits of 'normality', as it takes the curve's mean (μ) for a certain human capability as a dynamic value. Thus, it is open to human diversity and change. Moreover, it aims to promote the idea that revisions need to be done to the curve's parameters from time to time, based on how human capabilities are distributed (objective facts), rather than just on people's desires and perceptions of well-being (more subjective facts).

Despite the fact that some transhumanists have argued that such an approach would be morally arbitrary; I believe that the use of a certain percentage based on human statistics, as a political 'tool', would allow us to be able to set limits in the usage of resources that are limited and that need to be more fairly distributed. I acknowledge that much work still needs to be done and many questions still remain open, but I consider it could be a good starting point.

Considering that this approach tries not to get entangled in the therapy-enhancement distinction, it does not argue for a ban of those applications that could be used to enhance certain human capacity; but rather, it makes them attainable only as we cover certain priority cases. The approach is not against enhancement, but rather, it tries to: first, avoid the exacerbation of enhancements which could aggravate inequalities in society or promote a different capability divide (posthuman vs. human); second, to encourage policies that help us deliberate about our priorities; third, to give *incentives* to those that crave for posthumanity to support the distribution of implants that are focused in helping people to attain the basic set of capabilities before moving on to promote atypical human capabilities; and finally to give us time to develop better arguments and tools, such as educating people about these issues, for handling the new changes to come.

It is possible that certain groups – like the transhumanists- put political pressure in what we as a society decide to consider or not as a priority. Moreover, the priorities for a certain group of people might not be the same as for another group. For instance people with certain impairments might have different priorities than people without them. People in certain countries might have a priority for human implants that replace limbs that have been lost, while in other countries the priority can be implants that improve memory. That is why we should also acknowledge that a deeper understanding of the reasons to use implants instead of other alternatives is required; and of the meaning, purposes and reasons of the capability or capabilities to be enhanced.

Justice requires that science and technology be in balance with society's needs and not simply following human desire. Technoethics can definitely help us to shape our future as we merged with our technology. Technology has all the features to help humankind find appropriate-engineered solutions to material challenges and technical problems. But in the end, it is us, as humankind, who will have to decide which areas are the ones we should prioritize and start focusing on them.

CONCLUSION

Technology is playing and will continue to play an important role in the way we build our future. In this paper, I have argued for a different approach when handling technology-based human applications that are somewhere in between therapy and enhancement, using the idea of justice in the distribution of human implants. Particularly, those human implants that could help us reach the stage of posthumanity. An approach that focuses on those areas that are more important to tackle, not because the interests of greedy corporations tell us that those areas are important; but rather, because our humanness tell us they are morally more important than other areas. We need to be cautious in not promoting 'new-divides' that keep reinforcing current economic and power paradigms. Moreover, considering the pace of the changes we are seeing with technology, technoethics becomes a crucial player to assure that ethical reflection does not stay on the bookshelf, but instead, that society, politicians and policy makers really grasp the importance of addressing topics such as human enhancement and posthumanity.

ACKNOWLEDGMENT

I am grateful to Professor John Weckert for his critical review of the manuscript.

REFERENCES

ASUR (Arizona State University Report). (2006). *Policy implications of technologies for cognitive enhancement*. Phoenix, AZ: Arizona State University.

Barry, J. (1991). Silence is golden? *Miami Herald*, 8.

Bostrom, N. (2008). Why I want to be a posthuman when I grow up. In Gordijn, B., & Chadwick, R. (Eds.), *Medical Enhancement and Posthumanity* (pp. 107–137). New York: Springer.

Coenen, C., Schuijff, M., Smits, M., Klaassen, P., Hennen, L., Rader, M., & Wolbring, G. (2009). *Human enhancement study*. European Parliament.

Daniels, N. (1992). Growth hormone therapy for short stature: Can we support the treatment/enhancement distinction? *Growth: Genetics & Hormones,* 8S1.

de Botton, A. (2005). *Status anxiety*. New York: Vintage Books.

DeGrazia, D. (2005). Enhancement technologies and human identity. *The Journal of Medicine and Philosophy*, *30*, 261–283. doi:10.1080/03605310590960166

Fukuyama, F. (2002). *Our posthuman future, consequences of the biotechnology revolution.* London: Profile Books.

Greely, H. (2005). Regulating human biological enhancements: Questionable justifications and international complications. *University of Technology. The Sydney Law Review, 7,* 87–110.

Greenemeier, L. (2008). Nanotech to regrow cartilage and soothe aching knees. *Scientific American Journal.* Retrieved June 17, 2008, from http://www.sciam.com/article.cfm?id=nanotech-cartilage&sc=WR_20080617

Habermas, J. (2003). *The future of human nature.* Cambridge, UK: Polity Press.

Harris, S. (2007). *Enhancing evolution: The ethical case for making better people.* Princeton, NJ: Princeton University Press.

Hayles, K. (1999). *How we became posthuman: Virtual bodies in cybernetics, literature, and informatics.* Chicago: University of Chicago Press.

Hockenberry, J. (2001). The next brainiacs. *Wired Issue 9.08.* Retrieved February 18, 2007, from http://www.wired.com/wired/archive/9.08/assist.html

Hodgins, D., Bertsch, A., Post, N., Frischholz, M., Volckaerts, B., Spensley, J., Wasikiewicz, J., Higgins, H., von Stetten, F., & Kenney, L. (2008). Healthy aims: developing new medical implants and diagnostic equipment. *Pervasive Computing,* 14-21.

Just health: Meeting health needs fairly. (2008). Cambridge, UK: Cambridge University Press.

Kass, L. (2003). Beyond therapy: Biotechnology and the pursuit of happiness. *A Report by the President's Council on Bioethics.* Retrieved February 21, 2007, from http://www.bioethics.gov/reports/beyondtherapy/beyond_therapy_final_webcorrected.pdf

Kurzweil, R. (2005). *The singularity is near: When humans transcend biology.* New York: Viking Penguin.

Luppicini, R., & Adell, R. (Eds.). (2008). *Handbook of research on technoethics.* Hershey, PA: IGI Global.

Nussbaum, M. (2008). *Women and human development: Capabilities approach.* Cambridge, UK: Cambridge University Press.

Nussbaum, M., & Sen, A. (Eds.). (1993). *The quality of life.* Oxford, UK: Oxford University Press. doi:10.1093/0198287976.001.0001

Parens, E. (2006). Creativity, gratitude, and the enhancement debate. In Illes, J. (Ed.), *Neuroethics: defining the issues in theory, practice and policy* (pp. 75–86). Oxford, UK: Oxford University Press.

Rawls, J. (1971). *A theory of justice.* Cambridge, MA: Harvard University Press.

Roco, M., & Bainbridge, W. (Eds.). (2002). *Converging technologies for improving human performance: Nanotechnology, Biotechnology, Information Technology and Cognitive Science.* Arlington, VA: National Science Foundation/Department of Commerce.

Sandel, M. (2004). The case against perfection. *The Atlantic Monthly, 293*(3). Retrieved January 19, 2007, from http://www.theatlantic.com/past/docs/issues/2004/04/sandel.htm

Shipman, M. (2008). *NC State finds new nanomaterial could be breakthrough for implantable medical devices. North Carolina State University.* Retrieved November 19, 2008, from http://news.ncsu.edu/releases/nc-state-finds-new-nanomaterial-could-be-breakthrough-for-implantable-medical-devices/

Simonite, T. (2007). Neural 'extension cord' developed for brain implants. *New Scientist.* Retrieved January 19, 2007, from http://www.newscientist.com/article/dn10997

Smith, M., & Morra, J. (Eds.). (2006). *The prosthetic impulse: from a posthuman present to a bicultural future*. Cambridge, MA: The MIT Press.

Why NBIC? Why human performance enhancement? (2008). *Innovation: The European Journal of Social Science Research, 21*(1), 25-40.

Wolbring, G. (2005). *The triangle of enhancement medicine, disabled people, and the concept of health. Health Technology Assessment Initiative Series*. Retrieved December 5, 2008, from http://www.ihe.ca/documents/hta/HTA-FR23.pdf

ENDNOTES

[1]   Here I am using the term medical norm referring to the "quasi-statistical concepts of normality" that Norman Daniels has suggested (Daniels, 1992).

[2]   For more on this see http://www.cyberkineticsinc.com and http://www.brown.edu/Administration/News_Bureau/2001-02/01-098.html.

[3]   For more on this see: http://www.time.com/time/specials/2007/article/0,28804,1733748_1733756_1735285,00.html. or http://www.ted.com/index.php/talks/aimee_mullins_prosthetic_aesthetics.html

[4]   Digital divide here refers to what the Asian Development Bank defined as the "division of the world between those who have access to new information and communications technology and those who do not". See Asian Development Bank (2002). Digital divide: Determinants and policies with special reference to Asia (ERD Working Paper Series No 27). Philippines: Economic and Research Dept., Asian Development Bank.

This work was previously published in International Journal of Technoethics, Volume 1, Issue 4, edited by Rocci Luppicini, pp. 39-48, copyright 2010 by IGI Publishing (an imprint of IGI Global).

Chapter 20
The Functional Morality of Robots

Linda Johansson
Royal Institute of Technology, Sweden

ABSTRACT

It is often argued that a robot cannot be held morally responsible for its actions. The author suggests that one should use the same criteria for robots as for humans, regarding the ascription of moral responsibility. When deciding whether humans are moral agents one should look at their behaviour and listen to the reasons they give for their judgments in order to determine that they understood the situation properly. The author suggests that this should be done for robots as well. In this regard, if a robot passes a moral version of the Turing Test—a Moral Turing Test (MTT) we should hold the robot morally responsible for its actions. This is supported by the impossibility of deciding who actually has (semantic or only syntactic) understanding of a moral situation, and by two examples: the transferring of a human mind into a computer, and aliens who actually are robots.

INTRODUCTION

Technoethics focuses on the ethical aspects of technology in society, and attempts to devise principles to guide technological development in particular in relation to emerging new technologies that give rise to new ethical issues. Increasingly autonomous and intelligent robots represent one

of these new technologies. Autonomy in robots raises questions about robot morality, and about how we can make sure that the autonomous robots behave ethically, in some sense (Bekey, 2005; Allen, Smit, & Wallach, 2006; Andersson, 2008; Andersson, Anderson, & Armen, 2004; Allen, Varner, & Zinser, 2000).

This is relevant for ongoing technological development. Today there are robotic research programs where internal "ethical governors" and

DOI: 10.4018/978-1-4666-1773-5.ch020

"guilt systems" are being developed, and there are discussions on potential "pull the trigger-autonomy" of unmanned aerial vehicles in war (Arkin, 2009).

It has sometimes been argued that a robot can never be held responsible for its actions. No matter how advanced it is it can never be autonomous; since it is always programmed by a human there is no question of a robot having alternative possibilities. Robots also seem to lack mental states, which are considered necessary in order to be an agent.

This paper argues that we do not need to know what goes on in a robot, in terms of being programmed or possessing mental states. If a robot can pass a so called Moral Turing Test, than we can hold it morally responsible for its actions.

An objection to the whole idea of trying to find criteria for whether a robot might be morally responsible, is the "what would be the point"-objection, that is, that it would be pointless to hold a machine responsible. We cannot punish a robot; it would be useless to send it to prison, for instance. If it misbehaves, we would simply turn it off or destroy it. But in a longer perspective, with robots becoming more advanced, this issue cannot be ignored. The potential responsibility of robots might have an impact on liability when something goes wrong. If the robot is considered responsible, we may not be able to punish it, but its responsibility may have implications for the responsibility of others, such as programmers. The ascription of responsibility to robots may also have influence on decisions whether and how to use such robots. There might also be implications for how robots should be programmed "ethically".

The idea of morality as a human *construction* in a moral community is a useful assumption when investigating matters regarding robot morality. Moral responsibility can be expected to be a central notion in the moral community since the whole point of morality is to promote right actions and prevent wrong actions. Members of the moral community might be moral agents or moral receivers, i.e., agents whose well-being is

morally relevant but who cannot be held morally responsible.

The paper is outlined as follows. First, the moral community is described in terms of its members and how members decide whether other members are agents (which are a part of the other minds problem). The solution to the other minds problem seems—in this community—to be functionalistic; that is, we look at other humans' behaviour and assume that their mental states are what caused their outward behaviour. Then the moral community is discussed focusing on the case for robots. I argue that the nature of morality—the way humans actually behave in moral matters—supports the idea that *the passing of a moral Turing Test* (MTT) is a necessary and sufficient criterion for being held morally responsible. Support for this idea also comes from the so called "*deceiving robot-aliens*"*-example*. In summary I will conclude that the "functional morality" of robots allows us to hold them responsible. We have no reason to be biased towards nonorganic potential agents.

THE MORAL COMMUNITY

In order to decide whether we can hold *robots* morally responsible we should begin by considering when we hold *humans* morally responsible. On what criteria do we—or do we not—hold humans morally responsible?

Whom do we consider morally responsible? Not children, at least not very young children, and not animals, for instance. The same goes for the severely mentally ill, which is why we often test the mental health of defendants who are tried in court. Consider, for instance, a child hitting another child, not realizing that the other child feels pain—or someone who is mentally ill, and believed that he was fighting trolls and not innocent humans. The reason for not holding such people morally responsible is that we doubt their ability to properly understand what they do and what the consequences might be, or their ability to perceive reality. That is, their mental capacities are not fully developed, or damaged. Some sort of mental capacity, including understanding, seems necessary in order to be morally responsible.

A *moral* agent is someone who can initiate a *moral* action. In order to be a moral agent, and perform *moral* actions (actions that are either right or wrong) it is necessary to have a certain understanding of what is important to the moral community. That is, (M1): to be able to discern morally relevant information. This includes the ability to, for instance, discern motives, foresee consequences, and predict the reactions of others, (M2) make moral judgments based on that information, and then (M3) initiate an action based on the judgment. (M1) and (M2) are connected to the possession of internal states, which are for instance *desires* (to act on what is good), and *beliefs* (about what is good for humans, what is important for humans etc.).

Moral agents comprise a proper subgroup of the members of the moral community. All members of the latter are entitled to be treated "morally". But only the moral agents can be blamed for their actions since only they are morally responsible for their actions. A member who cannot be held morally responsible—a moral receiver—is someone who does not have the capacity to fully understand what is morally relevant in a situation, and therefore cannot initiate moral actions in the sense mentioned above (where there has to be an awareness of motives and/or consequences). Nevertheless, the moral receiver has moral *value*; the moral receiver is entitled to benefit from the good judgment of the moral agents, even though the receiver is not an agent him- or herself. The value is derived from being sentient and able to feel pain, for instance. Young children, the mentally ill, and some animals belong to this group. It is usually assumed that all moral agents are automatically moral receivers, but that does not have to be the case if robots are agents.

(Moral) situations need to be interpreted, in the sense that one has to filter the relevant in-

formation. That is, there is an issue of handling the *non-moral* facts. A situation might consist of an infinity of aspects, and we are most likely unable to process this infinity of potential data. Actually, some argue that morally relevant data can be considered a *subset* of possible data that must be chosen by some method. The idea would be that (relevant) data therefore would not be the same thing as the "brute reality"—but instead something already filtered and processed. Bernd Carsten Stahl (2004) suggests that this processed data is the result of cognitive processes as well as social constructions. He claims that information (in this area) should be defined as *data with meaning*, and in order to grasp meaning, we need some sort of understanding.

Let us say that we see someone pushing a lady from the sidewalk, or giving her a Heimlich manoeuvre. We need to know if this was done in order to harm her, or to save her from some danger. In a hospital we distinguish between cutting that is "wrong" (in order to kill someone) from cutting that is "right" (a surgeon cutting a patient during an operation). In order make a moral judgment this data has to be ordered, the relevant part must be processed, the irrelevant part discarded. There does not seem to be any algorithms to decide a priori which data is relevant and which is not. According to Stahl, human beings are able to make that decision because they are in the situation and they create the relevant reality *through interaction*. In order for a moral agent to participate in this social construct, the agent must have the capacity to decide which information is morally relevant and which is not.

That interaction gives meaning might, however, be questioned. First of all, one might wonder how "interaction" should be interpreted. Even not too advanced machines might "interact" with humans, if the term is used in a wide sense. Perhaps *consciousness* would be a better requirement. That is, to have a sense of self, and thereby, most likely, a sense of others.

A reason to focus on interaction might be that interacting is a way of developing into a moral agent, in the sense that children have to *learn* morality. It might also be a way of developing character traits. However, the training and developing of virtuous character traits is not only training to discern what is morally relevant in a situation. It also includes learning to control one's egoism and to weigh one's own self-interest against the self-interest of others. This is central for the human moral agents in the moral community, and seems to be an important part of most normative theories.

MORAL TRUTH

Is there such a thing as objective moral truth in the moral community? When the agents in the moral community make moral judgments, saying "this is right/wrong", are they stating some objective truth, or just expressing their own subjective view? According to cognitivism, a moral statement can be true or false, while non-cognitivists maintain that moral statements do not have truth values. According to the latter view, when people utter moral statements they are in fact expressing non-cognitive attitudes of approval or disapproval.

J.L. Mackie (1990) argues that even though we act as if cognitivism is true—we utter moral sentences in indicative form and try to convince others that we are right—and we act as if there are (objective) moral facts that our moral statements correspond to, thereby being true or false, we might still be in error regarding the existence of objective moral facts (Mackie, 1990).

If there are objective moral truths, we do not seem to demand of our fellow human moral agents that they have access to those facts. There is a lot of disagreement in moral matters. Even if some people might have an epistemological ability to discern those moral facts, the prevailing disagreement shows that there are also a lot of people who do *not* possess, or do not use, that ability. And more importantly, if there are moral facts that only some people are able to discern, then we have no agreed way of determining who actually has this epistemological ability. That is, we are not able to tell who is right. For the purposes of this paper there is no need to take a stand on whether there are moral facts or not. It is sufficient to note that either there are no moral facts, or, if they do exist, we lack the epistemological ability to discern them (or the ability to know who has the proper epistemological ability). However, members of the moral community *act as if* there are objective moral facts (as if the proper epistemological ability is present).

My point is that in evaluating whether or not to accept "new" (which is what robots would be) members into the moral community, we need to know how the already existing members *actually* behave. To do this, it is not necessary to assume that cognitivism is *true*, but it *is* necessary to know that humans *act as if* it is true, and move on from there. Note that the notion of a moral community also applies to specific areas, such as politics, business or law. In every area where moral issues are discussed, this can be observed. In every such area, humans act as if there is moral truth – not as if morality is an emotional attitude.

Let us return to the conditions for moral agency and responsibility. How do we decide that fellow humans pass the conditions? That is, on what do we base the assumption that the person standing before us fulfils the conditions necessary for being held morally responsible?

FUNCTIONALISM IN THE MORAL COMMUNITY

As mentioned above, one of the generally accepted conditions for agency is that the potential agent has mental states. How can we tell that another human being has mental states? And how can we tell that he or she understands? This touches upon *the other minds problem*.

The problem of other minds is the problem of how to justify the almost universal belief that other people have minds like our own. This includes two issues: an epistemological one (how can beliefs about mental states other than our own be justified?) and a conceptual one (how is it possible for us to form a concept of mental states other than our own?) (Hyslop, 2009).

One solution is to see the assumption that other humans have inner lives as the best explanation of their behaviour: the mental states of human beings are what cause them to behave as they do.

We know about ourselves that when we have a *desire* for chocolate, and a *belief* that there is a bar of chocolate in the kitchen, the combination of our desire and belief (mental states) causes us to go into the kitchen and reach for the chocolate. Therefore, when someone else reaches for a bar of chocolate, we infer that he had a desire and a belief (similar to the ones we have when we act in that way), causing the behaviour. The same goes for more complex behaviour. If someone acts in a certain way, say votes for a certain political party or candidate, we form beliefs about the mental states of that person.

Although this inference (from actions or speech to the actual existence of mental states in other people) cannot be proved, normal people seem comfortable with the "analogous defense" (Hyslop, 2009). Since we are describing the moral community—in terms of how normal people behave—we should, in this context, also accept this defense. If there is a certain output, we assume that this output is caused by a mental state.

One theory of mind that deals with the other minds problem in a way that suits the common opinion in the moral community is *functionalism*. According to functionalism regarding mental states, what makes something a mental state of a particular type is not its internal constitution but rather the way it functions, or the role it plays, in the system of which it is a part. Functionalism is similar to (philosophical) behaviourism, but there are differences. First, functionalism takes mental states to be real internal states, while behaviorism avoids talk of internal states (Kim, 2008). Second, functionalism provides more substance regarding theoretical power by constructing "input" and "output" for mental states" (Kim, 2006).

According to this theory, mental states are conceived of as inner states which are the means by which an organism responds to its surroundings. The different mental states are characterized by their various roles, their typical causes and effects. Functionalism was developing in the two decades before John Searle introduced his Chinese Room argument and was a major alternative to the identity theory that is implicit in much of Searle's discussion (Cole, 2009). According to functionalism a mental state *is* what a mental state *does*— the causal (or "functional") role that the state plays determines what state it is. Functionalists distance themselves both from behaviourist and identity theorists. In contrast with the former, functionalism holds that the internal causal processes are important for the possession of mental states, not just for the overt behaviour of the system as a whole.

One might ask whether a behaviourist account would be sufficient to delineate the criteria for being considered a moral agent. This does not seem likely since behaviourism completely avoids talk of internal states. It is not likely that we would consider someone (or something) a moral agent if we did not assume that it had mental states. The behaviour would not be enough (Cole & Foelber, 1984).

The Moral Turing Test

A functionalist method for deciding if another human agent is a moral agent is a so called moral Turing Test (MTT) (Allen et al., 2000). Analogously to the classic Turing Test, the MTT would be: "If two systems are input-output equivalent, they have the same moral status; in particular, one is a *moral agent* in case the other is (Kim, 2006).

A MTT can be constructed by restricting the standard TT to conversations about morality. A human and a robot would sit behind a screen, and the interrogator would ask questions about morality. If human interrogators cannot identify the machine at above chance accuracy, the machine is, on this criterion, a moral agent. Note that the idea is *not* that the robot has to come up with "correct" answers to moral questions (in order to do that, we would have to agree on a normative theory). Instead, the criterion is the robot's ability to fool the interrogator, who should be unable to tell who is the human and who is the machine. Let us say that we ask "Is it right to hit this annoying person with a baseball bat?" A (human or robot) might say (print) no, and B (human or robot) might also say (print) no. Then you ask for reasons for their respective statements.

MTT is similar to the way in which we decide whether humans are moral agents or not, in the sense that we check their reasoning and perceptive abilities before deciding if it seems to be the case that they "think" or "understand". If someone hallucinates, we know this via their reasoning. If they say "no" to the question above, and give the reason "because that person is a ghost", we might not consider them to be moral agents, since there appears to be something wrong with their perceptive or intellectual abilities. The point is that the only way we have access to the potential mental states of other agents is via their reasoning and behaviour.

Another example can be taken from the legal area. We do not hold people legally (or morally) responsible if they do not reason and act in a manner that we expect from moral agents. If a person on trial talks incoherently, or talks of ghosts or goblins, we automatically infer that there is something wrong internally with that person's mental states, and the court will decide that a psychiatric evaluation should be made. Such evaluations are usually based on the person's utterances and other behaviour in situations created for diagnostic purposes.

In a MTT there is a question of convincing the interrogator that you should be considered a moral agent—or not. Imagine a person on trial, who is unable to feel empathy or moral emotions. The interrogator might not always be able to detect this; the person without empathy may well seem perfectly normal since he might have learned how he should explain his actions in order for normal people to accept him. Then the interrogator might suggest that the person is normal, and might be sent to prison rather than psychiatric care. One might also imagine this going the other way; a person on trial convincing the interrogator that he *is* mentally ill, in order to avoid a death sentence, for instance. It is, however, a fact that we do not feel a need to actually look inside a person's head in order to check his mental status; we deem it sufficient to talk to the person, listen to his statements and the arguments he provides.

THE CASE FOR ROBOTS

It seems that the requirement of mental states is the most problematic for robots. It has been claimed that since they have no mental states, they can have no intension to act (Johnson, 2006). Another problem connected to this has to do with their capabilities of understanding.

Based on the reasoning in one of the most extensive debates in philosophy: the (understanding in the) Turing Test vs. the (understanding in the) Chinese Room it can be argued that there are different types of understanding: *semantic* and *syntactic*—and that meaning comes from semantic understanding (Presont & Bishop, 2002). I will not enter that debate here, but will just make a few points.

First, the division between semantic and syntactic understanding is not entirely clear. It is suggested that humans have semantic understanding since we understand the *meaning* of symbols, and that machines can never have semantic understanding. But it is not easy to prove that what we have is actual semantic understanding rather than syntactic understanding. And vice versa it is not easy to disprove that an advanced robot has semantic understanding.

We do not need to distinguish between syntactic or semantic understanding in order to ascribe either (moral) understanding or the ability to be a moral agent. This is an empirical fact: consider how we decide to treat our fellow humans as moral agents based on how they *behave* and how they give reasons for their moral statements. To do that we need not ascribe semantic or syntactic understanding to them.

Second, and more importantly for the case of robots as moral agents, it is sufficient that they can *deal* with the information of a situation, in the sense that they can pass a MTT. Then we actually do not need to decide whether it (or we, or other minds) have semantic or syntactic understanding. A robot may be considered a moral agent even with the (common) assumption that it (or machines) does not actually have the mental states that might be a prerequisite for being a human moral agent. If someone or something passes a MTT there is no need for additional proof that the internal states are mental.

Imagine an example with a human soldier, and a robot soldier. They have both made a mistake. An enemy solider laid down his weapon and raised his arms, which is a sign of surrender. But the enemy soldier kept a grenade in his hand, which both the human and the robot failed to see, and this caused the death of fellow soldiers. When asked, afterwards, why they did not shoot the enemy, the human and the robot provide similar explanations. Weapons on the ground and hands above one's head indicate surrender (the robot has different signs of surrender programmed into it) and after surrendering, an enemy should not be shot. There is no difference here between the human and the robot; the possibly semantic understanding of the human soldier, and the possibly syntactic understanding of the robot soldier, leads to the same conclusions and actions, and therefore, in many cases, it can be argued that it does not matter whether understanding is semantic or syntactical.

It might be argued that we would not accept robots as moral agents because there is a crucial difference between us and robots. We are organic, and they are not, and many claim that morality is a human or organic enterprise in the sense that you need emotions, empathy or the kind of understanding that only social interaction might bring, in order to be part of the moral community. There seems to be a common assumption that only organic brains can have the proper mental states for moral agency. But this is biased, and I will attempt to show it by two examples.

Imagine, in the future, that we will be able to transfer a human mind into a robot (a computer). Not the brain per se, since it is organic, but the contents of the brain in terms of all the functions, memories, personality and the sense of self. The idea is that everything would be intact, and identical to the contents of the person's mind, but that this content would be transferred into a machine. There would be nothing organic left. This may seem farfetched and too science fictional, but in principle it is possible; most cognitive scientists and philosophers agree that there is no such thing as an immaterial soul. And the point is: if the mind of a person is intact, but transferred into a machine, we would be biased if we because of that reason alone—the fact that the mind was no longer organic—would not hold the transferred person morally responsible for her actions.

Let us imagine another example, with aliens coming to earth. We can speak to them, also in moral matters. We realize that they seem to have an idea of morality similar to ours, since they make moral statements such as "that is wrong" when someone is causing pain to a sentient being, for instance. We would most likely accept these aliens as moral agents—based on their passing a MTT. But what if it would, after a while, turn out that these aliens are actually robots? If we decided to consider them as moral agents at first, while we believed them to be organic, why would anything change, regarding their moral ability, if we realized that they were *not* organic? There does not seem to be any plausible reason for this.

To say that you need to be made out of organic material, and have an organic brain, in order to be a moral agent, is prejudiced. If you pass a MTT, that should be sufficient.

FUNCTIONAL MORALITY

To sum up, I suggest that if a robot passes the MTT, it might be held morally responsible. If it would pass that test, its behavior would be "as if moral beliefs are true of false", that is, the way humans behave in moral matters. To accept this is, however, to accept a sort of moral *functionalism*.

Robots just need to *act* as other moral agents: make moral judgments and give reasons for those judgments.

A possible objection to the functional morality of robots, and the use of a MTT, is to ask what is special about morality. If a robot can be a moral agent if it passes a MTT, as I suggest, would that mean that a robot can be religious, for instance, in case it would pass a "religious Turing Test"? And imagine other areas, where you put another prefix to the TT. It might be easy to accept that a machine "thinks" (beats human Chess-players) but not so easy to accept robots as love partners, and maybe the idea of a robot as a moral agent would fall somewhere in between.

There are a lot of interesting problems to investigate here, but the discussion on whether or not robots can be held morally responsible does not depend on clarifying them. If we accept that robots cannot love, or cannot be religious, this has no direct bearing on whether they can be moral agents.

An interesting way to assess the MTT is to look at human psychopaths. Do we accept psychopaths acting "as if" they are moral agents even though they lack empathy? And in that case, is there still a difference compared to how we would feel about

a robot passing a MTT? It might be so, probably because of biological bias. And also, we seldom know if we are standing in front of a psychopath. They can function very well in society and act as "normal" human beings and as moral agents. Not all psychopaths commit crimes and many of them have learned how to behave in order to be accepted, even though they lack empathy. Note that empathy has two components: a perceptive and a cognitive one. Psychopaths do go to prison, but people with severe mental illness, whom we consider to have no contact with reality, do not. We draw the distinction by assessing behaviour and statements, i.e., by the method used in the MTT.

CONCLUSION

The nature of morality, that is, the way human moral agents behave in moral matters, is what we should look at when deciding to accept new members in terms of moral agency and responsibility, into the moral community. When we decide whether the humans we are dealing with are moral agents or not, we look at their behaviour, listen to the reasons they give for their judgments and then decide if we think they have understood the situation properly. This means that we apply MTT and consequently embrace functionalism when deciding whether others should be considered moral agents. I suggest that we should do the same for robots, and that if a robot passes a MTT, it should be considered a moral agent, without us requiring additional proof that its internal states are actually mental. This is supported by the impossibility of deciding who actually has (semantic or only syntactic) understanding, and by the conclusions shown above to follow from the example of aliens who actually are robots.

REFERENCES

Allen, C., Smit, I., & Wallach, W. (2006). Artificial Morality: top down and bottom up and hybrid approaches. *Ethics and Information Technology, 7*, 149–155. doi:10.1007/s10676-006-0004-4

Allen, C., Varner, G., & Zinser, J. (2000). Prolegomena to any future artificial moral agent. *Journal of Experimental & Theoretical Artificial Intelligence, 12*(3), 251–261. doi:10.1080/09528130050111428

Andersson, S. L. (2008). 'Asimov' three laws of robotics' and machine meta ethics. *AI & Society, 22*, 477–493.

Andersson, Y., Anderson, S., & Armen, C. (2004) Towards Machine Ethics. In *Proceedings of AAAI workshop on agent organizations, theory and practice*, San José, CA.

Arkin, R. C. (2009). *Governing Lethal Behavior in Autonomous Robots*. Boca Raton, FL: CRC Press. doi:10.1201/9781420085952

Bekey, G. (2005). *Robots: From biological inspiration to implementations and control*. Cambridge, MA: The MIT Press.

Cole, D. (2009). The Chinese Room Argument. In E. N. Zalta (Ed.), *The Stanford Encyclopedia of Philosophy*. Retrieved from http://plato.stanford.edu/archives/win2009/entries/chinese-room/

Cole, D. J., & Foelber, R. (1984). Contingent Materialism. *Pacific Philosophical Quarterly and Personalist (The) Los Angeles, 65*(1), 74-85.

Hyslop, A. (2009). Other Minds. In E. N. Zalta (Ed.), *The Stanford Encyclopedia of Philosophy*. Retrieved from http://plato.stanford.edu/archives/win2009/entries/other-minds/

Johnson, D. G. (2006). Computer Systems: Moral Agents but not Moral Agents. *Ethics and Information Technology, 8*, 195–204. doi:10.1007/s10676-006-9111-5

Kim, J. (2006). *Philosophy of Mind*. Boulder, CO: Westview Press.

Mackie, J. L. (1990). *Ethics – Inventing Right and Wrong*. London: Penguin Books.

Preston, J., & Bishop, M. (Eds.). (2002). *Views into the Chinese Room*. Oxford, UK: Clarendon Press.

Sparrow, R. (2004). The Turing Triage Test. *Ethics and Information Technology, 6*, 203–213. doi:10.1007/s10676-004-6491-2

Stahl, B. C. (2004). Information, Ethics and Computers: The Problem of Autonomous Agents. *Minds and Machines, 14*, 67–83. doi:10.1023/B:MIND.0000005136.61217.93

Wallach, W., & Allen, C. (2009). *Moral Machines – Teaching Robots Right from Wrong*. New York: Oxford University Press.

This work was previously published in International Journal of Technoethics, Volume 1, Issue 4, edited by Rocci Luppicini, pp. 65-73, copyright 2010 by IGI Publishing (an imprint of IGI Global).

Chapter 21
Cyber–Terrorism and Ethical Journalism:
A Need for Rationalism

Mahmoud Eid
University of Ottawa, Canada

ABSTRACT

Terrorism has been a constant threat in traditional and contemporary societies. Recently, it has been converged with new media technology and cyberspace, resulting in the modern tactic, cyber-terrorism, which has become most effective in achieving terrorist goals. Among the countless cyber-terrorist cases and scenarios of only this last decade, the paper discusses four cyber-terrorism cases that represent the most recent severe cyber-terrorist attacks on infrastructure and network systems—Internet Black Tigers, MafiaBoy, Solo, and Irhabi 007. Regardless of the nature of actors and their motivations, cyber-terrorists hit very aggressively causing serious damages. Cyber-terrorists are rational actors who use the most advanced technology; hence, the critical need for the use of counter-threat swords by actors on the other side. Given that terrorist goals are mostly dependent on the media's reactions, journalistic practices are significant and need to be most effective. A major tool that can help journalists in their anti- and counter-terrorist strategies with cyber-terrorists is rationalism, merged with the expected socially responsible conduct. Rational behaviour, founded in game theory, along with major journalistic ethical principles are fundamental components of effective media decision-making during times of terrorism.

A THREAT: TERRORISM

Threats to global citizens emanating from various terrorist groups around the world are increasingly widespread. No country is excluded from terrorists' potential plans, and both transnational and internal terrorist attacks are possible everywhere as long as the roots of terrorism cannot be effectively expunged. Most noticeable in the late 20th and early 21st centuries are those threats that come from Al-Qaeda, exemplified by bombings and multiple deaths in Dar es Salaam and Nairobi (1998), New York (2001), Bali (2002), Istanbul (2003), Madrid (2004), London (2005), and

DOI: 10.4018/978-1-4666-1773-5.ch021

Sharm Al-Sheikh (2005). Al-Qaeda first emerged to challenge the incumbency and authority of rulers in various Middle Eastern countries, and then its attention shifted from the domestic to the global: a war against the West with a wider goal of having a global balance of power between the West and the world of Islam. America's recent "war on terrorism" has made the West in general and North America in particular a major target of terrorist attacks. Even countries with strong foreign relationships and international reputations of peacekeeping, which might possibly reduce potential *external* or *transnational* terrorist attacks, still cannot guarantee that they will have any bearing in the face of potential *national* or *internal* terrorism.

The convergence of both *national* and *transnational* terrorism becomes a very dangerous threat. Transnational terrorism is a "type of non-state actor that is becoming more important" (Nye, 2005, p. 229). If external threats of terrorism are dangerous and require a rational response from policy decision-makers, it is also true that *internal* extremist groups can become more dangerous if policy decision-makers do not seriously address the issues with which these groups are concerned. Some argue, for instance, that "most terrorist attacks start from a racially, ethnically, or religiously motivated conviction that certain categories of human beings are not worthy of moral standing or consideration" (Ignatieff, 2004, p. 94). If it is conventional for counter-terrorism policymakers to regard terrorists as either mad or wicked, terrorists may, for example, see themselves as "freedom fighters, or fighters in a holy war or whatever. Thus, to execute a captured terrorist might have the very opposite effect from that which the authorities desired in that it creates a martyr and brings new people into the movement" (Nicholson, 1996, p. 169).

From another viewpoint, terrorism is sometimes described as the absolute last weapon of the oppressed.[1] The argument that the *internal* terrorism in United Kingdom has occurred as a result of the country's policies towards some Muslim countries in the Middle East may be partially correct, but it does not tell the whole story. September 11, 2001 (9/11) showed that the global villagers entertain profound misperceptions about, and abhorrence for, each other: "Living in a largely mediated world, they are hostage to the images of 'the other' received through the mass media. A growing global apartheid is tearing them apart into opposing camps" (Tehranian, 2002, p. 59). Hence, such apartheid seems to be one of the key factors behind global terrorism.

TERRORISM AND NEW TECHNOLOGIES: THE BIRTH OF CYBER-TERRORISM

The concept of cyber-terrorism was born in the mid-1980s, when Barry Collin, a senior research fellow at the Institute for Security and Intelligence in Palo Alto, California, USA, coined this hyped-up, techno-phrase by referring to the convergence of cyberspace and terrorism (Berner, 2003; Denning, 2000; Matusitz & Minei, 2009; Matusitz, 2009, 2005; Mitliaga, 2001). Although there are many different concepts of terrorism and no one agreed-upon definition of the term to date, most would acknowledge the existence of cyber-terrorism, i.e., the use of information and communications technologies to facilitate any or all forms of terrorism. Cyber-terrorism is the intentional use of threatening and disruptive actions, or attacks waged through computers, the Internet, and technology-based networks or systems against information and data, infrastructures supported by computer systems, programs, and networks in order to cause harm or to further ideological, political, or similar objectives, influence an audience, or cause a government to change its policies (Corzine & Cañas, 2008; Denning, 2000; Matusitz, 2005, 2008, 2009).

Terrorists have always been pioneers in embracing the newest communication technologies and using them in conjunction with the available media.[2] Much easier than the traditional media, new media technologies allow terrorist organizations to transmit their messages more efficiently. "The network of computer-mediated communication … is ideal for terrorists-as-communicators: it is decentralized, it cannot be subjected to control or restriction, it is not censored, and it allows access to anyone who wants it" (Tsfati & Weimann, 2002, p. 319). In today's world, "technology is putting into the hands of deviant individuals and groups destructive powers that were once reserved primarily to governments…. [It] has made the complex systems of modern societies more vulnerable to large-scale attack" (Nye, 2005, p. 229). Although the Internet, "relying on widely separated but interconnected computer systems, was originally designed as a military solution to the threat of communication disruption due to nuclear attack" (Briggs, 2004, p. 453), individuals or groups can now use cyberspace, computers, and information technology, especially the Internet[3], to threaten, terrorize and cause harm to both governments and civilians.

Modern terrorists also rely heavily on cyberspace[4] to communicate messages, implement operations, and achieve goals. Cyberspace provides a way for terrorists to inflict massive damage, cause psychological impact, and gain media appeal, all while remaining anonymous (Matusitz & Minei, 2009, p. 162). The wide spread of information and networking technology into virtually every corner around the globe is spawning new opportunities for terrorists to cause havoc through the Internet (Nakra, 2003, p. 3).

A keyboard for a terrorist is much more valuable than a bomb. In our growing era of cyberterrorism, a cyber-terrorist cannot only conduct the types of attacks to which we have grown accustomed, such as remote bombing, but are increasingly able to deliver horrific destruction from a distance. For example, it is possible, through the use of the Internet, to hack into the processing control systems of a cereal manufacturer, change the levels of iron supplement, and consequently kill the children of a nation enjoying their breakfast. Info-terrorists no longer need to enter an office or a home to steal or distort the information. Without leaving a single trace behind, info-terrorists can steal and tamper with information, create new and corrupt electronic files, block access to information by authorized users, and so on.

Cyber-terrorism is a very attractive option for modern terrorists for several reasons. First, it is cheaper than traditional terrorist methods; the terrorist needs only a personal computer and an Internet connection. Second, it is more anonymous than traditional terrorist methods as terrorists use online nicknames or log on to a website anonymously, making it very hard for security agencies and police forces to track down the terrorists' real identity. Third, it uses the Internet as an ideal vehicle to disseminate terrorist propaganda and hate speech, glorify the heroes and martyrs of the movement's cause, facilitate communication between members and sympathizers, plot terrorist acts, retrieve strategic and tactical information, recruit new members, and raise funds. Fourth, the variety and number of targets are enormous as cyber-terrorists can target the computers and computer networks of governments, individuals, public utilities, private airlines, and so on. Fifth, its ability to target, usurp, or tap into nearly any database or control system can be devastating and unpredictable. Sixth, it can be conducted remotely, spanning regional, state, and even international jurisdictional boundaries—a feature that is especially appealing to terrorists because it requires less physical training, psychological investment, risk of mortality, and travel than conventional forms of terrorism. Finally, cyber-terrorism has the potential to directly affect a larger number of people than traditional terrorist methods, thereby generating greater media coverage, which is ultimately a major goal for terrorists, as journalists and the public alike are fascinated by practically any kind of computer attack. (Breen, 2008; Corzine &

Cañas, 2008; Denning, 2000; Matusitz & Minei, 2009; Nacos, 2006; Weimann, 2005).

CYBER-TERRORISTS: CASES AND SCENARIOS

Computer-based technologies and the Internet are used in almost every governmental, business, organizational, personal, and home environment around the world. Computers even control major military and corporate networks and information. These practices amplify the dangerous capabilities of cyber-terrorists, whose strikes alter computer systems. Cyber-terrorists are potentially a few mouse clicks away from compromising important hospital databases, penetrating a top-secret federal computer system and stealing or erasing data, damaging files or changing information in order to destroy infrastructure targets and cause a disruption in the federal computer network, destroying the actual machinery of the information infrastructure, breaching dams, disrupting monetary systems, damaging the mass media, shutting down power grids, disseminating false information, sabotaging operations, and threatening to divulge confidential information or system weaknesses. In addition, cyber-terrorist attacks against computers and the Internet can be as simple as malicious software, computer viruses, computer network worms, DOS attacks, stolen passwords, insider collusion, and organized floods of electronic traffic that overwhelm computers. Unlike the traditional tactics of terrorism (i.e., bombings, assassinations, suicide missions, hijackings, kidnapping, missile attacks, and mass disruption/mass destruction), cyber-terrorism is a modern tactic of terrorism, which targets computer systems and attempts to manipulate and corrupt such systems to attain varying levels of criminal destruction of property, political change, and public fear. While the terrorists' three main goals are attracting attention, getting their demands recognized, and winning respect or gaining legiti-

macy, goals of cyber-terrorists vary from causing computer disruptions for the sake of mischief to damaging Internet sites used by political groups demonstrating moral or ethical points to the world (Breen, 2008; Eid, 2006a; Matusitz & Minei, 2009; Matusitz, 2005; Nacos, 2006).

Numerous terrorist organizations have entered cyberspace and created Internet sites. These include Hamas (the Islamic Resistance Movement), the Lebanese Hizbollah (Party of God), the Egyptian Al-Gama'a al Islamiyya (Islamic Group), the Popular Front for the Liberation of Palestine, the Palestinian Islamic Jihad, the Basque ETA movement, the Irish Republican Army, the Colombian National Liberation Army, the Liberation Tigers of Tamil Eelam, the Armed Revolutionary Forces of Colombia, the Popular Democratic Liberation Front Party in Turkey, the Kurdish Workers' Party, and the Japanese Red Army. Geographically, most of the organizations that have turned to the Internet are based in Third World countries (in South America, East Asia, and the Middle East), and only a few are located in Europe. Terrorist websites usually include information about the history of the organization and biographies of its leaders, founders, heroes, commanders or revered personalities, information on the political and ideological aims of the organization, and up-to-date news. While avoiding the violent aspects of their activities, Internet terrorists usually stress two issues: freedom of expression and political prisoners. The contents of their websites generally attempt to solicit money for their various causes, disseminate coded messages, approach potential supporters, address their enemies, and gain international public attention (Eid, 2006a; Gordon & Ford, 2003; Nacos, 2006; Tsfati & Weimann, 2002).

Scenarios of cyber-terrorism are countless. They range from "slow degradation of important but non-critical systems to wholesale broad attacks on critical infrastructure systems and anything in between them" (Mishra, 2003, p. 452). However, most cyber-terrorism attack scenarios involve operations that seek to corrupt government databases, disable delivery of essential services, or circumvent a government's cyber security measures in order to extort and hold for ransom access and control of these systems until the attackers' demands are met (Corzine & Cañas, 2008, p. 6).

During the late 20th century and the beginning of the 21st, there have been numerous severe cyber-terrorist attacks on security and financial infrastructure and network systems. For example, in 1995, a Russian computer geek, Vladimir Levin, was the first person to hack into a bank to extract money. He hacked into Citibank and robbed millions of dollars, transferring them to his accounts in the U.S., Finland, Holland, Germany and Israel. In 1999, the Melissa virus, written by David Smith, was the first of its kind to wreak damage on a global scale. Posted to a sex newsgroup, Melissa spread to more than 300 companies across the world completely destroying their computer networks, causing damages amounting to nearly $400 million.

This paper focuses on four cyber-terrorism cases that represent the most recent severe cyber-terrorist attacks on infrastructure and network systems—namely, *Internet Black Tigers*, *MafiaBoy*, *Solo*, and *Irhabi 007*. These cases include different types of terrorist actors (groups and individuals), motivated by different reasons (ethnic, religious, political, military, and financial), and using different scenarios of cyber-terrorism (e-mail bombs, Internet hacker attacks, military computer hacking, and website materials of radical militant ideology for terrorist recruiting, fund raising, planning, and operations). The following are brief descriptions of the four cyber-terrorism cases.

In 1998 the first cyber-terrorist attack against a country's computer systems occurred when an offshoot group of the ethnic Liberation Tigers of Tamil Eelam (LTTE), known as the Internet Black Tigers (IBT) adopted new tactics in their quest for independence towards a Tamil Eelam goal. LTTE is a guerrilla group representing the minority Tamil community, fighting for an Eelam,

or homeland in the northern and eastern provinces of Sri Lanka.[5] Its terrorist tactics are mainly suicide commandos, both men and women, some in their early teens, for individual assassination as well as mass attacks. The IBT organized and conducted what are known as the first "Email bombings"[6] and cyber-attacks to be reported by U.S. intelligence authorities crediting a terrorist group. They have swamped Sri Lankan embassies in Seoul, Ottawa and Washington, D.C., with thousands of electronic mail messages; successfully managing to crash the embassies' mail servers. Their strategy consisted of over 800 mass-emails a day for approximately two weeks. The emails contained the following message: *We are the Internet Black Tigers and we're doing this to disrupt your communications.* Although no physical harm was generated compared to usual LTTE acts of killing and bombings, the IBT did generate a significant amount of fear in the embassies. Nonetheless, despite the disruption and media attention the IBT attacks caused and received, their actions have been encouraged in hopes that it may distract from routine violent strikes custom to the LTTE, and receive higher attention (Berner, 2003; Denning, 2000, 2001; Joshi, 1996; Mishra, 2003; Thomas, 2001).

In 2000, between February 6 and February 14, Valentine's Day, a 15-year-old Montreal youth named Michael Calce, known under the Internet alias MafiaBoy, hacked into some of the largest websites in the world, including CNN, Yahoo, Amazon, eBay, Buy.com, E*trade and Excite, by gaining access to 75 computers in 52 networks, and ordered a Denial of Service (DoS) attack on them, causing panic everywhere from the White House to suburbia and around the world. U.S. law-enforcement authorities initially estimated the DoS attacks caused a total of 1.7 billion dollars in damages to commercial websites. The teenager was tracked through cyberspace by a team of Federal Bureau of Investigation (FBI) and Royal Canadian Mounted Police (RCMP) investigators to his home in an affluent west-island suburb.

He was charged as a juvenile in one of the most dramatic hacking assaults in Internet history. The alleged hacker has been investigated by the RCMP in connection with a series of attacks that are thought to have caused hundreds of millions of dollars of damage. The attacks were seen as the most serious security breaches in the history of the Internet and triggered a police hunt led by the FBI and the U.S. Justice Department. The attacks took place through the planting of "zombie programs" in numerous computers in several U.S. states that were activated remotely to bombard the target websites with fake requests that overloaded computer servers and denied access to legitimate users. Known as a packet kiddie, this type of hacker is more like a vandal than a programmer, taking advantage of software written by more sophisticated hackers to mount their attacks. MafiaBoy used an online tool supplied by another hacker to launch attacks against those websites. The incident, nonetheless, appeared to have been an unfortunate combination of teenage vandalism and hubris—an eager boy seeking to demonstrate his technical prowess and hence gain the esteem of his peer group (Alden & Kehoe, 2000; Alleged "MafiaBoy" faces..., 2000; Bridis & Chipello, 2000; Chipello, 2001; Harrison, 2000; Mohay, Panichprecha, & Tickle, 2009; Scott, 2000).

Between February 2001 and March 2002, an avid UFO (Unidentified Flying Object) conspiracy theorist from England named Gary McKinnon, going by the codename Solo, committed the biggest military computer hack of all time by breaking into 97 U.S. military and NASA computers, threatening national defence and security at a critical time in the weeks following the 9/11 attacks. His attack left the military network vulnerable to intruders. All of his acts were committed from the relative comfort of his then girlfriend's flat in Wood Green, North London, UK. The only direct link between his acts and the United States were bytes of data electronically transferred over the Internet. He extracted the identities of certain accounts and

associated passwords and then installed software called "Remotely Anywhere". This enabled further access and the ability to alter data without detection. He also installed further "hacking tools" that allowed him to scan over 73,000 United States Government computers. Among them were 53 Army computers that controlled its Military District of Washington network, and 26 Navy computers including United States Naval Weapons Station Earle, New Jersey. He also saved data onto his own computers, including files containing account names and passwords. His actions affected the integrity, availability and operation of programs, systems, information and data on the computers, rendering them unreliable. The cost of repair was said to total over 700,000 U.S. dollars. Solo has admitted infiltrating secure systems, but maintains he was motivated only by curiosity about UFOs and a desire to expose UFO secrets that were being concealed. He said, UFOs "have been reverse-engineered.... Rogue elements of Western intelligence and governments have reverse engineered them to gain free energy, which I thought was very important, in these days of the energy crisis" (Hacker Gary McKinnon loses..., 2009). Solo's supporters characterize him as a harmless eccentric (Arnell & Reid, 2009; Britain: Trial of an alien..., 2009; Dombey, Murphy, & Parker, 2009; Murphy, 2009).

In October 2005, British officials arrested a 22-year-old Moroccan-born student and new immigrant resident of the United Kingdom named Younis Tsouli, better known by his Internet pseudonym, Irhabi 007 ("Irhabi" means terrorist in Arabic, and "007" is a reference to the fictional British secret agent James Bond), in his west London flat. Irhabi 007 has been described as one of the most notorious *cyber-Jihadists* in the world (Cornish, Hughes, Livingstone, 2009). His activities included setting up websites and web forums in support of Al-Qaeda, and distributing video material filmed by the Iraqi insurgency. Assisted primary by two other co-conspirators,

22-year-old Waseem Mughal and 19-year-old Tariq Al-Daour, he allegedly posted tutorial videos on how to create car bombs and other such destructive instructions on the web page "You Bomb It". Along with such material, the website was also used for marketing, distribution, research, fundraising, recruiting, and, on occasion, operations. He used his hacking skills to break into and subvert computer networks in order to distribute video files of terrorist attacks, and to use the proceeds of common credit card fraud to set up Jihadi websites as well as train others involved in his plans. He is a classic example of a cyber-terrorist who used the Internet to spread radical, militant ideology that is central to the radicalization, recruitment, and planning stages of domestic and international terrorist cells. However, his websites were being shut down either when hosts realized they had been hijacked or when cyber-trackers or officials spotted the sites and shut them down. This meant that Irhabi 007 had to continually set up new websites to host the material. Al-Daour, with no evidence that he ever met in person with Irhabi 007 but only connected through cyberspace, was the moneyman who funded these activities. On his computer drives police found details of 37,000 credit cards, including security codes, which were linked to more than 2.5 million euros worth of fraudulent transactions (Blitz, Burns, & Fidler, 2005; Block & Solomon, 2006; Experts say West can't..., 2007; Maher, 2007; Solomon & Patrick, 2006).

CYBER-TERRORISM AND DECISION-MAKING: A NEED FOR GAME THEORY

Given these ever-increasing cases and scenarios of cyber-terrorism, computer security has become more important than ever to such organizations as government agencies, banks, retailers, universities, schools, and the wide range of goods and service providers, which all use the Internet as an integral part of conducting their daily business. Evidently, the interactions between the cyber-terrorists and the computer security agents take the form of conflict situations, where opponents seek to gain their best interests and benefits while avoiding or minimizing their losses. A hacker on the Internet may wish to attack a network and the network administrator has to defend against this attack. "The attackers can gain rewards such as thrills for self-satisfaction or transfers of large sums of money into their bank accounts; meanwhile, the administrators can suffer damages such as system downtime or theft of secret data" (Lye & Wing, 2005, p. 72). Cyber-terrorists aim to cause damage to the computer system that they attack. This damage can take many forms. For example, Matusitz (2009, p. 277) explains that any action undertaken by the computer network to strengthen its security system against attacks generates benefits for the cyber-terrorists because it imposes costs on the computer network. Also, any move taken by the cyber-terrorists that causes damage to the computer network increases benefits for the cyber-terrorist (e.g., self-glorification as the opponent suffers). On the other hand, the response from the computer network against a cyber-terrorist action can be twofold: retaliation (offensive) or conciliation (collaborative). Collaboration between the attackers and the defenders can contribute to the shrinking of the cyber-terrorist network by reducing the number of members, because the computer network can make it appear that the conciliation was not the result of the actions taken by the cyber-terrorists. As a result, some members may feel that the cyber-terrorist attacks in question have not carried the impact they had hoped. Retaliation can also increase winnings for both sides because it expends resources.

This battle between computer security experts and cyber-terrorists has been researched and explained through game theory (e.g., Hensgen, Desouza, Evaristo, & Kraft, 2003; Matusitz, 2009). As conflict situations between rational actors, cyber-terrorism cases need to be managed by their decision-makers within the parameters of game theory in order to maximize the benefits and minimize the losses. The decision-making process is better enhanced within game theory structure, so that players make effective decisions (i.e. select better choices or strategies). In fact, a deeper consideration of game theory helps understand how rational thinking can be useful for decision-makers, especially in times of conflicts (Eid, 2008). Game theory[7], a branch of pure mathematics, helps understand social situations that involve the interaction of individuals, as it explains how individuals' decisions are interrelated and how those decisions result in outcomes, and develops methodologies that apply in principle to all interactive situations (Flanagan, 1998; Heap & Varoufakis, 1995; Morrow, 1994; Shubik, 1954). Game theory recommends a rational course of action and then describes the consequences of such conduct, as it tells us what would happen if the recommended behaviour rules were followed (Nicholson, 1970).

In analyzing the security of computer networks, the interactions between attackers and network administrators can be presented as a two-player general-sum stochastic game (e.g., Lye & Wing, 2005), with strategies that can be helpful for administrators to enhance the security of their network. As Matusitz (2009, p. 277) explains, stochastic simply means random, a process whose behaviour is non-deterministic; a system's subsequent state is influenced both by predictable actions of the process and by randomness. After solving the stochastic game, the expected attacker behaviour is then manifested in the transitions between states in the system model by influencing the transition rates based on a probability distribution. Eventually, the corresponding stochastic process is employed to calculate security measures of the system. This is the case in any evolutionary game such as a chess game, when player A (e.g., a computer security agent) does not know the next move of player B (the cyber-terrorist)

and vice-versa. Player A only needs to act when an attack on the computer network is suspected. It is fair to assume that both players know what each other are capable of doing. However, they do not know each other's next move.

The need for game theory becomes more crucial in cyber-terrorism situations, given that it is a post-modern theory. Conventional strategies of conflict situations are useless when opponents wage attacks in a post-modern fashion using the most advanced technology and cyberspace tools. Under the principles of game theory, each player is assumed to be rational; all players wish the outcome to be as positive or rewarding as possible. The cyber-terrorist and the cyber forensics expert not only engage in real-time game play but also use tactics that are not conceivable in conventional conflict. Not only can cyber-terrorists make multiple moves from the same location (e.g., launch numerous viruses with just a few keystrokes); they can also make multiple moves simultaneously (as if they were composed of multiple selves). While in most conventional situations players alternate moves, in cyberspace this is not true anymore. A cyber-terrorist can easily launch rapid multiple simultaneous attacks. The possibilities in cyberspace and cyber-terrorism are almost unlimited and very complex. The fragmentary aspect of the Internet and communication in cyberspace give each player more autonomy to create their own environment and identity. Therefore, the interactions between the cyber-terrorists and the computer security agents are to be viewed as a post-modern two-player (or more) game, with decision-makers (who have opposing or joined interests) follow specific objectives and take into account both their skills and expectations of the other player's (decision-maker's) behaviour. The game theory structure helps explain what strategies both players can use and how computer security agents can use the outcomes (or payoffs) of the game to improve the security of their network (Matusitz, 2008, 2009).

GAME THEORY AND COMMUNICATION: A NEED FOR RESPONSIBLE JOURNALISM

Communication plays a central role in game theory in order for players to reach the desired outcomes. The strategic interaction between players in a given game requires making decisions, i.e., selecting choices among strategies. The outcome of the game depends on such choices (decisions). If there is no communication between two players, then no cooperation can be formed, and this can lead to negative outcomes for both players, as it is the case in the Prisoners' Dilemma Game. However, if they can communicate and engage in cooperative behaviour, the outcome would be quite different, as is the case in Eid's (2008) Communication Game, where a modified prisoners' dilemma game illustrates how Canada and the Arab World, during the 2003 War on Iraq, have communicated to play a more effective role during the crisis than that which has been imposed on them (prisoner's dilemma situation) due to their relations to the main adversaries in that crisis (U.S. and Iraq). Eid (2008) has demonstrated the media's involvement in a group of various major games (conflict situations) in the U.S.-Iraqi crisis to examine their rational performance, and to provide game-theoretic-based encouragement that may motivate journalistic practices towards ethical conduct during situations where conduct is frequently unethical.

Modern terrorism is highly dependent on the attention of the media. Thus, "modern terrorism can be understood as an attempt to communicate messages through the use of orchestrated violence" (Tsfati & Weimann, 2002, p. 317). As Former British Prime Minister Margaret Thatcher once said, "publicity is the oxygen of terrorism" and that terrorists "understood this and acted accordingly" (Nacos, 2006, p. 208). Terrorists need to publicize their attacks in order to generate fear; therefore, unlike criminals, terrorists usually claim responsibility for their actions and are in direct

or indirect contact with media representatives (Mishra, 2003, p. 444). Terrorists in this era are much more aware of their relationship to the media and understand how they can benefit the most from using them. Moreover, they are even more aware of avoiding "the use by the media"—the other side of the relationship. There are many incidents in history when the media were used by terrorists and their sympathizers. On the other hand, "terrorists themselves also feel 'used' by the media which pick up their action, but offer no guarantee of transmitting their message" (Schmid, 1989, p. 559). However, modern terrorists are more effective than the media in such a relationship. Terrorists overcome this obstacle and maximize their benefit from this relationship with the media. Osama bin Laden, for example, used to provide Al-Jazeera with videotapes to broadcast without any distortion of his messages. However, as the media became more aware of their role in communicating terrorist messages, Bin Laden no longer enjoys this benefit as the media have stopped conveying his messages in their unaltered form. He is still able to publish these on-line if traditional media should not give him exactly what he asks for.

For the media then to enhance their role in such a relationship with terrorists, it is fundamental to be involved in the conflict (game) between terrorists and policymakers, or cyber-terrorists and security computer agents, in a way similar to both adversaries. That is, the media should be also following the rules of the given game (case or scenario of terrorism), positioning themselves in a separate game against one of the adversaries, or joining an existing game being in support of a player. The media can be positioned as one player in a game with cyber-terrorists as their adversary, or be in support of policymakers in their adversarial relationship with cyber-terrorists. In either case, they need to be aware of the rules of the specific game, which vary from a game (a terrorist case or scenario) to another. This requires an understanding of the rational choices (decisions) among the various strategies available for them as one player, vis-à-vis those strategies available for terrorists.

In addition to being aware of the rationality of the decision-making process, ethics and responsibility are key fundamentals to the effective performance of the media: "communication cannot be effective without being ethical and socially responsible" (Wright, 1996, p. 521). Journalism, as in most other professions, has codes of ethics in order to guide its personnel (including media owners, managers, editors, and journalists). Journalistic codes of ethics are useful and necessary while greatly benefiting the common good of society. They attempt to instil moral balance to the interests of media personnel, the publics, and policymakers. However, it is often difficult to find journalism personnel who adhere to, or are obliged to adhere to, these codes. Journalism personnel's responsibility to the common good of society has proved largely inadequate and deficient. Reasons vary from simple to complex and justifications go further to the extreme of the philosophical perspective that suspects the very possibility of the existence of ethics. But given the dangerous role of journalism in society, there is a necessity for ethical journalism in order to enhance the communication performance of the media, most significantly in times of terrorism.

The need to consider the ethical component of a decision becomes practically relevant when we consciously confront a choice or decision and know that our action will have a potentially harmful impact on another person or persons. Digging deeper into the organizational structure of mass media where such decisions are made, as well as the nature of duties assigned to media personnel in various levels of management, sheds light on the significance of news-writing as a decision-making process. Journalistic decisions, whether simple or complex, and whether made by the writer, news sources, or editors, help shape news-writing and determine what the final product will look like. News-writing involves decision-making, as writers have to make decisions as they

write. It involves, in the simplest way, making compromises between one mode of expression and another, and deciding which facts to include and exclude in a story. But the process is not as simple as this: "the writer, like it or not, becomes a ruthless decision-maker, sometimes discarding the very items that seemed essential only a few hours before and choosing the form and style that will most effectively present the information in the space allowed" (Dennis & Ismach, 1981, p. 109). It becomes important to decide whether the news story presents sufficient information, and to recognize the criteria of effective journalism.

Considering this while covering acts of terrorism highlights the volume of decisions that need to be made in the context of news-writing. Looking into some journalistic guidelines[8] for covering acts of terrorism explores that there are twelve most frequently stated major principles or cautions; all of which require decision-making. These guidelines suggest that news personnel, during a terrorist event, should do the following: 1) assign experienced staff members to the story; 2) approach the story with care and restraint; 3) report demands of the terrorist(s) after paraphrasing them, instead of presenting them directly; 4) cover the event in a thoughtful and conscientious manner; 5) maintain communication with authorities to seek guidance; 6) consult officials before making publishing decisions; 7) consider recommendations carefully and obey instructions by authorities; 8) avoid interfering in the duties of authorities; 9) do nothing to jeopardize lives; 10) avoid sensationalizing beyond the innate sensation of the story itself; 11) avoid providing a platform for the terrorist propaganda; and 12) avoid using inflammatory catchwords or phrases, or reporting rumours.

It is very important to note here that such guidelines are contingent to terrorist events, as they require different decisions from those in normal situations (i.e., when no severe stress situations such those of terrorism, conflicts, crises, wars, etc.). From a rational perspective, and according to the rules of game theory, each social interaction situation is presented as one specific game with unique rules. This means that journalists can make different decisions following different guidelines than those presented above in order to maximize effective communication in different situations. For example, although in normal coverage of governmental politics the media are encouraged by the rationality of the Game of Truth to question and threaten to verify information in announcements made by government officials in order to push them toward telling the truth (Eid, 2006b), in terrorist events the media should follow different rules (based on the different game) and cooperate, somewhat blindly, with policymakers who are in control of playing the game with terrorists. Any deviance by the media from the policymakers' announcements and strategies may cause escalations and negative outcomes.

The significance of the role of the media during acts of terrorism requires a sense of responsibility. In general, ethical journalism requires adherence to journalistic principles and cornerstones that contribute to the achievement of effective journalism. These include truth telling, accuracy, fairness, balance, verification, and maintaining context (e.g., Eid, 2008; Elliott, 2003; Gordon, 1999; Harris & Spark, 1997; Hindman, 1997; Kittross, 1999; Kovach & Rosenstiel, 2001). However, responsibility as an overriding ethical principle may require in some situations, including acts of terrorism, that some of those ethical principles be rationally considered according to the rules of the game (terrorist event). This is to the extent that sometimes policymakers consider irresponsible journalism as a form of terrorism.[9] Therefore, if abiding by, for instance, telling the truth, which is absolutely the right thing to do to obtain the best payoffs in any social interaction and even in any severe stress situation (Eid, 2006), harm may be caused to policymakers who are rational players in a game with terrorists. This may consequently cause harm to any civilians involved and/or the whole society; therefore, it is rationally respon-

sible to coordinate the truthful information with policymakers rather than with the publics (who are affected by the outcome of the game) or with the adversaries (terrorists) to ensure that adhering to a major ethical principle does not infringe on rational decision-making, leading to an *effective* performance that is a hybrid of *ethical* and *rational* performance.

ETHICAL JOURNALISM AND RATIONALISM: EFFECTIVE DECISION-MAKING

Rationality is a major concept for effective communication and decision-making. Rationality exists in both behavioural decision theory and mathematical decision theory. Rational behaviour, a basic assumption in game theory, can mean many things in our everyday languages including reasonable, thoughtful, wise, just, or sane behaviour or action. However, for game theory scholars, rational behaviour have a more focused and centred meaning than the broad or common meanings of the term rationality. Rational behaviour in game theory is goal-directed towards *more* desired outcomes rather than *less* desired outcomes (e.g., Morrow 1994). The focus in the rational-choice approach is on how individuals' attempts to achieve their goals are constrained by one another's actions and the structure of the game. For journalism personnel, effective communication and decision-making during times of severe stress becomes crucial in order to achieve desired goals of not only the media, but most importantly the whole society given the significant role of the media.

The Crisis Decision-Making Model for Media Rational Responsibility ($CD\_M^3\_R^2$) is a pioneer model suggested by Eid (2008) as a media decision-making model that contributes to rendering the performance of the media decision-makers *effective*, as a consequent result of being *rational* and *responsible*. Through this model, Eid provides recommended actions that may be required of journalism personnel during their news-writing process in times of severe stress situations. The four main components of the model are the media's: rational thinking, responsible conduct, crisis decision-making and final acts. Basically, the components "rational thinking" and "responsible conduct" are two weights or forces fundamentally necessary for creating the balance in the model. That is, *rational* and *responsible* aspects of the model are crucial to achieving its main purpose and to making it *effective.*

The CD_M^3_R^2 component "rational thinking" consists of six consecutive and successive tasks, each of which again contains consecutive and successive actions. Consecutive and successive mean that they are implemented in a sequential nature, but at the same time are also subject to re-implementation as many times as is necessary in order to achieve the component of rational thinking during the severe stress situation. Also, the actions involved in each task are of the same nature. The six tasks are: 1) distinguishing the situation among the different severe stress situations; 2) studying the situation; 3) recognizing actors; 4) searching strategies; 5) learning outcomes; and 6) suggesting goals. There are certain actions that need to be taken in order to fulfill each of these tasks. First, to distinguish a situation from other similar severe stress situations, the situation should be investigated, and its characteristics tested. In so doing, media decision-makers need to clearly understand the political policies of their adversaries in the situation, the adversaries' real drivers, primary objectives, and the instruments needed to achieve these objectives. This investigative effort enables media decision-makers to avoid misinterpretations, and to recognize the logic behind the adversaries' decisions. Then, testing the characteristics of the situation to clearly identify what the situation really is helps in knowing how to approach it according to the appropriate rules. Second, to study the situation effectively, the different levels of structuring the situation should be

understood, and the situation itself and its developments should be defined mathematically as specific types of games with specific rules that should be followed. Third, to recognize actors included in the situation according to its game structure, major players in the game should be defined and the media organization should position itself as a player. Fourth, to search for strategies for playing the game, or for participating in the situation, the strategy of each player participating in the game should be realized, and possible strategies should be studied carefully and fully understood. Fifth, to learn about the possible choices for each player in the situation, the payoff matrix of each game should be constructed to include outcomes of each choice, and consequently the preferable choice should be determined. Finally, to suggest rational goals, the dimensions of each desired outcome should be checked, and consequently a set of the most desired outcomes should be prepared.

The CD_M^3_R^2 component "responsible conduct" consists of four cyclical tasks, each of which contains actions; two of these tasks maintain their cyclical nature while the other two have a consecutive and successive nature. Cyclical means that they have no specific order in which they must be implemented and that they continue until achieving the responsible conduct during the situation. Also, the actions involved in each of the four tasks have the same nature as the tasks themselves. The two tasks of a cyclical nature are: 1) balancing various responsibilities; and 2) emphasizing ethical principles; while the two tasks of the consecutive and successive nature are: 1) confronting major effects on decision-makers; and 2) focusing on facts. In order to fulfill each of these tasks, there are actions that need to be taken. First, to balance various responsibilities and interests, the media decision-makers should show responsibilities towards, or serve the interests of, themselves, colleagues, subjects, sources, the public(s), the profession, their employer or organization, and authorities. Second, to emphasize ethical principles, media decision-makers should adhere to six major ethical principles (independence, truth, accuracy, fairness, integrity, and serving the public interest), as well as three others (objectivity, balance, and maintaining context), which intervene with the six principles. Third, to deal with any major effects on decision-makers, media decision-makers should minimize negative effects, and maximize positive effects. The negative effects include: narrowing of options, over-reliance on experts, taking refuge in value judgments, poor mental performance, overloaded communications, meddling in lower levels, reduced team performance, and lack of a long term view. The positive effects include: increased responsiveness, enhanced innovation, and improved flexibility. Finally, to focus on facts, media decision-makers should carefully go through the processes of searching, defining, verifying, and sticking to facts. For example, in searching for facts the media decision-makers should investigate the origins of the facts and collect them from various sources before defining them because once they verify the facts and are confident of their reliability they will stick to them.

Pertaining to cyber-terrorism, the media should go through the tasks of both components of CD_M^3_R^2, rational thinking and responsible conduct, in order to be effective in making decisions that can either help the policymakers in their interactions with cyber-terrorists, avoid being used by cyber-terrorists for their own interests, or use counter-terrorism strategies directed against cyber-terrorists as their adversaries. For the first component, rational thinking, during the interactions (games) between cyber-terrorists and computer security agents or policymakers, the media may position themselves either in support of one side (i.e., policymakers) in the same games, or as an independent adversary against one side (i.e., cyber-terrorists) in separate games. If they choose the former option, they will likely achieve effective performance by following or enforcing the same strategies as the policymakers. Should they choose the latter option, they must then understand the nature and rules of the new games, depending on each case or scenario of cyber-terrorism.

In cyber-terrorism cases such as the IBT, MafiaBoy, Solo, and Irhabi 007, the media do not have similar strategies when playing the games (i.e., interacting in conflict situations) with cyber-terrorists. In fact, their strategies are determined based on how the goals of cyber-terrorists target the media. In other words, these four cyber-terrorism cases have targeted the media in different ways. IBT and MafiaBoy sought to attract the media's attention, although for different reasons—distract from routine violent strikes custom to the LTTE and receive higher attention (IBT), or demonstrate technical prowess and hence gain the esteem of peers (MafiaBoy). However, Solo and Irhabi 007 did not intend to attract the media's attention, but were driven by non-media related motivations—curiosity about UFOs and a desire to expose UFO secrets that were being concealed (Solo), or spreading radical, militant ideology that is central to the radicalization, recruitment, and planning stages of domestic and international terrorist cells. In the two cases where the media's attention was targeted by cyber-terrorists (IBT and MafiaBoy), the media are positioned in games with strategies different from those in their games with cyber-terrorists who did not aim at attracting the media's attention (Solo and Irhabi 007).

For the IBT and MafiaBoy games, the media may find themselves with strategies that can range between full coverage of the cyber-terrorist attacks to no coverage at all, with a wide range of coverage intensity in-between the two extremes. Strategies of cyber-terrorists (IBT and MafiaBoy) may include attracting the media's attention, using the media to disseminate specific helpful information to cyber-terrorists, maximize fear among the public, and so on. Strategies of both the media and cyber-terrorists will differ according to the players (IBT or MafiaBoy), resulting in different games with different outcomes (or payoffs). As for the Solo and Irhabi 007 games, the media may find themselves with the same strategies as in the cases of IBT and MafiaBoy. However, their payoffs for using the same strategies (full coverage or no coverage) are different in their games with Solo and Irhabi 007. Given the fact that strategies of cyber-terrorists (Solo and Irhabi 007) do not focus on attracting the media's attention, as was the case for IBT and MafiaBoy, the media's strategies will result in different outcomes in these different games. For example, if the media choose the strategy "full coverage" in games like those played with IBT and MafiaBoy, they will receive the worst outcomes (payoffs of the matrix) given the fact that more intensive media coverage results in achieving more desired goals for IBT and MafiaBoy. If the media use the same strategy "full coverage" in games like Solo and Irhabi 007, they will receive the best outcomes given the fact that the more intensive media coverage results in weakening the performance of Solo and Irhabi 007, by either conveying clear warnings to potential cyber-terrorists who may be in severe trouble due to careless personal curiosities (i.e., Solo), or educating the publics to avoid being victims of potential similar incidents (i.e., Irhabi 007).

For the second component, responsible conduct, the media should balance their responsibilities towards all actors involved in the cyber-terrorism case. The highest weight in this balance should be given to the responsibility toward the actor(s) who are in most need of help, information, and protection of rights and interests. The responsibility toward informing the public is most important in a cyber-terrorism case such as Irhabi 007; while toward authorities in cyber-terrorism cases such as IBT and Solo, and businesses in a cyber-terrorism case such as MafiaBoy. In doing so, the media should emphasize major ethical principles that are most useful both in achieving the most important responsibilities towards actors involved in the cyber-terrorism cases, and in achieving the media's goals in each situation. Ethical principles such as accuracy, truth, and serving the public interest are ideal for a cyber-terrorism case such as Irhabi 007, when accurate

and truthful information provided to the public will help them avoid being victims of innocently funding terrorism. Independence and integrity can be the most ethical principles used by the media in their relationship with businesses when covering a cyber-terrorism case such as MafiaBoy, when the media should highlight that one of their main objectives is to warn businesses of Internet hackers based purely on social responsibility, without looking for any form of potential profitable return. Objectivity and balance are ideal ethical principles for the media during a cyber-terrorism case such as Solo in order to emphasize that not all information technology professionals are driven by similar motivations and that the majority should follow the ethical standards of their profession. Maintaining context is key ethical principle for the media to use during a cyber-terrorism case such as IBT in order to give a background for authorities and the public, showing that IBT deliberately aimed at distracting from the usual terrorist events.

During cyber-terrorism cases the media should minimize negative effects on decision-makers while maximizing positive effects. For example, the sensational coverage of Solo with emphasis on his fears of extradition to the United States may cause negative effects on decision-makers. The over-reliance on experts to explain the performance of MafiaBoy as less dangerous than more sophisticated hackers may lead to negative effects by motivating more teenagers to attempt to reach a higher level of hacking than MafiaBoy. The extensive communications explaining how Irhabi 007 has used a variety of tools to achieve his goals may not help decision-makers convey simple and easy-to-understand information to the public on how to protect themselves from similar potential dangers of using their credit cards online or engaging in online discussions with anonymous users. Providing the most recent information in advanced innovations and technologies with regard to web servers may maximize the positive effects on policymakers in a cyber-terrorism case such as IBT, when computer network administrators may find better solutions for computer security.

Finally, a major point of strength for the media during cyber-terrorism cases is the providence of information to both the policymakers (who need to use information as a sword vis-à-vis cyber-terrorists) and the public (who need to be protected against false information provided by cyber-terrorists). Information that comes from terrorist attacks has a different nature than information stemming from normal situations; it has similar characteristics to those of the terrorist situation itself. Therefore, it must be searched out, produced, and dealt with differently by media decision-makers; it should be accurate, clear, rational, fast, de-escalating, constructive, and responsible. Therefore, it is crucial for the media to focus on facts when providing information in such situations. They should actively seek information, carefully dig into the roots of information, objectively gather the information from various sources, consistently verifying the information, and strictly adhere to facts in providing the information to both the policymakers and the public.

ETHICAL RATIONALISM: A COUNTER-THREAT SWORD

Throughout the history, numerous terrorist events have been committed by individuals, groups, and organizations (including governments), on national, regional, and international levels. The recent past, the present, and the future are times when technology and cyberspace have been interwoven with almost every aspect of our daily lives. Terrorism is not an exemption; hence the birth of cyber-terrorism. With the appealing characteristics of new technology and cyberspace, acts of cyber-terrorism have become more effective as a modern tactic of terrorism in achieving terrorist goals. Cyber-terrorists continue to be pioneers in embracing the newest communication technologies to achieve their goals. The number

of cyber-terrorism cases and scenarios is countless. As discussed in this paper with regard to the cyber-terrorist cases of IBT, MafiaBoy, Solo, and Irhabi 007, regardless of the nature of actors and their motivations, cyber-terrorists hit very aggressively and cause serious damage.

With such threat by rational actors who use the most advanced technologies, there must be constant efforts by policymakers and any other actors facing against cyber-terrorists. Defences by anti-terrorism strategists or offences by counter-terrorism strategists should also be most advanced. As a key actor in traditional and modern terrorism, the media are required to cope with such events and perform anti- and counter-terrorism strategies in effective ways. In fact the media are most influential, given that terrorists goals are heavily dependent on the media's reactions. It is a major achievement for terrorists when their acts are widely covered by the global media, disseminating fear. Media coverage of acts of terrorism serves as the oxygen with which many terrorists live and flourish. This fact does not mean that the media should not cover the terrorist events; quite the opposite, but with restraint and caution. Therefore, it is clear that the media are in need of assistance in the form of tools, techniques, and methodologies in order to enable them to be more effective in the face of rational actors who use advanced tools. The most significant tool aiding journalists in their games with cyber-terrorists is rationality in their practices, and rationalism as a philosophy of thinking.

Given their responsibility in society, and the public's expectations of ethical media practices, journalists are also required to merge ethical conduct with such rationalism—i.e., following the path of ethical rationalism. Ethical rationalism is "the doctrine that reason is the road to right action.... [A] right moral action results from knowledge and reason. If one wishes to find out what action is good, one must reason... furthermore, moral action will result in happiness and the good life" (Lee, 1971, p. 2). The intertwinement of ethical and rational conduct leads to an effective performance. Journalism personnel are in critical need of rational thinking and responsible conduct during instances of cyber-terrorism.

Game theory has been used as helpful methodology to structure strategic interactions between terrorists or cyber-terrorists and policymakers or computer security agents. However, there is also a critical need for using game theory with regard to media interaction with terrorists and cyber-terrorists. This rational approach will enhance the performance of the media to the level of their rational adversary (terrorists), helping them makes the most effective decisions. The ultimate goal of effective media decision-making can be reached by both rational and responsible (ethical) conduct as suggested by the CD_M^3_R^2 model (Eid, 2008). Game theory, its rational behaviour assumptions, as well as major journalistic ethical principles are all included in the model. Following the rational and responsible components, the media can be effective in making decisions that can either help the policymakers in their interactions with cyber-terrorists, avoid being used by cyber-terrorists for their own interests, or use counter-terrorism strategies directed against cyber-terrorists.

REFERENCES

Alden, E., & Kehoe, L. (2000, April 20). Montreal youth is charged over web attacks. *Financial Times (North American Edition)*, 1.

Alexander, Y., & Latter, R. (Eds.). (1990). *Terrorism and the media: Dilemmas for government, journalists and the public*. Washington, DC: Brassey's.

Alleged "MafiaBoy" faces new charges in Canada. (2000, August 7). *Wall Street Journal*, 1.

Arnell, P., & Reid, A. (2009). Hackers beware: The cautionary story of Gary McKinnon. *Information & Communications Technology Law, 18*(1), 1–12. doi:10.1080/13600830902727822

Berner, S. (2003). Cyber-terrorism: Reality or paranoia? *South African Journal of Information Management, 5*(1), 1–4.

Blitz, R., Burns, J., & Fidler, S. (2005, November 5). Men remanded on charges brought under Terrorism Act Security. *Financial Times (North American Edition)*, 2.

Block, R., & Solomon, J. (2006, June 6). Politics & economics: London case led terror arrests in Canada; Multinational investigation yielded suspects' roundup; Morphing threat via web. *Wall Street Journal*, 8.

Breen, G.-M. (2008). Examining existing counter-terrorism tactics and applying social network theory to fight cyberterrorism: An interpersonal communication perspective. *Journal of Applied Security Research, 3*(2), 191–204. doi:10.1080/19361610802135888

Bridis, T., & Chipello, C. J. (2000, April 20). How Mounties got their man in hacker case. *Wall Street Journal*, B1.

Briggs, W. (2004). North America. In de Beer, A. S., & Merrill, J. C. (Eds.), *Global journalism: Topical issues and media systems* (pp. 430–464). Boston: Pearson.

Britain: Trial of an alien; Britain, America and extradition. (2009, August 8). *The Economist, 392*(8643), 51.

Chipello, C. (2001, January 19). MafiaBoy admits to charges linked to web-site attacks. *Wall Street Journal*, B2.

Cornish, P., Hughes, R., & Livingstone, D. (2009, March). *Cyberspace and the national security of the United Kingdom: Threats and responses* (A Chatham House Report). London: Royal Institute of International Affairs.

Corzine, J. S., & Cañas, R. L. (2008, April 10). *The cyber-terror threat*. Washington, DC: Office of Homeland Security & Preparedness, Intelligence Assessment.

Denning, D. E. (2000). Activism, hacktivism, and cyberterrorism: The Internet as a tool for influencing foreign policy. *Computer Security Journal, 16*(3), 15–35.

Denning, D. E. (2001). Cyberwarriors: Activists and terrorists turn to cyberspace. *Harvard International Review, 23*(2), 70–75.

Dennis, E. E., & Ismach, A. H. (1981). *Reporting processes and practices: Newswriting for today's readers*. Los Angeles, CA: Wadsworth.

Dombey, D., Murphy, M., & Parker, G. (2009, August 1). Hacker fails in US extradition battle. *Financial Times (North American Edition)*, 2.

Eid, M. (2006, October 30). *Telling the truth in the media; Mathematically approved. Journalism Ethics for the Global Citizen*. Retrieved on September 29, 2009, from http://www.journalismethics.info/feature_articles/telling-the-truth.htm

Eid, M. (2006a). Cyber-terrorism in the information age: Actors, communications, tactics, targets, and influences. In *Proceedings of Information-MFCSIT, 06*, 39–42.

Eid, M. (2006b). Mass media and the puzzle of information in the course of playing crises. *INFORMATION: An International Interdisciplinary Journal, 9*(1), 83–100.

Eid, M. (2008). *Interweavement: International media ethics and rational decision-making*. Boston: Pearson.

Eid, M. (2009). On the way to the Cyber-Arab-Culture: International communication, telecommunications policies, and democracy. In Ricardo, F. J. (Ed.), *Cyberculture and new media* (pp. 69–98). Amsterdam, The Netherlands: Rodopi.

Elliott, D. (2003). Balance and context: Maintaining media ethics. *Phi Kappa Phi Forum, 83*(2), 16–21.

Experts say West can't stop web radicalization; From behind a computer keyboard at his London home, student Younes Tsouli used the Internet to spread al Qaeda propaganda, recruit suicide bombers and promote web sites that encouraged the killing of non-Muslims. (2007, November). *CIO Insight*, 87.

Flanagan, T. (1998). *Game theory and Canadian politics*. Toronto, Canada: University of Toronto Press.

Gordon, A. D. (1999). Truth precludes any need for further ethical concerns in journalism and public relations. In Gordon, A. D., & Kittross, J. M. (Eds.), *Controversies in media ethics* (pp. 73–80). New York: Longman.

Gordon, S., & Ford, R. (2003). Cyberterrorism? *Symantec Security Response*. Retrieved September 29, 2009, from http://www.symantec.com/avcenter/reference/cyberterrorism.pdf

Hacker Gary McKinnon loses extradition appeal. (2009, July 31). *Informationweek – Online*.

Harris, G., & Spark, D. (1997). *Practical newspaper reporting*. Oxford, UK: Focal Press.

Harrison, A. (2000, April 24). Analysts: MafiaBoy only amateur copycat. *Computerworld, 34*(17), 6.

Heap, S. P. H., & Varoufakis, Y. (1995). *Game theory: A critical introduction*. New York: Routledge. doi:10.4324/9780203199275

Hensgen, T., Desouza, K. C., Evaristo, J. R., & Kraft, G. D. (2003). Playing the "cyber terrorism game" towards a semiotic definition. *Human Systems Management, 22*(2), 51–61.

Hindman, E. B. (1997). *Rights vs. responsibilities: The Supreme Court and the media.* Westport, CT: Greenwood Press.

Ignatieff, M. (2004). *The lesser evil: Political ethics in an age of terror.* New York: Penguin.

Joshi, M. (1996). On the Razor's edge: The Liberation Tigers of Tamil Eelam. *Studies in Conflict and Terrorism, 19*(1), 19–42. doi:10.1080/10576109608435994

Kittross, J. M. (1999). The social value of journalism and public relations requires high-quality practices reflecting ethical considerations that go beyond truth and objectivity to accuracy and fairness. In Gordon, A. D., & Kittross, J. M. (Eds.), *Controversies in media ethics* (pp. 80–89). New York: Longman.

Kovach, B., & Rosenstiel, T. (2001). *The elements of journalism: What newspeople should know and the public should expect.* New York: Crown Publishers.

Lee, W. (1971). *Decision theory and human behavior.* New York: John Wiley & Sons.

Lye, K., & Wing, J. M. (2005). Game strategies in network security. *International Journal of Information Security, 4*(1/2), 71–86. doi:10.1007/s10207-004-0060-x

Maher, S. (2007). Road to Jihad: Almost impossible to regulate, the web is a gift for a new generation of young extremists. *Index on Censorship, 4*, 144–149. doi:10.1080/03064220701740590

Matusitz, J. (2005). Cyberterrorism: How can American foreign policy be strengthened in the information age? *American Foreign Policy Interests, 27*(2), 137–147.

Matusitz, J. (2008). Cyberterrorism: Postmodern state of chaos. *Information Security Journal: A Global Perspective, 17*(4), 179-187.

Matusitz, J. (2009). A postmodern theory of cyberterrorism: Game theory. *Information Security Journal: A Global Perspective, 18*(6), 273-281.

Matusitz, J., & Minei, E. (2009). Cyberterrorism: Its effects on health-related infrastructures. *Journal of Digital Forensic Practice, 2*(4), 161–171. doi:10.1080/15567280802678657

Mishra, S. (2003). Exploitation of information and communication technology by terrorist organisations. *Strategic Analysis, 27*(3), 439–462. doi:10.1080/09700160308450099

Mitliaga, V. (2001). Cyber-terrorism: A call for governmental action? *16th BILETA Annual Conference.* Retrieved October 9, 2009, from http://www.bileta.ac.uk/01papers/mitliaga.html.

Mohay, G., Panichprecha, S., & Tickle, A. (2009). Sub-project 1: Probabilistic packet processing to mitigate high-rate flooding attacks. *Review of Techniques for Mitigating Network Flooding Attacks.* Retrieved March 1, 2010, from http://iaw2009.iitm.ernet.in/files/sp1.pdf.

Morrow, J. D. (1994). *Game theory for political scientists.* New Jersey: Princeton University Press.

Murphy, M. (2009, January 24). Hacker wins right to legal review. *Financial Times (North American Edition),* 4.

Nacos, B. L. (2006). *Terrorism and counterterrorism: Understanding threats and responses in the post-9/11 world.* New York: Longman.

Nadarajah, S., & Sriskandarajah, D. (2005). Liberation struggle or terrorism? The politics of naming the LTTE. *Third World Quarterly, 26*(1), 87–100. doi:10.1080/0143659042000322928

Nakra, P. (2003). Info-terrorism in the age of the Internet: Challenges and initiatives. *Journal of Competitive Intelligence and Management, 1*(2), 1–10.

Nicholson, M. (1970). *Conflict analysis*. London: The English Universities Press.

Nicholson, M. (1996). *Causes and consequences in international relations: A conceptual study*. London: Pinter.

Nye, J. S. (2005). *Understanding international conflicts: An introduction to theory and history*. New York: Pearson.

Ryan, R. (2003). When journalism becomes "terrorism": Perle goes on offensive against investigative reporting. *Extra!* May/June. Retrieved March 1, 2010, from http://www.fair.org/index.php?page=1143.

Schellenberg, J. A. (1996). *Conflict resolution: Theory, research, and practice*. Albany, NY: State University of New York Press.

Schmid, A. P. (1989). Terrorism and the media: The ethics of publicity. *Terrorism and Political Violence, 1*(4), 539–565. doi:10.1080/09546558908427042

Scott, R. (2000, May 1). Inside the world of "MafiaBoy". *Maclean's, 113*(18), 37.

Shubik, M. (1954). Introduction to the nature of game theory. In Shubik, M. (Ed.), *Readings in Game theory and political behavior* (pp. 1–11). New York: Doubleday & Company.

Solomon, J., & Patrick, A. O. (2006, June 8). Terror probe widens with two arrests in Britain. *Wall Street Journal*, p. A2.

Tehranian, M. (2002). Peace journalism: Negotiating global media ethics. *The Harvard International Journal of Press/Politics, 7*(2), 58–83.

Thomas, J. L. C. (2001, January 12). Ethics of hactivism. *SANS-GIAC Practical Repository*. Retrieved October 5, 2009, from http://www.dvara.net/HK/Julie_Thomas_GSEC.pdf.

Thomassen, N. (1992). *Communicative ethics in theory and practice* (Irons, J., Trans.). New York: St. Martin's Press.

Tsfati, Y., & Weimann, G. (2002). Terror on the Internet. *Studies in Conflict and Terrorism, 25*(5), 317–332. www.terrorism.com. doi:10.1080/10576100290101214

Van de Voorde, C. (2005). Sri Lankan terrorism: Assessing and responding to the threat of the Liberation Tigers of Tamil Eelam (LTTE). *Police Practice and Research, 6*(2), 181–199. doi:10.1080/15614260500121195

Weimann, G. (2005). Cyberterrorism: The Sum of All Fears? *Studies in Conflict and Terrorism, 28*(2), 129–149. doi:10.1080/10576100590905110

Wright, D. K. (1996). Communication ethics. In Salwen, M. B., & Stacks, D. W. (Eds.), *An integrated approach to communication theory and research* (pp. 519–535). New York: Lawrence Erlbaum Associates.

ENDNOTES

[1] Terrorism can only be justified, according to Thomassen (1992, pp. 219-222), if: 1) it is used against a form of power that uses illegitimate violence; 2) the situation excludes all other possibilities for action; 3) it is only directed against those who are responsible for the practice of illegitimate violence; 4) its sole aim is to neutralize those people as practitioners of violence and not to harm them further; and 5) one has taken precautions against unwanted side-effects or has seen to it that these are at any rate kept within restricted limits.

2   For example, the Brazilian Marxist revolutionary Carlos Marighella, who became the idol of many left-wing terrorists far beyond Latin America, recommended in the post-World War II period the use of copying machines to produce large numbers of propaganda pamphlets and manifestoes. Also, as broadcasting transmitters became lighter and easy to transport, groups with direct or indirect involvement in terrorism established their own radio and television facilities. In the early 1990s, the Lebanon-based Hezbollah organization started its own television station, Al-Manar. In Colombia, left- and right-wing terror groups have utilized mobile radio transmitters. The Revolutionary Armed Forces of Colombia have broadcast over an increasingly large number of channels (Nacos, 2006, p. 230).

3   Members of Al-Qaeda, for example, rely heavily on the Internet to spread their propaganda and have used it to plan and coordinate their operations; most notably the 9/11 attacks. "Former FBI Director Louis J. Freeh told the Citizens Crime Commission of New York, when Ramzi Yousef (the mastermind of the World Trade Center bombing) was being tracked in the Philippines, he *left* behind a laptop computer that itemized plans to blow up (11) U.S. airliners in the Western Pacific on a particular day. All of the details and planning were set forth in that laptop computer. While part of the information was encrypted and difficult to decode, it revealed for the first time how sophisticated terrorists utilized computers for planning their operations" (Nacos, 2006, p. 237).

4   Cyberspace is one of the most significant technological developments of the late twentieth century. Since William Gibson published his 1984 science fiction novel *Neuromancer*, the word cyberspace has become common parlance. The term is used synonymously with other phrases such as cyberia, virtual space, virtual worlds, dataspace, the digital domain, the electronic realm, the information sphere, virtual reality, computer networking, and the Internet (Eid, 2009, pp. 69-70).

5   This is one of the longest-running and most intractable conflicts in the world. Sri Lanka has been besieged by ethnic separatism, nationalism, and an enduring ethnic conflict between its Sinhalese majority and the Tamil minority for decades. The LTTE are the strongest militant nationalists and fiercest terrorist group in Sri Lanka. It claims that it is spearheading an armed struggle for political independence for the Tamils as a response to institutionalized racism and violence against the Tamil people by a Sinhala-dominated state. That it, it is waging a national liberation struggle. The Tamil Diaspora of the 1980s, the extensive use of political propaganda, and the involvement of the group in arms procurement and massive fundraising activities have enabled the LTTE to increase its strength in Sri Lanka and its presence throughout the world. As a result, the Tamil Tigers have transformed their insurgent group into an international terror network that seems to have no limits today. On the other hand, describing itself as a democracy, the Sri Lankan state denounces the LTTE's violence as a challenge to its authority, unity and territorial integrity. Thus, the state's military response is rationalized as fighting terrorism (Nadarajah & Sriskandarajah, 2005; Van de Voorde, 2005).

6   E-mail bombs take the form of sending thousands of messages at once, distributed with the aid of automated tools. The effect can be to completely jam a recipient's incoming e-mail box, making it impossible for legitimate e-mail to get through. Thus, an e-mail bomb is also a form of virtual blockade. Although e-mail bombs are often used as a means of

revenge or harassment, they have also been used to protest government policies (Denning, 2000, p. 17, 2001, p. 74).

[7] Game theory rests on some basic assumptions regarding the way the interests of different individuals may be related to each other, which can be analyzed mathematically: 1) games always involve two or more players, each with an opportunity to choose between alternatives; 2) each available alternative is fully known to each player; 3) all possible outcomes that might occur to any player may be expressed in terms of numerical measures of utility; and 4) each player will make those choices that will provide the maximum expected utility (Schellenberg, 1996, p. 112).

[8] There are four media guidelines for covering terrorism enclosed in the appendix (139-143) of the 1990 *Terrorism and the Media*, edited by Yonah Alexander and Richard Latter. The media guidelines are those of CBS News Standards, *The Courier-Journal* and *The Louisville Times, The Sun-Times* and *Daily News* Standards for Coverage of Terrorism, and the United Press International.

[9] Senior Pentagon adviser Richard Perle abruptly announced his resignation on March 27, 2009 as chair of the Defense Policy Board, an influential Pentagon advisory panel. Perle had shortly before his resignation described the Pulitzer-winner journalist Seymour Hersh as a "terrorist", and threatened to sue Hersh for libel in Britain, simply because he has considered Hersh "widely irresponsible". Hersh's report in the *New Yorker* on Perle's messy finances was the first of a series of embarrassing stories that threatened Perle's considerable access to power (Ryan, 2003).

This work was previously published in International Journal of Technoethics, Volume 1, Issue 4, edited by Rocci Luppicini, pp. 1-19, copyright 2010 by IGI Publishing (an imprint of IGI Global).

Compilation of References

Wood, D., & Ball, K. (Eds.). (2006, September). A Report on the Surveillance Society. London: Surveillance Studies Network.

Abram, S. (2004). IP authentication and passwords – on life support and NOT expected to make it. *Information Outlook, 8*(8). Retrieved from ProQuest Educational Journals.

Abrapia. (2006). *Programa de redução do comportamento agressivo entre estudantes.* Retrieved February 19, 2007, from http://www.bullying.com.br/Bconceituacao21.htm

Academic Integrity. (2009). Retrieved March 1, 2009 from http://demo.flvs.net/webdav/navbar/integrity.htm.

Ach, J. S., & Siep, L. (Eds.). (2006). *Nano-bio-ethics. Ethical dimensions of nanobiotechnology.* Münster: NoE Nano2Life.

Aftab, P. (2010 a). *Stop Cyberbullying: What is cyberbullying, exactly?* Retrieved February 8, 2010, from http://www.stopcyberbullying.org/what_is_cyberbullying_exactly.html

Aftab, P. (2010 b). *Stop Cyberbullying: Why do kids cyberbully each other?* Retrieved February 8, 2010, from http://www.stopcyberbullying.org/why_do_kids_cyberbully_each_other.html

Ajzen, I. (1991). The theory of planned behavior. *Organizational Behavior and Human Decision Making Processes, 50*, 179–211. doi:10.1016/0749-5978(91)90020-T

Ajzen, I. (2002). Residual effects of past on later behavior: Habituation and reasoned action perspectives. *Personality and Social Psychology Review, 6*, 107–122. doi:10.1207/S15327957PSPR0602_02

Alden, E., & Kehoe, L. (2000, April 20). Montreal youth is charged over web attacks. *Financial Times (North American Edition)*, 1.

Alexander, P. J. (2002). Peer-to-peer file sharing: The case of the music industry. *Review of Industrial Organization, 20*, 151–162. doi:10.1023/A:1013819218792

Alexander, Y., & Latter, R. (Eds.). (1990). *Terrorism and the media: Dilemmas for government, journalists and the public.* Washington, DC: Brassey's.

Alleged "MafiaBoy" faces new charges in Canada. (2000, August 7). *Wall Street Journal*, 1.

Allen, C. (2004). *Tracing the Evolution of Social Software Evolution.* Retrieved September 9, 2009 from http://www.lifewithalacrity.com/2004/10/tracing_the_evo.html

Allen, E. I., & Seaman, J. (2008) Staying the course: online education in the United States, 2008. *The Sloan Consortium.* Retrieved from http://www.sloan-c.org 11/13/2008.

Allen, P. J., & Roberts, L. D. (2010). The ethics of outsourcing online survey research. *International Journal of Technoethics, 1*, 35-48.

Allen, C., Smit, I., & Wallach, W. (2006). Artificial Morality: top down and bottom up and hybrid approaches. *Ethics and Information Technology, 7*, 149–155. doi:10.1007/s10676-006-0004-4

Allen, C., Varner, G., & Zinser, J. (2000). Prolegomena to any future artificial moral agent. *Journal of Experimental & Theoretical Artificial Intelligence, 12*(3), 251–261. doi:10.1080/09528130050111428

Allen, P. J. (2008). Rip, mix, burn ... sue ... *ad infinitum*: The effects of deterrence vs. voluntary cooperation on non-commercial online copyright infringing behaviour. *First Monday*, *13*(9). Retrieved from http://firstmonday.org/htbin/cgiwrap/bin/ojs/index.php/fm/article/view/2073/2025.

Allhoff, F., & Lin, P. (Eds.). (2008). *Nanotechnology and society: Current and emerging issues*. Dordrecht: Springer.

Allhoff, F., Lin, P., Moor, J., & Weckert, J. (2007). *Nanoethics: The social and ethical dimensions of nanotechnology*. Hoboken, NJ: Wiley.

Allhoff, F., & Lin, P. (2006). What's so special about nanotechnology and nanoethics? *The International Journal of Applied Philosophy*, *20*(2), 179–190.

Altschuller, S., & Benbunan-Fich, R. (2009). Is music downloading the new prohibition? What students reveal through an ethical dilemma. *Ethics and Information Technology*, *11*, 49–56. doi:10.1007/s10676-008-9179-1

American Psychological Association Policy and Planning Board. (2009). How technology changes everything (and nothing) in psychology: 2008 annual report of the APA Policy and Planning Board. *The American Psychologist*, *64*, 454–463. doi:10.1037/a0015888

American Psychological Association. (2002). *Ethical principles of psychologists and code of conduct*. Retrieved from http://www.apa.org/ethics/code2002.pdf

Anderson, A., Allan, S., Petersen, A., & Wilkinson, C. (2008). Nanoethics: News media and the shaping of public agendas. In R. Luppicini & R. Adell (Ed.), *Handbook of research on technoethics* (pp. 373-90). Hershey, New York: Idea Group Publishing.

Anderson, A., Petersen, A., Wilkinson, C., & Allan, S. (2009). *Nanotechnology, risk and communication*. Houndmills: Palgrave Macmillan.

Anderson, A., Petersen, A., Wilkinson, C., & Allan, S. (2005). The framing of nanotechnologies in the British newspaper press. *Science Communication*, *27*(2), 200–220. doi:10.1177/1075547005281472

Andersson, Y., Anderson, S., & Armen, C. (2004) Towards Machine Ethics. In *Proceedings of AAAI workshop on agent organizations, theory and practice*, San José, CA.

Andersson, S. L. (2008). 'Asimov' three laws of robotics' and machine meta ethics. *AI & Society*, *22*, 477–493.

Andrews, D., Nonnecke, B., & Preece, J. (2003). Electronic survey methodology: A case study in reaching hard-to-involve Internet users. *International Journal of Human-Computer Interaction*, *16*, 185–210. doi:10.1207/S15327590IJHC1602_04

Aranti, L. (2007, February 26). Teens can multitask, but what are costs? *Washington Post*, p. A1.

Arbona, S. I. (1998, Jan.). Commercial Agriculture and Agrochemicals in Almolonga, Guatemala. *Geographical Review*, *88*(1), 47–63. doi:10.2307/215871

Arciniegas, G. (1944). *The Green Continent*. New York: Alfred A. Knopf.

Arkin, R. C. (2009). *Governing Lethal Behavior in Autonomous Robots*. Boca Raton, FL: CRC Press. doi:10.1201/9781420085952

Armitage, C. J., & Conner, M. (2001). Efficacy of the theory of planned behaviour: A meta-analytic review. *The British Journal of Social Psychology*, *40*, 471–499. doi:10.1348/014466601164939

Arnell, P., & Reid, A. (2009). Hackers beware: The cautionary story of Gary McKinnon. *Information & Communications Technology Law*, *18*(1), 1–12. doi:10.1080/13600830902727822

Arquilla, J. (1999). Ethics and information warfare. In Z. Khalilzad, J. White, & A. Marsall (Eds.), *Strategic appraisal: the changing role of information in warfare* (pp. 379-401). Rand Corporation, Santa Monica, CA, USA.

ASUR (Arizona State University Report). (2006). *Policy implications of technologies for cognitive enhancement*. Phoenix, AZ: Arizona State University.

Atkinson, R., & Flint, J. (2001). Accessing hidden and hard-to-reach populations: Snowball research strategies. *Social Research Update, 33*. Retrieved from http://sru.soc.surrey.ac.uk/sru33.html

Australian Bureau of Statistics. (2008). *Household use of information technology, Australia, 2007-08* (Catalogue Number 8146.0). Canberra, Australia: Author. Retrieved from http://www.abs.gov.au/Ausstats/abs@.nsf/mf/8146.0

AVANCSO. (1994). *Impacto ecológico de los cultivos hortícolas no-tradicionales en el altiplano de Guatemala.* Guatemala, Instituto AVANCSO.

Bailey, M., Cooke, E., Jahanian, F., Xu, Y., & Karir, M. (2009, March). A survey of botnet technology and defenses. *Proc. Conf. for Homeland Security: Cybersecurity Applications and Technology.*

Bakan, J. (2004). *The Corporation.* New York: Free Press.

Baker, J. D. (2007). Open source survey software. In Reynolds, R. A., Woods, R., & Baker, J. D. (Eds.), *Handbook of research on electronic surveys and measurements* (pp. 273–275). Hershey, PA: IGI Global.

Baldacci, A. (2006, July 12). Lost connection: Is technology isolating us? *Chicago Sun-Times.*

Bamberg, S., Ajzen, I., & Schmidt, P. (2003). Choice of travel mode in the theory of planned behavior: The roles of past behavior, habit and reasoned action. *Basic and Applied Social Psychology, 25,* 175–187. doi:10.1207/S15324834BASP2503_01

Bandura, S. (1995). *Self-Efficacy in Changing Societies.* New York: Cambridge University Press.

Baptista, C. (2004). *A fragilidade da experiência: Erving Goffman e os quadros da interacção.* Unpublished doctoral dissertation, Universidade Nova de Lisboa, Portugal.

Barchard, K. A., & Williams, J. (2008). Practical advice for conducting ethical online experiments and questionnaires for United States psychologists. *Behavior Research Methods, 40,* 1111–1128. doi:10.3758/BRM.40.4.1111

Bardone, E., & Magnani, L. (2006). The Internet as a moral mediator. The quest for democracy. In *Computing, Philosophy, and Cognition* (pp. 131-145). London, College Publications.

Barlow, J. P. (1990). A declaration of the independence of Cyberspace. http://www.eff.org/~barlow/Declaration-Final.html

Baron, R. M., & Kenny, D. A. (1986). The moderator-mediator variable distinction in social psychological research: Conceptual, strategic, and statistical considerations. *Journal of Personality and Social Psychology, 51,* 1173–1182. doi:10.1037/0022-3514.51.6.1173

Barry, J. (1991). Silence is golden? *Miami Herald,* 8.

Bates, J. M., & Demos, T. C. (2001, Sep.). Do We Need to Devalue Amazonia and Other Large Tropical Forests? *Diversity & Distributions, 7*(5), 249–255. doi:10.1046/j.1366-9516.2001.00112.x

Bateson, G. (1972). *Steps toward and ecology of mind.* Novato, CA: Chandler.

Bateson, G. (1955). A Theory of Play and Fantasy. In *A.P.A. Psychiatric Research Reports, II,* 177–193.

Bateson, G. (1989). *Metadiálogos.* Lisboa, Portugal: Gradiva.

Bates, S. C., & Cox, J. M. (2008). The impact of computer versus paper-pencil survey, and individual versus group administration, on self-reports of sensitive behaviors. *Computers in Human Behavior, 24,* 903–916. doi:10.1016/j.chb.2007.02.021

Bauer, K. (2007). Wired patients: Implantable microchips and biosensors in patient care. *Cambridge Quarterly of Healthcare Ethics, 16*(3), 281–290. doi:10.1017/S0963180107070314

Bayles, W. (2001). Network attack. *Parameters. US Army War College Quarterly, 31,* 44–58.

Beauchamp, T. L., & Childress, J. F. (2008). *Principles of Biomedical Ethics* (6th ed.). New York: OUP.

Beck, L., & Ajzen, I. (1991). Predicting dishonest actions using the theory of planned behavior. *Journal of Research in Personality, 25,* 285–301. doi:10.1016/0092-6566(91)90021-H

Behe, M. (2007). Design for Life. *New York Times.*

Beiderniki, G., & Kerschbaumer, A. (2007). Comparison of online survey tools. In Reynolds, R. A., Woods, R., & Baker, J. D. (Eds.), *Handbook of research on electronic surveys and measurements* (pp. 264–272). Hershey, PA: IGI Global.

Bekey, G. (2005). *Robots: From biological inspiration to implementations and control.* Cambridge, MA: The MIT Press.

Belsey, B. (2005). *Cyberbullying: An emerging threat to the "always on" generation.* Retrieved January 16, 2007, from http://www.cyberbullying.ca/pdf/feature_dec2005.pdf

Belsey, B. (2010). *Always on, always aware.* Retrieved April 30, 2010, from http://www.cyberbullying.org

Benfield, J. A., & Szlemko, W. J. (2006). Internet-based data collection: Promises and realities. *Journal of Research Practice, 2*, 1–15.

Bennett-Woods, D. (2008). *Nanotechnology, ethics and society.* Florida: CRC.

Bensley, L. S., & Wu, R. (1991). The role of psychological reactance in drinking following alcohol prevention messages. *Journal of Applied Social Psychology, 21*, 1111–1124. doi:10.1111/j.1559-1816.1991.tb00461.x

Bentham, J. (1907). *An introduction to the principles of morals and legislation.* Chicago: Library of Economics and Liberty. Retrieved November 3, 2009, from http://www.econlib.org/library/Bentham/bnthPML18.htm

Bentham, J. (1995). *The panopticon writings.* London: Verso. Retrieved October 16, 2009, from http://cartome.org/panopticon.htm

Beran, T., & Li, Q. (2005). Cyberharassment: A study of a new method for an old behavior. *Journal of Educational Computing Research, 32*(3), 265–277. doi:10.2190/8YQM-B04H-PG4D-BLLH

Beran, T., & Li, Q. (2007). The relationship between cyberbullying and school bullying. *Journal of Student Wellbeing, 1*(2), 15–33.

Berkowitz, L. (1964). *Aggression.* Philadelphia, PA: Temple University Press.

Berman, P. (2002). The globalization of jurisdiction. *University of Pennsylvania Law Review, 151*(2), 311–545. doi:10.2307/3312952

Berne, R. W. (2006). *Nanotalk: Conversations with scientists and engineers about ethics, meaning, and belief in the development of nanotechnology.* Mahwah, NJ: Lawrence Erlbaum Associates.

Berner, S. (2003). Cyber-terrorism: Reality or paranoia? *South African Journal of Information Management, 5*(1), 1–4.

Best, S. J., & Krueger, B. S. (2004). *Internet data collection.* Thousand Oaks, CA: Sage.

Best, S. J., & Krueger, B. S. (2008). Internet survey design. In Fielding, N., Lee, R. M., & Blank, G. (Eds.), *The SAGE handbook of online research methods* (pp. 217–235). London: Sage.

Biernacki, P., & Waldorf, D. (1981). Snowball sampling: Problems and techniques of chain referral sampling. *Sociological Methods & Research, 10*, 141–163.

Biersteker, T., & Eckert, S. (2008). *Countering the financing of terrorism.* London: Routledge.

Bijker, W. E. (1997). *Of Bicycles, Bakelites, and Bulbs: Toward a Theory of Sociotechnical Change.* Cambridge, MA: MIT Press.

Binik, Y. M., Mah, K., & Kiesler, S. (1999). Ethical issues in conducting sex research on the Internet. *Journal of Sex Research, 36*, 82–90. doi:10.1080/00224499909551971

Birnbaum, M. H. (2007). Designing online experiments. In Joinson, A., McKenna, K., Postmes, T., & Reips, U.-D. (Eds.), *The Oxford handbook of Internet psychology* (pp. 391–403). New York: Oxford University Press.

Bissett, A. (2004). High technology war and 'surgical strikes'. *Computers & Society, 32*(7), 4.

Black, J. K. (March 1st, 1993). Limits of Boom-and-Bust Development: Challenge of the Amazon. *USAToday, 121*(2574), 34, 3p, 3 bw.

Black, T., & Mohr, J. (2004). Are we ready for another change? Digital signatures can change how we handle the academic record. *College and University, 80*(1). Retrieved from ProQuest Educational Journals.

Black, J. (Ed.). (1997). *Mixed News: The Public/Civic/Communitarian Journalism Debate.* Mahwah, NJ: Lawrence Erlbaum.

Blauner, R. (1964). *Alienation and Freedom.* Chicago: University of Chicago Press.

Blitz, R., Burns, J., & Fidler, S. (2005, November 5). Men remanded on charges brought under Terrorism Act Security. *Financial Times (North American Edition)*, 2.

Block, R., & Solomon, J. (2006, June 6). Politics & economics: London case led terror arrests in Canada; Multinational investigation yielded suspects' roundup; Morphing threat via web. *Wall Street Journal*, 8.

Boccaccio, A. (2008). *Where Madness Follows.* Retrieved January 18, 2009 from www.boccacciophoto.com/amazongold/.

Bocij, P. (2003). Victims of cyberstalking: An exploratory study of harassment perpetrated via the Internet. *First Monday, 8*(10). Retrieved January 30, 2010, from http://firstmonday.org/htbin/cgiwrap/bin/ojs/index.php/fm/article/view/1086/1006

Bok, S. (1986). *Secrets.* Oxford, UK: Oxford University Press.

Bonetto, A. A., & Wais, I. R. (1990). Powerful Paraná. *The Geographical Magazine, 62*(3), 1–3.

Borg, S. (2005, November-December). Economically complex cyberattacks. *IEEE Security and Privacy, 3*(6), 64–67. doi:10.1109/MSP.2005.146

Bostrom, N. (2005). A history of transhumanist thought. *Journal of Evolution and Technology, 14*(1).

Bostrom, N. (2008). Why I want to be a posthuman when I grow up. In Gordijn, B., & Chadwick, R. (Eds.), *Medical Enhancement and Posthumanity* (pp. 107–137). New York: Springer.

Bourhis, R., & Leyens, J.-P. (1994). *Stéréotypes, discrimination et relations intergroupes*. Brussels, Belgium: Mardaga Editores.

Boyer, M. (2006, August 22). Colleges work to combat cyberstalking. *Fox News*. Retrieved January 14, 2010, from http://www.foxnews.com/story/0,2933,209395,00.html?sPage=fnc.college101

Brabham, D. C. (2008). *Review of a book: Organized networks: media theory, creative labour, new institutions.* Retrieved November 24, 2008, from http://rccs.usfca.edu/bookinfo.asp?ReviewID=535&BookID=288

Braga, J. L. (2007). *Comunicação, disciplina indiciária.* Paper presented at the GT "Epistemologia da Comunicação," Anais do XVI Encontro da Compós, Curitiba, Brasil.

Bredin, D. (1996). Transforming images: Communication technologies and cultural identity in Nishnawbe-Aski. In D. Howes (Ed.), *Cross-cultural consumption. Global markets, local realities* (pp. 161-177). London and New York: Routledge.

Breen, G.-M. (2008). Examining existing counter-terrorism tactics and applying social network theory to fight cyberterrorism: An interpersonal communication perspective. *Journal of Applied Security Research, 3*(2), 191–204. doi:10.1080/19361610802135888

Brehm, J. W. (1966). *A theory of psychological reactance.* New York: Academic Press.

Brehm, S. S., & Brehm, J. W. (1981). *Psychological reactance: A theory of freedom and control.* New York: Academic Press.

Brey, P., & Soraker, J. H. (2009). Philosophy of Computing and Information Technology. In Gabbay, D. M., Meijers, A. W., Woods, J., & Thagard, P. (Eds.), *Philosophy of Technology and Engineering Sciences* (*Vol. 9*, pp. 1341–1408). New York: North Holland. doi:10.1016/B978-0-444-51667-1.50051-3

Bridis, T., & Chipello, C. J. (2000, April 20). How Mounties got their man in hacker case. *Wall Street Journal*, B1.

Briggs, W. (2004). North America. In de Beer, A. S., & Merrill, J. C. (Eds.), *Global journalism: Topical issues and media systems* (pp. 430–464). Boston: Pearson.

Bristow, J. (2005, July 12). Moving Images. *Spiked*. Retrieved June 15, 2009, from http://www.spiked-onlein.com/index.php?site/article/865/

Britain: Trial of an alien; Britain, America and extradition. (2009, August 8). *The Economist, 392*(8643), 51.

Brown, A. (2008, September 28) The New Pornography of War. *The Guardian*. Retrieved December 12, 2009, from http://www.guardian.co.uk/world/2005/sep/28/afghanistan.comment

Brunsman, B. J. (2006, July 13). Ugly or not, cell phone tower likely coming to Pierce Park. *Cincinnati Inquirer*.

Buchanan, E. A., & Hvizdak, E. E. (2009). Online survey tools: Ethical and methodological concerns of Human Research Ethics Committees. *Journal of Empirical Research on Human Research Ethics; JERHRE, 4*, 37–48. doi:10.1525/jer.2009.4.2.37

Bunge, M. (1977). Towards a technoethics. *The Monist, 60*(1), 96–107.

Burlakova, E. B., & Naidich, V. I. (2006). *20 years after the Chernobyl accident: past, present and future*. New York: Nova Sciencia.

Bynum, T. (2008). *Computer and Information Ethics*. Retrieved December 4, 2008, from http://plato.stanford.edu/entries/ethics-computer/

Bynum, T. W., & Rogerson, S. (Eds.). (2004). *Computer ethics and professional responsibility*. Malden, MA: Blackwell.

Cadili, S., & Whitley, E. A. (2005). On the interpretative flexibility of hosted ERP systems. *The Journal of Strategic Information Systems, 14*(2), 167–195. doi:10.1016/j.jsis.2005.04.006 Callén, B. (2006). *Tecnología.política hecha por otros medios. Una comprensión del tecnoactivismo desde Riereta.net*. Universitat Autònoma de Barcelona, Proyecto de investigación para doctorado.

Callon, M. (1994). Four models for the dynamics of science. In S. Jasanoff, G.E. Markle, J.C. Petersen, and T.J. Pinch (Eds.), *Handbook of science and technology studies* (pp. 29-63), Los Angeles, CA: Sage.

Callon, M. (1997). Society in the making: the study of technology as a tool for sociological analysis. In W.E. Bjiker, T.P. Hughes, & T. Pinch (Eds.), *The social construction of technological systems* (pp. 83-106). Cambridge, MA: MIT Press.

Callon, M., & Latour, B. (1992). Don't throw the baby out with the bath school! A reply toCollins and Yearley. In A. Pickering (Ed.), *science as practice and culture* (pp. 343-368). Chicago and London: The University of Chicago Press.

Callon, M., Lascoumes, P., & Barthe, Y. (2009). *Acting in an Uncertain World: An Essay on Technical Democracy*. Cambridge, MA: MIT Press.

Camera Phones Incite Bad Behaviour. (2003, September 7). *Associated Press*. Retrieved June 19, 2009, from http://www.wired.com/print/culture/lifestyle/news/2003/07/59582

Campbell, M. (2005). Cyberbullying: An older problem in a new guise? *Australian Journal of Guidance & Counselling, 15*(1), 68–76. doi:10.1375/ajgc.15.1.68

Carlat, D. (2007). Diagnosis, Conflict of Interest. *New York Times*. Retrieved September 6, 2009 from http://www.nytimes.com/2007/06/13/opinion/13carlat.htmlEpstein, S. (2004). *Impure Science AIDS, Activism, and the Politics of Knowledge*. Berkeley, CA: University of California Press.

Carlson, S. (2002, June 7). Trending the Net: Computer discipline offices offer a human touch when investigating student complaints. *The Chronicle of Higher Education, 35*.

Carroll, A. B. (1991, July-August). The pyramid of corporate social responsibility: Toward the moral management of organizational stakeholders. *Business Horizons, 34*, 39–48. doi:10.1016/0007-6813(91)90005-G

Carruso, J. B., & Salaway, G. (2008, October). *The ECAR Study of Undergraduate Students and Information Technology, 2008*. Retrieved May 18, 2010, from http://net.educause.edu/ir/library/pdf/ERS0808/RS/ERS0808w.pdf

Carvalhosa, S., Lima, L., & Matos, M. (2001). *Bullying - a provocação/vitimação entre pares no contexto escolar português*. Retrieved March 8, 2007, from http://www.scielo.oces.mtces.pt/pdf/asp/v19n4/v19n4a04.pdf

Carver, C. S., & Scheier, M. F. (1981). *Attention and Self-Regulation*. New York: Springer Verlag.

Case, D. O. (2000). Stalking, monitoring and profiling: A typography and case studies of harmful uses of Caller ID. *New Media & Society, 2*, 67–84. doi:10.1177/14614440022225715

Castro, D., Bennett, R., & Andes, C. (2009). *Steal these policies: Strategies for reducing digital piracy*. Retrieved from http://www.itif.org/files/2009-12-15.DigitalPiracy.pdf

Cavalier, R. (2004, June 2-5). Instantiating deliberative democracy. Project PICOLA. European Conference Computing and Philosophy (E-CAP2004_ITALY), Abstract, Pavia, Italy.

CEPAL-United Nations Economic Commission on Latin America and the Caribbean (November 2000), Cepal News.

Ceruti, M. (2001, March). Mobile agents in network-centric warfare. *Proc. 5th International Symposium on Autonomous Decentralized Systems* (pp. 243-246).

Chadwick-Jones, J. K. (1969). *Automation and Behavior: A Social Psychological Study*. London: Wiley.

Chaker, A. M. (2004, January 24). Schools move to stop spread of 'cyberbullying'. *Pittsburgh Post-Gazette*.

Chang, M. K. (1998). Predicting unethical behavior: A comparison of the theory of reasoned action and the theory of planned behavior. *Journal of Business Ethics*, *17*, 1825–1834. doi:10.1023/A:1005721401993

Chapell, M. S., Hasselman, S. L., Kitchin, T., Lomon, S. N., MacIver, K. W., & Sarullo, P. L. (2006). Bullying in elementary school, high school, and college. *Adolescence*, *41*(164), 633–648.

Charlesworth, A. (2008). Understanding and managing legal issues in Internet research. In Fielding, N., Lee, R. M., & Blank, G. (Eds.), *The SAGE handbook of online research methods* (pp. 42–57). London: Sage.

Charmaz, A. B. A. K. (2007). *The SAGE Handbook of Grounded Theory*. Thousand Oaks, CA: Sage Ltd.

Chernofsky, E. (2008, October 16). Is that Cellphone Kosher? *BBC News*. Retrieved July 6, 2009, from http://news-bbc.co.uk/go/pr/fr/-/1/hi/world/middle_east/7636021.stm

Chipello, C. (2001, January 19). MafiaBoy admits to charges linked to web-site attacks. *Wall Street Journal*, B2.

Chizawsky, L. L. K., Estabrooks, C. A., & Sales, A. E. (in press). The feasibility of web-based surveys as a data collection tool: A process evaluation. *Applied Nursing Research*.

Cho, H., & LaRose, R. (1999). Privacy issues in Internet surveys. *Social Science Computer Review*, *17*, 421–434. doi:10.1177/089443939901700402

Christoff, P. (2005). Green Governance and the Green State: Capacity Building as a Political Project. In R. Paehlke & D. Torgerson (Eds.), *Managing Leviathan* (pp. 289-310). Ontario, CA: Broadview Press Ltd.

CIEL-The Center for International Environmental Law. (2004). *CIEL Helps Protect the Rights of Indigenous Communities Displaced by the Ralco Dam along the Upper BíoBío River in Southern Chile*. Retrieved January 18, 2009 from http://ciel.org/Tae/Ralco_Aug04.html.

Clapp, J. (2005). Responses to Environmental Threats in an Age of Globalization. In R. Paehlke & D. Torgerson Eds.), *Managing Leviathan* (pp. 271-288). Ontario, CA: Broadview Press Ltd.

Clark, A. (2003). *Natural-born cyborgs. Minds, technologies, and the future of human intelligence*. Oxford and New York: Oxford University Press.

Cloud, D. S. (2005, June 22). The struggle for Iraq: Insurgents. *New York Times*, pp. A1, A10.

Coenen, C., Schuijff, M., Smits, M., Klaassen, P., Hennen, L., Rader, M., & Wolbring, G. (2009). *Human enhancement study*. European Parliament.

Cole, D. (2009). The Chinese Room Argument. In E. N. Zalta (Ed.), *The Stanford Encyclopedia of Philosophy*. Retrieved from http://plato.stanford.edu/archives/win2009/entries/chinese-room/

Cole, D. J., & Foelber, R. (1984). Contingent Materialism. *Pacific Philosophical Quarterly and Personalist (The) Los Angeles, 65*(1), 74-85.

Colonna, L. (2008). Nuevo foco de conflicto con Uruguay. *LANACION.com*. Retrieved January 18, 2009 from http://www.lanacion.com.ar/politica/nota.asp?nota_id=988139&origen=premium

Cook-Deegan, R. M. (1994). *The Gene Wars: Science, Politics, and the Human Genome*. New York: Norton.

Corbin, J., & Strauss, A. (2008). *Basics of Qualitative Research: Techniques and Procedures for Developing Grounded Theory* (3rd ed.). Thousand Oaks, CA: Sage.

Cornish, P., Hughes, R., & Livingstone, D. (2009, March). *Cyberspace and the national security of the United Kingdom: Threats and responses* (A Chatham House Report). London: Royal Institute of International Affairs.

Corrêa, E. S. (2008). Reflexões para uma epistemologia da comunicação digital. *Observatório, 4*, 307-320. Retrieved October 10, 2008, from http://obs.obercom.pt/index.php/obs/article/view/116/142

Cortellazzi, L. (2006). *Bullying: humilhar, intimidar, ofender, agredir*. Retrieved March 26, 2007, from http://www.eep.br/noticias/docs/bullying.pdf

Corzine, J. S., & Cañas, R. L. (2008, April 10). *The cyber-terror threat*. Washington, DC: Office of Homeland Security & Preparedness, Intelligence Assessment.

Couper, M. P. (2000). Web surveys: A review of issues and approaches. *Public Opinion Quarterly, 64*, 464–494. doi:10.1086/318641

Crabb, P. B. (1992). Effective control of energy-depleting behavior. *The American Psychologist, 47*, 815–816. doi:10.1037/0003-066X.47.6.815

Crabb, P. B. (1996a). Answering machines take the 'answering' out of telephone interactions. *Journal of Social Behavior and Personality, 11*, 387–397.

Crabb, P. B. (1996b). Video camcorders and civil inattention. *Journal of Social Behavior and Personality, 11*, 805–816.

Crabb, P. B. (2000). The material culture of homicidal fantasies. *Aggressive Behavior, 26*, 225–234. doi:10.1002/(SICI)1098-2337(2000)26:3<225::AID-AB2>3.0.CO;2-R

Crabb, P. B. (2003). Technology and self-regulation: The case of alarm clock use. *Social Behavior and Personality, 31*, 343–348. doi:10.2224/sbp.2003.31.4.343

Crabb, P. B. (2005). The material culture of suicidal fantasies. *The Journal of Psychology, 139*, 211–220. doi:10.3200/JRLP.139.3.211-220

Craig, A., Goold, A., Coldwell, J., & Mustard, J. (2008). Perceptions of roles and responsibilities in online learning: a case study. *Interdisciplinary Journal of E-Learning and Learning Objects V4*.

Crawford, S. (2002). Evaluation of web survey data collection systems. *Field Methods, 14*, 307–321.

Crews, C. W., Jr. (2003). Monitoring biometric technologies in a free society. *USA Today, 132*, 2698. Retrieved from ProQuest Educational Journals.

Crews, C. W., Jr. (2007). Cybersecurity and Authentication: the marketplace role in rethinking anonymity – before regulators intervene. *Springer Science and Business Media, 20*. Retrieved from ProQuest Educational Journals.

Crisp, R., & Slote, M. A. (1997). *Virtue Ethics*. Oxford and New York: Oxford University Press.

Cronan, T. P., & Al-Rafee, S. (2008). Factors that influence the intention to pirate software and media. *Journal of Business Ethics, 78*, 527–545. doi:10.1007/s10551-007-9366-8

Crowdsourcing. (2009, July 12). *The Guardian*. Retrieved July 13, 2009, from http://www.guardian.co.uk/technology/crowdsourcing

Cuhls, K. (2003). From forecasting to foresight processes - new participative foresight activities in Germany. *Journal of Forecasting, 22*(2-3), 93–111. doi:10.1002/for.848

Cummings, B. J. (1995). Dam the Rivers; Damn the People: Hydroelectric Development and Resistance in Amazonian Brazil. *GeoJournal, 35*(2), 151–160. doi:10.1007/BF00814061

d'Astous, A., Colbert, F., & Montpetit, D. (2005). Music piracy on the web: How effective are anti-piracy arguments? Evidence from the theory of planned behaviour. *Journal of Consumer Policy, 28*, 289–310. doi:10.1007/s10603-005-8489-5

Daniels, N. (1992). Growth hormone therapy for short stature: Can we support the treatment/enhancement distinction? *Growth: Genetics & Hormones*, 8S1.

Daniels, N. (1985). *Just Healthcare: Studies in Philosophy & Health Policy*. Cambridge, UK: Cambridge University Press.

Davis, R. A. (2001). *What is Internet addiction?* Retrieved March 12, 2009, from http://www.internetaddiction.ca/internet_addiction.htm

Dawkins, R. (1989). *The selfish gene*. Oxford: Oxford University Press.

de Botton, A. (2005). *Status anxiety*. New York: Vintage Books.

DeGrazia, D. (2005). Enhancement technologies and human identity. *The Journal of Medicine and Philosophy*, *30*, 261–283. doi:10.1080/03605310590960166

Deleuze, G., & Guattari, F. (1987). *A Thousand Plateaus*. Minneapolis, MN: University of Minnesota.

Denning, D. (1999). *Information Warfare and Security*. Boston, MA: Addison-Wesley.

Denning, D. (2007). The ethics of cyber conflict. In K. Himma, & H. Tavani (Eds.), *Information and computer ethics*. New York: Wiley.

Denning, D. E. (2000). Activism, hacktivism, and cyberterrorism: The Internet as a tool for influencing foreign policy. *Computer Security Journal*, *16*(3), 15–35.

Denning, D. E. (2001). Cyberwarriors: Activists and terrorists turn to cyberspace. *Harvard International Review*, *23*(2), 70–75.

Dennis, E. E., & Ismach, A. H. (1981). *Reporting processes and practices: Newswriting for today's readers*. Los Angeles, CA: Wadsworth.

Departamento Nacional de Infra-Estrutura de Transporte. (2001). Retrieved January 18, 2009 from https://gestao.dnit.gov.br/menu/rodovias/mapas.

Department for Environment. Food and Rural Affairs (DEFRA) (2007). *Characterising the potential risks posed by engineered nanoparticles, Second government research report*. London: DEFRA. Retrieved May 5, 2009, from: http://www.defra.gov.uk/environment/nanotech/research/pdf/

DeVoe, J. F., Kaffenberger, S., & Chandler, K. (2005). Student Reports of Bullying. Results of 2001 *School Crime Supplement to the National Crime Victimization Survey*. Washington, DC: US National Center for Education Statistics. Retrieved November 26, 2009, from http://nces.ed.gov/pubs2005/2005310.pdf

Diamond, J. (2005). *Collapse: How Societies Choose to Fail or Succeed*. New York: Penguin.

Dickerson, D. (2005). Cyberbullies on campus. *Toledo Law Review, 37*(1). Retrieved January 14, 2010, from http://law.utoledo.edu/students/lawreview/volumes/v37n1/Dickerson.htm

Dillard, J. P., & Shen, L. J. (2005). On the nature of reactance and its role in persuasive health communication. *Communication Monographs*, *72*, 144–168. doi:10.1080/03637750500111815

Directorate for Science, Technology and Industry, Organisation for Economic Co-Operation and Development. (2009). *OECD key ICT indicators*. Retrieved September 20, 2009, from http://www.oecd.org/sti/ICTindicators

Dombey, D., Murphy, M., & Parker, G. (2009, August 1). Hacker fails in US extradition battle. *Financial Times (North American Edition)*, 2.

Dorf, J., & Johnson, M. (2007). Restoration component of business continuity planning. In H. Tipton, & M. Krause (Eds.), *Information security management handbook* (6th ed.) (pp. 645-1654). CRC Press.

Duden, B. (2003). *Ivan Illich. Beyond Medical Nemesis (1976): The Search for Modernity's Disembodiment of "I" and "You."* Paper presented at the Bremen Symposium "Ivan Illich zum Abschied". Retrieved September 9, 2009 from http://www.pudel.uni-bremen.de/pdf/Iv_tra_b.pdf

Duggan, M. (2001). More guns, more crime. *The Journal of Political Economy*, *109*, 1086–1114. doi:10.1086/322833

Dunnigan, J. (2003). *How to make war. (4th ed.)*. New York: Quill.

Dusek, V. (2006). *Philosophy of Technology: an Introduction*. New York: Wiley Blackwell.

Dzindolet, M. T., Pierce, L. G., Beck, H. P., & Dawe, L. A. (2002). The perceived utility of human and automated aids in a visual detection task. *Human Factors*, *44*, 79–94. doi:10.1518/0018720024494856

Eckley, T. (1999). Remote Authentication: the Obvia solution. *Library Computing, 18*(2). Retrieved from ProQuest Educational Journals. eCampus Proctoring Policy (2008). Retrieved from http://www.troy.edu/academics/aop/documents/AOP_08-19-08-01.pdf April 14, 2009.

ECPAT International. (2005). *Violence in Cyberspace against children*. Retrieved February 10, 2006, from http://www.ecpat.net/eng/publications/Cyberspace/PDF/ECPAT_Cyberspace_2005-ENG.pdf

Eid, M. (2006, October 30). *Telling the truth in the media; Mathematically approved. Journalism Ethics for the Global Citizen*. Retrieved on September 29, 2009, from http://www.journalismethics.info/feature_articles/telling-the-truth.htm

Eid, M. (2006a). Cyber-terrorism in the information age: Actors, communications, tactics, targets, and influences. In *Proceedings of Information-MFCSIT*, *06*, 39–42.

Eid, M. (2006b). Mass media and the puzzle of information in the course of playing crises. *INFORMATION: An International Interdisciplinary Journal*, *9*(1), 83–100.

Eid, M. (2008). *Interweavement: International media ethics and rational decision-making*. Boston: Pearson.

Eid, M. (2009). On the way to the Cyber-Arab-Culture: International communication, telecommunications policies, and democracy. In Ricardo, F. J. (Ed.), *Cyberculture and new media* (pp. 69–98). Amsterdam, The Netherlands: Rodopi.

Elliott, D. (2003). Balance and context: Maintaining media ethics. *Phi Kappa Phi Forum*, *83*(2), 16–21.

Ellul, J. (1954, 1964). *The Technological Society*. New York: Vintage Books.

Englander, E., Muldowney, A. M., & McCoy, M. (2009). Cyberbullying and information exposure: User-generated content in post secondary education. *International Journal of Contemporary Sociology*, *46*(2), 213–230.

Entertainment Media Research (in association with Olswang). (2007). *The 2007 digital music survey*. Retrieved from http://www.entertainmentmediaresearch.com/reports/EMR_Digital_Music_Survey2007.pdf

Epitectus. (1952). *The Discourses of Epictetus* (G. Long trans.). Chicago: Encyclopaedia Britannica.

Ericson, N. (2001). *Addressing the Problem of Juvenile Bullying*. Washington, DC: U.S. Government Printing Office.

Ess, C., & the The AIOR Ethics Working Committee. (2002). *Ethical decision making and Internet research: Recommendations from the AOIR ethics working committee*. Retrieved August 31, 2009, from http://www.aoir.org/reports/ethics.pdf

Ess, C. (2007). Internet research ethics. In Joinson, A., McKenna, K., Postmes, T., & Reips, U.-D. (Eds.), *The Oxford handbook of Internet psychology* (pp. 487–502). New York: Oxford University Press.

European Commission. (2005). *EU Stand-By Initiative*. European Union.

Evans, J. R., & Mathur, A. (2005). The value of online surveys. *Internet Research*, *15*, 195–219. doi:10.1108/10662240510590360

Experts say West can't stop web radicalization; From behind a computer keyboard at his London home, student Younes Tsouli used the Internet to spread al Qaeda propaganda, recruit suicide bombers and promote web sites that encouraged the killing of non-Muslims. (2007, November). *CIO Insight*, 87.

Fearnside, P., & Barbosa, R. I. (1996). Political Benefits as Barriers to Assessment of Environmental Costs in Brazil's Amazonian Development Planning: The Example of the Jatapu Dam in Roraima. *Environmental Management*, *20*(5), 615–630. doi:10.1007/BF01204135

Fearnside, P., & Barbosa, R. I. (1996). The Cotingo Dam as a Test of Brazil's System for Evaluating Proposed Developments in Amazonia. *Environmental Management*, *20*(5), 615–648. doi:10.1007/BF01204135

Feigelson, M. E., & Dwight, S. A. (2000). Can asking questions by computer improve the candidness of responding? A meta-analytic perspective. *Consulting Psychology Journal: Practice and Research*, *52*, 248–255. doi:10.1037/1061-4087.52.4.248

Felten, E. (2010, January 29). *Census of files available via BitTorrent*. Retrieved from http://www.freedom-to-tinker.com/blog/felten/census-files-available-bittorrent

Ferguson, D. A. (1994). Measurement of mundane TV behaviors: Remote control device flipping frequency. *Journal of Broadcasting & Electronic Media*, *38*, 35–47.

Ferguson, T. (2004). The first generation of e-patients. *British Medical Journal, 328*, 1148–1149. doi:10.1136/bmj.328.7449.1148

Ferrier, S. (2002, April). Mapping Spatial Pattern in Biodiversity for Regional Conservation Planning: Where to from Here? *Systematic Biology, 51*(2), 331–363. doi:10.1080/10635150252899806

Finn, J. (2004). A survey of online harassment at a university campus. *Journal of Interpersonal Violence, 19*(4), 468–483. doi:10.1177/0886260503262083

Fishbein, M., & Ajzen, I. (1975). *Belief, attitude, intention and behavior: An introduction to theory and research.* Reading, MA: Addison-Wesley.

Fishbein, M., Hennessy, M., Kamb, M., Bolan, G. A., Hoxworth, T., Iatesta, M., & Zenilman, J. M. (2001). Using intervention theory to model factors influencing behavior change: Project RESPECT. *Evaluation & the Health Professions, 24*, 363–384. doi:10.1177/01632780122034966

Flanagan, T. (1998). *Game theory and Canadian politics.* Toronto, Canada: University of Toronto Press.

Florentine, M., Hunter, W., Robinson, M., Ballou, M., & Buus, S. (1998). On the behavioural characteristics of loud-music listening. *Ear and Hearing, 19*, 420–428. doi:10.1097/00003446-199812000-00003

Floridi, L., & Sanders, J. W. (2003). The method of abstraction. In M. Negrotti (Ed.), *Yearbook of the artificial. Nature, culture, and technology. Models in Contemporary Sciences* (pp. 177-220). Bern: Peter Lang.

Floridi, L. (Ed.). (2010). *The Cambridge Handbook of Information and Computer Ethics.* Cambridge, UK: Cambridge University Press.

Forsberg, B. (2005, May 23). *Restrictions placed on Camera Phones, More Places say they may violate Privacy, Security.* San Francisco, CA: SFGate. Retrieved July 19, 2009, from http://www.sfgate.com/cgi-bin/article.cgi?f=/c/a/2005/05/23/BUG7KCSLRE1.DTL

Fotion, N., & Elfstrom, G. (1986). *Military ethics: guidelines for peace and war.* Boston: Routledge and Kegan Paul.

Foucault, M. (1979). *Discipline and punish: The birth of the prison (1975).* Translated by A. Sheridan. New York: Vintage Books.

Foucault, M. (1975). *Vigilar y Castigar.* Madrid: Siglo XXI.

Foucault, M. (1976). *Historia de la sexualidad: La voluntad de saber.* Madrid: Siglo XXI.

Foucault, M. (1995). *Discipline and punish: the birth of the prison.* New York: Vintage Books.

Fox, R. J., Crask, M. R., & Kim, J. (1988). Mail survey response rate: A meta-analysis of selected techniques for inducing response. *Public Opinion Quarterly, 52*, 467–491. doi:10.1086/269125

Frank, D. (June 4, 2002). Our Fruit, Their Labor and Global Reality. *The Washington Post* (p. B5).

Fratto, M. (2003). Are biometrics the answer? *Network Computing, 14*(3). Retrieved from ProQuest Educational Journals.

Freedom House Dismayed by new regulations, increasing censorship on video-sharing websites. (2009, April 2). Washington, DC: Freedom House. Retrieved July 15, 2009, from http://www.ifex.org/china/2009/04/03/freedom_house_dismayed_by_new_regulations/

Fricker, R. D. Jr, & Schonlau, M. (2002). Advantages and disadvantages of Internet research surveys: Evidence from the literature. *Field Methods, 14*, 347–367. doi:10.1177/152582202237725

Friedland, L. (2003). *Public Journalism: Past and Future.* Dayton, Ohio: Kettering Foundation Press.

Fromm, E. (1955). *The Sane Society.* New York: Holt, Rinehart and Winston.

Fukukawa, K. (2002). Developing a framework for ethically questionable behavior in consumption. *Journal of Business Ethics, 41*, 99–119. doi:10.1023/A:1021354323586

Fukuyama, F. (2002). *Our posthuman future, consequences of the biotechnology revolution.* London: Profile Books.

Furnell, S. (2002). *Cybercrime.* Boston: Addison-Wesley.

Furtive Phone Photography Spurs Ban. (2003, April 4). *BBC News*. Retrieved June 19, 2009 from http://news-votebbc.co.uk/mapps/pagetools/print/news.bbc.co.uk/1/hi/technology/2916353.stm

Gaiser, T. J., & Schreiner, A. E. (2009). *A guide to conducting online research*. London: Sage.

Galván, J. M. (2003). On technoethics. *IEEE Robotics & Automation Magazine*, *10*(4), 58–63.

Gandy, O. (1998). Coming to Terms with the Panoptic Sort. In Lyon, D., & Zureik, E. (Eds.), *Computers, Surveillance and Privacy*. Minneapolis, MN: Minnesota University Press.

Gardam, J. (2004). *Necessity, proportionality, and the use of force by states*. Cambridge, UK: Cambridge University Press.

Gearhart, D. (2009). Preparing students for ethical use of technology: a case study for distance education. In U. Demiray & R. C. Sharma (Eds.), *Ethical Practices and Implications in Distance Learning*. Hershey, PA: Information Science Reference.

Genus, A., & Coles, A. (2005). On Constructive Technology Assessment and Limitations on Public Participation in Technology Assessment. *Technology Analysis and Strategic Management*, *17*(4), 433–443. doi:10.1080/09537320500357251

George, J. F. (2002). Influences on the intent to make Internet purchases. *Internet Research*, *12*, 165–180. doi:10.1108/10662240210422521

Gibson, J. J. (1986). *The ecological approach to visual perception*. Boston: Houghton-Miffin.

Glaser, B. G., & Strauss, A. L. (1999). *Discovery of Grounded Theory: Strategies for Qualitative Research*. Piscataway, NJ: AldineTransaction.

Glaser, J., Dixit, J., & Green, D. P. (2002). Studying hate crimes with the Internet: What makes racists advocate racial violence? *The Journal of Social Issues*, *58*, 75–90. doi:10.1111/1540-4560.00255

Goffman, E. (1986). *Frame Analysis: An Essay on the Organization of Experience*. New York: Northeastern Press.

Goldberg, I. (1999). *Internet addiction disorder*. Retrieved December 14, 2008, from http://www.uml.edu/student-services/counseling/internet/netdisorder.html

González-Barahona, J. M. (2004). El software como servicio. O de cómo producir programas libres y no morir en el intento. En V. Matellán et al. (Eds.), *Sobre Free Software. Compilación de ensayos sobre Free Software. Grupo de Sistemas y Comunicaciones*. Madrid: Universidad Rey Juan Carlos.

González-Barahona, J. M. (2004). Free Software, monopolios y otras yerbas. En V. Matellán et al. (Eds.), *Sobre Free Software. Compilación de ensayos sobre Free Software. Grupo de Sistemas y Comunicaciones*. Madrid: Universidad Rey Juan Carlos.

González-Barahona, J. M. (2004). La imparcialidad de los estados y la industria del software. En V. Matellán et al. (Eds.), *Sobre Free Software. Compilación de ensayos sobre Free Software. Grupo de Sistemas y Comunicaciones*. Madrid: Universidad Rey Juan Carlos.

Gordon, S., & Ford, R. (2003). Cyberterrorism? *Symantec Security Response*. Retrieved September 29, 2009, from http://www.symantec.com/avcenter/reference/cyberterrorism.pdf

Gordon, A. (2002). Product review: SurveyMonkey.com—Web-based survey and evaluation system. *The Internet and Higher Education*, *5*, 83–87. Retrieved from http://www.SurveyMonkey.com. doi:10.1016/S1096-7516(02)00061-1

Gordon, A. D. (1999). Truth precludes any need for further ethical concerns in journalism and public relations. In Gordon, A. D., & Kittross, J. M. (Eds.), *Controversies in media ethics* (pp. 73–80). New York: Longman.

Gosling, S. D., Vazire, S., Srivastava, S., & John, O. P. (2004). Should we trust web-based studies? A comparative analysis of six preconceptions about Internet questionnaires. *The American Psychologist*, *59*, 93–104. doi:10.1037/0003-066X.59.2.93

Gostomski, C. (2005, November 13). Ironing out the kinks. *Morning Call*, p. A32.

Gracián, B. (2003). *Oráculo manual y arte de la prudencia*. Madrid, Spain: Cátedra.

Greely, H. (2005). Regulating human biological enhancements: Questionable justifications and international complications. *University of Technology. The Sydney Law Review, 7*, 87–110.

Greenemeier, L. (2008). Nanotech to regrow cartilage and soothe aching knees. *Scientific American Journal.* Retrieved June 17, 2008, from http://www.sciam.com/article.cfm?id=nanotech-cartilage&sc=WR_20080617

Greenfield, D. N. (1999). Psychological characteristics of compulsive Internet use: A preliminary analysis. *Cyberpsychology & Behavior, 2*, 403–412. doi:10.1089/cpb.1999.2.403

Grint, K., & Woolgar, S. (1997). *The Machine at Work: Technology, Work and Organization.* New York: Polity Press.

Gross, J. (1999, November 5). A long-distance tether home. *New York Times*, pp. B1, B10.

Groves, R. M., Cialdini, R. B., & Couper, M. P. (1992). Understanding the decision to participate in a survey. *Public Opinion Quarterly, 56*, 475–495. doi:10.1086/269338

Grunwald, A. (2005). Nanotechnology – a new field of ethical inquiry? *Science and Engineering Ethics, 11*(2), 187–201. doi:10.1007/s11948-005-0041-0

Gutman, R., & Rieff, D. (1999). *Crimes of war: what the public should know.* New York: Norton

Haas, T. (2007). *The Pursuit of Public Journalism: Theory, Practice and Criticism.* New York: Routledge.

Habermas, J. (2003). *The future of human nature.* Cambridge, UK: Polity Press.

Hacker Gary McKinnon loses extradition appeal. (2009, July 31). *Informationweek – Online.*

Hall, A. (1994). Grassroots Action for Resettlement Planning: Brazil and Beyond. *World Development, 22*(12), 1793–1809. doi:10.1016/0305-750X(94)90174-0

Haraway, D. (1991). A Cyborg manifesto: Science, technology, and socialist-feminism in the late twentieth century. In D. Haraway, *Simians, cyborgs and women: The reinvention of nature* (pp. 149-181). New York: Routledge.

Haraway, D. (1991). *Ciencia, Cyborg y mujeres. La reinvención de la naturaleza.* Madrid: Ediciones Cátedra.

Haraway, D. (1992). Las promesas de los monstruos: Una política regeneradora para otros inapropiados/bles. *Politica y Sociedad, 30*, 121–163.

Hård, M., & Jamison, A. (2005). *Hubris and hybrids: A cultural history of technology and science.* New York: Routledge.

Hardt, M., & Negri, A. (2000). *Imperio.* Barcelona: Paidós.

Harmon, A. (2004, August 26). Internet gives teenage bullies weapons to wound from afar. *New York Times*, p. A1.

Harris, G., & Spark, D. (1997). *Practical newspaper reporting.* Oxford, UK: Focal Press.

Harris, J. (2007). *Enhancing Evolution: The Ethical Case for Making Better People.* Princeton, NJ: Princeton University Press.

Harrison, A. (2000, April 24). Analysts: MafiaBoy only amateur copycat. *Computerworld, 34*(17), 6.

Harris, S. (2007). *Enhancing evolution: The ethical case for making better people.* Princeton, NJ: Princeton University Press.

Harson, A. (1995, November 25). Student's expulsion over e-mail raises concern. *Los Angels Times.* Retrieved December 11, 2007, from http://mr.caltech.edu/media/time.html

Hartman, B. (2005, September 28). Did Troops Trade Photos of War Dead for Porn? *ABC News.* Retrieved July 13, 2009, from http://abcnews.go.com/Technology/IraqCoverage/story?id=1166772&page=1

Harvey, M., Treadway, D., Heames, J. T., & Duke, A. (2009). Bullying in the 21st century global organization: An ethical perspective. *Journal of Business Ethics, 85*, 27–40. doi:10.1007/s10551-008-9746-8

Hawkins, D. L., Pepler, D. J., & Craig, W. M. (2001). Naturalistic Observations of Peer Interventions. In *Social Development.* Retrieved January 29, 2009, from http://www3.interscience.wiley.com/journal/119028433/abstract?CRETRY=1&SRETRY=0

Hayles, K. (1999). *How we became posthuman: Virtual bodies in cybernetics, literature, and informatics.* Chicago: University of Chicago Press.

Heap, S. P. H., & Varoufakis, Y. (1995). *Game theory: A critical introduction*. New York: Routledge. doi:10.4324/9780203199275

Heersmink, R., van den Hoven, J., van Eck, N. J., & van den Berg, J. (2011). A Bibliometrical Study of Computer and Information Ethics. *Ethics and Information Technology*.

Hellweg, E. (2003, September 10). The Kazaa conundrum. *CNN Money*. Retrieved from http://money.cnn.com/2003/09/10/technology/techinvestor/hellweg/index.htm

Hensgen, T., Desouza, K. C., Evaristo, J. R., & Kraft, G. D. (2003). Playing the "cyber terrorism game" towards a semiotic definition. *Human Systems Management*, *22*(2), 51–61.

Herrick, J. (2005). *Humanism: An Introduction*. Amherst, NY: Prometheus Books.

Hewson, C. (2007). Gathering data on the Internet: Qualitative approaches and possibilities for mixed methods research. In Joinson, A., McKenna, K., Postmes, T., & Reips, U.-D. (Eds.), *The Oxford handbook of Internet psychology* (pp. 405–428). New York: Oxford University Press.

Hewson, C., & Laurent, D. (2008). Research design and tools for Internet research. In Fielding, N., Lee, R. M., & Blank, G. (Eds.), *The SAGE handbook of online research methods* (pp. 58–78). London: Sage.

Hewson, C., Yule, P., Laurent, D., & Vogel, C. (2003). *Internet research methods: A practical guide for the social and behavioural sciences*. London: Sage.

Hildebrandt, T., Langenbucher, J., Carr, S., Sanjuan, P., & Park, S. (2006). Predicting intentions for long-term anabolic-androgenic steroid use among men: A covariance structure model. *Psychology of Addictive Behaviors*, *20*, 234–240. doi:10.1037/0893-164X.20.3.234

Himma, K. (2004). The ethics of tracing hacker attacks through the machines of innocent persons. *International Journal of Information Ethics*, *2*(11), 1–13.

Himma, K. E., & Tavani, H. T. (Eds.). (2008). *The Handbook of Information and Computer Ethics*. New York: Wiley. doi:10.1002/9780470281819

Hindman, E. B. (1997). *Rights vs. responsibilities: The Supreme Court and the media*. Westport, CT: Greenwood Press.

Hoch, D., & Ferguson, T. (2005). What I've Learned from E-Patients. *PLoS Medicine*, *2*(8). doi:10.1371/journal.pmed.0020206

Hockenberry, J. (2001). The next brainiacs. *Wired Issue 9.08*. Retrieved February 18, 2007, from http://www.wired.com/wired/archive/9.08/assist.html

Hodgins, D., Bertsch, A., Post, N., Frischholz, M., Volckaerts, B., Spensley, J., Wasikiewicz, J., Higgins, H., von Stetten, F., & Kenney, L. (2008). Healthy aims: developing new medical implants and diagnostic equipment. *Pervasive Computing*, 14-21.

Hogan, T. P. (1983). Psychology and the technological revolution. *Canadian Psychology*, *24*, 235–241. doi:10.1037/h0080747

Hollis, D. (2007). New tools, new rules: international law and information operations. In G. David, & T. McKeldin (Eds.), *The message of war: information, influence, and perception in armed conflict*. Temple University Legal Studies Research Paper No. 2007-15, Philadelphia, PA, USA.

Holmes, B. (2003). *Vers une scission dans l'Empire?* Retrieved from http://infos.samizdat.net/article.php3?id_article=211

Hongladarom, S. (2005, January 7-9). The digital divide, epistemology and global justice. The 2nd Asia-Pacific Computing and Philosophy Conference, Chulalongkorn University, bangkok, Thailand.

Hong, S.-M., & Faedda, A. (1996). Refinement of the Hong Psychological Reactance Scale. *Educational and Psychological Measurement*, *56*, 173–182. doi:10.1177/0013164496056001014

Hook, C. (2004). *Transhumanism and posthumanism. Encyclopedia of Bioethics*. New York: Macmillan Press.

Horrigan, J. (2009, June). *Home broadband adoption 2009: Broadband adoption increases, but monthly prices do too*. Washington, DC: Pew Internet & American Life Project. Retrieved from http://pewinternet.org/Reports/2009/10-Home-Broadband-Adoption-2009.aspx

Horst, S. (2007). *Beyond Reduction: Philosophy of Mind and Post-reductionist Philosophy of Science.* Oxford, UK: Oxford University Press.

Horton, R. (2004). Vioxx, the implosion of Merck, and aftershocks at the FDA. *The Lancet, 364,* 1995-1996. *Integrity in Science.* (n.d.). Retrieved September 6, 2009 from http://www.cspinet.org/integrity

House of Lords Select Committee on Science and Technology. (2000). *Science and society: Third report.* London: HMSO.

Howcroft, D., Mitev, N., & Wilson, M. (2004). What We May Learn from the Social Shaping of Technology Approach. In Mingers, J., & Willcocks, L. P. (Eds.), *Social Theory and Philosophy for Information Systems* (pp. 329–371). New York: Wiley.

Howes, D. (Ed.). (1996). *Cross-cultural consumption. Global markets, local realities.* London and New York: Routledge.

Hrubes, D., & Ajzen, I. (2001). Predicting hunting intentions and behavior: An application of the theory of planned behavior. *Leisure Sciences, 23,* 165–178. doi:10.1080/014904001316896855

Hughes, J. (2004). *Citizen Cyborg: Why Democratic Societies Must Respond to the Redesigned Human of the Future.* Boulder, CO: Westview Press.

Hunt, G. (2006). The global ethics of nanotechnology. In G. Hunt & M. Mehta (Ed.), *Nanotechnology: Risk, ethics and law* (pp. 183-95). London: Earthscan.

Hunt, G., & Mehta, M. (Eds.). (2006). *Nanotechnology: Risk, ethics and law.* London: Earthscan.

Hutchins, E. (1995). *Cognition in the Wild.* Cambridge, MA: MIT Press.

Hyslop, A. (2009). Other Minds. In E. N. Zalta (Ed.), *The Stanford Encyclopedia of Philosophy.* Retrieved from http://plato.stanford.edu/archives/win2009/entries/other-minds/

I.C.L.E.I. (2008). *Local Governments fro Sustainability.* Retrieved January 18, 2009 from http://www.iclei.org/index.php?id=iclei-home&no_cache=1.

Iannone, A. P. (1987). *Contemporary Moral Controversies in Technology.* London and New York: Oxford University Press.

Iannone, A. P. (1989). *Contemporary Moral Controversies in Business.* London and New York: Oxford University Press.

Iannone, A. P. (1994). *Philosophy as Diplomacy. Essays in Ethics and Policy Making* Atlantic Highlands, NJ and Anherst, NY: Humanities Press and Humanity Books. Atlantic Highlands, NJ: Humanities Press.

Iannone, A. P. (1999). *Philosophical Ecologies: Essays in Philosophy, Ecology, and Human Life.* Atlantic Highlands, NJ and Anherst, NY: Humanities Press and Humanity Books.

Iannone, A. P. (2005). Pollution entry. In C. Mitcham (Ed.), *Encyclopedia of Science, Technology, and Ethics.* New York: Macmillan.

Iannone, A. P. (2008). *Papeles del gobierno, los mercados, y la cultura cívica en programas de desarrollo comunitario estadounidenses.* Publication of the School of Administrative and Economic Sciences. Lima, Perú: Universidad Inca Garcilaso de la Vega.

Ibrahim, Y. (2009). The New Risk Communities: Social Networking Sites and Risk. *International Journal of Media and Cultural Politics, 4*(2), 245–253. doi:10.1386/macp.4.2.245_3

ICRC (International Committee of the Red Cross). (2007). *International humanitarian law – treaties and documents.* Retrieved December 1, 2007 from www.icrc.org/icl.nsf.

Ignatieff, M. (2004). *The lesser evil: Political ethics in an age of terror.* New York: Penguin.

InfoTrends/CAP Ventures Releases Worldwide Mobile Imaging Study Results. Study Projects Nearly 900 Million Camera Phone Shipments Worldwide by 2009. (2005, January 10). *Business Wire.* Retrieved July 3, 2009, from http://www.businesswire.com/portal/site/google/index.jsp?ndmViewId=news_view&newsId=20050110005831&newsLang=en

International Federation of the Phonographic Industry. (2008). *IFPI digital music report 2008.* Retrieved from http://www.ifpi.org/content/library/DMR2008.pdf

James, L., & Nahl, D. (2000). *Road Rage and Aggressive Driving*. Amherst, NY: Prometheus.

Jemmott, J. B., Jemmott, L. S., Fong, G. T., & McCaffree, K. (1999). Reducing HIV risk associated sexual behavior among African American adolescents: Testing the generality of intervention effects. *American Journal of Community Psychology*, *27*, 161–187. doi:10.1007/BF02503158

Jenetzko, D. (2008). Nonreactive data collection on the Internet. In Fielding, N., Lee, R. M., & Blank, G. (Eds.), *The SAGE handbook of online research methods* (pp. 161–173). London: Sage.

Jensen, E. (2003). Unexpected consequences from knock-on effects: a different standard for computer network operations? *American University International Law Review*, *18*, 1145–1188.

John, O. P., Naumann, L. P., & Soto, C. J. (2008). Paradigm shift to the integrative big-five trait taxonomy: History, measurement, and conceptual Issues. In John, O. P., Robins, R. W., & Pervin, L. A. (Eds.), *Handbook of personality: Theory and research* (3rd ed., pp. 114–158). New York: Guilford Press.

Johnson, D. G. (1994). *Computer ethics* (2nd ed.). Englewood Cliffs, NJ: Prentice Hall.

Johnson, J. (1984). *Can modern war be just?* New Haven: Yale University Press.

Johnson, D. G. (2006). Computer Systems: Moral Agents but not Moral Agents. *Ethics and Information Technology*, *8*, 195–204. doi:10.1007/s10676-006-9111-5

Johnson, D. G. (2007). Ethics and technology "in the making": An essay on the challenge of nanoethics. *NanoEthics*, *1*(1), 21–30. doi:10.1007/s11569-007-0006-7

Joinson, A. N., Paine, C., Buchanan, T., & Reips, U.-D. (2008). Measuring self-disclosure online: Blurring and non-response to sensitive items in web-based surveys. *Computers in Human Behavior*, *24*, 2158–2171. doi:10.1016/j.chb.2007.10.005

Jones, A., Kovacich, G., & Luzwick, P. (2002). *Global information warfare*. Boca Raton, FL: CRC Press.

Jonsen, A. R., & Toulmin, S. (1988). *The abuse of casuistry. A history of moral reasoning*. Berkeley and Los Angeles: University of California Press.

Jordon, G. (2006). Apologia for transhumanist religion. *Journal of Evolution and Technology*, *15*(1).

Joshi, M. (1996). On the Razor's edge: The Liberation Tigers of Tamil Eelam. *Studies in Conflict and Terrorism*, *19*(1), 19–42. doi:10.1080/10576109608435994

Joss, S. (2002). Toward the Public Sphere--Reflections on the Development of Participatory Technology Assessment. *Bulletin of Science, Technology & Society*, *22*(3), 220–231. doi:10.1177/02767602022003006

Joss, S., & Belucci, S. (Eds.). (2002). *Participatory Technology Assessment: European Perspectives*. London: University of Westminster, Centre for the Study of Democracy.

Just health: Meeting health needs fairly. (2008). Cambridge, UK: Cambridge University Press.

Kaboré, B. (2005, May 29-30). Vie privée, identité et vol d'identité. *Technology and Changing Face of Humanity, Conference*. Canadian Jacques Maritain Association. The University of Western Ontario, Canada.

Kaczmirek, L. (2008). Internet survey software tools. In Fielding, N., Lee, R. M., & Blank, G. (Eds.), *The SAGE handbook of online research methods* (pp. 236–254). London: Sage.

Kant, E. (1785). *Fundamental principles of the metaphysic of morals*. (T. K. Abbott, Trans.). Retrieved October 13, 2009, from http://www.gutenberg.org/dirs/etext04/ikfpm10.txt

Kass, L. (2003). Beyond therapy: Biotechnology and the pursuit of happiness. *A Report by the President's Council on Bioethics*. Retrieved February 21, 2007, from http://www.bioethics.gov/reports/beyondtherapy/beyond_therapy_final_webcorrected.pdf

Kass, L. (1971). The new biology: What price relieving man's estate? *Science*, *174*, 780. doi:10.1126/science.174.4011.779

Kearns, C. A., Inouye, D. W., & Waser, N. M. (1998). Endangered Mutualisms: The Conservation of Plant-Pollinator Interactions. *Annual Review of Ecology and Systematics*, *29*, 83–112. doi:10.1146/annurev.ecolsys.29.1.83

Keeter, S., & Taylor, P. (2009). The Millenials. *Pew Internet Research*. Retrieved May 20, 2010, from http://pewresearch.org/pubs/1437/millennials-profile

Keller, H. E., & Lee, S. (2003). Ethical issues surrounding human participants research using the Internet. *Ethics & Behavior*, *13*, 211–219. doi:10.1207/S15327019EB1303_01

Kelley, B. (2007). Criminalisation: Applying a Living Standard Analysis to Non-Consensual Photography and Distribution. *QUT Law and Justice Journal*, *2*(7), 464–476.

Kiesler, S., Siegel, J., & McGuire, T. W. (1984). Social psychological aspects of computermediated communication. *The American Psychologist*, *39*, 1123–1134. doi:10.1037/0003-066X.39.10.1123

Kim, J. (2006). *Philosophy of Mind*. Boulder, CO: Westview Press.

Kindberg, T., Spasojevic, M., Fleck, R., & Sellen, A. (2005, April 2-7). *I Saw This and Thought of You: Some Social Uses of Camera Phones*. Paper Presented at CHI '05, Portland, OR.

Kipnis, D. (1984). Technology, power, and control. *Research in the Sociology of Organizations*, *3*, 125–156.

Kipnis, D. (1991). The technological perspective. *Psychological Science*, *2*, 62–69. doi:10.1111/j.1467-9280.1991.tb00101.x

Kitahara, R. T., & Westfall, F. (2007). Promoting academic integrity in online distance learning courses. *MERLOT Journal of Online Learning and Teaching*, *3*(2).

Kittross, J. M. (1999). The social value of journalism and public relations requires high-quality practices reflecting ethical considerations that go beyond truth and objectivity to accuracy and fairness. In Gordon, A. D., & Kittross, J. M. (Eds.), *Controversies in media ethics* (pp. 80–89). New York: Longman.

Kjølberg, K. L., & Wickson, F. (2007). Social and ethical interactions with nano: Mapping the early literature. *NanoEthics*, *1*(2), 89–104. doi:10.1007/s11569-007-0011-x

Klein, A. (2008, February 11). Police Go Live Monitoring D.C. Crime Cameras. *The Washington Post*. Retrieved July 1, 2009, from http://www.washingtonpost.com/wp-dyn/content/article/2008/02/10/AR2008021002726_pf.html

Knapp, K., & Boulton, W. (2007). Ten information warfare trends. In L. Janczewski & A. Colarik (Eds.), *Cyber Warfare and Cyber Terrorism* (pp. 17-25). Hershey, PA, USA: IGI Global.

Kolakowski, L. (1999). *Freedom, Fame, Lying and Betrayal: Essays on Everyday Life* (pp. 124–125). London: Penguin Books.

Kovach, B., & Rosenstiel, T. (2001). *The elements of journalism: What newspeople should know and the public should expect*. New York: Crown Publishers.

Kraft, E. M. (2010). Juicycampus.com: How was this business model culpable to encouraging harassment on college campuses? In Shariff, S., & Churchill, A. (Eds.), *Truths and myths of cyber-bullying: International perspectives on stakeholder responsibility and children's safety* (pp. 65–103). New York: Peter Lang Publishing.

Kraut, R., Olson, J., Banaji, M., Bruckman, A., Cohen, J., & Couper, M. (2004). Psychological research online: Report of the Board of Scientific Affairs' Advisory Group on the conduct of research on the Internet. *The American Psychologist*, *59*, 105–117. doi:10.1037/0003-066X.59.2.105

Kremen, C., Williams, N. M., & Thorp, R. W. (2002, December 24). Crop Pollination from Native Bees at Risk from Agricultural Intensification. *Proceedings of the National Academy of Sciences of the United States*, *99*(26), 16812–16816. doi:10.1073/pnas.262413599

Krim, J. (2007, July 7). Subway Fracas Escalates Into Test of the Internet's Power to Shame. *The Washington Post*. Retrieved July 2, 2009, from http://www.washingtonpost.com/wpdyn/content/article/2005/07/06/AR2005070601953.html?referrer=emailarticle

Krishnamurthy, S. (2005, January 7-9). Internet booths in villages of India. *The 2nd Asia-Pacific Computing and Philosophy Conference* (pp.1-28), Chulalongkorn University, Bangkok, Thailand.

Kuhnhauser, W. (2004, January). Root kits: an operating systems viewpoint. *ACM SIGOPS Operating Systems Review, 38*(1), 12–23. doi:10.1145/974104.974105

Kurzweil, R. (2005). *The singularity is near: When humans transcend biology.* New York: Viking Penguin.

Kuzma, J., & Besley, J. (2008). Ethics of risk analysis and regulatory review: From bio- to nanotechnology. *Nano-Ethics, 2*(2), 149–162. doi:10.1007/s11569-008-0035-x

Kwong, T. C. H., & Lee, M. K. O. (2002, January). *Behavioral intention model for the exchange mode internet music piracy.* Paper presented at the 35th Hawaii International Conference of System Sciences, Maui, HI.

Laclau, E., & Mouffe, C. (1985). *Hegemonía y estrategia socialista: Hacia una radicalización de la democracia.* Madrid: Siglo XXI editores.

LaFrance, M. (1996). Why we trust computers too much. *Technology Studies, 3*, 163–178.

Lafuente, A. (n.d.). *El megachute tecnológico.* Retrieved September 6, 2009 from http://weblogs.madrimasd.org/tecnocidanos/archive/2008/01/20/82705.aspx

Langenderfer, J., & Linnhoff, S. (2005). The emergence of biometrics and its effect on consumers. *The Journal of Consumer Affairs, 39*(2). Retrieved from ProQuest Educational Journals.

Large, D. (2003). *The ecological philosophy.* Newcastle upon Tyne, UK: Newcastle Philosophy Society. Retrieved June 15, 2008, from http://www.newphilsoc.org.uk/Ecological/DavidLarge.PDF

LaRose, R., Lai, Y. J., Lange, R., Love, B., & Wu, Y. (2005). Sharing or piracy? An exploration of downloading behavior. *Journal of Computer-Mediated Communication, 11*, 1–21. doi:10.1111/j.1083-6101.2006.tb00301.x

Latest Abu Ghraib Pictures Threaten to Inflame Anger in Iraq. (2006, February 16) *USA Today.* Retrieved July 12, 2009, from http://www.usatoday.com/news/world/iraq/2006-02-16-prison-abuse_x.htm

Latour, B. (1987). *Science in action: How to follow scientists and engineers through society.* Cambridge, MA: Harvard University Press.

Latour, B. (1988). *The pasteurization of France.* Cambridge, MA: Harvard University Press.

Latour, B. (1999). *La esperanza de Pandora.* Barcelona: Gedisa.

Latour, B. (2002). Morality and Technology: the end of the means. *Theory, Culture & Society, 19*(5-6), 247–260. doi:10.1177/026327602761899246

Latour, B. (2007). *Reassembling the Social: An Introduction to Actor-Network-Theory.* Oxford, UK: OUP.

Lau, E. K. W. (2003). An empirical study of software piracy. *Business Ethics (Oxford, England), 12*, 233–245. doi:10.1111/1467-8608.00323

Laurance, W. F. (Mar. 29, 2004). Forest-Climate Interactions in Fragmented Tropical Landscapes. *Philosophical Transactions: Biological Sciences, 359*(1443), Tropical Forests and Global Atmospheric Change, 345-352.

Laurance, W. F., Cochrane, M. A., Bergen, S., Fearnside, P. M., Delamônica, P., & Barber, C. (2001, Jan. 19). The Future of the Brazilian Amazon. *Science. New Series, 291*(5503), 438–439.

Law, J. (1993). *Modernity, myth, and materialism.* Oxford: Blackwell.

Law, J., & Hassard, J. (1999). *Actor Network Theory and After.* New York: Wiley Blackwell.

Ledbeater, C., & Miller, P. (2004). *The Pro-Am Revolution: How enthusiasts are cha.nging our economy and society.* London: Demos.Martison, B. M., Anderson, M. S., & De Vries, R. (2005). Scientists behaving badly. *Nature, 435*, 737–738.

Lederberg, J. (Ed.). (1999). *Biological weapons: limiting the threat.* Cambridge, MA: MIT Press.

Lee, R. (1998). Romantic and electronic stalking in a college context. *The College of William and Mary Journal of Women and the Law*, 373-409.

Lee, R. M., Fielding, N., & Blank, G. (2008). The Internet as a research medium: An editorial introduction to 'The Sage Handbook of Online Research Methods. In Fielding, N., Lee, R. M., & Blank, G. (Eds.), *The SAGE handbook of online research methods* (pp. 3–20). London: Sage.

Lee, R., & Jose, P. D. (2008). Self interest, self restraint and corporate responsibility for nanotechnologies: Emerging dilemmas for modern managers. *Technology Analysis and Strategic Management*, *20*(1), 113–125. doi:10.1080/09537320701726775

Lee, W. (1971). *Decision theory and human behavior*. New York: John Wiley & Sons.

Lenhart, A., & Madden, M. (2005, November 2). *Teen content creators and consumers*. Washington, DC: Pew Internet & American Life Project. Retrieved from http://www.pewinternet.org/Reports/2005/Teen-Content-Creators-and-Consumers.aspx

Leo, A. (2006, July 26). Teen killed over cell phone dispute. *Connecticut Post*.

Lettice, R. (2004, November 10). Saudi ministers urge removal of camera phone ban. *The Register*. Retrieved July 5, 2009, from http://www.theregister.co.uk/2004/11/10/saudi_camera_phone_ban/

Levin, A. M., Dato-on, M. C., & Rhee, K. (2004). Money for nothing and hits for free: The ethics of downloading music from peer-to- peer web sites. *Journal of Marketing Theory and Practice*, *12*, 48–60.

Levy, P. (1995). *Qué es lo virtual?* Barcelona: Paidós.

Lewenstein, B. V. (2006). What counts as a social and ethical issue in nanotechnology? In J. Schummer & D. Baird (Ed.), *Nanotechnology challenges: Implications for philosophy, ethics and society* (pp. 201-16). London: World Scientific.

Libicki, M. (2007). *Conquest in cyberspace: national security and information warfare*. New York: Cambridge University Press.

Limayem, M., Khalifa, M., & Chin, W. W. (1999, December). *Factors motivating software piracy: A longitudinal study*. Paper presented at 20th International Conference on Information Systems, Charlotte, NC.

Lin, T.-C., Hsu, M. H., Kuo, F.-Y., & Sun, P.-C. (1999, January). *An intention model-based study of software piracy*. Paper presented at 32nd Hawaii International Conference on System Sciences, Maui, HI.

Lindner, R. (1997). Global logo, local meaning. *Focaal*, *30/31*, 193–200.

Loch, K. D., & Conger, S. (1996). Evaluating ethical decision making and computer use. *Communications of the ACM*, *39*(7), 74–83. doi:10.1145/233977.233999

Louv, R. (2005). *Last Child in the Woods*. Chapel Hill, NC: Algonquin.

Luppicini, R. (2009). Technoethical Inquiry: From Technological Systems to Society. *Global Media Journal - Canadian Edition*, *2*(1), 5-21.

Luppicini, R., & Adell, R. (Eds.). (2008). *Handbook of research on technoethics*. Hershey, PA: IGI Global.

Lye, K., & Wing, J. M. (2005). Game strategies in network security. *International Journal of Information Security*, *4*(1/2), 71–86. doi:10.1007/s10207-004-0060-x

Lyon, D. (2001, November 21). *Terrorism and Surveillance, Security, Freedom and Justice After September 11 2001*. Retrieved July 16, 2004, from http://privacy.openflows.org/lyon_paper.html

Lysonski, S., & Durvasula, S. (2008). Digital piracy of MP3s: Consumer and ethical predispositions. *Journal of Consumer Marketing*, *25*, 167–178. doi:10.1108/07363760810870662

Mackie, J. L. (1990). *Ethics – Inventing Right and Wrong*. London: Penguin Books.

Madden, M. (2004). *Artists, musicians and the Internet*. Washington, DC: Pew Internet & American Life Project. Retrieved from http://www.pewinternet.org/Reports/2004/Artists-Musicians-and-the-Internet.aspx

Magnani, L. (2001a). *Abduction, reason, and science. Processes of discovery and explanation*. New York, NY: Kluwer Academic/Plenum Publishers.

Magnani, L. (2001b). *Philosophy and Geometry. Theoretical and historical issues*. Dordrecht: Kluwer Academic Publishers.

Magnani, L. (2002). Epistemic mediators and model-based discovery in science. In L. Magnani & N.J. Nersessian (Eds.), *Model-based reasoning* (pp. 305-329).

Magnani, L. (2006). Mimetic minds, meaning formation through epistemic mediators and external representations. In A. Loula, R. Gudwin, & J. Queiroz (Eds.), *Artificial Cognition Systems* (pp. 327-357). Hershey, PA: Idea Group Inc.

Magnani, L. (2007a) *Morality in a technological world: Knowledge as a duty.* Cambridge: Cambridge University Press.

Magnani, L. (2007b). Semiotic brains and artificial minds: How brains make up material cognitive systems. In R. Gudwin & J. Queiroz (Eds.), *Semiotics and Intelligent Systems Development* (pp.1-41). Hershey, PA: Idea Group Inc.

Magnani, L., & Nersessian, N. J. (Eds.). (2002). *Model-based reasoning. Scientific Discovery, Technology, Values.* New York, NY: Kluwer Academic/Plenum Publishers.

Mahar, D. J. (1976, August). Fiscal Incentives for Regional Development: A Case Study of the Western Amazon Basin. *Journal of Interamerican Studies and World Affairs, 18*(3), 357–378. doi:10.2307/174962

Maher, S. (2007). Road to Jihad: Almost impossible to regulate, the web is a gift for a new generation of young extremists. *Index on Censorship, 4*, 144–149. doi:10.1080/03064220701740590

Mandia, K., & Prosise, C. (2003). *Incident response and computer forensics.* New York: McGraw-Hill / Osborne.

Manovitch, L. (2003). New Media from Borges to HTML. In Wardrip-Fruin, N., & Montfort, N. (Eds.), *The New Media Reader.* Cambridge, MA: The MIT Press.

Maramark, S., & Maline, M. B. (1993). *Academic dishonesty among students: issues in education.* Washington, DC: Office of Educational Research and Improvement. Eric Document reproduction service no. ED360903.

Martins, M. L. (2006). A nova erótica interactiva. In *Revista de Comunicação e Linguagens (No. 37).* Braga, Portugal: ICS.

Marx, G. T. (1994). New telecommunications technologies require new manners. *Telecommunications Policy, 18*, 538–551. doi:10.1016/0308-5961(94)90064-7

Marx, K. (1993). *Grundrisse: Foundations of the Critique of political Economy.* New York: Penguin Books Ltd.

Mason, S. (2007). Authentic digital records: laying the foundation of evidence. *The Information Management Journal.* Retrieved from ProQuest Educational Journals.

Matusitz, J. (2008). Cyberterrorism: Postmodern state of chaos. *Information Security Journal: A Global Perspective, 17*(4), 179-187.

Matusitz, J. (2009). A postmodern theory of cyberterrorism: Game theory. *Information Security Journal: A Global Perspective, 18*(6), 273-281.

Matusitz, J. (2005). Cyberterrorism: How can American foreign policy be strengthened in the information age? *American Foreign Policy Interests, 27*(2), 137–147.

Matusitz, J., & Minei, E. (2009). Cyberterrorism: Its effects on health-related infrastructures. *Journal of Digital Forensic Practice, 2*(4), 161–171. doi:10.1080/15567280802678657

Maurstad, T. (2003, April 12). Callers seek less privacy, opt for cell phones instead of stalls. *Dallas Morning News.*

McCabe, D., & Pavela, G. (2000). Some good news about academic integrity. *Change, 32*(5). Retrieved from ProQuest Educational Journals.

McCarthy, P., Sheehan, M., Wilkie, S., & Wilkie, W. (1996). *Bullying: causes, costs and cures.* Brisbane, Australia: Beyond Bullying Association Inc.

McFarlane, M., Bull, S. S., & Rietmeijer, C. A. (2002). Young adults on the Internet: Risk behaviors for sexually transmitted diseases and HIV. *The Journal of Adolescent Health, 31*, 11–16. doi:10.1016/S1054-139X(02)00373-7

McGinn, R. (2008). Ethics and nanotechnology: Views of nanotechnology researchers. *NanoEthics, 2*(2), 101–131. doi:10.1007/s11569-008-0040-0

McGregor, S. E. (1976). *Insect Pollination of Cultivated Crop Plants.* Washington, D.C.: U.S. Department of Agriculture–Agricultural Research Service.

McIlwraith, R., Jacobite, R. S., Kubey, R., & Alexander, A. (1991). Television addiction: Theories and data behind the ubiquitous metaphor. *The American Behavioral Scientist, 35*, 104–121. doi:10.1177/0002764291035002003

McLeod, C. (2003, August). Sneaky Cameras. *Press Council News, 15*(3). Retrieved June 19, 2009, from http://www.presscouncil.org.au/pesite/apcnews/aug03/cameras.html

McNiff, E., & Varney, A. (2008, May 14). College Gossip Crackdown: Chelsea Gorman Speaks Out: Juicy Campus' Cruel Online Postings Prompt Government Investigation. *ABC News.* Retrieved May 20, 2010, from http://abcnews.go.com/2020/Story?id=4849927&page=1

McQuade, S. (2007). We Must Educate Young People About Cybercrime Before They Start College. *Chronicle of Higher Education, 53*(14), B29. Retrieved January 13, 2010, from http://chronicle.com/article/We-Must-Educate-Young-People/23514/

McYntire, S. (2005). *Environmental Science and Technology.* Retrieved September 9, 2009 from http://www.climateaudit.org/?p=333

Mel, H., & Baker, D. (2000). *Cryptography decrypted* (5th ed.). Boston, MA: Addison-Wesley Professional.

Mill, J. S. (1998). *Utilitarianism.* Oxford and New York: Oxford University Press.

Milne, G. R., & Culnan, M. J. (2004). Strategies for reducing online privacy risks: Why consumers read (or don't read) online privacy notices. *Journal of Interactive Marketing, 18*(3), 15–29. doi:10.1002/dir.20009

Miranda, J. B. (2002). *Teoria da Cultura.* Lisbon, Portugal: Século XXI.

Mishra, S. (2003). Exploitation of information and communication technology by terrorist organisations. *Strategic Analysis, 27*(3), 439–462. doi:10.1080/09700160308450099

Mithen, S. (1996). *The Prehistory of the Mind. A Search for the Origins of Art, Religion, and Science.* London: Thames and Hudson.

Mitliaga, V. (2001). Cyber-terrorism: A call for governmental action? *16ᵗʰ BILETA Annual Conference.* Retrieved October 9, 2009, from http://www.bileta.ac.uk/01papers/mitliaga.html.

Mnyusiwalla, A., Daar, A. S., & Singer, P. A. (2003). Mind the gap: Science and ethics in nanotechnology. *Nanotechnology, 14*, R9–R13. doi:10.1088/0957-4484/14/3/201

Moffat, A. S. (1999, July 16). Crop Engineering Goes South. *Science, 287*, 370–371. doi:10.1126/science.285.5426.370

Mohay, G., Panichprecha, S., & Tickle, A. (2009). Subproject 1: Probabilistic packet processing to mitigate high-rate flooding attacks. *Review of Techniques for Mitigating Network Flooding Attacks.* Retrieved March 1, 2010, from http://iaw2009.iitm.ernet.in/files/sp1.pdf.

Molander, R., & Siang, S. (1998, Fall). The legitimization of strategic information warfare: ethical considerations. *AAAS Professional Ethics Report, 11*(4). Retrieved November 23, 2005 from www.aaas.org/spp/sfrl/sfrl.htm.

Monahan, T. (2006). Counter-Surveillance as Political Intervention. *Social Semiotics, 16*(4), 515–624. doi:10.1080/10350330601019769

Monk, A., Carroll, J., Parker, S., & Blythe, M. (2004). Why are mobile phones annoying? *Behaviour & Information Technology, 23*, 33–41. doi:10.1080/01449290310001638496

Moor, J. H., & Bynum, T. W. (Eds.). (2002). *Cyberphilosophy.* Maldem, MA: Blackwell.

Moor, J. H. (1985). What is computer ethics? *Metaphilosophy, 16*(4), 266–275. doi:10.1111/j.1467-9973.1985.tb00173.x

Moor, J. H. (1997). Towards a theory of privacy in the information age. *Computers & Society, 27*, 27–32. doi:10.1145/270858.270866

Moor, J. H. (2008). Why we need better ethics for emerging technologies. In Hoven, J. V. D., & Weckert, J. (Eds.), *Information Technology and Moral Philosophy* (pp. 26–39). Cambridge, UK: Cambridge University Press. doi:10.1017/CBO9780511498725.003

Morais, T. (2007). *Cyberbullying em crescendo*. Retrieved May 31, 2008, from http://www.miudossegurosna.net/artigos/2007-04-04.html

Morrow, J. D. (1994). *Game theory for political scientists*. New Jersey: Princeton University Press.

Moss, J. (2005, January 7-9). Fixing the digital divide; sustaining or undermining local values? *The 2nd Asia-Pacific Computing and Philosophy Conference,* Chulalongkorn University, Bangkok, Thailand.

Mouffe, C. (1992). Feminism, citizenship and radical democratic politics. En J. Butler & J. Scott (Eds.), *Feminist theorize the political* (pp. 369-384). New York: Routledge.

Muir, B. M. (1994). Trust in automation: Part I. Theoretical issues in the study of trust and human intervention in automated systems. *Ergonomics*, *37*, 1905–1922. doi:10.1080/00140139408964957

Mulligan, M., Card, D., Laszio, J., & Peach, A. (2003). *European broadband strategies: Reducing subscriber churn and adding consumer value with digital music services*. New York: Jupiter Research.

Murphy, M. (2009, January 24). Hacker wins right to legal review. *Financial Times (North American Edition)*, 4.

Murphy, R. R. (2000). *Introduction to AI robotics*. Cambridge, MA: MIT Press.

Myerscough, S., Lowe, B., & Alpert, F. (2006). Willingness to provide personal information online: The role of perceived privacy risk, privacy statements and brand strength. *Journal of Website Promotion*, *2*, 115–139. doi:10.1080/15533610802104182

Nacos, B. L. (2006). *Terrorism and counterterrorism: Understanding threats and responses in the post-9/11 world*. New York: Longman.

Nadarajah, S., & Sriskandarajah, D. (2005). Liberation struggle or terrorism? The politics of naming the LTTE. *Third World Quarterly*, *26*(1), 87–100. doi:10.1080/0143659042000322928

Nakra, P. (2003). Info-terrorism in the age of the Internet: Challenges and initiatives. *Journal of Competitive Intelligence and Management*, *1*(2), 1–10.

Nansel, T., Overpeck, M., Pila, R., Ruan, W., Simmon-Morton, B., & Scheidt, P. (2001). Bullying behaviors among U.S. youth: Prevalence and association with psychosocial adjustment. *Journal of the American Medical Association*, *285*(16), 2094–2100. doi:10.1001/jama.285.16.2094

Nardin, T. (Ed.). (1998). *The ethics of war and peace*. Princeton, NJ: Princeton University Press.

NASA. (2008). *Visible Earth, A Catalog of NASA Images and Animations of Our Home Planet*. Washington D.C.: NASA. Retrieved on January 18, 2009 from http://visibleearth.nasa.gov/view_rec.php?id=16728.

National Center for Victims of Crime. (2010). *Cyberstalking*. Retrieved May 20, 2010, from http://www.ncvc.org/ncvc/main.aspx?dbName=DocumentViewer&DocumentID=32458

National Conference of State Legislators. (2010). *State Electronic Harassment or "Cyberstalking" Laws*. Retrieved April 20, 2010, from http://www.ncsl.org/default.aspx?tabid=13495

National Crime Prevention Council. Cyberbullying FAQ for Teens. Retrieved May 18, 2010, from http://www.ncpc.org/topics/cyberbullying/cyberbullying-faq-for-teens.

National Health and Medical Research Council. (2007). *National statement on ethical conduct in human research*. Retrieved from http://www.nhmrc.gov.au/publications/synopses/e72syn.htm

Neumann, P. (1995). *Computer related risks*. Reading, MA: ACM Press.

Neves, J. P. (2008). *Algumas considerações provisórias acerca das redes sociais na Internet e o conceito de dependência*. Retrieved November 2, 2008, from http://www.socialsoftware.blogspot.com

Neves, J. P. (2006). *O apelo do objecto técnico*. Oporto, Portugal: Campo das Letras.

Newton, L. H., & Dillingham, C. K. (1993). Watershed. Belmont, CA: Wadsworth.

Nicholson, M. (1970). *Conflict analysis*. London: The English Universities Press.

Nicholson, M. (1996). *Causes and consequences in international relations: A conceptual study*. London: Pinter.

Noammy, P. C. (2004, March 2). Cameraphones and Worries Over Possible Misuse. *The Jakarta Post*. Retrieved July 3, 2009, from http://www.thejakartapost.com/print/108533

Norman, D. A. (1999). *The Invisible Computer*. Cambridge, MA: The MIT Press.

Nosek, B. A., Banaji, M. R., & Greenwald, A. G. (2002). E-research: Ethics, security, design and control in psychological research on the Internet. *The Journal of Social Issues*, *58*, 161–176. doi:10.1111/1540-4560.00254

Nozick, R. (2003). *Anarchy, State, and Utopia*. Oxford, UK: Blackwell Publishing Ltd.

Nussbaum, M. (2008). *Women and human development: Capabilities approach*. Cambridge, UK: Cambridge University Press.

Nussbaum, M., & Sen, A. (Eds.). (1993). *The quality of life*. Oxford, UK: Oxford University Press. doi:10.1093/0198287976.001.0001

Nye, J. S. (2005). *Understanding international conflicts: An introduction to theory and history*. New York: Pearson.

O'Connor, H., Madge, C., Shaw, R., & Wellens, J. (2008). Internet-based interviewing. In Fielding, N., Lee, R. M., & Blank, G. (Eds.), *The SAGE handbook of online research methods* (pp. 271–289). London: Sage.

O'Neil, D. (2001). Analysis of Internet users' level of online privacy concern. *Social Science Computer Review*, *19*, 17–31. doi:10.1177/089443930101900103

Office for National Statistics. (2009, August 28). *Internet access: Households and individuals*. Retrieved from http://www.statistics.gov.uk/pdfdir/iahi0809.pdf

Office of Technology Assessment. (1996). *OTA Archive* (On-line). Retrieved from http//www.access.gpo.gov/ota/

Okabe, D. (2004). *Emergent Social Practices, Situations and Relations through Everyday Camera Phone Use*. Paper Presented at the International Conference on Mobile Communication, Seoul, Korea.

Olewus, D. (2001). Peer harassment: A critical analysis and some important issues (introduction). In Juvonen, J., & Graham, S. (Eds.), *Peer harassment in school: The plight of the vulnerable and victimized* (pp. 3–20). New York: Guildford Press.

Olsen, F. (2001). Michigan deactivates Internet program linked in several stalking incidents. *The Chronicle of Higher Education*, *47*(7), 34.

Olsen, J. B., Pedersen, S. A., & Hendricks, V. F. (2009). *A Companion to the Philosophy of Technology*. New York: Wiley Blackwell. doi:10.1002/9781444310795

Olweus, D. (1991). Bully/victim problems among schoolchildren: basic facts and effects of school based intervention program. In Pether, D., & Rubin, K. (Eds.), *The development and treatment of childhood aggression*. Hillsdale, NJ: Erlbaum.

Ong, A. D., & Weiss, D. J. (2000). The impact of anonymity on responses to sensitive questions. *Journal of Applied Social Psychology*, *30*, 1691–1708. doi:10.1111/j.1559-1816.2000.tb02462.x

Opinion of the Supreme Court of the United States for Metro-Goldwyn-Mayer Studios Inc. *et al.* (2005, June 27). Retrieved from http://www.eff.org/IP/P2P/MGM_v_Grokster/04-480.pdf

Opinion of the United States Court of Appeals for the Ninth Circuit for Metro-Goldwyn-Mayer Studios Inc. *et al.* (2004, August 19). Retrieved from http://www.eff.org/IP/P2P/MGM_v_Grokster/20040819_mgm_v_grokster_decision.pdf

Orbell, S., Blair, C., Sherlock, K., & Conner, M. (2001). The theory of planned behavior and ecstasy use: Roles for habit and perceived control over taking versus obtaining substances. *Journal of Applied Social Psychology*, *31*, 31–47. doi:10.1111/j.1559-1816.2001.tb02480.x

Orrego Silva, J. P. (1997). In Defence of the Biobío River. In A. D. Usher (Ed.), *Dams as Aid: A Political Economy of Nordic Development Thinking* (pp. 153-170). London: Routledge.

Orr, J. (1934). *English Deism: Its Roots and Its Fruits*. Grand Rapids, MI: Eerdmans Press.

Paine, C., Reips, U.-D., Stieger, S., Joinson, A., & Buchanan, T. (2007). Internet users' perceptions of 'privacy concerns' and 'privacy actions'. *International Journal of Human-Computer Studies*, *65*, 526–536. doi:10.1016/j.ijhcs.2006.12.001

Palácios, M., & Rego, S. (2006). Bullying: mais uma epidemia invisível? Retrieved April 5, 2007, from http://www.scielo.br/pdf/rbem/v30n1/v30n1a01.pdf

Pallister, M. (March 2,1999). Banana Workers Toil in a Pear-Shaped World. *The Herald* (Glasgow), p. 13.

Parens, E. (2006). Creativity, gratitude, and the enhancement debate. In Illes, J. (Ed.), *Neuroethics: defining the issues in theory, practice and policy* (pp. 75–86). Oxford, UK: Oxford University Press.

Parker, A. (2004). *The true picture of peer-to-peer filesharing*. Retrieved from http://web.archive.org/web/20041022013828/www.cachelogic.com/research/index.php

Parker, A. (2005). *P2P in 2005*. Retrieved from http://web.archive.org/web/20060808053516/http://www.cachelogic.com/research/p2p2005.php

Parker, D., Manstead, A. S. R., Stradling, S. G., Reason, J. T., & Baxter, J. S. (1992). Intention to commit driving violations: An application of the theory of planned behavior. *The Journal of Applied Psychology*, *77*, 94–101. doi:10.1037/0021-9010.77.1.94

Parker, D., Stradling, S. G., & Manstead, A. S. R. (1996). Modifying beliefs and attitudes to exceeding the speed limit: An intervention study based on the theory of planned behavior. *Journal of Applied Social Psychology*, *26*, 1–19. doi:10.1111/j.1559-1816.1996.tb01835.x

Pascal, B. (1963). Pensées. In B. Pascal (Ed.), *Œuvres Complètes*. Paris: Éditions du Seuil. Retrieved October 23, 2009, from http://www.ccel.org/ccel/pascal/pensees.txt

Patchin, J. W., & Hinduja, S. (2006). Bullies move beyond the schoolyard, - A preliminary look at cyberbullying. *Youth Violence and Juvenile Justice*, *4*(2), 148–169. doi:10.1177/1541204006286288

Paullet, K. L., Rota, D. R., & Swan, T. T. (2009). Cyberstalking: An exploratory study of students at a mid-Atlantic university. *Issues in Information Systems*, *10*(2), 640–648.

Peace, G., Galletta, D. F., & Thong, J. Y. L. (2003). Software piracy in the workplace: A model and empirical test. *Journal of Management Information Systems*, *20*, 153–177. Retrieved from http://www.jmis-web.org/.

Pearson Government Solutions. (2006). *Enabling a paperless student loan process using electronic signatures*. Retrieved from ProQuest Educational Journals.

Peden, B. F., & Flashinski, D. P. (2004). Virtual research ethics: A content analysis of surveys and experiments online. In Buchanan, E. (Ed.), *Readings in virtual research ethics: Issues and controversies* (pp. 1–26). Hershy, PA: IGI Global.

Peirce, C. S. (1931-1958) (CP). *Collected Papers*. In C. Hartshorne & P. Weiss (Eds.) (Vols. I-VI) & A.W. Burks (Ed.). (Vols. VII-VIII). Cambridge, MA: Harvard University Press.

Pepitone, J. (2006, February 8). Kicked in the face: Freshmen claim Judicial Affairs threatened expulsion for creation of Facebook group critical of TA. *The Daily Orange*. Retrieved January 13, 2010, from http://www.dailyorange.com/media/paper522/news/2006/02/08/News/Kicked.In.The.Face.Freshmen.Claim.Judicial.Affairs.Threatened.Expulsion.For.Crea-1603618.shtml?norewrite

Perkins, D. (2003). *King Arthur's round table. How collaborative conversations create smart organizations*. Chichester: Wiley.

Perrow, C. (1984). *Normal Accidents*. New York: Basic Books.

Persson, R., Garde, A. H., Hansen, A. M., Orbaek, P., & Ohlsson, K. (2003). The influence of production systems on self-reported arousal, sleepiness, physical exertion and fatigueconsequences of increasing mechanization. *Stress and Health*, *19*, 163–171. doi:10.1002/smi.967

Petersen, A., Anderson, A., Allan, S., & Wilkinson, C. (2008). Opening the black box: Scientists' views on the role of the news media in the nanotechnology debate. *Public Understanding of Science*. Published 1st October via Online First.

Petersen, A., & Anderson, A. (2007). A question of balance or blind faith?: Scientists' and science policymakers' representations of the benefits and risks of nanotechnologies. *NanoEthics*, *1*(3), 243–256. doi:10.1007/s11569-007-0021-8

Petersen, A., Anderson, A., Wilkinson, C., & Allan, S. (2007). Nanotechnologies, risk and society. *Health Risk & Society*, *9*(2), 117–124. doi:10.1080/13698570701306765

Petraitis, J., Flay, B. R., & Miller, T. Q. (1995). Reviewing theories of adolescent substance use: Organizing pieces of the puzzle. *Psychological Bulletin*, *117*, 67–86. doi:10.1037/0033-2909.117.1.67

Picard, R. W. (1997). *Affective computing.* Cambridge, MA: MIT Press.

Pickering, A. (1995). *The mangle of practice. Tome, agency, and science.* Chicago and London, The University of Chicago Press.

Pinheiro, L. (2007). *Bullying: o perfil da vítima.* Retrieved October 12, 2008, from http://sites.google.com/site/bullyingemportugal/

Pinheiro, L. (2009). *Cyberbullying em Portugal: uma perspectiva sociológica.* Braga, Portugal: Universidade do Minho. Retrieved December 12, 2009, from http://repositorium.sdum.uminho.pt/bitstream/1822/9870/1/tese.pdf

Plato,. (1953). *The Dialogues of Plato (B. Jowett trans.).* London: Oxford University Press.

Platt, J. (1973). Social traps. *The American Psychologist*, *28*, 641–651. doi:10.1037/h0035723

Preston, J., & Bishop, M. (Eds.). (2002). *Views into the Chinese Room.* Oxford, UK: Clarendon Press.

Project NEThics. (2009). Retrieved January 24, 2010, from http://www.nethics.umd.edu/

Putnam, R. D. (1993). *Making democracy work: civic traditions in modern Italy.* Princeton, NJ: Princeton University Press.

Quantum Market Research. (2003, July). *Understanding CD burning and Internet file sharing and its impact on the Australian music industry: Key quantitative findings prepared for ARIA* (Project No. 23006). Retrieved from http://www.aria.com.au/pages/documents/AriaIllegalMusicResearchReport_Summary.pdf

Rabot, J.-M. (2009). Os videojogos: entre a absorção labiríntica e a sociedade. In *SOPCOM/LUSOCOM* (pp. 432-445). Retrieved May 13, 2009, from http://conferencias.ulusofona.pt/index.php/sopcom_iberico/sopcom_iberico09/paper/viewFile/463/462

Ramesh, S. (2009, March 23) Public Order Act Introduced to Examine New Realities in Managing Security. *Channel NewsAsia.* Retrieved December 12, 2009, from http://www.channelnewsasia.com/stories/singaporelocalnews/view/417146/1/.html

Rampton, S., & Stauber, J. (2001). *Trust Us, We're Experts! How Industry Manipulates Science and Gambles with Your Future.* New York: Tarcher/Putnam.

Ranum, M. (2004). *The myth of homeland security.* Indianapolis, IN: Wiley.

Rapoport, E. H. (1990, November-December). Vida en Extinción. *Ciencia Hoy*, *2*(10), 33.

Rawls, J. (2005). *A theory of justice.* Cambridge, MA: Harvard University Press.

Read, B. (2006, January 20). Think Before You Share Students' online socializing can have unintended consequences. *The Chronicle of Higher Education*, *52*(20), A38. Retrieved January 14, 2010 from http://www.usi.edu/stl/vpsa/forms/ThinkBeforeYouShare.pdf.

Reips, U.-D. (2008). How Internet-mediated research changes science. In A. Barak (Ed.), *Psychological aspects of cyberspace: Theory, research, applications* (pp. 268-294). Cambridge, UK: Cambridge University Press. Retrieved from http://gsb.haifa.ac.il/~sheizaf/cyberpsych/12-Reips.pdf

Reips, U.-D. (2007). The methodology of Internet-based experiments. In Joinson, A., McKenna, K., Postmes, T., & Reips, U.-D. (Eds.), *The Oxford handbook of Internet psychology* (pp. 373–390). New York: Oxford University Press.

Rennie, J. (2008, September). Here in the fishbowl. *Scientific American.*

Rentfrow, P. J., Gosling, S. D., & Potter, J. (2008). A theory of the emergence, persistence, and expression of geographic variation in psychological characteristics. *Perspectives on Psychological Science*, *3*, 339–369. doi:10.1111/j.1745-6924.2008.00084.x

Reser, J. P. (1980). Automobile addiction: real or imagined? *Man-Environment Systems, 10,* 279–287.

Resnik, D. B. (2007). *What is Ethics in Research & Why is It Important?* Retrieved December 29, 2009, from http://www.niehs.nih.gov/research/resources/bioethics/whatis.cfm

Retrieved April 17, 2009, from: http://pus.sagepub.com/cgi/rapidpdf/0963662507084202v1, Preston, C. (2006). The promise and threat of nanotechnology: Can environmental ethics guide us? In J. Schummer & D. Baird (Ed.), *Nanotechnology challenges: Implications for philosophy, ethics and society* (pp. 217-48). London: World Scientific.

Rico, M. N. (2000). *Desarrollo sustentable, Manejo de recursos de agua y género.* Paper presented at the 2000 Conference of the Latin American Studies Association, Miami, FL. Cited in Roberts (2003), p. 99.

Ricoeur, P. (1990). *Soi-même comme un autre.* Paris: Seuil.

Robb, J. (2007). *The U.S. and cyberwarfare.* Retrieved February 6, 2009 from globalguerrillas.typepad.com/globalguerrillas/2007/12/the-us-and-cyber.html.

Roberts, J. T., & Thanos, N. D. (2003). *Trouble in Paradise: Globalization and Environmental Crises in Latin America.* New York and London: Routledge.

Roberts, L. D., & Indermaur, D. (2003). Signed consent forms in criminological research: Protection for researchers and ethics committees but a threat to research participants? *Psychiatry, Psychology and Law, 10,* 289–299. doi:10.1375/pplt.2003.10.2.289

Robinson, K. M. (2001). Unsolicited narratives from the Internet: A rich source of qualitative data. *Qualitative Health Research, 11,* 706–714. doi:10.1177/104973201129119398

Robins, R. W., Tracy, J. L., Trzesniewski, K., Gosling, S. D., & Potter, J. (2002). Global self-esteem across the life span. *Psychology and Aging, 17,* 423–434. doi:10.1037/0882-7974.17.3.423

Robins, R. W., Tracy, J. L., Trzesniewski, K., Potter, J., & Gosling, S. D. (2001). Personality correlates of self-esteem. *Journal of Research in Personality, 35,* 463–482. doi:10.1006/jrpe.2001.2324

Roco, M., & Bainbridge, W. (Eds.). (2002). *Converging technologies for improving human performance: Nanotechnology, Biotechnology, Information Technology and Cognitive Science.* Arlington, VA: National Science Foundation/Department of Commerce.

Rogelberg, S. C., Spitzmueller, C., Little, I., & Reeve, C. L. (2006). Understanding response behavior to an online special topics organizational satisfaction survey. *Personnel Psychology, 59,* 903–923. doi:10.1111/j.1744-6570.2006.00058.x

Rogerson, S. (2000). Computer based harassment on college campuses. *Student Affairs nline: The Online Magazine about Technology and Student Affairs, 1*(1). Retrieved December 12, 2007, from www.studentaffairs.com/ejournal/Spring_2000/article5.html

Rohle, T. (2005). Power, reason, closure: critical perspectives on new media theory. *New Media & Society, 7*(3), 403–422. doi:10.1177/1461444805052283

Rome, E., Hertzberg, J., & Dorffner, G. (Eds.). (2008). *Towards affordance-based robot control.* Heidelberg, Germany: Springer Verlag. doi:10.1007/978-3-540-77915-5

Rother, L. (December 5, 1999). German Arciniegas, 98, Critic Of Latin American Dictators. T*he New York Times.* Retrieved January 18, 2009 from http://query.nytimes.com/gst/fullpage.html?res=9A02EED8153EF936A35751C1A96F958260&st=cse&sq=German+Arciniegas%2C+98%2C+Critic+of+of+Latin+American+Dictators&scp=1.

Roth, K. (2001). Material culture and intercultural communication. *International Journal of Intercultural Relations, 25,* 563–580. doi:10.1016/S0147-1767(01)00023-2

Roubik, D. W. (1995). *Pollination of Cultivated Plants in the Tropics.* Rome: Food Agric. Org. U.N.

Royal Society and Royal Academy of Engineering RS/RAE. (2004). *Nanoscience and nanotechnologies: Opportunities and uncertainties report.* London: Royal Society.

Rullani, E. (2005). Capitalismo cognitivo: ¿Un déjà-vu? En O. Blondeau et al. (Eds.), *Capitalismo cognitivo, propiedad intelectual y creación colectiva.* Madrid: Traficantes de sueños.

Rushmann, A. (2009). Photographers Tangle with Vague Rules in Transit Hubs. *The New Media & the Law, 33*(2), 34. Retrieved July 16, 2009, from http://www.rcfp.org/news/mag/33-2/photographers_tangle_with_vague_rules_in_transithubs

Ryan, R. (2003). When journalism becomes "terrorism": Perle goes on offensive against investigative reporting. *Extra!* May/June. Retrieved March 1, 2010, from http://www.fair.org/index.php?page=1143.

Sage, A. (2009, March 3). Happy Slapping Film Ban Will Gag Citizen Journalists. *The Times.* Retrieved July 5, 2009, from http://www.mail-archive.com/sustainablelorgbiofuel@sustainablelists.org/msg69077.html

Sandel, M. (2004). The case against perfection. *The Atlantic Monthly, 293*(3). Retrieved January 19, 2007, from http://www.theatlantic.com/past/docs/issues/2004/04/sandel.htm

Saner, E. (2009, February 25). I Felt Completely Violated. *The Guardian.* Retrieved June 16, 2009, from http://www.guardian.co.uk/lifestyle/2009/feb/25/women-upskirting/print

Sarason, S. (1984). If it can be studied or developed, should it be? *The American Psychologist, 39*, 477–485. doi:10.1037/0003-066X.39.5.477

Sarkar, S. (1998). *Genetics and Reductionism.* Cambridge, UK: Cambridge University Press.

Sauders, R. (2005). Happy slapping: transatlantic contagion or home-grown, mass-mediated nihilism? *The London Consortium Static, 1.* Retrieved April 30, 2010, from http://static.londonconsortium.com/issue01/saunders_happyslapping.pdf

Saxe, L., & Dougherty, D. (1985). Technology assessment and Congressional use of social psychology: Making complexity understandable. *Applied Social Psychology Annual, 6*, 255–280.

Sayer, P. (2006, June 3). France Bans Citizen Journalists from Reporting Violence. *Infoworld.com.* Retrieved June 15, 2009, from http://www.infoworld.com/print/27840

Schellenberg, J. A. (1996). *Conflict resolution: Theory, research, and practice.* Albany, NY: State University of New York Press.

Scheufele, D. A., Corley, E. A., Dunwoody, S., Shih, T., Hillback, E., & Guston, D. (2007). Scientists worry about some risks more than the public. *Nature Nanotechnology, 2*(12), 732–734. doi:10.1038/nnano.2007.392

Schmid, A. P. (1989). Terrorism and the media: The ethics of publicity. *Terrorism and Political Violence, 1*(4), 539–565. doi:10.1080/09546558908427042

Schmitt, M. (2002). Wired warfare: computer network attack and *jus in bello. International Review of the Red Cross, 84*(846), 365–399.

Schulze, H., & Mochalski, K. (2009). *Internet study 2008/2009.* Retrieved from http://www.ipoque.com/resources/internet-studies

Schummer, J., & Baird, D. (Eds.). (2006). *Nanotechnology challenges: Implications for philosophy, ethics and society.* London: World Scientific.

Schummer, J. (2004). Social and ethical implications of nanotechnology: Meanings, interest groups and social dynamics. *Hyle, 8*(2), 56–87.

Schweitzer, S. (2005, October 6) Fisher College expels student over website entries. *Boston Globe.* Retrieved January 13, 2010, from http://www.boston.com/news/local/articles/2005/10/06/fisher_college_expels_student_over_website_entries/

Scott, R. (2000, May 1). Inside the world of "MafiaBoy". *Maclean's, 113*(18), 37.

Seale, D. A., Polakowski, M., & Schneider, S. (1998). It's not really theft! Personal and workplace ethics that enable software piracy. *Behaviour & Information Technology, 17*, 27–40. doi:10.1080/014492998119652

Secchi, D. (2006). *A theory of docile society.* Submitted to Mind and Society.

Serres, M. (1994). *Atlas.* Madrid: Cátedra.

Shaffer, L. S. (1981). The growth and limits of recipe knowledge. *Journal of Mind and Behavior, 2*, 71–83.

Shapira, N., Goldsmith, T., Keck, P., Szabo, S., Lazoritz, M., Gold, M., & Stein, D. (2003). Problematic Internet use: proposed classification and diagnostic criteria. *Depression & Anxiety, 17*, 207-216. Retrieved December 27, 2008, from http://www3.interscience.wiley.com/journal/104539090/abstract

Shariff, S. (2008). *Cyber-bullying: Issues and solutions for the school, the classroom and the home*. New York: Routledge.

Sheeran, P., & Orbell, S. (2000). Using implementation intentions to increase attendance for cervical cancer screening. *Health Psychology*, *19*, 283–289. doi:10.1037/0278-6133.19.3.283

Shen, L. J., & Dillard, J. P. (2005). Psychometric properties of the Hong Psychological Reactance Scale. *Journal of Personality Assessment*, *85*, 74–81. doi:10.1207/s15327752jpa8501_07

Shen, L., & Dillard, J. P. (2007). Reactance proneness assessment. In Reynolds, R. A., Woods, R., & Baker, J. D. (Eds.), *Electronic surveys and measurements* (pp. 323–329). Hershey, PA: IGI Global.

Sherwin, A. (2006, October 17). Amateur Blogger 'Video Bloggers' Under Threat From EU Broadcast Rules. *The Times*. Retrieved July 15, 2009, from http://www.timesonline.co.uk/tol/news/world/europe/article603123.ece?print=yes&ra

Sherwood, J. (2009, January 28). US Considers Audible Warnings for Cameraphones 'Attention! Possible Voyeur Taking Pictures!' *The Register*. Retrieved July 6, 2009, from http://www.rehardware.co.uk/2009/01/28/cameraphone_alert_bill/print.html

Shim, S., Eastlick, M. A., Lotz, S. L., & Warrington, P. (2001). An online prepurchase intentions model: The role of intention to search. *Journal of Retailing*, *77*, 397–416. doi:10.1016/S0022-4359(01)00051-3

Shipman, M. (2008). *NC State finds new nanomaterial could be breakthrough for implantable medical devices. North Carolina State University*. Retrieved November 19, 2008, from http://news.ncsu.edu/releases/nc-state-finds-new-nanomaterial-could-be-breakthrough-for-implantable-medical-devices/

Shubik, M. (1954). Introduction to the nature of game theory. In Shubik, M. (Ed.), *Readings in Game theory and political behavior* (pp. 1–11). New York: Doubleday & Company.

Simon, H. (1993). Altruism and Economics. *The American Economic Review*, *83*(2), 156–161.

Simonite, T. (2007). Neural 'extension cord' developed for brain implants. *New Scientist*. Retrieved January 19, 2007, from http://www.newscientist.com/article/dn10997

Singer, E. (2004). Confidentiality, risk perception and survey participation. *Chance*, *17*(3), 31–35.

Singer, E., Von Thurn, D. R., & Miller, E. R. (1995). Confidentiality assurances and response: A quantitative review of the experimental literature. *Public Opinion Quarterly*, *59*, 66–77. doi:10.1086/269458

Sismondo, S. (1993). Some social constructions. *Social Studies of Science*, *23*, 515–553. doi:10.1177/0306312793023003004

Siwek, S. E. (2007). *The true cost of copyright industry piracy to the U.S. economy* (IPI Policy Report No. 189). Retrieved from http://www.ipi.org/IPI/IPIPublications.nsf/PublicationLookupFullText/23F5FF3E9D8AA79786257369005B0C79

Skinner, B. F. (1986). What is wrong with daily life in the Western world? *The American Psychologist*, *41*, 568–574. doi:10.1037/0003-066X.41.5.568

Skitka, L. J., Mosier, K., & Burdick, M. (2000). Accountability and automation bias. *International Journal of Human-Computer Studies*, *52*, 701–717. doi:10.1006/ijhc.1999.0349

Skitka, L. J., & Sargis, E. G. (2006). The Internet as psychological laboratory. *Annual Review of Psychology*, *57*, 529–555. doi:10.1146/annurev.psych.57.102904.190048

Smart, J. J. C., & Williams, B. (1973). *Utilitarianism: For and Against*. Cambridge, England: Cambridge University Press.

Smith, M., & Morra, J. (Eds.). (2006). *The prosthetic impulse: from a posthuman present to a bicultural future*. Cambridge, MA: The MIT Press.

Sollie, P. (2007). Ethics, technology development and uncertainty: an outline for any future ethics of technology. *Journal of Information. Communication & Ethics in Society*, *5*(4), 293–306. doi:10.1108/14779960710846155

Sollie, P., & Düwell, M. (Eds.). (2009). *Evaluating New Technologies: Methodological Problems for the Ethical Assessment of Technology Developments*. New York: Springer.

Solomon, J., & Patrick, A. O. (2006, June 8). Terror probe widens with two arrests in Britain. *Wall Street Journal*, p. A2.

Soto, C. J., John, O. P., Gosling, S. D., & Potter, J. (2008). The developmental psychometrics of big five self-reports: Acquiescence, factor structure, coherence, and differentiation from ages 10 to 20. *Journal of Personality and Social Psychology*, *94*, 718–737. doi:10.1037/0022-3514.94.4.718

Sparrow, R. (2004). The Turing Triage Test. *Ethics and Information Technology*, *6*, 203–213. doi:10.1007/s10676-004-6491-2

Sparrow, R. (2009). The social impacts of nanotechnology: An ethical and political analysis. *Journal of Bioethical Inquiry*, *6*(1), 13–23. doi:10.1007/s11673-009-9139-4

Spillius, A. (2009, May 14). Barack Obama Attempts to Block Alleged Torture Photos. *The Daily Telegraph*. Retrieved July 13, 2009, from http://www.telegraph.co.uk/news/worldnews/northamerica/usa/barackobama/5320559/Barack-Obama-attempts-to-block-alleged-torture-photos.html

Spitzberg, B. H., & Hoobler, G. (2002). Cyberstalking and the technologies of interpersonal terrorism. *New Media & Society*, *4*, 71–92. doi:10.1177/14614440222226271

Srivastava, S., John, O. P., Gosling, S. D., & Potter, J. (2003). Development of personality in early and middle adulthood: Set like plaster or persistent change? *Journal of Personality and Social Psychology*, *84*, 1041–1053. doi:10.1037/0022-3514.84.5.1041

Stahl, B. C. (2004). Information, Ethics and Computers: The Problem of Autonomous Agents. *Minds and Machines*, *14*, 67–83. doi:10.1023/B:MIND.0000005136.61217.93

Stalder, F. (2002, September). Privacy is not the Antidote to Surveillance. *Surveillance & Society*, *1*(1), 120–124. Retrieved April 16, 2007 from http://felix.openflows.com/html/priv_surv.html.

Stallman, R. (2005). *Bill Gates and other communists*. Retrieved September 6, 2009 from http://news.cnet.com/Bill-Gates-and-other-communists/2010-1071_3-5576230.html

Stelmaszewska, H., Fields, B., & Blandford, A. (2006). Camera Phone Use in Social Context. In *Proceedings of HCI 2006* (Vol. 2).

Stephan, S., Wütscher, F., Decker, M., & Ladikas, M. (2004). *Bridges Between Science, Society and Policy: Technology Assessment - Methods and Impacts*. New York: Springer.

Stern, S. E. (1999). Effects of technology on attributions of performance and employee evaluation. *Journal of Applied Social Psychology*, *29*, 786–794. doi:10.1111/j.1559-1816.1999.tb02024.x

Stern, S. E., Alderfer, R. R., & Cienkowski, H. A. (1998). From brain to pencil to calculator: An exploratory test of the effect of technological evolution on attitudes. *Journal of Social Behavior and Personality*, *13*, 503–516.

Stern, S. E., & Handel, A. D. (2001). Sexuality and mass media: The historical context of psychology's reaction to sexuality on the Internet. *Journal of Sex Research*, *38*, 283–291. doi:10.1080/00224490109552099

Stern, S. E., & Kipnis, D. (1993). Technology in everyday life and perceptions of competence. *Journal of Applied Social Psychology*, *23*, 1892–1902. doi:10.1111/j.1559-1816.1993.tb01071.x

Stern, S. E., Mullennix, J. W., & Wilson, S. J. (2002). Effects of perceived disability on persuasiveness of computer-synthesized speech. *The Journal of Applied Psychology*, *87*, 411–417. doi:10.1037/0021-9010.87.2.411

Stock, G. (2002). *Redesigning Humans: Choosing Our Genes, Changing Our Future*. Orlando, FL: Houghton Mifflin Company.

Strauss, A. C., & Corbin, J. (1997). *Grounded Theory in Practice*. Thousand Oaks, CA: Sage Publications, Inc.

Strickland, L. H. (1958). Surveillance and trust. *Journal of Personality*, *26*, 201–215. doi:10.1111/j.1467-6494.1958.tb01580.x

Sue, V. M., & Ritter, L. A. (2007). *Conducting online surveys*. Thousand Oaks, CA: Sage.

Sullivan, M. (2004, July 23). Law May Curb Cell Phone Camera Use. *PC World*. Retrieved June 19, 2009, from http://www.pcworld.com/printable/article/id,117035/printable.html

Sutcliffe, A. (2002). *IVF Children: The First Generation: Assisted Reproduction and Child Development*. Nashville, TN: Parthenon Publishing Group.

Sutton, S., McVey, D., & Glanz, A. (1999). A comparative test of the theory of reasoned action and the theory of planned behavior in the prediction of condom use intentions in a national sample of English young people. *Health Psychology, 18*, 72–81. doi:10.1037/0278-6133.18.1.72

Swierstra, T., & Rip, A. (2007). Nano-ethics as NEST-ethics: Patterns of Moral Argumentation About New and Emerging Science and Technology. *NanoEthics, 1*(1), 3–20. doi:10.1007/s11569-007-0005-8

Szoka, B., & Thierer, A. (2009, June). Cyberbullying legislation: Why education is preferable to regulation. *The Progress and Freedom Foundation, 16*(12). Retrieved April 29, 2010, from http://www.pff.org/issues-pubs/pops/2009/pop16.12-cyberbullying-education-better-than-regulation.pdf

Tamura, T. (2005, January 7-9). Japanese feeling for privacy. The 2nd Asia-Pacific Computing and Philosophy Conference (pp. 88-93). Chulalongkorn University.

Tappan, T. N. (2006). The road more travelled: Illegal digital downloading. *Tennessee's Business, 15*(1), 20–23.

Taylor, C. (2007, July 2). 1/3 of world population to have camera phones by 2011, firm says. *Electronic News*. Retrieved July 3, 2009, from http://www.allbusiness.com/electronics/computer-electronics/6365632-1.html

Tehranian, M. (2002). Peace journalism: Negotiating global media ethics. *The Harvard International Journal of Press/Politics, 7*(2), 58–83.

Tenner, E. (1996). *Why Things Bite Back*. New York: Knopf.

Teuteberg, H. J., Neumann, G., & Wierlacher, A. (Eds.). (1997). *Essen und kulturelle Identitä. Europäische Perspektiven*. Berlin: Akademie.

The Oracle. (2008). Retrieved from http://www.troy.edu/studentservices/oracle/2008-2009_Oracle.pdf April 14, 2009.

Thomas, A., Donnell, A. J., & Buboltz, W. C., Jr. (2001). The Hong Psychological Reactance Scale: A confirmatory factor analysis. *Management and Evaluation in Counseling and Development, 34*, 2-13. Retrieved from http://mec.sagepub.com/

Thomas, J. L. C. (2001, January 12). Ethics of hactivism. *SANS-GIAC Practical Repository*. Retrieved October 5, 2009, from http://www.dvara.net/HK/Julie_Thomas_GSEC.pdf.

Thomassen, N. (1992). *Communicative ethics in theory and practice* (Irons, J., Trans.). New York: St. Martin's Press.

Thompson, C. (2005, January). The BitTorrent effect. *WIRED Magazine, 13*(1), 150-153, 178-179.

Tonglet, M. (2002). Consumer misbehavior: An exploratory study of shoplifting. *Journal of Consumer Behaviour, 1*, 336–354. doi:10.1002/cb.79

Tonglet, M., Phillips, P. S., & Read, A. D. (2004). Using the theory of planned behaviour to investigate the determinants of recycling behaviour: A case study from Brixworth, UK. *Resources, Conservation and Recycling, 41*, 191–214. doi:10.1016/j.resconrec.2003.11.001

Tooby, J., & DeVore, I. (1987), The reconstruction of hominid behavioral evolution through strategic modeling. In W. G. Kinzey (Ed.), *Primate models of hominid behavior* (pp.183-237), Suny Press, Albany.

Tourangeau, R. (2004). Survey research and societal change. *Annual Review of Psychology, 55*, 775–801. doi:10.1146/annurev.psych.55.090902.142040

Tsfati, Y., & Weimann, G. (2002). Terror on the Internet. *Studies in Conflict and Terrorism, 25*(5), 317–332. www.terrorism.com. doi:10.1080/10576100290101214

Turow, J., & Hennessy, M. (2007). Internet privacy and institutional trust: Insights from a national survey. *New Media & Society, 9*, 300–318. doi:10.1177/1461444807072219

UNESCO. (2006). *The ethics and politics of nanotechnology*. Paris: UNESCO. Retrieved April 17, 2009, from: http://unesdoc.unesco.org/images/0014/001459/145951e.pdf

United Nations. (1998). *Kyoto Protocol to the United Nations Convention on Climate Change.* New York: United Nations. Retrieved January 18, 2009 from http://unfccc.int/resource/docs/convkp/kpeng.pdf United Nations Research Institute for Social Development-UNRISD (1995). States of Disarray: The Social Effect of Globalization. London: UNRISD.

United States Department of Justice. (2000). *The Electronic Frontier: The challenge of unlawful conduct involving use of the Internet. Report of the President's working group on unlawful conduct on the Internet.* Retrieved May 19, 2010, from http://www.justice.gov/criminal/cybercrime/unlawful.htm

Upendra, K., Singh, S., Kumar, V., & Verma, H. K. (2007). Online fingerprint verification. *Journal of Medical Engineering & Technology, 31*(1). Retrieved from ProQuest Educational Journals.

Uriell, Z. A., & Dudley, C. M. (2009). Sensitive topics: Are there modal differences? *Computers in Human Behavior, 25,* 76–87. doi:10.1016/j.chb.2008.06.007

Usher, A. D. (1997), Kvaener's Game. In A.D. Usher (Ed.), *Dams as Aid: A Political Economy of Nordic Development Thinking* (pp. 133-152). London: Routledge.

Valdez, V. J. (2005), Technology and civil society. *The 2nd Asia-Pacific Computing and Philosophy Conference.* Chulalongkorn University, Bangkok, Thailand, January 7-9, 2005.

Van de Voorde, C. (2005). Sri Lankan terrorism: Assessing and responding to the threat of the Liberation Tigers of Tamil Eelam (LTTE). *Police Practice and Research, 6*(2), 181–199. doi:10.1080/15614260500121195

van den Hoven, J. (2010). The use of normative theories in computer ethics. In Floridi, E. B. L. (Ed.), *The Cambridge Handbook of Information and Computer Ethics.* Cambridge, UK: Cambridge University Press.

van den Hoven, J., & Weckert, J. (2008). *Information Technology and Moral Philosophy* (1st ed.). Cambridge, UK: Cambridge University Press. doi:10.1017/CBO9780511498725

Van Eck, N. J., & Waltman, L. (2006). VOS: a new method for visualizing similarities between objects. In *Proceedings of the 30th Annual Conference of the German Classification Society, Studies in Classification, Data Analysis, and Knowledge Organization* (pp. 299-306).

Van Eck, N. J., Waltman, L., & van den Berg, J. (2005). A novel algorithm for visualizing concept associations. In *Proceedings of the Database and Expert Systems Applications, Advances in Data Analysis, Sixteenth International Workshop* (pp. 405-409).

Van Eck, N. J., & Waltman, L. (2009). Software survey: VOSviewer, a computer program for bibliometric mapping. *Scientometrics,* 1–16.

van Meter, K. M. (1990). Methodological and design issues: Techniques for assessing the representatives of snowball samples. In Lambert, E. Y. (Ed.), *The collection and interpretation of data from hidden populations (NIDA Research Monograph 98)* (pp. 31–43). Rockville, MD: National Institute on Drug Abuse, US Department of Health and Human Services.

Vargas Lloza, M. (2001, February). The Culture of Liberty. *Foreign Policy, 122,* 66–71.

Velasquez, M. G. (2001). *Business Ethics: Concepts and Cases* (5th ed.). Upper Saddle River, NJ: Pearson Education.

Verton, D. (2003). *Black ice: the invisible threat of cyberterrorism.* New York: McGraw-Hill Osborne Media.

Victorian Law Reform Commission Investigates Surveillance Cameras. (2009, March 30). *Herald Sun.* Retrieved June 19, 2009, from http://www.news.com.au/heraldsun/story/0,21985,25265948-661,000.html

Video Surveillance. (2007, December 18). *Privacy International.* Retrieved June 15, 2009, from http://www.privacyinternational.org/article.shtml?cmd%5B347%5D=x-347-559088

Violanti, J. M. (1998). Cellular phones and fatal traffic accidents. *Accident; Analysis and Prevention, 30,* 519–524.

Virginia Polytechnic Institute and State University. (2010). *Cyberstalking/Online Harassment @ Virginia Tech.* Retrieved January 31, 2010, from http://www.stopabuse.vt.edu/cyberstalking.php

Virno, P. (1994). *Virtuosismo y revolución, la acción política en la época del desencanto.* Madrid: Traficantes de Sueños.

Viseu, A. (2003). Simulation and augmentation: Issues of wearable computers. *Ethics and Information Technology, 5,* 17–26. doi:10.1023/A:1024928320234

Waldron, J. (1984). *Theories of Rights.* Oxford and New York: Oxford University Press.

Wallach, W., & Allen, C. (2009). *Moral Machines – Teaching Robots Right from Wrong.* New York: Oxford University Press.

Wallerstein, I. M. (1974, 1989). *The Modern World-System.* San Diego: Academic Press.

Walzer, D. (1977). *Just and unjust wars: a moral argument with historical illustrations.* New York: Basic Books.

Wang, H., & Gearhart, D. L. (2006). *Designing and developing web-based instruction.* Upper Saddle River, NJ: Pearson Merrill Prentice Hall.

Warwick, K. (2003). Cyborg morals, cyborg values, cyborg ethics. *Ethics and Information Technology, 5,* 131–137. doi:10.1023/B:ETIN.0000006870.65865.cf

Wayner, P. (2002). *Disappearing cryptography: information hiding: steganography and watermarking.* San Francisco, CA: Morgan Kaufmann.

Webgrafía (n.d.). Retrieved from http://www.gnu.org/gnu/manifesto.html

Weimann, G. (2005). Cyberterrorism: The Sum of All Fears? *Studies in Conflict and Terrorism, 28*(2), 129–149. doi:10.1080/10576100590905110

Weiser, M. (1991, September). The computer for the 21st century. *Scientific American,* 94–104. doi:10.1038/scientificamerican0991-94

Westwood, C. (1997). *The future is not what it used to be: conflict in the information age.* Fairbairn, ACT, Australia: Air Power Studies Center.

Whang, L. S.-M., Lee, S., & Chang, G. (2003). Internet over-users' psychological profiles: A behavior sampling analysis on Internet addiction. *Cyberpsychology & Behavior, 6,* 143–150. doi:10.1089/109493103321640338

Whitby, S. (2002). *Biological warfare against crops.* Houndmills, UK: Palgrave.

White Wolf Security. *Offensive operations in cyberspace.* Retrieved February 6, 2009 from www.whitewolfsecurity.com/publications/offensive_ops.php.

Whitehead, A. N. (1925). *Process and reality.* New York: Free Press.

Why NBIC? Why human performance enhancement? (2008). *Innovation: The European Journal of Social Science Research, 21*(1), 25-40.

Wikipedia. (2009). *Bullying.* Retrieved November 26, 2009, from http://pt.wikipedia.org/wiki/Bullying

Willard, N. (2007). *Educator's Guide to Cyberbullying and Cyberthreats. Center for Safe and Responsible use of the Internet.* Retrieved December 16, 2009, from http://cyberbully.org/cyberbully/docs/cbcteducator.pdf

Wilsdon, J., & Willis, R. (2004). *See-through science: Why public engagement needs to move upstream.* London: Demos.

Wingrove, T., Korpas, A. L., & Weisz, V. (2010). Why were millions of people not obeying the law? Motivational influences on non-compliance with the law in the case of music piracy. *Psychology, Crime & Law.* doi:10.1080/10683160903179526

Winner, L. (1987). *La Ballena y el reactor: Una búsqueda de los límites en la era de la alta tecnología.* Barcelona: Gedisa.

Winner, L. (1993). Upon opening the black box and finding it empty: Social constructivism and the philosophy of technology. *Science, Technology & Human Values, 18*(3), 362–378. doi:10.1177/016224399301800306

Winterman, D. (2005, April 7). Snapping the Dead Pope on a Camera Phone. *BBC News.* Retrieved July 2, 2009, from http://news.bbc.co.uk/1/hi/magazine/4415947.stm

Wolbring, G. (2005). *The triangle of enhancement medicine, disabled people, and the concept of health. Health Technology Assessment Initiative Series.* Retrieved December 5, 2008, from http://www.ihe.ca/documents/hta/HTA-FR23.pdf

Wood, S., Jones, R., & Geldart, A. (2007). *Nanotechnology, from the science to the social: The social, ethical and economic aspects of the debate*. Swindon: Economic and Social Research Council. Retrieved May 16, 2008, from: http://www.esrcsocietytoday.ac.uk/ESRCInfoCentre/Images/ESRC_Nano07_tcm6-18918.pdf

Woodall, P. (2002, November 25). Cell phone towers can be deadly magnet for birds. *Sun Herald*, p. A1.

Woodrow Wilson Project on Emerging Technologies. (2009). *Consumer products: An inventory of nanotechnology-based consumer products currently on the market*. Retrieved April 17, 2009, from: http://www.nanotechproject.org/inventories/consumer/

Wood, S., Geldart, A., & Jones, R. (2008). Crystallizing the nanotechnology debate. *Technology Analysis and Strategic Management*, *20*(1), 13–27. doi:10.1080/09537320701726320

Workman, T. (2008, October). How Digital Culture Shapes Student's Minds. The Real Impact of Virtual Worlds. *The Chronicle of Higher Education*, *55*(4).

Wright, A. (1990). *The Death of Ramon Gonzalez: The Modern Agricultural Dilemma*. Austin, TX: University Press.

Wright, D. K. (1996). Communication ethics. In Salwen, M. B., & Stacks, D. W. (Eds.), *An integrated approach to communication theory and research* (pp. 519–535). New York: Lawrence Erlbaum Associates.

Wright, K. B. (2005). Researching Internet-based populations: Advantages and disadvantages of online survey research, online questionnaire authoring software packages, and web survey services. *Journal of Computer-Mediated Communication*, *10*(3). Retrieved from http://jcmc.indiana.edu/vol10/issue3/wright.html.

Ybarra, M., & Mitchell, K. (2007). Prevalence and Frequency of Internet Harassment Investigation: Implications for Adolescent Health. *The Journal of Adolescent Health*, *41*(2), 189–195. doi:10.1016/j.jadohealth.2007.03.005

Young, J. (2008b, March 28). How to Combat a Campus-Gossip Web Site (and Why You Shouldn't). *Chronicle of Higher Education*. Retrieved May 19, 2010, from http://chronicle.com/weekly/v54/i29/29a01602.htm

Young, K. S., & Rodgers, R. C. (1998). *Internet addiction: personality traits associated with its development*. Retrieved December 18, 2008, from http://netaddiction.com/articles/personality-correlates.htm

Young, K. S. (2004). Internet addiction: A new clinical phenomenon and its consequences. *The American Behavioral Scientist*, *48*, 402–415. doi:10.1177/0002764204270278

About the Contributors

Rocci Luppicini is an associate professor in the Department of Communication at the University of Ottawa (Canada) and acts as the editor-in-chief for the International Journal of Technoethics. He is a leading expert in technology studies (TS) and technoethics. He has published over 25 peer reviewed articles and has authored and edited several books including, Online Learning Communities in Education (IAP, 2007), the Handbook of Conversation Design for Instructional Applications (IGI, 2008), and Trends in Canadian Educational Technology and Distance Education (VSM, 2008), the Handbook of Research on Technoethics: Volume I &II (with R. Adell) (IGI, 2008,2009), Technoethics and the Evolving Knowledge Society: Ethical Issues in Technological Design, Research, Development, and Innovation (2010), Cases on Digital Technologies in Higher Education: Issues and Challenges (with A. Haghi) (IGI, 2010), Education for a Digital World: Present Realities and Future Possibilities (AAP, in press). He is currently working on the Handbook of Research on Technoself: Identity in a Technological Society:Vol I &II (IGI, in preparation) to be released in 2012.

* * *

Evandro Agazzi (Bergamo, Italy 1934).- Having finished studies in philosophy at the Catholic University of Milan and physics at the State High school of the same city, he then went on to specialise at Oxford, Marburg and Münster. In 1963, he qualified for university teaching in Philosophy of Science and, in 1966, in Mathematical Logic. He has taught in the Faculty of Sciences at Genoa University, the State High School in Pisa and at the Catholic University in Milan. Since 1970, he has been Professor of the Philosophy of Science and, since 1983, of Theoretical Philosophy at Genoa University, where he is now Professor Emeritus. From 1979 to 1986 he also held the chair of Philosophical Anthropology, Philosophy of Science and Philosophy of Nature at Fribourg University in Switzerland. He has been a visiting professor at the Universities of Berne, Geneva, Düsseldorf, Pittsburgh and Stanford and is Doctor honoris causa at the Argentinain Universities of Cordoba, Santiago del Estero, Cuyo-Mendoza, of the University Ricardo Palma di Lima and at Urbino University. He has acted as chairman for the Italian Philosophical Society, the Italian Society of Logic and Philosophy of the Sciences, the Swiss Society of Logic and Philosophy of the Sciences, the International Federation of Philosophical Societies and the 'Institut International de Philosophie'. Of the latter two institutions he is now Honorary President. Currently, he is president of the Académie Internationale de Philosophie des Sciences. Bioetica. His works include (over 70 volumes and 800 articles) to name only a few: *Temi e Problemi di Filosofia della Fisica*, 1969; (with L. Geymonat and F. Minazzi) *Filosofia, Scienza e Verità*, 1989; *La Logica Simbolica*, 1990; *Il Bene, il Male, la Scienza*, 1992; *Cultura Scientifica e Interdisciplinarità* 1994; *Filosofia Della Natura, Scienza e Cosmologia*, 1995; *Le Geometrie Non Euclidee e i Fondamenti della Geometria*, 1998;

Paideia Verità Educazione, 1999; (with F. Minazzi) *Science and Ethics. The Axiological Contexts of Science*, 2008; *Time in the Different Scientific Approaches/Le temps Appréhendé à Travers Différentes Disciplines*, 2008; *Scienza* (interview by Giuseppe Bertagna), 2008; *Le Rivoluzioni Scientifiche e il Mondo Moderno*, 2008.

Peter Allen is a PhD candidate and Associate Lecturer in the School of Psychology and Speech Pathology at Curtin University of Technology in Perth, Western Australia. He is interested in the psychology of Internet behaviour, and is currently investigating the psychological aspects of online copyright infringement. Peter is co-author of the popular SPSS text, PASW Statistics by SPSS: A Practical Guide.

Andoni Alonso (Pamplona, Spain) Ph. D in Philosophy, from 1999 has been associate professor at the University of Extremadura. From 1996 to 1998 was Visiting Scholar at Penn State University and from 2003 to 2004 at Nevada University at Reno. He has published papers at *Technology and Culture, Argumentos de Razón Técnica, Isis, Isegoría*. Recent books *La nueva ciudad de Dios,* (Madrid, 2001) *Carta al Homo Ciberneticus,* (Madrid, 2002), *La quinta columna digital* (Madrid, 2003, Awarded by Epson Foundation) *and Diasporas in the New Media Age*, (Reno, 2010). His main field of interest is philosophy of technology especialized in new technologies of information and communication. Presently his work of research is on free software and knowledge and how these topics have to do with political and communitarian movements using the Internet. His present work can be accessed at www.quintacolumna.org.

Alison Anderson is Reader in Sociology, School of Law and Social Science, University of Plymouth, UK. She has researched and published widely on media and risk. Her most recent co-authored book is Nanotechnology, Risk and Communication (Palgrave, 2009) (with Alan Petersen, Clare Wilkinson and Stuart Allan). She is currently writing the single-authored book, Media, Environment and the Network Society (Palgrave, 2009), and editing a special issue of the Journal for Risk Research on new challenges for the study of media and risk. With Alan Petersen, she has recently conducted two projects on nanotechnologies: one, focusing on nanotechnologies and news media production (funded by the ESRC) and a second, on scientists' and policymakers' views on the benefits and risks of nanotechnologies, as applied to medicine and environmental sustainability (funded by the British Academy).

Keith Bauer works at the Jefferson College of Health Sciences. He earned his Ph.D. in philosophy/bioethics in 2002 from the University of Tennessee. From 2000-2001, he served as a fellow at the Institute for Ethics at the American Medical Association in Chicago. He has published in journals such as Ethics and Information Technology, The Cambridge Quarterly for Healthcare Ethics, The American Journal of Bioethics, and Theoretical Medicine and Bioethics. Dr. Bauer also holds a Master of Social Work degree. Present areas of research include electronically mediated communication, the distributive justice implications of ICT, online education, and transhumansim.

Mariana C. Broens received her bachelor degree in Law (1984, Catholic University of Parana - Brazil) and in Philosophy (1985, Federal University of Paraná – Brazil). In 1988 she obtained a scholarship to study in the University of Nantes – France and she received the Diplôme d'Etudes Approfondies in Logic and Anglo-Saxon Philosophy. Her PhD thesis (1996) The problem of the grounds of knowledge in the philosophy of Blaise Pascal, University of Sao Paulo, was supervised by Bento Prado Junior.

She is one of the coordinators of the research group on cognitive studies at the University of Sao Paulo State – UNESP. She is member of the Brazilian Society for Cognitive Science and the Brazilian Society for Philosophy of Mind. She is professor of Philosophy of Mind at the Department of Philosophy of the University of Sao Paulo State – UNESP – Brazil.

Laura Cabrera is a PhD research student in ethics and emergent technologies in the Centre for Applied Philosophy and Public Ethics at Charles Sturt University. Laura received a BSc in Electrical and Communication Engineering from ITESM University in Mexico City, and a MA in Applied Ethics from Linköping University in Sweden. Her current research focuses on nanotechnology and neurotechnology, human enhancement, posthumanity, and the ethical dimensions of emerging technology especially those connected to medical issues and individual/social perspectives.

Blanca Callén is a PHD student in Social Psychology at the Universitat Autònoma de Barcelona. She works as a researcher at the same department and is also a full member of the Group for Social Studies of Science and Technology (GESCIT). Her main research interest are power relations and political action in sociotechnical contexts.

Daniele Cantore received his post-graduate degree in Philosophy in 2010: *An Epistemological Approach to Biometrics. Identification, Verification, and Identity Issues.* He works with Lorenzo Magnani's group at the Computational Philosophy Laboratory of the Department of Philosophy (University of Pavia, Italy). He is interested in the area of ethical and epistemological problems of current technologies.

Peter Crabb received his Ph.D. in Social Psychology from Temple University in 1989. He is Associate Professor of Psychology and Coordinator of the Applied Psychology Program at Pennsylvania State University-Hazleton. His research examines the impact of technology on social behavior and the environment.

Miquel Domènech is Senior Lecturer in Social Psychology at the Universitat Autònoma de Barcelona. His research interests cohere broadly in the field of science and technology studies (STS), with a special focus on the relationship between technical innovations and power relationships.

Mahmoud Eid is Associate Professor at the Department of Communication, University of Ottawa, Canada. Dr. Eid is the editor of the Global Media Journal -- Canadian Edition. He is the author of Interweavement: International Media Ethics and Rational Decision-Making (2008), series editor of Communication Research Methods: Quantitative and Qualitative Approaches (2007) and Introduction to Communication and Media Studies (2008), and co-editor of The Right to Communicate: Historical Hopes, Global Debates and Future Premises (2009) and Introduction to Media Studies: A Reader (2007). His research interests, teaching experience, and publications concentrate on international communication, media ethics, terrorism, crisis management and conflict resolution, communication research methods, modernity, and the political economy of communication.

Josep M. Esquirol (Mediona, Spain, 1963).-Lecturer of Philosophy at the Universitat de Barcelona and director of the Foundation Ethics, Technology and Society. Among his Publisher books, *D'Europa als homes (From Europe to Men),*Cruïlla, 1994, that awarded him the Joan Maragall essay award; *La* *frivolitat política del final de la història* (*Political banality in the end of history*), Caparrós, 1998; and, more recently, *Uno mismo y los otros* (*Oneself and the others*, Herder, 2005, *El respeto o la mirada atenta* (*Respect or the attentive gaze*), Gedisa, 2006; and *El respirar dels dies (The breathing of days*), Paidós 2009. In 2002 he obtained the award to research granted by the Catalan Government.

Catherine Flick is a post-doctoral researcher in the Computer Science Faculty at the Facultés Universitaires Notre-Dame de la Paix, Namur, Belgium. Her interests are in ethics and philosophy of technology, particularly issues of informed consent and ethical governance.

Deb Gearhart is Director of eCampus, Troy University, USA. Previously Deb served as the founding Director of E-Education Services at Dakota State University in Madison, South Dakota and was there for the 11 years. Before joining Dakota State she spent 10 years with the Department of Distance Education at Penn State. Deb was an associate professor for educational technology at Dakota State University teaching at both the undergraduate and graduate levels. She has co-authored at textbook entitled Designing and Developing Web-Based Instruction and is editing another publication titled Cases on Distance Delivery and Learning Outcomes: Emerging Trends and Programs, due out in 2009 . Dr. Gearhart has earned a BA in Sociology from Indian University of Pennsylvania. She earned a M.Ed. in Adult Education with a distance education emphasis and an M.P.A. in Public Administration, both from Penn State. Deb completed her Ph.D. program in Education , with a certificate in distance education, from Capella University.

David Gick is a graduate student in the Communication department at the University of Ottawa interested in the relationship between science, technology, and social organization. His ongoing research investigates government policies of directed "innovation cluster" formation through examination of bibliometric indicators. He earned his B.A. from the University of Ottawa.

Maria Eunice Q. Gonzalez received her bachelor degree in Physics (1977, University of Sao Paulo State - UNESP, Brazil), and her master thesis in Logics and Philosophy of Science (1984, Artificial Intelligence and the methodology of scientific discovery, UNICAMP, Brazil). Her PhD thesis (1989, A cognitive approach to visual perception, University of Essex, UK, supervised by Noel. Sharkey and Peter Carruthers) dealt with aspects of the theory of information, and premises of the theory of self-organization, applied to neural networks. Since 1991, she is member of the Center of Logic and Epistemology (UNICAMP). In 1995 she started an interdisciplinary course (Masters and PhD) in Brazil in the area of Cognitive Science and Philosophy of Mind. In the same year she founded the Brazilian Society for Cognitive Science. She is professor of Epistemology and Ecological Philosophy at UNESP.

Philippe Goujon is a Professor in the Computer Science Faculty at the Facultés Universitaires Notre-Dame de la Paix, Namur, Belgium. His interests are in epistemology and ethics of information and communication technologies, with his main area of focus in reflexive ethical governance of ICTs.

Richard Heersmink is a researcher in computer and information ethics at the philosophy department of Delft University of Technology, the Netherland. His interests cover philosophy of information and communication technology, cognitive science and artificial intelligence.

Jeroen van den Hoven is professor of Moral Philosophy at Delft Technical University. Van den Hoven is Scientific Director of the 3TU.Centre for Ethics and Technology as well as Editor-in-Chief of Ethics and Information Technology (Springer). His interests cover ethics of information and communication technology.

A. Pablo Iannone, Professor of Philosophy, Central Connecticut State University, USA. He studied engineering, mathematics, philosophy and literature at the Universidad Nacional de Buenos Aires, received a B. A. in philosophy from U.C.L.A. and an M.A. and a Ph.D. in philosophy from the University of Wisconsin-Madison, and pursued graduate studies in business and economics at the University of Wisconsin-Madison and Iowa State. He taught at Canada's Dalhousie University, Perú's Universidad Inca Garcilaso de la Vega, and the U.S. universities of Wisconsin-Madison, Texas at Dallas, Iowa State, and Florida,. His publications include nine philosophy books, two literature books, and articles and reviews.

Yasmin Ibrahim is a Reader in International Business and Communications at Queen Mary, University of London. She writes on new media technologies and their social and political implications for societies. Beyond her interest in digital economies she is also interested in the use of the internet for political communication, political mobilisation and empowerment in repressed polities.

Veikko Ikonen (M.A., Design Anthropologist) is working as a senior research scientist at VTT (Technical Research Centre of Finland), Tampere, Finland. Ikonen's research interest is related to the development of Human-Driven Design approach in the area of smart environments and ambient intelligence.

Linda Johansson is a PhD-student in philosophy at The Royal Institute of Technology in Stockholm, Sweden. She is also connected to a research program on methods for dealing with the emergence of new technologies, with a focus on autonomous systems. This is in collaboration with The Royal Institute of Technology and The Swedish Defense Research Agency. Her main philosophical interests are robot morality, philosophy of mind, epistemology and metaethics.

Guiou Kobayashi received his B.S. in Electrical Engineering in 1982, from Escola Politecnica of the University of Sao Paulo, Brazil. His M.S. and Ph.D. degrees were also obtained from Escola Politecnica in 1991 and 1999, respectively, and were focused on Fault-tolerant Paralel Computer Architectures. More recently he started working on Fault-torelant distributed Sensor Networks, mobile computing, GIS, and RFID, directing his view for a broader perspective of Ubiquitous Systems. In 2006 he joined the first group of professors to build an entirely new university, the Federal University of ABC, at Sao Paulo, Brazil. His is currently assistant professor of Computer Science program and leader of Ubiquitous Systems research group at the Federal University of ABC. His is member of Computer Society of IEEE and ACM.

Ellen Kraft's research interest in cyberbullying evolved from teaching the courses Internet and Society and e-Commerce. She is an Assistant Professor of Business Studies at Richard Stockton College of New Jersey. During the fall 2008 Dr. Kraft began researching cyberbullying in higher education. She published "Juicycampus.com: How was this business model culpable of encouraging harassment on college campuses" in Truths and Myth of Cyber-bullying: International Perspectives on Stakeholder Responsibilities and Children's Safety edited by Shaheen Shariff and Andrew Churchill.

Antonio Lafuente (Granada, Spain) PH D in Phyisics, from 1987 Scientific Researcher Investigador at the Instituto de Historia del CSIC. From 1989 to 1990 was *Visiting Scholar* at the Berkeley University, California.Some of his last papers have been published at *Osiris, Social Studies of Science, Claves de Razón Práctica,Revista de Libros* and *Archipiélago*. Recent books: *Georges-Louis Leclerc, conde de Buffon* (1707-1788) (Madrid, 1999), *Los mundos de la ciencia en la Ilustración espanyola* (Madrid, 2003) and *El carnaval de la tecnociencia* (Gadir, 2007). Presently his research is on the connections among contemporary culture and the Enlightment using the notions of commons and heritage as key concepts. Also his interests go on how the frontiers among nature and artificial, private and public and expertise and layperson tend to disappear. His blog Tecnocidanos, beginning in 2005 gathers materials about these issues.

Daniel López is assistant professor in the Department of Psychology, Universitat Oberta de Catalunya. He is currently working on the implementation of new technologies in care settings like Home Telecare from an STS perspective (specifically ANT). His main areas of interest are: a) the emergence of new spatialities and temporalities of care ; b) the emergence of new practices of caring and security due to the increasing importance of technologies of accountability; and c) the enactment of hybrid forms of autonomy and independence.

Lorenzo Magnani, philosopher and cognitive scientist, is Professor,University of Pavia, Italy, and the director of its Computational Philosophy Laboratory. He has been visiting professor at the Sun Yat-sen University, Canton (Guangzhou), China and has taught at the Georgia Institute of Technology and at The City University of New York. He currently directs international research programs in the EU, USA, and China. His book Abduction, Reason, and Science (New York, 2001) has become a well-respected work in the field of human cognition. In 1998, he started the series of International Conferences on Model-Based Reasoning (MBR). The last book Morality in a Technological World (Cambridge, 2007) develops a philosophical and cognitive theory of the relationships between ethics and technology in a naturalistic perspective.

José Pinheiro Neves was born in Oporto (Portugal) in 1957, and he is graduated in Sociology in the "Instituto Superior de Ciências do Trabalho e da Empresa", Lisbon (Portugal). He has a Ph.D. from the University of Minho in 2005 about the technique at the present time: "Technical individuation in the actuality". Nowadays, he is a lecturer at the University of Minho (Portugal) and a researcher at the "Center of Research on Communication and Society" at the University of Minho. He published, in 2006, the book "The Appeal of Technical Object" based essentially on the work of Gilles Deleuze and Gilbert Simondon. He has several publications about the relationship between technique and social, the theory of actor-network, cyberbullying, and so on. More recently, Neves's research areas include new digital socio-technical networks. He is a member of the editorial boards of the journals "Communication and Society "and "Organizations and Work". Webpage: http://neves.paginas.sapo.pt.

Alan Petersen is Professor of Sociology and Discipline Convener, Sociology Program, School of Political and Social Inquiry, Faculty of Arts, Monash University, Clayton, Melbourne, Australia. He has researched and published extensively in the areas of the sociology of health and illness and sociology of new technologies. His most recent (co-authored) book is Nanotechnology, Risk and Communication

(Palgrave, 2009) (with Alison Anderson, Clare Wilkinson and Stuart Allan). With Alison Anderson, he has recently undertaken two projects on nanotechnologies: one, focusing on nanotechnologies and news media production (funded by the ESRC) and a second, on scientists' and policymakers' views on the benefits and risks of nanotechnologies, as applied to medicine and environmental sustainability (funded by the British Academy).

Luzia Pinheiro was born in the city of Viana do Castelo (Portugal) in 1986, graduating in sociology at the University of Minho, Braga (Portugal). In 2009 completed a Masters in Sociology at the University of Minho (Portugal) with a dissertation about the phenomenon of cyberbullying among Portuguese university students. Recently she was awarded with a doctorate fellowship by FCT (Foundation for Science and Technology, Portugal) for the project "Cyberbullying and cyberstalking" in the area of Communication and Information (Reference: SFRH/BD/62013/2009). She has several publications about cyberbullying and bullying. She has also organized information campaigns in primary and secondary schools about bullying and cyberbullying. Webpage: http://sites.google.com/site/luziapinheiro1986/.

J. A. Quilici-Gonzalez received the B.S., M.S. and Ph.D. degrees in Electrical Engineering from the Escola Politecnica of the University of Sao Paulo, Brazil, in 1996, 2001 and 2006, respectively. Since 2008 he is an assistant professor at the Federal University of ABC, Sao Paulo, Brazil. His research interests include run-time reconfigurable circuits, ubiquitous computing systems, machine learning and related ethical issues.

Michael Rader has a PhD in sociology and has worked for over thirty years as a researcher at the Research Centre in Karlsruhe, now the Karlsruhe Institute of Technology. His interests include technology assessment on information and communication technologies and he is involved in coordinating the work of several European Parliamentary Technology Assessment organisations for the European Parliament.

Lynne Roberts is a lecturer in the School of Psychology and Speech Pathology at Curtin Unviersity of Technology in Perth, Western Australia. Lynne has conducted and published research within the field of technoethics, with a particular focus on cyber-crime, cyber-victimisation and online research ethics. Her other research interests centre on social interaction online, online research methodologies and public attitudes to crime and justice. Details of Lynne's publications in these areas are available at http://psych. curtin.edu.au/staff_profile.cfm?id=25.

Neil C. Rowe is Professor and Coordinator of Research in Computer Science, U.S. Naval Postgraduate School where he has been since 1983. He has a Ph.D. in Computer Science from Stanford University (1983), and E.E. (1978), S.M. (1978), and S.B. (1975) degrees from the Massachusetts Institute of Technology. His main research interest is the role of deception in information processing, and he has also done research on intelligent access to multimedia databases, image processing, robotic path planning, and intelligent tutoring systems. He is the author of over 100 technical papers and a book.

Katherine Shepherd completed this research as part of her Bachelor of Psychology (Honours) at Curtin University of Technology in Perth, Western Australia. She currently works in the Disability Services field.

Bernd Carsten Stahl is Professor of Critical Research in Technology in the Centre for Computing and Social Responsibility at De Montfort University, Leicester, UK. His interests cover philosophical issues arising from the intersections of business, technology, and information. This includes the ethics of computing and critical approaches to information systems.

Steven E. Stern received his Ph.D. in Social and Organizational Psychology from Temple University in 1995. He is Professor of Psychology and Chair of the Division of Natural Sciences at the University of Pittsburgh at Johnstown. His recent research interests include the effects of cellular telephones on communication and relationships and reactions toward assistive technologies.

Francisco Tirado is Dr. Ph. in Social Psychology. He is a Lecturer in the Social Psychology Department of Universitat Autònoma de Barcelona and full member of the Group for Social Studies of Science and Technology (GESCIT). His main research interests are: a) power relations and political action in sociotechnical contexts and b) biopolitics and care technologies.

Kutoma J. Wakunuma is a Research Fellow at the Centre for Computing and Social Responsibility at De Montfort University, Leicester, UK. Her interests cover issues of diffusion of technologies and the social impact of ICTs in both developed and developing societies.

Jinchang Wang received Ph.D. in operations research / information technology at Georgia Institute of Technology in 1990. His research interests are in operations research, applied statistics, and intelligent machine systems. His dozens of research papers have been published in journals Mathematical Programming, ORSA Journal on Computing, Annals of Mathematics and Artificial Intelligence, Journals of Automated Reasoning, International Journal of Approximate Reasoning, Mathematical and Computer Modelling, Knowledge-based Systems, Computers and Operations Research, Journal of International Technology and Information Management, Journal of Combinatorial Optimization, etc. He is currently a Full Professor in Richard Stockton College of New Jersey, USA.

Sarah Wenglensky-Suggitt is a graduate student in the Communication department at the University of Ottawa interested in the organization innovation generating knowledge systems. Her ongoing research investigates the formation and structure of such knowledge systems within the Canadian economy. Sarah earned her B.A. in Communication from the University of Ottawa.

Index

A

academic integrity 178
affordances 56
Amazonic ecosystems 146
ambient intelligence (AmI) 73
analyticlal grid 69
anti-reductionist 240
anti-transhumanists 237
Aristotelian virtue 63
Association for Computing Machinery (ACM) 71
attentive gaze 21-24, 26
attribution 204
autonomous robots 254

B

Balance Hypothesis 153
Bateson, Gregory 139
bibliometrical analysis 73
Big Brother Watching 83
biometrics 177
    authentication 178
    enrollment 178
bio-psycho-social elements 239
BitTorrent 98
blogsphere 191
Bostrom, Nick 246
BrainTalk Communities 192
bullying 133
    between peers 134
    repetitive 133
    reversal roles 134

C

Campaña Ciudades por la Protección Climática
    (C.C.P.) 155
Chemistry Innovation Knowledge Transfer Network
    (CIKTN) 223

D

collateral damage 199
communities of knowledge 186, 193
Computer Emergency Response Teams (CERT) 201
computer security 269
cosmopoiesis 26
Crisis Decision-Making Model for Media Rational
    Responsibility (CD_M3_R2) 273
cyberattacks 195, 197-198, 201
cyber-blockades 204
cyberbullying 114, 116-117, 120
    stage 1 135
    stage 2 135
    stage 3 135
cyber-counterattacks 201
cyber-pacifism 205
cyberprivacy 1, 17
cyberstalking 114, 117-119
cyber-terrorism 263-264, 266
cyber-terrorists 263, 265-266
cyberwarfare 198
cyberweapons 195-196
    botnets 196
    rootkits 196
cyborgness 8
cyborgs 1-2, 240

D

damage assessment 200
decision-making 273
    rational thinking 270, 274-275, 278
    responsible conduct 263, 274-276, 278
Denial of Service (DoS) 267
deviance and image capture 86
Digital Hash Tables (DHT) network 98
Digital Rights Management (DRM) software 98
distance education 176
distributed cognition 1, 6, 17
distrust knowledge 186
docility 15